Black Baseball's
Last Team Standing

Black Baseball's Last Team Standing

The Birmingham Black Barons, 1919–1962

WILLIAM J. PLOTT

McFarland & Company, Inc., Publishers

Jefferson, North Carolina

ISBN (print) 978-1-4766-7788-0
ISBN (ebook) 978-1-4766-3603-0

Library of Congress and British Library
cataloguing data are available

Front cover: 1948 Black Barons who played in the last
Negro Leagues World Series. Willie Mays is at far right
(courtesy of Faye Davis and Birmingham Public Library Archives)

Printed in the United States of America

*McFarland & Company, Inc., Publishers
Box 611, Jefferson, North Carolina 28640
www.mcfarlandpub.com*

For Nancy and Atticus.
I could not ask for better teammates.

Table of Contents

Acknowledgments

As with any work of this kind, there are scores of people who deserve thank-yous for assistance over the years. Because of the overlapping content, the acknowledgments here are largely the same ones expressed in *The Negro Southern League: A Baseball History, 1920–1951*. My path to baseball research was first set by the late Lee Allen, historian at the National Baseball Hall of Fame and Museum. He provided invaluable assistance on my very first project, a detailed look at Ty Cobb's year with the Anniston Noblemen in the 1904 Tennessee-Alabama League. That particular project subsequently introduced me to two life-long friends and co-researchers, Ray Nemec and John Pardon, sadly both deceased. Lee, Ray and John were all founding members of the Society for American Baseball Research (SABR). Through them I was among the very first half dozen or so non-founders to join SABR in late 1971.

As noted elsewhere, Robert W. Peterson's *Only the Ball Was White* had a seminal effect on my work. He can be fairly referred to as the Father of Negro League Historians, since his 1970 effort brought so many of us into the field and sparked the formation of SABR's Negro Leagues Committee. The NLC annual meetings, now named the Jerry Malloy Negro League Conference, brought together a number of devoted and generous researchers. I developed friendships with many of those individuals, including Jerry Malloy himself, Larry Lester, Dick Clark, John Holway, Jim Riley, Leslie Heaphy, Lyle Wilson, and others. Over the years they helped shape and direct my research. My deepest regret is that so many of those colleagues died before seeing the results of their assistance to my projects.

When I was working on the Negro Southern League book, several SABR members provided important assistance by combing microfilm in their cities that I had been unable to obtain on interlibrary loan. Among them were Larry Phillips, Alden Mead, James B. Rasco, David Wade, Charles Kaufman, and Blake Sherry. I also thank local SABR friends Clarence Watkins, Jeb Stewart, Art Black, and David Brewer for their help and support.

When I began thinking about photos for this book, I realized I faced a difficult task on the early years. There are many photographs available from the 1940s, the decade or so I call "the Willie Mays and Piper Davis years." Images from the 1920s and 1930s are quite scarce.

A special thank-you to the Maffett family—Gloria Meredith Maffert, Marvin "Tip" Maffett, and Derrick L. Maffett, Sr.—for their help in getting the wonderful photograph of Buford "Geechie" Meredith. Thanks to Gregory Reese for connecting me with Harriet Bridgeforth Jackson, the daughter of Black Barons owner William "Sou" Bridgeforth. She provided the image of her father. And thanks to Denecise Williams Salters for her diligent but, alas, fruitless search for a photograph of her grandfather, Poindexter D. Williams.

As I noted in the previous book, I was fortunate to have employment situations in journalism and academia that often allowed my research to dovetail with my regular job. Admittedly, I probably occasionally took unfair advantage of that for the sake of research.

And as a retired journalist, I am indebted to the tireless work of three African American Birmingham journalists, whose work in the *Birmingham Reporter* and the *Birmingham World* was a pleasure to read and showcase in this book: Emory O. Jackson, William J. Moore, and Marcel Hopson. I had the pleasure of meeting Mr. Jackson early in my career.

Many librarians and archivists, whose names somehow never got recorded properly in my notes, simplified much of the research with interlibrary loans of numerous newspapers on microfilm. I am grateful to those at the Alabama Department of Archives and History and at Alabama State University for their years of accommodation. Equally important are the librarians at the Linn-Henley Research Library in Birmingham, the University of Montevallo's Carmichael Library, and the Harrison Regional Library in Columbiana, Alabama. In the latter facility, Kala Petric tirelessly pursued what at times had to seem an endless list of requests.

Finally, I am forever grateful to my family. I have been blessed with a wife, Nancy Wilstach, and four children who have all tolerated my extensive excursions into dusty bound volumes, microfilm readers, and more recently, Internet search engines, over the years.

Introduction

African Americans have played baseball almost as long as Caucasians. Whether the game was picked up from co-workers in the North or former masters in the South, they embraced it with the same enthusiasm as their white counterparts. Indeed, as early as 1886 there was a tentative effort in the South to organize a league of black baseball teams.[1]

Viable Negro leagues came into existence in 1920 with the formation of the Negro National League and the Negro Southern League. Those two circuits were comprised of sixteen black professional teams playing out a regular schedule over the course of the spring and summer. It was a prelude to a phenomenon that would, over the next four decades, see many other leagues come and go with scores of different teams in what has generically become known as the Negro leagues. In addition, there were dozens of independent barnstorming teams bound by no strictures of league, just by whatever means could get them to the next town and the next game.[2]

There is a general assumption that black baseball came to an end in 1960 "when the Birmingham Black Barons and the NAL (Negro American League) called it quits, ending the existence of the Negro Leagues after forty years."[3] However, in fact, there was an anemic effort to keep both the Black Barons and the NAL afloat for two more years. Both of those seasons concluded with playoffs favoring Birmingham, hence the title of *Black Baseball's Last Team Standing*. Those final years are detailed in the concluding chapter of this book.

I daresay there are not many Negro leagues researchers who did not have the same seminal experience that I did in 1970, opening the pages of Robert W. Peterson's *Only the Ball Was White* for the first time and discovering a whole new world. Not only that, but also a world that was waiting for further exploration and future discoveries.[4] Those discoveries are best summed up with two paragraphs from my book *The Negro Southern League: A Baseball History 1920–1951*:

> In 1971 a number of these researchers, all plodding along independently at first, came together through the Society for American Baseball Research, particularly the Negro Leagues Committee. This committee brought about an extraordinary sharing of information and encouragement. As the NCL grew, conferences became a part of its annual agenda. Thankfully at a conference in Harrisburg, Pennsylvania, in 1998, I was able to personally thank Bob Peterson for the profound influence his work had on my life.
>
> Although I was an active member of the Negro Leagues Researchers and Authors Group that compiled many Negro leagues records through a grant from the National Baseball Hall of Fame and Museum at Cooperstown, the greatest focus of my work was always black baseball in the South. To my knowledge no one else has done any serious research on the Negro Southern League. It was this minor league that gave early impetus to the Birmingham Black Barons, Nashville Elite Giants, Memphis Red Sox and several other teams that are now commonly known in black baseball lore. It also

provided the first formal professional experience for future Hall of Famers such as "Satchel" Paige and "Turkey" Stearnes.

Since Peterson's groundbreaking work, there have been scores of books written on the Negro leagues, including many team histories. Among them is *Black Barons of Birmingham: The South's Greatest Negro League Team and Its Players* by University of Alabama–Birmingham political science professor Larry Powell.[5] This book included dozens of excellent interviews with players from the 1940s and 1950s, particularly those dramatic years when "Piper" Davis, Willie Mays, Artie Wilson and Dan Bankhead made Negro American League pennants seem almost commonplace. But there was comparatively little from the 1920s and 1930s. The current work is an effort to fill in that gap as well as covering the final days of the Black Barons.

The history of the Birmingham Black Barons is inexorably tied to the Negro Southern League and the Birmingham industrial baseball leagues. Most of that research and published writing has focused, however, on the 1940s and the Negro World Series matchups with Negro National League champions. This book examines the 1920s and 1930s as closely as those later years, acknowledging the Negro Southern League's important role in the team's development. The NSL gave a home to professional ball in Southern cities that could not field teams at the NNL level. The core of the first Black Baron teams was the industrial league. It was a spawning ground for ball players for decades. In 1945, Emory O. Jackson, writing in the *Birmingham World*, noted a number of players who traced their roots to the YMCA Industrial League. They included Ed Steele, Art Wilson, Lorenzo "Piper" Davis, Freddie Shepard, Willie "Wing" Young, Jimmy "Schoolboy" Newberry, and Herman Bell of Birmingham; Jim Canada and John Henry Oliver of the Memphis Red Sox; Johnny Cowan of the Cleveland Buckeyes; and Felix "Chaser" Manning and Harry Barnes of the Atlanta Black Crackers.[6]

Also, this history of the team is much more about baseball than the sociology of Jim Crow, which has been well documented. Nor is there an attempt here to identify the "Black Ty Cobb," the "Black Babe Ruth," and the like. Such comparisons are meaningless, involving as they do players from different eras and, indeed, different worlds. They also suggest that what these black players did, and who they were, was not enough. This book instead is about everyday baseball players, many of whom became stars in the time, place, and circumstances that they found themselves in. Consequently, my primary resources were newspaper reports on the games as they were played. It should be noted that no official, completely reliable set of final standings was ever published for any year in the Negro Southern League. The same can be said for most years in the Negro National League and the Negro American League.

In attempting to locate and compile statistics and standings for the Black Barons, I encountered the same difficulties that I did in my research for *The Negro Southern League*. Although standings were frequently published during the season, it is rare to find a set that can be proven mathematically (i.e., the total number of wins for all teams equals the total number of losses). Consequently, when pennant winners are declared, they are often based on narratives from reporters rather than substantiated numbers. It was not unusual for the season to open with great fanfare followed by two or three months of sustained activity, then a withering away as revenues apparently diminished. Some clubs would simply disappear from media notice while others would spend more days barnstorming than playing a regular league schedule. The Black Barons were no exception to this pattern.

Reporting of games was often sporadic. In some years the local white press gave substantial coverage to teams, even printing box scores. In other years the local team was fortunate to get a paragraph and a line score after a game. There was also a dearth of first and last names of players in the articles. Also, box scores were as likely to list the team's star infielder Buford "Geechie" Meredith as "Geechie" as by his last name, "Meredith." This was a common practice in all cities, making the compilation of definitive rosters difficult. Attaching results to the published schedule was another difficulty. Many games were not reported at all, others were reported a day or two late, with the actual date of the game uncertain. Sometimes completely different scores of the same game were reported in different newspapers. And occasionally schedules were changed without notice.

For the Black Barons and the Negro American League, there was an added difficulty. Beginning in the 1940s, games between two teams were played in multiple cities. For example, in 1948 a series between Birmingham and Memphis was played in three states in as many days. They played in Houston on June 1, New Orleans on June 2, and Birmingham on June 3. In 1950 Birmingham played a series with the New Orleans Eagles. The schedule was: July 1, Birmingham; July 2, Tuscaloosa, Alabama; July 3, Clarksdale, Mississippi; and July 4, Pine Bluff, Arkansas. With such arduous travel schedules, it is understandable why many games were never reported, thus making the compilation of a comprehensive list of games for each season quite challenging at times.

There was a positive change in the 1940s and 1950s, for a time. The Howe News Bureau, a national statistical service, handled Negro American League statistics from 1944 to 1958. Although this put them in the hands of a professional firm, they were still dependent upon teams submitting information in a timely manner. The Howe figures for 1946, 1947, and 1952 are quite sparse, perhaps reflecting poor cooperation from the teams. Unfortunately, the late historian and statistician Ray Nemec says four of the fifteen years (1951, 1955–57) are missing altogether. "It seems that when Howe moved from Chicago to Boston, they did not bring any of the 1950s stats with them. From what I have heard, I think they may have been destroyed."[7]

Sporadic reporting was not confined to the white press. Although standings were more likely to be published in newspapers such as the *Chicago Defender* and the *Pittsburgh Courier*, it is quickly evident that the standings were frequently awash with errors and omissions. And sometimes there was a curious, for better explanation, lack of interest on the part of the black press. For example, when the Negro American League was formed in 1937 with the Chicago American Giants as a founding member, the coverage in the *Defender* was noticeably spare. Many games were reported only in brief stories with no box score. The newspaper's primary sports coverage that year was heavyweight boxing champion Joe Louis.

These shortcomings did not go unnoticed by the fans. One of them, Raymond Drake, wrote a piece in 1929 for the Associated Negro Press syndicate, decrying inadequate publicity and statistics for black baseball. Drake called "Negro baseball publicity" a joke. In his vitriolic piece he wrote:

> The proof of this statement is the fact that some weeks one does not hear from some of the clubs of the various leagues at all. When a certain club wins a game it is immediately sent to the newspapers, but when the same club drops a game—it never gets to the papers. And this happens in a city where organized baseball is supposed to be [played]. Still other clubs have been known to go almost an entire season and fail to report the results of their games to league headquarters, making it impossible to keep any trace of their games with any degree of accuracy. Consequently, at the close of the season the league officials had to guess at the standing of the club in question. Nice publicity, this! Such business-like methods....

Another bad feature of baseball publicity is that where ball players are dropped from the roster of a club and no mention of it is made in print. The fact becomes known at the points where the player in question appears with some other club. In the meantime, the fans had been wondering where he had gone. The general public probably never knows what becomes of most of the ball players who leave one club for some other club. There are instances where a ball club has been changed almost completely overnight and no announcement made of it to the press.

In Drake's view, those shortcomings reflected a symptomatic lack of respect for the fans by the owners. He said the owners' attitudes likely contributed to waning attendance in some areas.[8]

Those issues remained unresolved until Howe's services were contracted.

In 1941, expanding on Drake's criticisms, Lucius "Melancholy" Jones, sports editor of the *Atlanta Daily World*, wrote this blistering indictment:

Negro baseball is depressing to observe—particularly the professional brand among sepia performers…. Let us tell of the major shortcomings at one sitting. Among them these:
    (1) Absence of authentic box scores, game and attendance records.
    (2) Absence of college baseball, a natural "feeder" for the Negro leagues.
    (3) Total disrespect of player contracts and league canon and by-laws.
    (4) Excessive play of politics attendant in matters of the leagues.
    (5) Dishonesty of owners, managers, and higher officials.
    (6) Jumping of clubs by star players for "more … pay."
    (7) Laxity of enforcement of the rules regardless to who is affected.
    (8) Inadequate publicity, press cooperation, and general write up of games.[9]

Jones went even further, tearing down one of the game's biggest stars. He called Satchel Paige the worst club jumper and rules-breaker of all. In fact, by late July of that season Paige had already played for four different teams, including one in each league.[10]

Given those scenarios, it should be noted that I have taken some liberties with compiling results and a comprehensive roster for the Black Barons. For example, research has clearly shown that a box score listing a shortstop as "Geechie" is referring to the same shortstop listed as "Buford" or Meredith" on other days. Poor Meredith, one of the all-time great Birmingham players, was not free from this even among those who should have known better. When the NNL office released rare first-half batting averages in 1929, Geechie and Meredith were listed as separate Birmingham players. It was an extraordinary error, considering that Meredith had been playing for nearly 10 years, half of them in the Negro National League.[11] Consequently, when I felt such nomenclature was unequivocally correct, I have used the correct identification and avoided an endless succession of "*sics*" throughout the narrative. Obviously, this relies also on my forty-plus years' experience as a Negro leagues researcher. When first names of players were excluded from game accounts but substantiated in other research, they were included here.

Since the primary resource for this work has been contemporary newspapers, I have drawn from them fully within the context of their times. No effort has been made to clean up or put in politically correct terms some of the obvious racist overtones of those times. This is a book of history, and it should reflect as accurately as possible the events covered within the context of their times. It should be obvious that such reporting in no way represents my feelings.

On the other hand, I found that even among the white press, a majority of the sports writers simply reported on baseball games with no particular regard for the color of the players. Frequently, white writers were extremely praiseworthy of the caliber of play they witnessed at black games. That was as surprising a discovery as was running across black writers who crossed the line of political incorrectness. In 1946, an *Atlanta Daily World* writer, commenting on a pitcher's ineptness, wrote that "he was wilder than Comanche squaw with her first bottle of gin." Emory O. Jackson, writing in the *Birmingham World*, often referred to players by skin tone, referring to Birmingham third baseman Johnny Britton as "lemon-skinned."[12] Leo Berdine, a Black Barons pitcher, had the nickname of "Eight Rock." This derogatory term for "a very black Negro" originated in Harlem and apparently had some common usage in the 1920s.[13] Appellations such as "our dusky–skinned boys," "sooty-baseball," "the tar-dipped horsehiders," and "the tan-skinned Barons." were common in the *Birmingham World*. Marion Jackson once called the white Birmingham Barons "the milk-skinned Barons."[14]

Despite Jim Crow and its accompanying problems, Negro leaguers never considered themselves anything less than baseball players. And like their white counterparts, they responded to the culture of the game. On August 20, 1920, play was stopped at most Negro league games for three minutes in honor of Ray Chapman, the Cleveland Indians second baseman, who had died after being hit by a pitch a few days earlier.[15]

Black baseball players played the game "according to Hoyle," reported the *Birmingham News* later that season as the city hosted a convention for World War I veterans of the Rainbow Division. Urging the visitors to take in a doubleheader between the Black Barons and New Orleans, the writer said: "Don't think you will go out and see a gang of raw-boned negroes attempting to play a game of the national sport."[16] In Atlanta, the Black Crackers were accorded the traditional custom of seeing the home team's name in capital letters in league standings.[17]

Nonetheless, some white spectators expected to see a "show" at a black ball game, and there were players who were more than willing to provide it. Birmingham first baseman Mathews Taylor "kept the fans in an uproar throughout the game with his funny one-handed work around the initial sack. He's a comedian worth seeing," reported the *Birmingham News* after a doubleheader. But showman or not, Taylor played errorless ball and had two hits, one of them a triple, for his afternoon's work.[18]

In New Orleans, a film company announced plans to show up at a Negro Southern League game to film a comic movie. The producers were much taken with "buxom cook ladies whose rooting for the Caulfields has been of considerable amusement for the white fans." Years later in Atlanta, a *Daily World* writer had good news to report on the bigotry front: "Every colored fan will be glad to know that the management has responded to the request for an overhead roof under the left field bleachers. No longer may colored people approach the left field bleacher in fear of being spit upon by the men above."[19] Management of the white Atlanta Crackers obviously found black patrons' money good enough to counter that appalling indignity.

The Birmingham Black Barons trace their history to 1919, when Henry Vance or Zipp Newman, Birmingham sportswriters, used a variation of that name in reporting on a game played by Birmingham industrial league ball players against an Atlanta team. Although there were three years in the 1930s when there was no team by that name, the Birmingham Black Barons became one of the storied names in Negro leagues baseball, operating from 1919 through 1963. When the Negro American League was in its death throes in the early 1960s, the Birmingham team hung on until the end, likely winning the final pennants. I have come to think of them as the black baseball's Last Team Standing.

1

The "Bold"/"Coal"
Black Barons (1919)

On July 8, 1919, a sportswriter in the *Birmingham News*, possibly Henry Vance but more likely Zipp Newman, reported that "The Bold Black Barons from Edgewater [had] shut out the copper colored Giants from Chattanooga" on the previous afternoon.

It was the first appearance in print of the name Black Barons, a name that became synonymous with some of the greatest baseball players in the country, albeit ones who often toiled in relative obscurity. Marcel Hopson, writing about the team's 40th anniversary in 1959 in the *Birmingham World*, attributes the naming to Newman.[1]

Vance was the senior writer on the sports staff in 1919, but Newman, at the age of 25, had been named the new sports editor, the youngest in the South at the time. Emory O. Jackson, in the *World* in 1942, wrote that the "name has stood undamaged since it was carboned [*sic*] from the white Barons by the lamented Uncle Joe Rush by in the '20s."[2] Interestingly, one of Newman's personal scorebooks for white Birmingham Barons games he covered is in the Alabama Department of Archives and History. In the book, sandwiched between those Southern Association games, is a Black Barons game that Newman covered on June 7, 1920. That would be further evidence of Newman's interest in the black team.

In 1948, when the Black Barons were about to win the Negro American League pennant, Jackson reminisced about the "Original Black Barons" and other early players on the team in his "Hits and Bits" column. He again attributed the name's origin to Newman, but reported that hotel man Joe Rush "incorporated the name." Rush had taken over the club in 1923 after the original organizer, Frank M. Perdue, and his partner L.S. "Kid Wonder" Sharp had a falling out and went to court over the ownership.[3] Regardless of the specificity, it remains that the Black Barons became the home team eventually to such names as Satchel Paige, "Mule" Suttles, "Double Duty" Radcliffe, Artie Wilson, Willie Mays, and "Piper" Davis, players widely known in all baseball circles.

Although the term "Black Barons," playing off the name of the white team, was the whimsy of the sportswriter, it was a name that quickly stuck. Following that first usage, Black Barons surfaced frequently that summer, referring to at least two black Birmingham industrial league teams that played against each other as well as against outside opponents. It was widely used for the industrial league Ensley team and occasionally for Edgewater. In 1920, the name became fully connected with a single, specific team.

As the name was shared by various teams, so were the players. Some 29 names of players have been gleaned from line scores and box scores of games played in Birmingham in 1919 by "Arthur Coar's Famous Black Barons." About a dozen of them were regulars on the

Ensley roster. At least eight also played with Acipico and four with Edgewater. In addition, there was considerable uniform changing going on among other industrial league teams. Shortstop Charles "Twosides" Wesley, pitcher Sam Streeter, and catcher Poindexter Williams played for both. All three were later prominent Birmingham Black Barons. Compiled rosters suggest other players, for whom only first names are available, were also moving from team to team. Indeed, at the end of the season the team that hosted the barnstorming Chicago American Giants was alternately referred to as the Black Barons and the All-Stars in the local press. And when the 1920 season got under way, the same duality of names was applied for a time to Birmingham's entry in the new Negro Southern League.

The muddle of names for the team that became one of the best known in the Negro leagues continued throughout the 1919 season. At various times, newspaper accounts referred to the black ballplayers as Birmingham's Coal Black Barons, the Bold Black Barons, the Coal Barons and Arthur Coar's Famous Black Barons. Occasionally, it was just Black Barons as Birmingham compiled an enviable record against other strong black Southern teams such as the Chattanooga Giants, Knoxville Giants, Montgomery Grey Sox, and Atlanta Cubs.

Baseball likely came to the state of Alabama during the Civil War or the subsequent Reconstruction era. Jack Langhorne, sports editor of the *Montgomery Advertiser*, wrote an essay in 1927 reporting that local teams were organized and played intra-city games in the spring of 1867.[4] Most prewar recreation centered on the horse. After the war, horses were scarce and needed far more for work than recreation, so "baseball served to help the populace forget the horrors of the war."[5]

Southern whites and blacks alike embraced the pastime. The Southern League, formed by famous Atlanta newspaper editor Henry Grady and other white businessmen in 1885, was the first professional league in the South.[6] That was followed by a similar effort to create a league for black baseball teams. In Jacksonville, Florida, the Southern League of Colored Baseballists was established with clubs located in Jacksonville, New Orleans, Memphis, Atlanta and Savannah.[7] Although the white league struggled for 15 years with a frequently changing lineup of clubs and some seasons that were never completed, a nucleus was established. It led, in 1901, to the formation of the Southern Association, which would become a minor league mainstay for more than 60 years and provide a home ballpark for many black baseball teams.

There was no comparable success story for black baseball until 1920. The 1886 Southern League of Colored Baseballists faded quickly. There was little formal organizational effort in black baseball until the founding of the Negro National League and the Negro Southern League in 1920.

One of the earliest references to black baseball in Birmingham is found in 1908 when the *Birmingham Reporter*, the local African American weekly newspaper, published a grainy front-page picture of the Birmingham Giants, a team scheduled to play a four-game series with a Memphis team at West End Park in mid–May. Thirteen players and a man in hat and suit are in the photograph. None are identified, but the extended caption under the picture provides some additional information:

> The Giants have won six out of nine games played this season and we expect to maintain that record against Memphis.
> The Memphis team has been greatly strengthened by the addition of "Dago" Davis, the big 110-pound twirler who was as with Brooklyn last season. He will likely pitch the opening game.
> 5 per cent net gate receipts will be given to the Boy's Reformatory at Mt. Meigs, Ala.[8]

The Mt. Meigs institution, near Montgomery, coincidentally is the reform school where "Satchel" Paige was sent a few years later.[9]

The suited man in the picture is likely Charles Isham "C.I." Taylor. The following year the Birmingham Giants were hosts to the barnstorming Leland Giants, self-proclaimed "colored champions of the world." By that time Taylor had lived in Birmingham for four years. He came to Birmingham in 1904 following service during the Spanish-American War and matriculation at Clark College in Atlanta.

He played on an undefeated baseball team in college. He had three brothers, who were also baseball players. Benjamin H. "Ben" Taylor played first base with the Birmingham Giants, ABCs, and Chicago American Giants. James "Candy Jim" Taylor was a pitcher, infielder, and manager for 40 years. He started with the Birmingham Giants and later returned to the city to manage the Black Barons. Jonathan Boyce "Steel Arm" Taylor, starting with the Birmingham Giants, had a 20-year career as a pitcher, manager, and coach.[10]

When the Leland Giants came to Birmingham in 1909, it was under the leadership of Rube Foster, already a recognizable name in black baseball and one destined for legendary status. Few results from the 1909 games have been found, but the series apparently spawned a lasting friendship and rivalry between two men who became major figures in the development of black baseball nationally.

Historian James Riley wrote: "Rube and C.I. were two men who had the ability to block everything out of their minds *except* for baseball. Rube was big, boisterous and jolly; C.I. was a slim, reserved teetotaler. Both had their own trademarks of baseball discipline. At times they feuded intensely and publicly. At other times they were congenial friends. Together they worked as sunshine and rain to grow the seeds of professional Negro baseball."[11]

In his description of Taylor, he wrote: "[C]ontemporaries said that C.I. trained the players and Rube signed them. On the field, the master builder ... was a strict disciplinarian and a great teacher who brought out the best in his players. At times he would put on a show for the fans by 'clowning' in the third-base coaching box by eating grass or jumping up and down and yelling about a pitcher's fastball offerings."[12]

William "Dizzy" Dismukes, who managed the Black Barons on two occasions, knew both of the pioneers. In 1928 he wrote a remembrance of them for the *Pittsburgh Press*. He said Foster had financial backing that enabled him to pay salaries rather than per-game rewards. Taylor, in his early days, lacked those resources, but he was an astute judge of baseball talent:

> C.I. could tell almost at a glance if an individual had the making of a ball player. Once decided on, C.I. had the patience of Job in polishing a player to the highest degree of efficiency....
>
> "There are so many people who get to a place and do not consider how they go there," was one of his pet phrases. But with C.I.'s club, if it won there was a meeting and the victory discussed as to whether the game was won on the merits of the club's play or if the opposition donated the game. If the team lost—a "how did we lose?" meeting was held.[13]

Off the field, Taylor was described as a gentleman, a businessman and a civic leader. Oscar W. Adams, in his "What Negroes Are Doing" column in the *Birmingham News*, said Taylor was "an expert cotton sampler and highly respected by all the citizens of the community. He started his baseball career here and gave Birmingham its first setting for a colored baseball team."[14] Oddly, Taylor is not listed in any Birmingham city directories from 1904 to 1909.

Excited by Foster's stories about black baseball in the North, Taylor took his Giants on a road trip later in 1909. Barnstorming, the Birmingham Giants worked their way to Indianapolis for a July series with Indianapolis ABCs.[15]

The Hoosier experience was so successful that Taylor moved to West Baden, Indiana, where he managed the West Baden Sprudels for the next five years. In 1914 he bought a half interest in the ABCs and moved to Indianapolis. The ABCs drew their name from the initials of the three founding owners. Later they secured the sponsorship of the American Brewing Company, whose initials were tailor-made for the team. Although the brewery folded in 1917 as the Prohibition movement was growing, the initials stuck, and the ABCs became a major name in black baseball.[16] Under Taylor's management, the team expanded its schedule, playing the best Negro teams in the country, developing intense rivalries with such clubs as the American Giants. He also returned to the South, barnstorming, spreading the gospel of black baseball among an appreciative audience. Birmingham was often on the ABCs' itinerary.

He died in 1922 at the age of 46. His widow Olivia and brother Ben took over the club.[17] The year after his death, a memorial game was played between Foster's American Giants and the ABCs to raise funds "for the erection of a national monument" in Taylor's memory. The ABCs won the July 26 game, 7–1, in Indianapolis. Other league teams were asked to play similar fund-raising contests during the season for the monument.[18]

If C.I. Taylor found regular black baseball financially untenable in Birmingham in 1908, it had apparently become occasionally profitable by March of 1915. The *Birmingham Reporter* noted that Taylor, who continued to winter in Birmingham, was bringing the ABCs to the South for spring training.[19] Games were scheduled in March at Delta View Park against the Talladega College team. "These are twelve of the best colored players ever gotten together, and baseball fans of Birmingham will miss the opportunity of their lives if they do see them in action," exhorted the *Reporter*.

Talladega was shut out twice, 10–0 and 7–0.[20] In April, the newspaper reported that Indianapolis had pounded Montgomery, 15–3, in the final game of another series at the park.[21] There was no mention in the newspaper of the Birmingham Giants or any other club representing the city. Community and factory teams exemplified the status of black baseball in Birmingham until after World War I.

The following spring a three-column advertisement appeared in the *Reporter*, announcing that the ABCs would play a three-game series with the Montgomery Grey Sox, described as "the colored champions of the South," at Tidewater Park in Birmingham.[22] Warming up, the ABCs defeated Birmingham Industrial High School, 13–3.[23] (An author's observation here on the spelling of the Montgomery team's mascot. Gray Sox, which was used in the 1916 coverage, was replaced by a more consistent Grey Sox in later years. For the sake of narrative consistency, the author has Grey Sox throughout the book except for the 1916 references.)

In 1919, Alabama and the nation were rebounding from World War I, and the devastating Spanish Influenza pandemic that had killed millions worldwide. Baseball, which had been played only sporadically during the war—the white Southern Association played an abbreviated 70-game schedule in 1918—was also recovering. Industrial Birmingham had not only the Birmingham Barons, local college, high school, and town teams, but also a strong contingent of factory and mine teams, representing corporations, particularly those in the iron and steel industry. Paralleling the white industrial league was a black league featuring teams such as Westfield, the Edgewater Cubs, Ensley T.C.I. Giants, Acipco Stars, and Bessemer Williams All-Stars.[24] The Black Barons appear to have been based in Ensley, but drew players from all of the black industrial league teams when playing out-of-town opponents. The 1919 industrial league teams featured a number of players who became Black Barons when owner Frank Perdue placed his team in the fledgling Negro Southern League in 1920.

As noted above, it is impossible to place a precise organizational structure of the Black Barons in 1919. The black industrial teams played numerous games among themselves and with occasional outside teams. There was no mention of the Black Barons until July, when the Atlanta Cubs came for a series with "Birmingham's Coal Black Barons." It was reported that both Edgewater and Acipco would play games with the visitors with no explanation of which might be the Black Barons.

On July 7, the Chattanooga Giants came to Birmingham and the *Birmingham News* reported the contest as a 5–0 shutout for "Big Boothe," who scattered the visitors' seven hits. Support for Pickens, the Chattanooga pitcher, was termed "of the loose variety," but the reporter, again probably Henry Vance, was complimentary of the fielding in general: "C. Norman, at short for the visitors, and Twosides of the local aggregation, at second, nabbed two fly balls in a sensational acrobatic manner, while Sellers made a running one-hand catch that was headed in the direction of deep right for three bags."[25]

Later, the *News* reported on the impending series with the Atlanta Cubs, "the champion negro team of the South" and "the greatest negro aggregation in the country." The series would determine the Southern championship. The glowing report on the Atlanta team said the Cubs had been on a road trip, "trimming the Eastern and Northern teams with ease." Indeed, the Atlanta team offered a $500 purse to any team that could beat them two out of three and $1,500 to the team that could take all three games in a series. A special section of the grandstand was being set aside for white patrons amidst an anticipated "largest crowd of negro spectators that ever witnessed a game at Rickwood."[26]

As the series neared, the hype increased:

> Every negro fan in Birmingham is planning to be present…. Tickets for the battle were placed on sale early this week and the demand for them has been astounding. It will be recalled that the negroes of Birmingham are liberal patrons of the Barons and when negro teams get together there is no holding them.
> A crowd that will tax the capacity of the stands is expected to witness the struggle….[27]

While there was no clarification on just who the Black Barons might be, there was some on the process. Edgewood and Acipco would each play Atlanta once. The Birmingham team scoring the most runs would play the rubber game for a shot at the purse. Edgewater got the first assignment and found it a day of frustration as a pitcher named Smith threw a two-hit shutout for the visitors. Henry Vance's colorful, albeit racist, lead read: "The Coal Black Barons, possessing a sprinkling of high yellows on the team, hung-up nine consecutive doughnuts Monday afternoon while their opponents, the Atlanta Cubs, registered a couple of tallies and won the ball game."[28] Acipco was scheduled to play the second game against the Georgia visitors and perhaps that happened, but the game report referred to the team only as the Black Barons, and the lineup in the box score was practically identical to the one in the first game.

The Black Barons scored in the second game, but the Cubs won 5–2. Vance, again warming to his subject, wrote: "The Coal Black Barons have just about as bright a future as their name implies…." The Atlanta pitcher was "Wing" Maddox, a one-armed wonder who played outfield when not on the mound. Maddox, who would later play for Birmingham and several other teams, "proved beyond the question of doubt that he had a vast assortment of stuff packed away in his good right arm." One bright spot for the locals was the attendance. Some 5,000 fans, including a smattering of whites, witnessed the contest, "one of the best crowds attending a ball game at Rickwood since the opening of the season."[29] The white Barons, who finished the 1919 Southern Association season in seventh place with a dismal 59–77 record, were likely not filling the stadium seats.[30]

Finally, on the third day Birmingham was victorious. With Sam Streeter pitching, they won, 3–0.[31] The series ended with a double-header on July 24. "Ensley" won the opener, 5–2, then dropped the nightcap, 3–2. Sol DeJarnette hurled both games for Birmingham.[32]

DeJarnette pitched a masterful game in August when Birmingham beat the Knoxville Giants, 3–2, in a pitchers' duel with John "Steel Arm" Dickey, who struck out 15 Black Barons. Like Wing Maddox, Dickey, too, eventually wore a Birmingham uniform.[33]

As the Labor Day holiday approached, the growing interest in black baseball reached a high level. Coming to town for a double-header was Montgomery for a series billed as the state championship. The Grey Sox were reported to "have made a cleaning of all the teams around the Capital City and are known as the Black Belt Champions." A single game was scheduled the following day. "That is if a third game is necessary," reported the *News*. "Local negro fans allow that a third game won't be necessary as the Black Barons are going to cop. However, there is a difference of opinion in Montgomery...."[34] A railroad excursion was expected to bring as many as 500 Montgomery fans to Birmingham. Anticipating "a monster crowd," officials said "a big reservation of seats" had been set aside for white patrons. The projection was for 6,000 spectators.[35]

The guess was nowhere near reality. Birmingham swept the double-header, 6–2 and 5–2, before a crowd estimated at 12,000, of whom some 1,500 were white. The reporter said it was probably the largest crowd that ever saw "a negro game anywhere."[36]

Birmingham had picked up Smith, the hard-throwing Atlanta pitcher, and he beat Montgomery, 8–1, in the third game. It was reported after the game that Rube Foster's Chicago Giants were coming to Birmingham later in the month for a series.[37] Meanwhile Acipico demanded another crack at the "Black Barons" and got it. Acipico took a double-header, 6–2 and 3–0, before 6,000 fans, "the largest Monday crowd seen at Rickwood this year." Umpire for the games was Carlton Molesworth, manager of the Birmingham Barons.[38]

The Chicago series was scheduled for September 16–18. Birmingham Barons catcher John Peters predicted good baseball for local fans: "I have seen the Chicago Giants play every season, and take it from me, they can beat about half of the teams in the Southern League [*sic*]. Why, they even give the major league clubs a close battle. Rube Foster, the star pitcher of the team, is one of the best pitchers I ever saw." Peters's boss, Molesworth, had a positive comment about the local players, describing the Black Barons' unidentified catcher, likely either Poindexter Williams or John Cason, as "the best negro backstop he ever saw."[39]

In the two games reported, the visitors won, 8–6 and 5–0.[40] That was expected to be the end of the 1919 season, but a final series was arranged with Atlanta in late September. For the Black Barons it was a chance to make up for the poor showing in July, and they took advantage of the opportunity. Behind the pitching of Smith, formerly with Atlanta, and Gordon Zeigler, the Black Barons ended their season with three straight wins.[41]

In the spring of 1920 a newspaper story reported that the "Black Barons" had won 46 out of 54 games in 1919 with three of the eight losses coming from Chicago. While the figures are questionable, there is no doubt that by the end of the season the name Black Barons was a readily identifiable pairing of Birmingham's black community and baseball.[42]

While the industrial teams continued to draw well in their own right, a special fan base was being established for the evolving amalgam. Industrial league games had drawn 4,000 and 5,000 fans. The first game at Rickwood Field between black teams that year drew 3,000 for a June 11 contest between Acipco and Edgewater. It was a charity event for the benefit of "the Old Folks and Orphans Home."[43]

Those kinds of numbers led to the speculation that the Labor Day games with the Montgomery Grey Sox would pull as many as 6,000 spectators. No one was prepared for the 12,000 who showed up, a number so staggering that it had taken on hormonal growth within months: "Birmingham holds the record for the greatest crowd that ever witnessed a baseball game in the South. The record of 15,000 beats the attendance record of the Southern League held by Atlanta with something like 14,000 paid admissions. This record was made last year when the Coal Barons played the Montgomery Grey Sox a doubleheader on July 4th [sic] at Rickwood Field."[44] As late as 1923, the crowd was placed at 14,038, "which was the record for white or black in the South until 15,064 paid to see the Crackers and Lookouts over in Atlanta this year."[45] Regardless, it was evident that black baseball had a following in Birmingham.

2

The Negro Southern League (1920–22)

1920

The large crowds of African Americans who turned out to support the "Black Barons" in 1919 were going to receive a special treat that would further their baseball enthusiasm in 1920.

The impetus was germinated in February 1920 in Kansas City. A group of black baseball men, owners of ball clubs and successful businessmen, gathered at the Paseo YMCA at the behest of Rube Foster, generally recognized as the father of black league baseball.[1]

Foster, Frank Leland, C.I. Taylor, and others who loved the game, laid the foundation at the meeting for the formation of the Negro National League. It would become the dominant black baseball organization for decades, providing a competitive format for team owners and players.[2]

That fledgling organization was centered in the Midwest, but within weeks it was joined by the Negro Southern League. Three years later, the Eastern Colored League was formed.[3]

"For the first time in the history of the national pastime the colored people are attempting organized baseball, and its success is largely assured by the number of representative men behind the movement," reported Louis R. Lautier in the *Atlanta Independent* of the NSL formation.[4]

Attending the organizational meeting in Atlanta were Frank M. Perdue and L.L. Barber of Birmingham.[5] The city became a member of the Negro Southern League for nine of the league's twenty scattered years of operation, winning three championships. In 1923 the Black Barons were so dominant that the league essentially folded at the halfway point for lack of competition.[6]

Taking advantage of the ballparks available in white Southern Association cities, the 1920 NSL located six of its eight teams in those sites. Normally, the black clubs would play on the dates that the white clubs were on the road. It was from this arrangement that the late Chris Fullerton, first executive director of the Friends of Rickwood Field, drew the title for his book on the Black Barons, *Every Other Sunday*.

Baseball was the national pastime, prompting scholar Jacques Barzun's often-quoted line, "Whoever wants to know the heart and mind of America had better learn baseball." Baseball games, white and black, drew crowds. Negro teams gained access to nice facilities and white ballpark owners picked up revenue on days when their teams were out of town.

Providing white seating became commonplace. "The seating capacity is being greatly enlarged to accommodate white persons," the *Montgomery Advertiser* reported.[7] In Atlanta, it was noted, "Special seats are being prepared for the white fans who attend."[8] In Knoxville, on one occasion, half of the fans were believed to be white.[9]

Perdue was elected president of the NSL. Other officers were R.H. Tabor, Nashville, vice president; Prof. W.M. Brooks, Knoxville, secretary; and W.J. Shaw, Atlanta, treasurer. The entry fee for franchises was set at $200 with an additional $25 assessment for league promotion. Committees were formed to draft the constitution and by-laws. An Atlanta sporting goods dealer, obviously sensing a business opportunity, urged the league to adopt the A.G. Spalding baseball as the official league baseball and promised to sponsor a trophy to the winning club.[10]

C.I. Taylor was an interested observer and supporter. The *Chicago Defender* wrote that Taylor was "a deeply interested participant in the final arrangements, and his words of wisdom went a long ways towards encouraging options on franchises."[11]

Opening Day was April 29 with eight clubs, six of them in Southern Association cities. In addition to Birmingham, there were the Atlanta Black Crackers, Jacksonville Stars, Knoxville Giants, Montgomery Grey Sox, Nashville White Sox, New Orleans Caulfield Ads, and Pensacola Giants.

Although no winners were reported, President Perdue announced that, like its white counterpart, the NSL would present trophies for the best attendance on opening day. The clubs were divided into two divisions. The larger city division grouped Birmingham with Atlanta, Nashville, and New Orleans; the smaller city division was Jacksonville, Knoxville, Montgomery, and Pensacola.[12] Opening Day was a major event in the black communities of all cities. The mayor of Pensacola threw out the ceremonial first pitch, and owner A.J. Kerr promised a wool sweater to the first Giant hitting a home run.[13] Crowds of 1,200 in Montgomery and "nearly 5,000" in Birmingham were reported.[14] In Atlanta, "all wounded soldiers, white and colored," were admitted free.[15]

Birmingham opened on the road at Montgomery. The Grey Sox won, 7–2, at Southside Park. Both lineups were dotted with familiar Birmingham industrial league names. The winning pitcher was Sam Streeter, the former Edgewater/Ensley/Black Barons pitcher of 1919. The losing battery was former Acipco hurler Gordon Zeigler and catcher John Cason. Juanelo Mirabel pitched Birmingham to a high-scoring 15–8 win in second game. Harry Salmon lost, 6–3, in a seven-inning third game, shortened by rain.[16]

The first home game was on May 3. Some local media continued to use the name All-Stars, although the *Birmingham News* was more often going with "Coal Barons," even "Coal Black Barons." In the *Birmingham Reporter* it was generally All-Stars. Curiously, the *Reporter*, its columns filled with civic, social, and church news, ignored the team until late May. There had been coverage of C.I. Taylor's ABCs having spring training in Birmingham, but there was virtually no mention of the Black Barons until May 29, nearly a month into the season. Nor did Oscar W. Adams mention the team in his Sunday "What Negroes Are Doing" column in the *Birmingham News*.

Interestingly, the *News* used Black Barons in the headline and All-Stars in the report on the first home game. However, by the end of the season, it was usually Black Barons. Name confusion was not limited to the local team. One Birmingham newspaper called the New Orleans team the Browns rather than Caulfield Ads the entire series.

On Opening Day, May 3, the Birmingham lineup represented a cross-section of 1919 industrial league teams. Among the players were Buford "Geechie" Meredith (Acipco), ss;

John Kemp (Acipco), rf; Charles "Twosides" Wesley (Edgewater), rf; Miles (Ensley), 2b; and B. Rosella (Ensley), cf.

Although there was obviously enormous interest in the team in the black community, there was no information on what pregame activities and promotions were planned for Opening Day that first season. The *Birmingham News* wrote simply, "A big crowd of negro fans is expected to take in the opening game. Last year the Black Barons drew out the largest crowd that witnessed a game in Birmingham."[17] There was no report on attendance the following day, the figure of 5,000 coming from a New Orleans paper a few weeks later. In future years, Opening Day would be a major event in the black community, featuring an array of dignitaries, parades, and other activities.

Whatever the crowd, Birmingham's first home game was a disappointment. New Orleans took a 3–0 lead and held on to win, 5–3. "Chief" Lewis, a 45-year-old right fielder, drove in two runs with a single. Meredith with three hits and Wesley with a triple were the hitting stars for Birmingham.[18] Forrest "One Wing" Maddox, the one-armed pitcher-outfielder, was on the Birmingham roster but did not play.

Birmingham won the second game, 12–11, with a ninth-inning rally the next day. The game was almost called before it got that far, though. New Orleans, objecting to an umpire's call, pulled the players off the field and started packing up its equipment in the top of the eighth inning. The dispute was resolved and play resumed. The winning run came when Willie Dozier reached second on a muffed bunt. The first baseman then threw wild to home and Dozier scored the winning run, having circled the bases on a bunt.[19]

Maddox was scheduled to pitch on Wednesday. "Wing, the one-arm wonder of the All-Stars ... uses no glove and has as much speed and control as any of his teammates. It will be worth the price of admission to see this marvel work," reported the *News*. The double-header was rained out.

It is unlikely that Maddox ever appeared in a Birmingham uniform in 1920. He started the season in Atlanta and shut out Knoxville, 1–0. By late May he was with Knoxville, where he joined John "Steel Arm" Dickey, the league's premier pitcher in its inaugural season.[20] When Knoxville came to Birmingham in late June, there was no mention of him having played with the Black Barons earlier.[21] He did eventually appear in a few games with Birmingham in 1923. He never advanced beyond the NSL, dying in 1929 of tuberculosis at the age of 30.[22]

After the New Orleans games, the Black Barons disappeared for a week. There was no report on the team until it went to Nashville in mid–May, losing two of three games there. The two teams then came to Birmingham for a series.[23]

The homecoming was not a completely happy occasion, though. The first game was rained out. Then, despite a nine-strikeout performance by Zeigler, Nashville won the second, 6–4. Zeigler gave up only four hits and one walk, but Birmingham fielders committed four errors.[24] Birmingham won the third game on Salmon's 1–0 shutout, scoring the winning run in the ninth.[25]

After a series in New Orleans, Birmingham returned home against Pensacola. The Black Barons, as they were now increasingly called, stole eight bases in the 7–6 opening win. Zeigler pitched a three-hitter in the second game and Bob McCormick hit a home run, the first ever reported for a Black Baron in a league game at Rickwood.[26]

Entering the New Orleans series, Birmingham (6–5) was reported to be in fifth place. Montgomery (10–2) and Knoxville (11–4) were the frontrunners. The standings from the *Atlanta Constitution* are not mathematically correct, with totals of 64 wins and 62 losses.[27]

State of Georgia death certificate for Forest "Wing" Maddox, who died of tuberculosis at just 30 years old.

In early June, Gordon Zeigler and "Steel Arm" Dickey faced off in an extraordinary game. After 12 innings, both pitchers deserved Dickey's nickname as both went the distance. Dickey, who struck out 10, won the marathon, 2–1.[28]

Well, maybe. That was according to the *Birmingham News.*

Neither the *Knoxville Sentinel* nor the *Knoxville Journal* reported the game the same way. They listed the same two pitchers but reported the score as 4–0 in a regular, nine-inning game.[29] There is no plausible explanation for these discrepancies, and a similar reporting anomaly occurred in July, again over another pitching duel between Zeigler and Dickey.

However, there is no such uncertainty over Zeigler's pitching when Birmingham opened a home series with league-leading Montgomery. Zeigler and Sam Streeter wowed 3,500 fans at Rickwood with a 17-inning pitching battle. Birmingham won, 3–2, on an error, a hit, a walk, and a pinch-hit single by Salmon, who was scheduled to relieve Zeigler in the 18th inning. Streeter gave up 12 hits and walked two while Zeigler surrendered nine hits and three walks. Each struck out 12.[30] Streeter earlier in the season had thrown 20 consecutive strikes in a game against the barnstorming Chicago Black Sox.[31] A native of New Market, Alabama, Streeter played professionally for nearly two decades.[32]

The following day, Mirabal won, 10–0, holding the Grey Sox to just three hits. Kemp had three hits for Birmingham while Meredith, Wesley, and Matthew Taylor each had two. Meredith, the leadoff man, scored three times and was developing into an outstanding infielder. Better known by his nickname "Geechie," his play drew the following from one writer: "Shortstop Geecher [*sic*] played a nifty game for the local team. He fielded in faultless style and if there's a better shortstop in the league … he hasn't shown up at Rickwood this season."[33]

Meredith extended his reputation in the final game of the series, making "two circus catches in the last half of the ninth" to preserve a 2–1 lead and Birmingham's sweep of the first-place team. With the potential tying run on second, a Montgomery batter hit a short Texas leaguer into the left-center field. "Geechee [*sic*] ran back, turned a pair of somersaults and came up with the ball in his glove. He repeated the gymnastics when Patton hit a similar ball."[34]

Saul "Rareback" Davis, left, and Buford "Geechie" Meredith. An outstanding infielder, Meredith played with the Black Barons for 11 years. He was killed in a mining accident before the 1932 season (courtesy Gloria Meredith Maffett, Marvin "Tip" Maffett, and Derrick L. Maffett, Sr.).

Meredith was a fixture in black Birmingham baseball for more than a dozen years. Except for one year each in Memphis and Nashville, he was with the Black Barons every year until his untimely death in a mining accident in 1932. Meredith, of all of the Birmingham residents who played with the Black Barons, was the only one listed in the city directories as "ball player." All of the others were identified by their regular jobs. For example, Frank Perdue was a laborer and Elijah Juran was a miner.[35]

Despite those spectacular performances and good crowds, which the *Birmingham News* reported at 3,000 to 5,000 fans per game, Manager Perdue was not pleased with his team's overall performance. When he brought them home to face Montgomery, there were a lot of new faces and also a new language. He had signed several Cubans to make the Black Barons more competitive.[36] The players were from a barnstorming team called the Cuban Giants.[37]

Box scores soon listed Jiminez, Cardenas, Montalvo, Perez, and Rodriguez as well as pitcher Juanelo (Mirabel). Rodriguez, often called Roderiz in box scores and game accounts, was a strong addition to the pitching staff. But the new players were not able to stop the onslaught of the Knoxville Giants. They came into Rickwood and took three straight, two

The State of Alabama death certificate for Buford "Geechie" Meredith, a great Birmingham infielder who was electrocuted in a mining job accident.

of them on shutouts.[38] Other losses followed, but Zeigler continued to be a strong pitcher. On July 6, again at Knoxville, he lost a reported 16-inning duel with Bud Force, giving up only eight hits.[39] And again, the game accounts in the Knoxville newspapers reported just a nine-inning game.[40]

That Knoxville series opened with an 8–0 Birmingham win behind the two-hit pitching of Mirabel. The Black Barons seemed to play Knoxville better in Tennessee than in Alabama, also getting a win from Rodriguez.[41] Knoxville won a game on the hitting of "Wing" Maddox, who had two singles and a double in four at bats.[42] The winning pitcher was "Bun" Moore, a left-hander who won fifteen straight games in June and July.[43]

His teammate "Steel Arm" Dickey had a phenomenal string of 25 straight victories during the season, although some of them obviously were against semipro and town teams. His string was finally stopped on July 29, appropriately by Montgomery.[44]

The Montgomery–Knoxville rivalry was hard fought all season. Knoxville newspapers accused Montgomery players of frequent "beefing" over umpiring. Twice in Knoxville, Montgomery left the field in protest.[45] "This thing of leaving the field in protest to decisions has become the favorite outdoor sport of the Alabama leagues. When they are not playing baseball they are protesting decisions and the strange part of it is that they get away with that sort of stuff in Knoxville," reported the *Journal and Tribune*.[46]

Birmingham hovered around .500, finishing in fourth place. There were fine performances along the way. Harry Salmon, Gordon Zeigler, and Conrado "Red" Rodriguez pitched consecutive shutouts against Nashville. Salmon had three hits in his win.[47] Rodriguez threw a seven-hitter against Montgomery, only to lose 2–1 in the 13th inning. The following day he was called to the mound again, losing 1–0 as Streeter held the Black Barons to a single hit.[48] In a Labor Day morning–afternoon double-header, Rodriguez pitched both games, beating Montgomery, 5–2 and 3–0.[49] In a 5–1 win at New Orleans, centerfielder Rosella "raced into left field and with his back to the ball pulled down with one hand what would have been a three-base drive."[50]

Although many of the white patrons went to see good baseball, there was also an element that found the behavior of some Negro ball players comical. After one game it was reported Matthews Taylor, the Birmingham first baseman, "kept the fans in an uproar throughout the game with his funny one handed work around the initial sack. He's a comedian worth seeing."[51]

The pennant race was largely between Montgomery and Knoxville. There was a lot of squabbling over won-lost records and the place of forfeits in the standings. One set of standings showed Knoxville (55–21) clearly the pennant winner over Montgomery (47–39).[52] A few days later, another set had Montgomery (48–40) the winner over Knoxville (34–30).[53] Neither set was mathematically provable. Birmingham's record was 43–39 in both.

When Montgomery went to Knoxville in late August for a three-game series, it was reported that the clubs were in a battle for first place. However, "The league is so jumbled and accurate reports are so difficult to obtain that it cannot be said which team is leading at present, although it is known that the clubs are not separated by a wide margin."[54]

It was later announced that Knoxville and Montgomery would play a new thirteen-game series to settle the pennant. The winner of this extended series would then play the NNL winner "in a world's championship series."[55]

The thirteen-game series never materialized, and on September 6, Knoxville newspapers declared the Giants as champions. A club representative was reported en route to Chicago to arrange the "world" championship series.[56]

The Chicago American Giants won all three games from Knoxville, then played two games each with Montgomery and Birmingham, winning those as well. The day after Chicago won the second Montgomery game, the *Knoxville Sentinel* reported that League President Frank Perdue had declared Montgomery the pennant-winner, apparently drawing previously mentioned forfeits into the picture.[57]

Based on 40 published box scores, Birmingham's leading hitters were left fielder John Kemp (.284), first baseman Mathews Taylor (.273), and shortstop Buford "Geechie" Meredith (.248). Black Barons hit a total of 34 extra base hits, but only one home run, the blast by Bob McCormick on May 28. Mirabal (7–4) was the leading pitcher. Recording five wins each were Rodriguez, Salmon, and Zeigler.[58]

Combing the box scores with an additional 37 line scores, one gets a broader picture of Birmingham pitchers. Rodriguez was 12–3, throwing four shutouts. In July he pitched 35 consecutive scoreless innings. After 1920 he returned to barnstorming teams. A native of Tampa, Mirabel played with a number of Cuban-connected teams over the years. He was just 19 years old when he joined the Black Barons, compiling a 10–6 record with three shutouts.[59] Salmon (5–6) and Zeigler (7–10) were both better pitchers than their records reflected. Zeigler struck out 69 batters in 88 innings and had three shutouts.

Despite the fourth-place finish, Birmingham's first venture into league ball was an unqualified success. There was a strong fan base, drawing 3,000 to 5,000 spectators for every game. In July, when the Rainbow Division of World War I veterans held its reunion in Birmingham, the visitors were urged to take advantage of a Black Barons home game: "Don't think you will go out and see a gang of raw-boned negroes attempting to play a game of the national sport. They play it according to Hoyle."[60]

The season ended on Labor Day with Rodriguez's double-header wins over the pennant-winning Grey Sox, a satisfactory conclusion to the Black Barons' first professional season.[61]

1921

Buoyed by the successes of the 1920 season, the Negro Southern League sent 10 teams to the field for 1921. Back for another year were Birmingham, Knoxville, Montgomery, and New Orleans. Gone were Atlanta, Jacksonville, Nashville, and Pensacola. New teams were the Bessemer Stars, Chattanooga Tigers, Gadsden Tigers, Memphis Red Sox, Mobile Braves, and Nashville Elite Giants.

Memphis would become Birmingham's oldest and most continuous rival. Nashville also became a strong presence in Negro league baseball.

With a fourth-place finish in 1920, the Birmingham Black Barons had shown they could compete with the best professional teams in the South.

But before spring training even started, the team faced a major threat to their season. A delegation of white women approached the Birmingham City Commission in February to protest the team's playing at Rickwood Field. Presenting a petition signed by approximately 75 residents of the area adjacent of the ballpark and the street car line serving it, the women said they were fearful of the crowds attending the games. "These games are always played in the afternoon when the men are away from home, and the ladies and children have absolutely no protection and are forced to contend with them [baseball fans]. They are boisterous, disrespectful, scrapping among themselves, loitering, and lounging on the sidewalks monopolizing the entire street," read the petition.[62] The council, perhaps responding to the obvious economic boost from the games, took no action on the women's request.

In the off-season Manager Frank Perdue had picked up two of the better starting pitchers from the previous year, Forest "Wing" Maddox and John "Steel Arm" Dickey. His opening day lineup included veterans and newcomers for whom no first names were found:

Will Holt, rf-cf	Bob McCormick, ss
J.H. Russell, ss	Harry Salmon, rf
Grimes, c	Gray, 1b
Smith, cf-2b	"One Wing" Maddox, lf
Geechie Meredith, 3b	John "Steel Arm" Dickey, p[63]

Grimes, who finished the season with Atlanta, was replaced at catcher by Larry Brown. A Pratt City native, Brown, then just 17, had played with amalgamated Black Barons in 1919, launching a career of more than thirty years. Although he played with a number of clubs, including Indianapolis and Chicago, he is mostly associated with Memphis, sometimes as manager.[64]

Historian James Riley rates him as one of the great Negro leagues catchers: "An outstanding receiver with a quick release and an arm to be envied, Larry Brown was a master behind the plate. In the field, whether smothering dirt balls or handling pop flies, he was tops but was noted for the peculiar practice of not removing his catcher's mask on pop-ups." He played in three championship series and in six East-West All-Star games during his career.[65] Obituaries erroneously called him a former Black Barons manager.[66] He was only with Birmingham in 1921, apparently signing with Indianapolis after the local team folded in August.

Despite a slow start—losing two and tying one at Montgomery—the Black Barons were contenders early on.

Their home opener was against the defending champions. Two singles and an error gave Montgomery an early run. After that, Dickey allowed just four hits, winning 8–1, striking out four. Holt was the hitting star with three doubles and a single and "came within a hair's breadth of beating the throw on a grounder on his last appearance at the plate."

Maddox, the one-armed pitcher-outfielder, started in left field and had two hits. It was his only appearance with Birmingham at Rickwood that year. By late May he was back in Knoxville. Meredith handled six chances without an error at second base. For Montgomery, future Hall-of-Famer Norman "Turkey" Stearnes made "two nice throws to the plate."[67]

Birmingham won the second game, 7–1, behind the five-hit pitching of Rudolph, an otherwise unidentified player. This is likely Rudolph Ash, a right-hander with Pensacola in 1920. He was listed as Rudolph in every box score the previous season. McCormick at shortstop handled nine of 10 chances perfectly. The afternoon was enlivened by a disagreement between Birmingham left fielder Smith and Montgomery third baseman George Scales. "It took two umpires and four players to keep the belligerents off each other and both were ejected from the battle. Meredith and Montgomery's Marion Cunningham "were both spiked during the course of the game, but neither seriously enough to stop playing."[68]

Birmingham extended its winning streak to three in a row, defeating New Orleans, 5–3, the next day. Harry "Fish" Salmon was the winning pitcher, but the highlight was the fielding of the Ads' Percy Wilson. "He saved his mates at least five wild throws and many runs by his acrobatic and leaping stunts, while he was the pivot on two fast double plays."[69]

New Orleans ended Birmingham's excellent start, 10–5, getting 12 hits off of Juanelo Mirabel and Dickey.[70]

Despite a poor start, Mirabel was a good pitcher. His career spanned at least 14 years with various teams. He had "a three-quarters overhand delivery, excellent control, a sinking fastball and a baffling curve."[71] A few days later the Cuban right-hander carried a no-hitter in Memphis into the ninth inning before giving up a hit. Birmingham won, 4–0.[72]

A month into the season, the leaders were Montgomery (18–7), Birmingham (16–8), Chattanooga (11–9), and New Orleans (11–10). Among the new teams, Mobile (9–12) was the best. Gadsden (5–15) and Bessemer (5–17) were struggling. Last was Knoxville (3–18), the 1920 runner-up. The standings were not mathematically balanced, with totals of 93 wins and 122 losses.[73]

Obviously ten teams diluted the talent. Gadsden lasted barely a month before folding. W.J. Shaw's Atlanta team came in to fill the slot. The Black Crackers had started the season in the new Negro Southeastern League, where they totally dominated play.[74] Both Bessemer and Mobile had dropped out by August. A Mobile player, identified only as center fielder Hill, was a notable power hitter, hitting several home runs while the Braves were in the league.[75] Bessemer had a good pitcher in Moss, who threw a one-hitter against Nashville and shut out New Orleans.[76]

"Steel Arm" Dickey, the best pitcher in the league in 1920, was the early mainstay for Birmingham in 1921 and later one of the tragic figures of black baseball. In 1923, he was stabbed to death, reportedly while trying to break up a fight in Etowah, Tennessee.[77]

After his excellent Opening Day start, Dickey continued to pitch well. In mid–May he threw a one-hitter against Knoxville, striking out eight and walking one. The shutout came just a few days after a rare bad game. The *Birmingham News* reported the bad outing as an anomaly: "Dickey showed the world he is right once more and supporters who had worried because of his poor showing last week can cease their sighs. The huge portsider was never in better form. His dazzling fast one had the opponents stepping into the bucket, and every time they got set for a fast one, he would dish up a slow curve and another strike would be registered. His repertoire of stuff was bewildering and he certainly exhibited the reason he won 25 games in a row last year."[78]

But Birmingham could not keep him. He jumped to Mobile briefly and then settled in with Montgomery, leading the Grey Sox in their battle with Nashville for the pennant. The seeming indifference of coaches and athletes to contractual agreements was not uncommon in the Negro leagues. When NSL directors met in Montgomery in June the following year, one of the concerns was talent raids by the Negro National League: "A report coming from several managers as to the way the major league clubs were sending scouts this way, and in several cases, trying to induce players signed by the Southern league to jump contracts for a few dollars more was read...." The league secretary was instructed to contact NNL President Rube Foster with a formal protest and a request for fair play in the matter of contracts.[79]

There was occasional dissatisfaction with officials on the field, too. In May, Birmingham lost, 5–4, in Mobile and a reporter wrote: "The game was a slowly played one, being held up every few minutes by the bad decisions of the umpires. The Black Barons played a stellar game all the way through, but failed to score several times on account of bad decisions at the plate."[80]

After a time on the road, the Black Barons returned home in early June for a series with Atlanta. Birmingham was still playing well despite a rash of injuries, notably outfielder Smith, sidelined with arm troubles.

Dickey was expected to open the Atlanta series, but he had pitched his final game with Birmingham. One Birmingham sportswriter tried to put a positive spin on the loss: "This may seem, at first thought, a terrible blow, for the big lefthander has a wide reputation and is undoubtedly of the highest caliber. At the same time, pitchers are not the principal need of the local team at present."[81] Birmingham still had three capable right-handed starters—Salmon, Mirabel, and Ash. The writer called the loss of Smith, cleanup hitter and a good fielder, a bigger loss for Birmingham. The team had a capable infield but uneven outfield.

Birmingham played as a contender well into July, then hit a losing streak that dropped them under .500. They finished the month in last place with a 29–41 record.[82]

When league-leading Montgomery came to Rickwood for a series, the lineup had changed again in search of a consistent winning combination: "McCormick on second is the same old steady workhorse that he is at any position. Russell on short has proven a sensation, while curiously enough, he was only a fair to middling third sacker, and Meredith is taking care of third in good shape, though he would make fewer bobbles if he would throw quicker. He stops to sight, sets himself and takes careful aim before he throws and the result is disastrous sometimes. If he would scoop 'em up and throw with same motion he would not have time to think of making a poor throw and consequently wouldn't."[83]

Catcher Francesco Cardenas, a good hitter, had been moved to the outfield. Brown was behind the plate and the pitching staff now was centered around Harry Salmon, Pickens (no first name), and the Juran brothers, John and Eli.[84]

The highlight of the season came on July 26 when John Juran became the first Black Baron to throw a no-hitter in league play. Beating Atlanta 4–0, he struck out three, walked one and hit two opposing batters. Only one man reached third, and that was because of two successive throwing errors. In the first inning, all three Atlanta batters popped out to Brown.[85]

Shortly after that, the season appeared to disintegrate.

In early August, Montgomery swept all four games of a home-and-homes series. Birmingham was then to play Nashville, but the game was inexplicably canceled and no more was heard of the team until September. The last reported game was a 2–0 loss at Montgomery on August 7.[86] On August 21, the *Montgomery Advertiser* reported that Brown, Salmon, and J.H. Russell were all now with the Grey Sox.[87]

Birmingham was plagued with injuries in 1921. Meredith was out "with a badly sprained ankle" in May.[88] Smith, the cleanup hitter, was lost to arm trouble about the same time.[89] Will Holt, the capable outfielder, broke his leg in mid–June and was lost for most of the season.[90]

The Black Barons, "almost tied in the race," resurfaced for a Labor Day double-header with Nashville. A special train bringing fans from Nashville was expected to boost attendance.[91] There was no logical explanation for how Birmingham, last at 29–41 at the end of July, could possibly be in fourth place with a 61–56 record in September.[92] If the games were played, they went unreported.

Still, there were some seasonal highlights. Holt, despite missing much of the season, led the league with a .387 batting average. First baseman Gray hit .338 and stole 21 bases. Salmon (8–4) was the top pitcher, followed by Ash (7–5) and Mirabel (6–2).

Just as in 1920, the pennant winner was a matter of conjecture. The *Montgomery Advertiser* reported that the Grey Sox had won the pennant for the second year in a row with a final record of 80–32–3.[93] However, standings published in Nashville in mid–September had the Elite Giants (72–46) as the pennant winners and Montgomery (69–50) second. Montgomery was going to Nashville for a five-game series to decide the championship.[94] The Grey Sox manager had offered "a new $20 bill" to each player if they could take the series.[95] It was a useless offer, as Nashville won four straight games. The *Banner* declared the Elite Giants as Negro Southern League champions, and it would be hard to argue otherwise. They won the four games with strong pitching performances by four different pitchers: "Bullet" Cooper, "Kid" Billings, Lawrence Graves, and Eddie Noel. Ironically, Noel, who pitched the fourth win, had been with the Grey Sox earlier in the season.[96]

1922

Manager Frank Perdue returned for a third season when spring training began in 1922. There were again both old and new teams in the NSL. Returning were Birmingham, Chattanooga, Knoxville, Memphis, Montgomery, Nashville, and New Orleans. Gone were Atlanta, Bessemer, Gadsden, and Mobile. The newcomer, rounding out the participants to eight teams, was the Louisville Stars.[97]

For the first time, Birmingham's actual spring training site was ascertained. It was at Smith's Park, a race track and park ground developed by Joseph Riley Smith in 1879. A physician, Smith was the second white child born in Jefferson County.[98]

Returning Black Barons included Geechie Meredith, second base; Bob McCormick, third base; "Black Babe Ruth" Tubbs, right field; Watson, catcher; and Johnny and Eli Juran, pitchers. "Tubbs is known throughout the Southern baseball as the 'Smoky Babe Ruth,' and is a wicked stick wielder … his hitting is expected to prove a tower of strength to the Birmingham team. His home runs last year featured many of the games here and the fans are always pulling for the slugging gardener," reported the *Birmingham News*.[99]

New infielders were first baseman George McAllister and shortstop Miles (sometimes called Miller). New outfielders were "Sellers" and "Mitchell." Sellers was actually George "Mule" Suttles, a Negro leaguer for nearly three decades. His correct name never appeared in a box score during his tenure with Birmingham. Mitchell is likely Robert Mitchell, who had a twin brother, George. Both later played for the St. Louis Stars.[100]

Another perplexing question of identity concerned two pitching brothers, Eli and Johnny, whose surname often appeared as Juran, Duran, and Durant. Adding to the confusion were newspaper stories with a bewildering assortment names such as B. Duran, E. Durant, J. Durant, M. Durant, B. Juran, and D. Juran. Finally, more than 30 years later, clarification was found in an article in the *Birmingham World*, which identified the brothers correctly as Johnny and Eli Juran. Brief profiles of the brothers follow in the next chapter.

Opening Day was April 30. Perdue started lefthander Johnny Juran. Memphis Manager Chick Cummings countered with Carl Glass, also a lefty. The two pitchers battled for 12 innings before the Red Sox won, 2–1, when McAllister booted a grounder by Glass. The Memphis pitcher struck out 22, including all three he faced in the bottom of the 12th to preserve the win. Juran struck out 12 in the loss.

For white patrons, the inning-by-inning score of the Birmingham Barons at Memphis Chicks game was posted on the scoreboard throughout the game. At one point, it was noted that both games were tied 1–1.[101]

Birmingham's hard luck continued two days later when the team went to Memphis for the Red Sox home opener. Memphis won, 4–0, then took three more in the following days. The Black Barons faced a similar fate in Nashville, dropping to 0–7 before finally winning in Chattanooga. Although they regrouped and played respectable ball for a while, the disappointing start foreshadowed the overall season. It was the team's worst start until the 1928 squad began 0–8.

The first home stand started equally badly. New Orleans won, 14–9, at Rickwood, scoring seven runs in the second inning. Birmingham used three pitchers. The reporter complimented the team for rallying at the plate, but noted that the real highlight of the game for Birmingham was its glove work: "The fielding feature of the afternoon was a one-handed catch by Sellers [*sic*] in deep left field in the sixth. He sprinted towards the fence and snagged the ball while on the run. When he came in he was peppered with a deluge of coins from the stands and realized quite a nifty amount from the dusky fans, it taking about ten minutes for him to collect the offering. Jurand [*sic*] on first for the Black Barons made three nice catches of fouls, going over to the first base bleachers on each occasion and taking the ball out of the stands."[102]

In mid–May the team put a small winning streak together and moved up in the standings. Standings on May 28 were Memphis (17–7), New Orleans (13–10), and Birmingham (12–10).[103] They continued to get good pitching from Johnny Juran. On May 22 he beat Montgomery, 4–3, scattering eight hits over 11 innings. His shutout chances were spoiled by his teammates' nine errors.

In late June, Birmingham reportedly had a 12-game winning streak from both league and exhibition foes, but only three wins over Montgomery can be confirmed. When they prepared to host Nashville in a three-game series, the *News* reported that if Birmingham won two out of three, it would take over the league lead.[104] Actually, Memphis, not Nashville, was in first place at the time.[105] It was a moot point. Nashville won the opener, 7–6, and two days later swept a double-header. Birmingham's brief run for the top, if there was such a run, was over.

It was also nearly over for the Negro Southern League, which would last only about another month. It had been a tough year for black baseball in the South. In early June, President Perdue had sent out a notice that the New Orleans Crescent Stars would replace the Ads as the city's representative in the league.[106] Near the end of the month, the *Chattanooga Times* reported that the white Lookouts of the Southern Association "has barred the negro team from Andrews field pending payment for use of the same, and a decision as to just who has the right to run the club." There were reports of managerial disarray within the Chattanooga Tigers organization.[107]

Standings published July 1 were Memphis (27–10), Nashville (23–13), and Knoxville (22–13). Birmingham was 16–17. But standings just a few days later showed greatly different numbers. They had Memphis with a phenomenal 38–13 record, followed by Nashville and Birmingham at 27–20 each.[108]

Nashville (47–24) was first on July 30 in the final set of standings published. Trailing were Knoxville (44–27) and Memphis (42–27). Birmingham (29–41) was in last place.[109] Again the standings lacked mathematical integrity with totals of 302 wins and 253 losses.

Although Birmingham's wins and losses increased in each new set of standings, no games for the Black Barons were reported after a July 4 double-header with Montgomery.

Despite the standings, the *Commercial-Appeal* in August referred to the Red Sox as "winners of the Negro Southern League pennant."[110] It further reported that the Red Sox would soon take on Dallas in a seven-game series to determine "the negro championship of the south."[111] One game with the Texans was reported with the Red Sox winning, 6–2, at Dallas on September 9.[112]

The league folded, but several teams continued to play independent ball into fall, barnstorming in the East and the Midwest. Montgomery arranged a series of games with the Augusta, Georgia, team, called champions of the Southeastern Negro League.[113] Nashville and Memphis also continued traveling and playing well into September.

For the defunct Black Barons, there had been few highlights. With only one box score and handful of line scores, no meaningful statistics could be compiled for the team.

In September, the *Chicago Defender* said the 1922 league blew up "partly through mismanagement and lack of baseball experience." A new Negro Southern League reportedly was being organized out of New Orleans.[114]

3

Playing in
Two Leagues (1923)

The 1923 season was a landmark occasion for the Black Barons and the Memphis Red Sox. Both started the season with a bang, sweeping series after series from the other clubs in the Negro Southern League. At times, it seemed that they could only lose to each other. By early July they totally dominated the league and were ready for an extraordinary, seldom-heard-of move—leaving one league and joining another in mid-season. It was the beginning of the black major league experience for both clubs.

But the Negro Southern League had looked to the 1923 season with the usual ebullient spring optimism. Opening Day was set for April 30 with six clubs. Members besides Birmingham and Memphis were Chattanooga, Mobile, Nashville, and New Orleans. Two additional clubs were expected to be added during the first week of the season.[1]

However, as the season progressed, no new teams joined the league. In fact, Chattanooga was likely not a member at all, leaving just five viable teams playing each other and independent teams like the Atlanta Black Crackers, Pensacola Stars, and 24th Infantry team from Fort Benning, Georgia.

The Black Barons opened spring training in Ensley, then played exhibition games in Georgia and Arkansas. Club President Joe Rush, who had acquired the team from Frank Perdue, predicted great things, in fact foreseeing the best team in the club's history.[2]

Oscar W. Adams, in his "What Negroes Are Doing" column, said Rush was "appealing to friends everywhere, white and colored alike, to turn out on the day that Memphis reaches Birmingham and see the boys as they put on some of their scientific work and give Memphis the thrashing that she surely will get when she meets the Birmingham aggregation."[3]

Birmingham's manager was catcher Poindexter Williams. He announced his starting lineup:

Charles "Two Sides" Wesley, 2b	C.B. "Bob" Miller, 3b
Buford "Geechie" Meredith, ss	George McAllister, 1b
John Kemp, cf	John Mitchell, rf
George Sellers, lf	Harry "Fish" Salmon, p[4]
Poindexter Williams, c	

It was a creditable lineup with several future stars. The best was leftfielder "Sellers"—actually George "Mule" Suttles, still rarely called by his real name. In a 26-year career, Suttles was noted for his power, swinging a 50-ounce bat, but he could hit for average, also.[5] McAllister, Meredith, Miller and Mitchell were holdovers from the 1922 club.

For Opening Day, black businesses were asked to give their employees half a day off to attend the game. Back from its spring training travels, the team had been working out on "what is known as the Tidewater Diamond back of the Terminal Station."[6]

Rush's prediction of a good team was no exaggeration. The Black Barons shut out Memphis, 4–0, in the opener before a Rickwood Field crowd reported at 8,500. Wesley, Miller, Mitchell and Kemp each had two hits, and Meredith had a triple. Salmon did not pitch, however. The shutout was thrown by Jimmy Durant or B. Juran, depending on whether the game was reported by the *Birmingham News* or the *Birmingham Age-Herald*.[7] In a sense, both were correct. The pitcher was actually John "Bubber" Juran. An explanation follows.

In the 1920s, the Black Barons had a pair of brothers named Juran, both pitchers. One was Eli (pronounced Eely).[8] The other was often only identified except by the initial "B." Unfortunately, sloppy reporting throughout the season further complicated the situation. At various times the names Juran, Durand and Durant with an assortment of initials appeared in box scores and line scores.

The correct surname name was Juran, and the brothers were Eli and John. Most of the other assorted first names and initials were reporting errors. The issue was clarified by the chance discovery of a 1959 article in the *Birmingham World*, headlined "Remember Famous Juran Bros. Of Black Baron Fame??" From the un-bylined reminiscence, the following was discerned about the brothers:

> **Eli Juran** was a left-hander, sometimes called "Eagle" Juran. He died in Buffalo, New York, in 1955. He played first base and occasionally outfield as well as pitching.[9]
>
> **John Juran**, a right-hander, was the oldest, known among family and friends as "Bubber" or "Bubba." He lived in Pratt City in 1959. He was born in 1900 and played early ball with Ensley in the industrial league.
>
> **Both brothers** played with the Black Barons at various times from 1921 to 1926. John definitely, and Eli possibly, left Birmingham to play with the barnstorming Pullman Colored Giants of Buffalo, New York, in 1925.[10] John's best year was 1923, when he was said to have pitched 20 complete games without a loss. In 1921 he pitched a no-hitter against the Atlanta Black Crackers. He suffered a stroke in 1931, which seriously affected his right arm and shoulder.

In attempting to identify the two brothers in the various newspaper reports, the author has settled on the following: Johnny Juran incorporates all "B" notations by virtue of his nickname "Bubber." He was also called Buck occasionally. It seems logical that the occasional "Jimmy" first names are simply a sportswriter's mistake for Johnny. Obviously, the "E" notations are for "Eli" or "Eagle," his nickname. There is no satisfactory means of determining which brother was referenced by the occasional initials "D" and "M." While the names may have been questionable, the talent of the Black Barons was not. They defeated Memphis,16–4 and 4–3, in the next two games.[11]

The New Orleans Caulfield Ads fared a little better, dropping the opener, 6–2, and splitting a double-header. A pitcher named Dougherty, who relieved an ineffective Harry Salmon, struck out 10 in 8.1 innings.[12] The Ads managed an 8–8 tie in a game called because of darkness. The *Age-Herald* said rumors were afloat among Birmingham's black community that the New Orleans manager had brought some Crescent City mysticism to Birmingham, casting a voodoo spell to keep the Black Barons from winning the second game. He had been seen "chewing his roots and spitting his juice on the grounds."[13]

The "magic," perhaps, worked the next day. After five straight wins, the Black Barons finally lost, falling to the Ads, 8–6, in the first game of a double-header. The visitors appeared to have Birmingham's number in the second game also, batting around and scoring four runs in the first inning. Birmingham responded with an eight-run inning, eventually winning 13–6.[14]

After the excellent home stand, Birmingham went to New Orleans and Memphis. They lost only one game on the trip. Among the wins were three consecutive shutouts of the Red Sox in Memphis, spoiling the dedication of Lewis Athletic Park, "one of the most modern negro amusement parks in the country." The $10,000 facility included tennis courts, croquet grounds and a playground for children as well as the baseball stadium.[15]

Back at Rickwood Field on May 21, they swamped Nashville, 16–0, behind the tight pitching of Gordon Zeigler. The *News* reported it as the team's 16th win in 18 games. Birmingham got 17 hits off two pitchers. Suttles had four hits including a home run. Wesley also homered. The shutout was Birmingham's fourth in a row. Two more followed against Nashville, 5–0 and 3–0, and one against the Atlanta Black Crackers, 6–0, stretching the string to seven straight.

It would likely have reached eight in a row except for either an umpire's poor decision or a miscue by Salmon in the May 26 game with Atlanta: "In the sixth Godley led off with a single to right, stole second and third and came home when Umpire Montgomery called a balk on Salmon, who was getting ready to cut one loose at the plate when his field captain called for a halt to determine the number of outs. There was no balk; the umpire refused to change his decision the third time, having ruled at first that Salmon did not balk when Atlanta players argued he did. It's a pity that the ruling had to come when it did, as it took away the locals' chance for a record," reported the *News*. It was the first run scored against Birmingham since May 13. The string of 68 shutout innings was 14 innings shy of the world record established by Portland of the Pacific Coast League in 1913. Interestingly, the writer made no distinction between records held by white or black teams; it was just baseball.[16]

The Atlanta pitcher was "Wing" Maddox. He pitched a creditable game, trailing by only 3–1 after the disputed balk call. According to the game account, the ruling infuriated the Black Barons, who turned four hits, two errors, a walk, and a hit batsman into a seven-run seventh inning.

By the next Birmingham home stand in early June, Maddox was wearing a Birmingham uniform. In the opener against New Orleans, he was in center field and unquestionably was the star of the Black Barons' 9–3 win: "Maddox, the one-armed wonder of the locals, hit three times in four trips to the plate, getting a base on balls in his fifth appearance. Also handled two putouts in center with ease. This lad is really a wonder, both at bat and afield, his bunting exhibition being fine Wednesday." He also stole a base.[17]

In the second game he had a single, sacrifice hit and stolen base. He sat out the third game but returned to center field in the fourth, went two for three at bat, and had an astonishing day afield, starting two double plays and spearing a Texas Leaguer that appeared bound to be a hit for a New Orleans batter.[18]

After a two-week road trip that included Nashville and Memphis, Birmingham returned home for non-league games with Pensacola and the 24th Infantry team from Camp Benning, later renamed Fort Benning.

Meredith got nine hits in 14 at bats, and Pensacola lost three straight. In the third game, Maddox made his long-awaited pitching appearance with Birmingham. It was not a pretty performance—seven runs and 20 hits—although he did get the 8–7 win. Meredith, who had five hits, broke an 11th-inning tie with a single as darkness neared. "It was a game replete with thrills of may [*sic*] kinds," the *News* reported. "The sensation alone of watching

Forrest "Wing" Maddox, one-armed pitcher and outfielder, a popular player in the 1920s (courtesy Robert Reeves).

a one arm man pitch 11 innings of real baseball was well worth the visit to Rickwood. Although Maddox allowed the visitors 20 hits, he kept them scattered. Birmingham also committed three errors, so only four of the seven runs were earned. And Maddox struck out four and walked none. He also had two hits in five at bats. Mule Suttles had a home run with two men on in the seventh."[19]

The 24th Infantry Regiment was an all-black unit well known athletically as well as militarily throughout the South during the 1920s and 1930s. Several of the unit's baseball players, showcased in exhibition games with Negro league teams, later secured positions with those teams.[20] For the Birmingham series, the soldiers also brought along a 60-piece military band.[21] Birmingham won two out of three from the soldiers.[22]

A home stand with Memphis closed out the first half. Four games were split, with Birmingham winning two shutouts. One of the Jurans threw a four-hitter, and Salmon held the visitors to two hits, striking out six and walking one.[23]

The *News* reported on July 10 that the Black Barons would be idle until the second half of the season got underway on July 19. That changed dramatically a few days later.

On July 15, black businessman A. Brown Parkes announced that "major league" baseball was coming to Birmingham. Joe Rush had gone to Chicago in pursuit of a Negro National League franchise. He obtained the Reading, Pennsylvania, club, reportedly for $10,000, a move said to be "occasioned by the lack of competition in the Dixie League." Including exhibitions, the Black Barons reportedly had a 54–6 record against Southern teams and had once had a string of 63 [*sic*] consecutive scoreless innings, "a mark which has only been once been bettered in professional baseball."[24]

Birmingham's record, compiled from regular season results, showed 29 wins and 12 losses between April 30 and July 15. Memphis (18–16) was second, with 13 of the losses coming against the Black Barons. Nobody else in the league was above .500. Birmingham won nine of its ten league series. One was the split with Memphis.

The Reading reference is puzzling. No NNL Reading franchise is mentioned in any of the Negro leagues literature. Birmingham and Memphis may have been simply added to the league.

Without Memphis and Birmingham, the Negro Southern League quickly disintegrated.[25]

Although Birmingham switched from playing NSL teams to preparing for a home stand against the Milwaukee Giants and Toledo Tigers, they were not formally admitted into the NNL until August. Obviously, there was more involved than simply buying a struggling franchise. Rush persuaded Rube Foster that Birmingham was not only worthy but also could compete. In addition, he had to persuade Foster and other club owners that a ban of Sunday baseball in Birmingham would not be an economic problem. "He claims and backs up his claims with figures, that Monday will draw just as many fans to the park as he could get there on Sundays," reported the *Pittsburgh Courier*.[26] While a vote of the league directors was awaited, the other NNL clubs began playing games with Birmingham and Memphis.[27]

Rush urged local fans to show their support. "According to Rush, it is now up to the fans locally to support the team in order to defray the enormous expenses which the local management has incurred in bringing a better brand of baseball to its patrons. The left side of the grandstand will be reserved for white patrons, it is announced, each afternoon, and it is expected that strong delegation will witness the games between the locals and their stronger foes," the *Birmingham News* reported.[28]

The NNL's other teams were Milwaukee, Toledo, Kansas City, Detroit, Chicago, Indianapolis, St. Louis, and Cuba.[29]

A crowd of up to 10,000 was predicted for the opening game with Milwaukee on Thursday, July 18. No precise figure, but "a large crowd" saw an exciting ball game that had a *Birmingham News* reporter exalting: "Seldom has the old park seen such a fiercely waged battle as was fought within the confines of its walls Thursday. The game was featured by the wonder fielding of the diminutive Black Baron shortsmith, Geechie, and the hitting of Wesley, the local keystoner." The *Chicago Defender* reported that as many as 500 of the spectators were white people.[30]

Milwaukee went ahead, 2–0, in the first inning, leaving the Black Barons with "a scared and hurt look, while the many fans present, both white and black, settled back and said, 'Well, these big leaguers are out of the Black Barons class.'"[31] They were wrong. Birmingham fought back, moving ahead 4–3 in the eighth. Milwaukee tied it again in the ninth. The game was called because of darkness after 10 innings, a 4–4 tie in Birmingham's major league debut. *The Chicago Defender* said the opening game was "a society event," and the outcome was "a surprise to even the most loyal followers of the home team."[32]

The reporter had generous praise for Buford Meredith: "The work of Geechie at short for the Black Barons was a revelation to all who have seen shorters work on the local diamonds. He made many pretty plays and accepted ten chances with only one bobble, his many difficult stops making up for the one error. One of his plays, the prettiest that the writer has ever seen on a baseball diamond, came in the sixth inning when on a dead run he reached to the ground behind second, scooped up the ball and tossed it to Wesley at second, all in one motion." Wesley had a triple, two singles, and two runs scored.[33]

On Friday, Birmingham won its first NNL game, beating Milwaukee 4–3 behind the six-hit pitching of "Fish" Salmon. The right-hander handcuffed the Giants with his sidearm delivery. Meredith and Wesley had two hits each, and center field John Kemp had a triple.[34]

On Saturday, they played a double-header before a crowd estimated at 7,000. The visitors walloped the Black Barons, 9–1, in the opener, but received a like trouncing in the second game, falling 12–3. Birmingham ended its first series with two wins, a loss and a tie.

The *Birmingham Age-Herald* took particular notice of the white spectators:

> One whole section was reserved for white fans, and there was no room available to accommodate those who attended. Many were forced to stand, as the crowd kept getting larger and larger, and the grandstand was filled more and more.
>
> Rickwood officials announced that from now on a special section of the park will be reserved for white fans, who are showing an unusual amount of interest in the Black Baron games. There will be a ticket window for whites only, as well as a special entrance gate.[35]

A later report indicated that the number of white spectators may have been as high as 1,000.[36]

After the game, Milwaukee left for Memphis and St. Louis before returning to Birmingham for another series the following week. The Black Barons had been scheduled to play Toledo next, but the series was postponed. A telegram from Foster stated that the NNL had not had time to revise the schedule to totally accommodate the new member. A quick resolution was expected, but Birmingham was idle until Milwaukee returned.[37]

The second series also opened on a Thursday with 2,000 fans watching Milwaukee take a commanding 7–2 lead. Eli Juran gave up seven hits and seven walks and committed two fielding errors. It was a performance that caused a reporter to ask:

> [T]he writer wonders why a pitcher with seemingly the good arm that the Eagle has should allow himself to get in hole after hole as he did Thursday. After striking out as many men as he did during the game we cannot but wonder why he was so wild at other times. It seems to us that if he should give a little more thought to his hurling, put a spirit of fight in his heaving and remember that each ball pitched counts … otherwise he might, as one fan so aptly put it, "go back to cleaning cars." We are always for local athletes no matter what their creed or color, but we do want to see them try their best, when they really have something.[38]

But the writer was pleased with the way the Black Barons came from behind, scoring three in the eighth, two in the ninth and one in the tenth to win, 8–7. "Despite all of the criticism, it was a great game…. Fans who failed to turn out are missing some real baseball games," he added.[39] The *Age-Herald* noted that the white grandstand "was packed."[40]

Milwaukee won the next game, 8–1, and left town with 2–3–1 record against the Black Barons.

Birmingham soon found the caliber of opponents in the NNL to be tougher than those in the Negro Southern League, though.

Following Milwaukee were home series with the Toledo, St. Louis, and Chicago, sandwiched among a three-week road trip. As the team awaited Toledo, the *Birmingham News* said the local club needed a backup catcher. Poindexter Williams had been out with an injury, and the writer found his replacements less than satisfactory. He also recommended adding a couple of "real, experienced pitchers."[41]

With Birmingham exhibiting decent pitching and hitting but "rotten fielding," Toledo won two out of three. Only Salmon was able to salvage a win, hurling a four-hit shutout in the second game. He struck out six and walked none, beating Robert McClure, 1–0, in an exciting game. Meredith singled, advanced to second on a sacrifice, and came home on Kemp's single for the only run.

The inconsistent play did not dampen the enthusiasm of the crowds, however. With St. Louis coming in next for a five-game series, Rickwood officials were counting turnstiles. "In order to handle the crowds anticipated ... circus seats will be erected inside the bleachers and extra reservations for white fans will be made. Large crowds have been seeing the games with the Toledo team, but the largest gate receipts of the year are expected to result from the St. Louis series."[42]

When St. Louis came to town, according to the *Birmingham News*, the Black Barons "saw stars galore." The visitors took a 4–0 lead, then held off Birmingham's ninth-inning rally. The team failed to hit except in the ninth and had spurts of bad fielding. McAllister had an error at first and the usually reliable Meredith committed two at shortstop. The writer asked the fans not to get down on the Black Barons, promising a revival. The game was delayed for five minutes in the third inning to allow silent prayers to be offered for the recovery of President Warren G. Harding, who had suffered a heart attack in San Francisco.[43]

The return of the Black Barons to the victory column was delayed another day. Harding died on Thursday, and the game of Friday, August 3, was called off, becoming part of a Saturday double-header.

With Wesley, Meredith, Suttles, and Kemp getting two hits apiece, the Black Barons defeated St. Louis, 7–1, in the first game. Curtis Greene scattered eight hits. The second game was called because of darkness with the scored tied at 5–5.[44] A Monday double-header ended with similar results, a 7–6 Birmingham win and a tie because of darkness.[45]

St. Louis capitalized on poor Birmingham fielding to win the final game, 12–7, gaining a split in the series. A new pitcher, David Watson, started for the Black Barons, but lasted less than two innings. One of the Jurans relieved him. In the fourth inning, a Star hit a home run over Suttles's head in left field, prompting Juran to walk off the mound. "He was promptly fined and fired by Manager Rush."[46] The firing was apparently just a moment of pique on Rush's part, because the Jurans continued to pitch the rest of the season.

Afterward Birmingham boarded a train for a 10-day road trip to Memphis and points north.[47] They won three of four in Memphis, the only games reported.

Their return home was eagerly awaited because the opponent was Chicago. It was an occasion hyped by Henry Vance in a rare bylined article on black baseball in the *News*.[48] The veteran sportswriter wrote that four years earlier, when the American Giants came to Birmingham, a southern baseball attendance record was set with 14,362 paid admissions. It was the high-water attendance mark in the South until 1923, when the Atlanta Crackers drew more than 15,000 for their Southern Association opener. He predicted an outpouring of fans that might eclipse the Atlanta record.

Vance wrote that in their previous meeting, Birmingham had a mediocre team while Chicago was a powerhouse. The 1923 series offered a very strong Birmingham club. Adding to the excitement was a Poindexter Williams factor:

> It's a grudge affair in the truest sense of the word, too. For two years Poindexter Williams caught for Rube Foster's Chicago team. During that time he became recognized as the greatest negro catcher in the game. Poindexter had ambitions and he signed to manage the Birmingham club. Rube Foster waxed angry over his resignation. He waxed angrier when he realized that Poindexter was making as big a name as a miracle manager over the country as he himself was. Poindexter had worked won-

ders with the Birmingham club, even though he had been out of the game for two months now with a broken leg. The doctor has intimated that Poindexter can get back in the game against the Chicago team Monday, and Poindexter is straining at the leash. He wants to show his old boss what a real ball club looks like.[49]

Vance extolled the Birmingham lineup, citing the pitching of Salmon, Greene, and Duran [*sic*]. He said the Birmingham outfield was composed of all six-footers—Kemp, Sellers [*sic*], and Mitchell. "Kemp, in center … is heralded as 'the Tris Speaker of colored baseball.' Kemp plays close in and races toward the fence for alleged hits—he gets 'em, too. Kemp is a great hitter as well as a fielder."[50]

But Vance's greatest accolades were reserved for the infield, particularly shortstop Meredith. "Geechie's fame as a shortstop has spread all over the country. If he could successfully bleach his complexion, the chances are that he would get a job with any major-league outfit in the country."[51]

The *News*, which gave the Black Barons excellent coverage at times in the 1920s, published the expected starting lineups the day before the game, just as it would have for white teams.[52]

The *Age-Herald* reported that the Birmingham team had "been working smoothly" in recent weeks with six regulars hitting over .300. They listed McAllister (.385), Meredith (.377). Wesley (.328), Kemp (.325), Suttles (.323), and Mitchell (.317). McAllister was the team's doubles leader. Meredith led in triples, stolen bases, and errors. "Geechie has more errors than any other local player. This is due to his fast work at short, which necessarily causes errors occasionally," the paper reported, noting that all of the numbers were for the 15 league games only. Wesley had the lone home run for Birmingham.[53]

For Birmingham, the series was disappointing, but there had to be exhilaration in the first game. The *Birmingham News* reported: "Ruben Foster and his famous American Giants of Chicago, blew into Birmingham Monday afternoon to answer the call that has gone up from all over the Negro National League for someone to go down and administer a spanking to that little Birmingham team that is making so much noise in negro baseball circles. And so they came all dressed in their brand-new spanking clothes only to find that the Black Barons possessed a spank in each hand themselves, and it was all the Chicago team could do to knot the score in the seventh inning just as darkness called the game. The tally card read 1 to 1."[54]

Birmingham scored in the second and Chicago tied it. The visitors threatened several times "only to have Salmon pick them off the bags or some of the other Rushmen catch them napping." Kemp was the only Black Baron with two hits, but Suttles was robbed of two hits, according to one writer.[55] Poindexter Williams, still recovering, did not play.

Before a crowd of 8,000, a jazz band had added to the excitement and was scheduled to return for the next game. Anticipating an even larger crowd, officials said extra seats would be put in if necessary.[56]

Chicago, capitalizing on four Birmingham errors, won the second game 6–0. It was the first shutout of the season against the Black Barons. Although Lewis Means continued to catch for the Black Barons, Williams did finally make an appearance as a pinch-hitter.[57]

Rain on Wednesday turned Rickwood into a "mud lake," producing field conditions that the wily Rube Foster took advantage of. In the seventh a bunt showed Foster the difficulty that third baseman Bob Miller had getting to the ball. "The Giants leader saw his chance and for the rest of the game had his cohorts bunt and bunt until they had bunted Miller off the hot corner and bunted the game into the win column for the Chicagoans.

The visitors made Miller look pitiful … and finally Joe Rush had to send him to second and put Wesley on third in an attempt to stop the disastrous attack." Birmingham committed six errors, and Chicago won, 11–5.[58]

After the disappointing series, the Black Barons entrained to Dallas for an exhibition tour before resuming league play over the Labor Day weekend. The Texas jaunt was reported to be a shopping trip for owner Rush, who was "paddling all over the eastern end of the Longhorn state … with his money bags at his side buying up a choice lot of Texas tossers with which to strengthen the weak links in his baseball machine."[59] There was no report on the games played, but Birmingham did return home with new players.

The new personnel included pitcher Fred Daniels, outfielders Ruben Jones and Frank Dugan, and a catcher named McGhee, reportedly an Indianapolis ABCs player. In addition, Rush had swapped Meredith and Miller in the infield. "The former has taken Miller's place at third while Miller has gone to short. Miller was too slow on rollers and bunts, but is a reliable fielder. Geechie is fast and can handle a slow ball well."[60]

Two of the newcomers had an immediate impact in the morning-afternoon Labor Day games against Toledo. With the visitors leading 3–0, Daniels came on in relief, limiting Toledo to just one more run in eight innings. Jones had two hits, the Black Barons rallied for a 4–4 tie in 11 innings. In the afternoon game, Salmon pitched a seven-hit shutout.[61]

A double-header the next day resulted in Toledo winning the first game 8–4, then sinking "into the gutters of defeat and demoralization" as the Black Barons handed out a 13–2 whipping in the second. Daniels, making his first start and second appearance with the club, got the win. The new outfield of Jones, Suttles, and Kemp was praised for both fielding and batting.[62] The infield was still porous at times, and new shortstop Leroy Stratton was expected to shore up that position while Meredith, although hobbled by leg injuries, worked at third base.[63]

Toledo tied the series, winning the final game, 6–1. Stratton played an errorless game at third, but Williams was still unable to catch.[64] Means was described as a good receiver but lacking a strong throwing arm.[65]

The Black Barons rested, healing wounds, and preparing for five games with the Cuban Stars, one of the stronger teams in the league.

Fred Daniels again proved to be a quality addition. Facing the Cubans in the opener, he grew careless when the Black Barons got an early lead, but held on to win, 7–6. Suttles had the fielding gem of the day, hauling in a Texas leaguer to left to start a triple play. Meredith returned to form, playing errorless ball at shortstop and getting two hits. "The return of Geechie boosts the Black Barons stock 50 per cent, as the diminutive shortstopper is a whiz when he is going right," reported the News.[66]

The series went to the Cubans, three games to two. For Meredith, who had appeared to be back on track, the final game was an absolute disaster. He committed five errors at shortstop, negating Salmon's pitching.[67]

The Black Barons had found the competition at the "major league" level much stiffer than the NSL. After they had made a good start, winning some series and holding their own in others, weaknesses took their toll. Following the Cuban Stars series, they hosted 1922 NNL champion Kansas City and then closed out with Chicago.

Daniels's two-hit pitching and Meredith's double up the middle propelled them to an impressive start against Kansas City. The 3–1 win was a fitting tribute to Grand Trustee K.L. Quincy on Elks Day at the ballpark.[68]

Unfortunately, that was one of the few highlights of the final two weeks. Kansas City won the second game, 7–0.[69] The third game was an 8–4 loss as the Monarchs took advantage of catcher Lewis Means's weak arm. "The visitors were like wildmen on bases, and Means ... after six unsuccessful attempts to stop them, gave up in disgust and finally walked from the field, amid the whoops and angers of the spectators. He was replaced by Geechie, second baseman, who caught a fair game," reported the *Birmingham News*.[70]

Chicago won all four, two of them shutouts, at Rickwood. The losses left Birmingham with a 15–23 record in league games, a disappointment after the early success. Still, for Birmingham's black fans, it had been a good season, a memorable one. The team's .394 winning percentage was better than Milwaukee (.304) and St. Louis (.385).[71] And the Black Barons had been dazzling in the Negro Southern League, completely dominating all opponents.

4

Full Time in the NNL (1924)

Buoyed by the respectable performance of his team in its major league debut and the widespread acceptance of the team by the Birmingham community, owner Joe Rush set out to make the 1924 season even more successful. Spring training opened under the direction of a high-profile manager, Sam Crawford, who piloted Kansas City to the 1923 Negro National League pennant. Crawford's career started as a pitcher in 1910 and spanned 28 years.[1]

Among the early arrivals were pitcher Fred Daniels and outfielder Reuben Jones. Newcomers included Lefty Gray, a pitching sensation from Cleveland; Sylvester Foreman, a catcher from Kansas City; and Ames Thompson of Milwaukee, "who bears a good reputation as a player de luxe."[2] Rush then bought infielders Newt Joseph and Dewey Creacey from Kansas City. He planned to field a team of "experienced players handled by a first-class manager and will either play ball or move on to make a place for men who will play the game."[3]

The NNL pre-season lineup for 1924 was Birmingham, Kansas City, Chicago, Detroit, St. Louis, Memphis, Cleveland, and the Cuban Stars.[4] While most held steady, there were early franchise changes.

Birmingham's final roster had many players from the year before. At first was George McAllister, "one of the best negro first basemen to ever take the diamond in Birmingham. Bad throws are his meat and his ability to scoop them out of the dirt is remarkable." McAllister, field captain the year before, was said to have a good head for the game and an excellent clutch hitter. "Small but lightning-like" Buford "Geechie" Meredith was back at shortstop. Mule Suttles, the power hitter (still most often called Sellers) returned in the outfield. Others were third baseman Leroy Stratton, pitcher Harry Salmon, and catcher Poindexter Williams. Manager Crawford was in center field, filling in for Jones, who broke a leg in practice. Newcomers included outfielder James Thompson and pitcher Sam Streeter.[5]

Birmingham opened away with a 13-inning tie and a 6–3 loss at Memphis. The home opener was on April 28, a festive occasion. Most of the "colored businesses housed along Sixteenth, Seventeenth and Eighteenth Streets will close at noon, Monday, to allow their employees to attend the game," the *Birmingham News* reported. Some speculated that the crowd might set a new record for Rickwood Field attendance. The visiting Cuban Stars were expected to face "the greatest bunch of colored ball players that ever represented a Southern city."[6]

A crowd of 10,600, including a brass band, filled the stands at Rickwood Field as the Black Barons won, 6–3. The attendance was said to be a thousand more spectators than saw the white Barons' opener a few days earlier. It was also said to be the second largest crowd to ever see a black baseball game in Birmingham.[7]

Left-hander Sam Streeter pitched well, striking out six. Birmingham scored five runs in the third inning on five hits and an error. While the victory had fans excited, much of their conversation was on the sudden termination of Manager Crawford. An apparent disagreement with Joe Rush led to his dismissal.[8]

The Tuesday game was rained out, forcing a double-header on Wednesday. Birmingham won both games, 9–3 and 6–1. Salmon was never in danger after the Black Barons scored five runs in the fourth. In the second game, left-hander Bill McCall pitched masterfully, yielding five hits and struck out nine, including four in a row. Estaban Montalvo of the Cubans, sometimes called the black Babe Ruth, had only one hit in 12 at bats in the series. He had played left field for Birmingham in 1920. The crowd was reported at 4,000.[9]

The Cuban Stars went to Memphis for a series, then returned to Birmingham. The Black Barons apparently were idle during the interim. Meanwhile, there was speculation on the after-effects of Sam Crawford's dismissal. Would the team perform with the same dominance it had shown against the Cubans? "Back of it all was the master hand of Crawford, who is recognized throughout the country as being the best negro manager," an unidentified reporter wrote. "From all facts available to the press, the manager was fired because he wished to enforce discipline amongst the players. Force them to keep training or catch air. For such a thing he should have been congratulated, it seems he was fired and the public is wondering why."[10]

The writer's concern seemed well-founded the following day. The Cubans beat the Black Barons, 6–2, taking advantage of five Birmingham errors to beat right-hander Robert Poindexter.[11] Poindexter, sometimes confused in box scores with catcher Poindexter Williams, had a brief but flashy career. He spent four seasons with Birmingham. Armed with a good curve and spitball, he seemed headed toward a promising career. However, a drinking problem and a penchant for the wild side brought about his demise. Details of his tragic end follow in Chapter 9.[12]

Birmingham won the second game, 6–5, in 11 innings. After Montalvo tied the game with a two-run homer, Birmingham won it on a single, a double and a throwing error.[13]

A new feature was introduced at Rickwood Field with the Cuban Stars series. Via a telegraph ticker service, results of ongoing major league and Southern Association games were available at the ballpark. Inning-by-inning results were posted on the scoreboard in right field.[14]

Birmingham's next series was in Indianapolis, where they won two and tied one.[15]

The *Birmingham News* reported the team's return home with a colorful flair. The manager of the white Birmingham Barons in 1924 was Stuffy Stewart. A clever sportswriter penned, "The Stuffirino Carbon Copies will return to Birmingham."[16] The home stand opened with St. Louis. The Black Barons were in second place, just half a game behind Kansas City.[17]

It was a great homecoming for the home team and a huge disappointment for Stars manager Candy Jim Taylor, returning to his baseball roots. Birmingham won the first game with McAllister driving in two runs on a triple. Some 5,000 fans, again including a lively brass band, witnessed the game. "Spectacular fielding kept the crowd in a continuous uproar with the band breaking out with weird shrieks of Eighteenth Street jazz," reported the *News*. When McAllister lashed his game-winning triple, the band started playing W.C. Handy's "St. Louis Blues" to the delight of the crowd.[18]

St. Louis won the second game, but Birmingham took the series. They won the third game on good pitching by Streeter and also hitting by Streeter and Suttles, both of whom had triples. Meredith hit a home run in the second game, his second of the season at Rickwood. Four Birmingham errors contributed to the loss.[19]

Sam Crawford had been replaced by Charles "Twosides" Wesley, whose local playing career dated to 1919. He was capable in both the infield and outfield, but usually played second base. In the common jargon of the day, the team was soon referred to as the Wesleys.[20]

Indianapolis followed St. Louis. Birmingham won a rain-shortened first game, 4–1 on McCall's pitching. In the fifth, with two men on base and one out, Indianapolis walked John Thompson to set up a possible double play with Suttles, the next batter. "Nothing gives the negro fan more pleasure than to see a pitcher walk Thompson to get to Mule," reported the *Birmingham News*. "Sellers [*sic*] all but took the shortstop's hands off with a torrid grounder, Shepherd getting Thompson at second while Geechie was scoring."[21]

Birmingham won the second game, 10–6, with Harry Salmon making his first start in a month. Sidelined with chills and fever, "he had lost about 16 pounds and lacked stamina toward the middle of the game to continue." He pitched five innings and gave way to Poindexter.[22]

The ABCs won the third game, but Birmingham took the series with a 7–2 win in the first game of a double-header. The second game was tied when it was called so Indianapolis could catch a train. It was the fourth consecutive series won by Birmingham.[23]

It became six series in a row after Birmingham won three out of four at Memphis, then returned home to win four straight from the Red Sox at Rickwood. Only Kansas City (14–3) and Detroit (10–3) were playing better than Birmingham (12–4), according to June 8 standings.[24]

The first game with Memphis was one of the best-pitched ever at Rickwood. Streeter shut out the visitors, 1–0, giving up only three hits in 12 innings. He struck out eight and walked none. Suttles singled over second to score Meredith, who had tripled to lead off the 12th inning.[25]

Birmingham made it three straight, sweeping a double-header, 11–0 and 5–3. McCall's four-hit shutout in the first game gave Birmingham pitchers 26 consecutive scoreless innings against Memphis. The Red Sox ended their drought in the second inning in the second game.[26]

With a six-game winning streak, the team embarked on a nearly month-long road trip where a new reality was encountered. They lost six out of seven games to league-leading Kansas City and Chicago. In Chicago, about 400 former Birmingham residents turned out to support the boys from home. They presented owner Joe Rush with a large basket of flowers.[27]

Detroit was the only happy venue. Birmingham won all three with the Stars and split two with an independent team in Sturgis, Michigan. Then, it was three straight losses to Cleveland in neutral Chicago.

Road-weary, they returned to Rickwood on July 7, still in third place. Unfortunately, the home stand opened with Kansas City (26–5), now far out front in the standings.[28]

The *Birmingham News* reported that the Black Barons would have a new manager and some new players on their return home. None of them were named, but about a week later, William "Dizzy" Dismukes, formerly of the Indianapolis ABCs, was the manager.[29]

Birmingham took a 3–0 lead in the first inning, but it quickly evaporated as Kansas City won the first game, 8–3. Newt Joseph awed the crowd with a pair of massive home runs over the right and center field walls. "His first long drive cleared the right field wall with plenty of room to spare while his second home run vanished over the center-field wall. It was one of the longest wallops ever seen at Rickwood and cleared the fence by ten feet," wrote a reporter.[30]

Kansas City also used home runs to win the next two games, 3–1 and 15–5.[31] Although Birmingham salvaged the fourth game, Hurley McNair hit his third home run of the series. Altogether, the Monarchs hit eight in the series.[32]

Since the sensational start in May, Birmingham had now lost four out of five series, dropping near .500. The team needed a serious shot of adrenalin and got it in Memphis, where they won two out of three on a short road trip.[33]

Returning home, they beat Chicago, 6–4. Poindexter gave up 11 hits but spaced them adequately and struck out seven. He also hit a three-run homer.[34]

But the best the Black Barons could do was a four-game split. Chicago won the next two games despite Leroy Stratton's fine fielding, "standing like an 18-carat diamond in a tray of pearls."[35] Birmingham won the finale on Poindexter's three-hit shutout.[36]

The split showed an inconsistency that marked the rest of the season. They dropped four straight in Chicago, then won two out of three in St. Louis, where Streeter pitched a one-hit shutout, not surrendering the hit until two were out in the ninth.[37]

Back home, Rickwood Field did nothing to improve the situation for Birmingham, although it was a good venue for former Montgomery Grey Sox slugger "Turkey" Stearnes. They lost three of four to Detroit. Stearnes, who was inducted into the National Baseball Hall of Fame in 2000, had eight hits, four of them for extra bases, in 15 at bats.[38] In the first game, Poindexter got no support in a 2–0 loss.[39] Birmingham won the second game, 3–2, due in part to the hidden ball trick. Streeter had attempted to pick the runner off but struck third baseman John Richardson on the chin with the ball. While Richardson was being checked out for possible injury, Geechie Meredith slipped the ball back into the third baseman's glove, enabling him to tag the runner when play resumed.

Birmingham bats were embarrassingly cold, scoring only four runs in four games. In fairness, three infielder starters were out of the lineup most of the series. Wesley had a twisted ankle, McAllister a wrenched knee, and Stratton a bad leg. They were expected to return to the lineup for the upcoming series in Memphis.[40]

Only McAllister did so, batting leadoff and getting a hit in each game. The opener was an exciting pitching battle between the two managers. Each gave up seven hits, but Dismukes surrendered one run to two by Memphis skipper Carl Glass. In a split doubleheader the next day, Meredith hit a home run.[41]

The two clubs then moved to Birmingham for a series. Having two-thirds of the injured infielders, McAlister and Stratton, back did not help the Black Barons. Harry Salmon, who had been released after his lengthy illness, showed up in a Red Sox uniform and showed up his former teammates. He struck out seven in a 14–4 win. The second game, tied 4–4, was called because of darkness after seven innings.[42]

Away again, Birmingham lost three straight to Kansas City, took three out of four from lowly Cleveland, and then dropped a series at Detroit. During the Cleveland series, played in Chicago again, there was yet another managerial change. Owner Joe Rush and Dizzy Dismukes came to a "parting of the ways." Birmingham took the field on Sunday under Joe Hewitt, and "Dizzy sat in the box seats in citizen's clothes."[43]

In earlier September, long out of the pennant race, the Black Barons returned to Birmingham to close out the season against the Cuban Stars and the independent Atlanta Black Crackers. Birmingham (28–37) was in sixth place. Kansas City (51–17) and Chicago (46–

22) were the frontrunners.[44] Again the standings lacked mathematical integrity (251 wins and 229 losses), but the order of finish and the teams' performance levels seemed basically correct.

Birmingham's slide from contender to sixth place can be attributed in some measure to injuries. Salmon, Wesley, McAllister, Stratton, and Jones were all out at various times in the season.

At home and at full strength again, Birmingham came alive, beating the Cubans, 8–3 and 10–6, on Labor Day. Birmingham batters ripped three pitchers for 29 hits. Suttles drove in four runs with two doubles in the morning game and two singles in the afternoon. Reuben Jones and John Richardson each hit a home run in the afternoon contest.[45]

Streeter threw a four-hitter as Birmingham then made it three straight. The visitors won the final double-header. Williams and Thompson had home runs, but fielding was spotlighted on both sides. "[Angel] Alfonso, the midget Cuban shortstop, turned in one of the greatest performances ever seen at Rickwood in handling 19 chances out of 20 attempts. He cut off no less than a half dozen hits by spectacular stops and throws. Mule Sellers [*sic*] stood the cash customers on their collective ear twice with circus catches of long drives to deep left. He robbed Alfonso of a triple in the first inning of the second game by snaring a line drive in a cart wheel turn. In the fifth he went almost to the fence to get Sierra's line drive," reported the *Birmingham News*.[46]

The season was supposed to end with Memphis. Instead, three home games were scheduled with the Atlanta Black Crackers, to be followed by four in Atlanta.[47] According to the *Birmingham News*, the Black Barons "had a picnic" with the Atlanta club, winning 9–6, although "they could have made it 20 or 25 just as easy." Suttles drove in four runs with two singles and another home run over the right field fence. He also pitched a scoreless inning.[48]

The double-header scheduled the next day was abbreviated because the first game was also considered a laugher like the one the day before. Facing no real opposition, Birmingham won, 9–4. There were so few spectators that the second game was canceled, as was the series in Atlanta. "In order to keep the score down the Black Barons kept swapping positions throughout, the comedy of Mule Sellers [*sic*] featuring the shifts. There are enough feathers scattered round the home plate, beaten out of the Atlanta catcher's mitt, to pad an elephants' mattress," reported the *News*. Every Birmingham player except Joe Hewitt played at least three positions in the game.[49]

5

A Season of Struggle (1925)

Undaunted by the devastating collapse in the middle of the previous season, the Black Barons management opened spring training camp enthusiastically in nearby Gadsden, Alabama, in mid–March.

With exhibition games already set, new Manager William Patterson worked to whittle a 22-player roster down to the 15 allowed by league rules. Owner Joe Rush accelerated the process, announcing that veteran first baseman George McAllister and infielder/manager Charles "Twosides" Wesley had been sold, to Chicago and Memphis, respectively. But he also purchased three new players from Texas: left-handed pitcher Charles Beverly, third baseman Saul Davis, and a catcher named Henderson.[1]

There were other changes as they looked for a settled lineup. "Geechie" Meredith moved from shortstop to second baseman with Leroy Stratton taking over at short. McAllister was replaced at first by Curtis Green, "said to be better than McAllister." The catcher seemed likely to be Bobby Roth from various New Orleans teams.[2]

Birmingham opened at home with four games against Rube Foster's Chicago American Giants, three in Birmingham and one in Gadsden.[3]

Elaborate preparations were made for Opening Day. A.H. Parker High School's 40-piece band provided music. The Birmingham Civic and Commercial Association urged black businesses to declare a half-day holiday so workers could go to the game. As usual, "a section of the grandstand will be roped off for white patrons." Last year the team reportedly played before more than 6,000 white fans during the season.[4]

The projected lineup was Poindexter Williams, 1b; Buford Meredith, 2b; Saul Davis, 3b; Leroy Stratton, ss; George "Mule" Suttles, lf; James Thompson, cf; Reuben Jones, rf; Bobby Roth or Henderson, c; Robert Poindexter or Sam Streeter, p. The pitching staff was composed of three left-handers—Streeter, Beverly and Charles Robertson—and three right-handers—Poindexter, Harry Salmon, and Fred Daniels.[5]

Manager Patterson intended to remain in Gadsden until Monday morning, then journey to Rickwood around noon. Meanwhile, Cristobal Torrienti, the heavy-hitting Cuban right fielder with Chicago, was already in Birmingham in advance of the team and went to Gadsden a couple of days earlier to get "a line on the Black Barons."[6]

The game was delayed an hour because of Chicago's late arrival. For Birmingham, it would have been better if the visitors had not arrived at all. Chicago battered the Black Barons, 15–6, before an estimated 10,000 fans, the third largest ever for a black baseball game in the city. Chicago ripped Poindexter and Beverly for 17 hits, five by Torrienti. Floyd "Jelly" Gardner hit a home run.[7]

For Birmingham, Williams and Suttles each had two hits, and Thompson nailed a runner at home plate from center field. The late start caused the game to be called after eight innings because of darkness.[8]

Things got no better. Chicago won all four games, outscoring the locals 36–16 in three games at Rickwood. In the second game, Birmingham committed eight errors. Poor fielding also cost Birmingham the final game. Six of the nine runs off Robertson and Poindexter were unearned.[9]

Birmingham then made a swing to St. Louis and Indianapolis. There was one bright spot in St. Louis. In a 10–3 win, Suttles, Stratton and Thompson all hit home runs. Thompson's blast was a grand slam.[10]

On May 15, the *Birmingham News* reported that the team would come home with a new manager. In a telegram from Chicago, Joe Rush announced that he had hired Sam Crawford as manager, luring the veteran away from Chicago. Whatever difficulties the two men had the previous year, they were of an accord now. "In getting Crawford back, Rush has obtained one of the most successful negro managers in the country," the story read. "It was under Crawford's regime that the Kansas City Monarchs won their first pennant in the Negro National League." Rush said Crawford's first move was to obtain former Chicago teammates first baseman Willie Ware and outfielder Roy Tyler.[11] Neither showed up in subsequent box scores, however. Patterson remained as secretary and bookkeeper.[12]

Reaching Birmingham, Crawford announced that he had signed three new players, one of them a badly needed shortstop. They didn't arrive in time to help in the opener, a 10–2 loss to Kansas City.[13]

The second game was a lot closer but with no better result. Kansas City scored six runs in the ninth inning, winning, 12–11. Birmingham had 19 hits but also six errors, three of them by Arthur Jones at shortstop. The game was punctuated by continuous arguments by players with umpires.[14]

Birmingham committed five more errors and Kansas City won the third game, 5–1.[15]

Next up on the long home stand were St. Louis and Memphis. Finally, Birmingham fans had something to cheer about. With former Kansas City star Newt Joseph at shortstop, the porous infield was greatly improved. Birmingham won its first series, taking two out of three from the Stars and also the Red Sox.

Manager Crawford started the rubber game with St. Louis, giving up only two runs in the first five innings. Another new pitcher, John Finner, preserved the win. Suttles hit a home run.[16]

A six-run inning gave Memphis the opening game, but Birmingham won a doubleheader and the series. The first game was a forfeit, sparked by the Red Sox leaving the field in a disagreement with the home plate umpire over a pop fly in the second inning. Indeed, they had left the stadium altogether when they were informed of possible dire consequences: "[I]f they did not return they would be barred from Rickwood in the future." The players returned and played the second game, which Birmingham won, 5–3. The double-header was not the only thing Memphis lost. According to the *News*, the team faced a $375 fine on the forfeit and Manager Dizzy Dismukes was assessed $350.[17]

The poor start had Birmingham (4–18) in last place by early June. Kansas City (19–7) and St. Louis (14–7) were the leaders.[18]

Encouraged by four wins in six games, the Black Barons embarked on a 20-game road trip to Memphis, Detroit, Chicago, and Kansas City. It was a total disaster, three wins in 20 games. Not only was every series lost, but also frequently in an embarrassing manner.[19] The only positive was Poindexter's 1–0 shutout of Chicago.[20]

After the horrible road trip, the Black Barons showed some signs of scrappiness, winning six out of 11 games from Memphis in a long home-and-home series. Beverly pitched a complete game and Suttles homed in an 8–3 win to start the series. They won all four at home, but lost five of seven in Memphis.

The Cuban Stars opened the second half in Birmingham, winning 9–4 in a game halted by rain in the ninth inning.[21] Rain shortened the series to two games. Birmingham won the second one, 6–2, on Salmon's five-hitter. Suttles hit a home run over the right field wall.

Standings on July 11 had Birmingham (14–33) still last. Kansas City (31–9) and St. Louis (31–14) remained the leaders.

The struggling Black Barons had probably their best road trip of the season after the Cuban Stars games, although it was different from what was originally planned. They were scheduled to host the 24th Infantry team from Fort Benning for three games. Birmingham canceled the games after getting a guaranteed offer of all travel expenses if they would play five games in Chicago and two in Indianapolis.[22]

The Chicago series opened with a rain-halted tie. The next day Robert Poindexter earned a spot in the Black Barons record book with a no-hitter, according to a special dispatch in the *Birmingham News*. However, the *Chicago Defender*, in its detailed account of the game, said Poindexter pitched a one-hitter, crediting Jelly Gardner with a single in the seventh inning: "Stratton let Gardner's rap get through him and mess up his thumb." After Poindexter loaded the bases with two walks, he started a double play, nailing Gardner at the plate for the first out. The box score shows Gardner with two hits, but the game account reports only one. Apparently, whoever reported the game to the *Birmingham News* felt that Stratton, a notoriously weak fielder in 1925, had committed an error on Gardner's at-bat in the seventh. (In the appendices, the author credits Poindexter with a no-hitter.) Chicago won the third game, which was marked by an unseemly row. Manager Crawford, Beverly, and Salmon "were chased from the park by the umpires and police." Whatever sparked the row was not explained.[23] The next three games also went to the American Giants.

The two games in Indianapolis were split.[24]

Crawford was highly critical of the Chicago series, citing "unsportsmanlike tactics" by the American Giants. He said his team could take Rube Foster's team in a square situation. He offered a thousand-dollar side bet for such a matchup.

Meanwhile, they had to go home and face Kansas City again. It was a memorable occasion as the Black Barons took their first series from the champions.[25]

The Monarchs hit Salmon hard in the first inning of the opener, scoring three runs on a single, two doubles, and a homer. But Birmingham chipped away, gradually taking the lead and winning, 10–6.[26] Birmingham, perhaps to the wonderment of all, made it two in a row the next day, winning 4–1 on Poindexter's seven-hitter. He got stronger as the game advanced, striking out the first two men the ninth.[27]

The Monarchs showed they were still the Monarchs in the third game, crushing Birmingham, 13–0, as Bill "Bullet" Rogan pitched a one-hit shutout. He faced only 28 batters, striking out eight. Still, Birmingham had taken the series.[28]

They traveled again after the Kansas City series, dropping most games at St. Louis and Detroit.[29] As with the previous road trip, there was at least one remarkable highlight. In early August, Rube Foster traded his half-brother, pitcher Willie Foster, to Birmingham. Starting the fourth game against Detroit, the left-hander became possibly the second Black Barons pitcher to throw a no-hitter in less than a month.[30] The real oddity, though, is that it appears to be the only game that Foster ever played in with Birmingham. He is in no other box scores or line scores, suggesting that Rube Foster perhaps only loaned his younger brother to Birmingham for a day.

Birmingham owner Joe Rush, disgusted with his team's play, suspended Salmon, Robertson, and Thompson without pay and sent them home from Chicago. At the same time he traded infielder Stratton to Chicago for three pitchers, presumably to fill the spots vacated by Salmon and Robertson.[31] Whatever the circumstances, Rush traded away one of the team's steadiest players.

August 8 standings showed Birmingham (4–5) creeping out of the cellar in the second half, thanks to Indianapolis (2–10). The standings were just one game off mathematical accuracy. Chicago (11–3) and St. Louis (10–3) were leading, with Kansas (5–4) uncharacteristically in third place.[32]

After Detroit, six losses in seven games, the Black Barons took a break from league play to host the Houston Black Buffaloes of the Negro Texas League and the 24th Infantry. Birmingham won four out of six from the Texans. Poindexter pitched a six-hit shutout in the opening game. "Poindexter, in addition to pitching a good game, turned in an exhibition of fine fielding, handling eight chances. He started two double plays by snagging line drives," the *Birmingham News* reported.[33]

In mid–August, the third effort to get the 24th Infantry soldiers to Birmingham was successful. Two previous tries had been canceled at the last minute, one reportedly because NNL President Foster would not allow it. This was a few days after the ruckus in Chicago that had so aggravated Crawford.[34] It was also suggested that Colonel Waite C. Johnson, the commanding officer, was reluctant to sanction a Birmingham series because of the intensity of the 1924 series, "several cracked skulls, a broken leg and bruises too numerous to relate resulting from the intense rivalry."[35]

The soldiers came Birmingham with a 23–1 record, most of the games having been played on the military base. the *Birmingham News* predicted a competitive opponent.[36]

The prophecy appeared true when the soldiers drubbed the Black Barons, 16–7, in the opener. However, the *News* qualified the win: "Sympathy cost the Black Barons a ball game they should have had no trouble winning…. The Black Barons piled up a seven-run lead in the first innings, got to feeling sorry for the soldiers who showed a case of stage fright, let down and were never able to regain their top form."[37] Crawford gave up 13 hits, and Birmingham made seven errors. The winning pitcher, Columbus Vance, was a future Black Baron, joining the team in 1927.[38]

Birmingham won the second game, 8–0, behind the pitching of a left-hander named Stephenson, another late-season roster addition. Stephenson allowed only two runners as far as second base and the Black Barons, for a change, did not commit an error.[39]

The third game showed a clear delineation between professional and amateur players. Birmingham had 20 hits in a 16–4 romp. "The soldiers were so completely outclassed that they were recalled to camp," the *Birmingham News* reported.[40]

It would have been a good way for a disappointing season to end for the Black Barons. Unfortunately, there were still nearly three weeks to go against NNL opponents. The results were not good.

Detroit, which had wrested the second-half lead away from Kansas City, won three out of five at Rickwood. Two former Birmingham sandlot players, Norman "Turkey" Stearns and Clarence Smith, each had eight hits in five games, Birmingham helped with 23 errors. George McAllister played in three games for the Stars, giving "his usual demonstration of fancy fielding."[41]

Memphis also won three of five at home. Crawford pitched a three-hit shutout for a 2–0 win, but the Red Sox were dominant, winning the final game, 14–1.

There were more off-the-field problems, too. Rush fined Salmon and Meredith $50 each. Salmon was suspended indefinitely for "being drunk" and exhibiting behavior "unbecoming a ballplayer." Meredith, "for failure to co-operate with the club and for booting grounders … was put out of the ball park during the Barons last stand at Memphis and not allowed to see the game finished. When the youngster proceeded to tell both Owner Rush and Manager Sam Crawford where to go the place wasn't a cool one."[42]

The season came to a merciful end on the road with a succession of losses at Kansas City and Memphis. Manager Crawford disbanded the team in Memphis, and said he was returning to Birmingham to begin planning for the 1926 campaign.[43]

6

Satchel Paige and the Revival of the Negro Southern League (1926)

While the Black Barons struggled in the Negro National League, the Negro Southern League totally foundered. With Birmingham and Memphis, likely its strongest franchises, playing in the NNL, the NSL was unable to function in 1924 and 1925. Nashville and other former members either played independent ball or did not operate.

In March 1926, the NSL was resurrected at a meeting in Birmingham. Principals in the organization included Black Barons owner Joe Rush.[1] Bert M. Roddy of Memphis was elected league president.[2]

The rebirth of the league was a boon for Birmingham. The Black Barons played good baseball from the beginning, eventually defeating the Memphis Red Sox in a championship playoff. But that pennant was far from reality in March. In fact, if the Black Barons were in the league, they might face a boycott from their own fans.

Birmingham, although in the organizational forefront, suddenly appeared to be a questionable member. Henry O. Ruffingood wrote in the *Birmingham Reporter* that rumors had Rube Foster taking control of the team. Foster was reportedly sending Sam Crawford to Birmingham to take charge of the team and secure Rickwood Field for the season. It was hinted that Joe Rush could not come to terms with the Birmingham Barons for continuing to play home games at the park.[3]

Arriving in Birmingham for discussions about the issue were NNL Secretary J.J. Gilmore, NSL Secretary Professor Johnson, and Memphis club President R.S. Lewis.[4]

Gilmore, Crawford and W.N. Crisby [*sic*; Kritzky is the correct spelling], a white businessman, showed up at a meeting at the Elks Rest. Kritzky said he had taken over the Black Barons, and they would operate at Rickwood under his direction with Crawford as manager. Kritzky then left the meeting and Gilmore, representing him, spoke at length. Gilmore praised Kritzky and "ridiculed Negro management, Negro umpires and Negro base ball leaders in general."[5]

Oscar W. Adams Sr., offended by Gilmore's remarks, responded. He was critical of relinquishing control of a reputable black business "made so by sacrifices of the Negro people … and Joe Rush and his family." Adams said he was not willing "to sit idle while a Negro was double-crossed and mistreated."[6]

Hotel owner Rush had owned the Black Barons for several years and was generally credited with making the team known and respected nationally.[7] Adams observed:

I don't believe that Joe Rush is having a fair deal in this matter. Through his efforts Birmingham has received hundreds of thousands of dollars throughout the country in advertising and reputation. I am not willing to see him sacrificed and his business turned over to a white man on the simple ground that he is not able to secure Rickwood Park. We have millions of dollars in the banks of Birmingham, and I believe that Negroes of the South are loyal enough, brave enough and have enough business sense to build their own parks … if the Southern white people will not permit us to use their parks, but are willing to hand them over to Northern people. It approaches a scandal and disgrace upon the race and I am not willing to be idle while it goes on.[8]

Shortly after the rancorous gathering, NSL President Roddy came to Birmingham to personally intervene. He emerged from meetings with Birmingham Barons General Manager Billy West and Kritzky with an agreement for the Black Barons, through the NSL, to use the field. Kritzky relinquished all previous claims and said further negotiations with Rube Foster had been canceled.[9]

The near disaster averted, the NSL got busy with setting a schedule and other preparations for the season. Along with Birmingham and Memphis, the league lineup was the Albany (Georgia) Giants, Atlanta Black Crackers, Chattanooga White Sox, Montgomery Grey Sox, Nashville Elite Giants, and New Orleans Caulfield Ads.[10]

The Birmingham club's officers were Oscar W. Adams, president; H. Strawbridge, treasurer; and R.T. Jackson, secretary. Clarence Smith was the field manager.[11] He began spring training in Gadsden with 22 players seeking 16 roster spots.

Smith was a veteran ball player, starting his career with the Columbus Buckeyes in 1921. He came to Birmingham from the Detroit Stars. At 5'10", 185, he hardly seems a large man by today's standards, but he was commonly referred to as "Big Smith" in the press.[12] Primarily an outfielder, he was capable of playing almost any position. Indeed, he spent spend a great deal of the 1926 season shoring up the Birmingham infield as well as managing.

Among the players in camp were catcher Poindexter Williams, pitchers Harry "Fish" Salmon and Charles Beverly, and infielder Buford "Geechie" Meredith.[13]

In an interview with the *Birmingham Reporter*, Smith exuded confidence: "I feel that we can say to the fans in the Southern League that they may look forward to a real ball playing team such as has never been witnessed in the South. All my men are in good form now and we have two more weeks before the opening day. Our six pitchers are stars and they are anxious for a game."[14]

Birmingham opened away, playing in Chattanooga and Memphis. The *Birmingham Reporter* indicated that about 50 Birmingham fans were expected to greet the team in Memphis, traveling to Tennessee in a special rail car. In the first game at Chattanooga, the Black Barons faced a lanky young pitcher who would later become one of the most colorful and best-known baseball players of all time. He was Leroy "Satchel" Paige. In his debut with the Black Lookouts, Paige squeezed by Birmingham, 5–4, giving up only four hits.[15]

The losing pitcher was Leo Birdine, another player of name confusion. His career, 1925–1932, included stints with the Black Barons, Memphis and other teams. His name was spelled Burdine as often as Birdine. An ancestry.com search proved both spellings incorrect. After fruitless scrolling for workable Birdine or Burdine names, up popped Leo Berdine on an Alabama marriage license. The spelling was quite clear in the neat, cursive script of the courthouse clerk. The spelling was corroborated by a listing in the 1930 city directory. Subsequently, the author has used the Berdine spelling throughout this book.[16]

Salmon pitched Birmingham to a win in the second game, 6–2. Paige pitched in relief in the third game and found the Black Barons much harder to tame this time. Birmingham won, 13–9, rocking Paige for six runs and 11 hits.[17] The Black Barons lost two out of three at Memphis, returning home with a 3–4 record.[18]

Reports from around the South indicated widespread support, with good attendance, for the new league. Birmingham observers projected as many as 20,000 at Rickwood. "Parties have already given notice from as far as Montgomery, Tuscaloosa and other Alabama cities of their intention to be present on the opening day. The white people are giving cordial support through the press and in various enterprises for Negroes are employed. Some … believe that there will be at least 2,000 white people in the grand stand Monday."[19]

Black businesses were asked to grant employees a half holiday to attend the opener. White businesses were also asked "to let their employees off for a few hours."[20]

An advertisement in the *Reporter* listed the following 14-player roster: "George McAllister, first base; 'Geechie' Meredith, second base; [Curtis] Harris, third base; Saul 'Dixie'

Newspaper advertisement promoting Opening Day in 1926. From the *Birmingham Reporter*, 8 May 1926.

Davis, short stop; John Kemp, center field; Clarence Smith, right field; Joe 'Goose' Mitchell, left field; Poindexter Williams and Lewis Means, catchers; Harry Salmon, Charles Beverly, Juran, Calhoun and Bird Eye [sic], pitchers." Bird Eye was Leo "Eight Rock" Berdine. Juran and Calhoun's first names are not known. Not listed was third baseman J. Perry Oden, but he made his mark in the home opener nevertheless.[21]

Threatening weather shortened the game to five innings. The *Birmingham Reporter* called the turnout 14,000. "The white people responded in fine style at all the games and they have congratulated the club for its fine baseball season and expressed themselves as being willing to give full co-operation," reported the black newspaper. The *Birmingham News* put the attendance at about 8,000.[22]

Despite the weather, it was a festive day, including a celebrity first pitch by the bishop of the African Methodist Episcopal Church and assorted prizes for the first players to achieve various levels of play. "No doubt the greatest sensation in baseball circles in Birmingham was when Bishop B.G. Shaw … pitched the first pitch for the season. The fourteen thousand people yelled as if they would burst their throats and this gave the club a clean and perfect setting to begin the season with," said the *Reporter*.[23]

Webb Oden received a new Stetson hat from civic leader P.D. Davis for hitting the season's first home run at Rickwood. McAllister and Meredith received $25 and $10 in gold, respectively, for being the first Black Barons to score runs. The cash awards came from the Drennan Motor Company and businessman H.A. Hatcher.[24]

Paced by McAllister's three hits, Oden's home run, and tight pitching by Salmon, Birmingham won the rain-shortened game, 5–1. They gave fans a little more for their money the following day, playing a full nine innings as Berdine not only pitched a seven-hitter but also hit a two-run homer. Birmingham beat Memphis a third straight time in a 10-inning game decided on a two-out single by McAllister.[25]

At the end of the first two weeks, Birmingham (6–4) was third behind Albany (7–1) and New Orleans (6–3).[26] Albany, the next opponent, was managed by Big Bill Gatewood, a veteran ball player who had been pitching since 1905. He was a tall right-hander with a perfected spitball and emery ball. He is credited with giving James "Cool Papa" Bell his nickname. In 1927 and 1930, he played for Birmingham.[27]

In Albany, Birmingham moved into a tie for first place as Salmon and Berdine each won. The other games were rained out.[28] They returned home to play Nashville and the 24th Infantry.

Birmingham bats boomed against Nashville. They scored 23 runs and 28 hits, winning the first two games, 11–5 and 12–7. They closed the series with an 8–2 win.[29] They then won four straight from the soldiers.[30]

A couple of days later, Chattanooga came to town, boasting a respectable team and their new pitching sensation, Paige. The Mobile native made his Birmingham debut on May 31 in one of the finest pitching duels ever seen at Rickwood. It was an era when pitchers had endurance and bullpens were more of an afterthought than the results of strategic planning.

Birmingham scored in the second when Mitchell doubled and came home on a hard hit by Williams. Chattanooga tied it in the third. Birmingham won it, 3–2, on Mitchell's triple in the bottom of the 11th.[31]

Both Paige and Salmon pitched all 11 innings. Salmon struck out five and Paige three.[32] The match-up showed Paige to be a pitcher to be watched, but it also showed he was fallible. He showed flashes of greatness his rookie year but finished under .500 in wins. In statistics compiled by the author, his record was 11–12. He started 20 of 27 games, completing 19, and throwing one shutout.

Birmingham won the other games, 6–4 and 5–2, finishing the first month of the season contending for the lead.

Attendance was reported to be good throughout the league, even among clubs struggling on the field. When school ended, there was speculation that some teams like Atlanta and Montgomery would be strengthened by college players. In fact, both signed local college athletes.[33]

After sweeping Chattanooga, Manager Smith was exuberant about his team's chances for the pennant. "My men are in fighting form.... If the fans will give us support, we will give them as good a team as there is in America today among Negro players. Birmingham is a wonderful city with many possibilities, and there is no reason why they should not have an up-to-date baseball club among the Negro People. They have it in the Black Barons. It is up to the public to show their appreciation."[34]

However, Atlanta and Montgomery, bolstered by new players, threw off early season lethargy and suddenly emerged as winners.

"For weeks these two outfits have struggled valiantly to remain in the cellar, with Montgomery, by the hardest, holding the last place," reported a writer for the Associated Negro Press with a bit of sarcasm. "So consistently did these teams lose that fans and teams began to think the real purpose of Atlanta and Montgomery in the league was to contribute to the won column of the other members of the circuit...."[35]

Standings in early June were Birmingham (16–4), Albany (14–6), and New Orleans (14–7).[36]

Despite a strong finish, Albany was a close second to Birmingham, which sewed up the first half with a four-game sweep of Montgomery at Rickwood. Local fans were disappointed in not getting to see one-armed "Wing" Maddox pitch. Maddox had replaced Henry Hannon as Grey Sox manager, playing outfield when not pitching. He did not play at all in the series, apparently because of injury. "With Manager Maddox on the bench with an injured arm, the Montgomery Grey Sox went down in defeat to the tune of 8–2 in the opening game with the Elites Saturday," the Associated Negro Press reported.[37]

The sweep clinched the first half for Birmingham, making two shutout losses to Albany the final week inconsequential. One of the Albany wins was a no-hitter by Gatewood. Only three Black Barons reached base, two on errors and one on a missed third strike.[38]

Albany disputed Birmingham's claim to the first-half title, citing several forfeits that they felt belonged in the Giants' win column. League officials did not agree, and Birmingham was first-half champions.[39]

Manager Smith's analysis of the first-half title mirrored what any manager might say today: "Good pitching and timely hitting are responsible for the success of the team. The boys struck their stride after the first week and came up to expectations of the management and the fans in every department of the game."

Optimism was high at the league's mid-season meeting in Memphis. President Roddy expressed concern only over the state of umpiring. In most cities, the umpires were local men, hired for the day or the series. Obviously, the competency level could vary widely not only from city to city but even day to day. The *Albany Herald* reported on the umpiring problem early in the season: "At the end of the first game the white fans attending took up a collection to put Umpire Jones behind the plate to look 'em over. The umpires working before him had not been giving the satisfactory service Jones puts out. Following this move on the part of the hundreds of white fans attending, the president of the league announced that travelling umpires will be employed by the colored Southern League as is the case with all other good baseball loops."[40]

Another problem—one that always plagued black baseball leagues—was poor statistical reporting. The *Chicago Defender*, which attempted to run standings, line scores and even some box scores each week, lamented poor cooperation from the ball clubs under the headline "MAYBE THEY'RE CRIPPLED OR MAYBE CAN'T WRITE." The *Defender* writer noted: "Birmingham, Albany, New Orleans, Chattanooga, Montgomery and Atlanta haven't got men who can keep score by innings—a thing any 10-year-old boy can do—then add the batteries, place a special delivery stamp on letter after game and mail it to us."[41]

When the second half started, Albany still looked like the team to challenge Birmingham. The black press reported that all of the teams had been strengthened, and no one could be discounted. Memphis had acquired William "Steel Arm" Tyler from Chicago. In his first start, he shut down New Orleans on two hits.[42]

Montgomery, with the addition of Alabama State players, was more competitive also, under Manager "Wing" Maddox. A *Birmingham News* writer said Maddox "is considered the most sensational and scientific baseball player in negro baseball circles."[43]

Pete Cleage, first baseman with Chattanooga, recalled Maddox in an interview many years later: "You never saw anything like it. He had his left arm missing, so he wore the glove on his right hand. He would catch a fly ball, throw it up a foot or two in the air and sling his glove off, then catch the ball again as it came back down and throw it back into the infield. And he had an awfully strong arm. I've seen him cut down a lot of runners at home plate. He was a pretty good hitter, too, and a great bunter. He could really handle the bat on a bunt."[44]

A New Orleans writer said the arm was missing just below the shoulder. "When chasing flies, he makes his catch with one hand, slips the glove under his stump, and heaves the ball into the infield. His agility is amazing…. Maddox, as a pitcher, possesses a fine collection of curves and his speed and control, considering the lack of balance caused by his handicap, is remarkable."[45]

Claude Walker of Knoxville, as a small boy, saw Maddox play. "He was a good batter and he had speed. He'd choke up on the bat and I've seen him stretch a long single into a double."[46]

New Orleans, under Manager Fred Caulfield, remained a contender. They had the league's first legitimate power hitter in Roy "Red" Parnell, who pitched and played the outfield. On June 10 he pitched the Ads to a 7–4 win at Rickwood in the first game of a doubleheader. He also hit a home run, evoking the following description from a sportswriter: "Parnell hit one of the longest home runs of the year when he parked the ball over the centerfield fence just to the right of the Chero-Cola board."[47] He was credited with five home runs during the first two weeks of the season.[48] Parnell became a Black Baron in 1927 and 1928.

Still, everyone was chasing Birmingham, which had an outstanding lineup and the best pitching staff in the league. In a series, it was hard for anyone else to fill a rotation to equal Salmon, Beverly, and Berdine. In July, they added Robert Poindexter, "considered the best curve ball pitcher in negro baseball."[49] One sportswriter described Salmon and Berdine as being "on a par with any that the Southern Association can produce." The writer said both were quite capable of winning games for the Birmingham Barons.

In the same article, the reporter praised the NSL in general: "The baseball played by the Negro Southern League teams at Rickwood this year has been very good, and they deserve a better support than they have been getting. The white fans of the city, as a whole, are not aware of the class of baseball being exhibited by the negro teams at the 'Wood."[50]

If Birmingham had a weakness, it was at shortstop. Saul "Dixie" Davis had started most games, but others filled in occasionally. Frustrated at Davis's performance, Smith eventually dealt him to Memphis, getting a player named Williford in return. At the time of the trade, Davis was hitting .263, but had committed 22 errors in 137 fielding chances. Williford, in six games, hit an anemic .105 and committed four errors in just 20 chances. This forced Smith often to play shortstop himself. Finally, it was announced in early July that the shortstop they needed had been found in newcomer DeWitt Owens. Subsequent box scores show Owens making his share of errors, but there were flashes of brilliance. In the final regular season game against New Orleans, he handled nine chances with only one miscue. "He stabbed Breaux's grounder back of second and threw him out at first for the star play of the game," reported the *Birmingham News*.[51]

In late July the Black Barons started a Nashville-Memphis road trip with a five-day visit to St. Louis where they took on the NNL team. Harry Salmon beat the Stars, 8–3, in the opener, but St. Louis came back to take the series three games to two.[52]

Birmingham found second-half competition tougher. Nashville, near the bottom most of the first half, managed to split four games. Then, Memphis won four out of five and took over first place. Birmingham bounced back in a home stand with Nashville as Salmon struck out 13 in a win. Memphis continued to win also, taking series from New Orleans and Chattanooga. In early September, Memphis locked up the second half with a five-game sweep of Albany.

The highlight for Birmingham down the stretch was yet another fine performance by Salmon. Against Albany on August 28, he pitched an 8–0 no-hitter. Facing only 29 batters, he struck out seven and walked two.[53]

With two clear first- and second-half winners, a playoff between Birmingham and Memphis ensued. The best-five-out-of-nine series was to open with four games in Memphis, then move to Birmingham for four more. If a ninth game was necessary, the league would determine where it would be played. Additionally, the NSL winner was to play a Negro Dixie Series with a Dallas, Texas, team. The winner of that series would then likely play the Negro National League champion.[54]

Neither of those last two grandiose plans ever materialized, but the Negro Southern League playoffs was a big success, especially for pitchers. A total of ten games were played. Three of them were ties, called by darkness. Three games were decided by 1–0 scores and two ended 2–0.

Clarence Smith added former Black Baron Reuben Jones, a good outfielder, and left-hander James Jeffries to the roster for the playoffs.[55] Memphis's stretch drive, now under the leadership of Charles "Twosides" Wesley, another former Black Baron, had already been strengthened by the addition of pitcher Bill "Emery" Drake and two players from the 24th Infantry team, outfielder Findall Williams and pitcher-outfielder Nat Trammell. Drake, a twelve-year veteran, was "a smart pitcher who used a good curve, good control, and a variety of 'trick' pitches, including the emery ball."[56]

With the emery ball, the ball was roughed up with sandpaper before delivery to the batter. Like the spitball, it had been disallowed but never really went away. In one playoff game, it was noted that "there was no little argument over Drake using an emery ball. The umpires searched Drake's clothing for the sandpaper and after the search Drake allowed his third baseman and shortstop to doctor the ball."[57]

The series opened on Saturday, September 11, before a huge crowd in Memphis. Birmingham took a 2–0 lead in the first inning, only to see Memphis come back and tie the game in the ninth. The umpires halted the contest because of darkness after 12 innings. Salmon and "Steel Arm" Tyler pitched all twelve innings.[58]

The following day Berdine won, 9–4, despite giving up 11 hits and two walks. Meredith led Birmingham hitters with a double and a triple.[59]

On Monday, Birmingham took a two-game edge with a 1–0 win by Jeffries over Drake. Williams doubled and scored the only run, a heartbreaking defeat for Drake, who allowed only three hits and struck out 12. Jeffries gave up seven hits.[60]

That brought the series to an excited Birmingham. A special train excursion brought Memphis fans to Birmingham. "This will mean that the Memphis Red Sox will have many rooters at Rickwood Field Monday and Tuesday." Manager Smith said the series showed a promising future for the Negro Southern League.[61]

Rain washed out the opener, but a large crowd was at Rickwood Field the next day for a brilliant pitching battle between Drake and Poindexter. Drake gave up only four hits and one walk while striking out three. Poindexter surrendered six hits but fanned seven and walked none.

In the 9th, Drake issued his only walk to McAllister, who moved to third on Meredith's sacrifice and Reuben Jones's fielder's choice out. At this point, Manager Smith challenged Drake's alleged use of an emery ball.[62] The umpire gave Drake a new ball to throw, and Smith promptly whacked it to center to drive in the only run of the game. That gave Birmingham three wins to none for the Red Sox.[63]

The second game in Birmingham was another deadlock. Salmon was on the mound for Birmingham and Tyler for Memphis. Tyler, who pitched like "a blazing comet," carried a 2–1 lead into the ninth inning. Hits by Jones and Smith tied the game. The umpires deemed the light too dim to start another inning. The 2–2 tie eliminated the possibility of the Black Barons winning the pennant before a home crowd. After Game 6, scheduled for September 23, a crew of workmen was to start preparing Rickwood Field for the football season.[64]

But if they couldn't treat the home fans to the pennant, the Black Barons at least made sure their followers would know that only one game was needed when the series returned to Memphis.

Jeffries pitched a six-hitter to beat Memphis, 2–0, in Game 6. The Black Barons broke up Reb Willis's no-hitter in the fifth, scoring a run on an RBI single by Webb Oden. Jones added an insurance run in the sixth with a home run over the right field wall. Memphis had opportunities, but Birmingham's defense was flawless. "Fancy fielding featured the Black Barons' defense," reported the *News*, "Geechie's work standing out like a sore thumb. The little second baseman had a field day in the final game." Meredith handled eight chances perfectly, making two putouts and contributing six assists.[65]

After a rainout on the first day back in Memphis, the Black Barons saw another frustrating tie in Game 7. Berdine and Drake each pitched beautifully for 11 innings before darkness ended the game with no score.[66]

Then, Memphis tightened the series. Behind the pitching of Willis and Trammell, Memphis got back-to-back shutouts in Games 8 and 9. Willis struck out ten and held the Black Barons to just two hits in his 2–0 triumph. Trammell gave up nine hits but won, 1–0.[67]

That was as close as Memphis would get. Game 10 was a decisive triumph for Birmingham. With Smith getting three hits and scoring four runs, and Williams adding two more hits, one a triple, Birmingham thrashed Memphis, 9–3, for the championship. Jeffries held the Red Sox to just four hits.[68]

Again, there was a reference to a possible series with Dallas, champions of the Negro Texas League, but it never materialized.[69]

Manager Clarence Smith's ability to play anywhere was a key to his team's success. Although primarily the team's center fielder (31 games), he also played left field (8), second base (6), shortstop (5), third base (3), and first base (2). Despite frequently changing positions, he never seemed to lose his rhythm for hitting. His .355 batting average was the team's best. He also led in runs scored (52), hits (82), doubles (16) and stolen bases (38). It is one of the best all-around seasons by any Black Baron.

Other starters hitting over .300 included Berdine (.310) and McAllister (.306). After joining the club in August, Jones hit a remarkable .500 (23 hits in 46 at bats) in 11 games.

Birmingham also had one of its all-time great pitching staffs. Salmon (16–3) had a no-hitter and two shutouts. Berdine (15–5) threw four shutouts. Salmon struck out 83 and walked 14 in 125 innings pitched. Poindexter (6–5), who joined the team mid-season, pitched two shutouts and had complete games of 10, 11 and 12 innings among his 13 appearances.

Economically, it is likely that the NSL had one of its most successful years in 1926. The success can probably be attributed to a timely congruence of baseball-hungry fans, sound financial backing of the individual clubs, strong league leadership, and a good collection of players throughout the league.

The 1926 season was a strong year for Negro baseball in general. Three other leagues were operating simultaneously: the reorganized Negro National League, the Eastern Colored League, and the Interstate League.[70]

The success of the 1926 season became a springboard for both Birmingham and Memphis to return to the "major leagues" in 1927. Both returned to the Negro National League, where they played for the next four years.

7

Birmingham Returns to the Majors (1927)

Spring training in 1927 saw the Black Barons changing both leagues and managers. Birmingham and Memphis returned to the Negro National League. The new manager was Reuben Jones. The durable outfielder played with Birmingham from 1923 to 1925, and rejoined the team late in 1926 to help win the Negro Southern League pennant.[1]

He started playing baseball in Texas in 1910, eventually managing the Tillotson College team in Austin. The school was so poor it could not afford uniforms. Jones offered to mortgage a couple of his grandfather's mules to get money for uniforms. He played with the Austin Black Senators and Dallas Black Giants before coming to Birmingham.[2]

The 1926 championship had local fans excited about the league change. "Quite a few fans have visited the training camp at Gadsden, and predict a wonderful year.... Manager Jones is able to select from out of his large number of men in training. From all indications Jones is going to find it difficult in weeding his men down to the 15, the number to be carried under the rules of the National League."[3]

With nearly 30 prospects, Jones said he expected to "spring some surprises." He said in an interview, "I am encouraged over the way the men are working and the wonderful sportsmanlike spirit exhibited among the fellows. I've been in the game for a few years and I believe I am prepared to say that Birmingham is going to have the best baseball club this year in its history.... We are in this fight to win. I fear no comers, my men are trained to fight hard, steady and cautiously."[4]

The first look at the team came in mid–April in an exhibition series with the Chicago Royal Giants. It was a disappointing look for four innings. The visitors jumped out to a 9–0 lead, and everybody had to be wondering about Jones's prediction for a great team. A 6-foot-6, 225-pound right-hander named Tar Baby Pryor held Birmingham at bay while Chicago scored freely. Then, the Black Barons came to life, storming back for a wild 12–11 victory before "one of the largest crowds to ever see a negro exhibition game at Rickwood." James Thompson's two doubles and Red Parnell's home run sparked the comeback.[5]

Pitchers suffered equally the next two games, which Birmingham won, 12–11 and 11–10. In the second game, they came within three batters of batting around twice in a nine-run fifth inning. Parnell hit another home run and also drove in a run with a triple.[6] Shortstop John Hamilton had two triples in the third game.[7]

Although the rookie pitchers had performed poorly, the three Birmingham wins had local supporters excited about the season opener with the Cuban Stars. As usual, the community set its sights on an unrealistic Opening Day attendance of 20,000. Letters were sent out to fraternal and civic organizations, urging their support. Birmingham School Super-intendent Dr. C.B. Glenn authorized black principals to excuse any boy or girl who brought a parental request to attend the game. Bleacher seat prices were reduced for children. The chamber of commerce supported an effort to turn out a bigger crowd than the Chicago America Giants would have in their opener. Black businesses were urged to close at 2 o'clock so employees could attend the game, and trains were expected to bring interested fans from Tuscaloosa, Montgomery, Anniston, and Gadsden.[8]

Support also came from Masonic Grand Master W.T. Woods, Exalted Ruler J.E. Kelley of the Elks, and President P.D. Davis of the Birmingham Civic and Commercial Association. Davis also offered a new Stetson hat to the first Black Baron to hit a home run. The expected starting lineup for Birmingham:

John Hamilton, 2b	George McAllister, 1b
James Thompson, cf	Reuben Jones, lf
Red Parnell, rf	John Oden, 3b
Poindexter Williams, c	Harry Salmon or Leo Berdine, p.[9]
Dewitt Owens, ss	

Before more than 10,000 fans, the Black Barons won, 5–4, in 10 innings. Manager Jones hit a solo home run for the winning margin and made "two sensational falling catches" in left field. Sam Streeter pitched a complete game.[10]

The next two games were divided in Gadsden. They returned to Birmingham for the final two games, both of which the locals won. A 13-inning Thursday game was decided by Meredith's sacrifice fly. Every Birmingham player had at least one hit in the 9–2 Friday game. Salmon held the Cubans to eight hits. Outfielders Thompson, Jones, and Valetin Drake of the visitors all made breathtaking catches.[11]

Birmingham finished the first week on top in the standings and attendance. The Rickwood Opening Day crowd was about 3,000 more than Chicago's and double every other city.[12]

Although Cleveland was projected to be a stronger opponent, Birmingham won four out of five. Poindexter pitched superbly in the opener, giving up seven hits, striking out six. Parnell had three hits, and Owens hit a three-run homer before another large crowd. The *Birmingham News* called it a snappy game with both teams "out throat cutting, hustling all the way."[13]

Birmingham blew a five-run lead in the second game, but Streeter retired 13 straight batters in relief in the 7–5 win. New first baseman John Shanks hit safely his first three times at bat and handled 11 chances in the field without an error. Hamilton and Parnell both homered.[14]

Cleveland won the third game and Birmingham the next two, including Streeter's 4–0 shutout. Spoony Palm starred in the last game with a triple and a home run.[15]

William J. Moore, writing in the *Birmingham Reporter*, was lavish in his praise of several players and the great start:

> Our hats off to Mgr. Jones and his men for their wonderful playing. They outguessed and outplayed the visitors in every department of the game. The pitching we received without a doubt for the series was the best we have witnessed this year, and is what the fans want to see. No loafing.
> We cannot help but speak of Williams' wonderful work behind the plate in the series just closed. His handling of the pitchers in these games again causes us to say we believe him to be one of the best receivers in the league, and how he can hit that pill down the right field line in a pinch. Merdith

[*sic*] played as one inspired and if you didn't know better you would have thought that the manager had warned him about his job....

That Alexander is one sweet fielder. He can get them from either side. Those who missed seeing the play he made on a ball in the second game Thursday missed seeing one of the great plays made in the history of Rickwood....

McAllister's playing around first base is wonderful. He is best fielder of low thrown balls we have seen in this circuit. At the bat he can drag them and put on the hit and run with the best.[16]

Still in first place, Birmingham (8–2) made its first road trip, 23 days, with stops in Memphis, Chicago, Kansas City, and St. Louis. Fred Daniels's four-hitter won the first game at Memphis, 6–0. Birmingham won with three out of five and its third straight series.[17] Then, a downturn. Both Chicago and Kansas City won three out of five.[18]

Despite Birmingham's obvious improvements, Kansas City was still a nemesis, getting shutouts in the first two games. Birmingham won two on strong pitching by Streeter and Salmon. Streeter, in relief, struck out nine. Salmon had a two-hit shutout.[19]

At St. Louis, the Black Barons encountered a strong team that fielded such stars as Cool Papa Belle, Willie Wells, and George "Mule" Suttles. The Stars won the opener and Birmingham the second game. On Sunday, the Stars got 32 hits, sweeping a double-header, 12–4 and 11–3.[20]

Both teams boarded a train immediately afterward, hurrying to Birmingham to resume competition on Monday afternoon at Rickwood Field. A.G. Bennings, Birmingham secretary and business manager, said the teams, traveling together, would reach Birmingham at 2:40 p.m. and go straight to the ballpark from the station. Birmingham fans were eager to see the Stars and welcome the team home.[21] Birmingham had dropped out of first place on the road. Standings through June 9 were Chicago (20–10), Detroit (19–11), and Birmingham (22–16).[22]

A new pitcher, left-hander John W. Johnson, was with the team. Also, owner Joe Rush was after George Hubert Lockhart, athletic director at Alabama State and former Bacharach Giants star.[23] The anticipated signing of Lockhart was reportedly frequently throughout the 1920s, but "Prof" never appeared in a Birmingham uniform. Oscar Adams reminded his readers that Mule Suttles—his name correctly spelled—was an Edgewater boy, coming home.[24]

Birmingham won the first game, 5–2, on Streeter's "stingy" pitching in tough situations. He struck out nine and had three hits, one a triple.[25]

But St. Louis won three out of the next four to take the series. In the second game Birmingham outhit the Stars, 17–13, but lost, 9–8. Nine players, including Suttles, had two or more hits in the game. Meredith and McAllister had triples and Palm a home run. Suttles doubled and homered as St. Louis won the third game, 11–4.

The concluding double-header was split. For Birmingham, Jones hit a two-run homer and Parnell had four hits. Suttles, who hit two home runs, was walked intentionally three straight times, a total of eight in the series, a clear indication of respect for his bat.[26] The grueling series drained the Black Barons. Without any rest, they played and lost two games with the 24th Infantry.[27] The soldiers left town with two wins but also two fewer players. Jones signed pitcher Columbus Vance and outfielder Findall Williams. Of course, Jones was limited to using them only when they could get away from the base on leave. Both were available when Kansas City came to Birmingham two days later. Vance, a left-hander, pitched a seven-hitter, winning 6–2. He struck out five and walked two.[28]

In a remarkable turnaround from the two previous series, Birmingham swept the

Monarchs. In a 9–3 win by Poindexter, Parnell had three hits, including a home run, while five other players had two hits each.[29]

Salmon won the third game, 6–1, as Jones and Hamilton hit home runs. Birmingham fielding was excellent. "Meredith galloped all around the keystone and took in drives from every angle. Manager Jones flagged a few flies on the dead run."[30]

In the series-ending double-header, Parnell's three-run homer won the first game, 9–7. Salmon won the second, 4–2, with a four-hitter. Chuffy Alexander, replacing Meredith at second, "pulled play after play of sparkling fielding."[31]

The sweep moved Birmingham into third place. They won their sixth straight game two days later as they started a 20-game road trip in Memphis. Other stops were Chicago, St. Louis, and Detroit.[32]

Memphis won the next three, sending Birmingham on to Chicago with a losing streak.[33] The first game in Chicago sidelined three Birmingham players—Salmon, Poindexter, and Williams—with unspecified injuries. Chicago won all four games, and Birmingham's losing streak was seven.[34]

St. Louis won the Saturday and Sunday games easily, 10–2 and 4–0.[35]

The Monday game lasted only two innings after a near-riot halted play. The *Birmingham Reporter* detailed the donnybrook for local fans. With the scored tied 1–1, Satchel Paige was pitching for Birmingham. Pinch hitter Mitch Murray apparently dodged a close pitch, which struck his bat, the ball caroming and injuring his hand. Bat in hand, Murray started toward the mound. A spectator allegedly yelled to Paige, "You have nothing to defend yourself with. Run, boy, run!" Paige broke for the dugout, Murray in pursuit. The latter threw his bat, striking Paige in the side.

Several St. Louis players went over to the Birmingham dugout then. A woman in the stands shouted "Murder! Murder!" and the whole park was in an uproar. Manager Jones and the Black Barons left the field. Police officers began manhandling Birmingham players. A fan with an open knife got on the field, heading for "Geechie" Meredith. Some measure of order was apparently restored with Umpire Donaldson declaring that Paige could not finish the game. When Jones demanded to know why, Donaldson called the game. Jones said he would play the game under protest if he could put in another pitcher. Donaldson agreed to the pitcher but not the protest, and the game was stopped.

The "Special to the Reporter" article on the melee chastised Murray for his poor sportsmanship, especially for attacking the unarmed pitcher with a bat. "It is to be remembered that Paige is a young fellow, nearly six feet, about 21 years old, and

The baseball legend Leroy "Satchel" Paige, whose Birmingham career spanned 1927 to 1940 (courtesy Faye Davis and Birmingham Public Library Archives).

throws the fastest and hardest ball in the circuit. On this occasion, he was throwing hard, fast and wild," the writer concluded.[36] Paige had been acquired from Chattanooga by Birmingham in mid-season. They also added Bill Gatewood.

The Black Barons won the final two games in St. Louis, then headed on to Detroit, where they lost four out of five games.[37] Afterward, they returned home for exhibition games with Chattanooga.

They came home to criticism from sports editor Moore, always a strong booster. He took the team to task for poor play. "It is not our policy to knock any one or try to run the Black Barons through these columns, but we feel that too long have we held our peace and that the loyal fans of this city are being treated unfair [sic] when the material that is the Black Barons is allowed to waste as it has during the first half of the season," he wrote. Moore suggested that poor management in both the front office and on the field was responsible for Birmingham's first-half slide after a fine start.[38]

Two weeks later there was more criticism. He said the 1926 team, although playing in the Negro Southern League, had played better. Moore blamed the manager for the current second- division spot. "If I managed the team and made the poor showing that team made I would resign at once, for I would feel that I had been a failure in every respect as a manager," he wrote. "If I stayed, then I would be the manager of my team. When I put a fine on a player that would remain [or] … you surely invite another breaking of training rules." He challenged Manager Jones to prove the first-half problems were not his responsibility.[39]

Relentlessly, Moore resumed his attack the following week, writing, "It is not material that the Black Barons need but … use of that which they have." He said Jones, who had been playing left field, belonged in right field. "No better evidence of that will ever be shown than in Monday's game when a Chicago runner scored from third on a short hit to left center that he caught and made no attempt to throw the runner out. The way he plays ground balls he is never in position to throw at a runner until he has made two or three extra steps and almost invariably the runner beat the throw." Moore also criticized the batting order and decisions on when to remove pitchers and use relievers.[40]

The second half opened with two exhibition victories against Chattanooga, the start of a 12-game winning streak. A special guest at the first Chattanooga game was NNL President Judge W.C. Hueston of Gary, Indiana. Hueston spent two days in Birmingham and praised the city for its economy and race relations: "I am surprised to note the cordial relations existing here between the races. It may be yet that the problem of our people is going to be solved in this section. And with the steady improvements for education, police protection and fairer decisions in court, one cannot doubt as to what the future will be." He also praised Rickwood Field and the crowd support for the local team.[41]

In the 12-game run, Birmingham had eight league victories and two ties, all against Memphis.[42] It began with a 6–4 win at Rickwood. Salmon scattered nine hits, and Williams had three hits, including a game-tying home run and a two-run double.[43]

Six games were then played in Memphis, adding four more wins and two ties to the streak. "Satchel" Paige made several relief appearances in the Memphis games. One of the ties was 12 innings, called because of darkness.[44]

And it ended at Rickwood. The Chicago American Giants, getting off the train about 15 minutes before game time, rushed straight to Rickwood and won the opener, 9–7. They won again the next day, 4–3. Birmingham then won a 12-inning game, 4–3. Poindexter, had a pinch-hit double for the winning run. Sam Streeter and Chicago's Willie Foster pitched complete games, yielding 12 and 10 hits respectively. Manager Jones was put out of the game for arguing with the umpire.[45] The closing double-header was a Chicago win and a tie.[46]

Despite losing that series, Birmingham (16–5) remained in first, followed by Detroit (13–10) and Chicago (14–11).[47]

The Chicago series was followed by one against Detroit, which was coming off impressive wins at St. Louis and Memphis. The Detroit series brought hometown boy Norman "Turkey" Stearnes back to Birmingham.[48]

The first game went to Birmingham, 5–4, decided in the ninth on an error by the Detroit catcher. Stearnes celebrated his return with a home run. Meredith tripled for Birmingham.[49]

Birmingham won the second game, 12–11. Eight players had two or more hits in the game. The two wins in a row moved the Black Barons five games up on the Stars.[50]

Detroit regained ground in a rain-shortened third game. Manager Jones argued futilely with Umpire Montgomery to have the contest stopped at the top of the fifth inning, "but the ump didn't think that the downpour was great enough to warrant this, so the battle went to the sixth." Detroit won, 5–4. An unreported doubleheader was likely rained out.

Birmingham broke from league play to host Nashville. The NSL leader won 4–2.[51] The Black Barons ended the series with two wins.[52]

That sent Birmingham on to Kansas City, where the Monarchs waited for their chance to regain first place.

Sports editor Moore, no longer caustic, was elated over the improved Black Barons and thanked the owners for giving the city a winning team again. He was even kind to Reuben Jones, who had been taken ill. "We are indeed sorry to know that Manager Jones is ill and unable to be with the team during the winning spurt, but the very fact that they are on the winning side should make it easier for him recover and join the team on their return home in first class condition," Moore wrote. He said an unidentified but capable veteran outfielder would take Jones' place.[53]

Birmingham's strong second-half run continued with a 2–1 victory in the opening game in Kansas City. Salmon staved off a ninth-inning rally by the Monarchs. With the bases loaded, he retired the next three batters.[54]

Kansas City was unable to gain any ground in the Sunday double-header. They won the first game, 6–1, but Birmingham won the second, 7–5. Paige struck out 11, but needed relief help from Poindexter.[55]

Birmingham went a long way toward sewing up the second-half pennant in the fourth game. They scored two in the ninth inning to tie the game and went ahead, 4–3, in the tenth on Chuffy Alexander's single. Poindexter retired the Monarchs in the bottom of the tenth.[56] The Black Barons won the fifth game, 11–3.[57]

But there were still two more stops on the road trip. Both contributed to a quick letdown from the Kansas City euphoria. Birmingham lost four out of five in both St. Louis and Chicago. Suddenly the standings were reversed. The American Giants took over first and Birmingham fell to third.[58] St. Louis claimed second.[59]

Returning home, the Black Barons knew their chances were still very good. They would wrap up the season against second-division Memphis and the Cuban Stars, while Chicago closed with first-division Detroit and Kansas City.[60] Chicago would either win both halves or face Birmingham in a championship playoff.

The countdown for Birmingham began with a Labor Day morning-afternoon tripleheader against Memphis. Anticipating a large crowd, the management signed up the Tuggle

Institute band for entertainment during the afternoon game. Children under 16 were admitted for half price.[61]

It was a near-perfect day for Birmingham. After battling the Red Sox to a 2–2 tie in the morning game, the Black Barons swept the afternoon double-header on excellent pitching by Streeter and Paige. Streeter won a three-hitter, 8–1. Paige threw a seven-inning one-hitter in the nightcap, facing only 22 men. He struck out 10 and hit a single and a triple.[62]

Back in second place, the Black Barons faced the Red Sox in another double-header, and again won both games.[63] Columbus Vance, on leave from Fort Benning, won 2–1 in the first game, giving up the lone run on two errors. Paige again was brilliant in the seven-inning nightcap, giving up one hit and striking out nine in the 10–0 shutout. Jones hit a home run.[64]

Thanks to Memphis, which Birmingham dominated all season—16 wins and two ties in 23 games—the Black Barons went into the final series against the Cuban Stars back in first place by a hair. The odds were good, with Chicago facing third-place Detroit. According to the *Birmingham News*' assessment, Chicago needed a combination of five wins and two Birmingham losses to win the second half. On the other hand, Birmingham could pull it out with five wins and just one Chicago loss. More good news for Birmingham was the return of the injured Red Parnell to the lineup.[65]

Harry Salmon scattered eight hits to beat the Cubans, 5–1, in the opener. Double plays in both the eighth and ninth innings helped preserve the win.[66]

In the second game, Satchel Paige was dominant. His second straight shutout was a four-hitter, accompanied by 12 strikeouts and no walks. New center fielder "Pinky" Ward had two singles and a home run. The *Birmingham News* said the Black Barons were three wins away from the championship.[67]

And then it was one. As Chicago lost in Detroit, Sam Streeter beat the Cubans, 3–1. Streeter held them to five hits, retiring the side in order five times. He also benefited from tight fielding.[68]

The next day, the Black Barons made the Chicago outcome a moot point. Thompson's single in the ninth scored Jones from second, giving the locals a 6–5 triumph in the first game of the double-header. Paige limited the Cubans to six hits in the nightcap as Birmingham coasted, 6–2, locking up the second-half pennant.[69]

It was an exciting conclusion to Birmingham's best season in the Negro National League. It offset the disappointing slide in the first half and brought the first NNL playoff to Birmingham. Unfortunately, the good news on the field would end there. Chicago, with a lineup full of experienced post-season players, cut the Southern upstarts no slack. They won two games in Birmingham, then wrapped up the title at home.

But pre-playoff enthusiasm was high. Frank A. Young, longtime sportswriter with the *Chicago Defender*, had said if Birmingham won the second half, it would "increase the enthusiasm in the league 40 per cent" because it would bring a new element to a league largely dominated by two teams, Chicago and Kansas City. He predicted a bigger payday with Birmingham in the playoff, and added that the Black Barons' success "would give other teams more spirit to try, would cause colored men to invest money in the league."[70]

The *Birmingham Reporter* said Birmingham fans were "all het up and still heating, looking forward to the contest such as has never been witnessed before in the Magic City." The American Giants came to town to play a Southern team that had achieved a new level.[71]

On the eve of the opening game at Rickwood Field, it was reported that Big Bill Gatewood was now managing the Black Barons, "filling in for the still-ill Reuben Jones." There was no explanation of Jones's ailment. He had played in the Cuban Stars series, getting three hits in six at bats.[72]

The first playoff game was a repetition of Chicago's last trip to Birmingham. The American Giants, half an hour late getting to the ballpark, were unfazed by the travel problem. Buck Foster scattered six hits as the visitors won the opener, 5–0. They scored all of their runs in the first three innings.[73]

Birmingham led 2–0 in the second game, but the visitors knocked Paige out of the box in the fourth inning. Birmingham regained the lead in the seventh, and Poindexter appeared to be in control. Then, Chicago scored six runs before an out was made in the ninth. The final score was 10–5.[74]

While the *Birmingham News* account suggested nothing but superior play by the visitors, William J. Moore in the *Reporter* questioned the umpiring. He took arbiter Donaldson to task for ball-and-strike calls in the explosive ninth inning, and also for not removing Willie Powell from the game after he was apparently caught doctoring the ball with a foreign substance. "When it looked like the Barons would stage a rally, it was Donaldson who nipped the rally, not the Chicago Americans." Moore was disturbed also by a call at first base, saying the fielder's foot was not on the bag.[75]

Although Birmingham won the third game, 6–3, at Rickwood, the American Giants made short work of the Black Barons in Chicago. They took the third game, 6–4, then closed out the series with a 7–2 win.[76] As the Birmingham players dispersed, the American Giants prepared for a World Series date with the Atlantic City Bachrach Giants. Chicago won the series five games to three.[77]

Moore lamented Birmingham's failure to win the playoff, but said that Chicago was overall a much better team. Still, on behalf of himself and "thousands of fans" in Birmingham, he thanked Manager Bill Gatewood and Captain Sam Streeter for their services and the great showing that the team made during the second half. Buoyed by those memories, he was already looking toward 1928: "The past season is history. Start building now and next season to give the fans of this city a winning baseball team, a team that will not shut up and quit when certain teams are met. We can have one but the time to start is now, not next spring."[78]

8

Misplaced Optimism (1928)

After two exciting, pennant-winning seasons in a row, Birmingham fans went into the 1928 campaign with a great deal of optimism. It was a misplaced emotion as the Black Barons—despite showing promise at times—foundered often, putting together both winning streaks and losing streaks. The team was beset by injuries, losing key players for long periods of time. Among them were catcher Poindexter Williams, broken leg sliding into a base; outfielder "Chuffy" Alexander, broken collarbone diving for a line drive; and pitcher Harry Salmon, broken hand after being hit by a batted ball.[1]

There were also pre-season difficulties. Pitcher Sam Streeter was "sent home for breaking training rules" as the team set up camp at Fort Benning in Georgia. Streeter did not return. He joined the Homestead Grays in Washington.[2] Satchel Paige "had a slight misunderstanding" and left spring training, although this was quickly patched up.[3]

The injuries, coupled with extraordinarily inconsistent play on the field, resulted in a fourth-place finish for a team with some very talented players.[4]

R.T. Jackson, formerly club secretary and a Negro National League board member, had moved up to president.[5] Poindexter Williams was the new manager, replacing Reuben Jones, who played briefly. A number of men who had played well in the 1927 second half returned. Among them were infielders George McAllister, Buford Meredith, and DeWitt Owens. Pitchers included Salmon, Paige, Robert Poindexter, and Leo Berdine. The outfielders were Alexander, James Thompson, and Roy "Red" Parnell.[6]

Newcomers included pitcher Jim Willis, catcher William Perkins, and former Birmingham pitcher Jim Jeffries. Lost from the previous year were Streeter and catcher Clarence Palm. Because of Poindexter Williams's broken leg, the loss of the competent Palm again made catching a weak position.[7]

The new team beat Ft. Benning, 4–3, in the only home exhibition game.[8] Afterward, they played in Kentucky and Illinois, working their way into St. Louis for the NNL opener on April 28.[9]

Rarely has the optimism of spring training been dashed so quickly. If the Black Barons were disheartened after losing the first two games to the St. Louis Stars 7–5 and 8–5, they had to be crushed by the third game, a 20–2 shellacking.[10] The Stars then swept a doubleheader, sending the team on to Chicago with a 0–5 record. It got no better there. The horrible start got to eight losses before Birmingham finally won the last game of the series.[11]

Birmingham played the entire Chicago series under protest, claiming that left fielder Nat Rogers was the property of Memphis and should not have been playing. They also protested that the Chicago team had 17 players in uniform when league rules clearly limited squads to 16 players.[12]

From Chicago, they returned south for a four-game series in Memphis. Gaining a four-game split there, the Black Barons limped into Birmingham for their first home games. Manager Poindexter Williams had "sustained a broken leg for the fourth time" sliding into home at Memphis. The *Birmingham Reporter* said the injury occurred at second base, where Williams was about to slide but changed his mind. He snagged a spike on the second base bag and broke his ankle.[13]

Fearing Williams might be out for the season, an immediate search began for a new catcher. Charley "Twosides" Wesley was named interim manager.[14] The *Birmingham News* reported that local fans were excited about the home opener and "bent on showing the Black Barons that a few reverses will not turn them against the team." The crippled Williams said the players were in "fine condition" and would challenge Memphis. He praised two newcomers who had performed well on the dismal road trip—catcher-outfielder Bill Perkins and infielder Ray Sheppard.[15]

But with a crowd of 7,500 watching, Buster Jackson outpitched Jeffries and Memphis won the first game, 4–1.[16] The next day Salmon won by the same score. He held the visitors to four hits, striking out eight. Meredith tripled and Thompson doubled.[17]

Birmingham made it two in a row with a rain-shortened 9–5 win. Poindexter started but gave way to Paige in the fourth. Paige gave up only two hits, facing just 10 batters in the last three innings. He struck out five, walked one, and had two hits at bat, one a triple.[18]

The other games were rained out, but Birmingham had a two-game winning streak when Cleveland came in on May 23. When the series ended, the winning streak was seven games. In the 7–6 opener, home runs were hit by McAllister, Parnell, and Jones, who also doubled home the winning run in the bottom of the ninth.[19]

The second game was rained out, forcing back-to-back double-headers. The surging Black Barons won all four games.

Poindexter and Paige won on Wednesday. Jones continued his hot streak with three hits, but the *Birmingham News* reporter said fielding was the real star: "Some of the best fielding of the year was seen in the first game…. Geechie and Parnell made sensational running catches, which saved the Black Barons from a closer victory." The Thursday games were won, 9–6 and 9–5. Strong bats offset spotty pitching. Meredith had six hits in eight at bats, and Parnell had a home run.[20]

However, inconsistency returned against Detroit at Rickwood Field the next weekend. Birmingham, which countered the eight-loss start with seven straight victories, fell apart against the Stars. In the first game, Detroit scored twice in the eighth inning, and won 5–4 on a throwing error.[21]

The tough loss seemed to open a floodgate of Detroit runs. They won the second game, 7–2. Future Hall of Famer Norman "Turkey" Stearnes had six hits, two of them triples, in a double-header sweep, 17–6 and 7–3.[22]

A league press release puzzled over Birmingham's showing: "The Birmingham Black Barons [which] from past performances should be near the top has flopped…. The club which is about the same that won the last half of the 1927 race has not been able to get going. Something must be wrong with the Barons."[23]

Sports editor William Moore was very specific in identifying the problem: finding a replacement for Poindexter Williams. "The present catching staff won't make the grade and there is no need of the Black Barons management trying to put such on the fans," he wrote in his column. "We need a catcher who can receive and throw. At present we do not have such. Both are hard workers but cannot measure up to the standard required to remain

[in] this league. Bad catching causes the whole team to look bad and several of the times when the pitchers blow up, it is because of faulty receiving…. There is no need of waiting on Williams, to our way of thinking, for this season he is through. Give us a catcher or we perish."[24]

Although management said they were looking for another catcher, they stuck with Bill Perkins the entire season. A fill-in name Mead or Mean (both names were in game accounts) was tried but did not last long. This was likely Lewis Means, who had been with team earlier. Ironically, Perkins was Satchel Paige's favorite catcher throughout his career. The two became a battery in Birmingham that year and the relationship lasted for decades. They were both suspended for a while in 1937 for jumping to Santo Domingo in the Dominican Republic. Described as slow and lacking mobility, Perkins had a strong arm and wore a chest protector with the words "Thou shalt not steal."[25]

Moore also chastised the Black Barons for failing to hustle:

> [W]e feel we owe it to the public to speak of the way our boys run hits out. Somewhere some one [*sic*] must have put it into their heads that [when I get a hit] that I can just trot down to first base [as] it belongs to me and it [is] against the rule for me to go any further on that particular hit. Thus, on several occasions had we run the hit out to first base we could have gone on to second because the outfielder or whoever was making the play, played the ball bad…. Ball games are won by keeping awake, heads up baseball, and if we are going to play like school boys we are sure to find that on the bottom of the league standing we shall be.[26]

Moore's comments were perhaps reinforced a few days later when Birmingham released Reuben Jones and announced that Jim Willis had jumped the club. "The reason assigned for the release of Jones was for the good of the club, as he felt there were some rules of the club that he did not feel he could obey," said the *Birmingham Reporter*. "Willis became displeased or dissatisfied because of his inability to win in this league, and decided to go where he could have an easy time and not work quite so hard."[27]

Hard-hitting outfielder James Thompson was suspended without pay for 10 days for breaking training rules.[28] Soon afterward the club traded him to Chicago. "Thompson, who was on the outs with the Baron management because of his failure to stay in condition, has been of very little service to the Barons this year, and hence, there was nothing left to do but trade him," said the *Birmingham Rep*orter.[29] In return Birmingham got infielder "Red" Haley, who only appeared in one box score.[30]

A bright spot was the hitting of "Geechie" Meredith. Early in the Detroit series he was batting .500 in home games with 17 hits in 34 at-bats.[31]

Birmingham (14–10) prepared to host Chicago the following week. Over the years, the locals had struggled against the always strong American Giants.

Continuing their streaky play, the Black Barons won the first three contests. Meredith powered a double-header victory to open the series. He had five hits, including a two-run triple and a game-winning single. McAllister won an abbreviated second game with a two-run homer. Poindexter and Paige, who had been battered by Detroit, pitched well.[32]

In a second double-header, Salmon won the first game, scattering nine hits. Chicago won the nightcap, 7–1, although Meredith had two hits, giving him 10 for the series.[33]

Away again, Birmingham won three of five in Cleveland and Detroit, then lost four of six in Chicago and four of five in Kansas City. That pretty well set the pattern for the remainder of the season. There was one highlight in Chicago: Robert Poindexter threw a seven-inning no-hitter.[34]

It was, perhaps, the highlight of a brief and troubled career for Poindexter, who had a drinking problem. He was reportedly drunk when he shot Memphis Red Sox teammate J.C. McHaskell in 1929. McHaskell subsequently lost both legs, ending his career.[35] Poindexter spent four of his six NNL years with the Black Barons. He was a mainstay on the pitching staff in 1924–25 and again in 1927–28. In between he helped Chicago win the 1926 pennant. In 1929 he returned to Chicago, but soon dropped down to an independent team. Despondent, he attempted suicide. The effort failed, but his career was over.[36] Just over a year later, he was stabbed to death in an altercation in Washington, D.C., where he was playing sandlot baseball. He was 36 years old.[37]

But in 1928, Poindexter had a lot of good games left in his arm. In July, he pitched two outstanding games against some of the NNL's best. He beat future Hall of Fame pitcher Chet Brewer and Kansas City, 3–2, in a classic pitching battle.[38] A week later he held Mule Suttles hitless in five trips to the plate. Suttles, playing first base for St. Louis, had 43 home runs at the time.[39]

Despite the disappointing season overall, Birmingham had other good baseball players who had their moments. Paige won games with both his arm and his bat. He enabled the Black Barons to split the series with St. Louis, throwing a four-hit shutout (also blanking Suttles) and striking out nine. He started and ended the game with strikeouts, retiring the last 15 batters in a row. His second-inning single (one of his two hits) resulted in the go-ahead run.[40]

In August, Salmon pitched a fine four-hit shutout against Cleveland. Parnell and McAllister, criticized often in game stories for their fielding, backed Salmon superbly. "Parnell cut a home run off Hall's bat in the fifth when he jumped up in front of the negro bleachers and plucked a line drive out of the air. McAllister made one fancy play after another, playing the best defensive game of the season."[41]

Some former Black Barons played well, too. Detroit shortstop Grady Orange and center fielder "Turkey" Stearns caught the eye of the *Birmingham News*. "Orange's brilliant throwing featured the defense of the stars. The former Black Baron wiped out three runs by getting his men at first on eyelash decisions," read one report.[42] Stearns hit two home runs in the game. "He poled his first home run in the negro bleachers in the fourth with one on and shot his second home run into the upper tiers of the negro grandstand with two on in the sixth."[43] In the same game, two different Black Barons were credited with "a terrific wallop that landed in the coal pile in right." The game story attributed the blow to Parnell, but the box score credited McAllister.[44] In fact, it was a feat that could have been accomplished by either.

Memphis arrived for the final home stand in August, and the Black Barons were winners again. They had just won three straight in Memphis.[45] At Rickwood, Paige won the first game and Salmon the second, extending the streak to five games. The second game was played in just 67 minutes. Salmon pitched a 3–0 six-hitter.[46]

The series concluded with a double-header, but only one game was played. With a storm rapidly approaching and Birmingham up 4–3 in the seventh, the Red Sox left the field. The win in the abbreviated game gave the Black Barons six in a row.[47]

Finishing the season away, they extended the streak to seven in the first game at Chicago, but lost the series three games to two.[48] The season ended with a four-game split in Detroit. In the victories, William Nash, an industrial league lefthander, and Paige each pitched four-hit games.[49]

So a season that began with promise ended with disappointment, not only in the playing but also in dwindling attendance and the inability of management to maintain order on the field. Throughout the season there was criticism of players constantly arguing with umpires. "Either the umpires are afraid of the players, or they do not know the rules, to know when a player oversteps his bounds. Something is wrong when on almost each decision some player protests the ruling of the umpire and appeals to some other for a change," wrote Moore. He admonished management to make some changes before next year.[50] He blamed on-field wrangling partly for the attendance drop.

When the final standings had Detroit edging out Birmingham for fourth place, Moore had further admonitions:

> The fans of this city have been loyal. No city in the league gets any better average attendance than that given the Black Barons. There seems to be a fixed understanding that the pennant must go to one or two places each year. Give us a manager such will not be the case any longer. If there is such a thing as a ring we will surely break it up.
>
> Wake up, owners, the fans have received promises long enough. Start building next year's team now and so when the bell rings the Barons will be off with the bunch.[51]

No Birmingham position players were among the league leaders, but several did hit over .300 for the year: Ray Sheppard (.331), Red Parnell (.326), and Charlie Wesley (.315). Paige (13–4) was among the top pitchers. His 112 strikeouts were second only to the 118 by Bill Foster of Chicago.

9

A Season with
Few Highlights (1929)

The Black Barons again set up spring training at Fort Benning. The 1929 outlook for the Negro National League was mixed. Cleveland was gone, leaving just seven teams.[1] Eventually, the Nashville Elite Giants came in.[2]

Management said the Birmingham team had "strengthened considerably" over the winter and was ready for a pennant run. R.T. Jackson was back as president and Charles "Twosides" Wesley as manager. He had taken over in 1928 when Poindexter Williams was injured. Early returnees included Satchel Paige, Ray Sheppard, Buford Meredith, Samuel Thompson, Harry Salmon, Webb Oden, Anthony Cooper, and Leo Berdine.

Promising newcomers included Dave Thomas, a hard-hitting first baseman formerly with Mobile; and Edward Roussell, Porter Dallas, and left-handed pitcher Robert "Black Diamond" Pipkin, all from New Orleans.[3] Catcher Bill Perkins, counted on as a backup, was a holdout. "Williams is good but his leg is liable to go back on him at any moment as he has had one of them broken twice and there is no way to tell just how they will show up under a hard campaign."[4]

Little was reported on the exhibition season. The Black Barons opened the regular season in Memphis, losing 2–0 as Carl Glass bested Harry Salmon in a tightly pitched game. Salmon's single was the only Birmingham hit. And more bad news: Poindexter Williams was injured again, this time a finger that would keep him sidelined for several days.[5] Memphis won three straight before Birmingham salvaged a five-inning win.[6]

Opening Day at Rickwood Field was with the Cuban Stars. It was one of only three home series during the first half of the season due to schedule conflicts with the Birmingham Barons. Birmingham City Schools Superintendent C.B. Glenn announced that any boy bringing an excuse from home would be released early in order to attend the game. Nothing was said about girls who might want to go. The price of admission was 20 cents.[7]

Despite the weak start in Memphis, the *Birmingham News* said the Black Barons "have a strong team and are expected to be a leading contender." A large crowd was expected for Monday's opener. Birmingham did not allow Sunday baseball at the time.[8] A player identified only as L. Thomas replaced Williams at catcher. Expected to lead the visitors was former Black Baron Estaban Montalvo, "who is considered the Babe Ruth of negro baseball."[9] Sadly, the great Cuban's career was brief. He died of tuberculosis in 1930.[10] Montalvo did not appear in any of the games in Birmingham. Apparently his health had already deteriorated because he is not listed on any roster for 1929.[11]

The expected Birmingham lineup:

McAlister, 1b	Sheppard, ss
Meredith, 2b	Cooper, lf
D. Thomas, rf	L. Thomas, c
Roussell, cf	Paige, Salmon, Berdine, or Pipkins, p[12]
Dallas, 3b	

Paige, who did not play in Memphis, started and was in top form. Although he gave up two runs and nine hits, he struck out 17, at least one in every inning but the sixth, and five of the last six batters he faced. Birmingham won, 6–2. Roussell had a triple, single, and stolen base in his Birmingham debut before 6,000 or 10,000, depending on the newspaper.[13]

Rain reduced the series to just three contests. It was so cold on the final day that the managers agree to play seven- and five-inning games. Birmingham won both on the pitching of Berdine and Paige. "Geechie" Meredith hit a two-run homer. Paige, who had a rough outing, won the game with a triple, driving in two runs. Despite the weak start, he struck out seven, giving him 24 total in 14 innings.[14]

Paige's strong strikeout performances continued a few days later in Nashville. He struck out 18 batters in a 15-inning 8–6 win. That gave him 42 strikeouts in 29 innings. The Nashville series was also plagued by rain, but Birmingham won two games and moved on to Chicago with a five-game winning streak.[15]

They won three out of five in Chicago and two out of three exhibition games from the Postum team in Battle Creek, Michigan.[16] The record in NNL games was 9–5.

Detroit cooled them off. The Stars, led by Alabamians Norman "Turkey" Stearnes and Ted "Double Duty" Radcliffe, swept the series. Each hit a home run with men on base as the Stars drove Paige from the mound in the 13–8 second game. Birmingham pitching was also clobbered in a double-header, 16–5 and 9–8. Detroit had 41 runs and 53 hits in the series.

Although some felt the team was affected by Detroit's cold weather, personnel changes ensued.[17] Anthony Cooper, who had failed "to get in condition and remain so," was released. He was replaced by outfielder Clarence Smith, who had managed the team in 1926. A.J. Dykes, an infielder from Texas, was put at second base, with the popular Meredith becoming a substitute. "The letting out of Cooper served notice on several more players who are on the ragged edge that they must get into condition and remain so or expect the same as Cooper received," William J. Moore reported.[18]

Signing Smith was a positive in another disappointing season. His bat was spectacular even when the rest of the team was faltering.

The weather in Detroit was not an anomaly. Midway through the first half of the season, NNL President William Hueston said that the league had "been beset with the worst playing conditions … since the institution of the league ten years ago." Four out of six series had been affected. "This has affected our league in many respects," Hueston continued. "First … two-thirds of our playing area is in the northern section of our country, and to be handicapped at the beginning of the season with rain and cold weather for four weeks means that it has been impossible for our teams to be in the best playing condition."[19]

With the bad weather, attendance was down, Hueston appealed for fan support, noting that the league provided not only good sport but also "employment to several hundred young men, each playing season at a cost to the joint team owners of well over $200,000."[20]

In St. Louis, Harry Salmon stopped Birmingham's slide with a 3–0 shutout, but Paige faltered, giving up 12 hits in a 6–3 loss. Other pitchers suffered, too. St. Louis won two out of the final three games, scoring 36 runs.[21]

Sports editor William Moore, as usual, pulled no punches in assessing the team's struggles. "Only two regulars above .300…. D. Thomas is just about hitting his weight and Roussell, who was expected to fill Parnell's shoes, is way down. One only needs to look at Roussell to see that he is overweight and badly out of condition…. Roussell should be told to get in shape to play or be suspended until he is." Moore added that other players were also out of shape and should be disciplined. "The owners owe it to the fans that the players give their best and not shirk on the job. The Barons' players are just as good as any others in the league, judging from the performance thus far, but the shirking must be cut out and now."[22]

As they moved on to Kansas City, the news broke of Robert Poindexter's shooting of Memphis teammate J.C. McHaskell. From the hospital, the first baseman was interviewed by the Associated Negro Press. "Robert was somewhat low spirited over his punk pitching, and I tried to sympathize with him…. I told him tomorrow (Friday) was Ladies Day at the Stars' park and he should pitch better with the girls all there. Somehow he took offense at that. He thought I was 'joshing' him, so he pulled out his pistol and shot me in the foot," said McHaskell."[23]

The injury was not considered serious at the time.[24] A few days later, "McHaskell celebrated his return to the Sox lineup by getting three singles out of five trips to the plate."[25] He appeared to remain healthy. In the season-ending double-header at Rickwood Field, he had four hits in eight at bats for the day.[26] However, a later infection required amputations that ended McHaskell's career.[27]

Birmingham and its shell-shocked pitchers arrived in Kansas City to conclude the long road trip. The outcome was similar to Detroit. The Monarchs swept, most games by handy margins. If there was a highlight for Birmingham, it was Salmon's tough 1–0 loss in the second game.[28]

The *Birmingham News* put a more positive spin on the road trip on June 9, the day before Memphis was to arrive in town: "Reports are that everything from rain to freezing weather was encountered but in spite of all this the Black Barons came through with a record of 13 wins and 16 losses."[29] Documented games show the record at 17–18, including several exhibition games, not bad for such a difficult three weeks.

Meanwhile, Wesley added two new players, Julian Bell and Eppie Hampton. "Bell is a hurler and is considered one of the best in the league. Hampton, formerly of the Twenty-Fourth Infantry, will be added to the receiving staff," the newspaper reported.[30] Poindexter Williams had recovered from his finger injury. The *News* praised his hitting, but called him "somewhat slow on the bases and the new man will likely see plenty of action."[31] The writer also extolled the virtues of Clarence Smith. "His powerful bat is expected to put fear in opposing pitches while his work on defense should be above reproach from his past record."

"One of the largest Monday crowds of the year" saw the Black Barons win the opener, 7–4, behind good hitting. Thomas and Smith hit home runs, Pipkin doubled, and Meredith tripled. Memphis's Nat Rogers made an on-the-run one-handed catch of a line drive to deep left field. Appreciative Birmingham fans "showered the visitor with small change."[32]

For William Moore, it was a treat to see Smith in a Birmingham uniform again:

> With him the winning of the ball game is something serious and not a plaything…. Smith is in the game every moment, no matter how far behind he is or how far out in front, he plays the same kind of game—out to win. His opponents respect him, and they watch him very closely for they never

know just what he will pull off. Smith belongs to the old school that believed in fighting until the last. Smith is full of tricks and pulled several in the game Monday to the delight of the large number of fans who follow his every move from the very start of the game. As we see it Smith is one of the smartest Negro's [*sic*] playing ball today and it is worth a great deal to any club to have him a member of their club.

We only trust that a few more of the Barons will catch his spirit and fight and if so the Barons will not only win more games but will attract large crowds, as the fans like to see a fighter, a hustling player, one who puts his all in every game. Clarence Smith is such a ball player.[33]

After losing the second game, Birmingham closed the series with double-header wins. Paige, returning to form, struck out 15 batters in the first game, which went 11 innings before George McAllister singled in the winning run. Bell pitched a two-hit shutout in the nightcap.[34]

With a week off between league games, the Black Barons played a series of exhibition games. They won two out of three in Chattanooga, and then met the Miami Giants in Gadsden.[35] The Florida team won the first game, 8–6. Perhaps the loss was a wake-up call for Birmingham. The Black Barons won the next two, 18–0 and 17–2. Unfortunately, shortstop Ray Sheppard, the team's leading hitter with a .384 average, fractured a leg in one of the games.[36] He was trying to score from third on a squeeze play when he caught his spike on home plate.[37]

Resuming league play, Birmingham won three out of four in Chicago. Salmon threw a five-hit shutout, striking out seven. He also scored the first run on a single, followed by Meredith's triple. Meredith scored when McAllister dropped a bunt in front of the plate. "Geechie brought the fans to their feet with a nose dive into the plate." Former Black Baron Saul Davis was thrown out of the game "for kicking up too much fuss" over a call at second base.[38]

In fourth place, Birmingham went to St. Louis next. Surprisingly, they managed to remain in fourth despite a disastrous road trip.

With Pipkin and Berdine giving up 20 hits and teammates committing six errors, they were swamped by the Stars, 21–8, in the first game. St. Louis then swept a double-header to end first-half play.[39]

Kansas City won the first half. At the break, Kansas City catcher Tom Young (.433) was the leading batter. Meredith (.326) was Birmingham's best. Former Black Baron Mule Suttles (13) led the league in home runs.[40]

Poor fielding was an ongoing problem for the Black Barons in 1929. While the team was third in batting in the first half (.287), it was next to last in fielding, committing 50 errors.[41] William J. Moore frequently voiced his unhappiness over the fielding. He wrote that a game with St. Louis "was lost when McAllister played a hit to rightfield [*sic*] more like a blind man than a ball player."[42] On another occasion he said a Kansas City loss came "when McAllister made his usual daily error."[43] When Birmingham won a Detroit series, he attributed success to the fact that there were only four errors in five games.[44]

Birmingham opened the second half in Chicago. Not even Kansas City could excite the local fans as much as Chicago did. "For years even when the games were played at the old slag pile, the coming of the Chicago boys created more interest than any other ball club," wrote the *Birmingham Reporter* earlier in the season. "Thus it is today, and when the Chicago Americans blow in town ... the fans will be out in large numbers."[45]

But this series was in Chicago, and it forecast the rest of the year for Birmingham. They were without shortstop Ray Sheppard, a key player all year. "Just how much he meant to the team can be realized now as the team goes into action each day. Ray's timely hitting, his hustling spirit is sorely needed as the club hit road Tuesday night for the second half of the schedule," lamented Moore.[46] Chicago won all five games.[47]

The Black Barons then managed splits with Detroit and the Cuban Stars, but were swept by Kansas City.[48] The second half start was 5–13. They finished in fifth place, often playing well against St. Louis but poorly against the rest of the league.

Back home, they faced Kansas City, runaway winner of the first half. The visitors won the first two games. A double-header was to end the series. "After three hours of arguing and fussing," the Monarchs won the first game, 8–7, as the Black Barons blew a six-run.[49] "The Barons started to playing loosely and Satchel started loafing and the Monarchs soon tied the score. In the 8th Joseph hit a home run with what finally turned out to be the winning score. The Barons played very loosely in the field and performed at times like school boys," wrote William Moore.[50] The first game took so long to complete that the second was called at the end of the third inning to allow the Monarchs to catch a train.[51]

There were some second half highlights:

- In July, the erratic Satchel Paige struck out 17 batters in a 6–2 win at Detroit. He allowed the Tars only two hits.[52]
- On August 7, St. Louis beat Birmingham, 4–2, at Rickwood with former Black Baron Clarence Palm getting timely hits off Satchel Paige. The pitcher settled down, though, striking out future Hall-of-Famer Mule Suttles twice. "The sight of Mule striking out gave the dusky fans a big kick. They whooped and yelled," reported the *Birmingham News*.[53]
- The following day, Suttles showed why Cooperstown was in his future. He was four for five with two doubles, a triple and a home run. He added three more hits, including another triple, in a concluding double-header game.[54]
- The final road trip to Detroit, August 17–20, displayed sensational batting. Detroit won the first two games by scores of 5–4 and 12–11. Birmingham took the next three, 9–2, 17–16, and 16–13. Altogether the two teams scored 105 runs and 142 hits.[55]
- The season ended at Rickwood with a Labor Day double-header against Memphis. Paige scattered eight hits to win the first game, 6–2. He got another win in relief of Julian Bell in the second game.

10

Return to the Negro National League (1930)

With the Negro Southern League still dormant, Birmingham returned to the Negro National League in 1930. It was difficult to assess the prospects for baseball teams with jobs falling as the Great Depression set in.

The first league meeting was held in Detroit in January. The session opened with all in attendance standing "for a moment in respectful attitude, hoping that Rube Foster should be early restored to good health."[1] Foster, suffering from mental health problems, had been committed to a state mental institution in Illinois in 1926. He was now in his fourth year of institutionalization. He died there in December of 1930.[2] His obituary ran on the front page, not the sports section, of the *Pittsburgh Courier* where a creative headline writer penned, "Diamond Magnate Called 'Out.'"[3]

Birmingham was represented at the meeting by R.T. Jackson. Judge W.C. Hueston was reelected president.[4]

The tough economy was reflected in another league meeting in March. Several clubs complained of financial losses when traveling to the South, and the issue threatened to bounce Birmingham and Memphis from the league. It was said that both had "an inability … to draw in their home cities after July 4." Moses Walker of Detroit said that he received only $400 for a trip to Birmingham the previous year and had to pay player salaries, travel expenses and other costs out of that sum. Tom Wilson was reported to be "up against it with his Nashville club." Walker and others also objected "to going into the hole simply to carry out a schedule in the second half."

However, their case was successfully pled by Oscar Adams and R.T. Jackson for Birmingham and Dr. W.S. Martin for Memphis. Both clubs retained their status, along with Chicago, the Cuban Stars, Detroit, Kansas City, Nashville, St. Louis, and the Louisville Black Caps.[5]

President Hueston saw many positives going into the new season. He noted that in the 11-year history of the NNL, no organized ball league below Class A had lasted as long. He estimated that total salary expenditures for players and others would top $300,000, "in these days of race non-employment an item not to be overlooked." In addition, there was a new $100,000 stadium in Detroit and a new $75,000 grandstand in Nashville. The Martin family in Memphis owned a park valued at $75,000, and owners in St. Louis possessed a facility valued at $150,000.[6]

Information on the 1930 season was slow coming. In mid–March, sportswriter William Moore expressed his frustrations: "Tried several times to get some definite information concerning the outlook for this year's team, and the only reply is not decided just yet. It is reported that several of the players have received contracts from other clubs and will pull out in a few days to join those clubs. If there is to be a team it is surely time that those in charge let the fans know just what is doing. The fans of this city have been as loyal as any fans in any city and they should be given a good team or not any at all. To have such a team, it cannot be gotten over night...."[7]

Finally, Moore reported that the team was headed to spring training at Fort Benning.[8] Clarence Smith, the 1926 manager and 1929 outfielder, was manager again. Enjoying nice weather, the team was "rounding into shape with some of the men showing mid-season form." Second baseman Otto Mitchell was "fielding and hitting like a fiend," left-hander Herman Andrews was looking good, and first baseman James West, "a big, strapping young man weighing about 180 pounds," was challenging Dave Thomas. Other players noted were Claude Johnson at third base, William Perkins and Robert Smith behind the plate, and Terris McDuffie in the outfield.[9] Moore called the signing of Perkins "a master stroke," citing his ability as a catcher, good hitter, and fan favorite.[10]

Atlanta sportswriter Ric Roberts, who occasionally wrote a column for the *Chicago Defender* called "Under Southern Skies," said the base's amenities made it a popular spot with college athletes when their teams played against the all-black 24th Infantry. He said the government "spares no pains in vending out the very best food" and recreational activities such as swimming, fishing and tennis. This year, a Vitaphone had been installed and "a new picture is run each night." The Vitaphone was a film sound system used by Warner Brothers and its sister studio First Nation from 1926 to 1931. Roberts noted that McDuffie, Johnson, and pitcher Hy Vance were all former members of the soldier team. He had high praise for third baseman Johnson, who "is hitting the ball hard and fielding like a Trojan."[11]

Except for R.T. Jackson, neither the ownership nor the front office personnel were identified in any of the reports on the team. The *Birmingham World*, in a 1941 listing of owners and managers, gave the ownership of the team from 1926 to 1930 as J.C.B.B.A. (Jefferson County Black Barons Association).[12] It should be noted, though, that 1920–41 listings of owners and managers, appearing in Emory Jackson's "Hits and Bits" column, contained several errors.

From camp, it was reported that the team was expected to be "twice as strong" as last year. Drawing attention in the workouts was West, who was "cutting all kinds of capers around first base and each day finds West growing more and more in the eyes of Manager Smith." That posed a pleasant problem for Smith, who had power-hitting David "Showboat" Thomas back from 1929. "The question is what to do with two such infielders," posed Moore.[13] Thomas later played outfield some so West could be used at first base.

Another newcomer making a good impression was catcher Robert Smith, also a Birmingham industrial leaguer. "Gifted with a wonderful arm, he has been death to all would-be base stealers this spring. With a little more speed on the path Smith would cause Perkins to warm the bench now," wrote Moore.[14]

The Black Barons opened their exhibition season against Fort Benning, winning 16–6. Birmingham batters got 22 hits off three Benning pitchers. Harry Salmon, Sam Streeter, and Vance held the soldiers to nine hits.[15]

Opening Day was April 28 against the Cuban Stars at Rickwood. It was practically a brand-new Black Barons team. Only third baseman Claude Johnson, who had played briefly in 1929, returned in the infield. Local favorite Buford "Geechie" Meredith, equally good at second base or shortstop, had been enticed away by Nashville. It was one of only two seasons in Meredith's career when he was not in Birmingham.[16] Trying to fill the shoes "of one of the most popular players to ever wear a Black Barons uniform" was Otto Mitchell, a youngster out of Evansville, Indiana.[17] First baseman–outfielder George McAllister was now with Memphis.[18] A new outfielder, who would become a Negro leagues star, was Jimmie Crutchfield.[19]

The *Birmingham Reporter* published the following starting lineup:

Jimmie Crutchfield, cf	Terris McDuffie or Clarence Smith, lf
Otto Mitchell, 2b	Claude Johnson, 3b
David Thomas, 1b	Elmer Carter, ss
"Jabbo" Andrews, rf	Harry Salmon, Hy Vance or Sam Streeter, p[20]
William Perkins, c	

Despite tough times, a paid attendance of 8,000 was reported as Birmingham defeated the Cubans, 4–1. They made it four straight before the visitors won the final game.

Salmon, back for his fifth straight year and eighth overall with his hometown team, pitched a solid game. After giving up a run in the first inning, he pitched a shutout the rest of the game. He struck out eight batters, including five in a row. He drove in Birmingham's go-ahead run after Thomas had tied the game with a home run.[21]

Streeter, back after several years with other clubs, won the second game, 6–1. He struck out seven and had the winning RBI with a single in the eighth. Vance won the third game, 3–1, giving up only two hits and striking out nine. He scored on Mitchell's home run.[22]

The series ended with a double-header split. Herbert Gay won a 10-inning game, 3–2, on Johnson's home run. The visitors took the nightcap, 6–4.

It was one of the Black Barons' best starts.[23] It continued the following week when they won four out of five in Memphis and three out of four in Nashville. They returned home on May 19 in first place. Manager Smith said many of the Black Barons were "playing in mid-season form."[24]

In both Memphis and Nashville, the Black Barons were followed by the Kansas City Monarchs, who were traveling with a portable lighting system. The lights had been a sensation on a barnstorming tour through Texas. Anticipation was so great in Memphis that the Red Sox, who owned 3,000-seat Lewis Park, added 2,000 more, making sure there were plenty for white spectators.[25]

They played the first night baseball game in Nashville at Wilson Park rather than Sulphur Dell, the home of the white Nashville Vols. The equipment was designed to be dismantled easily and moved to another ballpark, giving the Monarchs an added plus for barnstorming trips.[26]

The equipment consisted of "positively the largest Electric power plant in the world on wheels." The lights were on telescoped poles and towers extending 40 to 50 feet in the air. Twenty-one large reflectors holding three bulbs each were arranged with six at first base, six at third base, and nine in the outfield.[27]

The *Tennessean* reporter was quite impressed with the electrical marvel, noting that although "the fans could not see the ball at all times as well as the players could … there was hardly a time that they [could not] follow the ball, even on the longest drives, some of which were 300 feet or more. The ball appeared larger on high flies in the artificial light that it does in the day time." Remarkably, only about a thousand spectators, white and black, turned out for the historic event.[28]

Entering the next home stand, Birmingham (11–3) led St. Louis (9–4).[29] The starting lineup was essentially the same as the first game.[30] Playing second base for Nashville was "Geechie" Meredith.

Strong pitching marked the return to Rickwood. Salmon struck out 12 in the five-hit, 4–1 opening win. There was also timely hitting and strong defense. "Crutchfield played a spectacular game in centerfield, thrice coming from deep center to snag high flies back of second," reported the *Birmingham News*. Thomas hit two home runs and Jabbo Andrews one as Birmingham swept all four games. They added two exhibition wins against Fort Benning and an Evansville, Indiana, team before beginning extensive travels to St. Louis, Kansas City, Chicago, Detroit, and Memphis.[31]

Meredith did not play in the first two games at Rickwood, but was at second base in both games of the Sunday double-header. He had two hits in the second game and handled five chances with one error.[32]

One of Meredith's infield replacements was playing well for Birmingham. Anthony "Runt" Cooper had been with the team in 1928 and at the start of 1929 before being traded to Memphis. When he returned in 1930, "very few thought that Cooper would fill the bill at short," wrote Moore. "Being fast with a good whip it has been the work of this fellow more than any one other thing that is responsible for the Barons leading the league today."[33]

Another key to Birmingham's successful start was Crutchfield. Moore wrote: "Very few pay any attention to the work of Crutchfield in center because he plays every play with so much grace and ease that the plays look simple. To our way of thinking, he is the surest outfielder to put his feet in Rickwood this season…. It is really a treat to watch him snag long fly balls. Off with the crack of the bat, he very, very rarely misjudges one. He seems to have the power to be able to run and turn just at the right spot…." Moore cited Crutchfield's speed and ability as a leadoff batter also, concluding, "Watch Cooper and Crutchfield, they are budding stars."[34]

Travel slowed Birmingham's excellent start. After two exhibition wins over the Reichart Giants in Evansville, there were three losses each in St. Louis and Kansas City. Birmingham pitching was crushed. St. Louis won, 14–3, 7–6, and 11–1.[35] The Monarchs won, 21–5, 7–3, and 6–0.[36]

As the team faltered, management quickly signed three new men and gave signals that Andrews, Mitchell, and Berdine might soon be released. William Moore was merciless regarding the pitcher:

> There will be no regret at the passing of Berdine, for everyone knows Berdine is through. The Baron owners should have been ashamed to impose Berdine upon the public. To bring Berdine back meant that three or four more old timers should have been brought in. It was a waste of money to pay his transportation around on the trip. Just as soon as they learn that friendship must be left out and let each man deliver or go, just so soon will the Barons have the class of team everyone would like to see here. The right road is started, the slogan should be, "Deliver or go," and each man drawing a salary will feel bound to stay in condition and give his best each and every day.[37]

Since there had been no previous reports criticizing Berdine's play or work habits, it is difficult to assess Moore's attack. Berdine been with the team since 1926, and Moore's farewell notwithstanding, Berdine was still with Birmingham in 1931, pitching and playing a utility role. (The author notes again that Moore and other writers were consistent in using the surname spellings of Burdine over Birdine.[38]) The correct spelling of Berdine never appeared in any newspaper. After his release by the Black Barons, Berdine went to Memphis briefly.[39]

Birmingham's new players were reported to be Dick Seay, a young second baseman from New Jersey, and Bynum, "a shortstop, who besides the ability to field, can slam the old horsehide around." There was also an unnamed pitcher.[40] Seay had a long Negro leagues career.[41] However, neither player appeared in a Birmingham box score in 1930. Two weeks after the anticipated personnel changes, Jabbo Andrews had two hits in a road win over Chicago.[42] Verifiable changes saw DeWitt Owens return at shortstop, J.G. Shackleford at third base, and legendary Satchel Paige back on the mound. These signings occurred in late June.[43]

Recovering from the St. Louis and Kansas City losses, Birmingham won two exhibition games in Springfield, Illinois, then three out of five games from the American Giants in Chicago. The *Chicago Defender* called Birmingham "a hustling ball club ... the best looking team in years." Streeter, Julian Bell, and Vance pitched well in the three wins.[44]

After splitting two with the Postum club of Battle Creek, Michigan, the Black Barons went into Detroit. With "some solid and resonant thumping of the apple," they won two out of five.[45] During the Detroit series, word came out of Washington, D.C., that Robert Poindexter had bled to death after being stabbed. It was almost a year to the date of his shooting of teammate J.C. McHaskell on June 26, 1929, a tragedy that destroyed both careers and led to their untimely deaths.[46]

In Memphis, Birmingham lost, 7–5, then won three in a row. Returning home on June 23, they hosted Memphis for five games. New standings were Kansas City (20–7), St. Louis (29–11), and Birmingham (20–13).[47]

Memphis, usually struggling against Birmingham, played well at Rickwood, winning three out of five games. Mid-series there was a dramatic change in personnel for both clubs. A five-player deal sent Jabbo Andrews, James West, and Harry Salmon to Memphis. Birmingham acquired outfielder Nat Rogers and right-handed pitcher Willie "Sug" Cornelius.[48]

Memphis won the opener, 11–6, then squeezed by, 6–5, in the second with the three ex–Black Barons all playing significant roles. Salmon, in relief, retired his old teammates in order. He came back in the fourth game to pitch a seven-hitter while Andrews drove in four runs with a home run, a double and a single. Cornelius gave up 12 runs, 14 hits, and four walks, losing to his former team, 12–4. Rogers, playing right field, had three hits in three games. And former Black Baron George McAllister had eight hits in the series.[49]

Although the first half was to end on June 26, standings in The *Chicago Defender* obviously included some second-half games: St. Louis (41–5), Kansas City (28–23), Memphis (19–16), and Birmingham (27–26).[50]

Birmingham opened the second half in Nashville, losing four, winning two. From there it was on to Chicago, Memphis, and Detroit. They broke even in Chicago and Memphis and lost three of five in Detroit. One of the wins at Memphis was a 4–0 four-hitter by "Fork" Cornelius.[51]

In the second half, Birmingham struggled to break even, but there were some highlights.

In their first home stand in mid–July, the Black Barons unveiled the recently signed and eagerly awaited Satchel Paige. He did not disappoint, striking out 12 batters in a seven-inning game as Birmingham won a double-header from Detroit. "Paige should have won the nightcap 1 to 0, but two misplays enabled the visitors to tie the score in the seventh, with Manager Smith's baser running finally winning the battle, 2–1 for the Black Barons. Smith went in to run for Rogers, stole second and got around on a wild pitch," reported The *Birmingham News*. Vance won the opener, 5–4, striking out seven.[52]

But Detroit won the next three games. In the concluding double-header, a pitcher named Ed Davis (probably a misidentified Albert "Gunboat" Davis) pitched two complete games, giving up a total of eight hits. It was believed to be the first "iron man" performance at Rickwood in about fifteen years. "Turkey" Stearns hit triples for key RBIs in both games.[53]

First-half winner St. Louis was next and treated the Black Barons about as rudely as did Detroit. They won the first game, 15–2. "Pasting the agate to all corners and crevices, the St. Louis Stars showed why they won the first half pennant ... when they hammered three Black Barons hurlers," reported the *News*. They scored six runs in the first as Vance failed to retire a batter. Every Detroit player had at least one hit. To make matters worse, David Thomas and Clarence Smith jumped the team "for reasons not quite understood." They were next with the independent Baltimore Black Sox.[54]

With Paige pitching, Birmingham won the second game, 5–0. He struck out 11, allowing only one runner to reach second base. Big Bill Gatewood, a pitcher for Birmingham in 1927, was brought in as manager to replace Smith, a move that drew immediate approval. "Gatewood ... had the locals hustling all the way, making several shifts that seemed to help the club. He has promised a winner and having won a pennant here, should be able to make good his promise," wrote a local reporter. Gatewood moved Owens from shortstop to first base, Perkins from first base to catcher, Cooper from left field to shortstop, and McDuffie from the bench to left field. Crutchfield hit a home run, and Paige thwarted the great Suttles. "Twice he fanned Mule Suttles and each time the fans roared. Once Mule was the pride of Slagtown."[55]

Still, St. Louis won the series, taking the third game, 9–4, while the fourth, after eight innings of spectacular pitching and fielding, ended in a 1–1 tie.[56]

Paige, whose pitching had been inconsistent in 1929, was magnificent in his return to Rickwood Field in 1930. Jumping from the Baltimore Black Sox back to Birmingham, he showed the stuff of his legend-making.[57]

In late July he threw a four-hitter against Louisville, striking out 10. He struck out the side in the first inning. He had two singles and a stolen base. The teams split a double-header. New first baseman Nat Trammell did a creditable job filling in place of Thomas.[58]

Paige pitched again a week later against Chicago. "'Satchelfoot' placed the ball wherever he desired Monday, and exactly 10 of his opponents went down swinging or listening to the umpires call the strikes. Paige was right Monday afternoon, and when he's right, you might as well chalk up a win for the Ebony Barons," reported the *Birmingham News*.[59] But the lanky pitcher was not infallible. A rocky start against Detroit in August evoked the following from a sportswriter: "Leroy (Satchel) Paige proved a mere brief case in the opening game Sunday, the Stars combing his delivery for 10 bingles top the verdict by a 7 to 2 count."[60]

With other Black Barons playing good baseball, also, Birmingham swept the Chicago series. Streeter won the second game, 3–1, and also the first game of a closing double-header. Cornelius won the nightcap, 3–2.[61]

With six wins in seven games, it looked as if the Black Barons were back on the winning path again. They would finish the second half with a road trip to St. Louis, Chicago, Detroit and Nashville, then close out the season at home on Labor Day against Nashville. Birmingham (8–10) was looking at the road trip from fifth place. The leaders were Detroit (11–3), St. Louis (14–6), and Kansas City (5–2) with no explanation for the wide disparity in the number of games played.[62]

The trip was marginally successful. Paige won in St. Louis but was involved in a major altercation in Chicago. Eddie Miller of the American Giants "threatened Satchel and chased him all over the diamond with a bat," reported the *Chicago Defender*. Miller and Birmingham catcher William Perkins were both ejected from the game.[63] It was the second time Paige had been chased by a bat-wielder in Chicago. The previous incident was in 1927 when Mitch Murray was the attacker.[64]

Birmingham lost all five games in Detroit, each one by a different pitcher.

Back home, they ended the season positively, beating Nashville twice on Labor Day. Streeter outdueled Jim Willis, 4–2, in the first game, and Paige won a three-hitter, 4–0, in the second. Uncharacteristically, he only struck out three. Perkins hit a two-run homer and stole two bases in the second game.[65]

For Paige, it was his final game as a Black Baron. Although he had multiple stops in in various cities and Latin American countries, his future would be largely with the Kansas City Monarchs until Cleveland Indians General Manager Bill Veeck defied all odds and put the ageless hurler in a major league uniform in 1948. In typical Paige fashion, he had jumped from Baltimore in the Negro Eastern League to return to Birmingham in the middle of the 1930 NNL campaign. His half season in Birmingham was a highlight for an otherwise dismal year for the Black Barons. Paige appeared in eight games at Rickwood Field, six of them as a starter. He won all six. Among the wins were two shutouts and four games with 10 or more strikeouts, a memorable conclusion to his Birmingham tenure.

11

Return of the Negro Southern League (1931)

There were a lot of changes in Negro leagues baseball in 1931. The Negro National League launched its season with just six clubs. Gone were Birmingham, Memphis, and Nashville, all returning to the resurrected Negro Southern League. The Eastern Colored League, shut down in 1930, was back, but with only four teams.[1] All of the actions forecast an even more difficult time in 1932.

The NSL planned an eight-team lineup. In addition to Birmingham, Memphis, and Nashville, the other clubs were the Chattanooga Black Lookouts, Knoxville Giants, Little Rock Black Travelers, Montgomery Grey Sox, and an unidentified New Orleans club. On the periphery, as an associate member, was Atlanta. However, when the season opened, there were only six teams.[2] Neither Atlanta nor New Orleans appeared in any standings during the season, and Little Rock actually joined the league for the second half of the season.[3]

Birmingham, Memphis, and Nashville were ripe for the NSL's revival. They wanted out of the NNL "because of the long jumps" for playing the Northern teams."[4] The league was reorganized at a Birmingham meeting. Charles Johnson represented the Black Barons. Real estate dealer R.T. Jackson, not connected to the team this year, was elected president.[5] "It is expected that more interest will be shown by followers of the Black Barons in the future as the team will appear here more often and will be one of the favorites to cop the flag," reported the *Birmingham News*.[6]

A preliminary schedule called for a split season, opening on April 24.[7] However, most reports indicated the season's start on the first weekend in May. Buford "Geechie" Meredith, after a year in Nashville, was back to manage his old team. Three other managers were former Black Barons: Larry Brown, Memphis; Jesse Edwards, Chattanooga; and Felton Stratton, Nashville.[8]

Spring training was at what one newspaper called Vinesville College, actually Miles Memorial College. The popular Meredith would play as well as be the manager. Frank Perdue was back as owner.[9]

The first preview of the team came in exhibition games with the Cuban Negro House of David. The team was "touring America under special permission of the United States Immigration Department, under heavy bond." It was said to be drawing good crowds "with its long whiskers, spectacular ability, and novel appearance on the diamond."[10] All of the players were under a five-year contract "to refrain from shaving during the baseball season."[11]

Returning Birmingham players were pitchers Harry "Fish" Salmon and Leo Berdine, infielders Anthony "Peewee" Cooper and Elmer "Willie" Carter, catcher Bill Perkins, and outfielders Terris McDuffie and C.F. "Jabbo" Andrews.[12] Newcomers were infielder Matthew "Lick" Carlisle and first baseman George McAllister, back after a year's absence.[13]

The *Birmingham News* writer extolled the ability of catcher Perkins, "the boy from down in Georgia, who first brought the Tenth [*sic*] Commandment to the ball diamond, 'thou shalt not steal' across his breast,' and he means every word of it." Overall, the writer said "a real pennant contending club" was expected.[14] Another newcomer was a young right-handed pitcher named Robert Veale. He finished the season in Montgomery rather than Birmingham. It was his only known season of professional ball, but he played for many years in the industrial leagues and his son, Robert "Bob" Veale Jr., later became a successful multi-sport athlete and major league pitcher.[15]

The Cubans came with impressive talent. The pitching staff was led by Luis Tiant, and like Veale, the father of a future major leaguer. His son, Luis Tiant, Jr., became a fixture with the Boston Red Sox.[16] It was only an exhibition game, but Tiant and Salmon fought a tough nine-inning battle that Birmingham finally won, 3–2. Tiant held the Black Barons to seven hits, striking out four. Salmon gave up nine hits and struck out four.[17]

Among the white spectators was Emile "Red" Barnes, a University of Alabama football star who also played baseball in the major leagues. Barnes, now with the Atlanta Crackers but out with an injury, was among the many amazed at the speed of Cuban shortstop Jose "Bunny" Vargas. "He came to bat four times and collected four hits and three stolen bases. He beat out three hits and stole base twice under perfect pegs. No faster human being has ever been seen on the satchels at the 'Wood."[18]

More than 4,000 turned out for the game, but the *News* writer said the House of David was "short on mustaches," with only two "full grown sets on the squad." And although there was a generous sprinkling of Latin names in the roster, there were some that were startlingly Anglo, such as Jim Mason, Frank Stevens, and Woodrow Wilson.[19] A curiosity was the description of Tiant as "a snaggled toothed old man." Born 1906 in Havana, he was only 24 years old in 1931, but he had false teeth by the time he was in his early 40s. "In his later years the aging veteran would sometimes be the subject of good-natured ribbing from younger teammates when he would go to sleep on the bus and his false teeth would fall out."[20] Perhaps, when he played in Birmingham, Tiant simply looked older than his years and had poor, uncared-for teeth.

The Cubans matched their reputation by winning the next three games. They also entertained the crowd with an exhibition of shadow ball. "It was better than slow motion," reported the *News*.[21] Shadow ball was a pantomime entertainment often performed by baseball teams, particularly black clubs. The stunt had players throwing an imaginary ball and making spectacular catches. In later years, the term also came to be a metaphor for the Negro leagues, playing in the shadow of the white leagues.[22]

If the Black Barons fared poorly against the Cubans, it was nothing compared to what happened to Montgomery the next day. The Cubans won the first game, 20–1, taking advantage of 10 Montgomery errors. The Grey Sox settled down but lost the second game also, 9–7.[23]

Birmingham opened the season in Montgomery. The Grey Sox were playing league ball for the first time in several years.[24] Montgomery won the first game, 6–4. H.C. Trenholm, president of Alabama State Teachers College, threw out the first pitch at his school's new 1,000-seat College Hill Park stadium.[25] The Black Barons won the second game, 12–1. Before returning home, they won two in Knoxville and lost four in Chattanooga.[26]

At Knoxville, the previously error-prone Black Barons played flawlessly. Salmon and Columbus Vance each pitched one-run games to give Birmingham a 4–2 record going into Chattanooga.[27] The Black Lookouts were not impressed, sweeping the series.[28]

Opening Day at Rickwood was on May 18 against league-leading Chattanooga. Schoolchildren were allowed in for 20 cents.[29] A sportswriter reported that Peewee Cooper, the Wenonah boy who had made the team in spring training, had so far been "scintillating at shortstop and the management is expecting everybody from Red Mountain to turn out to boost their favorite son." There were no details on the size of the crowd or opening game festivities, but there was a distressing report on Cooper. The young player suffered a scary injury in the first inning when he stepped into a fast ball. "The ball struck him at the base of his skull and knocked him out cold for a few seconds."[30]

Nevertheless, Cooper played the entire game, which Birmingham won, 5–3. Salmon outpitched Walter Calhoun for the win. Berdine, identified as J. Burdine, playing both right and left field, had three hits, one of them a triple. Carter "played a spectacular game around second," and Manager Meredith was behind the plate.[31]

Because of rain, only two games were played. Chattanooga won the second, 8–6.[32]

Birmingham then went to Memphis. Willie "Sug" Cornelius, back with the Red Sox, won the first game, 3–0. The Black Barons dominated the next three. They pounded Harry Cunningham for 17 hits in a 10–1 second game. Four Birmingham hitters had three hits each. A local sportswriter cited shortstop "Lick" Carlisle for fielding "sensationally, taking care of nine different chances without a bobble."[33] After splitting a Sunday double-header, the two teams moved to Rickwood Field for a series.

There were new faces in the lineup. Popular, speedy shortstop Peewee Cooper had been traded to Louisville for left-handed pitcher Jim Jeffries and an outfielder named Clark. A new catcher, Tommy Dukes, was from the Cuban House of David.[34] Memphis came in as an NSL contender and proved it, winning all three games. As sportswriter William Moore put it, "the Red Sox acted and played like a real ball club."[35]

A fourth game was played in Gadsden. Birmingham apparently barnstormed for a few days afterward, returning to Rickwood on June 1 for a series with Montgomery. In the opener, Birmingham had 12 hits but committed four errors and lost, 8–7. The only bright spot was Hank Anderson's home run, a 431-foot drive that bounced over the wall in right-center. It was the first time in Rickwood history for a ball to bounce over that wall.[36]

The Black Barons won a double-header the next day. Salmon pitched a six-hitter, and Vance hit a home run in the first game. Calhoun won a high-scoring, five-inning second game, 10–6.[37]

Although a fourth game was scheduled in Gadsden, the Black Barons actually went to Little Rock, Arkansas, where they played two games with Memphis. Both were one-run losses.[38] A second series was played in Little Rock on June 12–13, with Memphis again winning two one-run games.[39] When the first game drew 1,500 fans, including many whites, it caught somebody's attention. Club officials for the independent Little Rock Black Travelers (24–2) began negotiating for a second-half spot in the Negro Southern League.[40] In late June it was announced that Little Rock would, indeed, be in the league.[41]

Standings through June 12 saw the Black Barons (10–12) in fourth place. Nashville (14–6) led, followed by Memphis (13–7) and Chattanooga (12–12).

A week or so later, standings in the *Chicago Defender* had Memphis leading Nashville by half a game. Birmingham had improved to 12–12.[42]

The first Little Rock games opened a long road trip for Birmingham. Overall, it was not a bad trip. They won three in Memphis, lost two in Montgomery, dropped three of five games to Detroit, and then lost a double-header in Chattanooga.[43]

The Montgomery visit was historical. The June 17 game was the first "negro night game in Cramton Bowl." The Grey Sox had been scheduled to play an Indiana team in an exhibition, but for unexplained reasons drew the Black Barons instead. Montgomery won, 3–1, as Everett Nelson pitched a one-hitter. The following night, Montgomery won again, 9–6. Harvey Peterson, who had started the season with Birmingham, hit a home run for the home team.[44]

The quality of the lighting system is not known, but there were eight errors in the first game and fourteen in the second, seven by each team. The lights had been installed in 1927, and a high school football game became the first night football game played in the South. A former school superintendent recalled: "[We] used dishpans for reflectors and sent to California for the lamps. We drew 7,200 people from all over the South to see it."[45]

Birmingham concluded the trip in Memphis, where each team won a double-header.[46]

When the two teams went to Birmingham on Monday, it was for more night baseball. Rather than Rickwood Field, the games were set for July 6–7 at the new Fair Park facility. The lighting system, patterned after the one at Sulphur Dell in Nashville, had received a trial run from Birmingham amateur teams in June. The grandstand, with a capacity of 10,000, was expected to be nearly full for the NSL games.[47]

The Black Barons won the historic Monday night game, 2–1. Salmon gave up only five hits. Birmingham managed only four hits off Murray Gillespie, but one of these was a two-run homer by Meredith with Salmon on board. Meredith also hit a home run the second night as Birmingham won, 8–6.[48]

Strangely, there was no mention of the event in the local daily newspapers. Night baseball did not seriously arrive in Birmingham until 1936, when Birmingham Barons owner Rick Woodward installed lights at Rickwood Field. The first night game was played on May 21 of that year. The first five night games at Rickwood drew 43,000 fans.[49]

Another night series was set in mid–July with the Fort Benning team. "Night baseball has been a boon to the colored fans," *The Birmingham News* finally reported. "It has given them an opportunity to see baseball without having to lose any time off their jobs."[50]

By early July, Birmingham (20–19) had shown some improvement, rising to third in the standings. Nashville (22–11) still led with Memphis (26–16) in second. The league record was not balanced, with 110 wins and 119 losses.[51]

The standings were said to be final first-half numbers. However, in September playoffs began between Memphis, reported to have been the first-half winner, and Montgomery, the second-half winner. Nashville played a series with the Monroe Monarchs, winners of the Negro Texas league.

Although the Black Barons were not seriously challenging for the NSL pennant, Walter Calhoun gave the local fans something to cheer about in the Fort Benning series. He threw a no-hitter as the Black Barons won, 11–0.[52] It was the first Birmingham no-hitter since Robert Poindexter's in Chicago in 1928.

Although Calhoun's performance was in an exhibition game, there were three league no-hitters that year. Dawson of Knoxville lost a seven-inning game to Montgomery, 1–0, on an error. Homer Curry of Memphis threw two no-hitters, beating Little Rock, 12–0, and Birmingham, 3–1. Birmingham scored on an error.

Birmingham played generally break-even baseball throughout most of July and August, even splitting a series in Nashville. The *Nashville Banner* reporter praised "the spectacular catches" of Birmingham catcher Dukes, calling him one of the best "Negro receivers in the business."[53] However, in another series at Nashville in August, the writer was not so generous. Tom Anderson reported that a 13–8 Nashville win "featured about everything but good baseball." He wrote that Berdine, the Birmingham pitcher, "refused to take the game seriously. He grinned tooth-filled grins throughout the tilt." Nashville players were not immune to criticism. "There was Slim Henderson, Elite left fielder, who must be seven feet tall if he is an inch. Slim had a terrible time keeping off his own dogs. He got his number twenties tangled three or four times during the game, each time taking a full length sprawl over the landscape." Red Charleston, the veteran catcher, also took the game lightly, or simply had one of the worst games of his career: "He persisted in molesting the alien hitters until removed from the game after Birmingham base runners had pilfered six bags in one inning."[54]

In early August the Cuban House of David returned to Birmingham.[55] Two night games were played at Fair Park. The first game was a good one, featuring "two of the best pitchers in baseball." Tiant outpointed Salmon, 5–3. The Cubans won the second game, 8–4.[56]

Nashville, bolstered by the return of pitcher Jim Willis, who had been with the Cleveland Cubs, appeared to edge out Memphis for the pennant.[57]

But that was a matter of conjecture. Other sources said Nashville won both halves. According to The Commercial-Appeal, Memphis won the first half, and a greatly improved Montgomery team won the second half. On Saturday, September 12, they began a playoff series for the championship.[58] By September 21, they were tied with three wins each. A seventh game, scheduled that day to determine the championship, was canceled without explanation.[59]

A week earlier a Negro Dixie Series was played between reported NSL champion Nashville and the Monroe Monarchs, winner of the Negro Texas-Louisiana League.[60]

The series opened in Nashville on August 30 and the Elite Giants looked unbeatable. Right-hander Willis pitched a 1–0, 13-inning shutout. Nashville won the second game, 9–1.[61]

When the series moved to Monroe, the Monarchs won three games and the series.[62]

12

The Worst Season Ever? (1932)

Negro leagues baseball hit its lowest point in 1932. The Negro National League, which had launched organized black baseball in 1920, was defunct. The Eastern Colored League, which had failed to operate in 1930 and had struggled with just four teams in 1931, was dormant again. Taking its place was the East-West League, an Atlantic Coast-Midwest amalgam that saw 10 different teams from Baltimore to Detroit in action at various times.[1]

These circumstances resulted in a hybrid Negro Southern League, featuring teams from three different leagues. Representing the NNL were the Chicago American Giants, Cleveland Cubs, Indianapolis ABCs and Louisville Black Caps, a reconfiguration of the Louisville White Sox. From the NSL were Birmingham, Atlanta Black Crackers, Little Rock Black Travelers, Memphis Red Sox, Montgomery Grey Sox, and Nashville Elite Giants. Coming over from the Negro Louisiana-Texas League were the Monroe Monarchs.[2]

Chicago had a new owner, Robert A. Cole. He changed the name of the team to Cole's American Giants.[3] However, few newspapers ever referred to it as anything but the Chicago American Giants throughout the season.

Veteran catcher Poindexter Williams took the Black Barons to spring training at the Stockham Field in Birmingham. Williams had managed the team in 1928, but his second stint likely would not have occurred except for an off-season tragedy. Buford "Geechie" Meredith, the popular second baseman and all-around star who had been with the club since its inception in 1920, was killed in a mining accident in January. Meredith, a miner in the off season, was electrocuted when he came in contact with a live wire at Republic Steel and Iron Company's Sayreton mine on January 13, 1932. He was 31 years old, leaving behind his widow, Lillie Mae, and four young sons.[4]

Meredith had managed the Black Barons in 1931. "Last year he managed the Black Barons, and notwithstanding the financial condition of the country, he completed the season, coming out leader of the Southern League," recalled the *Birmingham Reporter*, somewhat charitably as Birmingham was far behind in both halves of the split season.[5]

In camp were first baseman George McAllister, outfielder Jim West, utility man Martin Oliver, and pitchers Alonzo Boone, Harry Salmon and Ernest "Spoon" Carter. Two newcomers were infielders Milt Laurent and Lenon Henderson. Laurent, a veteran of several New Orleans teams, replaced Meredith at second base. Henderson, one of several brothers from Chattanooga, played shortstop.[6]

Meredith's death seemed to foreshadow what became the worst season in Black Barons history. Although the team played better than .500 baseball, it was the shortest season ever for a Birmingham team. They played for a little over a month before apparently folding without warning or acknowledgment in the local press. It also was one of the poorest covered in the team's long history, making for limited documentation. Fewer than a dozen articles, including game reports, appeared in Birmingham newspapers. The team was also plagued by horrible weather.

The season opened in Memphis with a 7–3 win. In the four-game split, West, playing first base, had six hits in 15 at bats. Two hits were home runs.[7]

The home opener was with the Crawfords, a perennial power in the East. Although there was adequate pregame publicity, there were no reports on the series at Rickwood Field in the *Birmingham News*. According to the *Birmingham Reporter*, Pittsburgh won all three games.

After a disappointing start before the home fans, the Black Barons went on the road again, winning two exhibition games in Decatur, Alabama, then going on to Louisville for a league series. Birmingham swept a double-header on May 1. Boone gave up 10 hits but spaced them effectively to win, 7–3, in the opener. Birmingham won the second, 5–1, behind the pitching of Richard Cannon and Sam Bankhead.[8]

From Louisville they went to Chicago and lost three games. The home team had 26 runs and 36 hits against completely ineffective Birmingham pitching.[9] Somewhere on the trip, Birmingham lost hard-hitting first baseman Jim West. McAllister filled the position in Chicago. Later reports suggested that West had been released and picked up by Memphis.[10] That seems highly unlikely, given his performance with the Black Barons. A subsequent article credited West with three home runs in a game against Montgomery.[11] About the same time, the *Birmingham Reporter* said that George McAllister had been named manager of the Birmingham team.[12]

Birmingham won three out of four in Montgomery. A new pitcher named Jasper won the opener, 11–4, striking out six and yielding four hits.[13] Carter won, 3–2, on Saturday and they split a double-header on Sunday. Boone won the opener, but Montgomery beat Bankhead, 6–2, in the nightcap. Bankhead also pitched in a tie game on Monday. It was called for darkness after nine innings. He struck out 10.[14]

Bankhead, normally an infielder but an occasional starter, was the oldest of the five baseball-playing brothers from the mining community of Empire. They played at various levels from around 1930 through 1965. All except Garnett, the youngest, played for the Black Barons part of their careers.[15]

Sam Bankhead's career started with the Black Barons in 1929, although he didn't show up in a game account until 1931. As well as Negro leagues, he also played in the Mexican League and was an early integrator in the Canadian Provincial League.[16]

Fred, an infielder, was with the Black Barons in the late 1930s, and also with Memphis and the New York Black Yankees.[17] Dan, the third brother, was the most successful, making it to the major leagues with the Brooklyn Dodgers in 1947. In 1950, he was 9–5 with the Dodgers. He went to Mexico in 1954, playing there until 1965. Joe, whose career was brief, played for the Black Barons in 1948 and with Grand Rapids in the Central League.[18] Garnett also had a brief career with Memphis and the Homestead Grays. He was a pitcher when the Grays defeated Birmingham for the 1948 Negro World Series championship.[19]

In mid–May the team opened a home stand with Nashville, Monroe, and Indianapolis. Weather reports suggest that the entire Nashville series may have been rained out. The Monroe series started with a first-game rainout, followed by a 5–1 Birmingham victory that snapped Monroe's nine-game winning streak.[20] Boone held them scoreless until the last inning. Petway, a new right fielder, had two hits and drove in two runs. Monroe won two shutouts on Sunday. Dick Matthews bested Bankhead, 2–0, and Bill Nash lost a three-hitter, 1–0, on an unearned run in the nightcap.[21]

The next day, May 23, the Indianapolis ABCs game was rained out. Birmingham won a double-header the following day. Boone pitched a two-hitter to win the first game, 5–0. The *Birmingham News* reported that one of the hits was "of the scratch variety." In the second game, catcher Andrew Drake lined a home run to win it for Carter. In the second inning, with runners on first and second, shortstop Henderson speared. He stepped on second and threw to McAllister at first to complete the triple play.[22]

The two wins were likely the last local fans saw of the Black Barons in 1932. There was no report on the third game scheduled the next day. The team headed north. They lost a double-header to Pittsburgh on May 28 and split two double-headers with Cleveland on May 29–30. Those were the last games reported for the Black Barons in 1932. Birmingham's name was absent in the final first-half standings published a few weeks later.[23]

The Indianapolis series was the last time the Black Barons appeared at Rickwood Field for more than two years. In 1933 and 1934, teams representing the city were sometimes called the Black Barons, but at other times by such names as Foxes and Giants. It was not until 1935 that the name returned with clarity and certainty. As for 1932, the *Chicago Defender* reported on August 6 that the Birmingham Black Barons had defeated the Black Tars, 7–1, in Panama City, Florida.[24] On August 26, the *Birmingham News* reported that the Black Barons would play a three-game series at Fair Park against the Docena All-Stars. In both instances, it is likely that the "Black Barons" was just a remnant of the club that opened in the NSL, or was perhaps an industrial league team that appropriated the name Black Barons.[25]

But the Black Barons were not the only team in trouble in 1932. By June 5, Memphis, struggling with a 5–16 record, was in dire straits. The Red Sox were accused of playing men who actually belonged to another team. League President R.B. Jackson was considering dropping Memphis from the league.[26]

Because of the mixture of leagues represented, historians and researchers have accorded black "major league" status to the 1932 Negro Southern League. It was, with its eclectic membership, the only league to survive the season. Yet, by the end of the season, many teams had folded, and a peculiar series of playoffs was scheduled to determine the best team among the Negro leagues.[27]

By late June it as obvious that Chicago, Nashville, and Monroe were the best clubs in the league. Standings on June 29 showed Chicago (23–5) on top. Trailing were Monroe (23–6) and Nashville (20–12). Birmingham's final published record was 11–9.[28] It did not change between June 5 and June 26, about a week before the end of the first half.

Three different sets of standings, remarkably uniform, had newspapers agreeing that Monroe edged out Chicago for the first-half championship.[29]

But none of the standings were "official," and Monroe's title was yanked away about a month later. President R.B. Jackson released a statement explaining why: "Cole's American Giants are winners for the first-half, this team played and won more games, presenting the best attraction qualities, and above all, their individual respect for league affiliation is unsurpassed." Chauvinistic or not, Jackson attributed the previous numbers to "some few sports writers … [who] overzealously accepted reports of games won and averaged a percentage for publication."[30]

Jackson further said consideration needed to include "the use of the official league ball, using disqualified players, clubs missing their scheduled dates, clubs giving breach to some or all rules in base-ball."[31] Monroe challenged this arbitrary rearrangement of standings with "letters and telegrams" asserting it had protested two of its Memphis games. It was all to no avail, and the first-half title was awarded to Chicago.[32]

When league officials met in Nashville to plan the second half of the season, there were many problems on the table, "the cry of the depression and other hard luck stories" notwithstanding.[33] President Jackson, putting on a brave front, congratulated the survivors on their success and then moved quickly to plug up holes in the dam. These include franchise shifts. Atlanta was transferred to Columbus, Ohio; Birmingham to Lexington, Kentucky; and Little Rock to Kansas City. Associate memberships were accorded to Knoxville, Tennessee, and Alcoa, Tennessee.[34] Like the remnant of the Black Barons that had plodded on, Little Rock players did likewise. Manager Reuben Jones pulled together a group for barnstorming. "The Grays of Little Rock" were reported to be in Mexico City on July 30 for a seven-game series with a club called the Aztecs.[35]

There is no concrete evidence that Knoxville ever played any league games except with nearby Alcoa. After a reported reorganization, former owner J.A. Nance said that he had reclaimed the team and bolstered its roster, and was headed to Montgomery for a Fourth of July series.[36] However, there was no report on the series in Montgomery.[37] Also, the *News-Sentinel* reported that Nance and Floyd Holland had been "engaged in lawsuits over" the use of the name Giants.[38]

On July 23, Monroe reached Louisville for a series with the Black Caps, only to find that the team had disbanded. "The Louisville club gave out no news of its plans to quit until Monroe had arrived on the scene on Saturday and then the sign was displayed, 'no game today.' Quite a few fans were present, however, and appeared dissatisfied with sudden decision to quit cold. President Jackson was notified of the action by wire late Saturday night."[39]

In August, the *Montgomery Advertiser* reported that travel costs had taken their toll on the far-flung NSL: "[T]eams will not complete their original schedule but they will be kept together for special games in order to keep base ball going in their respective cities."[40] The *Chicago Defender* also reported that the league appeared to be on its last legs. "Although nothing has been received from the offices of Dr. R.B. Jackson … rumor coming from that section still persists that the second half of the pennant race may not be completed. Monroe, La., has had no league games for the past several weeks and Montgomery, Atlanta [*sic*] and Alcoa have already folded up." Atlanta, of course, had not played at all during in the second half. The situation in Memphis was described as "somewhat unsettled."[41]

Indianapolis Manager Candy Jim Taylor, writing in the *Chicago Defender*, ripped the whole situation, saying that with the exception of Chicago, Indianapolis, and Nashville, the league "had ceased to function since the first half, which ended on July 4." Disgusted with it all, Taylor said his ABCs would host one final series with the Elite Giants on August 21–22, then finish the season against "some of the best semipro teams in the state of Indiana."[42]

If the comings and goings of teams was peculiar during the regular season, it was perhaps a reflection of an equally extraordinary postseason. Three different playoff series were conducted for various championships.

First up was a return of the "Negro Dixie Series" with Monroe facing the Austin Black Senators. This came after Monroe had defeated the New Orleans Black Pelicans and/or Algiers Giants five out of seven games for the "Louisiana state championship."[43] The Dixie Series opened in Austin on August 20 with the Monarchs winning two out of three games.[44] The following weekend the series moved to Monroe, where Austin won the first game. Monroe won the next two, claiming its second Negro Dixie Series in as many years.[45]

While Monroe's apparent first-half title had been negated by President Jackson's ruling, dedicated local fans said "no news item from any papers in the country could make them believe that Monroe did not win the first half."[46] Yet the Monarchs watched as two other teams entered playoffs for the pennant. Chicago played Nashville for the championship. "Following this contest for league honors, the winners of the Southern League championship will challenge and play the decided winners of the east, namely New York [Black] Yankees, Homestead Grays and Pittsburgh Crawfords."[47]

The NSL situation was no more chaotic than the race among the eastern teams, where the winner would be determined by journalists: "President Jackson is now awaiting correspondence from the sports writers of the *Pittsburgh Courier, Chicago Defender* and *Philadelphia Independent* as to the decided and undisputed team."[48]

Nashville won two out of three at Chicago, but the American Giants eventually won the series four games to three. The series started on September 2 and did not end until October 2.[49]

The third playoff, billed as the "Negro World Series," was as confusingly reported as the others. It featured Monroe against the Pittsburgh Crawfords. Pittsburgh won it five games to one, with another game ending in a tie.[50]

The Negro Southern League's first Negro World Series appearance was disappointing, but without the NSL, the state of black baseball in 1932 would have been even more dismal.

13

Where Are the
Black Barons? (1933)

The year 1933 was something of a rebirth for black baseball after 1932's chaotic season. Although leagues had merged to find a path to survival, numerous clubs folded as the Depression sapped resources. At one double-header in Atlanta, a sportswriter noted that it was played "before a crowd of 500, almost 400 of which witnessed the game from the outside of the park," presumably unable to afford or unwilling to spend the price of admission.[1] Lagging attendance was a common theme throughout the season.

But in baseball, spring training always brings hope. The Negro National League returned with a seven-club lineup, among them the Nashville Elite Giants. It was a pivotal move for one of the South's perennial black teams. There were rumors that the team was relocating to Detroit.[2] Although that did not happen, by 1934 the Elite Giants were in Columbus, Ohio. Later they migrated to Washington and finally to Baltimore.[3]

The NSL was back with a lineup of more familiar cities such as Little Rock, Memphis, Monroe, Montgomery, and New Orleans. New teams were from Jackson, Mississippi; Shreveport and Alexandria, Louisiana; and Algiers, a suburb of New Orleans.[4]

There was a new president, Dr. J.B. Martin of Memphis. Martin and his brother B.B. Martin were Memphis dentists and businessmen. They owned the Memphis Red Sox and built Martin Park. The Red Sox were one of the few teams in the Negro leagues with their own ballpark.[5]

And what about Birmingham? Where were the Black Barons? The whereabouts of the Birmingham team in 1933 is murky territory. At various times, the city was represented by a team called the Black Barons, but also the Monarchs, and even the Foxes on one occasion.[6] It is entirely possible that the Black Barons name was used by writers based on past experience with Birmingham teams. One certainty, though, is that Birmingham was not a member of any league in 1933. Although the city was mentioned in preseason articles as a likely member of the Negro Southern League, and it played against familiar NSL and NNL opponents, the team never appeared in any standings.[7]

In mid–April the *Birmingham Reporter* announced the Birmingham Monarchs would be "playing games throughout the state and the South." Other teams were advised to contact management to schedule games.[8]

The team was organized under the presidency of Lige Frazier. Games were to be played at Fair Park, an obvious come-down from Rickwood Field. The identity of the original field manager is unclear, but pitcher George Nash was in the role by around May 20. By the last appearance of the team in late July, the manager was said to be a man named Springer.[9]

"With Nash in rare form and given sensational support by his teammates, the Birmingham Monarchs applied a coat of whitewash to the Atlanta Black Crackers," the *Birmingham Reporter* boasted after a 2–0 game in late April. Atlanta threatened only once when a bad throw sent a runner from second toward home. The Birmingham center fielder, possibly Hamp Johnson, cut him down with "a perfect peg" to home plate. Only "a handful of fans" were present for the game, which was over in an hour and a half. Sports editor William L. Moore wrote that Birmingham "played a good game in the field but look very weak at the bat."[10]

On May 4, the *Montgomery Advertiser* reported that the local Grey Sox would open their season on May 6 against the Monarchs. There was no mention of either team being in a league. Veteran pitcher-outfielder Terris McDuffie started for Birmingham. McDuffie, a native of Mobile, played more than 15 years in the Negro leagues, including several years with the Black Barons. He also played in the Mexican League and in the minors in the Texas League.[11]

Montgomery won the opener, 4–3. On Sunday the two clubs split a double-header, the Grey Sox winning the first game, 4–3, and Birmingham the nightcap, 8–0. A new pitcher named Rowe pitched the four-inning shutout.[12]

In May, the *Commercial-Appeal* reported that a weekend series with Monroe had been canceled. Instead, the Birmingham Black Barons would be in Memphis. The paper reported it as the fourth Negro Southern League series for the Red Sox, the others being Jackson, Algiers, and Alexandria.[13] Apparently, the Memphis writer assumed Birmingham was in the league because of past affiliations.

The first game, on Saturday, was a hitting battle with Memphis winning, 13–12.[14]

Memphis won a double-header on Sunday, then swept the series on Monday with a 12–7 pounding of Walter Calhoun and a reliever named Caldwell.[15]

It was the *Chicago Defender* that reported in May the hiring of pitcher George Nash as manager of the Monarchs. "Among the players he has to work with are Harris, Jackson, College, Field, Mills, Bryant and others."[16] None of these players were confirmed in box scores or game accounts. In the 13–12 loss to Memphis, the Birmingham lineup was: Howard, 2b; Nash, lf; Johnson, rf; Borden, ss; Smith, 1b; Caldwell, cf; M'wain [sic], 3b; C. Smith, c; Calhoun, p. George Nash was the losing pitcher the next day.[17]

After two weeks passed with no news of the Birmingham team, the *Birmingham Reporter* wrote that the club, with a "stronger lineup," would face Memphis at Fair Park on May 28. New players included Harry Barnes, Bozo Jackson, Walter Cooley, Joe Turner, and the Frazier brothers of Montgomery. Following the Memphis games, Birmingham would go to Atlanta for two games, then return home for a Thursday Ladies Day game with an unnamed opponent.[18]

No results were published for any of those games, if, indeed, they were even played. A week later the *Reporter* lamented the state of black baseball in Birmingham:

> If ever there was a question in the sport line, it is here in the Magic City. Baseball is at a low ebb. No one to back teams, hence no playing. Results, fans are suffering for the want of some place to go.
>
> What kind of management is this that will advertise a game and then when it is called off never say a word. The Monarchs sent copy for their game Sunday and in good faith we printed same. Sunday we found no game. We apologize to our readers.[19]

That was the last mention of the team in the *Birmingham Reporter*, although it did surface in Montgomery and New Orleans newspapers.[20]

A Birmingham team called the Foxes was to play in Montgomery on June 28. The game was rained out.[21] If others were planned, they were not mentioned in the newspapers. There was a reference to a Fourth of July game between the Grey Sox and "Birmingham Aspic, champions of the city league."[22]

On June 19, the *Times-Picayune* reported that the Birmingham Black Barons were coming to play the New Orleans Crescent Stars. Because of a travel delay, the Birmingham club did not arrive in time for a Saturday game or a double-header on Sunday. Instead, the Crescent Stars played another local team in the first game and then the late-arriving Black Barons in the second game. Nash pitched in the 1–0 loss, giving up just six hits and striking out 10. New Orleans won again on Monday and Tuesday.[23] The *Times-Picayune* said both teams were in the Negro Southern League.[24]

On July 29 the *Montgomery Advertiser* reported that the "Birmingham team" under Manager Springer was in town to play the Grey Sox. Birmingham reportedly had been touring Florida cities. Montgomery won a Sunday game, 3–1, beating another new Birmingham pitcher named Chatman.[25]

The following week, the "Black Barons" returned to New Orleans for another series with the Crescent Stars. Again, it was unclear if this really was the Black Barons or just a sportswriter's assumption. New Orleans won two games; one was rained out. The newspaper reports were short and without detail.[26]

No other reports of a Birmingham team were found in newspapers after that date.

A total of 15 results, including six box scores, were located for the season. Birmingham won only two of those games, although there was a possible third victory in a game against Atlanta for which no score was reported. The only box score for a win was a six-inning 2–0 shutout of Montgomery. M. Jones was the pitcher.

From the six box scores, infielder Bill Howard led the hitters with a .429 batting average (6 for 14 with a triple). Borden, who played three different positions, was 6 for 16, .375, and outfielder Hamp Johnson was 5 for 16, .313.

About 35 player names were gleaned from game reports and other newspaper stories, most of them from Memphis, New Orleans and Montgomery newspapers. With essentially no local coverage, only seven players were positively identified with first names. They were second baseman Bill Howard, outfielder Hamp Johnson, catcher Carl Smith, second baseman Martin Oliver, and pitchers Walter Calhoun, Terris McDuffie, and George Nash. It is possible to make an educated guess at some others within the context of previous and later seasons. The third baseman is likely Johnny Cowan, who had a long career with the Black Barons. This would have been his professional start. Another likely player is outfielder Willie Crawford. The most frustrating unidentified name belonged to a third baseman whose abbreviated name appeared in four box scores, three as "M'Sw'n" and one as "Mc'wain." A diligent search of Negro league rosters, with particular attention to such name possibilities as McSwain, McSwanson, and McElwain, produced nothing helpful.

As for the Negro Southern League, it opened with eight teams: Alexandria Giants, Algiers Giants, Jackson Bear Cats (sometimes called Senators and Black Senators), Little Rock Stars, Memphis Red Sox, Monroe Monarchs, New Orleans Crescent Stars, and Shreveport Cubs.[27]

Opening Day promotions reflected the difficult economic times. In Little Rock, five dollars' worth of nickels were dropped from an airplane and fans allowed to scramble for the loose change. In addition, 50 loaves of bread were dropped from a plane in a special contest for women only. Finally, five baseballs were to "be thrown over the park and the boy or girl under 12 years of age" returning the greatest number "will receive a prize of 50 cents." For perspective, theater admission at the local theater was ten cents matinee and fifteen cent nights.[28]

Monroe's season opened with a parade and prizes for the best decorated float or car. Local merchants had donated more than 50 prizes to be given away, including a grand prize diamond ring. Monroe management offered two promotions that topped the ones in Little Rock. The "first ball to be used in the game," with money attached to it, was dropped from an airplane. Boys under 12 were allowed to scramble for it. In the other promotion a "coop of chickens" would be turned loose in the park and would belong to anyone catching them.[29] The chicken chase "brought the fans to their feet in excitement," the local press reported, but left unanswered a burning question: what did people do with their chickens during the game?[30]

For Jackson, joining the Negro Southern League was a matter of pride for the African American community. Whites had previously managed its teams. "The negro lovers of baseball have been clamoring since the organization of professional negro baseball for a management of negroes from top to bottom. They claim that under the leadership of their own people, the management can and will get 100 per cent support."[31] Unfortunately, 1933 would prove to be a bad year for a new baseball venture, regardless of the management's ethnicity.

Within weeks, the club president issued a solemn statement: "We wish to assure the fans it will be impossible to continue in the Negro Southern League unless we get better attendance from the fans. We are herewith pleading to the fans both white and colored to help us stay in the circuit as it means much for the city of Jackson to be associated with progressive cities and towns of the south in the great national pastime."[32]

Problems were abundant in black baseball that year. At the July league meeting, W.M. Brown of Montgomery was welcomed as his team replaced Monroe, which had dropped out even before the first half ended.[33] The *Pittsburgh Courier* reported in October that only three of the Negro National League teams had completed the season's schedule.[34]

Memphis (32–10) was declared first-half winner, nine games ahead of second-place Algiers.[35]

Second-half play deteriorated rapidly. Fewer than two dozen second-half games were recorded in standings published as late as August 12. Memphis was still the best in the league, undefeated but having played only three league games.[36]

In August, Memphis announced an extended road trip to Missouri, Nebraska, Iowa, Oklahoma, and Colorado.[37] In Little Rock, the Stars were scheduled to play a seven-game series with Dubisson, a local semipro team, for the city championship.[38] These announcements obviously reflected a decrease in the number of certified league games being played.

There was little logic or explanation for the playoff lineups. The *Arkansas Gazette* reported in September that the Red Sox and the Little Rock Stars were beginning a seven-game series to determine the NSL champion. The newspaper suggested that Little Rock won the second half, although Memphis led in the only published standings. No results were located for these games.[39]

The New Orleans Crescent Stars played postseason series with the Houston Black Buffalos, Nashville, and Cole's Chicago American Giants. "The Crescent Stars feel that they have eliminated all the strongest teams in the South and feel sure that the winners of the Negro National league will chose [*sic*] them as their opponents in the world series," said a newspaper report in late August.[40]

The Crescent Stars won the first game with Houston, 5–1. Double-headers were scheduled for the next two days. "These games will determine the team that plays Nashville in the Negro Dixie Series. Reserve seats for white fans at all games," reported the *Times-Picayune*.[41] New Orleans won three more games from Houston, setting up the series with Nashville.[42]

The Dixie series was to open in New Orleans and continue "until one team has won four games and the right to meet the winners of the Negro National League in the Negro World Series."[43] That was puzzling, since Nashville was in the Negro National League.

New Orleans won all three games scheduled in the Crescent City.[44] In Nashville, the Crescent Stars wrapped up the title in the second game of a double-header. After dropping the opener, New Orleans won the nightcap, 2–1, and the "Negro World Series" matchup with Chicago.[45]

While the New Orleans–Nashville series was being played, yet another controversy was simmering over second-half standings. The *Chicago Defender* reported that Nashville, Chicago, and Pittsburgh had all claimed the NNL second-half title.[46] The article further stated that if Chicago was awarded the second half, there would be no need for a playoff since it also won the first half. The American Giants would then play New Orleans. Whatever the officials' decision was, a New Orleans–Chicago series followed a few weeks later.

The entire series was played in New Orleans. The first game was rained out. Chicago then won four out of five to claim the championship. In the second game, former Birmingham Black Baron George "Mule" Suttles hit a grand slam home run as the American Giants won 6–1.[47]

14

A New Season, a New Name (1934)

The Black Barons were still in limbo when spring training time arrived for the 1934 baseball season, but Birmingham was about to have league ball again. Perhaps equally exciting, both Birmingham and Atlanta had vacated blue laws that previously prohibited Sunday baseball.[1]

The Negro Southern League held its first 1934 organizational meeting in February in Memphis. It was believed to be "the largest gathering of Southern League Moguls" ever held. Eight city representatives and other black baseball individuals participated.[2] However, there was no mention of a Birmingham representative.

One of the teams said to be interested in the NSL was the Kansas City Monarchs. The consensus, though, was that "a better circuit should be formed to include a shorter mileage, larger population, and salary base to enable each team to finish with a little cash."[3]

Subsequent meetings were held in New Orleans and Nashville with optimistic owners anticipating improving business conditions.[4] In Nashville, Gus Greenlee, president of the Negro National League, talked about possible cooperative arrangements with Eastern teams. This time, Birmingham was represented, by Frank Perdue and Ludie Key.[5]

The lineup for the 1934 season was the Atlanta Athletics, Cincinnati Tigers, Louisville Black Sox, Memphis Red Sox, Monroe Monarchs, and Birmingham Giants. Although there were frequent newspaper references to the Black Barons, it was actually the Giants. The New Orleans Crescent Stars were awarded an associate membership.[6]

President Dr. J.B. Martin, determined to prevent players jumping clubs and player-raiding by northern teams, announced that he had affiliated the NSL with "the national body." Greenlee told Martin he would not seek three players who had tried out with his team the previous spring.[7]

The NNL had its own problems to deal with. Although there was an eight-team lineup for the new season, there was also the lingering knowledge that only three clubs had managed to complete their schedules in 1933.[8]

It is uncertain when the 1934 NSL season actually opened. The *Times-Picayune* had the opening on April 21 when the Crescent Stars hosted Birmingham.[9] The *Birmingham News* had the opening on May 20 when Memphis played the Giants "in the real opening of the Southern League schedule" at Rickwood Field.[10] Standings published in late June contained so few total games that the May 20 opening seems more likely.

As Opening Day approached, it became clearer that the Birmingham team was the Giants, not the Black Barons. One newspaper referenced the team as "formerly known as the Black Barons."[11] As the *Birmingham News* put it: "Birmingham Giants, alias Black Barons, will stage the opening of their 1934 season at Rickwood Field Friday afternoon at 3:30" in an exhibition series with Cleveland of the NNL.[12]

There was a similar name disparity in Louisville. Although the name Black Sox had been presented in preseason reporting, the team was usually called the Louisville Caps in game reports. There was also an amateur team in the city called the Louisville Red Caps.[13]

Confusing nickname or not, preseason hype for the Birmingham team was positive. "Frank Purdue and Ludie Keys are in charge of the colored team here this year, and they announce that they have corralled some of the greatest colored stars ever to appear locally in representing Birmingham this year. 'We'll give 'em a run for their money this year,' said the wily Frank, who should know what he's talking about, as he has been mixed up in the local baseball situation ever since colored teams of Birmingham started competing professionally."[14]

The manager was Bill "Thou Shalt Not Steal" Perkins, although his stay was short. Assisting him was veteran catcher Poindexter Williams. The workouts were on a diamond at 12th Street and 8th Avenue.[15]

The *News* predicted that "several hundred" white fans would attend the Cleveland games.[16] Both worked out at Legion Field, the football stadium, in preparation for the series.[17]

Two games were rained out, but local fans got a good look at the team in the two that were played. Birmingham won the first game, 10–0, with the following lineup:

Jerry Benjamin, cf	A. Matthew Jackson, ss
Matthew "Lick" Carlisle, 2b	Harvey Peterson, lf
Herman "Jabbo" Andrews, rf	Johnny Cowan, 3b
Bill Perkins, c	Walter Glover, p
John Washington, 1b	

Glover, a left-hander, gave up only five hits, striking out seven. Perkins had three hits and Benjamin two, while Washington hit a solo home run. The Cleveland first baseman was former Black Baron George McAllister. Cleveland won the second game, 4–3, but Birmingham appeared to have a respectable team for its return to league play.[18] It was a veteran lineup with several players destined for long careers in the Negro leagues.

Benjamin, a Montgomery native, had a sterling 17-year career, particularly with the great Homestead teams from 1937 to 1945.[19] Carlisle, a Wenonah boy, started with the Black Barons in 1931. Andrews started with them in 1930, and then played with various teams through 1943. Perkins had first played with the Black Barons in 1930. Jackson, Glover, and Peterson were all former Montgomery Grey Sox. Of the newcomers, Washington's career was relatively short, but Johnny Cowan made in to the white minor leagues in 1950. He was an industrial leaguer and played with the Black Barons three different times.[20]

The identity confusion of 1934 is with Birmingham pitchers. Various reports listed Bill Jones and C. Jones as pitchers, and historian James Riley places Arthur "Mutt" Jones on the team. Mutt started as a shortstop, playing that position for Birmingham in 1925.[21] Further, an outfielder named W. Jones also appeared in some box scores. "Bill" and "W" may be the same person. Regardless, it is impossible to determine just who played in some games.

After the Cleveland series, the Black Barons barnstormed through Georgia, reportedly winning all seven games played.[22]

Three of the Georgia wins were over the Atlanta Black Crackers. Birmingham crushed a makeshift Atlanta lineup, 15–2, in the opener, getting 17 hits. For the three Atlanta games, Birmingham had 29 runs and 43 hits. Andrews was called the Birmingham manager throughout the Atlanta series.[23]

The *Atlanta Daily World* was impressed with shortstop Matty Jackson. "He's easily one of the three greatest short fielders in the game today. He plays as deep as some left fielders, gobbles them up without a split second delay, and throws to first base like a shot out of a cannon. His stop and toss that ended the game Saturday was one of the sweetest fielding plays your scribe ever looked at. The drive looked like a sure hit past second, but Jackson dashed around and speared it up and heaved to first to nick his man by a hair," the paper reported.[24]

Back home, they played Kansas City, winning two out of three with good pitching. Glover bested the great Chet Brewer, and Bill Jones threw a four-hit shutout.[25] The performances impressed the sportswriter for the *Birmingham News*, who noted that the team was "hopping away to what looked like one of the greatest seasons in the career of colored baseball in Birmingham."[26] The winning pitcher in Kansas City's win was former Black Baron Charlie Beverly.[27]

Missing from any action in the Kansas City games was catcher-manager Bill Perkins. The receivers for the series were Paul Hardy and Martin Oliver. No Birmingham field manager was mentioned in any pregame or game stories the rest of the season. Other sources place Perkins elsewhere in 1934. The exhibition games were likely his only Birmingham appearances.[28] Perkins did play for Birmingham in 1928, 1930, and 1945.

That leaves unanswered the question: who was the Birmingham field manager in 1934? The *Atlanta Daily World* in April referenced "the managers of the Birmingham Giants."[29] In early May, sportswriter Melancholy Jones said Herman Andrews was the manager.[30] The *Chicago Defender*, in June, said two wins over Memphis "added some power to Walker and Keys in the steel city."[31] Later articles in various newspapers referred only to Walker and Keys, suggesting that they were possibly dual field managers. Charles Walker was the club secretary.

15

Return of the
Black Barons (1935)

The Negro Southern League held its 1935 organizational meeting in April at the Martin Building in Memphis and much was accomplished.[1] Represented at the meeting were Monroe, New Orleans, Cincinnati, Birmingham, Memphis, Atlanta, Louisville, and Claybrook, Arkansas. Umpires and an official baseball for league games were selected. Inter-league play with Negro National League teams was planned as well as a postseason championship series.

The season would open on May 15 and close on July 4. Dr. J.B. Martin of Memphis was reelected president. Milton H. Grey of Birmingham was elected first vice president.[2] The corresponding secretary was Burwell Towns Harvey, for 42 years a coach, athletic director, and science professor at Morehouse College.[3] He frequently umpired Negro Southern League games in the Atlanta area.[4]

The May 15 date notwithstanding, there was considerable confusion over Opening Day. The Memphis Red Sox said they were opening with the Atlanta Black Crackers on May 7. The opener in Atlanta was proclaimed for May 7.[5] For Birmingham it was April 29.[6]

The good news for Birmingham fans was that "the Black Barons will 'ride again' in the Magic City," wrote Wilson L. Driver in the *Atlanta Daily World*. Driver, in a breathless, difficult-to-understand, 122-word sentence, said in part that this team was "not the same Barons of years ago under the helm of 'Uncle' Joe Rush and others in the days when work was plentiful, money more plentiful, and crowds came from miles to watch the 'heroes of the diamond of the boom days' but a new Black Baron ... a younger, faster chap with just as much showmanship and more, besides that youthful energy that 'oldtimers' would give anything in the world to possess...."[7]

Working out at Sloss Field, Driver reported that the team would be "an aggregation of youngsters who have been outstanding on most of the semi-pro teams ... a bunch of youngsters who under the proper leadership should develop into one of the best teams in the Southern league." In one forgivable error, Driver named the Birmingham manager as Robert Poindexter, the disgraced pitcher who had shot his roommate some years earlier. In fact, it was Poindexter Williams, the veteran catcher.[8] Birmingham newspapers carried very little news on spring training.

When the "new Black Barons" opened with Atlanta, a starting lineup, full of those youngsters from the industrial league, was projected:

George McAllister, 1b	Good Black, 2b
Hamp Johnson, rf	W.H. Mays, lf
Cliff Carr, 3b	Fred Bankhead, ss
Jim Fields, cf	Bob Walker, p
Harry Bond, c	

Additional pitchers were Erwin Boyd, Jeff Posey, Wild Bill Mitchell, and George Nash. Utility players were Howard Smith and Lefty John Smith.[9]

Only McAllister, Johnson, and Nash had played with the club previously. Fred Bankhead was the second of the five Bankhead brothers to play professional baseball and the second to play with his hometown team. The most interesting name, though, was the No. 7 hitter, W.H. Mays. "Cat" Mays's son, Willie Howard Mays, Jr., would, of course, become one of the game's greatest players.[10]

Birmingham officials planned a regular "baseball jubilee" to kick off the new season. A preliminary game between industrial league teams Stockham and Acipco was set for 2:15 p.m., followed by the NSL game. African Methodist Episcopal Church Bishop B.G. Shaw was invited to pitch the first ball.[11]

Mitchell pitched a good game for eight innings, holding Atlanta scoreless on four hits, but it fell apart in the ninth. Atlanta scored three times to win, 3–2. Second baseman Sylvester Owens, who had not been listed in the earlier roster, had two hits for Birmingham in the leadoff position.[12]

The next day was better. Birmingham used an early 3–0 lead to give Bob Walker a 3–2 win. He pitched well, allowing just five hits and retiring the first eleven batters to face him. When he appeared to weaken in the ninth, Manager Williams brought in George Nash to save the win.[13]

The Claybrook Tigers, a newcomer to the NSL, were a black semipro team located in Claybrook, Arkansas, in southern Crittenden County. The town no longer exists, but in the 1930s it was home base for farming and logging operations of John C. Claybrook, who became one of the area's most successful black businessmen. He started a baseball team, built a stadium, hired outstanding players, and in the mid–1930s placed the team in the NSL. Among those outstanding players was Mobile native Ted "Double Duty" Radcliffe, a future Black Baron.[14]

The New Orleans Black Pelicans were expected to replace the Crescent Stars in 1935.[15] However, in early March, owner Allen Page chaired a committee that formed a Tri-State League composed of teams from various Louisiana and Mississippi municipalities, plus Mobile, Alabama.[16]

Atlanta was back after a two-year absence. The new manager was Sammy "Runt" Thompson, "short but stocky young second baseman who was voted the best keystoner in the NSL by Dixie sports writers in 1931 when he was with Memphis."[17]

Birmingham's excitement over returning to league ball was matched in Atlanta. The *Atlanta Daily World* sports editor, Ric Roberts, reported that management was working hard for the opener and a crowd of 5,000 was not unrealistic:

> This is only five percent [of Atlanta's 100,000 population] and does not seem to me a very ambitious figure to strive for. Atlanta was once a baseball town. Atlanta can be made a baseball town again if well organized, well groomed and well represented teams can be fetched in here.... If we are to ever enliven the dull summers that we have here; if we are to ever enjoy ball games from press boxes and reserved seats, now is the time to make preparation. Now is the time to see this new venture through. I have not seen so many illustrious ball players in Atlanta in a life time of sport hounding here.[18]

An estimated 3,500 black fans and 1,000 whites turned out for a June 2 double-header with Birmingham.[19] Crackers general manager Earl Mann apparently watched the turnstile count with glee: "Why, you played to far more fans than Little Rock or Knoxville are able to draw when they play the white Crackers here. We pledge you these grounds any day you have games billed and hope you can come out on Sunday dates when our team is out of town."[20]

Unusually, the Black Barons opened the season in Montgomery's Cramton Bowl against Nashville.[21] The game was sponsored by former Montgomery Grey Sox President William M. Brown, Nashville Manager Candy Jim Taylor, and Birmingham Business Manager Molton Gray, according to the *Alabama Journal*.[22] There was no report on the game's outcome, but the *Birmingham News* implied later that Nashville won it.[23]

They then played two games in Birmingham. Still billed as the Nashville Elite Giants, the team was now based in Columbus, Ohio. Owner Thomas Wilson was unable to return to the Negro National League in 1935 because other owners objected to the lengthy trips to Nashville. Wilson first moved the team to Detroit but was unable to secure a suitable ballpark there. Ultimately, it was Columbus for the 1935 season.[24]

Regardless of geography, it was still the Elite Giants and Candy Jim Taylor, whose connections with black baseball in Birmingham dated to the early 1900s and the original Birmingham Giants.[25] The Nashville lineup was filled with ex-Birmingham players, notably Red Parnell, Jim Willis, and Paul Hardy.

Nashville won the first game, 6–3. Birmingham third baseman Cliff Carr was four for four, but the Black Barons had trouble bunching their 12 hits for runs. A Friday game was canceled, leaving Birmingham (1–3) headed to New Orleans, where they lost a Sunday double-header.[26]

The Black Barons returned home on May 19 to host Memphis. The *Birmingham News* said the team was "away to one of the greatest seasons of colored baseball in the Birmingham district."[27] However, among reported games, they lost three at Memphis and won two of three in Atlanta. "Wild Bill" Mitchell and Jeff Posey each pitched four-hitters in the wins. In the 10-inning loss, Fred Bankhead hit a home run.[28]

World Sports Editor Ric Roberts offered a colorful description of Mitchell's performance. He was "a bow-legged and grinning molester … and the best our Black Crackers could do was dent him for four remotely occasioned base hits and three bases on balls. He was the real headache in this smearing of Gabby Stephens debut as manager. His crossfire and hook was [sic] something to see and after he got past the first inning, he hung eight straight horsecollars around our boys' necks."[29]

Roberts, always a knowledgeable and entertaining writer, had some interesting observations on first baseman George McAllister, who apparently had replaced Poindexter Williams as manager. Using the contemporary definition of the word "gay" as an expression of joy rather than sexual preference, he wrote: "Our moral for today's sermon, brethren, should be; 'Never get gay with an old gaffer; he may not like it.' Demonstrating the truth of this adage our Black Crackers tried to get gay with 42-year-old 'Grandpap' McAllister of the Birmingham Barons and barely escaped getting their ears pinned back by the old gaffer and his gang before 2,000 fans yesterday at Ponce de Leon Park."[30]

Roberts said the ruckus started in the first inning when some of Atlanta's young players suggested "with the carelessness of young squirts that he should be home with his pipe and slippers." McAllister "decided that something should be done, that these youngsters and Gabby Stephens should be taught a lesson of respect for their elders. He took things in his honey mitts and put himself in the lineup as an outfielder." Noticing that Atlanta pitcher Lefty Williams "couldn't field a lick," McAllister led off the sixth with a bunt that Williams botched. He then had the next batter, Howard, also bunt. Williams fielded the ball but threw it over the first baseman's head, and McAllister scored all the way from first. The strategy gave the Black Barons a 3–0 lead before "Black Rider" Brown stopped the rally. Atlanta eventually won the game, 4–3, but the venerable McAllister had three hits in his "personal insurrection."[31]

In Jeff Posey's 7–2 win in the third game, Roberts said Birmingham batters had "reduced our two bellowing bulls of Friday, Pitchers 'Lefty' Williams 'Black Rider' Brown, to muling [*sic*] calves."[32]

But the Memphis series at Rickwood cast doubt on the projected "greatest" season.

With big bats, Memphis won, 14–4 and 6–3. For Birmingham, "Cat" Mays, like his son later, played center field and was leadoff hitter for the Black Barons. He had one hit in nine at bats.[33] Additional games in Anniston and Gadsden were unreported.

The Black Barons returned to Atlanta on June 2. In the only game reported, Birmingham won, 5–4, although Jeff Posey gave up two home runs, one to Birmingham boy Ted Smith.[34]

Once again Birmingham's season appears to have disintegrated away from home. The June 2 win in Atlanta was the last locally reported game for the Black Barons in 1935.

But again, the real question may not be what happened to the Black Barons, but what happened to media coverage. As with other recent seasons, the team vanished from the pages of the *Birmingham News* and other local papers. But games and references to the team continued to show up periodically in other cities.

In mid–August, the *Montgomery Advertiser* said the Black Barons were scheduled to play the Grey Sox on August 28 in the final game of the season. Pyrus or Lloyd would pitch for Montgomery while Jones would pitch for Birmingham.[35] No pitcher named Jones appeared in any of the other Birmingham games for which results were located. On the day of the game, the projected Montgomery pitcher was Lloyd or Glover, while Birmingham's was Watson or Walker (presumably Bob Walker). The newspaper reported that the Grey Sox entered the game with a record of 28–11 while Birmingham was 43–16.[36]

Montgomery won, 4–1, and the two teams were said to be playing again that afternoon.[37] There was no report on the second game. It seems likely that the Birmingham team that played in Montgomery in August was an independent team that appropriated the Black Barons name or, perhaps, the newspaper referenced it from force of habit. There is no evidence to suggest that the NSL team still functioned in August.

Despite the organizational meetings in early spring, there is some question as to whether the Negro Southern League actually functioned as such in 1935. The league was to open the season with eight teams—Atlanta, Birmingham, Chattanooga, Claybrook, Memphis, Monroe, Montgomery, and New Orleans. But the *Atlanta Daily World* lineup listed Knoxville and Nashville instead of Claybrook and New Orleans.[38] The teams that actually played out, the teams that started and failed, and the teams that never seemed to start league play, are matters difficult to determine.

When Atlanta went to Montgomery for a May 29 game, there was no mention of the Grey Sox being in the NSL. Nor were any other games played in the capital city referred to as league games. In fact, in July, Grey Sox owner William M. Browne announced that the team had been reorganized and was "ready for engagements on the road." Interested parties were invited to contact him at his residence on O'Connor Street.[39]

In Chattanooga it was reported on June 23 that the Knoxville "colored nine" was com-ing to play the Black Lookouts. Knoxville was said to be in third place in the NSL "right behind the Lookouts."[40] But in September, when Chattanooga ended the season against a Knoxville all-star team, there was no mention of the NSL.[41]

When a league schedule should have been underway in earnest, Claybrook, Monroe, and New Orleans were traveling widely, playing games in several states. On May 26, Monroe began a road trip that stretched through Mississippi, Arkansas, Illinois, and Missouri.[42] In June, Atlanta embarked on a two-week road trip to various Florida cities. Then a day of rest before going north for games in Indiana and Illinois. Again, no reference to league play.[43] Much later it was explained that Atlanta had dropped out of the league at the end of the first half on July 4, "forced by the exigencies of enveloping financial chaos."[44]

To be sure, there were still other references to the league. In June the Claybrook Tigers were referred to as "the class of the Southern league." Ric Roberts reported that an effort was going to be made to get the Claybrook team to Atlanta.[45] It would seem that if both teams were in the league, the normal schedule would have provided such a matchup. At some point, the season went downhill, perhaps hastened by the unsettled league situation. Roberts reported in August that the white ballpark's owners were considering closing out the Black Crackers' season early: "In the first place, they are a bit peeved over the poor fan backing that we have given our Crackers. We hardly made it interesting for the office out there to realize regular expenses—it does cost money to run a ball yard."[46]

Unsurprisingly, there was no mention of a postseason series with the NNL champion. However, Monroe scheduled a Louisiana–Arkansas Negro championship series with the Athletics of Crossett, Arkansas.[47]

An all-star game surfaced in September, but it was surrounded by confusion. "For the past three years Southern cities have been asking for this game. Critics argue that stars which form the backbone of the National body have been drafted from Southern Colleges and semi-pros teams. These players performed throughout the season in the East or North of their home and the homefolk are denied an opportunity to see them."[48] The previous year's all-star games were not mentioned.

The NSL and NNL presidents met in Chicago to plan a series of games. The teams would be selected by the presidents with help from the managers. Also, the black press was expected to have some role in the selection and/or promotion of the games. The first contest was to be in Memphis on September 29.[49]

Managers were announced a week later, Oscar Charleston for the North and Reuben Jones for the South.[50] When rosters were announced, only one Birmingham player was listed: pitcher Ernest "Spoon" Carter as a utility man.[51]

Ric Roberts announced yet another South all-star team comprised only of players from the Black Crackers and Jacksonville Red Caps. Roberts said the team would play a North all-star team in a three-game series in Jacksonville and Atlanta.[52]

There was no mention of the earlier North-South teams selected for the game in Mem-phis.[53] The only game reported in the *Daily World* was the one of October 2 in which Roberts's South team won, 4–1, behind the pitching of Norman Cross, the star Black Crack-ers pitcher.[54] No Birmingham player was mentioned.

Abbreviated statistics based on ten box scores showed Birmingham's best hitters to be third baseman Cliff Carr and outfielder Hamp Johnson, both hitting .286. "Cat" Mays, the father of future star Willie Mays, batted .263. The top pitchers were Jeff Posey, 2–0, and Bob Walker, 1–1.

16

The End of an Era (1936)

Although it was another abbreviated Negro Southern League season, in 1936 the Birmingham Black Barons fielded one of their best teams ever. Leading the way was outfielder David Whatley.

The new manager for what would be Birmingham's last year in the Negro Southern League was Andrew M. Walker. Very little is known about Walker. No record of him as a player or manager turns up in any Negro leagues research resources. He was possibly a native of Perry County. When the Black Barons played a barnstorming game in Marion, the local fans honored Walker as a local boy come home.[1] However, the local newspaper, the *Marion Times-Standard*, took no notice of either the game or the homecoming.[2]

He was possibly a relative of Alfreda "Freddo" Walker, a Birmingham numbers racketeer. The numbers or "policy" game was imported from Memphis to Birmingham in 1929. It flourished for ten years or so, then lost some of its sway with the local community.[3] Wikipedia traces the numbers game history to the beginning of the Italian lottery in 1530. It was widespread in the United States in the 19th century, particularly in ethnic neighborhoods for Italians and Cubans. To play the game, a bettor picked three or four numbers that he hoped would match those drawn randomly by the "policy bank."[4]

The big bankers in Birmingham in the early 1930s were Berry "Woco" Jackson, J.B. Bobo, Hill Harris, and Walker. Walker was likely the kingpin: "In those days he was netting himself $750 a day. He put himself up an office in the 'Little Masonic Temple' building and in 1935–36 revived the Black Barons. It is said that the Black Barons operated under a three-man partnership, although Mr. Walker's name was associated as sole owner," wrote Emory O. Jackson in the *Birmingham World*.[5]

Jackson said Walker, in 1936, leased the Birmingham baseball team to Pittsburgh Crawfords owner Gus Greenlee. "This led to the third dismemberment of the Black Barons and the scattering of its players all over the Negro National League. The Pittsburgh Crawfords and the Homestead Grays signed most of them." According to Jackson, Walker claimed to have lost $8,500 through his ownership of the Black Barons. It was "hardly more than a hobby" for him. Jackson said that in 1936 Molton H. Gray and Gus Allen took over the club.[6]

Jackson's timeline is incorrect. The "dismemberment" occurred after the 1938 season. Also, only David Whatley was with Homestead the following year. No Birmingham player was with the Crawfords, then located in Toledo.[7]

Given the last name of owner Alfreda Walker and field manager Andrew W. Walker, there is a logical conclusion that the two men possibly were related. Since Manager Walker seems to have no baseball history before or after his two-year stint with the Birmingham club, is it possible he was a brother, a son, or some other relative given a nice job by owner Walker? For that matter, is it possible that Andrew and Alfreda Walker were actually that same person? Neither man appears in the Birmingham City Directory for the years 1936–38. United States Federal Census records for 1940, found on ancestry.com, list an Andrew M. Walker. The 54-year-old black male is identified as a teacher. The only Alfreda Walker in the 1940 census is a 21-year-old black male living in Barbour County.[8]

Jackson makes no reference to Andrew Walker in his discourse on Alfreda Walker. In fact, he writes that Anthony Cooper was manager of the club in 1935–36. That is incorrect. George McAllister was the 1935 manager and, of course, Walker was the 1936 manager. Cooper, who had played with Birmingham from 1928 to 1930, returned in only 1934. Jackson also gives a starting lineup for the Black Barons that does not match any of those years. His recounting of Black Barons history appears to rely on faulty memory rather than documented facts.

Regardless, A.M. Walker represented Birmingham at the Negro Southern League meeting in March, and he was the man in charge when the team began spring training at the Sloss industrial league diamond in "extremely cold weather." Rickwood Field was not yet available because of usage by white teams.[9]

"From the looks of things, we are going to be ready to start with a jambup [sic] ball club from opening day," Walker told the *Birmingham News*. "The team has ample financial backing this season, something that it has lacked woefully in other years and every indication points to the fact that the colored fans are hungary [sic] for baseball." Walker noted that large numbers of black fans had turned out for recent major league exhibition games at Rickwood Field.[10]

Once again the NSL was reorganized with a mix of old and new faces. When another confusing season wound down in late summer with the usual lack of final standings or even first- half/second-half playoffs, the Birmingham Black Barons had the best claim to the 1936 championship.

Unbeknownst to those participating, the NSL was playing its last season until after World War II. League meetings in March and April drew up a schedule, handled procedural matters, and considered applications from interested teams.[11] In addition to the normal Southern cities, there were "one or two clubs from above the Mason-Dixon line" showing interest in the league.[12] Represented by proxy were H.G. Hall of Chicago and DeHart Hubbard of Cincinnati.[13]

Plans were finalized at a Nashville meeting at which Thomas T. Wilson, owner of the Nashville Elite Giants, was elected president. Of course, by that time the Elite Giants were now located in Washington, D.C.[14]

A number of financial matters were set at the meeting. Each would-be member put up a "$100 forfeit" and each was pledged to contribute $25 toward league expenses. In addition, two per cent of the gross receipts were to be taken by the home team and sent to the league treasurer. Finally, guarantees of $25 for weekday games, $50 for Sundays and holidays, and $12.50 for rainouts were set for the visiting teams.[15] There was also a $500 per month salary limit set for each club.[16]

The May 2–July 5 schedule involved seven clubs: Birmingham, Chicago, Cincinnati, Hopkinsville, Memphis, Montgomery and Nashville.[17] It was totally invalid as none of the teams played games matching the dates and opponents.

In mid–April, the *Atlanta Daily World* reported potential league members as Atlanta,

Birmingham, Chattanooga, Dayton, Louisville, Memphis, Nashville, and New Orleans. The Pittsburgh Crawfords, Indianapolis, and St. Louis were said to be associate members.[18] On May 3, the lineup changed to Atlanta, Chattanooga, Cincinnati, Claybrook, Hopkinsville, Memphis, and Nashville. There was no mention of Birmingham.[19] Nevertheless, the newspaper reported the May 10 Nashville at Birmingham game as an NSL opener.[20]

When Atlanta swept three from Chattanooga, the club was said to be in first place in a 10-team league now comprised of Atlanta, Birmingham, Chattanooga, Chicago, Cincinnati, Hopkinsville, Knoxville, Memphis, Montgomery, and Nashville. No associate members were named.[21] The *Chattanooga Times* listed a 10-team league, but with Columbus, Ohio, instead of Knoxville.[22]

Nashville was the Black Vols, a new entity after the departure of the Elite Giants. Admission for games was 40 cents, with ladies admitted free on Monday.[23]

The oddball team was Hopkinsville, Kentucky, a city that not only had never been in the league but also did not even appear to be a regular barnstorming stop for other teams. Only one story about the Hopkinsville Athletics appeared in the *Kentucky New-Era*, the local daily newspaper. On June 8, the paper reported that the Athletics, "members of the colored southern league," won both games of a double-header from Chattanooga on Sunday. No players were mentioned for either team.[24] Some Hopkinsville scores showed up in other newspapers, but no players were identified.

As the Black Barons worked out, the pitching staff looked promising, especially right-hander Jack "Dizzy" Bruton. A native of Cordova, Bruton was said to have "a fast hop ball and good breaking curve." The 24-year-old had compiled a 15–8 record in Virginia in 1935.[25] "Pop-Eye Hollins, the old spinach-eater, is another right-handed pitcher who looks mighty good," the *Birmingham News* reported. "Pop-Eye has been performing for a semi-pro colored club in Walker County for the last several years and while with the Jasper club in 1935 he won 12 and lost only three games. Pop-Eye is a speed demon when it comes to pitching, working largely on the fairly authenticized [*sic*] theory that they can't hit 'em when they can't see 'em."[26]

Other prospects included: Robert Walker, a 14–4 industrial league pitcher from Edgewater and a semipro team in Cincinnati; Harry Barnes, right-hander with New York Zulu Giants in 1935 (his pitching record was not given, but he batted .320 that year. There may be confusion here because a Harry Barnes was a Birmingham catcher several years in the 1930s); Fred Bankhead, shortstop with New York Zulu Giants in 1935, hitting .320; Parnell Woods, a veteran third baseman; and Herman Howard, a left fielder and.350 hitter in the industrial league.[27]

And here, another round of player identification. No Herman Howard appeared in box scores or game accounts. There were numerous references to a left fielder named "Red" Howard. Also, occasional references to A. "Red" Howard, B. Howard, and Carl Howard. James Riley lists outfielder Carl Howard with the Black Barons in 1936, outfielder Herman "Red" Howard in 1937–40, and infielder (1b-3b) Bill Howard 1931–33.[28] It is likely that the first name with the initial "A" was a typographical error. The 1936 player is either Carl or Herman. According to baseball-reference.com, Herman "Red" Howard was a pitcher-outfielder, intermittently from 1932 to 1946. The Birmingham years were 1932 and 1940. William Howard played with Memphis and Jacksonville in 1937 and 1938, respectively. No Carl Howard is in that database.[29] The seamheads.com web page lists Herman "Red" Howard with Birmingham as a pitcher in 1937 and 1940.[30] All of this leaves the author with no clear opinion on the correct identity of the plethora of Howards on the 1936 Birmingham roster. In subsequent references in this chapter, "Red" is used as the identifier, as that was the most common name from game accounts.

The *Montgomery Advertiser* reported in mid–April that the Grey Sox would play an exhibition game against the Birmingham Foxes, which recalls one of the names applied to the Birmingham team in 1933. Whether this was a misnomer for the Black Barons or an independent team is unclear. Birmingham's possible pitchers were listed as Calhoun, Collins and Mitchell, all familiar names from previous seasons.[31] The game was canceled when Birmingham arrived late.[32]

Birmingham's home exhibition season opened with Chicago, but only one game was played because of cold weather. Although Pop-Eye Hollins lost the game, he apparently impressed Chicago Manager Dizzy Dismukes enough to be offered a contract with that club. The offer was negated since he was already under contract with Birmingham.[33]

Next up were Candy Jim Taylor's now-Washington Elite Giants. The visitors won a Sunday double-header before 3,500 excited but disappointed fans.[34] Exhibitions ended in early May.[35]

Near Opening Day, Walker said he had signed two new "winning pitchers" and was negotiating for several other players, including "a first-string catcher that should prove to be one of the greatest backstops in colored baseball."[36]

Birmingham faced the Nashville Black Vols in the opener. They looked to "enter the season with a better ball club and more ample financial backing than has been the case in the last five years." Club officials were hoping for a turnout of 5,000 fans for the May 10 double-header.[37] There were also new uniforms.[38]

Opening Day festivities included a 40-piece band and a first pitch ceremony. Rather than a minister or politician, popular choices for first pitch activities, the Black Barons selected the girl student at the Industrial High School (later A.H. Parker High School) graduating with the highest grade average for the last semester. The young lady was to "outfitted from head to foot in [a] new Spring ensemble."[39]

By the time Thelma Smith threw out the first pitch, the band had increased to 65 strong, and the fans were estimated at 2,000. Manager Walker presented a different lineup from those fans had seen in the exhibition games. It included Dewitt Owens in center field, Parnell Woods at third base, Fred Bankhead at second, and a Tarrant City boy named Wilson at shortstop.[40]

Jeff Posey pitched a five-hitter as Birmingham won, 4–1. He struck out seven and lost his shutout to an error in the eighth inning. "Whatley won the game before the notes of the Industrial High School band had faded out. Owens led off with a single. And the bases were loaded when Johnson walked Wood and hit Canada. David Whatley blasted a double into left scoring Owens and Wood."[41] It was the first of many games decided by Whatley. Owens and Woods, also, had two hits.

Whatley, a native of Griffin, Georgia, was apparently one of the unnamed players that Walker was seeking during spring training. He played with Birmingham for three years, picking up the nickname "Hammerman" for his power hitting. He also had the nickname "Speed" for obvious reasons.[42]

On Monday, Birmingham won, 5–1, with Dizzy Bruton on the mound. He scattered seven hits and struck out six. Again, the visitors' only run resulted from an error. Harry Barnes hit a home run.

After an off day, the Black Barons returned against "the weirdest array of baseball talent ever coming to Birmingham." The barnstorming New York Zulu Giants "wear grass skirts on the playing field, bedeck their ebon faces with war paint like savages, give vent to blood curdling yells, and speak on the playing field in an 'unknown tongue.' Many of 'em discard spiked shoes and play barefoot."[43] The Zulus had compiled a record of 133–38–3 last year.[44]

To the delight and amazement of the crowd at Rickwood, the first baseman Limpopo and right fielder Tanna did play barefooted, and the team "looked like something Barnum-Bailey brought back from Africa years ago. The Zulu Giants go in for a display of spears, shields and a tom-tom drum. And don't think they can't shake a mean skirt as well as play baseball," reported the *Birmingham News*. The visitors pushed Birmingham to the ninth inning before losing, 4–3. That got them "an undressing from their manager."[45]

They probably got a bigger one the next day because Birmingham crushed the Zulus, 11–2, recording their 11th straight victory. "Impo, short for Important or something like that, started on the mound for the Zulus and he stayed there, what time he wasn't dodging Black Baron wallops. The way the Black Barons were hitting yesterday afternoon, it wouldn't have mattered if the king of the tribe had been on the mound." Birmingham batters had 15 hits against the unfortunate Impo.[46]

The Black Barons extended their winning streak, including exhibitions, to 13 in Atlanta, beating the Black Crackers, 5–1 and 12–0, behind superb pitching from Jeff Posey and Jack "Dizzy" Bruton. Posey, practically invincible, limited Atlanta to one hit and drew praise from the Atlanta press: "Birmingham's star pitcher, Mr. Posey, was in town yesterday. He was master of ceremonies at Ponce de Leon Park where he helped worst the local Black Crackers. He brought along an impudent grin for the fans in the stands and a baffling change of pace that set our boys down in order. He stood out there in the mid-point of that snuff-colored pitcher's mound and slow-motioned our boys to death. He was deliberate and methodical with his stuff and Jack Thornton's desperate ninth inning two base clout was the one and only clean hit the Black Crackers got."[47]

Birmingham (14–4–1) returned home for exhibitions against industrial league teams. All four losses were in exhibition games with Negro "major league" teams. "Fact that the Barons have won all their games against Southern League competition seems to be sufficient proof that they have the best team in the history of colored baseball in Birmingham."[48]

After Birmingham swept two, Atlanta sports editor Ric Roberts had posed the question, "Are Those Big, Bad Black Barons Real?" "This is an argument I'm having with myself," wrote Roberts. "A few days ago I was very certain that no average Dixieland team would step into Atlanta and do very much to our Black Crackers of 1936. Birmingham came here and destroyed them before my eyes and, in doing so, gave them only one run in 18 bitter innings. What is worse still the fact that our boys got but 6 hits in that stretch of horror."

Roberts decried talk that the Birmingham roster was largely of industrial league and semipro players as "alarmingly inadequate," adding that they looked more like major leaguers. "I don't believe a third baseman like Birmingham has today [Armand Tyson] is a 'pick-up' from any sand lot. He looks better than any third baser to visit Poncey this spring."[49]

Beefing up its lineup, Atlanta ended the Birmingham winning streak, 8–6, in the first game. Poor fielding, particularly Jeff Posey's "in ability [sic] to field bunts," gave Atlanta an early lead. When the visitors realized Posey was having problems, the Black Crackers "made capital of bunting the ball around the infield."[50]

In the second game, Birmingham had 18 hits against two pitchers, winning 12–7. The big blow was a home run down the left field foul line by Whatley. The play of the game, though, was a foul ball that scored a Birmingham run. The Atlanta catcher and third base-man chased a foul ball in front of the Birmingham Barons' dugout. The catcher caught the ball for the out. "While they were discussing something, leaving both third and home uncovered, Parnell Woods scored. It brought more cheers than Whatley's zooming home run...."[51]

Birmingham made a mid-week trip to Atlanta for what was erroneously reported to be "the first game under the floodlights ever played by any two teams of the Negro Southern League." Actually, black teams had played night baseball as far back as 1930.[52] Tickets sales were said to be booming for the game.

The Black Barons made the trip to Atlanta in style, riding in their own team bus, another sign of new management and adequate financing.[53]

Atlanta, won, 7–2, as Roy Wellmaker gave up only one hit and struck out 14, six of them in a row.[54] The *Birmingham News* suggested that Birmingham's poor performance might be connected to playing under the lights. "They offered no alibi ... but it was pointed out that it was the first time the Birmingham Negroes had ever played under the floodlights. Night baseball is something a team has to get accustomed to and the Black Barons were jittery in the first few innings."[55]

On May 31, the Black Barons, "leading the Negro Southern League by a comfortable margin and playing the best ball of any Black Baron team in the history of Negro baseball in the Birmingham district," returned home for a double-header against Memphis.[56]

Manager Walker announced that he would start two brothers, Jack "Dizzy" Bruton and his brother, Pit "Daffy" Bruton, the nicknames obviously coming from white major leaguers Dizzy and Daffy Dean. Despite some losses, the *News* cited "four rip-roaring hit-ters" as keys to the team's success—third baseman Woods, right fielder Whatley, left fielder Howard, and catcher Barnes. "Not only is Whatley slamming the ball when the pitch arrives, but his pegs home and to third base have been nothing short of sensational all season. He throws from right field to home plate very much in the manner that the average catcher throws to second to nip a would-be base stealer. Wherever the Black Barons have played this season Whatley's powerful arm has been the topic of conversation."[57]

Birmingham won the double-header, then barnstormed through the Alabama Black Belt region, playing games in Selma, Greensboro, Marion, Uniontown, and Montgomery. The June 12 game at Marion was the aforementioned homecoming for Manager Walker.[58]

On June 14, Birmingham (23–6), still leading the league, returned home for a series against Montgomery. A double-header was scheduled for Sunday afternoon and a single game on Monday. The Monday game would be played at night, "the first Negro night base-ball game ever played in Birmingham," according to the *Birmingham News*. There was no reference to the 1931 games played at Fair Park. For the Monday game, extra seats that had been erected along the third base line for a circus were being left up in anticipation of a large crowd.[59]

Special sections were reserved for white patrons. "Many ... want to see Whatley," reported the *News*. "He has been nothing short of sensational this season, having been placed in the cleanup position of the batting order and having delivered there in wholesale lots with his hitting."[60]

This was no exaggeration of Whatley's work. Based on 11 box scores from May 10 to May 31, Whatley batted 45 times with 15 runs scored and 24 hits for a batting average of .533. Among his hits were two doubles, two triples, and two home runs. He had 14 RBIs. The extra base hit and RBI totals are for only 10 games as no summary was published with the May 18 box score. Whatley's ability to cut down runners heading for third or home was cited again.[61]

The Black Barons crushed the Grey Sox, 7–1 and 10–2, on Sunday afternoon. Dizzy Bruton gave up just two hits. Walker apparently changed his mind about the second game, starting a newcomer named Robertson instead of Pit Bruton. Whatley had three hits in seven at-bats, driving in two runs. Second baseman Johnny Cowan was four for eight with two triples.[62]

Once again night baseball did not agree with the Black Barons. "Lefty" Glover struck out 17 Birmingham batters as Montgomery won, 14–8. Glover struck out 10 of the first 12 batters he faced, but weakened in the eighth, giving up five runs. Whatley was one of three Black Barons with two hits.[63]

Following the Montgomery games, there was no report on the team again until they showed up in Memphis on the Fourth of July. In Memphis, they won three of the four games and apparently the first-half championship.

A second half schedule for July 12–August 10 included games for Atlanta, Birmingham, Chattanooga, Hopkinsville, Memphis, Montgomery, Nashville, and St. Louis. There was no explanation for the absence of Chicago, Cincinnati, and Claybrook. The schedule included many seemingly random open dates for the different teams. A press release indicated that local ballparks were unavailable on some dates. There is little evidence that most scheduled games were actually played. On July 12 the *Atlanta Daily World* referred to the local team as "the orphaned Atlanta Black Crackers."[64] It is unclear if this was a euphemism for the long road trip or a reflection on the demise of the NSL. In either case, when the team was in North Carolina in August, the newspaper noted, "It seems that the Black Crackers have found it possible to earn more dough while operating in foreign territory than at home." Ric Roberts said local interest had declined considerably after star pitcher "Snook" Wellmaker joined the Homestead Grays.[65] Birmingham opened the second half against Chattanooga. The *Birmingham News* reported that the Black Barons were 12–2 in league games during the first half.[66] An examination of scores against league teams shows 15 wins and four losses. It is possible some of those games were considered exhibitions. If the numbers in the *News* are correct—just 14 league games played—it would explain why the team was often away, likely barnstorming. It was a successful plan: "Placed on a sound financial basis at the very start of the season, the Black Barons have played every engagement on their schedule thus far, traveling to each road assignment in their own private bus." The team's overall record was reported at 23–6–1.[67]

On July 9, Birmingham won, 7–1, against Chattanooga. Pit Bruton started and got the win, pitching six innings, striking out seven. But new pitcher "Lefty" Glover, formerly with Montgomery, was the star in relief, striking out eight in just three innings. Whatley, Jim Canady and "Red" Howard each had two hits. Whatley, batting cleanup, drove in two more runs. Although his pace of May had slowed a bit, Whatley's play was still phenomenal. In 18 box scores from May 10 to July 9, he was batting .441 with 34 hits in 77 at bats. His totals included three doubles, three triples, two home runs, and 18 runs batted in.

After a game with Chattanooga, the Black Barons went to Jacksonville and were away from Birmingham until August 2. A July 24 game with Nashville was canceled. Apparently the Black Barons were victimized by a rumor of demise: "Reports were put into circulation that the team had broken up. This prevented the Barons from being able to get Rickwood as it had been let to the amateur clubs who were having their elimination games."[68]

During the long hiatus, only three games with Jacksonville were reported. In the first one, Glover, reinforcing the decision for his acquisition, allowed only four hits, winning, 11–1. He struck out nine. Red Howard had an inside-the-park home run.[69]

Finally at home again for a double-header against Memphis, the Black Barons were still said to be in first place.[70]

Birmingham won the opener, 10–2, and Memphis took the nightcap, 8–6. In the first game, Cowan, Bankhead, and Barnes each had two hits. In the second game, Tyson had two hits, and Whatley drove in two runs with a home run.[71]

Another two weeks away followed, with only two games at Jacksonville reported. When the Black Barons returned to Rickwood on August 16, it was to play the barnstorming New Orleans Cubans. Coverage was sparse, with no box scores. A short article credited Birmingham with two wins, 7–5 and 13–3. "Lefty" Glover pitched the first game, but the winning margin came on a two-run home run by "Dizzy" Bruton. Pit Bruton won the second game easily, with Howard and Owens providing big bats.[72]

Those were the last 1936 Black Barons results published in the *Birmingham News*. No final standings were published, but most reports indicated the Black Barons were the front-runner practically the entire season.

That championship run was due, unquestionably, to David Whatley. In 19 games for which box scores are available, Whatley had 31 hits in 77 at-bats for a .402 batting average. His three doubles, two triples, two home runs, 18 runs scored, and two stolen bases, added up to one of Birmingham's all-time greatest individual seasons.

Whatley had a lot of support, though. Birmingham had a team batting average of .308. Other high individual batting averages were compiled by Johnny Cowan, .391; Harry Barnes, .339; Jim Canaday, .338; Parnell Woods, .316; and Fred Bankhead, .314.

Pitching records are more difficult to ascertain because of confusion among the Bruton brothers. They had a combined record of 7–1. Pit and Dizzy Bruton were both 2–0, but a record of 3–1 is ascribed to an unidentified Bruton. Glover was 2–0 and Posey was 2–4.

There were some memorable moments for the NSL generally as it played out what would be its final season until 1945.

Nothing was more dramatic than when Atlanta's cheerful outlook was dampened by tragedy even before the first practice could be held. Less than three weeks before Opening Day, death struck popular restaurateur Percy Williams. He and W.B. Baker had brought the Black Crackers back to the forefront. The Atlanta club regrouped with a new slate of officers, Louis Means as field manager, and Tiny Smith, who had been an All-American end at Morris Brown College, the team captain.[73]

Montgomery opened play in a new facility on North Decatur Street. Festivities included submitting names for the park. The fan whose name was selected would receive five dollars.[74] The event was rained out and rescheduled for April 12, but there was no report on the outcome of either the game or the park naming.[75]

When Chattanooga had its home opener, it was a three-game sweep of the Hopkinsville Athletics. Simpson, who pitched the third game, struck out 18 visiting batters.

Atlanta pitcher Roy Wellmaker had one of the great NSL performances on opening day. He pitched a no-hitter against Chattanooga, striking out eleven and walking only two. He also hit a single and a home run at bat.[76]

On June 23, Atlanta likely set an NSL record, swamping Memphis, 29–2. Sam McKibben, writing in the *Atlanta Daily World*, said "the larruping Atlanta Black Crackers turned the Ponce De Leon Park diamond into a track and the game into a track meet." Atlanta had

29 hits off four pitchers when the game was called after eight innings. There was no box score, but the story credited James Kemp with two doubles and a triple. Two players hit home runs, and there were three consecutive triples at one point.[77] Memphis's only runs came on errors. It was such a joke that the *Daily World* noted, "The Atlanta boys had a merry evening, running the bases backward and once through the pitcher's box."[78]

17

The Negro American League (1937–38)

1937

In 1937, stability came to the Negro leagues. Southern and Midwestern cities formed the new Negro American League. The Negro National League became a largely Eastern circuit, thereby setting up a possible Negro leagues World Series.

The new NAL was comprised of Birmingham, Chicago, Cincinnati, Detroit, Indianapolis, Kansas City, Memphis, and St. Louis.[1] The St. Louis club would not finish the season in that city. In late June, hotel owner Allen Page announced that he had purchased the franchise and was moving the team to New Orleans. The New Orleans–St. Louis Stars played their first home game on July 7.[2]

With the new NAL, the Black Barons found a home for the remainder of their existence. To be sure, there would be problems, such as no team at all in 1939, a succession of new managers, and also numerous changes in ownership. Yet, the NAL years would be some of the richest for black baseball with such names as Piper Davis, Willie Mays, Artie Wilson, and Dan Bankhead waiting in the future.

As players dispersed for home or winter ball after the 1936 season, club owners began meeting to assess the season and plan for 1937. None was more important than the October gathering in Indianapolis to form the new NAL.[3] Birmingham was represented by A.M. Walker. Major R.R. Jackson of Chicago was elected president.[4]

The enigmatic Walker was back as manager for Birmingham's first season in the new league. Dr. B.B. Martin of Memphis, "after a couple of weeks working with refugees" during a Mississippi River flood crisis, turned his thoughts to baseball and met with Walker in Birmingham. The purpose was to put together "two of the strongest teams that have ever been in the South."[5]

Familiar names in the Birmingham training camp at Sloss Field included second baseman Fred Bankhead, pitchers Jack and Pit Bruton, outfielder David Whatley, third baseman Parnell Woods, and first baseman Elmer "Willie" Carter, an early 1930s Black Baron. Walker invited any interested ballplayer to come by for a tryout.[6]

The *Birmingham News* recognized the return of "major league" status: "Negro baseball in Birmingham is very much like steel production this district. It has reached a peak since the very beginning of the depression. The best the Black Barons could offer as the depression got under way was a franchise in the Negro Southern League. Today they hold a franchise in the Negro American League … big league status."[7]

The exhibition season opened with Candy Jim Taylor's Chicago American Giants. Before a reported 3,000 fans, Chicago won the first game, 8–7, and Birmingham the second, 10–9. The loss was attributed largely to errors.[8]

Opening Day was with Kansas City at Rickwood. While the Black Barons were training at Sloss Field, the Monarchs were working out in Monterrey, Mexico. They came into Birmingham with a 6–3–1 record in exhibition games. The Monarchs, reputation intact, swamped the home team, 7–1 and 10–1, in a double-header.[9]

The following weekend Birmingham was host to St. Louis under Dizzy Dismukes, the 1924 Black Barons manager. His third baseman was Bill Carter, another former Black Baron.[10] Birmingham treated Dismukes rudely, edging the Stars, 5–4, in the first game, and then crushing them, 19–3, in the second. Again, the crowd numbered about 3,000. David Whatley, the slugging star of 1936, showed the same form despite being identified as "Jim" in the newspaper. After collecting a hit in the first game, he went five-for-five in the second. He hit a double and a home run, scored five runs, and drove in four. Jack Bruton was the winning pitcher in the first game, thanks to flawless fielding by his teammates. A new pitcher named Fellows threw the second game.[11]

That was about as good as it would get for Birmingham in the new league. As the season progressed, they lost one series after another.[12] If they could play St. Louis every week, success was guaranteed. In July in St. Louis they split a double-header, winning the second game, 20–4.[13] In August they took a three-game series from the Stars at Rickwood.[14] This group of Stars was not the same team that Mule Suttles played for from 1926 to 1931. That team folded after the 1931 season. This was a new entity altogether.[15]

On the road, Birmingham lost three of four in Chicago and in Kansas City. Most NAL league series were Sunday double-headers with occasional Saturday and Monday contests. Most teams barnstormed from one series to the next. While there was good coverage of home games, there was little on the away games.[16]

Standings on June 5 had Birmingham (3–7) in seventh place. Kansas City (6–2), Chicago (9–3), and Cincinnati (7–4) were the leaders.[17]

Back home against Detroit, the Black Barons managed a split with another team that was also struggling. Elbert Eatmon and Fellows were shelled, 10–4, in the first game. Birmingham, behind Jack Bruton's seven-hit pitching, won the second, 8–3. Whatley had four hits, including another home run.[18]

After another road trip on which little news filtered back except for two one-run wins over Memphis, Birmingham returned home to host Cincinnati. At Memphis, the first game had added excitement for several hundred Birmingham fans who went up on an excursion train. Memphis teammates Floyd Kranson and R. Taylor were ejected from the first game after a brawl. Kranson had made "a bonehead play," and Taylor evidently kidded him about it. A fight ensued.[19]

Cincinnati was in third place. They showed why at Rickwood, sweeping the Sunday double-header, 9–8 and 5–0. The *News had* reported that the local team was "fighting it out for the second-place spot," but no standings substantiated that claim.[20] In early July, it was reported that Birmingham has been "in the first division in the league practically all season."[21] Published standings throughout the first half showed the opposite. Final first-half standings had Birmingham (10–17) in sixth place.[22] Reports of competitiveness were likely a management ploy to boost support. There is little to indicate that the team was ever over .500 the entire season.

Cincinnati was without Manager "Double Duty" Radcliffe. He was recuperating from being hit by a pitch the previous weekend. Third baseman Pee Wee Carter filled in.[23]

Two double-headers were scheduled with Indianapolis for July 4–5. Two were rained out, and two were split to end the first half.[24]

After a poorly reported road trip, Birmingham returned home with Chicago. The American Giants won both games, 6–0 and 11–7. Sloppy fielding cost Birmingham the second game, despite Birmingham home runs by Woods and Whatley. Woods's came with two on. Whatley's was described as "a Ruthian blow."[25]

Most of Birmingham's second-half schedule was away. There were five home stands in the first half but only three in the second half. The final league home stand was with St. Louis.[26] Birmingham continued its mastery of the Stars, winning three straight. Alonzo "Hooks" Mitchell pitched a seven-hitter and struck out seven to win the first game, 2–0. Bruton won the Sunday nightcap, 12–4. Whatley had three hits, including a triple and a home run. Birmingham won on Monday, 18–9, as the Stars committed 10 errors. Whatley was perfect at the plate—six hits in six at bats, three for extra bases.[27]

The season ended on the road with unreported series in Memphis and Kansas City. The final published second-half standings located so far showed Birmingham again in sixth place with only two league wins.[28] Chicago won the second half, but lost to Kansas City in the playoff. Spring projections for a Negro World Series with the NNL champion were unfulfilled.[29]

As in 1936, David Whatley led Birmingham hitters at a torrid pace. Already noted are his five-for-five and six-for-six performances. In 16 games at Rickwood for which box scores are available, Whatley was 29-for-71, a batting average of .408. He scored 12 runs, drove in 15, and stole two bases. Among his 25 hits were five doubles, four triples, and five home runs. With the exception of Lorenzo "Piper" Davis and Artie Wilson in the 1940s, it is unlikely that Birmingham has any other hitters who could match Whatley's first two years with the Black Barons.

Some other players had good years, too. Shortstop Clarence Lamar and third baseman Elmer Carter did well in early fan voting for positions in the East–West game.[30] Neither made the team, though.[31] Unfathomably, Whatley was not among the top four for an outfield position. On the East roster, though, was Mule Suttles, and on the West squad was Turkey Stearns. Alabama's native representation also included the two Radcliffe brothers.[32]

Lamar, Carter, and Whatley were selected for a series of North-South all-star games showcasing NAL players. The games were scheduled for Birmingham, Memphis, Atlanta, and Nashville, or St. Louis. NAL officials projected the games as the start of an annual event that would rival the East–West game. The North won the Rickwood game, 13–5, with three players getting four hits each against South pitching. Whatley, leading off, had two hits for the South.[33]

1938

When Birmingham opened spring training for the 1938 Negro American League season, it was under completely new management. The new owner was Henry L. Moore of Holly Springs, Mississippi.[34] Moore had previously owned the St. Louis Stars.[35] He hired as manager William "Dizzy" Dismukes, the 1924 manager.

A native of Birmingham, Dismukes had started playing baseball before World War I.

When he died in 1961, he had been in baseball for more than half a century, the last few years as a scout for the New York Yankees. In a memoir, he said he frequently skipped school to play ball. After spending a semester in the prep program at Talladega College, he joined the East St. Louis Imperials in August 1908. They paid him to play baseball, and it became his life.[36]

A submarine-style pitcher, Dismukes was a friend of C.I. Taylor. After Taylor's unexpected death in 1921, Dismukes managed the ABCs until 1924.[37] At the time, the Black Barons were foundering in the Negro National League. Dismukes was brought in to manage the club down the home stretch.[38]

Dismukes carried a certain amount of bravado. In 1936, Cum Posey, longtime owner of the Homestead Grays, wrote a series of reminiscences for the *Pittsburgh Courier*. Dismukes was the focus of one:

> In June, 1923, the writer [went] to Indianapolis in an effort to "steal" Oscar Charleston from the Indianapolis A.B.C.'s. Arriving at the ball park we found the A.B.C.'s stacked against rube Foster and his American Giants.
>
> Dismukes was opposing a young fast ball pitcher named Owens. The seventh inning found the score tied at 3 to 3....
>
> Owens was an easy out to start the seventh. "Jelly" Gardner doubled and stole third. Dismukes then deliberately walked Jim Brown and Torrienti, this brought Beckwith to the bat, the clean-up hitter. Dismukes stepped out of the box, moved Gerald Williams so close to third base it looked like two men were playing third. "Dizzy" then pitched one ball to Beckwith and without looking around walked to the bench. Beckwith hit a first bounce "screamer" directly to Gerald Williams. The double-play, Gerald to Day to Gant was just a formality.[39]

Spring training opened at Sloss Field. Back for another season was the sensational hitting outfielder David Whatley. Also in camp were second baseman Fred Bankhead, catcher Harry Barnes, third baseman Parnell Woods, and pitchers Jack Bruton, Alonzo "Hooks" Mitchell, and Elbert "Lefty" Eatman.[40] A newcomer was shortstop Lester Locket, an Indianan whose career lasted until 1950. He started with the Black Barons in 1938 and returned in 1941 for a six-year stint.[41] Any ballplayers who wanted to try out for the team were invited to contact Dismukes at the Rush Hotel on North Eighteenth Street.[42]

Returning for a second season in the NAL were Birmingham, Chicago, Indianapolis, Kansas City, and Memphis. Cincinnati, Detroit, and St. Louis were gone.[43] Fleshing out a seven-club league were the Atlanta Black Crackers and Jacksonville Red Caps. An eighth "affiliated" team was also supposed to be in the league.[44] Mounds, Illinois, was mentioned as a likely "associated member" and was represented at the league meeting.[45]

The Indianapolis club was not the same team as a year earlier, but rather an attempt to resurrect the ABCs. It was not successful. The franchise shifted to St. Louis in 1939–40, playing as a new version of the St. Louis Stars. The following year Atlanta moved to Indianapolis, playing as the ABCs.[46]

After a poorly reported exhibition schedule, the regular season opened at Rickwood against Chicago. Dismukes announced his starting pitchers as right-handers Jack Bruton and "Ishkooda" Dunkin(s), a new player with "a smoke ball that is faster than a light ray."[47] Dunkin(s), a local product, was with the Pittsburgh Crawfords in 1937. Later, in 1938, he was with Atlanta.[48] Baseball-reference.com lists an Escotta Dunkin with the Crawfords in 1937–38, the first name likely a variation of Ishkooda.[49] Bruton and Clifford Blackmon actually pitched and neither fared well as Chicago won, 5–0 and 6–1, before a crowd of 4,000. Whatley had two of Birmingham's three hits in the first game.[50]

Birmingham then went to Jacksonville for single games on Sunday and Monday. The Red Caps took advantage of five Birmingham errors to win 8–2 in the first game. They won, 6–4, on Monday.[51]

On the way home, the Black Barons stopped in Atlanta for a series with the team now called the Red Sox. The name came from a contest allowing citizens to make suggestions. More than 80 different names were submitted to the *Atlanta Daily World* sports editor. A high school student won the naming honor."[52] The honor was short-lived, however. League President R.R. Jackson wrote Atlanta club officials, requesting that the team drop "Red Sox" to avoid confusion with Memphis. Atlanta switched back to Black Crackers.[53]

In Atlanta, Birmingham lost three out of four games. Atlanta won a 2–0 shutout on Thursday night. A Sunday a double-header was split, Eatman's three-hit pitching giving Birmingham its only win.[54] Atlanta won a 10-inning game on Tuesday.[55]

The two teams then moved to Rickwood Field for three games, a double-header on Sunday and the season's first night game on Thursday night. The double-header was split. Atlanta won the first game, 7–5, halting a three-run, ninth inning rally by the Black Barons. Birmingham won the nightcap, 4–3. Eatman pitched and Whatley had two hits.[56]

Three former Black Barons were with Atlanta: pitchers William Ferrell, Bo Mitchell, and Red Howard. Atlanta won the Thursday night game, 6–4.[57]

Traveling, Birmingham lost a double-header to Indianapolis in Illinois, 10–4 and 4–0.[58] Losses continued to pile up. They fell to Kansas City, 5–1, although Whatley was 3 for 5. Then came a double-header at Memphis before "3,000 howling fans," about 500 of whom had come up from Birmingham. Although the Black Barons outhit the Red Sox, they committed two errors in each game. Still, they were described as "the most stubborn foes the Red Sox have encountered this season, and time after time, brought the hometown fans to their feet with sparkling plays."[59] Two more games were lost at Kansas City. Clifford Blackmon pitched well in the opener, losing when Kansas City scored four runs in the sixth, largely on walks and errors. Whatley hit a home run for Birmingham's only run in the nightcap.[60]

The standings at this point, although obviously missing some games, found Birmingham (2–8) decidedly in last place.[61]

They returned home on June 19 for a series with league-leading Memphis. Birmingham was somewhat crippled. Catcher Harry Barnes had split a finger in Kansas City, and first baseman Henry "Butch" McCall had been left behind in Kansas City, battling the flu.[62]

Memphis won a rain-shortened Sunday game, 3–2. Birmingham won on Monday, 8–7, in 10 innings. The fielding of a new shortstop, "Ground Hog" Cephus, and Whatley's hitting were keys. Cephus had handled eight chances perfectly in the 3–2 loss.[63] Singles by Whatley, Bankhead and Woods scored the winning run in the 10th.[64]

In June, NAL and NNL officials met to discuss mutual interests. Out of the meeting came a planned July interleague double-header in New York. The first game would be Homestead and Memphis, followed by Birmingham and Newark.[65] Four-team twin bills were popular with fans. One was scheduled at Birmingham.[66]

The superiority of the NNL was apparent. At Yankee Stadium, Newark beat Birmingham, 7–5, when Mule Suttles hit a three-run homer. Homestead trounced Memphis, 9–2, before a crowd of 18,546.[67] At Rickwood, Kansas City shut out Memphis, 7–0, and Baltimore defeated Birmingham, 6–2. The *Chicago Defender* reported that a "record crowd" saw the games, but the *Birmingham News* said it was about 4,000.[68]

In late June, Birmingham fans got a rare home double-header. The Black Barons took two from Jacksonville, 8–3 and 9–6. In the first game Birmingham trailed by two, but came back to win. The second game featured explosive innings for each club. Jacksonville scored six runs in the fourth after Birmingham scored five in the second.[69]

The next weekend they lost two in Chicago. The American Giants had a new look, with a shortstop and outfielder from Monroe, Louisiana. They replaced two Alabama-connected players. Tommy Sampson and Turkey Stearnes were released, the latter "for indifferent playing." Between games, another noted Alabamian, Olympic track star Jesse Owens, was bested in a 100-yard-dash by David Whatley, with Chicago's Edward "Pep" Young finishing third. However, Owens gave the two baseball players a 10-yard handicap.[70]

Memphis (21–5) edged out Kansas City (19–5) for the first-half championship, a rare title for the Red Sox.[71]

When the team returned to Rickwood on July 24, local fans were treated to a double-header sweep, but it was not with a league opponent. The victim was the Nashville Elites Juniors, a subsidiary of Thomas Wilson's Baltimore team. "Bo" Mitchell, who had started the season with Atlanta, and Samuel Burris, a rookie who had gone to spring training with Memphis, were the winning pitchers.[72]

They followed up the Nashville games with two wins at Indianapolis.[73] No other games were reported for a three-week period.

Birmingham's improved second-half play produced a 6–3 mid–August win at Memphis. Blackmon held the Red Sox to seven hits, and Whatley had three hits, including a double. Birmingham was flawless in the field.[74]

On August 21, Parnell Woods became the first Black Baron to play in the East–West Game, pinch-hitting in the sixth inning. Whatley, who was fifth in fan voting, was on the team but did not play.[75]

On the same weekend as the East–West Game, Birmingham was at home against Chicago. The Black Barons won, 15–11, in a Saturday night game played in nearby Leeds. Bankhead hit a home run. Barnes had three hits, scored three runs, and drove in three runs. On Sunday, at Rickwood, Chicago won both games, 11–3 and 4–1.[76]

The home season ended on Labor Day weekend with three losses to Kansas City. The Monarchs won, 12–9, in Leeds, then by 7–2 and 8–6 at Rickwood on Sunday. The scheduled Labor Day games were canceled "due to financial difficulties of the Black Barons."[77]

Those canceled games contributed to a muddle on who won the second half in the NAL. Kansas City owner J.L. Wilkinson claimed the pennant, saying games played on East–West weekend should be excluded. That being said, Kansas City (12–5) beat out Atlanta (16–7). In reporting those numbers, the *Chicago Defender* also a noted a number of claims to games won, games lost, games that should be counted, and games that should be discounted. President Jackson eventually ruled in favor of Atlanta.[78]

The standings were Atlanta (12–4), Chicago (17–7), and Kansas City (13–10), but with 63 total wins and 61 losses, they were not mathematically balanced.[79]

The ruling set up a playoff between Memphis and Atlanta for the 1938 championship. The series was to be two games in Memphis, one in Birmingham and three, if necessary, in Atlanta.[80]

Neal Robinson, who decided the East–West game with an inside-the-park home run, carried his magic home to Memphis. With two home runs, he powered the Red Sox to a 6–1 win in the opener. Radcliffe held Atlanta to five hits. The next night, Porter Moss gave up six runs but won, 11–6, giving Memphis a two-game advantage.[81]

The series ended there. Jackson announced few days later that he had declared a "no contest" in the series. His reason was the third game scheduled in Birmingham in Tuesday. Jackson reported that Memphis arrived at the park at 7 o'clock, but Atlanta did not show up until 8:30. Jackson said that was too late to start and asked the umpires to call off the game.

Reconciliation could not save the series. The Atlanta Crackers notified the Black Crackers that the park would be in use Wednesday through Friday, the nights scheduled for the Black Crackers' home games. Atlanta officials wanted the series delayed until Sunday, but Dr. B.B. Martin "refused to agree to this because of the heavy expense of keeping in his team in Atlanta."[82] The decision ended any chance that either Memphis or Atlanta would ever have to win a championship played out on the field. By virtue of the two games played, Memphis was awarded the 1938 pennant at the owners' winter meeting in December.[83]

Some final comments on outfielder David Whatley are in order. In his three years with the Black Barons, he was the club's most prolific batter. He started the current season batting third or fourth, but by June 12 had moved into the leadoff position. Even though he could hit for power, hence his nickname "Hammerman," Manager Dismukes apparently decided Whatley was more valuable to the team as an early base runner.

Frazier Robinson, who saw Whatley in a more competitive environment later with Homestead, described him as "a pretty fair hitter. He didn't hit the long ball but he could get on that base—bunt and drag the ball. He'd run over you if you get in his way." On racing Jesse Owens, Robinson said the Olympian "could beat him to first base but Owens couldn't beat him after he left first."[84]

On August 16, Birmingham score 10 runs in the first inning en route to an 18–9 win over St. Louis. Whatley not only hit for the cycle but also had a perfect six-for-six day at the plate. His hits included a home run, a triple and two doubles. It is one of the greatest individual hitting performances by a Black Baron. Whatley's three-year record at Birmingham is shown below, drawn from two sources—the author's compilations (1936 and 1938) and baseball-reference.com (1937). Baseball-reference.com did not report the number of games played but had significantly more at bats than the author was able to find.

	G	AB	R	H	2B	3B	HR	SAC	SB	BA
1936, rf	19	77	18	31	3	1	2	0	2	.403
1937, cf-rf	—	71	12	29	5	4	4	0	2	.408
1938, rf-cf	21	8	21	38	4	3	1	0	1	.442
Totals	—	23	51	98	12	8	7	0	5	.419

Although no box scores were published, three additional games can be added to Whatley's 1938 numbers because his performance was reported in the game stories. He went three for five on May 30 at Kansas City and five for eight in a double-header at Indianapolis on July 24. Those three games would boost his batting average to .465.

There are no box scores for the Labor Day weekend series with Kansas City. The name Whatley appears as a relief pitcher in the line score of a 12–9 loss.[85] His Birmingham career ended there. In 1939, there was no team in Birmingham.

Whatley spent the next five years with Homestead, hitting .308 with just four extra base hits, a far cry from his output in Birmingham. In 1944 the Grays released him, and he finished the year with the New York Black Yankees. Why such a brilliant ballplayer seemed to fizzle out after just a few years is unclear. Riley suggests that "his propensity for alcoholic consumption" was possibly a factor.[86]

18

Death and Resurrection
(1939–41)

1939

Although there had been reports of crowds of 3,000 and 4,000 fans attending Black Barons games at Rickwood in 1938, it apparently was not enough support financially. Henry L. Moore faded from the scene, and when spring rolled around in 1939 there was no black baseball in Birmingham except for barnstormers at Rickwood Field. The Negro American League had also lost Atlanta and Jacksonville, but added teams in Cleveland and St. Louis.[1]

Several teams from the two leagues played in Birmingham during the season. Former Black Barons owner Frank Perdue was the promoter for April games between the Homestead (now Washington) Grays and the Baltimore Elite Giants.[2] Later, he brought in the New York Black Yankees to play Baltimore and the Memphis Red Sox to play Baltimore and Kansas City. In September the Crawfords and Cleveland Bears were booked at Rickwood.[3]

1940

In 1940, after a year without local black baseball, Birmingham regained its franchise in the NAL. Coming to the rescue was Memphis mortuary owner Thomas H. Hayes, Jr. He purchased the remnants of the Black Barons and acquired the franchise from the league. After Birmingham failed to operate in 1939, the NAL considered the franchise forfeited by the previous owners. Hayes said he had also negotiated a deal with Bill McKechnie Jr., general manager of the white Birmingham Barons, for the use of Rickwood Field.[4]

Hayes hired a storied name to manage the new team—Candy Jim Taylor. There were also some former players at spring training. Herman "Jabbo" Andrews, a 1930 Black Baron and 1934 Birmingham Giant, was in camp. Dan Bankhead, third of the brothers, and Jack Bruton were among the pitchers. A newcomer at first base was Lyman Bostock, Sr., and at second base was Tommy Sampson. Both became well known during the 1940s. Two other signees were outfielder John Bissant and catcher Ernest Smith.[5]

Spring training was in Jackson, Mississippi. They worked their way home, playing exhibition games in Alabama, Georgia, and Louisiana.[6]

The new team had a formidable task for Opening Day on May 12. The opponent was defending NAL champion Kansas City. The champions would bring in such stars as Newt

Allen, Hilton Smith, and hometowner Norman "Turkey" Stearnes, now in his 18th year of baseball and still a threat with the bat.[7]

Hayes traveled to St. Louis to shore up the Black Barons. He picked up Emmett Wilson, "one of the fastest men in baseball," to play center field. Sampson, who had been out with a leg injury, was now expected to be ready for the opener.[8]

The return of baseball was a festive occasion with a number of "appropriate ceremonies" planned.[9] The team added to the festivities with its play.

Kansas City showed its championship caliber, scoring five runs in the first inning of a 6–0 win. But Birmingham bounced back, winning the second game, 5–3. Blanchette Moody held the Monarchs to five hits. Birmingham gave him four runs in the first inning.[10] Birmingham won the third game, 8–7, on Monday. In that game, Bostock had two singles and a double in four at bats. Sampson and Billy Nixon had triples.[11]

The name dilemma for 1940 is pitcher Blanchette Moody. The only Moody listed on the roster posted by baseball-reference.com is Frank Moody.

Abe Saperstein (left) founded the Harlem Globetrotters basketball team and was a business partner with Black Barons owner Thomas Hayes (right) for a number of years (T.H. Hayes Collection, Memphis and Shelby Room, Memphis Public Library and Information Center).

He is credited with eight plate appearances and a 1–3 pitching record. Riley also lists Frank Moody with Birmingham in 1940.[12] However, that name never appeared in Birmingham newspapers. Blanchette Moody was the starting pitcher throughout the season. An Internet search produced no hits for Blanchette Moody and only the single baseball-reference.com hit for Frank Moody.[13] Of course, it is possible that Blanchette was a nickname that Frank Moody picked up in his career.

Hayes must have been pleased with his investment. The estimated attendance of 8,500 for the double-header.[14]

St. Louis came in the following weekend and split a Sunday double-header. Earlier the Stars had won an exhibition game in Gadsden, 7–3. Manager Taylor attributed that loss to the absence of second baseman Sampson, still out with the leg injury. He told a reporter that Sampson "has one of those trick knees football players are often addicted to." Taylor said he held Sampson out to rest up for the Sunday games.[15]

Sampson played, but the Stars won, 6–4, in 10 innings. Birmingham obviously missed the power that David Whatley had provided during the 1936–38 seasons. Nixon, trying to compensate, had two doubles in the loss. Birmingham won the second game, 3–1, as "Red" Howard limited the visitors to five hits.[16]

After a largely unreported trip to the Midwest, Birmingham returned home with Memphis. The Black Barons had lost a Decoration Day (now Memorial Day) double-header in Chicago. Memphis extended the losing streak to five games starting with a Sunday double-header sweep, 3–2 and 7–0. The opener went 14 innings. They won again, 2–1, on Monday in Gadsden.[17]

The following weekend Birmingham made a better showing in Memphis, winning two out of three.[18]

St. Louis returned to Rickwood on June 16. It was an historic occasion for Candy Jim Taylor. That date in 1904 was said to be the day the Birmingham Giants, started by his brother C.I. Taylor, made their debut in the Magic City. Candy Jim had played third base, making only three errors in 55 games. The double-header was rained out, postponing Taylor's honors for a week.[19]

A week later, Cleveland was the opponent for the Jim Taylor Day ceremonies. Presentation of a loving cup was part of the special ceremonies. Threatening rain cut the crowd for the games, which were divided.[20]

Cleveland won the opener, 8–7, in 10 innings despite three Black Barons—Fred McBride, Tommy Sampson, and Buddy Allen—each having three hits. Birmingham won the second game, 5–4. The *Birmingham News* reported that "quite a few fans braved the threatening rains to see the games, which were considered among the best played at home by the Black Barons."[21] Rain fell on Monday, but Birmingham won on Tuesday in Anniston. Cleveland won on Thursday at Rickwood.[22] When they split a double-header in Atlanta the following Sunday, right fielder Nixon hit a grand slam home run in the first game and two triples in the second. By winning three of five from Cleveland, Birmingham was said to be in the NAL first division.[23]

Owner Tom Hayes with the Black Barons' bus, ca. 1940 (T.H. Hayes Collection, Memphis and Shelby Room, Memphis Public Library and Information Center).

A July home game with Toledo offered a lot of interesting features. First, the opponent was the Toledo Crawfords, formerly the Pittsburgh Crawfords. Founder Gus Greenlee had sold the team, which moved to Toledo, replacing the Indianapolis ABCs in the second half of the NAL season.[24] Two of the Crawfords came from the Birmingham industrial league—catcher James "Steelarm" Bell, "the best catcher to hit big-time Negro baseball" since Pepper Bassett, and outfielder John "Lefty" Smith, a batting leader with Stockham.[25] Also traveling with the team was Olympian Jesse Owens.

Owens, business manager of the Crawfords, continued his vaudevillian-type speed demonstration.[26] In Birmingham, he planned a 30-minute "athletic program," a race against Prince Mackerel, a race horse owned by A.G. Tsimpides, and competition with three local track athletes—Clifford Stanley and Augustus Blanks of Westfield High School and "Speed" Henderson of Brighton High School.[27]

Rain prevented Birmingham fans from seeing the Owens spectacle. The two teams went to Gadsden on Monday and then to Memphis, where they split a double-header. Following was a Midwestern swing that included games in Little Rock, Oklahoma City, and St. Louis. In Chicago, Birmingham lost three to the American Giants.[28]

Back home on July 28, a double-header was scheduled with Memphis. Second-half standings showed Birmingham (4–9) struggling. Chicago (6–0) and Kansas City (4–0) were tied for first.[29] Memphis won the opener and Birmingham the second. Exhibition games followed in Montgomery and Mobile, while awaiting the next league series with Kansas City.[30]

The league-leading Monarchs came to Rickwood Field on August 4. Birmingham won the first game, 6–4, but almost lost. Left-hander Eddie Sneed blew a 6–0 lead and "Red" Howard saved it in relief. Kansas City second baseman Newt Allen played left field in both games and had seven hits. Kansas City won the second, 7–1.[31]

Afterward there was no report on the team for two weeks. They were next seen at Rickwood on August 18 hosting Chicago in their final home stand. The games were played without two Birmingham stars. Parnell Woods and Tommy Sampson were in the East–West Game in Kansas City. Manager Taylor was a West coach.[32]

The Black Barons played good baseball, winning, 4–2 and 3–1. Sneed gave up 13 hits but pitched a shutout after the third inning. He struck out eight and had two hits, one a triple. Bankhead threw a four-hitter in the second game.[33]

Birmingham closed out play in New York, Philadelphia, and Chicago. No further results were reported locally. Historian John Holway placed Birmingham (9–11) fifth in the NAL.[34] Results compiled by the author present a record of 13–17. How the team fared financially is unknown. Only the 8,500 opening day attendance was reported.

It is interesting to note that although about 30 players appeared on the Birmingham roster during the season, the starting lineup was pretty consistent, with Lyman Bostock, 1b; Tommy Sampson, 2b; Samuel Burton, 3b; Ulysses Redd, ss; Jabbo Andrews, lf; Buddy Allen, cf; Billy Nixon, rf; and Paul Hardy, c. The pitching staff was steady with Dan Bankhead, "Red" Howard, Blanchette Moody, and Eddie Sneed. That consistency foretold glorious years ahead.

1941

As 1941 season plans unfolded, Candy Jim Taylor had moved to Chicago. Tom Hayes replaced him with another legendary figure, Winfield S. Welch. Although most of his playing career was spent with lower-echelon teams, particularly Louisiana clubs, Welch had a good reputation as a manager.[35] That certainly proved true in Birmingham over the next four years.

"Welch has established himself as one of the greatest managers and developers of young players in baseball," wrote a *Chicago Defender* reporter. Among the stars he tutored over 23 years were Johnny Markham, Robert Pipkins, Pepper Bassett, Goose Tatum, Lefty McKinnis, Buck O'Neil, and Al Gipson.[36]

Returning players included Dan Bankhead, Lyman Bostock, Lester Lockett, Paul Hardy, and Tommy Sampson. Some of them became the nucleus of the formidable Birmingham teams of the 1940s. Debuting at shortstop was Jesse "Hoss" Walker, who was with the team three years. Starting in left field was Reese "Goose" Tatum, the Harlem Globetrotters basketball star.[37]

Spring training was in Shreveport, Louisiana. Hayes announced the formation of a Knot Hole Club for boys, coordinated with E.Q. Adams, superintendent of the local Boys Club. All boys 14 years old and younger could get into Black Barons games free with their membership card.[38]

The six-team NAL was comprised of Birmingham, Chicago, Jacksonville, Kansas City, Memphis, and St. Louis. There was a renewed effort to have a postseason playoff with the Negro National League champion. Toward that goal, the two leagues agreed to a plan calling for one-third of the schedule to be interleague games.[39]

Birmingham fans' first look at the team was in exhibition games with the New York Black Yankees. The visitors won the opener, 5–1. Buster Markham threw a 4–0 shutout for Birmingham in the second game. An estimated 3,000 fans turned out despite threatening weather.[40]

The exhibition games presented a ticket dilemma. Team publicity director Levi Johnson announced that all season passes issued during the past week were being recalled. Apparently, "several passes were missing," and some showed up at the gate, saying they had purchased passes. Johnson said pass holders should contact the club for new credentials.[41]

That was not the only off-the-field problem. After a Sunday double-header in May, the *Birmingham World* lamented the "bottle problem" at Rickwood. The writer reported:

It was estimated that some 10 gallons of the liquid pep was checked at the Rickwood Park Sunday ... as some gro-craving [*sic*; grog-craving?] fans tried to carry in too much. It seems senseless that the drink

Catcher Paul Hardy, whose career with Birmingham spanned three decades (T.H. Hayes Collection, Memphis and Shelby Room, Memphis Public Library and Information Center).

addicts would need to have on their person quarts and gallons of whisky unless they have it for redistribution.

To try to cope with the bottle problem the park devised a system of checking at the gates all of the big bottles and letting the my-own supply size of the gay juice go by.

Unless something can be done to handle the bottle problem, Negro baseball will be imperiled at Rickwood. The management has been patient, has tried to invent plans of coping with it, has made appeals, but all this has fallen short of the spot. Half drunks, hell raisers, and the liquid bolds have no business being tolerated at baseball parks. Baseball managers and park attaches don't always like to have these kind of thing written for fear they woll [sic] endanger attendance.[42]

Except for an exhibition double-header with Newark, the interleague schedule never really materialized. No NNL teams came to Birmingham during the season, nor was there a "Negro World Series" in the fall. The Newark games were divided, with visitors taking the first game, 5–4. Birmingham won the second, 6–5, on Willie Nixon's two-run homer.[43] Among the Newark players was Monte Irvin, an Alabama native and future Hall of Famer. He had joined the Eagles after an outstanding all-round athletic career at Howard University.[44]

Opening Day was disappointing. Dizzy Dismukes and Kansas City won both games, 9–3 and 5–3. Birmingham pitchers gave up 25 hits. First baseman Lyman Bostock had two hits in the first game and another in the second for Birmingham.[45] The games were played before "a large crowd." Pregame ceremonies included remarks by Birmingham City Prosecutor Ralph Parks, representing Mayor Cooper Green. Britton McKenzie American Legion Post 150 and the Rosedale High School band handled the flag-raising and national anthem. Mrs. Matilda Folkes threw out the first pitch, which was "almost caught" by A.A. Johnson.[46]

Despite those losses, this was a Birmingham team destined for greatness. On the road, the Black Barons seemed to get their footing. They won double-digit shutouts over three state semipro teams. The 14–0 win over the Decatur Tigers was the team's eighth straight win. Over that span, Birmingham had collected 115 hits.[47] Additional road games were played with the Monarchs. Birmingham pitchers reportedly limited Kansas City to only six runs in seven games.[48]

Next up was a league series with Jacksonville. It opened in Anniston, with Birmingham winning, 5–3. At Rickwood Field on May 25, the Black Barons won a Sunday double-header, 7–2 and 6–5, then added a 5–1 win on Monday. McKinnis pitched a five-hitter in the first game. Lockett and Jesse Douglas each had three hits in the first game, including two doubles by the former and a triple by the latter. In the second game, Douglas had two more hits, as did Sampson and Nixon. Alfred "Greyhound" Saylor won the second game with a pinch-hit single.[49] Grady Jessup's win on Monday was the team's tenth straight.[50]

There was high praise for Manager Welch in the local press before a series with Memphis:

Welch has made a big hit with Magic City fans because of the aggressiveness he displays during the course of a ball game, and also because of the fact that he has displayed his willingness to gamble with young talent until it displays its worthiness of the gamble he has taken, or drops from the picture.

Many wondered when he succeeded Jim Taylor as the boss of the Black Barons. They have ceased to wonder about Welch. He has clearly demonstrated that he is Taylor's equal in strategy and also in the matter of disciplining his team members. They have learned to know that what Welch says goes, and if a team member willfully falls down on any assignment given him he is soon looking for another job.[51]

They split the Sunday double-header. Bankhead pitched a five-hitter, winning the first game, 9–2. Memphis won the second, 4–0. A Monday night game was promoted as "a benefit game for the Slossfield Recreational Center and a camp for underprivileged boys for Negroes."[52] There was no report on the outcome.

On Tuesday, they played in Gadsden with Birmingham winning, 3–1. McKinnis scattered seven hits. Memphis's lone score was on a home run by Manager "Double Duty" Radcliffe. The legendary Radcliffe also pitched, giving up seven hits but striking out 10.[53]

A road trip, paired with the St. Louis/New Orleans Stars, went unreported, but the Black Barons (14–7) returned home in first place for a series with Chicago (7–5). Kansas City (10–5) was second.[54]

Birmingham split the Chicago games, winning, 4–3, behind McKinnis. Although Bankhead gave up only four hits, Chicago won the second game, 4–0. The shutout was thrown by "Sug" Cornelius, who had pitched for Birmingham in 1930.[55]

After another mostly unreported road trip, Birmingham had a home-and-home series with Jacksonville, winning two in Florida before playing a Fourth of July double-header at Rickwood.[56] The holiday games, played before an estimated 5,000 fans, were both shutouts. Bankhead won the opener, 5–0, and Smokey Jarvis gave the visitors a 3–0 win the second game.[57]

After the holiday games, Birmingham played short series in St. Louis and Kansas City. Then, paired with Jacksonville, they traveled throughout the Midwest, upper Plains States, and Winnipeg, Manitoba.[58] In a game in Milwaukee, Markham pitched a four-hit, 1–0 win, and Bostock was four-for-four.[59]

Later in the summer, barnstorming with the Ethiopian Clowns, Bankhead struck out 17 batters as the Black Barons won, 3–0, in St. Paul.[60]

The East–West Game was played in Chicago on July 27. Three Birmingham players—first baseman Bostock, second baseman Sampson, and pitcher Bankhead—were on the West squad. Manager Welch was a West coach. Bostock singled and drove in a run. Bankhead pitched two scoreless innings in relief, but the East won the game, 8–3.[61]

Paul Hardy managed the team against Memphis in Welch's absence. Inning-by-inning results from Chicago were telegraphed into Rickwood during the games.[62] Memphis won the opener, 9–3, and Birmingham the second, 3–2.[63] To celebrate the Birmingham All-Stars, the two clubs played a free game on Tuesday night. The only payment was the taxes included in the ticket price. Memphis, incidentally, had five All-Stars.[64]

A week later, with the All-Stars back in the lineup, Birmingham beat Memphis, 7–2. Bankhead was the winning pitcher, Bostock had two doubles and a triple, and Sampson had a double and a triple. Fred Bankhead, Memphis third baseman, got two hits off his brother.[65]

On August 24, back home from the long Midwest and Canada trip, the Black Barons played Sunday games with St. Louis. Officials and fans proclaimed the occasion "Welch Day" in appreciation of the job he had done.[66]

Birmingham shut out the Stars in both games, 2–0 and 4–0. Bankhead held them to two hits in the first game, and McKinnis threw a four-hitter in the second game. Bostock tripled Lockett home with the lone run in the first game. Between games, Mrs. Larnie J. Williams and Timothy Smith presented a gift on behalf of appreciative fans.[67] Emory O. Jackson, somewhat reserved in writing about the event, nevertheless said he had become a Welch fan because of "his clean interest in baseball, not merely the Black Barons."[68]

Near the end of the season, Birmingham played a lengthy barnstorming series with the Miami Ethiopian Clowns. The trip brought the two teams to Birmingham for a double-header in late August. Markham pitched a 2–0 shutout in the first game. In the nightcap, Bostock had a double, a triple and two singles as Birmingham won, 9–2. The fielding star of the first game was Edward Steele, one of three industrial league players "inserted into the patched-up Black Barons lineup." He hauled in a long fly in right field and with a perfect throw nailed a runner trying to go from second to third after the catch.[69] It was the beginning of a career that saw Steele play a decade with the Black Barons.

According to the *Birmingham News*, the Black Barons won both halves. Thus, there was no need for a Negro American League playoff.[70] However, various other sources credit the pennant to Kansas City, with a pitching staff that included Satchel Paige and Hilton Smith.[71]

Six months later there was still uncertainty. As the Black Barons went to spring training in spring of 1942, Emory O. Jackson reported that both Birmingham and Kansas City were still claiming the second-half pennant.[72] However, when Kansas City came to Birmingham for an early June double-header the following season, the *Birmingham World* said he Monarchs were "winners of three successive pennants in the Negro American League."[73]

The author's calculations, based on reported games, give the Black Barons a 28–14 NAL record and a 47–23–1 overall record.

They closed out one of their best seasons ever with September exhibition games against local industrial league teams.[74]

Pennant or not, the 1941 season was a high mark for Birmingham, which just two years earlier had no team at all. Lyman Bostock (.400) was the leading hitter, followed by Paul Hardy (.364). Baseball-reference.com credits Dan Bankhead with a perfect 4–0 record while John Holway gives him 6–1.[75]

Few, while basking in the afterglow of a fine season, could anticipate that in just a few weeks the world would change dramatically. The catalyst, of course, was the Japanese attack on the Pearl Harbor Naval Base on December 7, 1941.

19

The War Years (1942–45)

1942

Tom Hayes selected Algiers, a New Orleans suburb, as the site for 1942 spring training for the Black Barons. The manager was Winfield S. Welch again.[1] It was a time of great uncertainty, just months after the nation was plunged into World War II. Both black and white ballplayers were enlisting in the military or preparing for a likely draft notice. Despite the uncertainties, baseball tried to be as normal as possible.[2]

There was also another touch of the unusual in 1942. Pittsburgh Pirates President William K. Benswanger announced that his team would offer tryouts to three black players. The lucky trio were Roy Campanella and Sam Hughes of the Baltimore Elite Giants and Dave Barnhill of the New York Cubans.

"Negroes are American citizens with American rights. I know there are many problems connected with the question but after all, somebody has to make the first move," said Benswanger. Despite the fact that no black had played in the major leagues in more than half a century, Commissioner Kenesaw M. Landis said there was no rule against Negroes in Organized Ball.[3] J.L. Wilkinson, co-owner of the Kansas City Monarchs, said there were at least 25 players in the Negro National League and the Negro American League capable of playing with the white boys.[4]

Nothing came of the tryouts but disappointment. Baseball was still five years away from Jackie Robinson.

At a joint meeting in Chicago, officials of the Negro American League and the Negro National League attempted to improve the image of black baseball. They accepted a resolution by NNL President Tom Wilson to ban all league clubs from playing the Ethiopian Clowns. Wilson said eastern club owners "had long been of the opinion that the painting of faces by the Clowns players, their antics on the diamond and their style of play was detrimental to Negro league baseball."[5] The resolution notwithstanding, the Black Barons played a team called the Ethiopian Clowns in August and September.

Dan Bankhead again anchored the Birmingham pitching staff after spending the winter playing in Puerto Rico. Because of wartime transportation restraints, it took Bankhead three weeks to return home. When he landed in New York, he told an interviewer it had also cost him $175 for the return trip.[6]

Also back were Lester Lockett, Tommy Sampson, Buster Markham, and Goose Tatum. Leroy Morney was seeking a spot after a year in Mexico. Industrial league infielder Charlie West got a tryout, too.[7]

The NAL lineup was set with Birmingham, Chicago, Jacksonville, Kansas City, Memphis, and the Cincinnati/Cleveland Ethiopian Buckeyes.[8]

Owner Hayes appeared to be doing very well with his various business interests. The *Birmingham World* reported that Hayes was going to buy an airplane: "He has been flying for seven years, although he has not soloed and has not been licensed. The other day a friend of his flew down to Memphis and let him, Hayes, steer the iron bird. Hayes was so delighted that he made plans to buy a plane."[9]

The first exhibition games were a double-header with Kansas City. Some 8,000 fans turned out to see Birmingham win the opener, 2–1, and Kansas City the second, 8–6.[10]

The wartime manpower drain was obvious. Lyman Bostock was in basic training at Fort McClellan in Anniston. Ulysses Redd was now a corporal at Fort McDill in Tampa.[11] However, Bostock did play occasionally when he was able to get furloughs.[12] It was a common practice during the war.

Jacksonville opened the season at Rickwood Field. A "brilliant ceremony" and more than 9,200 paid admissions marked the day. The overall crowd was estimated at more than 10,000. There was somberness as well as festivity. The Parker High School band, directed by Wilbert Robinson, played for the pregame flag raising by members of Britton McKenzie American Legion Post No. 150. Coreania Hayman, head of the music department at Daniel Payne, Jr. College, sang the National Anthem. In keeping with the wartime climate, Laura Washington sang "He is 1-A in the Army and He is 1-A in My Heart."[13] Olympic track star Ralph Metcalfe, now director of United Service Organizations activities at Fort McClellan, was selected to throw out the first pitch, but was unable to attend.[14] The ceremony was performed by *Birmingham World* editor Emory O. Jackson, who threw "a perfect strike" to Parker Principal W.B. Johnson.[15]

The Red Caps brought an ex–Black Barons contingent—Manager Herman "Jabbo" Andrews, shortstop Clarence Lamar, and third baseman Parnell Woods. Birmingham won the first game, 9–2, and Jacksonville the nightcap, 6–3. Bankhead pitched brilliantly for eight innings, holding the Red Caps to six hits. Shortstop Joseph Spencer had three hits in the first game. Andrews had a good homecoming with two hits and two "excellent running catches" in left field in the opener. He won the second game with a two-run pinch-hit single.[16]

Although it was not reported locally, Opening Day brought a $25 fine for Tom Hayes by NAL President Dr. J.B. Martin. Memphis claimed that Birmingham center fielder Lloyd "Ducky" Davenport was their property. "Hayes, who was officially notified on the matter prior to the game, placed his team in a position where it is subject to suspension from the league," reported the *Chicago Defender*. The issue must have been resolved to Memphis's satisfaction because Davenport remained with Birmingham throughout the season.[17]

Taking advantage of a furlough, Lymon Bostock was at first base.[18] Playing part-time, Bostock and others often didn't have regular uniforms but were accommodated when they were able to play. He was not listed on the 17-man roster published in the *Birmingham World* in early June. The roster was interesting because it was one of the earliest showing assigned uniform numbers. The sharing of a number by two pitchers could be a typographical error or could indicate a shortage of uniforms:

Player	No.	Pos.	Player	No.	Pos.
Sampson	1	2b	Morney	12	lf
Bradford	2	rf	Miller	20	ss
Davenport	3	cf	T. Radcliffe	8	c

Player	No.	Pos.	Player	No.	Pos.
Lockett	4	3b	McKinnis	10	p
Warren	5	1b	D. Bankhead	25	p
Tatum	17	lf	Markham	26	p
Spencer	7	ss	Pipkin	14	p
Hardy	18	p	Saylor	11	p
Gipson	18	p	W.S. Welch	19	mgr.[19]

Bostock, whose career spanned seventeen years, spent five of them with the Black Barons. He played in the 1941 East–West All-Star Game. His son, Lyman Bostock, Jr., was an outstanding player with the California Angels when he was shot to death in Gary, Indiana, in 1978.[20]

Bostock secured leave five times for home double-headers during the season. The rest of the time the position was filled by several players, most often in the first half of the season by Luther Gilyard. Then, he entered the Army in early July in Oklahoma. Gilyard is another case of identity frustration. He is often confused with Luther Gillard, who, in fact, may actually not be another player but Gilyard. Historian James Riley and baseball-reference.com list both as Birmingham players in 1942. However, Gillard only appeared in box scores while Gilyard is mentioned in game stories, suggesting that the former may be a spelling error.

Additionally, both are shown by both Riley and baseball-reference.com as being with the same teams at the same time in 1934, 1937–39, and 1942. Again that suggests the two players are actually the same person. Baseball-reference.com has no biographical information on Gillard. It is available on Gilyard. He was born in Fort Smith, Arkansas, in 1910 and died in Detroit in 1976.[21] In the 1930 United States Federal Census, Gilyard was living in Oklahoma with a brother. That fits with his having enlisted in the military in Oklahoma.[22] The author includes only Luther Gilyard in the comprehensive Birmingham roster.

On May 17, Candy Jim Taylor and Chicago came in for two games. Among his pitchers was former Birmingham player Gentry Jessup. The *Birmingham News* reported Birmingham in second place behind Kansas City, with Chicago third. The local writer said Birmingham would be in first place except Kansas City had played fewer games due to cold weather.[23] The games were split. Chicago won, 6–4, and Birmingham won, 3–0. Bankhead held the visitors to four hits before an estimated 8,000 fans. Bostock had two hits in the first game.[24]

Birmingham was away the next two weeks, playing Detroit and Kansas City in various cities. They returned to Birmingham on June 7 with Kansas City. The Monarchs were in second place behind Birmingham, according to the *Birmingham News*. If the Black Barons won both games, they would have "too big a bulge on the percentage table to overcome." A split would also keep them close to the first-half title.[25]

With Robert "Black Diamond" Pipkin on the mound, Birmingham won the first game, 12–2. Pipkin, in at least his 14th season of baseball, gave up seven hits while the Black Barons had 17, including three each by the pitcher, Lester Lockett and "Double Duty" Radcliffe. Kansas City won the second game, 5–4.[26]

For the next three weeks it was "several thousand travel-weary miles" for Birmingham. "Traveling by bus, and bumping along in some areas where gas was mighty hard to get, the Black Barons were successful in playing every engagement their booking called for when they left on their longest road trip of the year, and they hung up an enviable road record in spite of the fact that they had to be forever on the move."[27]

In addition to the usual Jim Crow–dictated difficulties with food and lodging, there were also wartime restrictions. The U.S. government rationed certain products that were in short supply during the war. These included such commodities as gasoline, automobile tires, sugar, meat, shoes, and nylon. Coupon books were issued to families to ensure that everyone had a fair share of the rationed goods.[28] Consequently, quotas might be used up, even though there was money available. Some items, such as gasoline and tires, were hard to find in some areas.

When the team returned home against Memphis on June 28, a large crowd was expected. On previous Sundays, Birmingham had averaged more than 6,000.[29] In the first game, Gready McKinnis beat Porter Moss, 2–1, in a pair of four-hitters.

The following weekend brought a unique pair of Saturday–Sunday double-headers. On Saturday, July 4, Birmingham played Jacksonville and then on Sunday, Kansas City. The Monarchs played in Memphis on the Fourth. The two days of games would decide the first-half championship.[30]

There were personnel changes going into the weekend. Outfielder Sammy Harris, Jr., from Cincinnati, and shortstop Jesse Walker, from the Ethiopian Clowns, were signed. Manager Welch said signing Walker enabled him to switch Leroy Morney to third base, replacing Lockett, who was now in service. With so much on the line, Welch elected to throw right-handers Buster Markham and Al Gipson at the Red Caps. The pitching situation was complicated by Bankhead, who had fallen out of favor. Welch said that he had "disposed of Dan Bankhead temporarily." He said the pitcher was not in shape, so he had been suspended and loaned to a St. Paul, Minnesota, club.[31]

A split with Jacksonville gave Kansas City the first-half flag. Markham held the Red Caps to six hits, winning 7–2. Jacksonville won the nightcap, 2–1, shutting down a seventh-inning rally by Birmingham. Pitcher Al Gipson grounded out with the bases loaded to end the game.[32]

Birmingham and Kansas City started the second half even, splitting a double-header. Wielding big bats, the Monarchs won, 11–5. Five of their 17 hits were for extra bases, including three home runs. Birmingham got homers from Davenport and Morney. McKinnis won the second game, 2–1.[33]

The team was away the next two weeks, mostly playing the Cincinnati/Cleveland Buckeyes in various Midwestern cities.[34] They returned home with a 12-game winning streak to face Memphis on July 19. The Memphis second baseman was Fred Bankhead, brother of the Birmingham pitcher.[35]

The games were divided. Willie Hutchinson's 8–0 shutout ended the streak. It was the first time the Black Barons had been shut out all year. Morney drove in four runs as Birmingham won the nightcap, 6–5.[36]

The following day they played in Memphis to benefit the Miss Memphis Scholarship Contest for young black women. Right-hander and Morehouse College graduate Felix "Chin" Evans shutout the Black Barons, 4–0, "using a tantalizing cure [sic] and drop ball that kept heavy hitters of the Birmingham club confused."[37]

From Memphis, they traveled up the East coast, playing the Homestead Grays, Baltimore Elite Giants, Philadelphia Stars and other teams in various cities. On July 26, they played the New York Black Yankees in Yankee Stadium, losing 5–2. Birmingham's pitcher was Pipkin. The left-hander, who had started in the 1920s, played with Birmingham in 1928–29 and briefly in 1940. Reportedly, he "lost his arm" in 1931 but remarkably had gotten it back in the early 1940s.[38]

While they were gone, the Ethiopian Clowns came to Birmingham to play the local industrial league all-stars. The Clowns pitcher was Dan Bankhead. After being sent to St. Paul for "an infraction of club rules," he gravitated to the Clowns.[39] The Clowns won both games, 7–5 and 9–3. Bankhead pitched the first game.[40]

On August 16, the Cincinnati/Cleveland Buckeyes came to town. Several Birmingham players were in Chicago for the East–West Game. On the West team, managed by Welch, were "Ducky" Davenport, Tommy Sampson, Gready McKinnis, and James Hardy. A "direct wire" was arranged to bring East–West results to Rickwood during the local games.[41] Although the boss and four stars were away, the team played well, beating the Buckeyes, 5–2 and 3–0. In the first game, Morney hit a two-run homer, and Rube "Rocky" Ellis held the visitors to five hits. In the five-inning second game, Pipkin gave up only four hits. Bostock had two hits. The first game started more than an hour late because part of the Cincinnati team encountered highway difficulties traveling by private car.[42]

The following Sunday, Birmingham hosted the Ethiopian Clowns. The Clowns won the first game, 5–4, and the second ended in a 2–2 tie. If Dan Bankhead played, it was under one of the contrived player names such as Khora or Yahodi.[43]

In mid–September it was announced that the Black Barons added a legendary name to their roster. James "Cool Papa" Bell, arguably the fastest man to play in the Negro leagues, was to play center field. He and pitcher Willie Ferrell, a 1937 Black Baron, had both spent most of the 1942 season with Chicago.[44] The roster additions bolstered a club that had lost seven men to military service, but still managed to finish second in the Negro American League. Kansas City again was champion.

Whether Bell or Ferrell actually played for Birmingham cannot be substantiated through game reports. No box scores were published after the announcement.

On September 20, the New York Cubans were at Rickwood for "Manager Welch Day" and "Player Appreciation Day." Owner Hayes promised his players an appreciative bonus, a cut of the gate.[45] New York won the first game of the double-header, 14–5. Birmingham won the second game, although the score was not reported.[46]

In late September the team had an additional dose of bad luck after losing the pennant. While they were traveling in Indiana, the team bus was wrecked. There were no serious injuries, but the bus was totaled.[47] They finished the trip by train, returning to Birmingham to close out the 1942 season with victories over the Ethiopian Clowns and the Negro American League All-Stars.

The Clowns' star was "Peanuts" Nyasses, a much-ballyhooed pitcher-infielder-comedian. Nyasses, like most of the other odd-named players, was no foreigner at all. In an interview with the *Chicago Daily News*, he confessed to being Eddie Davis of Jackson, Mississippi. He chose the name "Peanuts" because it sounded clowny and the name "Nyasses" because it sounded Ethiopian.

Picking up the story, the *Birmingham News* reporter wrote: "If readers want the lowdown on the pitching ace who will work against the Black Barons in one game of Sunday's twin bill, it's simply this: He has never been to Ethiopia, and up until several years ago he thought 'Abyssinia' was short for 'I'll be seeing you.' Instead of seeing the light of day for the first time in Addis Ababa, he rode in on the stork's back in Jackson, Miss., where he grew up and sold pop and peanuts until he turned to baseball for a career."[48]

Birmingham breezed through the two games, beating the Clowns and prodigal Dan Bankhead, 6–1 and 3–1.[49] It was Bankhead's last game before the hometown fans. He left for the Army on October 10. He was the eighth Black Baron lost to military service that season.[50] More than 100 Negro league baseball players are known to have served in the military during World War II.[51]

1943

Winfield Welch returned as Birmingham manager in 1943. He also received a promotion with the job, adding general manager to his duties.[52] When the Black Barons played Chicago at Cramton Bowl in Montgomery, he was described as "Whistler" Welch because instead of using traditional hand signals with his batters, he whistled his instructions. For the Montgomery game, he was said to be "brushing up on some new signs."[53]

When Welch and owner Tom Hayes talked contract in February, it was during a brief break from Welch's winter job: road manager for the Harlem Globetrotters basketball team. For Hayes, the hire was a natural. Welch had produced two competitive teams and had earned league recognition for himself. He managed the West team in 1942 after serving as a coach the year before.[54]

But there was great uncertainty about the future of baseball in wartime. In March, Negro American League President Dr. J.B. Martin said that, "unless stopped by the government," the league would continue to operate. "Team owners feel that as long as the fans want baseball, they shall have it. There will be fewer games this year but larger attractions and the owners will be financially better off than playing many games during the week with smaller attractions."[55]

Martin noted that some teams would have trouble getting players. He opposed players holding defense or other jobs and trying to play baseball on weekends. He doubted their ability to keep in condition.[56]

There were also transportation problems. A devastating blow was delivered when the Office of Defense Transportation announced a ban of privately owned buses, often used by bands and baseball teams. There had already been a restriction for "non-essential service" charter service vehicles. Martin and Negro National League Secretary Cum Posey made a hasty trip to Washington, D.C., to confer with the ODT director, emerging with a view that the situation was not as bad as originally believed.[57]

Yet, the ODT ruling was typical of many sacrifices facing teams and citizens alike during the war. For example, the *Chicago Defender* announced that scorers of baseball games and reporters of other sports had to have their material into the newspaper's office before noon on Mondays in order to make the following Saturday's edition. "We are at war. Munitions, guns, tanks and food have priority over newspapers," read the announcement.[58]

White teams faced the same problems, and some saw that as an opportunity for blacks in Organized Ball. Richard Robinson, an Associated Negro Press writer, noted that the white player shortage might seemingly offer an opening. However, he wrote that black owners were opposed to the prospect. "Negro owners were not anxious to lose the stars who proved drawing cards in an unprecedented successful session last year," he wrote. "It is asking a great deal to expect the Negro club owners to give up such an opportunity in order to enrich major league club owners, who in the past, have ignored Negroes in every way."[59]

The NAL's six-team lineup was Birmingham, Chicago, Cincinnati, Cleveland, Kansas City, and Memphis.[60] Cincinnati was the former barnstorming Ethiopian Clowns.[61]

Birmingham's trained at Sloss Field "under war time conditions" rather than out of state this year.[62] It was a camp with great expectations. "Manager W.S. Welch's powerful squad will settle for nothing less than the Negro American League's world series championship for this season," reported the *Pittsburgh Courier*.[63]

There was good reason for the optimism. Birmingham, projected to be "the class of the league," had returning pitchers Gready McKinnis, Alvin Gipson, John Markham, and Alfred Saylor. New prospects included Jimmie Lee Newberry, Leo Reed, and Jonas Miles. Reed and Miles did not stick, but Newberry became a mainstay.[64]

The first exhibition games at Rickwood Field brought in Kansas City and Satchel Paige. McKinnis, "who has hopped away to what looks like his greatest season in baseball," was designated to face Paige in the opener. Welch announced the following lineup:

Tommy Sampson, 2b	Piper Davis, lf
Lester Lockett, 3b	Jesse Walker, ss
Leroy Morney, 1b	Paul Hardy, c
Clyde Spearman, rf	Gready McKinnis, p[65]
Ed Steele, cf	

The Black Barons won both Sunday games, 4–2 and 3–2, before a reported crowd of 10,000.

It was Satchel Paige Day in honor of the ever-popular former Black Baron. Welch presented him with a $100 War Bond "as a token of appreciation of the Birmingham club." After that it was all business against the Mobile native. McKinnis pitched a complete game. His teammates drove Paige from the mound in the sixth inning. He was frequently in trouble. He struck out Piper Davis with bases loaded to get out of one jam, but not the others.[66] Buster Markham yielded only five hits in the seven-inning second game.[67]

Kansas City won on Monday, 14–9. That was the debut of Newberry. He was pulled after the Monarchs scored four runs in the fifth inning. Kansas City added seven runs in the sixth. "Lax base running and critical errors" were keys in the loss.[68]

Birmingham made it three out of four in a Thursday Ladies Night game. Spearman hit a walk-off home run to win it 6–5 in the eleventh inning.[69]

The final exhibitions were with Chicago, now managed by Ted "Double Duty" Radcliffe. Chicago won two games played in Montgomery. Sunday games at Rickwood were divided. A Montgomery sportswriter wrote that McKinnis "looked extremely good" in the Friday night loss.[70]

During spring training, a major squabble erupted among NAL and NNL owners and officials. Memphis and Chicago asserted that Homestead and Philadelphia had raided their rosters. NAL President Martin said the players must be returned or there would be no East–West game.[71] Philadelphia Manager Homer Curry was charged with giving Memphis players a $25 pay raise, $50 train fare, and a $100 bonus when they reached Philadelphia. Responding, Cum Posey said the NAL had broken an agreement between the two leagues.[72]

The controversy dragged on into June, with a total of twelve players allegedly in inappropriate uniforms. Finally, an agreement was reached in late June with most of the players returning to their original teams.[73]

Opening Day, May 16, for Birmingham was at Cincinnati, two weeks before the home opener.

At Cincinnati, the teams played two 10-inning games with each winning one.[74] The following weekend the Black Barons split at Memphis. Porter Moss beat Gipson, 2–1, in the opening game. In the nightcap, Markham won a 10-inning three-hitter, 1–0.[75]

Memphis came in for Birmingham's first home games. The Black Barons had won eleven of thirteen exhibition games and were shooting for the Opening Day attendance record, topping 9,000 in Kansas City and 4,000 in Cincinnati.[76] An elaborate pregame program included music by the Lincoln High School and Fairfield Industrial High School bands. A black American Legion post was in charge of the flag-raising ceremony. FIHS principal E.J. Oliver threw out the first pitch. The starting lineup:

Felix McLaurin, cf	Piper Davis, ss
Clyde Spearman, rf	Alphonse Dunn, 1b
Leroy Morney, lf	Paul Hardy, c
Lester Lockett, 1b	Buster Markham, p[77]
Tommy Sampson, 2b	

It was an auspicious start for the Black Barons, who won both games, 6–2 and 10–1, and probably the attendance trophy as well. According to the *Birmingham News*, the crowd was estimated at 12,000. McKinnis pitched the first game and Markham the second, giving up seven and five hits, respectively. Lockett worked "sensational shifts" at third base and had four hits in the first game.[78]

The following weekend, the new Cincinnati team was at Rickwood. "Ringling Brothers isn't docketed until Fall, the Clowns are already in town," reported the *Birmingham News*. "Sunday afternoon the Clowns, with all the comedy stunts known to baseball and some never exhibited locally before, will go into the rather serious pastime of trying to dethrone the Black Barons from a tie for top spot in the loop."[79]

Birmingham, sharing third place with Cleveland, swamped the Clowns, 13–0, in the opener, then won a 2–1 extra-inning game. The winning pitchers were McKinnis and Markham. Lockett hit a two-run home run in the first game. Spearman won the second game with a solo homer.[80] Birmingham won again on Thursday.[81]

The fast start whetted the local appetite for baseball. "In spite of inroads by the draft and enlistments by certain of his men, Welch has come up this season with one of the greatest teams to serve under the Black Baron banner. They enjoy one of the biggest early leads they have ever boasted over their constant rivals, the Kansas City Monarchs … it looks like a Black Baron year."[82]

After two days' rest, they hosted the independent Atlanta Black Crackers. A crowd of 4,000 saw Birmingham extend its winning streak to seven games. Gipson threw a three-hitter, striking out 15, as Birmingham won the first game, 5–0. Local batters got nine hits off Roy Wellmaker, who was on leave from the U.S. Army. Newberry came on in relief to preserve a 3–2 win in the second game.[83]

After a three-week road trip, called "the most sensational in their history," Birmingham returned home for a July 4 double-header with Chicago. Few details of the "clean-sweep road tour" were reported except that Kansas City had been beaten, 5–2, in Cincinnati. Birmingham batters again pummeled Satchel Paige.[84] Also, they beat the New York Cubans, 6–1, in a Chicago four-team double-header.[85]

McKinnis pitched well and Birmingham won the first game from Chicago, 5–1, clinching the first-half pennant. He was "in sight of a shutout" until an error allowed a Chicago run in the eighth. The Giants won the second game, 7–3, after Markham was forced to leave the game in the third inning because of the heat. Shortstop Davis had five hits in the two games.[86]

That was the entire home stand. Birmingham was off on another sparsely reported three-week trip. They were paired first with Kansas City, and then with the NNL New York Cuban Stars, mostly in the Southwest and Midwest."[87]

The Black Barons, "the real sensations of Negro major league baseball this year," returned home with the undefined league record for consecutive wins. They "vanquished the famous Satchel Paige" every time they faced him.[88]

Back home with the Cuban Stars, Birmingham lost its first doubleheader of the season, 11–2 and 2–1.[89] They recovered on Thursday night. Gipson, in first inning relief of the usually reliable McKinnis, held the Cubans to two hits, striking out eight. Sampson had three hits as Birmingham won, 7–4.[90]

Awaiting a Sunday set with Chicago, Birmingham played a Saturday night game to benefit the United Service Organizations (USO), a congressionally chartered nonprofit to provide morale boosting and recreational service for service members and their families. After a game between industrial league teams, the Black Barons defeated a team from Camp Sibert in Gadsden, 7–0.[91]

Chicago came in, leading the NAL, with Birmingham in second. Manager Welch missed the games. He was in Chicago for the East–West classic. Also on the West team were McKinnis, Sampson, and Lockett.[92] Although he did not specify who was in charge of the team in his absence, Welch left a revised lineup:

Leroy Morney, 2b	Jesse Walker, 3b
Clyde Spearman, rf	Herman Bell, c
Alphonse Dunn, lf	Al Saylor, 1b
Ed Steele, cf	Buster Markham, p[93]
Piper Davis, ss	

Bad weather spoiled the much-anticipated meeting of the longtime rivals. The first game was rained out. The second game started but only went six innings before additional deluges came. Birmingham won the abbreviated contest, 2–0, with Newberry allowing only two hits.[94]

The pattern for the season was to play a short home stand, then go away for two or three weeks. The trip after the Chicago games paired Birmingham with Cincinnati in the upper Midwest and Canada, followed by a four-team double-header at Wrigley Field. There was also a three-team double-header at Yankee Stadium with the New York Cubans and Black Yankees.[95]

But local fans were not completely without baseball. Tom Hayes arranged a special exhibition game at Rickwood, bringing in the Nashville Crawfords, "one of the fastest Negro baseball teams in the South," to play the Birmingham City League All-Stars. The Birmingham team crushed the visitors, smashing out 32 hits to win both ends of the double-header, 11–8 and 11–2.[96]

The following Sunday, Hayes brought in another opponent for the All-Stars. This one came with an old fan favorite. Managing the Panama City (Florida) Tigers was Charles "Twosides" Wesley, the former Black Barons infielder and manager whose career dated to the 1919 formative year. Other familiar faces included Sylvester "Good Black" Owens, a centerfielder under Andrew Walker; James "Neckbone" Davis, a former industrial leaguer; and George Young, a Montgomery boy.[97] A Sylvester Owens played second base with Birmingham in 1935. This could also be DeWitt Owens, who played multiple positions with Birmingham from 1936 to 1938.[98]

The All-Stars won both games from Panama City, 12–3 and 4–1. The winning pitcher in the first game was Nathaniel Pollard, who struck out 17. The hitting star was Sam Hairston with two hits. Wesley had two for the visitors, and was the only batter that Pollard failed to strike out.[99] Pollard, like Piper Davis, grew up in the Bibb County mining community of Piper. He became a regular with the Black Barons later.[100]

Meanwhile, the Black Barons remained away. Few results filtered into the local media, but when they did, they were noteworthy. In a double-header with Cleveland, Davis had seven hits in eight at-bats. The games were split with McKinnis winning the opener, 3–1, Birmingham's ninth straight win.[101] It was likely the longest road trip in team history. Not a single home game was played from August 2 until Game 6 of the NAL playoffs on September 19.

While the fans were awaiting the long homecoming, Hayes continued to fill the void at home. He scheduled a September 12 double-header between the City League All-Stars and the Jacksonville Red Caps with former Birmingham players Clarence Lamar and Rocky Ellis.[102]

That same day the Negro American League playoffs between Birmingham and Chicago were scheduled to begin in Chicago. Other games were set for Toledo, Columbus, and Dayton, Ohio; Montgomery, Alabama; and finally, Birmingham.

The Chicago game was rained out, moving the opener to Toledo on September 13. The American Giants scored two runs in the bottom of the ninth to win, 3–2. The winning hit was by "Double Duty" Radcliffe, scoring his brother Alex.[103]

Birmingham tied the series in Columbus, walloping the Giants, 16–5. Chicago won in Dayton, and Birmingham in Montgomery, bringing the two teams to Birmingham for the deciding contest.[104]

Officials announced that "extra reservations had been made for white fans … and indications were that the biggest crowd of the season would be on hand to see the Black Barons go gunning for a chance to meet the Homestead Grays" in a Negro World Series.[105]

Manager Welch's lineup:

Felix McLauren, cf	Jesse Walker, 3b
Tommy Sampson, 2b	James Lindsay, 1b
Clyde Spearman, rf	Herman Bell, c
Lester Lockett, lf	Gready McKinnis or
Al Gipson, p	
Piper Davis, ss	

Speculation among fans was that Welch might not use either of those pitchers. He might go to Markham, Saylor, or even Newberry, whose work had been "mighty good" in road games leading up to the playoffs.[106] Actually, it was none of those. He started right-hander John Huber, who had pitched for Chicago in 1942.

The first baseman presents another name quandary. Historian James Riley says James Lindsay was a first baseman for Birmingham in 1943. Also on the team was Leonard "Sloppy" Lindsay, an infielder who had earlier played for the Ethiopian/Cincinnati Clowns under the name of "Yahodi." Clark and Lester likewise list both players on their 1943 Birmingham roster.[107] Game reports offered no clarification of which player may have been in a game. Two postseason box scores list only one Lindsay, the first baseman. Although both first names appear in game reports, James was the one more often seen. It is also quite possible that there was only one Lindsay, Leonard, who was sometimes identified as James.

The winner would face the Homestead Grays, NNL champions, in the second Negro

World Series. There was also a personal note between the two managers. "Double Duty" Radcliffe was with Birmingham when the Chicago managerial spot became available. Welch reportedly helped Radcliffe get the job.[108]

A huge crowd was anticipated. Its size was never reported, but what a game sportswriter Jimmie Gibbs covered at Rickwood.

Radcliffe started Grady Jessup, a right-hander who had pitched for Birmingham in 1940. Jessup was masterful, holding the Black Barons to four hits. He struck out three and hit one batter but did not walk any. But Jessup's work was eclipsed by Huber's. It remains one of the all-time best at Rickwood Field. He faced only 28 batters, allowing Ralph Wyatt a leadoff single to start the game. Wyatt was subsequently thrown out attempting to steal second. Only one other batter reached first base, Radcliffe on a walk in the sixth. Huber then struck out two to end the inning. He had four strikeouts in the game, and Birmingham won, 1–0.

The game-winning run was scored in the second inning when Piper Davis was hit by a pitch and advanced to third on Leonard Lindsay's single. Hoss Walker's sacrifice fly to center field scored Davis.[109] With no box score, it is impossible to determine if both James and Leonard Lindsay played.

On the following morning, the Black Barons left for Washington, D.C., for a workout at Griffith Stadium prior to the first World Series game. Like the regular season and the NAL playoffs, most of the games were played away. Birmingham fans did not see their team in the series until Game 9 on October 7. The Washington manager was Candy Jim Taylor. The series format was best of seven, but a total of ten games were played.[110]

The NAL championship win over Chicago was costly, however. Although he played the entire game, backup catcher Herman Bell was injured. The club had already lost regular catcher Paul Hardy to the U.S. Army. Homestead management allowed Birmingham to get "Double Duty" Radcliffe from Chicago for the World Series.[111]

Interestingly, pitchers Huber and Saylor had done a bit of double duty themselves, filling in at catcher occasionally. For the World Series, though, neither was considered proficient enough to keep the club from going without a proven catcher. While Radcliffe is certainly the most notable player to both pitch and catch, there were a number of occasional practitioners in the Negro leagues over the years, including Birmingham's Bill Greason. A 1949 photo referred to his "Double Duty" activities in semi-pro ball, pitching the opener and catching the nightcap in doubleheaders.[112] However, it was Radcliffe who drew the original nickname from New York sportswriter Damon Runyan.[113]

Hall of Fame pitcher Warren Spahn (left) and "Double Duty" Radcliffe. They were guests at a sports memorabilia show in Montgomery, Alabama, on 17 August 1996 (author's collection).

Radcliffe was behind the plate for Al Saylor in Washington on September 21. The Black Barons used three unearned runs to beat the Grays, 4–2. Saylor pitched a five-hitter.[114]

Game 2 was in Baltimore two nights later. Although the Black Barons did not lose the game, they probably lost the World Series that night. The game ended in a 5–5 tie after 12 innings, called because of a local curfew. Birmingham led, 4–2, but allowed the Grays to tie the game in the seventh. Birmingham led, 5–4, after eight but again could not hold the lead.[115] Had Birmingham won that game, they would have been two games to none and definitely in control of the series.

When Game 3 was played in Washington, D.C., the following night, the Grays were able to tie the series with an 11-inning 4–3 win. Markham, who had held the home team to seven hits, gave up a leadoff single to Sam Bankhead to open the 11th. When Vic Harris laid down a sacrifice bunt attempt, James Lindsay appeared to have the lead runner nailed at second, but his throw sailed over Davis's head, putting runners on the corners. Josh Gibson was intentionally walked to set up a force play at any base. It worked on the first batter, but not the second. "Cool Papa" Bell singled down the first-base line to score the winning run.[116]

Perhaps inspired by the extra-inning win, the powerful Grays seemed to take charge of the series. Game 4 in Chicago produced the momentum that led to the championship. Right-hander John Wright pitched a 9–0 shutout. Although he gave up five hits and six walks, he kept base runners scattered and benefited from two double plays. Homestead had a six-run fifth inning. The normally dependable McKinnis and Huber were both ineffective, and Birmingham fielders made three errors.[117]

Still, the Black Barons did not go quietly. After an off day, the series moved to Columbus, Ohio. Although Josh Gibson hit a grand slam home run for the Grays, Birmingham held on for an 11–10 victory to tie the series at two games each.[118]

Game 6 was in Indianapolis and once again Wright was in charge. He shut out the Black Barons again, holding them to six hits. Like the game in Chicago, the Grays took an early lead, then blew Birmingham away with a big inning, a five-run seventh that put the game out of reach. The final score was 8–0.[119]

That brought the series finally to Rickwood on Sunday, October 3. For Homestead, it was a chance to wind up the series and claim the title. For Birmingham, it was an opportunity to even the series. For the Birmingham fans, it was a festive occasion. Among those attending was W.C. Handy, the famed composer of "The St. Louis Blues" and "The Beale Street Blues." Handy was described as "a rabid baseball fan."[120]

The *Birmingham News* covered the Negro World Series as thoroughly as it would a white championship, displaying an awareness of the game's historical significance: "It's rather a coincidence that the former manager of the Barons and the man who drove them to a pennant in 1943 should be dueling for the world's championship. W.S. Welch, who has worked wonders since he joined the Birmingham club, finds himself aligned against a man who was never able to win a pennant for the Black Barons, 'Candy Jim' Taylor. Yet today, the two maestros are battling tooth-and-toe-nail to see which club will wear the championship belt throughout 1944."

The following lineups were announced for the crucial game:

Birmingham	*Homestead*
Felix McLauren, cf	"Cool Papa" Bell, lf
Tommy Sampson, 2b	Jerry Benjamin, cf
Clyde Spearman, rf	Buck Leonard, 1b

Birmingham	*Homestead*
Lester Lockett, lf	Josh Gibson, c
Piper Davis, ss	Howard Easterling, 2b
James Lindsay, 1b	Sam Bankhead, ss
Jesse Walker, 3b	Jud Wilson, 3b
Ted Radcliffe, c	Vic Harris, rf
John Humber or Al Saylor, p	Johnny Wright, p[121]

With Huber pitching sensationally, the Black Barons evened the series at three games apiece. He yielded only three hits as Birmingham claimed a 1–0 win in 11 innings. In the bottom of the eleventh, Lindsay tripled and came home on Ed Steele's single. Both teams had scoring opportunities that were squelched by good defense.[122]

Game 8 was played in Montgomery two days later. Big Josh Gibson did not hit one of his legendary home runs, but his two singles and a double propelled the Grays to an 8–4 win and the world championship. The Grays overcame a 4–2 Birmingham lead with four runs in the eighth and two in the ninth.[123]

Although the series was officially over, three additional games were scheduled, two in Birmingham, one in New Orleans. The latter was canceled. The Black Barons won, 6–2, on Thursday behind Jessup's seven-hitter. On Sunday, the Grays brought the Black Barons' greatest season to a close with a 9–4 win. It was a rather one-sided game, but Birmingham fans got to cheer in the fifth when Felix McLauren and Ed Steele both hit home runs.[124]

Although there was an enthusiastic reception for the World Series in various cities, not everyone was pleased with the overall product. Wendell Smith, sports editor of the *Pittsburgh Courier*, said the series was run "in a rather slip-shod manner," particularly Chicago's loaning Radcliffe to Birmingham. "Although the Grays approved the move, there is no justification for it. Obviously the teams have ignored all eligibility rules by permitting a player from another team to compete in the series." Smith called for a black baseball commissioner. "It is hardly conceivable that an authority over both leagues would permit such tom-foolery."[125]

Smith was not finished. He also he railed against the cancellation of the game in New Orleans, calling it a "kick the pants" to the public." The move was made because several Birmingham players had been ordered to report to their draft boards. Even if so, Smith argued, no one bothered to notify Allen Page, the New Orleans promoter, until after the fact. Again, Smith called for a Negro baseball commissioner.[126]

1944

Winfield Welch opened spring training with a strong nucleus of players from 1943's championship run. Among them were Lester Lockett, Tommy Sampson, Leroy Morney, Ed Steele, Piper Davis, Al Gipson, Johnny Huber, Jimmie Newberry, Buster Markham, Al Saylor, and Gready McGinnis. Trying to join that solid lineup were first baseman Henry McCall, outfielder Leandy Young, third baseman Johnny Brittain, and pitcher Lafayette Nash. Brittain, actually Britton, had played with Cincinnati the year before.[127] Lafayette Washington, misidentified as Nash here, was later on the team.

Again, due to wartime limitations, the team trained in Birmingham with a shortened exhibition season. Five games were scheduled in Birmingham.[128]

Joining Birmingham for the 1944 Negro American League season were Chicago, Cleveland, Kansas City, Memphis, and the Cincinnati-Indianapolis Clowns.[129] The *Chicago Defender* reported that the Clowns franchise had been shifted from Cincinnati to Indianapolis "due to conflicting bookings in the Ohio city."[130] The team was variously called the Indianapolis Clowns and the Cincinnati Clowns.

The league voted to hire an outside firm for statistical services. Also, the owners agreed "to play an unspecified number of games to aid worthy causes during the season."[131] Games to promote war bond sales and various charitable endeavors were common. For example, Dr. W.S. Martin of Memphis sought charity help for "a training school and hospital for negro nurses."[132]

The contract with Howe News Bureau, which handled statistics for many white baseball leagues at the time, was something fans and sportswriters had sought for decades. "This forward step means that fans throughout the country will know now for the first time, what their favorite players are actually doing, and will also make it possible to determine just who is the best hitter, pitcher, fielder and leader in various departments in the game, which has never been determined before by actual facts and figures," wrote Wendell Smith in the *Pittsburgh Courier*.[133]

The arrangement worked well for the first half of the season. The *Courier* ran a weekly column called Diamond Dope. It contained standings for both leagues, the previous week's scores, and the upcoming games. Occasionally, it added individual player statistics. Unfortunately, the amount of detail faded during the second half, probably because so many teams were often barnstorming instead of playing league games. In September, Birmingham played at least eight games in various cities with the New York Cubans. A similar series with the Homestead Grays was played during the first half.

During spring training, word reached Birmingham that Charles "Twosides" Wesley, one of the original Black Barons, had died of a heart attack in Panama City, Florida. A native of Montgomery, Wesley had spent nearly twenty years in the Negro leagues.[134]

Birmingham's prospects looked bright again. In fact, the *Pittsburgh Courier* said it was "the club to beat … [and] confidence fairly oozes out of their every action."[135] The team was packed with veterans from a squad that just missed winning the world championship. Owner Tom Hayes, Jr., and Manager Welch "frankly admit they believe they have best ball club in Negro baseball this season and will win the world's championship."[136] And Ted "Double Duty" Radcliffe had joined the club, providing both experience and leadership at catcher. He was needed because Paul Hardy was still in military service.[137]

The exhibition season opened on a pleasant note. Some 4,000 fans turned out at Rickwood to see the Birmingham Barons beat Chicago twice.[138] The following weekend they beat Cleveland, 10–2, then lost two to the New York Cubans.[139] Games with Baltimore were rained out. The exhibitions ended with a sweep of the Ethiopian Clowns. Saylor pitched a 1–0 shutout in the 11-inning opener. Huber shut down the Clowns, 9–1, in the second game. Some 6,000 fans saw Birmingham finish with a 5–1 record.[140]

As Opening Day neared, there was encouraging race relations news out of St. Louis. The National League Cardinals and American League Browns announced that they would have open seating, regardless of race, in 1944. St. Louis was the last major league city to do away with race-restricted seating.[141]

Birmingham opened in Chicago, winning a double-header, 5–3 and 7–2, behind the pitching of Saylor and Gipson. Lockett was the batting star, driving in seven runs in two games.[142] Working their way home, they beat Chicago in Dayton and St. Louis in Knoxville.[143]

Opening Day at Rickwood Field was on Sunday, May 14. Emory O. Jackson, writing in the *Birmingham World*, celebrated the fifth season under Hayes's ownership, noting that the team had prospered during his tenure.[144]

Entertainment included "torrid baseball music" by the Fairfield Industrial and Parker High School bands. A local American Legion post and a Masonic organization, the George Ruffin Council, handled flag-raising activities, and all servicemen were admitted free.[145]

The music was fine, but the flag-raising was a problem. Both groups thought they were in charge of the ceremony. Molton H. Gray, commander of the Masonic group, "brought a long list of names, his council roster, under the impression they should be passed into the game free. The gateman, backed by the Black Baron management, balked on the idea of letting in the proposed number." The Legionnaires, fewer in number and also in uniform, made a more favorable impression. The flag-raising was turned over to them. But there were more problems to come. Instead of someone singing the national anthem as the flag was raised, a bugler played "Taps." "Everybody after this point seemed to be lost, even the flag-raisers. Mr. Downey's speech was interrupted by music, forcing him to give up for a while." The unfortunate Mr. Downey was not further identified, and the newspaper reporter gave everybody involved an equal share of the blame.[146]

But things went very well on the field. An estimated 11,000 turned out for the double-header. Birmingham won both games. The Black Barons scored five runs in the first, and coasted to a 7–2 win on Saylor's six-hitter. In the second, Gipson shut out the Monarchs, 3–0. The fielding was spectacular with five of the seven double plays recorded taking place in the first game.[147]

The next weekend was in Cleveland with much different results. The Buckeyes won, 2–1 and 3–1. Birmingham salvaged a Wednesday night game, 5–2.[148] Birmingham won four of five from Cleveland as the teams barnstormed back to Birmingham.

On May 28 at Rickwood Field, Saylor won the first game, 3–2. Huber lost the second, 2–0. Ex–Black Baron Johnny Cowan made several key plays at second base for Cleveland. The shutout broke Birmingham's five-game winning streak. A pregame ceremony was held to hoist "a flag emblamatic [*sic*] of the 1943 Negro American League championship."[149]

In early Howe News Bureau statistics, Artie Wilson was the batting leader with a .414 average. Steele was listed at .304. Birmingham pitching records were Newberry (2–0), Saylor (4–1), Gipson (3–1), Washington (2–1), and Huber (0–1).[150]

The Black Barons left on a two-week road trip. It included a double-header shutout of the Philadelphia Stars at Yankee Stadium. Birmingham beat the NNL club, 9–0 and 13–0. Gipson and Dan Bankhead, apparently on leave from the Army, were the pitchers. Birmingham had a couple of games with Cincinnati, but was paired mostly with Homestead, playing in Philadelphia, Baltimore, New York, Washington, and Portsmouth, Virginia. A series with Memphis followed in Texas.[151]

In June, the white Barons played Camp Sibert from Gadsden in at a war bonds fund-raiser. Admission was free with a $25 war bond purchase. The *Birmingham World* urged blacks attending the game to record the serial number of the bond so it could be credited to the Negro War Bond Sale Division, headquartered at Smith and Gaston Funeral Home. The black bond sale had a million-dollar goal. The newspaper also urged Black Barons management to schedule a similar fund-raiser, noting that possible opponents were available at Fort Benning and Tuskegee Army Air Base.[152]

World War II involved the entire nation intimately. In addition to rationing, most families had at least one member in uniform. War bonds were one means of financing the war and also controlling inflation. Their purchase was also viewed as a patriotic, civilian contribution to the war effort, even though the interest rate (2.9 percent) was below market value.[153]

Winding up the long trip with Memphis, the Black Barons returned home for a three-team double-header on June 25. The games were with Fort Benning and St. Louis. Newberry beat the soldiers, 6–0, in the first game, striking out 12 and allowing only six hits. In the second game, Birmingham edged St. Louis, 9–8, scoring the winning run in the ninth.[154] The Stars, a loose remnant of the team that was a charter member of the NAL in 1937, were barnstormers in 1944.[155]

The Black Barons went to Atlanta on June 29. Promoting the game, Atlanta sportswriter J.C. Chunn said Birmingham had "a quarter of-a-million-dollar" infield. "That is to say that it would take that much to purchase Davis, at first base; Sampson, at second base; Art Wilson, at shortstop; Britton at third base, and Double-Duty Radcliffe, catcher."

From Atlanta, the Black Barons, first-half winners, went to Cleveland, where they split a double-header.[156] Pitcher John "Buster" Markham rejoined the team in late June, after spending some time in California. It was not explained if his California time was military or baseball related.

Birmingham spent almost all of July away. One notable event occurred in New Orleans. Promoter Allen Page designated the Kansas City–Birmingham game as an "honor" occasion for Winfield Welch, a Louisiana native. A large crowd witnessed the presentation of gifts to Welch. Birmingham won, 7–6.[157]

July 16 was a break in the long trip. They returned to Rickwood for a double-header with Kansas City. It was a pleasant homecoming for Satchel Paige, who pitched a four-hit shutout, winning 6–0. Birmingham, with 16 hits, won the second game, 9–5.[158]

In mid–July the black baseball world was stunned to learn that outstanding Memphis submarining right-handed pitcher Porter Moss had died from a gunshot wound. Although not a statistical leader, Moss was one of the steadiest pitchers in the league. The Red Sox, en route from Nashville to Memphis, were forced to take a train when their bus broke down. In the crowded, segregated car, an altercation broke out and a drunk fired a pistol shot that hit Moss in the abdomen. The bullet perforated the large intestine and lodged against his spine.

What ensued is sadly reminiscent of the death of blues singer Bessie Smith, who died because of the difficulty of getting medical help for a black person.[159] Moss was either denied help by whites or none was available at several small-town stops along the train's route. Each time they were told there was no ambulance available. Finally, they reached Jackson, Tennessee, where he was taken to a hospital. Perhaps because of the treatment delay, he died a few hours later.[160]

The assailant, "a small-town gun-man identified as Johnny Easley, 30, of Camden, Tenn.," was arrested later that day near his home.

"Thousands of Memphis baseball fans observed a hushed moment when the popular pitcher's death was announced during the game at Russwood Park," reported SNS, a black national news service.[161]

Late July standings were Birmingham (8–4), Chicago (8–5), and Cleveland (7–5).[162]

Sam Jethroe (.361) led hitters. Artie Wilson (.335) was second. Jethroe also led in hits, runs, total bases, and doubles. Birmingham pitching records were Saylor (12–3), Gipson (8–5), Newberry (4–3), Washington (2–2), Huber (1–2), and Markham (2–0).[163]

On Sunday, July 30, the Black Barons came home for a few days, playing Chicago in a Sunday double-header and a Thursday night game in Montgomery. This was the NAL's second-half format of Sunday double-headers and barnstorming the rest of the week. The *Birmingham News* said the Black Barons "have become the greatest drawing in all Negro baseball. The Black Barons now draw better on the road than the famed Kansas City Monarchs. They are averaging better than 6,000 at home. Hence, they are making an effort to return home any Sunday the white Barons are on the road. The Black Barons did not do that last year."[164]

A July appearance at Crosley Field in Cincinnati drew 8,000 fans, lending credence to the *News*' assertion.[165]

On the road or at home, the first-half champions continued to win. Chicago was defeated, 3–2 and 7–1, at Rickwood. Gipson won the opener and Saylor the nightcap, striking out 10. Wilson made "a leaping one hand" catch to start a double play and stop a potential Chicago rally in the first game. Lockett broke out of a long hitting slump with four hits.[166]

At home for the third consecutive Sunday, Birmingham split a double-header with Memphis on August 6. Steele homered, but Verdell Mathis won the first game, 4–3. Markham won the second game, 2–1. Traveling together, they played in Montgomery, Dallas, Houston, and Little Rock during the week.[167]

The 12th East–West Game was held in Chicago in August. Six Black Barons were on the West squad. Joining Manager Winfield Welch were catcher Ted Radcliffe, first baseman Piper Davis, second baseman Tommy Sampson, shortstop Artie Wilson, and pitcher Alvin Gipson. Welch opposed "Candy Jim" Taylor of the East. W.J. Moore of Birmingham was an umpire for the classic.

The West won, 7–4. Verdell Mathis was the winning pitcher. Satchel Paige, who would have pitched for the East, boycotted the game because of a disagreement over the distribution of gate proceeds. Luther A. Townsley of the Associated Negro Press said "it is unlikely that the results would have been different." One of the batting stars was Radcliffe, who hit a two-run homer. "When the veteran Radcliffe tried to take his seat in the players' dugout after his home run drive, he was lifted to the shoulders of his teammates, showered with money and given $50 in war bonds. Nearly 50,000 fans knew he had sealed the doom for the East," wrote Townsley.[168]

Howe News Bureau standings that weekend were Birmingham (15–9) and Chicago (13–10). Birmingham's team batting average was .298.[169]

Individual statistics had Cleveland outfielder Jethroe (.357) still ahead of Wilson (.340). They were tied in runs scored with 47. Ed Steel (4) was in a three-way tie in home runs. Al Saylor (14–4) had the most wins. Former Black Baron Gready McKinnis, now with Chicago, threw a no-hitter, shutting out Kansas City, 4–0.[170]

In early September, when Birmingham split two games with Cincinnati in Indianapolis, the *Birmingham News* declared that the Black Barons had won both halves.[171]

The Homestead Grays won out in the NNL. The Negro Leagues World Series was to open in Birmingham on September 17. Game 2 would be in New Orleans, Game 3 in Birmingham, and Game 4 in Pittsburgh. The remainder would be in Washington.[172]

"For the first time in the history of Negro baseball, a world series will be conducted in a manner pleasing to both owners and fans," reported the *Chicago Defender*. Among the pluses were appearance guarantees by each club. A certified $1,000 check was put up by the Birmingham and Homestead owners. Should both teams fail to appear as required, the money would be given to a charity. Additionally, the league presidents appointed an Arbitration Commission composed of "three outstanding Negro sports writers [to] rule on all disputes or protests which may arise during the series." The members were Frank A. "Fay" Young of the *Defender*, Wendell Smith of the *Pittsburgh Courier*, and Sam Lacy of the *Baltimore Afro-American*.[173]

The first game at Rickwood Field came just hours after the Black Barons traveled all the way from losing a Saturday double-header in Cleveland. It was an even worse week for Birmingham off the field. Four players were injured in an automobile wreck. Tommy Sampson was driving a car with three other players when they were hit head-on by a drunk driver. John Britton hurt his thumb; Leandy Young had a hip injury; and Pepper Bassett was bruised and shaken up. Sampson was seriously injured, remaining in critical condition for several days. One writer, saying it was a miracle any of the players survived the wreck, projected that the accident might end Sampson's career.

Suddenly, a World Series championship that seemed within Birmingham's grasp was now unlikely. Pittsburgh sportswriter Wendell Smith said Birmingham's "battered ball club" would be facing a Homestead team "with the strongest lineup they've had all year." Analyzing the teams, Smith said Birmingham had the edge in pitching but suffered in the infield after the wreck. Homestead's outfield of James "Cool Papa" Bell (.380), Jerry Benjamin (.306), and Dave Hoskins (.343) was superior. The Black Barons had only one outfielder, Ed Steele (.306) hitting over .300.[174]

Manager Welch said he would try to offset Sampson's loss by moving Piper Davis, with his great throwing arm and ability to pivot on double play balls, from first base to second. Morney would replace Davis at first. At shortstop he had Wilson, perhaps the best in either league at that position, although his hitting had not been up to par. Radcliffe was back behind the plate despite having missed time with a broken finger.[175]

He also got agreement from the Grays to add Collins Jones, a local boy, to the roster as a utility man for the series since four of his eighteen series-eligible players were out with injuries from the wreck. Jones, an infielder, had played with Cincinnati the previous year. He appeared in the first game as a pinch runner and scored a run.[176]

Welch's patched-up lineup:

Felix McLauren, cf	Double Duty Radcliffe, c
Artie Wilson, ss	Leroy Morney,1b
John Britton, 3b	Lester Lockett, lf
Piper Davis, 2b	Al Saylor, p[177]
Ed Steele, rf	

Among the Grays were Montgomery native Jerry Benjamin, a 1934 Black Baron, and Sam Bankhead, oldest of the brothers and a 1931–32 Black Baron.

Playing before a huge crowd of 12,449, the Black Barons were obviously sub-par. Homestead dominated from the start, winning 8–3. As Wendell Smith put it, the Grays won the first game by "blasting Johnny Markham and the battered Birmingham Black Barons into complete submission." Birmingham got 11 hits off Roy Wellmaker, but the old Atlanta pitcher kept them well spaced. Josh Gibson, Buck Leonard, and Dave Hoskins hit home runs off Markham.[178]

Birmingham fared no better in New Orleans as Homestead won, 6–1. Al Saylor pitched a tight game until the ninth, when the Grays scored four runs.[179]

By the time Game 3 was over on September 21, the Grays had a commanding three-game lead. They won 9–0 at Rickwood Field. Radcliffe's single in the second inning was Birmingham's only hit. Earl Bumpus started for Birmingham. Although he struck out six and kept the ball inside the fences, he gave up 11 hits, six walks, and three wild pitches.[180]

Three all-time greats, from left: Ed Steele, Piper Davis, and Artie Wilson (courtesy NoirTech Research).

The Grays seemed likely to close out the series in Game 4 at Pittsburgh on Saturday, September 23, but Birmingham finally resembled the team that had dominated the NAL. Huber threw a three-hitter, shutting out the Grays, 6–0. It was the first time Birmingham had been ahead in a series game. The fielding highlight was by centerfielder McLauren. He turned a somersault hauling in a 430-foot Gibson drive but held on to the ball.[181]

Wendell Smith attributed Birmingham's win to Welch, whom he described as "baseball's No. 1 psychologist, a [radio quiz show host] 'Mr. Anthony' and 'Dale Carnegie' rolled into one." Smith said a teary-eyed Welch pleaded with the Black Barons "to go out there and beat hell out of 'em." Smith continued: "He pleaded to them as an innocent man pleads for his life, like a father to a wayward son, or like a man who has lost his last penny in a stock market swindle. And, it worked! They blasted two Homestead Grays' pitchers for six runs, fielded like champions and had plenty of fight. The personable Birmingham manager was grinning from ear to ear after the game. Unfortunately for Birmingham, Mr. Welch didn't have enough tears for all five games."[182]

The following day, the Grays wrapped up the series before their home fans at Griffith

Stadium. It was possibly the best game of the series. Washington won, 4–2. Roy Wellmaker was again the winning pitcher.[183] Although the series was over, the two teams scheduled a double-header in New York on October 6 with the Grays winning both, 5–2 and 8–5.[184]

Birmingham's downfall was poor hitting, attributable in some measure to the automobile accident. "The loss of Tommy Sampson … was a blow to the morale of the ream," wrote Chicago sportswriter Fay Young. "Johnny Britton played in three games of the series with his hand bandaged, and Art Wilson's wrist was ailing. Pepper Bassett and Young were so badly injured that neither donned a uniform, even in Birmingham. Sammy is still in the hospital with a broken hip and two fractured ribs." Even so, Young said Birmingham "wasn't hitting when hits were needed, and you can't win ball games without hits."[185]

1945

A hallmark of the war years for Birmingham was the retention of key personnel, despite the manpower shortage. More than 100 Negro league ballplayers served in the military during World War II. Seven Black Barons either enlisted or were drafted right off the roster: Dan Bankhead, Lyman Bostock, Sr., Bill Greason, Paul Hardy, Nat Pollard, Ulysses Redd, and Joe Scott. Team alumni who served included Matthew "Lick" Carlisle, Elmer Carter, Jimmie Crutchfield, Bill Perkins, Goose Tatum, and Jimmy Zapp.[186]

Yet during those years there was more roster stability from year to year than probably any other time in Black Barons history. Keeping that nucleus of good players together typified the managerial skills of Winfield S. Welch. In 1945, five men were in their fifth year with the club: Buster Markham, Al Gipson, Lester Lockett, Ed Steele and Al Saylor. Piper Davis and Felix McLauren were back for the fourth consecutive year.

At the Negro American League meeting in Chicago, the owners decided on a first half to open May 6 and close on July 4. The second half closing was not announced.[187] Toward the war effort, the league agreed on a 25 percent curtailment of travel, and also said it would not take on any additional associate members. The six members were Birmingham, Chicago, Cincinnati, Cleveland, Kansas City, and Memphis.[188]

The travel reduction is hard to comprehend. For example, Birmingham and Chicago played in Chicago, Milwaukee, St. Paul, Minneapolis and Racine, Wisconsin, in mid–June. That was followed by Birmingham and the New York Cubans at Toledo, Detroit, Indianapolis, and Columbus, Ohio.[189]

For spring training, Welch announced that pitchers were to report on March 20, the other players a week later. He already had contracts from Art Wilson, Johnny Huber, Jimmie Newberry, and Ed Steele. Wilson was the 1944 NAL Rookie of the Year. Missing was second baseman and team captain Tommy Sampson, still not fully recovered from automobile wreck injuries. Meanwhile, he had been loaned to the independent St. Louis Stars as bench manger.[190] To fill the critical second base position, Welch talked about possible trades and also tryouts for two Texas infielders, Eugene Reed and Edward Stone. Neither of them made the team.[191]

Added to that mix of veterans were third baseman John Britton, and catchers Ted "Double Duty" Radcliffe, Pepper Bassett, and Herman Bell. With the addition of Bassett late in the 1944 season and the return of Bell from military service, Radcliffe would probably pitch in 1945. It was easy to see why Birmingham was again expected to be a contender.[192] In fact, Welch outright predicted victory: "The Birmingham Black Barons are in great shape and, in my book, certain to win the Negro American League championship for the third year in a row."[193]

Britton had been obtained in a trade that sent Jesse "Hoss" Walker to Cincinnati. The Clowns wanted Walker as manager. Birmingham got a good infielder, who had also been part of the Clowns comedy routines. Britton's shtick was wearing a wig over a clean-shaven head. After an apparent bad call by the umpire, he would yank off his hat and throw it on the ground. This was followed by yanking off his wig. It was said to be a crowd favorite.[194]

A seven-game exhibition schedule was announced, four contests at Rickwood Field and three away.[195] The first game was against the New York Cubans in a New Orleans war bond appeal.[196] Most exhibitions were unreported.

Opening Day was Sunday, May 4, with Cleveland at Rickwood. Pregame ceremonies included music by the Parker High School band and a flag-raising by black veterans.[197] Emory O. Jackson, in his "Hits and Bits" column in the *Birmingham World*, was wary of the flag-raising choice. Citing two previous debacles, he recommended the Boys Scouts instead.[198] Jackson's concerns proved not to be unfounded: "Unit Commander Archie Williams' Legionnaires showed improvement in their flag-raising ceremony. But James 'Seaboard' Story came near marring it with his taps blowing, take that bugle away from him."

"Prof. E.J. Oliver's opening pitch was wild," wrote Jackson. Not only that, but fans started throwing pillows at some point during the game and the "police were helpless."[199]

There were some positives. "Squalling commercials over the public address system has been cut out." The ballpark announcer, J.B. Sims, was pushing "a good conduct campaign among the fans," apparently referencing drunkenness and rowdiness in past years. It was further noted that the fans now rose during the seventh inning stretch. It was not reported if fans sang "Take Me Out to the Ball Game."[200]

On the field, the Black Barons divided the games with Cleveland. The Buckeyes won the opener, 4–0. Birmingham won the nightcap, 9–3, with Earl Bumpus pitching a four-hitter.[201] Two Montgomery games were also split. The defending NAL champions began their first long road trip with a 2–2 record.[202]

The travels lasted three weeks and included a double-header loss at Kansas City and two wins from Memphis in Indianapolis.[203] A witness to the Indianapolis games was Donnie Bush, president of the white Indianapolis American Association

Catcher Herman Bell, a fixture with the Black Barons from 1945 to 1950 (T.H. Hayes Collection, Memphis and Shelby Room, Memphis Public Library and Information Center).

club. Bush, a former major leaguer, had high praise for the Black Barons: "That's a great ball club, and it's full of hustle. They'll win practically all the close ones with that sort of dash."[204]

During the trip, Radcliffe became ill and spent some time in the hospital. By May 20 he was back with the team, although again it was said that he would not do any catching this year.[205] By early June, he was no longer with the club, having been traded to Kansas City.[206]

Birmingham returned home against "Hoss" Walker and Cincinnati on May 27. The team was still hurting at second base without Sampson.[207] "Birmingham has felt the loss of Tommy Sampson ... keenly, and Manager W.S. Welch is still casting around desperately for an experienced player to plug that gap," wrote one sportswriter.[208]

But the home stand was a good one. The Black Barons won, 6–5 and 7–4, on Sunday. They split two in Montgomery during the week.[209]

The following Sunday, they were beaten twice by Kansas City.[210] In fairness, the club had a rash of injuries. As was often the case in the 1940s, when there were problems, the solution was usually Piper Davis: "When Winfield Welch sees a real emergency, he usually calls on Piper Davis to fill the bill, and Piper usually comes through with colors flying. Forced to play a patched-up lineup against the Kansas City Monarchs, he has thrown Piper in at second base and the Alabama-bred Negro looked like he was born and raised at the keystone."[211]

Lorenzo "Piper" Davis was one of the Black Barons' all-time best players, as well as a manager in both black baseball and the integrated minor leagues (courtesy Faye Davis and Birmingham Public Library Archives).

Against Kansas City, Welch had to put pitcher Saylor at first base. A bright spot was Steele, who had five hits.[212]

Birmingham played a much stronger game on Wednesday night. Newberry held the Monarchs to seven hits in 10 innings, but Birmingham batters fared little better. The game was a scoreless tie, called around midnight "after numerous protested decisions and near fist fights between the players." Umpire W.J. Moore's calls on balls and strikes were a particularly contentious issue. Kansas City took a 1–0 lead in the top of the eleventh. With Birmingham threatening to tie it in the bottom of the inning, another protested decision brought the game to an unsatisfactory close. A scuffle broke out between Davis and Kansas City catcher Chico Renfroe. When players on both sides rushed to join the melee, the game was called, reverting to the score at the end of the last completed inning.[213]

The following night they played in Nashville, beginning a month-long road trip for Birmingham. They played somewhat better away, winning a double-header from Chicago at Wrigley Field. Newberry threw a six-hit shutout in the first game, and Willie Young and Buster Markham teamed up to win the second. Young held Chicago to four hits in the first four innings, and Markham completed the 5–3 win.[214] Young brought back memories of "Wing" Maddox from the 1920s. Young was born without a right hand. He fielded much as Maddox did, catching the ball, shoving the glove under the bad arm, and extracting the ball with the left. Most of Young's career was in the Birmingham industrial league, although he did play a year or two in the Negro Southern League as well as one season with the Black Barons.[215]

The second game was played amid discord. After Britton hit a double to give Birmingham a 5–3 lead, "the game was held up for several minutes" while Chicago players argued that it was a foul ball. Earlier in the game, Chicago outfielder John Smith "kicked himself out of the game ... when he proceeded to abuse [umpire] Virgil Blueitt over a called strike. There were no police in either dugout and no protection for the umpires. Smith refused to go, and it took some persuasion on the part of his teammates before he finally decided to allow the game to proceed."[216] Birmingham played without pitcher Huber, who broke his ankle on May 27. Shortstop Wilson played in Chicago although he had suffered a broken nose in the same game.[217]

There was a consequence to the bickering. The following weekend a similar melee ensued when Memphis played the American Giants. Soon after, park management announced that there would be "no more Negro baseball at Wrigley field." Ostensibly the reason was a new rental fee of $5,000 per event. But "the recent fight at Wrigley field ... is believed to have hastened the decision of the Wrigley field management," reported the *Chicago Defender*.[218]

When Birmingham returned to Chicago in July, the games were at Comiskey Park.[219]

As usual, while the team was away, owner Hayes arranged for another black ball double-header at Rickwood. The June 24 benefit game matched the independent Chicago Brown Bombers with the Fort Benning Tigers. Part of the proceeds went to the black Elks Club to help take the Parker High School band to the Elks' convention in Pittsburgh.[220]

In September, Hayes arranged another double-header matching industrial league all-stars against a similar team from the resurrected Negro Southern League. Hayes, ever the skillful promoter, said if the local team won, he would give them a shot at the Black Barons the following Sunday.[221] The Negro Southern League, dormant since 1936, had reorganized in the spring.[222]

In June, Birmingham met the Cuban Stars before a crowd of 14,000 in New York. The Cubans won the first game, 4–0. The winning pitcher, holding Birmingham to six hits, was the great Luis Tiant, Sr., who was said to have first beaten the Black Barons in 1930 as a member of the original Cuban Stars. Tommy Louden's two-run homer for the Cubans broke Jimmie Newberry's 38-inning scoreless string. The Black Barons won the nightcap, 6–2, on Davis's grand slam homer.[223]

The box score from the April 29, 1930, game at Rickwood Field shows Tiant as the losing pitcher in a 6–1 Birmingham win.[224] Tiant's career spanned more than 20 years. His son, Luis Tiant, Jr., pitched in the major leagues for 19 years, most prominently with the Boston Red Sox. In 1975, after Tiant Sr. had not seen his son for fifteen years, Cuban leader Fidel Castro allowed him and his wife to leave Cuba to see their son pitch in the World Series.[225]

On July 1, back home for a series with Memphis, Newberry threw a five-hitter and Birmingham won the first game, 5–1. Earl Bumpus pitched a six-hit 7–3 win in the second game.[226] The next day, in Montgomery, Birmingham won, 7–2. Back at Rickwood on Tuesday, Birmingham won, 12–7. Davis hit a home run.[227]

The Fourth of July holiday games were played in Memphis. Birmingham made it five straight in the first game, beating the Red Sox 4–1 on John Huber's five-hitter. Memphis took the second game, 7–1. The games ended the first half of the season.[228]

For much of July and August, all reports on the Black Barons were culled from newspapers in other cities. A printer's strike shut down Birmingham's three daily newspapers. The *Birmingham World* was not affected by the strike, but it covered very few games in any detail. The range of the missing daily newspapers was from July 12 through August 15.[229]

Cleveland (31–9) won the first half with ease, threatened only by Birmingham (26–11). They were the only two clubs over .500 in the final first-half standings.[230]

The second half opened with yet another long road trip. Games were played in Arkansas, Kentucky, Indiana, Illinois, Ohio, Michigan, Tennessee, Delaware, and Virginia. In Portsmouth, Virginia, they lost to the New York Cubans, 4–3. The game was not pleasant for the Black Barons, but apparently it was a real treat for fans, according to writer Lem Graves, Jr., who wrote: "Long-suffering Tidewater baseball fans, who have endured some pretty sad baseball for most of this year, were partially rewarded for their faithfulness here at City Stadium Wednesday night when the New York Cubans and the Birmingham Black Barons staged a hum-dinger of a baseball fame. The Cubans won the thriller, 4 to 3, in the last half of the ninth inning."[231]

Virginia fans did not get to see Piper Davis play, though. On July 17, he was fined $50 and suspended indefinitely by League President Martin. Davis struck umpire Jimmy Thompson in a game at Cleveland the night before. "I am extremely sorry to have to deny Davis' services to the West team, to hurt Birmingham's chances of winning the second half but it is my duty, regardless of how painful it may be, to stamp out these uncalled for assaults on umpires by ball players in my league." Martin said he had tried to be lenient with the $50 fines, but he felt like owners were paying those fines, thus leaving the players basically unpunished. The suspension of Davis was obviously to be an example to other players.[232]

"I am backed by the fans who pay the freight," Martin continued. "Davis stands suspended and it not only means that he may not be able to play with his club the balance of the season but he will not have the suspension lifted until I am firmly convinced that he will deport himself like a ball player and a gentleman should."[233]

The Black Barons returned home on August 19 against Cleveland. In a pregame ceremony, the 1943 and 1944 pennants were raised to great enthusiasm before a crowd of 7,000. Unfortunately, Birmingham lost the first game, 9–2. The second game was called after nine innings, tied 4–4.[234] In Montgomery, Birmingham won, 8–4, but Tommy Sampson, finally back with the team, was spiked.[235]

The next road trip, poorly reported, included Louisiana, Mississippi, Illinois, Indiana, New York, Maryland, Missouri, and Tennessee. In mid–September in Chicago, they played well. Boone shut out the American Giants, 8–0.[236] The following day, they won twice. Newberry won the first game, 5–2. Frank "Groundhog" Thompson, a 5-foot-4-inch left-hander, threw a six-inning shutout in the second game. They were Birmingham's seventh and eighth straight wins, although the streak was too late to help the club make the playoffs.[237]

Back home on September 20 they played Chicago again. Despite two pennants in a row, the *Birmingham News* reported that the Black Barons had "failed to hit the target this year, due largely to injuries and players jumping the club." Johnny Britton went to Mexico for a short time. Piper Davis's suspension hurt the team's competitiveness, also.[238]

Cleveland won both halves, and went on to do something the Black Barons had not managed the previous two years. The Buckeyes beat the Homestead Gays in the Negro World Series. In the final second-half standings, Birmingham (13–19) was next to last.[239]

Most of the season was spent on the road, but Birmingham fans got to see their team again in the fall. The autumn schedule included three straight wins from the New York Black Yankees.[240]

On October 7, Artie Wilson, Ed Steele, and Herman Bassett were named starters for the South squad in a North–South All-Star game in New Orleans. The North team won, 7–1. Wilson and Bassett were hitless and Steele did not play.[241]

Meanwhile, the war was over. Germany had surrendered on April 29, signing an unconditional surrender document on May 7. Japan surrendered on August 15 after two of its cities had been destroyed by atomic bombs.[242]

The baseball world could look forward to a return to peacetime seasons in 1946.

20

Two Seasons with
Tommy Sampson (1946–47)

1946

It was a grateful nation, a grateful world, and a grateful baseball community that looked toward spring training in 1946. The war was over. Soldiers, many of them ballplayers, were returning to their homes and families.

For black Americans there was also an historic milestone. A young man, who had played shortstop for the Kansas City Monarchs in 1945, was embarking on a bold venture that would change baseball forever. Leaving the Negro American League and joining the Brooklyn Dodgers' Montreal farm club was all-round UCLA athlete Jackie Robinson. Just one year later he would be wearing Dodger blue.[1]

The signing of Robinson signaled an effort to establish a more cooperative relationship between Organized Baseball and the Negro leagues. But there was tension in that relationship. Cum Posey, co-owner of the Homestead Grays, told the *Pittsburgh Courier* that white baseball had long criticized the practice of the Negro leagues of allowing club owners to serve in league positions such as president. Baseball Commissioner A.B. "Happy" Chandler said a few weeks later that Negro baseball need to get its house in order.[2]

Posey, one of the founding fathers of Negro leagues baseball, would not live to see Robinson's debut and the promised cooperation between his colleagues and Organized Baseball.

He died of lung cancer in March. Hundreds of people, including the mayor of Pittsburgh, paid their respects at the funeral service. Sports Editor Wendell Smith wrote a 36-line poem titled "Game Called" in honor of his friend.[3]

Robinson was not the only ballplayer trying to cut through baseball's racial fabric in 1946. Another who tried with much less success was Eddie Klep, a young white ballplayer from Erie, Pennsylvania. His failed try at integration happened at Rickwood Field with hardly anyone in Birmingham being aware of it.

As for the 1946 season, it was one of changes for Birmingham. In January, the *Chicago Defender* reported the resignation of Winfield Welch as Black Barons manager. His four-year run had been the most competitive in Black Barons history. In 1942 they challenged the Kansas City Monarchs, finishing second. They won pennants in 1943 and 1944. And despite numerous injuries and other problems, they were contenders for much of the 1945 season. On a personal level, Welch managed twice in the East–West All-Star game.[4]

Owner Tom Hayes named popular infielder Tommy Sampson the new manager. It

The 1946 team in a Photograph taken at the ballpark in Memphis (T.H. Hayes Collection, Memphis and Shelby Room, Memphis Public Library and Information Center).

was a logical decision.[5] A native of Calhoun, Alabama, Sampson had one of the longest careers with the Black Barons, playing from 1940 through 1947. A six-year starter at second base, he had played in four consecutive East–West All-Star games.

He grew up in Raleigh, West Virginia, playing semipro baseball and working as a coal miner. A mining accident cost him his right index finger, which later "caused his throws to first base to break unnaturally, presenting a bit of a problem for some first basemen." He later played with teams in Virginia and North Carolina until he was discovered and signed by Birmingham in 1940. Under Manager Candy Jim Taylor his skills were refined. A third baseman in his younger days, he suffered an arm injury that impaired his throwing ability. Moving to second base gave him a shorter throw to first base. It was said that Sampson had such a strong arm that he made his throws to first underhanded, not having to come out of a crouch to throw.[6]

Training camp opened at Sloss Field with Hayes excited over the team's prospects: "The player situation has been greatly relieved by the return of ex-service men. We are bringing them in from as far as Chicago, Dallas and New York for a trial."[7]

There was a rumor early in the year that someone was forming an independent team in Birmingham that might drain away talent from the Black Barons. Indeed, the rumor was fueled when Ted "Double Duty" Radcliffe and Winfield Welch passed through the city in mid–January. It was immediately reported that they were in the city on a talent hunt.[8] But it was nothing more than a rumor.

The Negro American League lineup was the same as 1945 except that the home city of the Clowns was now Indianapolis instead of Cincinnati. The other clubs were Birmingham, Chicago, Cleveland, Kansas City, and Memphis.[9]

Sampson would be a playing manager, but Hayes cautioned that the second baseman's playing time might be limited: "Sampson will be able to serve as playing manager part of the time, but he may find the going too strenuous to be in there at second base every game. While he recovered from his auto accident, he, of course, is not as rugged a type of athlete as he used to be."[10]

Sampson opened camp with about 25 players, but said he expected about three dozen eventually. This lot would be pared down to 18 by Opening Day. He was assisted by Sam Rush, manager of the independent Hilldale, Pennsylvania, Yellowjackets. Rush said it was he who helped Sampson develop into a great second baseman.[11] The exhibition schedule included games with the 1945 Negro World Series champion Cleveland Buckeyes, Ethiopian Clowns, and Baltimore Elite Giants. As the Cleveland games neared, Lyman Bostock reported, back from military service. Piper Davis and Ed Steele were holdouts. New players "looking exceptionally good" included outfielders Edward Palmer and Howard Gay. Palmer was from the Birmingham industrial league. Gay had played "great ball" for the Great Lakes service team. Two outfield candidates were Malcolm Smith of Biloxi, Mississippi, and "Dandy" Green of Rushton, Louisiana.[12] There was talk that Davis might follow Winfield Welch to whatever new position he might take.[13]

Others in camp included Johnny Britton, Lester Lockett, Nathaniel Pollard, and Jimmie Newberry. However, Britton was reported to be "dissatisfied and desires to be either traded or released outright."[14]

There were also some sad departures. Sampson announced that pitchers Johnny "Buster" Markham and Al Saylor had been released outright. Frank "Groundhog" Thompson, another 1945 pitcher, had joined a new Cincinnati club.[15] Markham got on with an independent team later, but Saylor's career was apparently over.[16]

The exhibition season opened on Sunday, March 24. Reporting was sparse, but Birmingham won the opener "behind effective pitching," though it "lacked power at the plate" in the second game. Both scores were 6–1.[17] But the real drama of the day happened before a pitch was even thrown, making the scant reporting on the games even more remarkable.

Over the winter, Cleveland owner Ernie Wright had quietly signed Eddie Klep, a 25-year-old white left-handed pitcher, to a contract with the Buckeyes. Klep was with the team when they walked out on the field in Birmingham to warm up. Here is how the *Pittsburgh Courier* reported what happened:

> All went well until the word started spreading around that Klep—A WHITE MAN—was playing with the colored Clevelanders. So, on Sunday afternoon at Rickwood Field, while Klep was warming up prior to the Bucks' game with Birmingham's Black Barons, two of the town's "bulliest" cops approached Jimmie Jones, the club's press agent and asked:
> "Do y'all have a white boy on yo' team?"
> The answer was in the affirmative.
> "Git him out of here … and quick!" they demanded. "We don't have no mixin' down here!"
> When asked whether the white player could remain in the dugout, the cops answered gruffly:
> "No! He can't sit in the dugout or anyplace else with you. If you want to game to go on, git him off the field and out of them ball clothes or there won't be any game."[18]

Klep returned to the hotel and changed into street clothes. When he returned to the ballpark, he attempted to sit behind the Cleveland dugout but was ordered to move over to the white section.[19] Teammate Al Smith recalled that the next day, the Buckeyes went to Atlanta for an exhibition game and Klep was allowed to play.[20] It seems likely that Ernie Wright was simply making a point. In an article by publicist Jimmie Jones, Wright was quoted as saying: "If Branch Rickey and others of organized baseball can choose material of their liking in order to produce a winning ball club and without questions of race or color despite the Southern 'Jim-Crow' tradition, then why can't I do the same?"[21]

But while Jackie Robinson, a college graduate, was carefully chosen to break the Organized Ball color barrier, Eddie Klep was just happenstance. His career was brief and marginal. He had played mostly semipro ball in Pennsylvania and never went beyond that after the Cleveland experience. He appeared in one game for the Buckeyes in 1946, pitching seven innings against the Chicago American Giants in Grand Rapids, Michigan.[22] But his ex-wife, Ethel Kelp, said Eddie did love baseball. "That ball playing, that was his life…. That boy didn't work if he didn't have to. He had a bad drinking problem, and that didn't help any."[23]

Klep died in 1981 in a state institution in Los Angeles of conditions related to alcohol abuse. His remains were returned to Erie for burial in the family plot.[24] Asheville, North Carolina, singer-songwriter Chuck Brodsky immortalized Klep in "The Ballad of Eddie Klep" on his 1996 compact disc *Letters in the Dirt*.[25]

Just why there was no mention of the Klep incident in Birmingham papers is a matter of speculation. Since he was removed before the game, it is possible that the local writers were unaware of what happened. It is equally possible that they were well aware of it and chose not to report on it. A similar event in 1950 was covered by the local press.[26] Details of that incident are recorded in Chapter 22. However, by 1950, many black players had been signed by white league teams. Racial barriers were rapidly dropping.

When the next exhibition games arrived, it was obvious that Birmingham fans had accepted the changes with the team and put the disappointing 1945 finish behind them. A large crowd came to see the Indianapolis Clowns, still often identified as Cincinnati-based. The Clowns were managed by former Black Baron Jesse "Hoss" Walker. Sampson, experimenting with lineups to fill troublesome positions, moved Piper Davis to center field. Sterling Talley was given a shot at second base in his place.

Birmingham won both games, 3–2 and 3–1, before a crowd estimated at 6,500. It was a remarkable turnout given the fact that there was a major streetcar and bus strike under way. "Fans walked, trucked and autoed to the game in amazing numbers. This city is paralyzed by a transportation shutdown. It remains a mystery how so many came under such handicaps," reported the *Chicago Defender*.[27]

An encouraging exhibition performance came in Atlanta. Birmingham beat Baltimore, 4–3, and Atlanta, 9–2, in a three-team double-header.[28]

The final exhibition games were against the Chattanooga Choo Choos, managed by Felix "Chin" Manning, a popular former industrial league player. Two games were set for Rickwood Field. The pregame article also reported that Walter Bester, a Bessemer sandlot pitcher, had thrown a no-hitter for Birmingham against a Lanett team the previous week.[29] Only one of the Chattanooga games was reported, an 8–2 Birmingham win. With it, the team was said to have won five in a row and 18 of 21.[30]

Opening Day was in Cleveland on Sunday, May 5. Birmingham split a double-header with the defending champions, and then lost one in Toledo the following night.[31]

The home opener at Rickwood was set for Thursday night, May 9, rather than the traditional Sunday double-header. Cleveland, with former Black Barons Johnny Cowan and

Parnell Woods on the roster, was the opponent. Selected to throw out the first pitch was William "Sweet" Conley, a widely known Fourth Avenue bail bondsman.[32] "He has the heft and popularity to [do] a good job, both from the side of the gate and the plate. A better thrower might have been chosen, but not a better Black Baron booster," reported Emory O. Jackson.[33] The honor had originally been offered to the Rev. J.W. Goodgame, who turned it down. "It is understood that he will be in the midst of a revival, although this may not be the reason for his turn-down," wrote Jackson cryptically.[34] And again, the Parker High School band provided music. The flag-raising ceremony was handled by the Julius Ellsberry Veterans of Foreign Wars Post.[35] Birmingham Mayor Cooper Green proclaimed the event Black Baron Day in Birmingham.[36]

With 7,000 boisterous fans cheering them on, the Black Barons scored three runs in the first inning and two more in the second and won, 7–2. Jehosie "Jay" Heard, a new left-hander, held the Buckeyes to eight hits. Like so many Black Barons over the years, he came

Birmingham's strength during the 1940s was due, in some measure, to a stable of fine pitchers. Front row, from left: Nat Pollard, Jehosie Heard, Jimmie Newberry, and Bill Greason. Back row: Sam Williams, Alonzo Perry and Bill Powell (T.H. Hayes Collection, Memphis and Shelby Room, Memphis Public Library and Information Center).

out of the city industrial league. The *Birmingham World* reported a much bigger crowd, listing it "an estimated 11,000 fans."[37]

The following night Birmingham made it two in a row with a 4–3 victory.[38]

Another big crowd was expected for the Sunday double-header at Rickwood. Manager Sampson offered the following lineups:

Artie Wilson, ss	Lyman Bostock, 1b
John Britton, 3b	Pepper Bassett, c
Piper Davis, 2b	James Reynolds or Hamp Johnson, cf
Lester Lockett, lf	Jimmy Newberry, p
Ed Steele, rf	Nat Pollard, p[39]

It was three straight wins after Black Barons won the first game, 5–2. But Cleveland was not to be dismissed so lightly. Pounding out 19 hits off four Birmingham pitchers, the defending champions won the seven-inning second game, 15–2. Birmingham had only five hits. The next night they played in Gadsden.[40]

Birmingham's black community was staggered in mid–May by the sudden death of Oscar W. Adams. His ties to the ball club included serving as team president and on the Negro Southern League board of directors in 1926, but his baseball connections were a small part of his service. For 28 years he had written the "What Negroes Are Doing" column in the *Birmingham News*, chronicling church and social activities. He was scheduled to receive a gold watch as the newspaper's oldest employee at the end of the year. He had also been editor and publisher of the *Birmingham Reporter*, a black newspaper that folded around 1934 after 40 years of operation. He was both a state and local leader in the Knights of Pythias, an important fraternal group at the time.[41] His son, Oscar Adams, Jr., later became the first black elected to statewide office in Alabama, serving on the Alabama Supreme Court from 1980 to 1993.[42]

Birmingham's next series was in Memphis. The first game on Thursday night, May 16, was preceded by the coronation of the king and queen of the Cotton Makers Jubilee, a local festival. Composer W.C. Handy, with trumpet in hand, led the Jubilee parade from Handy Park to Russwood Park, home of the Red Sox. The Jubilee was a black counterpart to white Memphis's famous annual Cotton Carnival.[43]

The two clubs were battling for second place, two games behind Kansas City.[44] Memphis won a tight contest with Johnny Huber holding his old team to four hits.[45]

The Friday game was rained out, and they split a double-header on Sunday. Despite home runs by Piper Davis and Pepper Bassett, Memphis won the first game, 8–6. Birmingham won the second game, 9–4, with Nat Pollard on the mound.[46]

The next weekend, the Red Sox came to Rickwood. With the visitors was first baseman Olan "Jelly" Taylor, "after being a sensation in Army baseball, back on first with his famous floppy-eared glove." Taylor, a left-handed first baseman, was noted for his fielding, which sometimes included "comic antics and flashy glovework."[47]

The series opened on Sunday, May 26, with a Birmingham sweep, 7–6 and 6–5. Ed Steele was five-for-eight for Birmingham.[48]

As the first month of the season came to a close, Emory O. Jackson reported that the team was doing poorly at the plate, batting a weak .199, last in the league. Only Artie Wilson was hitting above .300. On the other hand, he said the team led the league in fielding, and the pitching "has held up better than expected."[49]

On Monday and Tuesday, the series moved to Montgomery and Atlanta, where Memphis won a pair of games. In Montgomery, they bombed the Black Barons, 20–8, then won, 7–5, in Atlanta.[50] On Wednesday night the two teams fought to a 13–13 tie in Gadsden. The game was called after nine innings, not because of weather or a curfew, but rather because of an equipment failure. The two teams hit two triples, six doubles, six home runs, and numerous foul balls. When the last home run or foul ball left the ballpark in the ninth, the umpires realized they had no more baseballs and the game was called.[51] Birmingham won the final game, 4–3, at Rickwood, scoring two runs in the bottom of the ninth.[52]

Back on the road, Birmingham won five straight from Chicago, most at neutral sites. After losing the opener on Sunday, they won the second game, 2–1. At neutral sites, they won 13–3, in Davenport, Iowa; 6–3, in South Bend, Indiana; 6–2, at Cincinnati; and 11–2 in Chicago. Davis and Steele hit home runs in the final game.[53]

Despite the 13- and 11-run outbursts against Chicago, the Black Barons were still not hitting well overall. Manager Sampson turned to "adventurous base-running" to get an edge, with the double steal becoming a frequent ploy.[54]

There were also injuries. Lyman Bostock was spiked on the ankle just as he seemed to be coming out of a hitting slump, and outfielder James Reynolds was "on the ailing list." Bostock had "an ugly six-inch long, inch-deep cut" that was not healing well, probably because he didn't get stitches to close the wound. Then Sampson, filling in for Bostock, was spiked in the Chicago series, and pitcher Al Gipson also fell ill.[55]

After the Chicago games, it was on to Memphis, where they lost a Sunday double-header. "Chin" Evans and Willie Hutchinson outdueled Jimmie Newberry and Nat Pollard. In Little Rock on Monday, Birmingham won, 9–6, on Freddie Shepard's three-run homer.[56]

After the Memphis games, Birmingham stepped away from league play for a series with the Montgomery Red Sox. When the Negro Southern League was revived in 1945, the only Alabama team was the Mobile Black Bears.[57] In 1946, league ball returned to Montgomery. The Montgomery Grey Sox were gone, but a new team owned by Jake Whatley gained a franchise as the Montgomery Dodgers.[58] Games were played at both Cramton Bowl and Hornet Stadium on the Alabama State campus. Obviously inspired by Brooklyn's signing of Jackie Robinson, Whatley appropriated the Dodgers nickname for his new team. It appears that Brooklyn, albeit likely flattered, was protective of the trademark. Whatley soon backed off and renamed his team the Red Sox, apparently a more generic name. A logical assumption is that the Brooklyn club's attorney requested the change.[59]

Birmingham faced the Red Sox in Jackson, Mississippi, Montgomery and Birmingham, winning three straight from a tougher-than-expected opponent. A fourth game in Gadsden was not reported.

On June 16, Birmingham played a double-header in Cincinnati and swept the home team, 7–3 and 5–4. Artie Wilson was four-for-six in the first game. The nightcap went 11 innings with the winning run coming on doubles by Freddie Shepard and Tommy Sampson. "Jay" Heard and Jimmie Newberry were the winning pitchers.[60] The two clubs then paired for an exhibition swing through Illinois and Indiana.

The Black Barons returned to Birmingham the following Sunday for two games with Chicago. Birmingham won the opener, 5–4, in 10 innings. Gipson, relieving Newberry, got the win. Chicago won the nightcap, 3–1. Birmingham's run came on a solo homer by Steele.[61]

The two clubs then played in Gadsden, Montgomery, and New Orleans before returning to Rickwood. There was no report out of New Orleans, but Birmingham won the other three games. After Birmingham won on Thursday night, the two teams went to Belvoir, Illinois.[62]

By dominating the Chicago series, the Black Barons (18–11) had moved up to second place behind Kansas City (19–5). A chance to take the lead came as Birmingham faced the league-leading Monarchs in a crucial series around the Fourth of July holiday.[63]

Birmingham's slim first-half hopes were decimated by the much stronger Monarchs, who won three out of four games. The Fourth of July game at Rickwood Field was a holiday only for Kansas City, which won, 15–1, getting 20 hits off Newberry, Curtis Hollingsworth and Gipson. Birmingham had only three hits.[64] Sampson, said to be hurting for outfielders, had obtained John Henry Thomas from the Mobile Black Bears. He was burned several times while playing too deep. The Monarchs "dropped several blows for hits."[65] And the team soon was hurting for a backup catcher as Herman Bell turned in his uniform. The reason was said be "a pay-ache." And, as if all of that weren't enough bad luck, Manager Tommy Sampson was fined $100 for his role in a fight with an umpire in Kansas City.[66]

After the Kansas City series, the Black Barons were gone for much of July. There were league games in Kansas City and Chicago as well as travels to the Northeast. In Syracuse, they were shut out twice by Cleveland. In New York City, they lost to the New York Cubans in a three-team double-header at the Polo Grounds.[67]

There was a brief return to Rickwood for a double-header with Winfield Welch's Cincinnati Crescents. Birmingham treated its former manager unkindly, beating the visitors, 4–0 and 4–2. Bostock hit a home run in the second game. Meanwhile, catcher Herman Bell, apparently not finding any other work, returned to the team after a week or so.[68]

Early second-half standings showed Birmingham in third place behind Indianapolis and Chicago, but just a half game out of first. Although no regular Birmingham player was hitting over .300, first baseman Bostock had shaken off his slump and raised his batting average to .294. Steele was leading the league in runs scored with 38.[69]

If there was any question of owner Hayes being well-heeled financially, it was probably dispelled by reports that he was flying from Memphis to Birmingham to watch Black Barons games. A licensed pilot, Hayes also flew at least once from Birmingham to Gadsden for a game.[70]

When they returned home on Sunday, August 4, for a double-header with Chicago, there were some new names on the roster. Lee Moody, an outfielder, had been acquired from Kansas City. They already added John Thomas, the outfielder from Mobile. The Chicago roster included "a Birmingham battery," pitcher Herman "Red" Howard and catcher "Jumbo" Tolbert. Howard played for Birmingham in 1937 and 1940. Tolbert played at Parker High School when it was known as Industrial High.[71]

The double-header was divided. Chicago won the first game, 7–3, and Birmingham the second, 2–0. Jehosie Heard gave up just one hit in the five-inning nightcap. Birmingham won four of the six games with Chicago, taking wins in Gadsden, Huntsville, and Montgomery. The other loss was at Rickwood in a 12-inning game.[72]

The home stand continued on Sunday, August 11, with the Cincinnati-Indianapolis Clowns. Nat Pollard threw a three-hitter to win the first game, 6–2. The Clowns won the second game, 7–5, although Pepper Bassett had a home run for Birmingham.[73]

Three Black Barons were selected for the annual East–West game. Actually, it was "games" again in 1946, with a Friday night contest played at Griffith Stadium in Washington, D.C., and the traditional Sunday afternoon game at Comiskey Park in Chicago.[74] The two-game format had been used in 1942, also. Selected from Birmingham were shortstop Artie Wilson, second baseman Piper Davis, and right fielder Ed Steele. The East won the Washington game, 6–3, and the West won in Chicago, 4–1. Wilson and Davis had a hit and scored a run in each game. Steele did not play.[75]

In August, the Black Barons played a special game with the industrial league all-stars. Gipson and Newberry combined for a 1–0 win, holding the stars to just two hits. The only run of the game came on a fourth-inning home run by Eddie Sampson. None of the newspaper stories suggested that he was related to Manager Sampson.[76] The following night they beat the All-Stars, 9–7, in Montgomery.[77]

Cleveland returned to Rickwood on August 18, winning the opener, 8–3. The second game was a 2–2 tie.[78] The following Sunday, Birmingham won two at Cleveland, 4–2 and 4–0. Pepper Bassett had a home run in the second game.[79] En route to Cleveland Birmingham played a game at Chattanooga, losing 4–0.[80]

Birmingham ended league play against Memphis. Going into the games, Birmingham was reported to be 14–11 but not a threat to league-leading Kansas City.[81] Double-headers with Memphis were scheduled in Birmingham on Sunday and in Memphis on Labor Day. At Rickwood, Birmingham won the first game, 1–0, as Nat Pollard beat Dan Bankhead, the former Birmingham star who was the winning pitcher in the East–West game. Memphis won the second, 4–2. Catcher Casey Jones hit a three-run homer to win the game. Pepper Bassett and Emanuel "Eddie" Sampson each homered for Birmingham.[82] Birmingham won both games at Memphis and also a Tuesday game in Little Rock.

But Kansas City was again dominant in the Negro American League, winning both halves of the season. They carried the Newark Eagles to the limit before losing the Negro World Series four games to three.[83]

On September 27, Birmingham beat Memphis, 3–0, in a seven-inning exhibition game at Rickwood. A new pitcher named Barney Higgins held the visitors to two hits.[84]

The Black Barons' season ended on Sunday, September 29, with a "post-season" double-header with Memphis. The two old rivals had missed the playoffs, but they could at least "determine the best Negro baseball club in Dixie," according to the *Birmingham News*.[85] C.L. Moore's Asheville Blues might have argued that point. Although they had lost a 5–3 decision to the Black Barons in July, the NSL champs had a phenomenal 48–12 record that included triumphs over non-league foes such as the Pittsburgh Crawfords and New York Black Yankees.[86]

Manager Sampson announced the following lineup:

Artie Wilson, ss	Eddie Sampson, cf
John Britton, 3b	Pepper Bassett, c
Piper Davis, 2b	Nat Pollard, p
Lyman Bostock, 1b	Jimmy Newberry, p
Ed Steele, rf	Jehosie Heard, p
Lee Moody, lf	Bill Powell, p[87]

The occasion was, also, a finally consummated "Tommy Sampson Day." Two other attempts to honor the manager had been rained out. Sampson was properly celebrated with Birmingham defeating the Memphis Red Sox, 5–4, in the first game and playing a six-inning 3–3 tie in the second. Sampson enjoyed his day. He had five hits, scored four runs, stole a base, and was errorless at third base. Freddie Shepard also had a great day with six hits in seven at-bats. Owner Hayes presented Sampson with a traveling bag and other gifts. Mrs. Ritta Williams, called the Black Barons No. 1 fan, paid tribute to Sampson, the umpires, management and players.[88]

But 1946 baseball at Rickwood was not completely over. On Sunday, October 13, the Dixie Dream Game was scheduled between North and South all-star teams from the Negro National League and Negro American League, respectively. Tommy Sampson, Britton, and Pollard were on the South roster. North players included former Black Barons Jerry Benjamin, John Thomas, and Sammy Bankhead. Thomas hit a home run as the North team won, 6–4.[89] The game, played before a sparse crowd, was delayed 35 minutes due a wrangle over the disbursement of gate receipts.[90]

Two Birmingham players, Artie Wilson and Ed Steele, were selected by promoter Abe Saperstein to play on a post-season all-star team. The team was to fly to Hawaii and play a 14-game series with island teams. Also on the roster were two of the Bankhead brothers, Fred and Dan.[91]

A final odd note on the 1946 season: Traveling secretary Freddie Shepard was pressed into service as an out outfielder late in the season, a position he had played for Birmingham the previous year. He was replaced in the front office by L.J. Graham of Memphis, a former USO worker and baseball player at Atlanta College.[92]

1947

With Tommy Sampson back as manager, the Black Barons stepped up their spring regimen. The team left Birmingham on March 9 for their spring training camp in Orlando, Florida. Daytona Beach and Tampa also sought to host the team. They traveled in style on "a new bus of the latest type so the Black Barons will make their 1947 tour with every comfort and convenience."[93] The bus developed unexplained trouble before going too far, however. The team stopped at Alabama State's Hornet Field in Montgomery for its first workout.[94]

The exhibition schedule included games with the Homestead Grays, Asheville Blues, Kansas City Monarchs, and Philadelphia Stars. The regular season was scheduled to open on Saturday, May 10, with the 1946 Negro American League champion Monarchs at Rickwood Field.

Returning players present in mid–April included Piper Davis, Artie Wilson, John Britton, Ed Steele, Pepper Bassett, Herman Bell, Bill Powell, Jimmy Newberry, Nathaniel Pollard, Curtis Hollinsworth, and Jehosie Heard. Trying out were first baseman Sam Williams, catcher Earl Ashby, and outfielders Eli Chism and Walter Thomas.[95] Gone was first baseman Lyman Bostock, traded to Chicago for Thomas.[96]

Pitcher William Powell, a mound mainstay from 1946 to 1952 (courtesy Faye Davis and Birmingham Public Library Archives).

Another newcomer seeking a position on the club was catcher Johnny Taylor, who had played with the Boston Blues, a team in the United States League. Also trying out were two local youths, Andrew Talbert and Elisha Perry; center fielder James Brizzle from Arkadelphia, Arkansas; and outfielder Norman Robinson from Baltimore.[97]

The 1947 Negro American League lineup would again be Birmingham, Chicago, Cleveland, Cincinnati-Indianapolis, Kansas City, and Memphis.[98] The *Chicago Defender* reported that a franchise had also been granted for the Detroit Senators. The ownership included Jesse Owens and Winfield Welch. The Cincinnati Crescents, owned by Abe Saperstein, sought a franchise, but it was denied.[99] Saperstein, nevertheless, was still involved in the league. He was business partners with Black Barons owner Tom Hayes, Jr., and handled much of the business end of the club.[100] The dual city franchise of Cincinnati-Indianapolis was a precursor of what would be commonplace when the Negro leagues began their downward slide in the 1950s.

Both the NAL and the Negro National League were to start play in May and end on September 15. Both leagues were to play the same number of games in split season schedules. Interestingly, the first- and second-half championships were irrelevant. The cumulative record would determine the pennant winner, thus eliminating league playoffs and starting the Negro World Series earlier.[101]

When owners met in Chicago in February, they voted to bar one familiar name from the season. It was Ted "Double Duty" Radcliffe, who had caught for the Homestead Grays in 1946. The banishment was because of Radcliffe's decision to leave the Grays five days before the season was over "to play in a foreign country." The *Chicago Defender* reported: "'Peck's bad boy,' as Doubleduty [*sic*] is known to Negro baseball owners, will not be allowed to play with any club in the leagues or against any non-league clubs even in any exhibition game or games."[102] Of course, Radcliffe, ever resourceful, played baseball anyway, joining the barnstorming Harlem Globetrotters.[103]

Birmingham's lengthy exhibition season opened on March 23 with a home game against Cleveland. It stretched through April 30 with league play beginning on May 4. In a game at Rickwood Field, center fielder Sam Hill, a Hooper City High School graduate in spring training with Chicago, celebrated his homecoming with a 350-foot home run. Catcher "Pepper" Bassett countered for Birmingham with a 375-foot blast.[104]

Later in the month, Birmingham defeated Homestead, 6–4, for their seventh win in eleven spring games. There was a scary moment pitcher Jimmie Lee Newberry was "hit on the head by one of Relief Pitcher Eugene Smith's odd pitches and had to be taken from the field."[105] There was no explanation for the "odd pitches" reference. The long exhibition schedule included games in Houston, Oklahoma City, Montgomery, and other cities.

In late April, the Black Barons hosted the Philadelphia Stars. It was announced that Tommy Sampson would play, "now ready for regular duties for the first time since he was injured in an automobile wreck in '45."[106] There was no report on the game itself, however.

On an odd note, a few days before the season opened, a former player was arrested by Federal Bureau of Investigation agents on a charge of draft-dodging. Willie Walter Crawford, 43, was said to have failed to answer an induction call at Knoxville on April 28, 1943. "FBI authorities said they had trailed Crawford (aliases 'Skeet,' 'Schoolboy' and 'Screwball') for four years, catching up with him in a baseball uniform at the Porter Mines" in Jefferson County.[107] A Willie Crawford was an outfielder with the Birmingham Giants in 1934.

Owner Hayes seemed determined to have a first-class operation in Birmingham. He announced that he was planning to hire a scout to look for talented prospects. This individual would complement a staff that included a full-time business manager and publicity department. Emory O. Jackson, writing in the *Birmingham World*, said Hayes had mastered the art of booking. He had secured several cities within a 125-mile radius of Birmingham as venues for games. He said Hayes had changed Birmingham from "a one-day-a-week baseball city to a two-day-a-week baseball city."

In addition, Hayes had developed a farm team for players "who are not ready for Black Baron duty." Veteran ball player and manager Reuben Jones was managing the "little Black Barons." Catcher Earl Ashby and outfielder James Brizzle were projected as players likely to be sent to the team "where they can get steady work." There was no information on the club's organization or schedule.[108]

Birmingham opened the season away, losing 9–4 at Cleveland on May 3. They won the second game at Covington, Kentucky, and a third game at an undetermined location.[109] Two other games were canceled because of yet more problems with the highly publicized new bus. "Leaving Cleveland, the team's bus caught fire, the players narrowly escaping serious injury. A woman trailed the bus for a half hour, honk-honking the danger but no one heard her horn. She finally succeeded in making the signal heard. Catcher Bassett's uniform was destroyed by flames. Shoes and handbags of other players were consumed by the fire."[110]

They returned home on May 9 for a rare Saturday home opener against nemesis Kansas City.

Hayes arranged the usual pomp and ceremony for Opening Day. Again, the Parker High School band, directed by George Hudson, performed and the flag was raised by members of the Julius Ellsberry Post of the Veterans of Foreign Wars. Savannah Crews sang the National Anthem. First pitch honors were accorded W.H. Hollins, president of the Birmingham Negro Business League.[111] Hollis made "a wild, batter-hitting pitch in throwing the first ball."[112] J.E. Lowery was master of ceremonies for the pregame activities and the teams were welcomed to the ballpark by Mrs. R. Williams, who was called the "No. 1 Black Barons fan."[113] Birmingham City Commission President Cooper Green proclaimed the date as Black Barons Opening Night and urged residents "to witness this opening game and help honor these baseball players."[114] The activities began with a parade starting at 16th Street and Fourth Avenue North. It was such a momentous occasion that owner Hayes brought in his 83-year-old father, Tom Hayes, Sr., his wife and daughter from Memphis.[115]

Birmingham won, 5–2. Bill Powell allowed nine hits but was in control, also striking out nine. The *Birmingham News* reported the crowd at 7,000. But the highlight was the return of Tommy Sampson at second base. He stabbed two line drives, starting double plays with both. Batting stars were Artie Wilson with three hits and Johnny Britton, Piper Davis and Sampson with two each.[116]

Kansas City played like the defending champions on Sunday, sweeping a doubleheader. The Monarchs won the first game, 6–4, and shut out the Black Barons, 8–0, in the seven-inning second game..[117]

On the road, Kansas City won, 9–4, at Jackson, Mississippi, and Birmingham won, 5–3, at Shreveport, Louisiana. Nat Pollard took a tough loss in Jackson when Walter Thomas "let three fly ball [*sic*] drop safe" and Ed Steele misplayed a ground ball. Sampson was said to be bringing back Lee Moody to help with the outfield problems.[118]

On Thursday night, they returned to Rickwood, where Birmingham won, 8–4. Alonzo Perry's three-run triple broke up a 4–4 tie.[119]

While Birmingham and Kansas City were battling at Rickwood, an old rival of both teams died in Nashville. Thomas Wilson, founder of the Nashville Elite Giants, suffered a heart attack "at his country home, in the suburbs of Nashville." He had moved the team several times, eventually to Baltimore. Although his primary interest was the Baltimore Elite Giants, he had been elected president of the revived Negro Southern League. He and Dr. R.B. Jackson, owner of the Nashville Cubs, were planning a trip east when death occurred.[120]

On Friday night, Birmingham won, 9–5, in Huntsville. "Squatty" Eli Chism and Piper Davis hit home runs. Davis also had two singles.[121] With the Huntsville victory, Birmingham had taken two of three from Cleveland and four of seven from Kansas City to start the season.

From Huntsville the Black Barons went to Indianapolis, where they split a double-header with the Clowns. As the clubs worked their way back to Birmingham, the Black Barons won three of five games. Birmingham was second in the league in hitting with a team batting average of .288. Although no Birmingham players were among the top five individual leaders, Davis (.367) led six teammates who were hitting about .300. Pitchers Newberry (3–0), Heard (2–0) and Powell (2–0) were all undefeated.[122]

But returning to Rickwood Field, they won a double-header despite very weak pitching. Nat Pollard won the first game, 7–5, giving up 11 hits. Birmingham won the second game, 21–10, with Alonzo Perry, Curtis Hollingsworth and Sam Williams giving up 13 hits. Of course, Birmingham did show fantastic offense in the two games, scoring 28 runs on 37 hits. Steele had seven of those hits.[123] On Wednesday, Indianapolis won, 13–8, but the number of hits was not reported.[124]

When Chicago came to Rickwood the following Sunday, Birmingham pitching suddenly was nearly perfect. Heard shut out the Giants, 3–0, in the opener, and Hollingsworth, getting his first start of the season, won the nightcap by the same score. Hollingsworth gave up only three hits, one of them "a fluke."[125]

After splitting games with the Clowns in Montgomery and Birmingham, the Black Barons went to Cleveland for their next series. On June 8, they lost the first game, 8–6, blowing a 5–0 lead. In the seven-inning nightcap, Nat Pollard won, 5–3.[126]

Cleveland won three straight games in Dayton and Buffalo. It was the first series Birmingham had lost all season, and it came against the team that now shared the lead in the pennant race. Birmingham's rookie pitchers Al Perry and Sam Williams performed well but had little support. Perry lost, 2–1, in Dayton. Williams lost, 3–0, on three unearned runs. The Black Barons "let 15 men dry up on the bases like the Negro vote in Wilcox county. Eleven men perished on base when Cleveland defeated Birmingham 8 to 5 Wednesday in Buffalo like the anti-lynching bill in the Senate." The colorful prose was from Emory O. Jackson's "Hits and Bits" column in the *Birmingham World*.[127]

Despite the disastrous series, Birmingham (16–8) and Cleveland (12–6) were tied for first as the Black Barons returned home against Memphis. An estimated 8,000 fans saw the visitors win the first game, 6–3 Birmingham had the bases loaded with two outs in the ninth. Dan Bankhead got Lee Moody to hit into a force play to end the game. Perry pitched and batted Birmingham to a 4–1 win in the nightcap. He tripled and scored a run and held the Red Sox to five hits.[128]

Moving to Memphis, Birmingham won four more times during the week. Most interesting was a two-city double-header. Birmingham won, 15–4, in a twilight game in Jackson, Tennessee, and then won, 10–4, that night in Memphis.[129]

An eight-day road trip carried them into the Midwest, playing Chicago and local teams in Indiana, Ohio, and Illinois. The Black Barons also played the Michigan City Cubs, a white team, but no report was found on that game's outcome. A Thursday night double-header closed the trip in Chicago.

Despite the publicity department set up by Tom Hayes and the contract with the Howe News Bureau for statistics, Emory O. Jackson wrote on June 6 that no standings had been released thus far into the season. He urged fans to write letters and complain. He also criticized the Black Barons and visiting teams for not hustling off the field and for "slowpoking" to the plate, thus dragging out games. Newberry was taken to task for an incident in which he tossed a bat at an umpire. Finally, Jackson chided the Birmingham team for poor third base coaching and base running.[130]

Although lacking published standings for confirmation, the Birmingham record was reported at 19–7. A shining light had been center fielder Norman "Bobby" Robinson, playing sensationally in the field and batting. 341. Two other Birmingham players getting good reviews were Piper Davis and Artie Wilson. Wendell Smith, sports editor of the *Pittsburgh Courier*, wrote that both were good enough to join Jackie Robinson in the major leagues.[131]

The *Birmingham World* was finally able to publish standings on June 17. They showed Cleveland (12–6) out front, followed by Birmingham (16–8) and Kansas City (14–10).

It was reported about this time that the Black Barons farm club had been disbanded "for lack of good, young baseball prospects." Sampson had sent veteran Jim Canada to the farm club at one time.[132]

Birmingham returned home on June 29 to start a series with Cleveland. The Buckeyes, now with a five-game lead over the Black Barons, featured center fielder Sam Jethroe, who was widely touted as destined for the major leagues.[133] Birmingham had been playing well, though, and the *Birmingham News* reported that eight players hitting over .300.[134]

Cleveland came in five games ahead and left the same way. Birmingham won a Sunday double-header but lost a Monday game in Montgomery, 7–2, and a Tuesday game at Rickwood, 12–10. In the latter, Sam Jethroe had three hits and two stolen bases. One of his hits was a grand slam homer off of Heard, who had relieved Newberry in the third inning. In the Sunday games, Birmingham had looked all-powerful, winning 8–3 and 14–0. Bassett had a home run.[135]

The series continued on the road, starting in Huntsville and including a stop in Dayton before they reached Cleveland for a double-header.

While the team was on the road, the *Birmingham News* addressed a rumor that the Philadelphia Phillies were scouting some of the Black Barons. By now, black fans were ecstatic over the play of Jackie Robinson with Brooklyn and Larry Doby with the Cleveland Indians. Some white club owners were licking their lips at the prospect of plucking great players from the ranks of the Negro leagues. When Bill Killifer, a veteran Cleveland scout, showed up in Birmingham in early July, the rumors began. Sportswriter Alf Van Hoose collared Killifer in his hotel room to test the tales. Killifer denied the report, saying he was in Birmingham "on a routine visit concerned mainly with checking on a young ball player he had seen play in the East last year." Also, he planned to spend some time with Eddie Glennon, general manager of the white Barons. They were friends from nearby towns in Pennsylvania.[136]

There was soon more speculation about Black Barons and the major leagues. On July 17 it was reported by the Associated Press out of St. Louis that the St. Louis Browns had obtained a 30-day option on the contract of "Piper" Davis. Jack Fournier, a Browns scout, had seen Davis play in Kansas City and was impressed. A Browns spokesman quickly said Davis had not been signed yet: "We have not signed him and he's not coming here. We have an option to buy him within 30 days if we want to. He'll stay with the Black Barons and we'll continue to scout him." At this time, the 27-year-old, 6-foot-2-inch Davis was playing first base and hitting .361.[137]

The report touched off joyous anticipation back home that Piper would finally get his shot. The Birmingham Negro Business League and the Housewives League, prominent local black organizations, began "planning a testimonial" for the Black Barons' star.[138]

On the Fourth of July, a Friday, Birmingham split two at Cleveland. Alonza Perry pitched a 5–0 shutout in the first game. Cleveland won a high-scoring nightcap 12–9.[139]

Standings published in mid–July showed the Buckeyes (29–16) still on top. Birmingham (29–21) was second and Kansas City (27–20) was third. The other three teams were all under .500. Shortstop Artie Wilson was the team's batting leader, hitting .370, followed by Piper Davis with .360. Pitching leaders were Curtis Hollingsworth and William Powell, both 4–0.[140]

Taking a break from league play, the Black Barons hosted the barnstorming Cuban LaPalomas on Sunday, July 6. Among its pitchers was John Huber, former Birmingham and Memphis player. The visitors won the first game, 5–4, Birmingham the second, 8–5, with Ed Steels and Pepper Bassett hitting home runs.[141]

After the LaPalomas games, the Black Barons went on a lengthy road trip to Kansas City and then the East Coast. They lost 10–9 in Kansas City on Thursday, July 10.[142] Among the other contests, they split a double-header with the Monarchs on Sunday, won a single game in Newark against the Eagles, and then lost a double-header to the Philadelphia Stars in Yankee Stadium.[143]

The 15th annual East–West All-Star Game was scheduled for July 27 at Comiskey Park in Chicago. Standings published earlier that week showed Cleveland (33–16) still maintaining its lead, but the second-place club was now Kansas City (29–20), Birmingham (29–23) having slipped to third.[144]

Piper Davis was the hitting star as the West defeated the East, 5–2. Davis had three hits in four at-bats to pace the winners. One of his hits was a double and he scored a run and drove in a run. Artie Wilson was hitless in four trips to the plate, but former Black Baron Dan Bankhead was the winning pitcher.[145] In the second game, played on Tuesday at the Polo Grounds in New York, the West won again, 8–2. This time Artie Wilson was the star, going four-for-four, scoring four runs and driving in another one. Davis was only one-for-five but he drove in two runs. Pepper Bassett also had a hit in the game.[146]

While Davis, Wilson, and Bassett were all-starring, the rest of the Black Barons were still playing regular games. They beat the Newark Eagles in Newark on Friday night. They split a double-header with the New York Black Yankees at Yankee Stadium on Sunday, and beat the New York Cubans there on Monday night. Headed back toward Birmingham, they lost to a team identified only as Cedarhurst on Tuesday.[147]

They returned home on Sunday, August 3, to face the Indianapolis Clowns. It was Piper Davis Appreciation Day, sponsored by the Birmingham Negro Business League. Playing for the Clowns was Sam Hairston, who had come out of the Birmingham industrial league, reportedly working his way on the Black Barons roster in 1944. Due to incomplete records, it is not clear how much Hairston actually played for the Black Barons. However, he became a fixture in Birmingham baseball history in later years, the patriarch of a major league dynasty. His son Johnny played in three games with the Chicago Cubs in 1969. Jerry Hairston, Sr., debuted with the Chicago White Sox in 1973. His two sons, Jerry Jr. and Scott, also made it to the majors.[148]

Sam Hairston's tenure with the Black Barons is likely but difficult to verify. According to a Society for American Baseball Research biography, he joined the Black Barons in 1944 to back up starting catcher "Double Duty" Radcliffe, who had broken a finger. Jerry Hairston, Sr., said he got a slightly different version from Radcliffe himself. Radcliffe said third baseman Johnny Britton was holding out for more money. Unhappy because he knew Britton was getting more money, he asked Sam Hairston, "Can you catch? You catch tomorrow. I'm going to be sick."[149] In fact, Radcliffe did have a broken finger in 1944.[150] Nevertheless, after a long playing and scouring career, the elder Hairston was named a coach for the Class AA Birmingham Barons and spent the last 12 years of his life in that role.[151]

Yet another Internet article on "Double Duty" Radcliff suggests that Hairston was likely with the Black Barons in 1943. Hairston relates that the team was without a catcher when Radcliffe broke a finger. Hairston said he told Welch he could catch and was sent down to warm up Lefty McKinnis. "He threw a shutout in Montgomery, Alabama. That's the first game I ever caught," he said.[152] The problem with that story is that in 1944 McKinnis was with the Chicago American Giants.[153] He pitched for Birmingham in 1941–43. The discrepancy could also be simply that Hairston's memory was faulty on who the pitcher was.

A native of Columbus, Mississippi, Hairston began playing baseball in the industrial league in 1942. After he was signed by Birmingham, whether in 1943 or 1944, he was quickly traded to Indianapolis for Pepper Bassett. Hairston played with the Clowns for six years, and then became the first black player signed by the Chicago White Sox. He eventually got into four games with the Sox in 1951, but spent most of his career in the minor leagues.[154]

The Hairstons are one of only four families that have had three generations in the major leagues. The others are the Boones (Ray, Bob, Bret, and Aaron), the Bells (Gus, Buddy and David), and most recently the Colemans (Casey, Joe Jr., and Joe Sr.). However, the Hairstons are one of only two families with five major leaguers. The other is the Delahunty family (Ed, Frank, Jim, Joe, and Tom).[155]

With a crowd of 10,000 packed into Rickwood Field, Piper Davis Appreciation Day was a big success. The Black Barons swept the double-header, winning 6–4 and 6–3. Bill Powell won the first game despite giving up 12 hits. A new pitcher, Arianthal Anderson, pitched a four-hitter in the second game.[156]

When the games were over, Birmingham made an incomprehensible leap to St. Louis, where they lost a 3–2 decision to the Kansas City Monarchs on Monday night. It was the start of a road trip that would culminate in a New York series with the independent Bushwicks. Heading north, Birmingham made it a clean sweep over the Clowns. The Black Barons won 11–1 in Memphis, and then 7–6 in Knoxville.[157] Despite these successes, they were still in third place headed into New York. Cleveland (39–18) seemed to have the pennant race in hand. Kansas City (33–21) was second and Birmingham (30–23) was third.[158]

The Bushwicks took a 2–1 win in 14 innings in the opener. Birmingham came back to win the second game, 4–2. There was also a pair of wins over the Baltimore Elite Giants as the team worked its way back South for another showing at Rickwood.[159]

The long road trip through the Northeast included stops for games with Lloyd's Athletic Club in Chester, Pennsylvania; the Bushwick Giants at Wood Haven, Long Island; and two games with the Baltimore Elite Giants.[160]

The team was scheduled to return to Rickwood on Sunday, August 17, for two games with Memphis. But the big news was not the games. Dan Bankhead, the former Birmingham sandlotter and Black Baron, had been sold the Brooklyn Dodgers. That raised speculation about a couple of current Black Barons: "It may be that Piper Davis and Art Wilson are rounding out their career as Black Barons during the month of September. It looked for a time some weeks ago as if the St. Louis Browns would exercise their option on the two and call 'em to St. Louis. Each is having the greatest season of his career, and Black Barons supporters believe that the pair may Spring-train in some major league camp, when the call to the baseball colors is sounded next March."[161]

Those games were actually played in Memphis instead of Birmingham. The Black Barons won the opener and the Red Sox the nightcap. On Monday, Birmingham won 5–4 in 12 innings. The following night they beat Memphis again, this time in Montgomery.[162]

As the season waned, and with it Birmingham's hopes for a pennant, the Black Barons hosted league-leading Cleveland (49–22) in late August. Standings published two days before the first game showed the Buckeyes far in front of the third-place local club. Although Birmingham (31–23) had lost only one more game than Cleveland, the Black Barons had won only 31 compared with 49 by the Buckeyes.[163]

In the Sunday double-header, Cleveland won the first game, 9–3. The second game was rained out. The series continued in Mississippi cities with Birmingham winning in Greenville but losing in Jackson.[164] The two teams returned to Alabama for two more games. Cleveland continued to win, 10–3 in Montgomery on Wednesday and 7–3 at Rickwood Field on Thursday.

Tommy Sampson's run of hard luck would not seem to end. He was forced to leave the team in August for an appendectomy. Piper Davis took over as interim manager.[165] It proved to be a permanent changing of the guard. Sampson and owner Tom Hayes had "an unspecified disagreement" later, and Sampson resigned as manager in the fall. Davis would manage the Black Barons for the next two years. Sampson would end his career with the Chicago American Giants in 1948 and the New York Cubans in 1949.[166]

With Cleveland gone, Birmingham found success again. Behind the hitting of catcher Pepper Bassett, they pounded the Memphis Red Sox, 18–6, in the first game of an August 31 double-header at Rickwood. Bassett had a home run, three doubles, and a single. Eli Chism and John Britton executed a perfect double steal to score Birmingham's first run. Catcher Casey Jones had a home run for Memphis, which committed eight errors. In the nightcap, shortened to five innings by the length of the first game, Jehosie Heard struck out five, winning 4–0.[167]

Cleveland won the pennant and met the New York Cubans in the Negro World Series. The opening game was rained out with the score tied in the top of the 7th. New York then won four of the next five to take the series. Although he did not finish the game, the starting pitcher for the Cubans in the last game was ageless Luis Tiant. The leadoff batter for the Cubans in every game was Minnie Minoso, whose major league career would eventually span five decades. He debuted with the Cleveland Indians in 1949 but spent most of his career with the Chicago White Sox. He was known affectionately as "Mr. White Sox," and the club brought him out of retirement for three games in 1976 and two in 1980, pushing his career across five decades. Although his last year in the majors was 1964, he continued to play professionally in Mexico for several more years. A seven-decades acclamation was provided by the St. Paul Saints of the independent Northern League. In 1993 and in 2003 he made appearances with the Saints, the latter at age 77.[168]

Although the official NAL season was over, fall baseball continued for the Black Barons.

On Sunday, September 14, a double-header was scheduled at Rickwood between Lloyd Bassett's All-Stars and the Indianapolis Clowns. There was no mention of the Black Barons and Piper Davis's whereabouts. However, the *Birmingham News* reported: "It was being noised about Saturday that some of the players in the All-Star lineup would actually be donning the uniform of the Black Barons for the '47 season." Indeed, the starting pitchers for the All-Stars were announced as Nat Pollard and Arianthal Anderson. Gates were to open at 1 p.m. to allow plenty of time for local fans to enjoy the antics of King Tut and Goose Tatum of the Clowns.[169]

Also it was reported that Bassett would add to the fun by doing his rocking chair stunt. Bassett had played with the Clowns in 1942–43 before joining the Black Barons. He was noted for catching part of the game sitting in a rocking chair behind home plate. Historian James Riley said Bassett actually developed the gimmick as far back as 1936 when he was with the Homestead Grays. Cum Posey, owner of the Grays, apparently came up with the idea.[170]

The Bassett team won first game, 9–4, and lost second, 3–0.[171]

Final statistics and standings released by the Howe News Bureau near the end of the calendar year contained good news for Birmingham fans. Although he had slipped badly for a time near the end of the season, shortstop Artie Wilson had surged back to the top of the batting race. With an average of .377, he edged out teammate Piper Davis, who hit .373. Wilson's numbers included 87 hits in 231 official at-bats. He had two triples, seven doubles and five stolen bases. The two were among the better fielders in the league, too. At second base, Davis committed only 10 errors in 235 total chances (.957); at shortstop, Wilson committed 17 errors in 319 chances (.949).[172]

While the 1947 season had been a success for both the Black Barons and Negro league baseball, there was a foreboding undercurrent for those willing to see it. More than 86,000 fans had turned out for the two East–West All-Star games, but Organized Ball still largely ignored the Negro American League and the Negro National League while accepting into its infrastructure the Cuban Winter League as an "unclassified" minor league. Sportswriter Marion E. Jackson chastised the Negro club owners for taking a lackadaisical approach to the lack of official recognition:

> These two "Orphan baseball leagues" have no parents in the horse hide profession, and appear to be relatively unconcerned about their illegitimacy.
>
> "Negro baseball born in sin and barn storming [*sic*], wild and tempestuous, dowdy and untamed has gone on its capricious way too long, not to let age and common sense catch up with it. Yet, common sense and statesmanship seem to be the most lasking [*sic*] quality in the leadership of two Negro Major leagues."[173]

21

Piper and Willie (1948–49)

1948

When the Black Barons reported to spring training in 1948, it was under the leadership of Piper Davis. Despite the contract option with the St. Louis Browns, the Black Barons star had never been given a chance at making the major league club or one of its farm teams. Owner Tom Hayes., Jr., named him as field manager, replacing Tommy Sampson.[1]

Hayes told the *Birmingham News* what happened with the contract. Hayes said that St. Louis had paid $1,000 for the option on Davis, "but the bad luck they had with Negro ball players who reported—their inability to come through—made them shy off the Davis deal." Hayes said he returned $500 to the Browns since Davis was never called up. "Hayes still thinks, as many others do around here, that Piper would have made the club if he had ever reported."[2]

Spring training was on the Alabama State Teachers College campus in Montgomery. Davis and Hayes had searched widely for new talent in the off-season. They found some at Grambling College. David Crawford was a 6-foot-3-inch, 185-pound first baseman, who batted .333. Pitcher "Boots" Moore was also a football player on the team that played in the Vulcan Bowl at Legion Field. None of the newcomers had much of a chance of cracking the veteran-studded Birmingham lineup, though. An exception was outfielder Jimmy Zapp, who had hit 11 home runs for the Atlanta Black Crackers in 1947.[3]

Looking at black colleges as a possible talent pool, Hayes said he would hold "a tryout camp for college stars." The camp was expected to draw players from such schools as Alabama State, Alabama A&M, Grambling, Lane College, Knoxville College, and Florida A&M. "All expenses will be paid candidates, and none will lose time from his classes. No contracts will be offered, except to seniors who are graduating. Lower classmen will be advised to finish school before they 'play for pay,'" Hayes said.[4]

Returning players included Ed Steele, John Britton, Artie Wilson, Herman Bell, Bill Powell, and Pepper Bassett. New prospects included first baseman Joseph Scott, catcher Otha Bailey, infielder Wiley Lee Griggs, pitcher Joe Bankhead, and outfielder Zapp.[5] Bailey was a promising semipro player from Huntsville. Griggs, a Birmingham boy, had played with Chattanooga in 1947. Bankhead was the fourth of the five baseball-playing brothers.[6]

At the Negro American League meeting in Chicago, the owners considered expansion requests from Nashville and New Orleans, but decided to "proceed with six clubs, not caring to venture out too far in 1948 as the season looked uncertain for such a move."[7] The lineup was Birmingham, Chicago, Cleveland, Indianapolis, Kansas City, and Memphis.[8]

A $6,000 salary cap was set in accord in a joint commitment with Negro National

League owners.[9] Despite 1947 end-of-the season reports "of unbelievable losses in profits, attendance and players," the owners pushed optimistically into the season. League President Dr. J.B. Martin said Jackie Robinson's success had bolstered the Negro leagues, increasing attendance and exposing the game to a wider audience.[10]

However, sportswriter Marion E. Jackson again urged the owners to address "musts" for the survival of the black game. These included timely publicity and statistical information, a cessation of umpire-baiting and other bickering, more hustle by the players, more timely starts for games, and umpires provided by the league, not the clubs.[11]

Despite the uncertainties, there were plenty of businessmen willing to invest in the game. The Negro Southern League returned with six regular members and two associate members, including clubs in Birmingham and Memphis.[12] The little-known Negro American Association, which consisted mostly of teams in the Carolinas and Virginia, announced that it was expanding to ten teams.[13]

The home exhibition season opened on March 28, with Birmingham doing what was rare in 1947. The Black Barons beat defending champion Cleveland, 12–8. Steele put the locals ahead in the first inning with a 407-foot home run. Zapp also hit a home run. Played on a cold Easter Sunday, the game drew only about two thousand fans. It was so chilly that a second game was canceled.[14] Birmingham clubbed the Buckeyes, 11–4, on Tuesday night before launching a multi-state exhibition road trip.[15]

Sportswriter Ellis Jones predicted the Black Barons would be "a stronger contender for the 1948 championship." The infield was second baseman Piper Davis, shortstop Art Wilson, and third baseman John Britton; Birmingham needed only a steady first baseman. The outfield was anchored by Steele, a power hitter with a strong throwing arm. There were two capable catchers, Pepper Bassett and Herman Bell. A veteran pitching staff included Alonzo Perry, Nat Pollard, and William Powell. Jones's enthusiasm was not unfounded. The 1948 team became possibly the greatest Black Barons team of all time.[16]

Opening Day was on Saturday, May 1, at home against Cleveland. At 5:30 p.m., a parade, led by the Parker High School band, formed in downtown Birmingham, then proceeded to the ballpark. Pregame ceremonies included a flag-raising by the Veterans of Foreign Wars, a welcome from Mrs. Retha Williams, and the first pitch by a "surprise" hurler.[17]

It was an exciting start. The Black Barons blasted Cleveland, 11–2. Powell pitched a complete game and Steele hit a two-run homer. For hitting the first home run of the year, Steele received a number of prizes from local merchants: Two chicken dinners from Porter's Club, one chicken dinner from the Brown Derby Café, two chicken dinners from the Afro Club, a diamond-studded watch from the Famous Record and Jewelry Store, five dollars from Davenport and Harris Funeral Home, five dollars from the Orange Bowl Drink Stand, and two dinners from Bob Reed's Blue Bird Inn. The crowd was estimated at from 8,000 to 10,000.[18]

Birmingham almost started the season without Steele. Over the winter he was traded to Memphis for catcher-outfielder Waymon "Red" Longley. However, Longley refused to leave Memphis, where he had been playing continuously since 1937. The deal was canceled, and Steele continued his Black Barons career that began in 1942.[19]

A Sunday double-header was split. Cleveland won the first game, 9–7, breaking a tie with two runs in the ninth. Bassett had two hits, but Cleveland got 13 hits off three Birmingham pitchers. Although Cleveland's Willie Grace was thrown out of the game by Umpire William Moore (the report did not specify why), Jimmie Newberry apparently got away with a major transgression: "Newberry threw plenty of illegal pitches during his six-inning stunt [*sic*] on the mound. Newberry has a tendency to use a spitter which has long since been outlawed. Several times he went to his mouth with his fingers and got away with it." In a five-inning second game, Wilson had threes hits and three runs.[20]

The *Birmingham News* reported on Monday that the Saturday paid attendance was 7,625 and Sunday's was 6,117. The discrepancy caused Ellis E. Jones to wonder if attendance figures were being "tampered with." He said it was obvious to him that the attendance was "better by a couple of thousand" than what the *News* reported. The "surprise" first-pitch honoree was not identified.[21]

Despite losing two of three at Rickwood, the Buckeyes were still a formidable opponent. On Monday night in Montgomery, they got 20 hits and won, 15–3. The team then barnstormed their way toward Cleveland for a series.[22]

Birmingham had big bats in Cleveland, winning the first game, 15–2.[23] They won two more games on the trip, then returned home with Indianapolis.[24]

Back at Rickwood, the Black Barons were welcomed by a crowd reported at 12,000. They rewarded the fans with a sweep of Indianapolis. Bill Powell pitched an eight-hit 5–0 shutout in the opener. Bassett homered, and Wilson had a double and a triple. Birmingham won the second game, 9–4.[25] There was a down side to the wins, though. Sometime on Sunday, thieves entered the team bus and made off with two catcher's mitts, a fielder's glove, a pair of spikes and several baseball caps.[26]

After the Sunday games, Birmingham released Joe Bankhead, youngest member of the ball-playing family, and he was not happy about it. The 21-year-old pitcher said the Black Barons never gave him a fair shot: "I wasn't given a chance by the Black Barons management. I wasn't allowed to work a single inning of league play despite the fact we have played 12 games since the season opened."

Bankhead said a messenger delivered the release notice at 10 a.m. on Monday morning despite the fact that he had a contract which called for a10-day notice. He said he received no advance warning, and he had not seen owner Hayes for several days. A Scott News Syndicate story credited Bankhead with worthy outings in several exhibition games.[27] Later, he joined the Harlem Globetrotters baseball team.[28] For a time he was with the white Grand Rapids teams in the Central League but had a mediocre season. He never played professionally again.[29]

After an off day, Birmingham beat the Clowns, 9–3, on Alonzo Perry's pitching and a 13-hit offense. Wilson had three hits again, one of them a triple. Davis and Zapp each had two hits, and Steele hit another home run. They also beat the Clowns in Huntsville and Montgomery for a five-game sweep.[30]

The series gave two local boys at opportunity to work out with the professionals. Mansfield Richardson, a three-letter athlete at Westfield High School, got a try at shortstop with the Clowns in Montgomery. Young Richardson "looked rather impressive. He should be ready in a couple of years with the right kind of training," reported Ellis Jones. Working out with the Black Barons was an 18-year-old Willie Mays. "He is reported to have declined a $300 offer from the Newark Eagles of the National league. Mays is said to be listening to Butch Huber, former Black Baron, on where and what to do. When school days are over, the young one might catch on with the Barons," wrote Ellis prophetically.[31]

Off the field, Newark Eagles owner Effa Manley made a highly critical statement about Jackie Robinson, the new hero of the black community. Robinson was quoted in *Ebony* magazine as saying Negro baseball need a house cleaning. He was critical of salaries and umpires. Manley retorted: "I charge Jackie Robinson with being ungrateful and more likely stupid. How could a child nurtured by its mother turn on her within a year after he leaves her modest home for glamour, success and good fortune? ... It is regrettable that someone has to jump on a man of whom most of us were proud."[32]

Howe News Bureau standings through May 17 had Kansas City (7–3) in first and Birmingham (8–5) second.[33] Working their way north, Birmingham continued to dominate the Clowns, winning in Nashville, Indianapolis, and Cincinnati. They were 14–5 headed into a series with Chicago.

The winning streak ended in Cincinnati, where Chicago won a double-header, 7–5 and 5–3. Bassett hit a two-run homer in the first game, but three errors contributed to the loss.[34]

The trip ended with wins at Nashville and Chattanooga. Bassett had a home run in Nashville.[35]

Gone for nearly a month, they opened a home series with Memphis. An intriguing note about the Friday night opener at Rickwood Field was the possibility of the great Willie Wells, Sr., playing alongside his 22-year-old son, Willie Wells, Jr. Papa Wells was playing third base for Memphis, having lost his old shortstop position to the youngster.[36]

Teenager Willie Mays in a Black Barons uniform (courtesy Faye Davis and Birmingham Public Library Archives).

The Friday night game was rained out, and there was no mention of the Wellses in the Sunday double-header. However, when Birmingham won, 11–4, on Thursday night, a box score showed father and son both playing. Wells, Sr., appeared as a pinch hitter in the ninth inning, getting a single and scoring a run. Wells, Jr., was at shortstop. For Birmingham, Davis had four hits with two doubles. Britton, Scott, and Steele each had two hits and Zapp homered.[37]

A new right-handed pitcher was Bill Greason. An Atlanta native and World War II veteran, in semipro ball he got the nickname "Double Duty" from alternating pitching and catching in double-headers. He spent two years in the Negro Southern League. Birmingham got him from the Asheville Blues.[38] Curtis Hollingsworth was released. Although he was 4–0 in 1947, he had not been effective as a reliever in 1948.[39]

Standings on June 1 showed Birmingham (15–7) close behind Kansas City (12–4).[40]

On Sunday, Birmingham won, 9–1, and lost, 5–4.[41] There was no report on a Monday game in Little Rock, but Birmingham won on Tuesday and Wednesday in Houston and New Orleans. Davis had three hits in Houston, and Steele hit an inside-the-park home run in New Orleans.[42]

Finally, the series fans anxiously awaited arrived. League-leading Kansas City came to town. There was exhilaration as the Black Barons took three games at Rickwood Field. Powell got his sixth win on Saturday night. On Sunday, before a crowd estimated at 7,500, they won, 4–3 and 5–4. Greason pitched a complete game, and Perry had a pinch-hit home run. The three victories moved Birmingham into first place.[43]

Powell was saluted by sportswriter Marcel Hopson, who wrote that the "elongated right hander" had been even more impressive than he was given credit. According to Hopson, the NAL statistics for 1947 gave Powell a 7–0 record, but in reality he was 19–0 including exhibition games. He attributed Powell's success to "a swift breaking curve ball carefully delivered from many angles." He also cited Powell's speed, understanding of the game, and unruffled performance under pressure.[44]

On the road, Kansas City won, 6–5, in Centralia, Illinois. Birmingham had triumphs in Memphis and Detroit. In the Detroit game, Basset and Wilson had four hits. Bassett's included a double and a homer. Newberry pitched a five-hitter, striking out 11. Davis hit a homer in Memphis.[45]

Pitcher Bill Greason, whose long career included a stint with the St. Louis Cardinals (T.H. Hayes Collection, Memphis and Shelby Room, Memphis Public Library and Information Center).

Birmingham, still in first place, went to Chicago with six players who were hitting over .300: Bassett, .444; Wilson, .382; Davis, .362; Perry, .346; Steele, .330; and Bobby Robinson, .305.[46]

The Giants won the opener, 4–3, ending Powell's winning streak. Greason won the second game, 3–1.[47] Most games on the trip were unreported.

The Black Barons brought Chicago back to Birmingham on June 20. They won the first game, but it took a while. Eight pitchers were used before Birmingham won, 13–12, in the 11th. Wilson and Davis each had four hits. Sixteen players were credited with RBIs in the 37-hit game. A crowd of 6,862 witnessed the three-hour and twenty-minute contest. Darkness halted the second game after three innings.[48]

Monday's game was nine innings, but it resembled Sunday's. The two teams produced 18 runs and 29 hits. Birmingham won, 12–6. Greason had a complete game despite giving up 13 hits and walking five. The hitting stars on Monday were Wilson, Steele, and Greason with three hits each.[49] Birmingham won two of three in other cities, then paired with Indianapolis.[50]

Most of the nine-game series went unreported, but the Black Barons won a Sunday double-header at Rickwood, 5–0 and 5–2. Greason pitched a four-hit shutout, and Powell threw a three-hitter. Wilson had five hits in eight at-bats.

Of greater interest in the second game, however, was the No. 8 hitter for the Black Barons. Appearing in a published box score from Rickwood for the first time was Willie Mays in left field. He was hitless in two times at bat.[51]

A benefit game for local Negro Boy Scouts was played at Rickwood on July 1. Birmingham beat the Clowns, 7–3, on Newberry's eight-hit pitching. Steele and Davis had home runs among their three hits apiece. The youth program received $865 from the proceeds, and the Clowns entertained the fans with a game of "imitation baseball" in which they hit, fielded and threw an imaginary baseball.[52]

Mays had been attracting attention for some time. He played football, baseball, and basketball in high school and was a regular in sandlot baseball games. In 1947 or 1948 he started going to Chattanooga on weekends, playing with the Choo Choos in the Negro Southern League.[53] In the author's research, Mays first turns up in a Chattanooga game in 1948. Piper Davis went there to watch the youngster. Davis said he cautioned Mays that playing pro ball on weekends would end his high school career if authorities found out, but he said he didn't care. When school was out, Mays joined the Chattanooga team, but by June he was wearing a Black Barons uniform and playing occasionally.[54]

Howe News Bureau standings for the first half showed Birmingham (38–14) solidly ahead of Cleveland (31–21) and Kansas City (24–18).[55]

Birmingham also led the league in team batting (.299) and team fielding (.958). Wilson, Bassett, Davis, and Perry were all hitting over .300.[56] Wilson (.406) was leading the league. He also led in hits. Davis (.380) was second and leading in total bases.[57]

On the Fourth of July, Birmingham closed out the first half, beating Memphis, 10–9 and 8–5. Steele hit a homer in the first game, and Davis hit one in the second. Davis's shot to center field traveled at least is 407 feet. Mays, still batting eighth, started in left field. He was hitless but played an errorless game in the field with four putouts. In the second game, Powell raised his record to 9–1.[58]

After winning the first half rather easily, Hayes celebrated by hosting a picnic and distributing $500 in bonus money among the players.[59]

The 1948 season was not only the Black Barons' best, but also probably its most efficiently managed: "Your Black Barons have quite an elaborate set up. It is composed of the 18-players team, the front office and aides, salaried and unsalaried. Tom Hayes, Jr., president-owner, is at the top of the set up. Lorenzo (Piper) Davis, is the manger; T.C. Eric Lincoln, road secretary; Charlie Rudd, bus driver; Roosevelt Atkins, trainer; Charles T. Mabry, local contact man; C.E. Williams, play-card distributor; W.W. Whetstone, P.A. (public address) man; Walton Lowry, official scorer; and Walter Jelks, the barber, works the scoreboards in the downtown area." That report by Emory O. Jackson also noted that the team had a bat boy and a mascot.[60]

Following the Rickwood games, the Black Barons paired with Memphis for a week. A notable win was Sam Williams's three-hit shutout in Greenwood, Mississippi.[61] They opened the second half with an exhibition game in Durham, North Carolina, then toured the Midwest and Northeast, ending up in Cleveland.[62] They lost three out of four there. In the only win, Bassett's two-run home run gave Newberry his 11th win.[63]

Second-half standings through July 19 showed a resurgence of Kansas City (6–2). Birmingham (4–3), Memphis (5–5), and Cleveland (4–4) followed.[64]

On July 9, a former Black Baron made major league history in Cleveland. Satchel Paige, at the age of 42, pitched two scoreless innings in his debut with the Indians.[65] It was, perhaps, even more extraordinary given a barnstorming appearance earlier in the season in New Orleans. Starting the second game of a double-header against the Harlem Globetrotters, Paige, "just a shadow of his former self, hurled three innings for the Kansas City Stars and was belted for five hits and one run," reported the *Times-Picayune*.[66] Obviously, Cleveland General Manager Bill Veeck knew Paige could still pitch.

Birmingham sportswriter Ellis Jones was in Philadelphia the following week when

Cleveland came in for a double-header. He got to Shibe Park about 5 o'clock in the afternoon, hoping to see Paige pitch. "Unaware of the weight the name Paige, the immortal, the legend, the mound wizard, still carries ... I was almost crushed to death trying to shove, ram, knife my way in. I missed out, coming away bruised and battered," he wrote. Fans had been standing in line since 10 that morning. Jones watched the game on a television in a café, seeing Paige get his first major league win in relief.[67]

Later that month, American League President Will Harridge ruled that Paige's "hesitation pitch" was illegal. The Washington Senators initiated the complaint. With runners on base, Paige would bring his hands above his head and fix the ball in his glove. Although there was no rule specifically prohibiting that action, Harridge instructed umpires to call the move a balk. If Paige was bothered by the ruling, he didn't show it.[68] He finished his season with a 6–1 record and 2.47 ERA.

On July 25, Birmingham returned home for a series with the Newark Eagles. One of the Newark stars was outfielder Monte Irvin. A native of Columbia, Alabama, Irvin had been seen as a likely player to break the Organized Ball color barrier. He had attended college for two years before signing with Newark. However, while he was in the army during World War II, Branch Rickey formulated his plans for Jackie Robinson. But the Hall of Fame was in his future. He signed with the New York Giants in 1949 and was in the majors in 1950.[69]

Irvin was hitless as the Black Barons won the first game, 9–2. Wilson had a single, double and triple. Zapp and Joe Scott hit home runs to back Perry's pitching. The second game was quite different. The Eagles had 20 hits, winning 14–4, and Irvin showcased his talents. He was four-for-five with two RBIs and a stolen base. Willie Mays, now batting third, had one hit, driving in two runs.[70]

Newark, the first-half winner in the Negro National League, got other victories in Tuscaloosa, Alabama, and Greenville, Mississippi. The Tuscaloosa game was played at Alberta City Park before a crowd estimated at 3,500. Tom Hayes was so impressed with the crowd that he planned two more games in Tuscaloosa.[71]

By late July, Birmingham continued to win, but trailed the Monarchs, who were playing well also. Wilson (.412) was chasing another batting championship. Davis (.373) and pitcher Powell (10–1) were among the leaders. Birmingham also led the league in hitting and fielding.[72] The *Alabaman Citizen*, noting those achievements, published another roster with uniform numbers:

2 Art Wilson, ss	10 Nat Pollard, p
3 Herman Bell, c	11 John Britton, 3b
4 Jimmy Zapp, lf	12 Norman Robinson
5 Jehosie Heard, p	13 Joe Scott, 1b
6 Sam Williams, p	15 Ed Steele, rf
7 Alonzo Perry, p	17 Jimmy Lee Newberry, p
8 Pepper Bassett	19 Bill Powell, p
9 Bill Greason, p	20 Piper Davis, 2b-manager[73]

Regrettably, Willie Mays's number was not on the list.

On July 31, Jimmie Newberry pitched a no-hitter as Birmingham beat Cleveland, 4–0, at Dayton, Ohio. It was the first Birmingham no-hitter in 17 years. Newberry was now 12–5. Pepper Bassett caught the game.[74] A week earlier, former Black Baron Dan Bankhead had pitched a no-hitter for Nashua in the New England League. He then won the second game in relief.[75]

An important home series with Cleveland came in early August. The teams were tied for third place. Birmingham won, 4–3, in Montgomery on Saturday night, then swept a Sunday double-header at Rickwood.

In Montgomery, Alonzo Perry (9–2) struck out 10. Newberry, with relief help from Greason, won the Sunday opener. Powell threw a three-hitter in the seven-inning night-cap.[76]

Sensational fielding by Mays and Griggs contributed to the win. "Mays pulled down [Chico] Renfroe's drive in left on a great catch in the fourth. And the crowd of 7,680 gave Griggs a thundering hand when he made a leaping stab of Renfroe's drive near second in the sixth with Buckeye runners on first and third." Mays started both games in left field. He batted seventh and fifth. He had one hit and scored twice.[77]

Mays starred on Monday night in Memphis. His pinch-hit double drove in the winning run in the 10th inning. Williams pitched a complete game.[78]

Birmingham made it five straight on Wednesday, beating the Buckeyes, 3–2, in Tuscaloosa. Greason struck out 12, and Mays hit a home run.[79]

They played a peculiar game at Rickwood on Thursday night. Birmingham won, 7–6. All 13 runs were scored in the first two innings. Both starters were out after just 1.2 innings. The Buckeyes got all six runs off Perry. Newberry held them scoreless afterward.[80]

Standings through August 5 showed Birmingham still in third place.

The New York Cubans came in for a series in mid–August, bringing with them former Birmingham managers Winfield Welch and Tommy Sampson and, also, Lyman Bostock. Welch was manager and Sampson played second base.[81]

The Cubans won on Saturday and Birmingham on Sunday. Powell gave up seven hits, two of them by Minnie Minoso. Wilson, Steele, Mays, and Scott each had two hits for Birmingham, one of Scott's being a home run.[82]

There was an unreported game in Tuscaloosa on Monday, followed by a Greason complete game in Montgomery and a Cubans win in Chattanooga.

At Rickwood on August 19, it was Black Barons Appreciation Night with players receiving many gifts. B.T. Warren, manager of Kent Tailors, was credited with the idea. Fans were invited to send gifts to the *Birmingham World* office for inclusion in a gift chest that would be equally distributed among all of the players. Other community leaders on the Appreciation Chest Committee were J.T. Walker, O.K. Cleaners; C.J. Greene, Atlanta Life Insurance Company; W. H. Hollins, Hollins and Shores Realty Company; Robert L. Williams, Bob's Savoy Café; Emory O. Jackson, the *Birmingham World*; and L.G. Blackus, Jefferson County School System.[83]

Columnist Emory O. Jackson announced that any member of the original Black Barons sending him his name and address would be given a lifetime pass to future games.[84] It is not known if any responded. By now a number of the "Original" players were deceased. Among them: Charles "Twosides" Wesley, Buford "Geechie" Meredith, and Gordon Zeigler. One who was still very much active in baseball, though, was Poindexter D. Williams, now a café owner. The former catcher was still a familiar figure at Rickwood Field and other ballparks as an umpire. He was not present for Black Barons Appreciation Night because he had been selected for a singular honor in Chicago. Williams was invited to the lead the parade on Rube Foster Day, a reunion of the pioneer's former players in Chicago. Williams had played on Foster's 1921 team.[85]

Gifts of money, jewelry and merchandise were solicited for the Appreciation Chest. As the event neared, it was announced that donations thus far included an 8 × 10 portrait of the team by Brown Studio, a cleaning and pressing job for each player by O.K. Cleaners, a $5 men's toilet kit from Temple Pharmacy, a suit of clothes from Kent's Tailors, and assorted cash.[86]

The event was a rousing success with each player getting to draw from the Appreciation Chest at least once. The baseball game that followed was less enjoyable. With Minoso getting two runs, two hits, and two runs batted in, New York won, 7–3. Mays had a triple and an RBI. Wilson was presented a trophy for his 1947 batting title.[87]

With three weeks remaining, it was likely that Kansas City would win the second half, necessitating a championship playoff. Through the games of August 11, the leaders were Kansas City (14–7), Memphis (19–12), and Birmingham (8–7).[88]

Although their second-half hopes were dim, Birmingham played good baseball the final weeks, winning seven straight games from Chicago. They came from behind twice to win a double-header in Chicago.[89] The other five games were in various Midwestern locations. The regular season closed in Memphis.[90]

The playoffs opened on Saturday, September 11. Birmingham entered the series without centerfielder Norman "Bobby" Robinson. He broke his ankle when he stepped in a hole chasing a fly ball in Springfield, Missouri, on September 1. He missed the remainder of the season. Manager Davis was expected to put rookie Mays in centerfield and move Zapp to left.[91]

Fans could not have asked for a better start. Birmingham won the first game, 5–4, an 11-inning marathon that ended when Mays drove in the winning run with a two-out single. Newberry, relieving Powell, got the win.[92] The Black Barons extended their series lead with a 10-inning, 6–5 victory on Sunday afternoon. With the score tie at 5–5, Ed Steele made a perfect throw to home plate from right field to cut down a runner. In the 10th, Bassett singled Davis home from second with the winning run. "Davis hit one of the longest balls in Rickwood history in the fourth inning—a terrific drive well above the right end of the 33-foot scoreboard which is 381 feet from home plate."[93] Davis, Wilson, and Mays all had three hits. Wilson had a double and a triple, Mays a double, and Davis the long home run. Greason won in relief of Perry. The *Birmingham News* reported the attendance for Saturday at 5,234 and Sunday at 7,539.[94]

After two days of rest, the Black Barons won Game 3 at Rickwood, 4–3, when Jimmy Zapp hit a home run in the bottom of the ninth. Powell won in relief of Newberry.[95]

Facing elimination, the Monarchs regrouped in Kansas City. They won, 3–1, on Sunday. The next night they fought to an unresolved 3–3 tie. On Tuesday, the Monarchs won, 5–3.[96]

That gave Kansas City a chance to tie the series at home in Game 7 on September 23. It was not to happen. Greason pitched a four-hitter, and the Black Barons won the NAL championship, 5–1.[97]

Art Wilson (.402) won the NAL batting championship again. Robert Boyd (.376) of Memphis was a distant second. Piper Davis (.354) was fifth and led in RBIs (69). Wilson also led the league in runs (78) and hits (134). Alonzo Perry (10–2) was the league's best pitcher.[98]

The Negro World Series with the Homestead Grays opened on Sunday, September 26. Although the games were frequently played in neutral sites, the opener was normally a home game for one of the participants. Game 1 in 1948 was played in Kansas City because neither Rickwood Field nor Griffith Stadium in Washington, D.C., was available.[99]

At Kansas City, Homestead won, 3–2. Birmingham took a 1–0 lead in the second, but

Homestead scored three times in the bottom of the inning. Newberry, the losing pitcher, struck out six and walked one.[100]

On September 29, the series moved to Rickwood Field for Game No. 2. Manager Davis announced the following lineup:

Artie Wilson, ss	Willie Mays, cf
Johnny Britton, 3b	John Scott, 1b
Eddie Steele, rf	Howard Zapp, lf
Piper Davis. 2b	Pepper Bassett, c

Birmingham pitchers would be Bill Powell (11–3), Jimmie Newberry (14–5), Alonzo Perry (10–2), and Bill Greason (6–4).[101]

Homestead won, 5–3, scoring all five runs in the sixth inning before a crowd of 4,159. The Grays' big inning included two doubles and a home run by Willie Pope. One of the doubles was by Luke Easter, who was signed by the Cleveland Indians a few months later. The Homestead rally was aided by a double play ball that got stuck in Wilson's glove.[102]

In a deep hole, Birmingham rallied to win Game 3 at Rickwood, 4–3. Mays drove in the winning run with two out in the ninth.[103]

But the euphoria was short-lived. The series moved to New Orleans for Games 4 and 5. Rickwood was unavailable because the white Barons were hosting Fort Worth in the Dixie Series.

In New Orleans, the "orphaned" Grays, playing the entire series on the road, put a quick, decisive damper on Birmingham's hopes, blasting the Black Barons, 14–1. Luke Easter hit a grand slam home run.[104] The next night, Ted Alexander pitched a three-hitter and Homestead won the championship, 8–2.[105]

For the third time in six years, Homestead had beaten Birmingham in the Negro World Series. The 1948 loss was particularly disappointing as Birmingham enjoyed home field advantage. "This series spotlights the plight of Negro baseball which is an orphan of white parks," wrote Emory O. Jackson.[106]

Local fans got one more chance to see the Black Barons and the Grays. They returned to Birmingham for a final exhibition game. Homestead won this game also, 10–6.[107] No one foresaw that the 1948 games were the final Negro World Series.

On October 12, Birmingham fans got to see the man whose success had so captivated black fans. A Negro National All-Stars team, featuring Jackie Robinson, beat the Black Barons, 3–0. Robinson "whiffed, singled, stole home, and fielded flawlessly" before an estimated 5,300 fans. One of his All-Star teammates was Brooklyn catcher Roy Campanella. He went hitless but thrilled the fans with his work behind the plate and general hustle. Newberry excited local fans when he struck out both major leaguers. Only one of the three runs by the All-Stars was earned.[108]

1949

Manager Piper Davis and the Black Barons went to spring training, hoping this would be the year they won it all.

If they did, it would not be quite the same, though. The Negro National League had folded. Three of its teams had gone under, and the three survivors moved over to a restructured Negro American League. Players from defunct New York Black Yankees and Homestead Grays were placed in a pool for drawing by NAL teams. Birmingham selected pitcher Wilmer Fields of the Grays, outfielder Arthur Heffner of the Black Yankees, and pitcher Ted Alexander of the Black Yankees.[109]

The NAL was set up with Eastern and Western divisions, whose champions would play in the Negro World Series.[110] Birmingham was in the West with Chicago, Kansas City, Memphis, and the Houston Eagles. The East Division was Baltimore, Indianapolis, Philadelphia, the New York Cubans, and the Louisville Buckeyes. Cleveland was now in Louisville and Newark in Houston.[111] Longtime Newark owner Effa Manley had decided to get out of baseball.[112]

Scott News Syndicate writer Marion E. Jackson said black baseball was surrendering

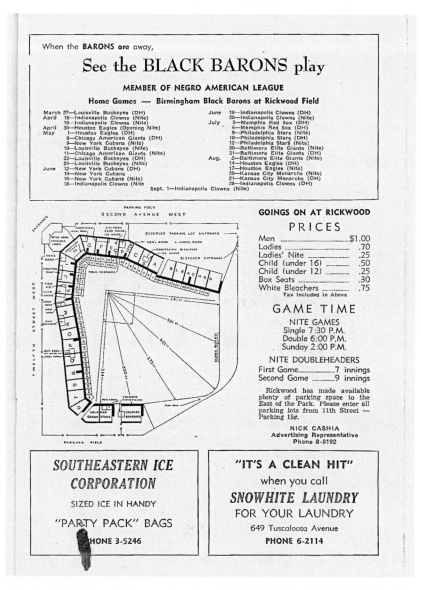

A page from the official scorecard of the 1949 Birmingham Barons of the Southern Association. It includes a large advertisement for the Black Barons with the home schedule (courtesy of the Friends of Rickwood Field).

territorial rights "on the East Coast of the United States without a semblance of a fight."[113] Indeed, black baseball was gone from Washington and Newark and reduced in New York.[114]

Opening Day was set for the weekend of April 30–May 1. New league President J.B. Martin waxed enthusiastically over the coming season. "Player and fan interest is expected to be greatest in the league's history … because the major leagues are accepting Negro players," penned one sportswriter. There was acclaim over Satchel Paige and Artie Wilson getting $15,000 salaries while Negro league pay had topped out at around $5,000 for the best players.[115]

Martin's enthusiasm notwithstanding, the Negro leagues were in trouble. Disbanded were such famous teams as the New York Black Yankees and even the world champion Homestead Grays. The Clowns' home had bounced between Cincinnati and Indianapolis for years. The Negro Southern League lineup was uncertain. The player pool was being depleted by Organized Ball's signings of stars.[116] Over the winter, Birmingham had sold Art Wilson to the Indians, and Chicago sold Jim Pendleton to the Cubs.[117]

Cuban Stars owner Alex Pompez was in the everything-is-rosy camp. He said selling players to Organized Ball assured black owners that they held a valuable recruiting franchise. Ed Gottlieb of the Philadelphia Stars was more circumspect, calling black ball's future "questionable." Elaborating, he said:

> More Negro youngsters will take up the game professionally, feeling they have a wonderful opportunity to make the big leagues, but fans must support the Negro American League if these players are to be developed and given their opportunity.
> Failure to do this will cause more owners to quit and may result in the dissolution of Negro organized baseball.[118]

The Jackie Robinson effect was spreading like a virus, sapping the star strength of the Negro leagues. Interest in local black baseball waned as Larry Doby, Satchel Paige, Jim Gilliam, and other stars made the transition. Attendance declined and coverage evaporated. Newspapers such as the *Chicago Defender* and the *Pittsburgh Courier* devoted more and more space to the integrators and less to the black teams and leagues. Columnists like Fay Young, Ric Roberts, Emory O. Jackson, and Marion E. Jackson wrote less about the players and teams left behind.

An article by Jackson showed the reality of black ball's future. "What everyone wants now more than anything else is minor league status," wrote Jackson. "They've petitioned Commissioner A.B. Chandler to give the Negro leagues minor league status. Yet, because of 'territorial rights' organized baseball has refused to grant this status." For the owners, survival was at stake when stars were often lost without compensation. "Jackie Robinson and other stars were signed without the Negro club profiting one cent from the deal," wrote Jackson.[119]

Speaking at the annual meeting of the National Negro Publishers' Association, Effa Manley issued a clarion call for support. "The success or failure of the teams to draw this year may determine the future of the Negro leagues," she said. "If we fail to support our Negro leagues in this critical period, we may be hastening the day when no Negros will be playing in the majors. The boys cannot make the jump from sandlot baseball into the big leagues without going through a period of development such as they are given in the Negro leagues."[120]

A white sportswriter, David J. Walsh of the International News Service, forecast the end that was rapidly approaching for black baseball:

> It seems that with the second emancipation, AD 1946, not even Negroes want to watch Negroes play baseball. That is, unless they happen to be playing it under big league auspices. The novelty of that is much too recent, for one thing, to have worn itself thin. For another, two Negro players—Robinson

and Newcombe—were given the National League's rookie-of-the-year award by vast plurality, thus greatly enhancing this particular situation.

For another thing: it costs no more for big league baseball at the general admission window that it does to see the Negro American League.[121]

When the East–West All-Star game, the showcase of black talent and a major African American social event, was played in Chicago in August, the attendance was down 11,000 from the previous year. There could be no more obvious sign of the black community's declining interest in segregated baseball.[122]

But the hearse had not arrived yet. Birmingham rushed into the 1949 season full of hope for an elusive championship and possible major league contracts. The Black Barons franchise was among the most enduring. Marion E. Jackson called Birmingham the best baseball city in the Negro leagues.

> Every club in the Negro American League wants to play in Birmingham because of the huge crowds, the roaring enthusiasm and of, course, the gate receipts, which top the returns of any park in the circuit. Baseball in this city is more than a pastime … it is a passion. Likewise some of the top players in the United Sates got their start playing here on the industrial leagues teams and sandlot league teams and the roster of the Birmingham Black Barons…. In addition to being a Birmingham ball club, the Black Barons are an Alabama institution. The teams regularly play in Tuscaloosa, Montgomery, Mobile and Gadsden, and folks in those cities take equally as much pride in them as the home folks.[123]

Owner Tom Hayes, Jr., interviewed in Atlanta, where he was making arrangements to play games in that city, urged the black community to support Negro leagues baseball. He said money going to black baseball clubs was money that stayed in the black community. Hayes shared some financial facts about the Birmingham club. "My own payroll is $11,000 a month. The players earn from $350 to $500 a month. They have nice homes and brand new cars. In addition to this we spend a great deal of money providing them with transportation, hotels, and food, all of which is provided by the management. We do all of this business with Negro enterprises," Hayes said.[124]

Spring training opened in March on the Alabama State campus in Montgomery. Emory O. Jackson reported that the team was in good condition, although some of the players "complained of soreness, stiffness, and such minor bruises which go with getting in shape." About 30 players were in camp.[125] There was a gaping hole at shortstop, where Artie Wilson had excelled for five years, but many clubs had opened a new season with a lot less talent. Birmingham's returning outfielders—Willie Mays, Ed Steele, and Norman Robinson—were of championship caliber. Of course, Mays, a senior in high school, would not likely make road trips until June.

Missing were pitchers Nat Pollard and Jehosie Heard. Pollard, bothered by a sore arm much of the previous season, had been moved to the club's front office as traveling secretary.[126] Heard was with Houston. Wilson was headed to San Diego in the Pacific Coast League, just a step away from the major leagues. Wilson had caught the interest of the New York Yankees earlier, but Hayes said the Yankees offered him a salary much lower than what he was making in Birmingham. "So, how did they expect him to sign? … Wilson wrote me and said that he would rather come back to Birmingham than go to Newark for less money than he was getting at home," said Hayes. Cleveland's entrepreneurial Bill Veeck had no such reservations.[127]

Returning veterans were Pepper Bassett, Herman Bell, John Britton, Bill Greason, Jimmie Newberry, Alonzo Perry, Bill Powell, Joe Scott, and Sam Williams. Davis was the NAL's

Manager of the Year in 1948 and Willie Mays was the Rookie of the Year.[128] Several players kept in shape playing winter ball. Bassett went to the Philippines, while Powell and Perry played in Puerto Rico.[129] Missing was outfielder Jimmy Zapp, who, surprisingly, had been released after the 1948 season. He was coaching basketball at a Nashville Catholic high school.[130] There was also a report that Tommy Sampson, driving a coal truck in Birmingham in the offseason, was considering retirement. After eight years with the Black Barons, he had played for the New York Cubans in 1948.[131]

New prospects included utility man Luther Branham, Puerto Rican shortstop Jose Burgos, infielders Frank Nesbitt and Mitchell June, and outfielders Arthur Turner, Clifton Fain, Frank Garrett, Willie Hill, and Alonzo Thomas. Hill was from Hooper City, and Thomas was described as 6–4, 222 pounds. A lot of pitching prospects were in the camp also. They included Willie Scruggs, William Rosser, Richard Watts, Kelly Searcy, Frank Marsh, Fred Jones, Oscar Harris, Nathaniel Booker, and William Hough.[132]

The exhibition season opened with Louisville at Alberta City Park in Tuscaloosa. The Buckeyes won, 4–1, taking advantage of Davis's experimentation with four rookie pitchers. Former Black Baron Parnell Woods had a double, a home run, and two singles. The home run was worth $20 as it cleared an advertising sign nearly 400 feet from home plate. For Birmingham, Mays tripled and also made two "grand catches," one at his shoe top and the other chasing down a long fly. One of the outfield candidates with Louisville was P.D. Williams, Jr., the son of Birmingham's old catcher.[133]

Houston came to town for Opening Day on Saturday, April 30. A crowd of 4,636 saw Birmingham win, 3–1. Perry pitched a complete game, and Davis had three hits, one a triple.[134] Pregame ceremonies were a mixed bag, according to Emory O. Jackson:

> The brief ceremonies were excellent despite the fact that the Fairfield I.H.S. band came one hour and ten minutes late. The welcome speech by Mrs. Herman Williams could not have been nicer, but it could have been shorter. Miss Savannah Crews sang the national anthem gloriously. But a few of the fans need to be taught American manners, baseball patriotism, and public culture with reference to singing the Star-Spangled Banner. We should try singing the national anthem again when the Black Barons play at Rickwood just to show ourselves we can make a hundred in fan behavior when we hear our country's theme song played or sung.[135]

Sunday's double-header was rained out. Games were divided in Atlanta on Monday and Tuesday. Newberry won, 5–4, in a complete game. Robinson hit two triples. At Rickwood on Thursday night, Powell struck out 11 in a 7–3 win.[136]

On May 8, Birmingham faced Chicago and a crowd of former Black Barons at Rickwood. They included Felix McLauren, Lloyd Davenport, Lyman Bostock, Paul Hardy, Alvin Gipson, Jessie Douglas, Gready McKinnis, and Manager Winfield Welch. The *Alabama Citizen* published a roster with uniform numbers:

1	Pepper Bassett, c	11	John Britton, 3b
3	Herman Bell, c	12	Norman Robinson, utility
4	Bill Powell, p	13	Luther Branham, lf
5	Willie Mays, cf	15	Piper Davis, 2b-manager
6	Sam Williams, p	17	J.L. Neve, p
7	Alonzo Perry, p	18	Bill Greason, p
8	Richard Watts, p	20	Edward Steele, rf
10	Joseph Scott, 1b	21	Jose Burgos, ss[137]

Pitcher J.L. Neve is actually Jimmie Lee Newberry.

The Black Barons won both games on a rainy night. Greason and Powell combined to win the first game, 6–2. The second, shortened by rain and curfew to five innings, was a 4–1 victory before a crowd estimated at 4,800. "Manger W.S. Welch, dubbed the 'smartest manager in Negro baseball,' made Pilot Piper Davis resort to all sorts of maneuvers before yielding. Birmingham had a patched-up, splashy lineup on the field which was constantly undergoing alterations," reported the *Birmingham World*.[138]

Davis, shifting players to meet given situations, had made the traditional "utility" player obsolete on the local club:

> He moved Branham to the outfield … and assigned Norman Robinson to a utility role. In the real sense there is no such player as a utility man on the team under fluid lineup pattern the local franchise is using.
>
> He shifted his lineup against the Houston Eagles.… In the shakeup, Alonza [*sic*] Perry, star right-hand pitcher, was inserted at first base in place of Joseph Scott, regular first baseman. And put in the clean up slot, Perry came through with a four-ply blow in the sixth inning. Edward Steele, pistol-armed right fielder, who was dropped from lead-off to second place in the batting order, had come through with three singles in four tries.[139]

Even by NAL standards, the second week in May offered a strange lineup of games. After Chicago, Birmingham faced the New York Cuban Stars on Monday, Louisville on Tuesday, Chicago again on Wednesday and Thursday, then concluded the week with Kansas City on Friday. They won four of the five games.

After the Kansas City game, they made a long jump to Cleveland, where they beat the Indianapolis Clowns, 8–2, on Sunday. They split games in Columbus and Zanesville, Ohio, and defeated a white team in Fairmont, West Virginia.

On May 22, Birmingham opened a home series with Louisville. "In the middle spot in the outfield will be arrow-armed Willie Mays, their school-going centerfielder. With Mays in the lineup the Black Barons are stronger. They missed him on their recent eastern tour," reported the *Birmingham World*. Birmingham won the double-header, 14–2 and 18–7. In the opener, Perry yielded only six hits and Birmingham batters got 14 off two pitchers. Scott and Davis each had three hits while Steele, Robinson, and Mays had two apiece. Mays, batting seventh, drove in four runs. Perry and Steele hit home runs.[140]

The second game was played under protest by Louisville after three Buckeyes were ejected from the game. Umpire H.L. Mosely booted Manager Alonzo Boone and two of his players for a combination of "doctoring" the ball and abusive language.[141]

Games were split in Montgomery and Columbus, Mississippi, prior to a Wednesday charity game at Rickwood. Proceeds were to benefit a fund drive for a Negro hospital in Birmingham. It was noted that only 574 of Jefferson County's 2,286 hospital beds were considered to be available

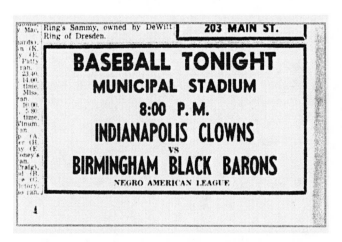

Advertisement from the *Zanesville (OH) Times Recorder*, 17 May 1949.

for blacks, even though the city had a black population of 34.7 percent. Local civic leader Howard Scott was chairing the hospital campaign. Club Lumiere, a women's organization, solicited fans at the ballpark. They club had previously used its annual Christmas dance to aid the hospital fund.[142]

Entering the game, Ed Steele (.418) was leading Birmingham batters with 23 hits in 55 at bats. But Steele was not the main attraction. "Fans will have a chance to see the sensational Willie Mays perform in the Black Barons center field," wrote the *Birmingham News*. "The 18-year-old Fairfield boy is a fine defensive player with a great throwing am. Many observers believe Mays is a cinch for future major league stardom. He is currently batting .345."[143]

Birmingham won, 5–3, as Williams gave up only five hits. Scott and Burgos each had three hits. Brilliant fielding plays were made by Burgos, Mays, and Robinson. "The highlight of the game was a sensational bare-handed catch by centerfielder Willie Mays in the seventh inning near the left center wall while speeding full throttle away from the plate."[144]

The Black Barons made it three in a row on Thursday, sweeping a double-header, 6–3 and 18–8. Davis had two doubles, a triple, three runs scored, five RBIs, and a stolen base in the second game.[145]

Launching a long road trip, the Black Barons won twice in Louisville, and then spent the next weekend in the East. They split a Sunday double-header with the Cubans at the famed Polo Grounds. Once again speculation about the major leagues was rampant. Mays, apparently on his first road trip after graduation from high school, hit an inside-the-park home run in the first game. "Several Black Barons are being eyed by major league scouts," wrote a *Birmingham News* sportswriter. "However, all offers to date have been rejected. Piper Davis, Willie Mays, Alonzo Perry, William Powell and Jimmy [*sic*] Lee Newberry are being watched by the ivory hunters. All are getting favorable reports."[146]

They participated in a four-team double-header in Philadelphia, losing to Baltimore, 11–8. Davis hit a grand-slam home run. They wrapped up the series with an unreported game in Chester, Pennsylvania, on Tuesday night, and met the Houston Eagles for a single contest in Petersburg, Virginia, on Wednesday. The Eagles won, 3–1. The result of the game in Chester was not given, but it was reported that Newberry broke his right arm in the game.[147]

Near the end of the eastern swing, Howe News Bureau standings put Birmingham (15–9) in second place behind Memphis (9–5) in the Western Division. In the East, New York (12–3–1) was first and Baltimore (11–7) second. Steele (.402) was the league leader in batting. He also led in runs scored and was tied with Davis for hits.[148]

Returning to Birmingham on June 11 for a game with the New York Cubans, Powell won a classic pitching battle, 1–0. He scored the only run and struck out 10.[149] A double-header was scheduled on Sunday. Birmingham won the first, 8–4, but the second was rained out. Steele had a home run and three RBIs.[150]

The next day, they played a double-header in St. Louis. Birmingham was in the midst of a plethora of roster changes. Pitchers Felix "Chin" Evans and Ernest "Spoon" Carter were signed to offset the loss of Newberry. Also, a sore arm sidelined Perry for a week. Rookie hurler Willie Scruggs was not immediately available because he had missed the team bus in Cleveland. Pitcher Nathaniel Booker was released with his spot expected to be filled by Ted Alexander, formerly of Homestead. Finally, Catcher Herman Bell and third baseman Johnny Britton were seeing limited action due to injuries.[151]

In St. Louis, New York won the first game, 3–1, in 11 innings. "Chin" Evans, who had last pitched for the Black Barons in 1934, shut out the Cubans, 3–0, on two hits in the night-cap.[152]

On June 19, Indianapolis was at Rickwood Field for a double-header. It was not a good day for pitchers. When the long afternoon ended, the two teams had recorded 36 runs and 43 hits off 14 pitchers. The Clowns used six in the second game. The collective hurlers walked 15 batters and hit one. Birmingham won the first game, 13–5. Bassett and Mays hit home runs with Mays driving in four runs. Indianapolis took the nightcap, 10–8. A good crowd of 7,057 was present.[153]

There was more high scoring on Monday night. The Clowns outhit the Black Barons 9–7, but Birmingham won the game, 9–5. Indianapolis used three pitchers for a total of 12 in two days. Greason pitched a complete game, striking out seven and walking four. Steele drove in three runs.[154]

On the road, they played in Alexander City; Columbus, Georgia; Montgomery; and Greenwood, Mississippi.[155] New standings had Birmingham (18–12) just a half game behind Kansas City (19–12). In the Eastern Division, New York (14–5) continued to lead Baltimore (22–12).[156]

Columnist Emory O. Jackson noted that four former Black Barons were now in the upper levels of Organized Baseball. Satchel Paige was in the major leagues with Cleveland. The other three were in AAA: Dan Bankhead, Montreal; Artie Wilson, Oakland; and Parnell Woods, San Diego.[157]

After Indianapolis, Birmingham picked up Kansas City for a week-long road series. It included a Sunday double-header in Kansas City, then solo games in other cities.[158]

The Black Barons won the first game, 5–3, to gain a little ground on the Monarchs, but lost four out of seven in the series.[159] Their first-half fate was sealed when they returned home and lost a Sunday double-header to Memphis, 6–3 and 14–2.[160]

Memphis's double victory was attributed to strong hitting—catcher Casey Jones had two home runs—and some "daffy base-running" by rookie Birmingham pitcher Richard Watts. In the second game, Watts walked to start the fifth inning. When Steele hit a line drive between left and center, Watts rounded second and was halfway to third base when he inexplicably stopped and reversed his journey. That put him and Steele on the same base and both were put out.[161]

Watts possibly thought Steele's drive had been caught and was trying to backtrack to prevent a double play. In any case, the blunder cost him his spot on the roster. Owner Hayes announced after the game that Watts had been released. That was not the end of his troubles. A few days later, a deputy sheriff had showed up at the ballpark to serve papers. The nature of Watts's legal problems was not given.[162]

On the Fourth of July, Birmingham and Memphis played three times. There was a holiday double-header at Rickwood and a night game in Tuscaloosa. At Rickwood, Memphis won, 5–4, and Birmingham, 8–7. The Black Barons lost the first game in spite of getting 15 hits off two Memphis pitchers. Piper Davis had four hits, one of them "a tremendous homer over the scoreboard."[163] A *Birmingham News* sportswriter, commenting on the Davis blow a few days later, wrote that the drive "cleared the scoreboard and took one short bounce, hitting the old concrete wall 467 feet from home plate."[164]

Curiously, the writer did not mention the fact that Birmingham Barons outfielder Walt Dropo had hit that same wall the year before. An "X" has been painted on the concrete wall to mark the spot. Dropo's ball reportedly hit the wall on the fly. A plaque commemorates the event.[165]

The series continued in Memphis with the Red Sox winning on Tuesday and Birmingham on Wednesday. Steele and Bassett both hit grand slam home runs on Wednesday.[166] Ending the series, Birmingham won, 5–1, at Greenwood, Mississippi, on Friday night. Williams struck out six and Branham had three hits, but the highlight was a triple play started by Davis in the sixth inning.[167]

On July 10, Philadelphia came to Rickwood, and the Black Barons got a much-needed win in the first game, but it wasn't easy. It took 10 innings for Birmingham to win, 13–12. Willie Mays had perhaps his best game so far. He was five-for-six, scored two runs, and drove in two. The second contest was rained out, as was a Monday game.[168]

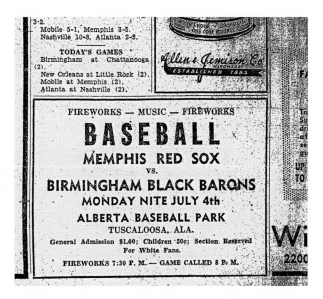

Advertisement from the *Tuscaloosa (AL) News*, 4 July 1949.

In July, Piper Davis was named manager of the West squad in the annual all-star classic. Birmingham players announced were shortstop Jose Burgos and pitcher Alonzo Perry. But catcher Herman Bell and pitcher Bill Greason also played.

On July 22, the New Orleans Creoles came to Birmingham, bringing with them Toni Stone, the young woman who had earned a spot at second base. Birmingham won, 4–0. The game report did not mention Stone.[169]

Stone had a most unlikely connection to one of white baseball's colorful characters, Charles Evard "Gabby" Street, the catcher who once caught a ball thrown from the top of the Washington Monument. A native of Huntsville, Street's career as a player, manager, coach, and broadcaster ran from 1904 to 1951. In 1936–37, while managing a minor league team in St. Paul, he frequently held baseball clinics for boys at the ballpark. Stone, who lived near the ballpark, kept hanging around, badgering him to let her go to the camp. He ran her off, not knowing she was already playing on a Catholic boys' team. Finally, one day he gave her a chance and was impressed

Advertisement from the *Greenwood (MS) Commonwealth*, 8 July 1949.

with her throwing, fielding, and batting. Remembering her saying that her family couldn't afford to buy her equipment, on her fifteenth birthday, he gave her a pair of baseball shoes. What is more remarkable is that Street, often called "Old Sarge" because of his demeanor, not only he let his natural sexism slip, but also his racism. Street was a member of the Ku Klux Klan. His nickname "Gabby" came not from being a chatterbox, but from an epithet that he used routinely to get the attention of black males.[170]

After the New Orleans game, Birmingham split a double-header in Memphis. Playing in Mississippi towns later in the week, Birmingham won in Jackson and Memphis in Columbus. Davis hit home runs in both games.[171]

The series ended with single game at Rickwood. The Black Barons won, 6–5, scoring the winning run in the ninth. Davis was five-for-five, and Mays was four-for-six as Birmingham smashed 16 hits off Sam Woods and former Black Baron Frank "Groundhog" Thompson. Mays's single decided the game.[172]

On July 30, Baltimore opened a series in Birmingham. The Eastern team totally dominated the Black Barons, winning seven of nine games over a ten-day stretch. Birmingham fans were happy, though, to see Jimmie Lee Newberry, who had been out for some time with a fractured arm, back on the mound. He started the first game of a double-header, pitching five innings before needing relief help.[173] Birmingham won, 7–3, with Scott and Davis hitting home runs.[174]

Although Perry lost the second game, 4–3, his record stood at 13–4. That was good enough for an Organized Ball contract. On Tuesday morning he flew to California to join the Oakland Oaks in the Pacific Coast League. Waiting there were two former Black Barons, Artie Wilson and Parnell Woods.[175]

Perry's break did not pan out well. He appeared in twelve games as a first baseman and outfielder, getting just three hits in 15 at bats.[176] On the mound, his big problem had been a lack of control, finding himself often behind hitters, wrote Doc Young in the *Chicago Defender*.[177]

He was back with the Black Barons in 1950, then returned to the Pacific Coast League again in 1951. But that was as far as he was going. He spent the rest of his career in Mexico. Historian James Riley said Perry's failure to move up may, in some measure, have been related to the fact that he was "often in trouble with the law."[178] Wilson got to the majors briefly with the New York Giants in 1951, but Woods was too old to make it. It is odd that Oakland even gave him a chance, as he was 37 years old when they signed him.[179]

Barely a week later, Manager Piper Davis got his second chance in Organized Ball. On August 15, General Manager Joe Cronin announced that the Boston Red Sox had signed Davis to a contract with its Scranton farm club. Davis would report to spring training with the Red Sox in 1950. Having hit .350 the year before, Davis was having an even better year in 1949, batting .397 at the time of his signing.[180]

The game at Rickwood Field the day before Davis's signing was another interesting battle of current and former Black Barons. Chicago Manager Winfield Welch was in town with Lyman Bostock, "Double Duty" Radcliffe, Felix McLauren, Lloyd Davenport, Tommy Sampson, John Huber, Gready McKinnis, and Alvin Gipson. The pre-game article contained a prophetic sentence: "Piper is having such a great year as a player that it is doubtful Prexy-Owner Tom Hayes will be able to keep him."[181]

However, Davis did not leave immediately. He managed in the East–West All-Star Game on August 14. The East won, 4–0. Davis, playing second base, got one of the West's two hits. Burgos played shortstop, Bell pinch hit, and Greason pitched three shutout innings. Major league Baseball Commissioner "Happy" Chandler threw out the first pitch.[182]

Going into the East–West game, Davis (.402) continued to lead the league in hitting, well ahead of Memphis first baseman Robert Boyd (.384). In the standings, though, Birmingham (8–5) lagged behind Kansas City (12–7).[183]

Unlike the Major League All-Star Game, which was considered the season's midpoint and a day off for those players not participating in the game, non–All-Star Negro leaguers played on. Using "makeshift lineups," Birmingham and Chicago met at Rickwood Field.

Birmingham won the opener, 8–7, and Chicago the second, 7–0. Henry Bayliss, filling in at shortstop, had two hits, one of them a double that sealed the win. Sampson and Jess Douglas hit home runs for Chicago.[184]

Birmingham had a chance to gain on Kansas City the next weekend. But the Monarchs won, 7–3, on Saturday and then swept a Sunday double-header. Birmingham could muster only five hits in each game.[185] Birmingham won at Memphis, Tuscaloosa, and Montgomery, that one a 15-inning game. The Monarchs won in Columbus, Mississippi. In August 26 standings, Birmingham had dropped to third place. Davis (.392) had slipped slightly but continued to lead the NAL in batting.[186]

The regular season ended with Indianapolis at Rickwood on August 29. Birmingham won the first game, 2–1, on Powell's five-hitter. The second was rained out. The final game was on Monday. Indianapolis won, 13–12, getting 21 hits off four Birmingham pitchers.[187]

With the loss, Birmingham fell to fourth place, three games under .500 for the second half of the season. In addition, Piper Davis (.385) lost his lead in the batting race. Indianapolis catcher Len Pigg moved ahead with a .392 average.[188]

The regular season was over for the Birmingham team, but the players continued to pick up paydays with exhibition games. Throughout September and October they played lengthy series with Memphis, Cleveland, Indianapolis, and the New York Cubans. Games were played in Alabama, Georgia, and Mississippi.[189]

The most interesting series was with the Jackie Robinson All-Stars. On October 17, Bill Greason pitched a one-hitter to beat the All-Stars, 3–1, in Talladega. The All-Stars run was scored on two walks and an error. Robinson had a walk and three pop-ups in four at-bats. Also playing with the All-Stars were Larry Doby and Roy Campanella.[190]

Another Dodger, Don Newcombe, pitched for the All-Stars at Rickwood on Tuesday night. He threw a three-hitter as the Stars won, 9–3, before a crowd of 15,781. "The crowd filled all seats, the passages and overflowed on the playing field along the left and right field foul lines. Hundreds left before the game without attempting to battle the jammed-packed entrances into the park," reported the *Birmingham News*. Doby and Robinson each had two hits.[191]

In October, Hayes announced that Piper Davis would be replaced as manager for the 1950 season by Elander Victor "Vic" Harris, the former manager of the Homestead Grays.[192] Harris, who spent 23 years with the Grays, won nine consecutive Negro National League championships as player-manager from 1937 to 1945.[193] Owner Hayes was bringing in a heavyweight to lead the Black Barons.

The 1949 season reflected the continuing problems with Negro leagues baseball—desperate scheduling in multiple cities, the siphoning off of good players by Organized Ball, and diminishing attendance. It recalled Effa Manley's dire prediction that Negro baseball was at a crossroads.[194]

Journalist Luix Virgil Overbea, writing about falling attendance in Chicago, noted that same crossroads. His solution embraced a number of thoughts often expressed before, particularly box scores, statistics, rosters with player biographies, publicity, all of the things that most white clubs considered commonplace. "About the most difficult thing anyone can get on a Negro ball game is a bona-fide box score. A good baseball fan loves his box scores and statistics," he wrote.[195] Indeed, with the exception of the East–West All-Star game, the *Chicago Defender* did not print a single box score during the 1949 season.

But perhaps a bigger sign of deterioration was the attendance at the East–West Game. At 31,000, the game drew some 11,000 fewer fans than the year before. If black baseball's showcase event was slipping that badly, the outlook for the game overall had to be troubling to its supporters.[196] Actually the signs had been there the year before. Two days before the All-Star game, some 51,000 turned out at Comiskey Park to see Satchel Paige pitch in an American League game. An estimated 15,000 were turned away. On Sunday, the East–West game drew 42,099 fans.[197] As noted above, the *Chicago Defender* was perhaps contributory to the problem of declining interest. The nation's leading African American newspaper carried no Negro American League or Negro National League box scores throughout the season.

22

The Beginning
of the End (1950)

Spring training camp for the 1950 Black Barons opened on March 20, again at Hornet Stadium on the Alabama State campus in Montgomery.

Knowing that Piper Davis would be in spring training with the Boston Red Sox organization, owner Tom Hayes, Jr., began looking around for a new manager as the 1949 season closed. He found his man in Vic Harris.[1]

A native of Pensacola, Florida, the 45-year-old Harris had 27 years of professional baseball under his belt. He started in 1923 with the Cleveland Tate Tigers and the Toledo Tigers. He entered league ball with Chicago in 1924, and later moved over to Homestead, where he spent most of his career as player-manager. He was in the dynasty that won nine consecutive Negro National League pennants. He managed the 1948 team that beat Birmingham in the Negro World Series. When the Grays collapsed at the end of that season, he went to Baltimore for 1949.[2]

Another front-office change was the departure of Traveling Secretary Nathaniel Pollard. He was replaced by Joseph Atkins of Memphis, a Wilberforce College business administration graduate. Hayes announced the hiring in a speech before the Greater Birmingham Negro Business league.[3] Pollard, who had moved to the front office after a pitching arm injury, went to Atlanta, pitching briefly with the Brown Bombers in the Negro Southern League. He got a comeback spot with Birmingham in June.[4]

The Negro American League returned with the same 10 teams that played in 1949, again divided into East and West divisions. The only change was the relocation of the Buckeyes from Louisville back to Cleveland.[5] On the surface, things looked good. It appeared that stability had returned.

Beneath the surface, the erosion was continuing. The previous summer, when former Newark Eagles co-owner Effa Manley spoke to the black publishers' group at their annual meeting in Washington, D.C., she had laid out three criteria for Negro leagues survival:

(1) establish a firm relationship between the major leagues and the present Negro leagues.
(2) newspapers, fans, owners and everyone interested in the welfare of the game get together on a common basis.
(3) sportswriters on Negro publications evidence the same enthusiasms towards our Negro baseball leagues and the players competing in them.[6]

Unfortunately, none of those goals were really attainable. First of all, with its own viable minor league structure already in place and with the ability to negotiate directly with individual owners, major league baseball needed no "relationship" with the Negro leagues. How somebody performed in a game at Rickwood Field between Negro league teams could not match the interest in how major leaguers Jackie Robinson, Larry Doby, or Satchel Paige did on the same day.

Moreover, when baseball made inroads into television, opportunities for watching baseball were increasing, even for people nowhere near a major league park. James R. Walker and Robert V. Bellamy, Jr., authors of a book on television and baseball, concurred with a *Baseball Weekly* article that said television was second only to Jackie Robinson as the most impactful event in major league baseball history. Most early telecasts were regional, but in 1953 ABC launched the national *Game of the Week*.[7]

Manley's appeal for such disparate groups to come together in a vague, undisciplined effort to save Negro leagues ball was, at best, naïve. A cursory look at African American newspapers from 1946 to 1950 shows an ever-decreasing number of inches given to Negro leagues baseball alongside a comparable increase in space given the players who had crossed the color line. Yet the Negro leagues were still a livelihood for hundreds of players, owners, and ballpark employees. And they still had fans, albeit in smaller numbers. They were still more than a decade away from totally disappearing.

Harris had a nucleus of returnees to get him started in Birmingham. Among them were pitchers Bill Greason, Bill Powell, Sam Williams, and Jimmie Newberry. The catchers were Lloyd "Pepper" Bassett and Herman Bell. Norman "Bobby" Robinson, Willie Mays, Ed Steele, Wiley Griggs, and Henry Bayliss also returned. Among the new prospects were Frank Dixon, a pitcher from Florida, and shortstop Johnny Smith. Third baseman Johnny Britton was now with Indianapolis.[8] Griggs and Smith hoped to replace Piper Davis at second base.[9]

Hayes announced a two-day tryout session at Rickwood Field. He said he had "such a barrage of applications from promising youngsters that he decided to give them a look-over."[10]

Despite the losses of such regulars as Britton and Davis, the team appeared to be solid. They opened the exhibition season at Alberta Park in Tuscaloosa, trouncing Cleveland, 18–2.[11]

In their exhibition debut at Rickwood, they beat Cleveland, 7–6 and 1–0. In the second game, Birmingham failed to get a hit but scored the winning run on "a walk, an error and smart baseball" before a crowd of 3,500.[12] Mays got the first hit and run scored of the exhibition season, coming in on Steele's triple. Mays also made the fielding play of the day, pulling down an apparent home run ball 295 feet deep in centerfield, then whirling and nailing a base runner at the plate.[13]

By April 28, they had won 16 of 21 exhibition games, splaying across South Alabama, Georgia, and Mississippi.[14] Near Opening Day, the *Birmingham World* published the team's 18-man roster:

No.	Name	Pos.	Ave.
12	Norman Robinson	lf	.312
10	Johnny Cowan	2b	.204
21	Willie Mays	cf	.311
20	Edward Steele	rf	.311
7	Alonzo Perry	1b-p	.278

No.	Name	Pos.	Ave.
4	Andrew Watts	3b	1st year
8	"Pepper" Bassett	c	.295
3	Herman Bell	c	.194
2	Henry Bayliss	ss	.268
9	Jose Burgos	ss	.214
18	William Greason	p	.160
17	Jimmie L. Newberry	p	.268
19	William Powell	p	.187
6	Samuel Williams	p	.080
11	Frank Dixon	p	1st year
14	Curtis Hollingsworth	p	1st year
5	"Pijo" King	util of	1st year
13	Johnny Smith	util inf	1st year
15	"Vic" Harris	Mgr.	1st year[15]

Hollingsworth, of course, was not really a first-year player. He was just returning to Birmingham after two years' absence. He played with the team in 1946–47.

The regular season was to open at Memphis on Sunday, May 7, but the games were rained out. The two clubs played their first league game in Little Rock on Monday night with Birmingham winning, 7–4.[16]

On May 11, having lost two of three with Memphis, the Black Barons had their home opener. Writing in the *Birmingham World*, Emory O. Jackson noted Thursday was the traditional "off-night" for many domestic workers who might be able to attend the game. Pregame ceremonies included the first pitch by the Rev. J.W. Goodgame, pastor of the Sixth Avenue Baptist Church. His battery mate would not be one of the regular Birmingham catchers, but rather a Black Barons legend—Poindexter D. Williams, the popular 1920s catcher and manager. Jackson said Goodgame, in his younger days, "was one of the blazing slab artists of the South."[17]

James Grimes and the Fairfield Industrial High School band provided music, proud of the fact that FIHS senior Willie Mays was in the Black Barons lineup. Commander Freeman Cleveland and the W.B. Johnson Post of the American Legion raised the flag. Women also participated in the Opening Day ceremonies. Savannah Crews, gifted soloist and city school teacher, sang the national anthem. Mrs. Ruth J. Jackson, "the marvelous 'Mayor of Bronzeville,' was to greet the owners, managers, players, and fans "in her role as the 'brown queen of Birmingham.'" Mrs. Rheda Williams, "the Black Barons' number one fan," also offered greetings.[18] Later, it was reported that Mrs. Jackson had been unable to carry out her "duties," due to arm injury from a burn.[19]

Memphis, Birmingham's oldest and most continuous rival, was managed by Homer "Goose" Curry. His roster was said to be "sprinkled liberally with Cubans and other tanzy-tongued islanders."

Unfortunately for all of the dignitaries, the crowd of 4,918, and the Black Barons, the fun was quickly over. Memphis batters hit Jimmie Newberry for six runs in two innings. Four other Birmingham pitchers fared no better. It was 12–0 Memphis after three innings and 15–3 at the end. The only bright spot for Birmingham was Alonzo Perry's four hits and the game's only home run.[20]

Birmingham's dismal start was offset by a double-header split on Sunday. Indianapolis won the first game, 4–3. Perry, back with the Black Barons after a brief stint with Organized Ball, hit another home run. Birmingham won the nightcap, 7–3, with Newberry before a crowd of 4,142.[21] Birmingham made it two in a row on Monday night, winning 3–2 in 10 innings. Williams pitched a complete game, yielding six hits, striking out five. He struck out the side in the second inning. Bayliss was the hitting star with two singles and a double.[22]

Winning four of six from Indianapolis, Birmingham went to Houston, managed by former Black Baron "Red" Parnell.

They returned home with the Eagles on May 24. Greason pitched well, going 11 innings, but Houston won, 4–3, when Birmingham fielders committed two errors. Former Black Baron Jehosie "Jay" Heard won in relief for Houston.[23] Birmingham was also hampered by the absence of center fielder Willie Mays, who missed the game in order to receive his diploma from Fairfield Industrial High School.[24]

Mays atoned for his absence the next night, celebrating his graduation with a 370-foot home run. Newberry a pitched five-hitter as Birmingham won, 8–2. Mays then had three hits, one a triple, on Friday night. Williams threw a six-hitter, winning, 9–1.[25]

Rejoining the club was infielder Lorenzo "Piper" Davis. Having been released in Scranton, Pennsylvania, he went hitless in his return. Davis, despite obvious talent, was said to not have future with Boston Red Sox because of his age (31).[26] At the time he was released he was batting .333, with four home runs and 12 RBIs for a last-place club. According to a Scranton sportswriter, there was a "big storm" of public protests over the team's move.

Davis was released on May 29 after getting five hits in a double-header the day before. When the news of his release appeared in the newspaper, "fans began writing letters of protest, making telephone calls and sending telegrams." The protests were to no avail. Whether Davis's release was indeed an age decision or part of an unwritten Organized Ball quota on black players will likely never be known.[27]

Alvin E. White, writing from the American Negro Press syndicate, said that despite the success of Jackie Robinson, Larry Doby and other black players, there was an undercurrent of resentment against blacks by both the baseball establishment and writers:

> Not only has the general attitude of ball club owners remained against the hiring of Negroes, but there has not been much unbending on the part of the average baseball writers.
> And right on into the field of spectators, resentment against Negro ball players in the big leagues is still expressed by some of the die-hards.
> The towns where baseball attendance has dropped most are the towns where Negro ball players are unwanted.[28]

White criticized owners such as Connie Mack of the Philadelphia Athletics. He quoted the great pitcher Bob Feller as saying there were not enough "good negro ball players to make much difference."[29]

Two other former Black Barons who were sticking in Organized Ball, though, were pitcher Dan Bankhead and infielder Artie Wilson. Bankhead "has completely fooled the experts" who thought he was at least a year away from the major leagues, reported a newspaper article. Bankhead was off to a 4–1 start with Brooklyn.[30] Wilson, the 1949 Pacific Coast League batting champ who had been in a mild slump, broke out of it with 15 hits in 23 at bats and also fielded brilliantly for the Oakland Oaks.[31]

Enjoying a two-game winning streak, the Black Barons went back on the road. The trip started with an exhibition game against the Nashville Cubs of the Negro Southern League, then series with Memphis and Philadelphia.

Back at Rickwood, a double-header sweep extended a winning streak. Powell pitched a 2–0 shutout.[32] The return of "Piper" Davis played no small role in the surge by the Black

Barons. He "bolstered the defense and the plate power" after returning to second base with the club.[33]

In a 10–5 win in Huntsville, Willie Mays hit a three-run homer, prompting a reporter to write: "Mays may not be making many more appearances with the Black Barons, as it is known that several big league scouts are watching him closely."[34]

The 14-game winning streak was snapped by the New York Cubans in a June 11 double-header at the Polo Grounds in New York. That it had reached 14 games was quite remarkable, considering what had happened to the team the night before in Jersey City. The Black Barons' customized bus was destroyed by a fire. Lost with the vehicle was all of the team's equipment. Perhaps buying a few pieces and borrowing some from the Cubans, the Black Barons won the first game on Sunday afternoon, 7–5. The Cubans won the second, 9–7, ending the streak.[35]

Undaunted by those setbacks, they barnstormed with the Cubans, reaching Birmingham on June 17. Nat Pollard, his arm woes apparently at bay for the present, got his third win against one loss since rejoining the club.[36] Standings showed Birmingham (21–9) behind Kansas City (22–5) in the West while Indianapolis (15–11) led the East.[37]

It was evident that Davis was a key to Birmingham's success. In 12 games, he was batting .340. Clarence "Pijo" King at .318 was the only other player above the .300 mark. But Mays was still generating the buzz. As the Black Barons put together another winning streak (13 games), Mays raised his average to .289 in 20 games (a slow start—he was well over .300 a few weeks later). His 22 RBIs were second in the league.[38] The pitching leaders were Williams (5–1), Newberry (4–1) and Powell (5–2).[39]

The 1950 Black Barons with their team bus. Front row, from left: "Pepper" Bassett, c; Curtis Hollingsworth, p; Jimmie Lee Newberry, p; Bobby Robinson, of; John Cowan, ss; Henry Bayliss, 2b; Trainer; unidentified pitcher. Back row: John Atkins, business secretary; Sammy Williams, p; Bill Greason, p; "Pijo" King, of; Bill Powell, p; Dick Watts, 3b; Ed Steele, of; Alonzo Perry, 1b; Herman Bell, c; Russell (first name unknown), bus driver (courtesy of the Friends of Rickwood Field).

The rigors of the road perhaps caught up with the Black Barons. Although they won the Saturday night game, 7–1, they lost both games on Sunday, 2–0 and 16–4, before a crowd of 3,921. The losses pretty much doomed any chance of catching Kansas City for the first-half title.

There was also some more bad news. While they were playing the Cubans in the East, Newberry jumped the team. He signed on with the Winnipeg Buffaloes in the Manitoba-Dakota Baseball League.[40] Angry Birmingham owner Tom Hayes, Jr., said he had advanced Newberry money before the pitcher disappeared. Hayes said the action would result in Newberry's indefinite suspension should he decide to return to the NAL.[41] As it turned out, that was not an issue. Newberry compiled a 7–7 record with Winnipeg and was the star pitcher in the playoffs. He returned to Winnipeg in 1951 and then played in Japan and in the low minor leagues. He never returned to the Negro leagues.[42]

On June 22, the day that everybody was expecting arrived. Willie Mays was signed by a major league team. The New York Giants farm club at Minneapolis purchased his contract from Birmingham and assigned him to the Trenton, New Jersey, team in the Class B Interstate League. The purchase price, reported at $15,000, was "believed to be a record price paid for a Negro player." Of that sum, Mays was to get $5,000 and the Black Barons $10,000.[43]

Mays was batting .394 at the time. He had hit .311 the year before as an 18-year-old. Interestingly, the report on the sale indicated that center field might not be his best position. "Mays' future with the Giants may be as a pitcher. He has one of the most powerful throwing arms in baseball. At least two major league scouts thought of him only as a future pitcher," wrote the *Birmingham News*.[44] Fortunately, the Giants decided center field was the spot for Mays, who subsequently became arguably the game's all-time greatest outfielder. He was the seventh former Black Baron to cross the color line, following Satchel Paige, Dan Bankhead, Piper Davis, Alonzo Perry, Parnell Woods, and Art Wilson. Four of them were signed directly from the Black Barons.

The Mays news overshadowed what normally would have been an exciting baseball event at Rickwood. The New Orleans Creoles, featuring female Toni Stone at second base, were in town to play a semipro team called the Birmingham Black Eagles.[45] A reported 5,000 fans paid to see Miss Stone thrill the fans "with her diamond agility and playing ability." The Creoles won the game, 10–8.[46]

Meanwhile, the NAL pennant races continued. Kansas City (26–7) and Birmingham (23–9) were clearly the best in the West Division league. Indianapolis (17–13) was the only team over .500 in the East.[47]

In late June, local fans got another glimpse of their team that had been so dominant on the road. Hosting Cleveland at Rickwood, Birmingham slammed out 26 runs in winning 14–1 and 12–0. Powell and Greason were the winning pitchers. Steele had one of the strongest plate appearances in club history. He was seven-for-eight with two home runs, a triple, and three doubles, 17 total bases on the day. Alonzo Perry was five-for-nine with two homers. Davis was four-for-seven with a home run estimated at 400 feet.[48]

The biggest home series of the year came the following weekend with Kansas City. The series would likely determine the first-half championship between Birmingham (33–14, .702) and Kansas City (29–10, .743). The pregame article reported Birmingham's pitching records: Powell (8–3), Greason (8–4), Pollard (4–1), and Williams (7–3).[49]

When the final out was made on Tuesday night, Birmingham had won three of four games and seemingly taken the lead, 36–15, .705 to 30–13, .697.[50]

However, amid the usual NAL confusion over records and standings, it appeared that a single game win on July 4 had catapulted the Monarchs back into the lead and the first-half title. Standings in the *Birmingham World* were Kansas City (31–13, .705) and Birmingham (38–16, .703). Standings in *The Chicago Defender* were Kansas City (30–11, .732) and Birmingham (38–14, .731.)[51]

Sam Hairston (.464) of Indianapolis was the first-half individual batting leader. Second was "Piper" Davis (.448). Hairston, the dominant player in the NAL, also led in hits, total bases, two-base hits, home runs, and RBIs.[52]

Birmingham started the second half on the road, although no games were reported until they reached Baltimore in mid–July.[53] Likewise, there was a comparable drop in reporting by the *Chicago Defender*, which had published most Sunday double-header results during the first half.

While the team was gone, Marcel Hopson wrote a column, suggesting that Birmingham might have won the first half by four percentage points. Supposedly, the Howe News Bureau had failed to credit Birmingham with wins by pitchers who were released after playing in only one or two games.[54] However, there was no announced or published recalculation awarding the honors to Birmingham.

In Memphis in early July, the struggling Negro Southern League put together an all-star team for a game with the Red Sox. Memphis won the game, 6–5, before a crowd of 5,396 at Martin Park. Toni Stone played six innings for the all-stars, hitting a double and walking twice in three plate appearances. She handled two chances perfectly in the field.[55]

The Black Barons returned home in mid–July for single games with Baltimore. Two of the Baltimore players, pitcher Joe Black and second baseman James "Junior" Gilliam, would soon be in the major leagues. Birmingham's lineup:

Henry Bayliss, 2b	Clarence "Pijo" King, lf
Norman Robinson, cf	Jose Burgos, ss
Charles "Coot" Willis, cf	William Powell, p, 9–3
Piper Davis, 1b	William Greason, p, 9–4
Ed Steele, rf	"Rip" Collins, p, 1–1
Andrew Watts, 3b	Nathaniel Pollard, p, 5–1
Lloyd "Pepper" Bassett, c	Samuel C. Williams, p, 7–4[56]
Herman Bell, c	

Gilliam was in his sixth with Baltimore. Before the year was out, he was with Brooklyn's Montreal farm club. In 1953 he moved up to the majors, spending fourteen seasons with the Dodgers.[57]

By now, Willie Mays was having a terrific season with Trenton in the Interstate League. When it was over, he had a .353 batting average and .510 slugging percentage.[58]

Taking his place in Birmingham's center field were the veteran Norman "Bobby" Robinson and an industrial league rookie named Charles "Coot" Willis. The latter, 18, would later find his calling as an educator and as a civic and political leader, serving a number of years as mayor and city council member in Fairfield. Willis was also a 1950 Fairfield Industrial High School graduate. He and Mays were football, basketball and baseball teammates for Coach James McWilliams. But nobody was really capable of filling the young Mays's shoes. Willis's role was backup for Robinson in home games. He didn't travel when the team left town.[59]

The two games at Rickwood were an anathema for pitchers with Birmingham winning, 14–8, and Baltimore winning, 12–2.[60]

Starting a series with Indianapolis, Birmingham won, 6–4, on Saturday night. The Sunday games were split before a crowd was reported at 3,561.[61] The series continued on the road with stops in Little Rock, Columbus, Mississippi, and New Orleans. Birmingham then barnstormed with Baltimore and later Indianapolis for more than two weeks.

As the Black Barons returned to Birmingham on August 6 to play Chicago, rosters for the East–West game were announced. Davis, Greason and Bassett were among those selected.[62]

The Chicago manager was now Ted "Double Duty" Radcliffe. Other former Black Barons on the team were Joe Scott, Luther Branham, Jesse Douglass, and John Huber.[63]

Birmingham won both games. The star of the day was Alonzo Perry, who probably had no bigger day in his career. The big pitcher-turned-first-baseman had four home runs, two in each game. He also had a single in the first game. His RBI total for the day was 11, seven in the first game and four in the second.[64] The *Birmingham News* reported:

> The first two Perry homers went into the right field bleachers. The last one struck the next to top row—a 410-foot clout. This was considered a lengthy blow until Harry Rhodes of Chicago batted in the ninth inning.
>
> With the score tied, Rhodes hit a 0–2 pitch completely over the bleachers in right out into a dirt road back of the park. The ball travelled at least 450 feet.

Lost in all of the home run bashing was Herman Bell's key pinch-hit double in the bottom of the ninth, driving in two runs and sending the game into extra innings.[65]

It was an exciting day off the field in Birmingham, too. Traveling with the American Giants were three white players, pitcher Louis Chirban, shortstop Frank Dyll, and second baseman Stanley Hierko. Radcliffe said he was met at the gate by two uniformed and two plainclothes police officers, who told him the whites could not play. He sent the white players back to the hotel to change into civilian clothes.[66]

Like Eddie Klep in 1946, the barred players returned to the ballpark and watched the game from the white stands. The three were said to have played in Fairmont, West Virginia, on Friday, but missed the Birmingham-Chicago game at Cullman, Alabama, on Saturday night because of transportation difficulties. Radcliffe said the American Legion promoter of the Cullman game told him that the trio could have played in that city. Ironically, they were not there. The Chicago bus had broken down and the team had to go to Cullman in cars. There were not enough cars, so the three white players were left behind in Birmingham.[67] The fact that they were left behind probably says a lot about whether they were signed for the novelty or for their real baseball talent. Their American Giants' careers were brief.[68]

If bats boomed in the first game with Chicago on Sunday, they were absolutely thunderous in the Wednesday night game at Rickwood. The nine-inning game saw 37 runs and 39 hits as Birmingham won, 19–18, on Black Barons Appreciation Night. Seven players— Norman Robinson, Ed Steele, Jose Burgos, Clyde McNeal, Jesse Douglass, Art Pennington, and Joe Scott—had three hits each.[69]

While all of those runs and hits produced three wins for Birmingham, they didn't change the standings. Birmingham (5–6) was still in third place, trailing Memphis (11–1) and Kansas City (10–3) in the West. In the poorly reported East, it was Philadelphia (1–0) and New York (2–1). The Cleveland club had folded.[70]

If the standings were accurate for Houston, that hapless club remained winless after a weekend at Rickwood. Birmingham won a Friday night game in Tuscaloosa, then beat the Eagles three straight in Birmingham. The Sunday crowd was a disappointing 2,011.[71]

On August 16, the New Orleans Creoles returned to Birmingham, this time to play a pair of games with the Black Barons. The star attraction for the Creoles was still Toni Stone, the 5-foot-7½-inch female at second base. The 19-year-old's role was a reflection on the dwindling interest in black league ball. She was a gate attraction. But she was also able to play baseball, hitting a respectable .243 in 50 games that year.[72] Some 5,000 fans had turned out to see her when the Creoles played the semipro Birmingham Black Eagles in June. There had also been a crowd of more than 5,000 in Memphis in July when she was with the Negro Southern League all-star team.[73]

Birmingham won, 13–5 and 10–8. There was no mention of how Stone performed in the game reports. The two teams then went to Tuscaloosa for a single game and to New Orleans for a double-header.[74]

Birmingham lost two games in New Orleans, but it was missing four starters. The games were played on Sunday, August 20, the same day of the East–West All-Star game. Playing for the West were Perry, Steele, Bassett, and Powell in place of Greason, who had been mentioned earlier.[75] The Birmingham group played well as the West won, 5–3. Perry had three hits and two RBIs. Steele drove in a run with a triple, and Bassett also had a hit. Powell, the third West pitcher, closed the game with a save. He gave up a run and two hits but struck out four batters in three innings.[76]

Although still far back in the standings, the club had shown improvement in the weeks leading up to the East–West game. Birmingham (11–9) trailed Memphis (15–2–1) and Kansas City (18–8).[77]

The four All-Stars rejoined the club somewhere on the road. It was another of those trips whose results remained a mystery to the fans in Birmingham. "No details and scores of Black Baron games while they are on the current road trip," noted the *Birmingham World* on August 29. West Division standings published that day were Kansas City (21–9), Memphis (16–7–1), and Birmingham (13–10).[78]

Despite one report that said Memphis was the second-half champion in the West—and the club did play much better—the Monarchs won both halves, thus eliminating any need for a playoff in that division. No championship series was held between the East and West.[79] Sam Hairston (.424) ran away with the batting title. He was signed by the White Sox and sent to Colorado Springs in the Class A Western League in August. He had a game-winning hit in his first game.[80] Hairston also led the NAL in home runs, RBIs, hits, and total bases. Birmingham's best batter was "Pijo" King (.348). Alonzo Perry (.313) led in runs scored and total bases. His 14 home runs were second to Hairston's 17. Bill Powell (110) was second to Indianapolis's Raul Galata (120) in strikeouts.[81]

Although Kansas City won both halves and the sensational Willie Mays was lost to Organized Ball, Birmingham still had some highlights in 1950. The *Birmingham News* singled out several:

> In the last half of the season [Manager Vic] Harris trotted out one of the deadliest double play combinations in all Negro baseball. Jose Burgos starting most of them with Henry Bayliss in the pivot job and Perry at first turning in one end of couple killings....
>
> Ed Steele, out of the game for quite some time on account of illness, and playing sometimes when he should have been in bed, has been leading the club in extra base hits through the season's two halves.[82]

23

A New Division (1951)

Vic Harris's tenure with the Black Barons was just one year. When training camp opened in the spring of 1951, the new manager was veteran outfielder Ed Steele.

A native of Selma, Alabama, "Stainless" Steele joined the Black Barons at spring training in 1941, although he does not appear to have made the final roster. In 1942 he began a long career, primarily in right field. The 1951 season was his tenth consecutive year with the team. It was also his final one. The following year he signed a minor league contract with the Pittsburgh Pirates and logged playing time with the Hollywood Stars and Denver Bears.[1]

The 1951 season was also a milestone for Tom Hayes, Jr. It was his twelfth year of ownership, the longest tenure in club history. And, like Steele, it was his final season with Birmingham.

The Negro American League saw its ranks diminished. There were still East and West divisions, but with only four clubs in each. Birmingham moved to the East with Baltimore, Indianapolis, and Philadelphia. In the West were Chicago, Kansas City, Memphis, and the New Orleans Eagles. Gone were the New York Cubans and Cleveland, the latter folding before the 1950 season ended. New Orleans was the once-again relocated original Newark Eagles, this time moving from Houston.[2] Dr. J.B. Martin was re-elected president of the league. Hayes was vice president.[3]

Martin, putting on his best public relations face, issued a statement in which he predicted that the upcoming season would be the league's greatest postwar year:

> I believe that the 1951 season will be a success both financially and artistically. It will not be as good as the [pre] war years, but it will be better than any post-war period.
> Our league will have better players this year than in the past. Of course, the [military service] draft has taken some of our bright young prospects, but we have some good players left.
> The breaking in of Negro players into organized baseball has cut down on our post-war attendance, but with the tightening of the league, I expect a good season. All the owners may not agree with me, but I am sure the colored baseball fans will prove my case this season.[4]

The draft was a renewal of the Selective Service System to fill U.S. military ranks, a move necessitated by the Korean War.[5]

Hayes again held a tryout camp "for local talent" at Sloss Field. Each prospect was expected to provide his own uniform, shoes, and glove to participate.[6]

Spring training opened on April 9 with about 30 candidates on the Alabama State campus. It was obvious there would be a lot of new faces. Returning were Norman "Bobby" Robinson, Pepper Bassett, William Powell, Willie Collins, Clarence "Pijo" King, and Samuel Williams. Also, Nathaniel Pollard and John Huber sought to return to the Black Barons.[7]

There was a large group of new players seeking spots on the roster. Among them were Rufus Gibson, Lewis Gillis, John Henry Williams, Joe Chism, Douglas Pickins, Fred Clarke, Willie Lee Price, Felix Pines, Homer Garrett, Irwin Castille, Sim King, Willie Lee, Jr., Norris Cooley, Woodrow Means, David Williams, and Willie Boulware.[8] Castille, a 21-year-old shortstop from Lafayette, Louisiana, and Los Angeles, was called the "most promising first year player in years." It was predicted that he would make a bid for the major leagues.[9]

Hayes told Marcel Hopson, sports editor of the *Birmingham World*, that there was a lot of interest in the team outside of Birmingham. He said he had received inquiries from weekly newspapers for action shot photographs of Black Barons home games. Among the photographs requested were double-play put-outs, individual player close-ups, and slides into home plate. He invited interested photographers to attend the games and submit their work to Manager Steele for possible purchase.[10]

Steele planned to work the group hard for a week, then begin an arduous exhibition schedule to prepare them for life on the road. Between April 13 and Opening Day on May 4, they played in such far-flung locations as Aliceville and Anniston in Alabama, Hattiesburg and Greenville in Mississippi, Baton Rouge, and Little Rock.[11]

An earlier exhibition series with the Jacksonville Eagles gave local fans a look at the team.[12]

Hopson was impressed with Birmingham bats, particularly the long-range hits of King, Robinson, and Gibson. He also noted Bessemer resident King's "powerful throwing arm," and observed, "Gibson may not fill fully in the footsteps of Lorenzo 'Piper' Davis at second sack, but he has great promises ... rookie shortstop Joe Chisholm may not be a 'Artie' Wilson or Jose Burgos, but has promises of doing a good job at S.S. post.... Fans gave many approving nods at the performance of Rookie Catcher Patterson." A pitcher who caught his eye was rookie Roosevelt Lilly.[13]

But he also had some advice for officials, particularly the three umpires—William "Bill" Moore, H. Lovell Mosely, and Parker Austin. Railing against players that he called "creampuffs," Hopson asked the arbiters to take action against certain aspects of the game:

> [D]on't you think it is "cream puffish" when a base-runner gets on first base [and] too much time is wasted if a teammate or line coach has to go over to, or send someone to the dugout to get a jacket to wraparound the base runner before he makes his way around the bases to get (in many instances) "put out"? ... It doesn't make sense, it seems, when a base runner, in order to be more effective in his speed and lightness, needs a jacket.... It is obvious that he isn't going to freeze in June, July or August at Rickwood Field. A good-thinking player should want to be as light as possible (meaning less clothes on his body or his arms which steer his body for speed pick up) if he desires to score for his team.[14]

The last home exhibition game brought in Chicago, now under Winfield S. Welch.[15]

The two teams played a double-header with Birmingham winning the first game, 11–1, and Chicago the second, 9–8. Collins pitched a six-hitter and King drove in five runs in the opener. Steele played mostly rookies in the second game.[16]

Opening Day was on Friday, May 4, with New Orleans at Rickwood. Hopson wrote that local fans were "over-powered with much anxiety" awaiting the team's return.[17] The "rebuilt" Black Barons were expected to present a starting lineup with only two returning veterans, outfielders Steele and Robinson. Manager Jim Ford of the Eagles had pretty much the same team as last year. Among those players was catcher Otha "Bill" Bailey from Huntsville and former Black Barons Jehosie "Jay" Heard and Jessie Douglas.[18]

Wendell Smith, writing in the *Pittsburgh Courier*, projected Birmingham as the 1951 favorite. "The new manager, Ed Steele, has come up with three pitchers who are tabbed as future stars, Rip Collins, ex-Tuskegee ace; Len Collie, a small but effective southpaw; and Willie Price," he wrote.[19]

Festivities included a Friday afternoon parade, the Fairfield Industrial High School band under James Grimes, and "other colorful activities."[20] Hopson provided a rare demographic look at the ball club. Ten of the players were born in Alabama, including five from Birmingham. The average age was 25, height 5-foot-9, and weight 168.[21]

Birmingham won, 6–5, in 11 innings before a crowd of 3,554. Rookie John Henry Williams, pinch hitting for Griggs in the eleventh, drove in the winning run. His single brought in catcher Patterson, who had tripled. A left-hander named Pine or Kines started for Birmingham but lasted only four innings. He was replaced by Collins, who held the Eagles in check. Rookie right fielder Acie Griggs had three hits in six at bats and drove in two runs.[22]

In the Sunday double-header, Birmingham won the first game, 7–6, with rookie Leroy "Slim" Johnson, of Daphne in Baldwin County, pitching a complete game. New Orleans won the second game, 5–2. Patterson, Robinson, and Claiborne Cartwright each had three hits for Birmingham. The attendance was 3,464.[23]

The next weekend brought Kansas City to Rickwood. They were managed by Buck O'Neil, back for his fourth year. In later years, when the Negro leagues were being rediscovered and commemorated, O'Neil became a national spokesman for black ball.

The Birmingham lineup:

Irwin Castille, ss	Acie Griggs, cf
Claiborne Cartwright, cf	Joe Chism, 2b
Rufus Gibson, 3b	Jim Canada, 1b
Willie Patterson, c	Willie "Rip" Collins, Roosevelt Lilly,
Norman Robinson, lf	or Leroy Johnson, p[24]

Birmingham won, 4–3, on Saturday. Gibson hit a home run. Bill Greason, pitching two scoreless innings, was the winner in relief of Leroy Johnson. On Sunday, Birmingham won the opener, 5–0, behind Greason's two-hit pitching, picking up his second win in as many days. Patterson hit a home run and Gibson had three hits, one of them a triple. Kansas City won the nightcap, 8–2.[25]

Next up were the American Giants. Birmingham lost a double-header in Chicago, won a single game in Chattanooga, then returned to Rickwood for a Thursday night game. Greason pitched a complete game, winning 2–1, before crowd of 1,406. He struck out 12 and walked three.[26]

That weekend, the Philadelphia Stars, under future Hall of Famer Oscar Charleston, came in for a series.[27] On Sunday, they split a pair of high-scoring games, Philadelphia winning, 9–8, and Birmingham, 9–7, before a crowd of 3,899.[28]

Birmingham was 9–12 after the Sunday games. It was a record that got worse as the week progressed. Philadelphia won in Gadsden and Columbus, Mississippi, and again in Birmingham.[29]

A two-week road trip, paired with Philadelphia and Baltimore, included games in Buffalo, New York; Chattanooga, Tennessee; and Andalusia and Tuscaloosa, Alabama. They returned home on June 11 for a 10–5 win over Baltimore. Greason pitched shutout ball for six innings, then gave up five runs over the last three. Gillis had three hits. Gibson was shifted from second to shortstop. Castille moved to third, replacing Williams.[30]

The following Sunday, Memphis came to town and trounced the Black Barons, 13–2. Birmingham won the second game on an unexplained forfeit. The series continued on Tuesday, June 19, with a game to benefit the Miles College Development Fund (building expansion) drive. Activities included a performance by Prof. Ira Williams and Miles College Marching Band with "its curvaceous, charming, scintillating corps of band majorettes." Memphis won, 9–5. Birmingham's one bright spot was John Henry Williams, who had four hits and doubled home two runs in a ninth-inning rally.[31]

July opened with a series of at least 12 games against New Orleans. The travel itinerary started with a Sunday double-header in Birmingham and a single game in Tuscaloosa. From there it was on to Mississippi, Arkansas, Oklahoma, and Texas.[32]

At Rickwood Field, Birmingham won the first game, 19–6. New Orleans starter Clyde Golden had a game that must have given him nightmares for days to come. Not only was he battered for 13 hits but he also walked 17 batters. Williams and Robinson had three RBIs each while Castille and Greason each had two. One of Castille's hits was a solo home run. Greason pitched a complete game, striking out eight and walking one. Former Black Baron Jay Heard pitched New Orleans to a 7–5 win in the second game.[33]

The first half ended on the Fourth of July. The Black Barons, struggling with so many young players, finished second in the East but did not seriously challenge leader Indianapolis. Indeed, a writer in the *Pittsburgh Courier* noted, "The Black Barons are having one of their worst years in many seasons. They have hit only five round trippers, fewer than any club in the circuit." Kansas City edged out Chicago in the West.[34]

As the first half wound down, "Piper" Davis, now playing in the Pacific Coast League, happened to catch a game in Chicago between the American Giants and the New Orleans Eagles. He pointed out serious defects that he saw in Negro leagues baseball, defects that would hold talented young players back. He told Luix Virgil Overbea of the *Chicago Defender*:

> In Negro baseball, the players advance purely on natural talent and not much more. Their basic shortcoming is that they do not learn the fundamentals of the game. When I was playing with the Barons I really didn't know anything about the game. I have learned more in two years in white baseball than I learned all of my years in the colored leagues.
>
> If our league will pay such men as Ray Dandridge a reasonable amount of money, it would produce much better baseball. The best men in this league must spend a year or two in the minors to learn the fundamentals.[35]

Dandridge, possibly the best third baseman in Negro leagues history, was inducted in the National Baseball Hall of Fame in 1987.[36]

As the second half got started, so did voting for the 19th Annual East–West Game. Once again, fans could send in their choices for the starting lineups of the two teams. As the first wave of votes went in to the NAL headquarters in Chicago, four Birmingham players were among the East favorites. Jim Canada led at first base and Irwin Castille at shortstop. Ed Steele and Norman Robinson were among the top five in the outfield.[37]

But by now Birmingham had lost one of its best arms. Bill Greason was offered a contract by the Oakland Oaks of the Pacific Coast League. The Oaks, though, wanted Greason to start off with their Wenatchee, Washington, team in the Class B Western International League. Greason turned down the offer, opting for Jalisco, Mexico, which offered more money. He had played there in 1950.[38] Presumably, Birmingham could not match or better what Jalisco was willing to pay.

Few results were reported locally on the long road trip with New Orleans. The team returned home on July 15 to win a double-header from Philadelphia, 9–8 and 3–2. Steele was four-for-four in the first game, including a home run. Lilly pitched a complete game in the seven-inning nightcap.[39]

The following Sunday, in Durham, North Carolina, Birmingham beat the Southern All-Stars, 22–5, reportedly for its ninth win in a row.[40] It is not clear if this was a team of Negro Southern League all-stars or just a pick-up team. The latter is more likely because the NSL was largely a semipro operation with only four teams by 1951.[41]

They returned home in late July for two double-headers with Baltimore. Manager Steele released the following lineup, although it was missing a third baseman:

Wiley Griggs, 2b	Johnny Williams, ss
Acie Griggs, cf	Jim Canada, 1b
Ed Steele, rf	Ollie Staton, p
Louis Gillis, c	John Huber, p
Norman Robinson, lf	Roosevelt Lilly, p[42]

Canada was a veteran Negro leaguer and former Black Baron. He had played in Birmingham in 1936, 1937 and 1946. His career dated to at least 1933 with the Jacksonville Red Caps. He managed Chattanooga briefly in 1948, reportedly leaving the team because he hadn't been paid. He claimed to have recommended Willie Mays to Piper Davis. However, Tommy Sampson is also credited with recommending Mays to Davis.[43] Regardless, Mays was already well known at Fairfield Industrial High School and the city league. His "discovery" at Chattanooga was more likely simply word of mouth because of his playing professional ball there on weekends.

The Friday night games were rained out. Baltimore hit five home runs on Sunday, crushing Birmingham, 10–3 and 10–2. Henry Kimbro hit three homers and Doc Wesley two. The nightcap, mercifully for Birmingham and the crowd of 2,046, was called because of darkness after six innings by umpire Poindexter Williams.[44]

On August 8, the toll on Birmingham pitchers continued as Indianapolis shelled Willie Lee Price and Roosevelt Lilly for 19 hits, winning 15–0. Leander "Schoolboy" Tugerson of the Clowns pitched a no-hitter, striking out 14 and walking four.[45] It is the only known time that the Black Barons were a no-hit victim at home. Tugerson later had a year with Knoxville in the Mountain States League.[46]

Three Birmingham players were on the East roster for the East–West Game in Chicago. Steele had led all outfielders in the fan voting with 10,019. Robinson (7,923) was the backup outfielder in fourth place, and Lilly (8,117) made the pitching staff.[47]

Although declining, the classic still had appeal, drawing a crowd of 21,312. The East won, 3–1, "behind some fancy clutch pitching and Robinson's two run-scoring doubles." Steele also drove in a run with a triple.[48]

Indianapolis returned to Birmingham in mid–August. The Clowns won both games before the season's biggest crowd, reported at 4,522. Although Steele hit a home run, the Clowns won the first game, 8–5. Propelled by an eleven-run second inning, they walloped the Black Barons, 21–5, in the nightcap. Tugerson gave up four hits this time, but his teammates overwhelmed four Birmingham pitchers. The only highlight for Birmingham was a 350-foot home run by Lilly, pinch hitting for Steele in the fifth. In the nightcap, the Clowns scored 15 runs on 16 hits in the first two innings.[49]

Howe News Bureau standings had New Orleans (15–8) on top in mid–August. Indianapolis (14–10) and Chicago (10–6) followed. Birmingham was 6–13.[50]

Parnell Woods, the old Black Baron from the 1930s, had moved into the hitting lead with a .375 average. Birmingham's best batter was Steele, just two percentage points behind Woods at .373.[51]

Although they were not the final standings, the won-lost records released by the Howe News Bureau in late August placed Indianapolis (22–12) ahead of New Orleans (19–13). Birmingham (6–17) was last.[52]

As the season end neared, Birmingham returned home for a Sunday double-header with Memphis and a Labor Day game with Philadelphia. It was reported that Ed Steele was being scouted by two major league clubs.[53] His prospects were likely slim because of his age. If "Piper" Davis was deemed too old at 31, Steele was likely more so at 35. One former Birmingham player was doing well in Organized Ball, though. Although he was farmed out to the high minors, Artie Wilson had made the New York Giants' roster in spring training. He appeared in 81 games with Oakland in the Pacific Coast League.[54]

Birmingham won the two Memphis games, 15–11 and 4–3, but fell to Philadelphia, 10–4, on Labor Day before a pitiful crowd of just 751. The Philadelphia game was Steele's last one in the Negro American League. In 1952 he was in the Pacific Coast League. The Labor Day game was preceded by one involving two YMCA Industrial League teams. Ishkooda downed Rosedale, 11–7. Rogers Repp, who had a triple and two singles for the victors, was named most valuable player and presented "a colorful wrist watch" by Black Barons owner Tom Hayes, Jr.[55]

NAL statistics at that point had Birmingham seventh in team batting (.242) and last in fielding (.924). Indianapolis was hitting .312, and Kansas City was the best fielding team with a .958 percentage. Steele (.371) continued to lead Birmingham batters. Birmingham's best pitcher was Leroy Johnson (4–4).[56]

An interesting footnote to the 1951 season was the appearance of yet another black ball player in an integrated Southern setting. In August, Percy Miller, Jr., had debuted with the Danville Leafs in the Class B Carolina League. His reception by the fans was cordial, and his signing had been greeted by "more favorable comment" than unfavorable. "I don't see anything wrong with signing the Negro. I had three on a team of mine in Canada," said Danville Manager Bob Latshaw. But a black player in a previous all-white setting was still a novelty. As Durham Manager Ace Parker put it: "I think it's all right to play Negroes. I played with them in professional football and once the game is under way you don't realize that you have them on the team."[57]

24

New Leadership and a
Disputed Championship (1952)

Another season, another manager. Also, a new owner.

When spring training camp opened for the 1952 Black Barons, the new manager was George "Tubby" Scales. In his 30-plus years in baseball, Scales had never worn a Birmingham uniform, but he had played many games against the Black Barons, starting in1920 with the Montgomery Grey Sox. Over the years his career as primarily a second baseman had carried him to St. Louis, Homestead, Baltimore, and New York. A native of Talladega, Alabama, Scales was said to be one of the founders of the Black Yankees and was the team's first manager in 1932. Buck Leonard said no one could hit a curve ball better than Scales.[1]

The new owner was William "Sou" Bridgeforth, whose nickname was occasionally spelled "Soo" and "Suke."

A native of Tanner, Alabama, in Limestone County, Bridgeforth was a lifelong baseball fan. He was a wealthy Negro nightclub owner when he purchased the Baltimore Elite Giants for $11,000 in 1950. The club did not do well financially, so a year later he purchased the Black Barons from Tom Hayes and merged the front office personnel. Paul Jones was general manager of the Elite Giants and later the Black Barons. Bridgeforth moved the Elite Giants back to Nashville in 1951, which turned out to be the club's final year.[2]

Baseball was a calling for Bridgeforth. His father, Ike Bridgeforth, had attended Tuskegee Institute on a baseball scholarship. "Sou" played at Trinity High School in Athens, and was reportedly the winning pitcher in all 24 games that the school played in 1925. Starting out as a brick mason with an uncle in Nashville, he eventually became financially stable enough to buy the Baltimore team and launch his career as an owner. He died in 2004, but he has not been forgotten in his hometown. He was inducted into the Limestone County Sports Hall of Fame in 2009.[3]

With the sale of the team to Bridgeforth came an end to the greatest, most stable, and likely most storied period in the history of the Birmingham Black Barons. Thomas Hayes had formed a partnership with Abe Saperstein, founder of the Harlem Globetrotters, bringing astute management to the Birmingham team during the 1940s. Under the 12 years of Hayes's ownership, the team won three pennants, played in the Negro World Series three times, and maintained a roster of players that fans could identify with year after year. Beginning in 1948, the Black Barons produced nearly two dozen players who went on to Organized Ball, including eight who made it to the major leagues—Dan Bankhead, Bill Greason, Willie Harrell, Jehosie Heard, John Kennedy, Willie Mays, Willie Smith, and Artie Wilson.[4]

Chris Fullerton also lists Sam Hairston as a Black Baron who reached the majors.

Hairston, the first black to play with the Chicago White Sox, has a tenure with Birmingham in 1944 that is somewhat anecdotal and described in Chapter 20.

Ed Steele, whose 11-year tenure with the Black Barons is matched only by Buford "Geechie" Meredith, had gotten his opportunity in Organized Ball. Even though he was now 36 years old, he had been signed by the Hollywood Stars of the Pacific Coast League. He had a slow start, though, batting .213 with just two homers and 10 RBIs in 69 games. Because of his weak performance, he was farmed out to the Denver club in the Western Association, where he improved to .254 in 47 games. In July he was injured and subsequently released.[5]

But "Stainless" Steele's career was not over. He would eventually return to Birmingham for a while, and also played two seasons in Canada with Guelph, a semipro ball club. The Canadian semipro leagues became an alternative to the Mexican League for the Negro American League for black ball players who washed out of Organized Ball. Players such as Willie Wells, Leon Day, Lyman Bostock, Ray Dandridge, and "Double Duty" Radcliffe logged time in Canada in the early 1950s. Later, Steele managed the Detroit Stars for three years as the NAL neared its end.[6]

Scales was leading Birmingham in yet another scaled-down version of the Negro American League. Now there were only six teams. Besides Birmingham it was Chicago, Indianapolis, Kansas City, Memphis, and Philadelphia. Gone were the Baltimore Elite Giants and New Orleans Eagles. Baltimore had lost its home grounds the previous year and spent most of the season as a traveling club. Dr. B.B. Martin, co-owner of the Eagles with W.S. Young, said the team had lost money the past two years.[7]

In the off season, Indianapolis signed Toni Stone, who had broken the gender barrier at New Orleans in 1951. When the Clowns played a preseason exhibition game against the Uniontown, Alabama, Black Steers, she was given serious promotion as a player rather than just a novelty. "She's no 'weak sister' at the plate. At the moment her batting average is just under the .300 mark," reported the *Alabama Citizen*. "Miss Stone, a native of St. Paul, Minn., goes all out on all plays. She's every bit a fine girl, but when the going gets rough she'll rival any of the male players in toughness. On the difficult double-plays, when the base runner flashes his spikes, she holds her ground and completes the play."[8]

In early April, the Black Barons held tryout camps in Nashville and at the Stockham Valve ball field, then moved to the Alabama State campus in Montgomery for formal spring training activities.[9] Reported in camp were outfielders Norman "Bobby" Robinson, Jimmy Zapp, Sidney Bunch, Henry Kimbro, and Tom Hester; catchers Louis Gillis and Dan Black; first basemen Wesley Dennis and Jim Canada; shortstops Irwin Castille and Tommy Butts; utility man Frank Russell; second baseman Paul Parsley; third baseman Fleming Reed; pitchers Frank Thompson, Kelley Searcy, Willie Scruggs, Ted Robinson, Ulysses Holleman, and Ollie Staton; and George Carter, a rookie from Gallatin, Tennessee, whose position was not indicated.[10]

Others who reported over the next couple of weeks included Eddie Brooks, Frank Russell, Otha Bailey, and Frank Evans. Among the pitchers were Eddie Hancock, Bill Beverly, Fred Cain, Charlie Johnson, Paul Jenkins, and Ted Richardson.[11] At some point, the team added a notable infielder, Thomas "Pee Wee" Butts, whose career dated to the late 1930s with the Atlanta Black Crackers. Butts, a shortstop, was part of a great double-play combination with Baltimore in the 1940s. He never got a shot at Organized Ball, but his double-play partner, Junior Gilliam, did. In 1942, Lucius "Melancholy" Jones, sports editor of the *Atlanta Daily World*, called Butts "the best shortstop in the game."[12] Some of these players, notably Kimbro, Dennis, Russell, Evans, and Robinson, had been picked up from the demise of the Elite Giants.[13]

Catcher Otha Bailey, who spent eleven seasons, 1952 to 1962, with the Black Barons (courtesy NoirTech Research).

The exhibition season opened with Chicago. The visitors won the first game, 9–8, and Birmingham won the second, 5–3. The two clubs then barnstormed on an exhibition schedule through North Alabama, Tennessee, and Kentucky. Additional games were played with Kansas City and Memphis, most of which indicated a strong Birmingham team in 1952.

After compiling an 18–4 exhibition record and sweeping Memphis in its NAL opening double-header, the Black Barons opened the home season against the Red Sox at Rickwood Field. The *Pittsburgh Courier* reported that "veteran baseball observers are predicting that this year's aggregation might turn out to be one of the dark horses in the Negro American League pennant chase." The Fairfield Industrial High School band once again provided music for the Friday, May 16, opener. The first-pitch honors were given to E.W. Barker, executive secretary of the 18th Street YMCA.[14]

The Memphis manager was Homer "Goose" Curry. Sportswriter Marcel Hopson shared a Curry story that he had picked up from Luther Carmichael of the *Nashville Globe*. The incident had occurred during Sunday exhibition games between the Red Sox and Black Barons at Memphis a few days earlier. According to Carmichael:

> "Goose" Curry, manager of the Red Sox, is another Leo Durocher (of the New York Giants) with the umps. That voice of his is perfectly enchanting. And the fans like it.
>
> One of the notable traits of Mr. Curry is his ability to notice every little thing. For example, he complained to the umps that a crucifix chain and cross around the neck of young Mr. Kelly Searcey (Black Baron pitcher) was interfering with the hitting efficiency of the Red Sox batsmen. And the wrangling was on. Finally, George Scales (Black Baron manager) barged out and took said crucifix from Kelly's neck and bellowed: "play ball."
>
> Then Scales cracked back: "It's not that crucifix that's keeping your boys from hitting, Goose. It's simply that baffling speed that boy's throwing them."[15]

The projected Birmingham lineup for the opener:

Rufus Gibson, 3b	Irvin Castille, ss
Eddie Brooks, 2b	Otha Bailey or "Pepper" Bassett, c
Henry Kimbro, cf	Frank Thompson, p
Wesley "Doc" Dennis, 1b	"Pee Wee" Jenkins, p
Norman Robinson, lf	Theodore Richardson, p
Frank Russell or Sidney Bunch, rf	Kelly Searcy, p[16]

Thompson, the 5-foot-2-inch lefthander, had started his career with the Black Barons in 1945. He also played with the barnstorming Cincinnati Crescents, New Orleans Black Pelicans, Homestead, and Memphis. Historian James Riley describes him thusly: "Short and squat, he was built like a fire hydrant, and had a harelip, walleye, and chipped tooth. His physical appearance sometimes made him the object of ridicule. Josh Gibson kidded him about his looks and put him on his 'all-ugly' team."[17] His physical appearance no doubt spawned the nickname "Groundhog." But what Thompson lacked in stature he made up in ability, quite successfully pitching for 10 years.[18] Interestingly, throughout the 1952 season many newspaper accounts referred to the pitcher only as Frank Thompson; somehow usage of the denigrating nickname had lessened.

Birmingham won the opener, 4–3, with Richardson holding the Red Sox to six hits. He also scored the winning run, coming in on Castille's fly to center. Both pitchers had control problems. Richardson walked seven and struck out three. His opponent, Marshall Bridges, walked four and struck out one. Kimbro hit a triple and a single to pace the hitters. The opening night crowd was 3,155.[19]

The Sunday double-header was rained out. They played in Huntsville and Columbus, Georgia, then returned to Rickwood for a single game that went 11 innings. Birmingham won, 4–3, when Kimbro drove in Castille with the winning run. Richardson pitched the entire eleven innings, striking out thirteen and walking only two.[20]

Despite two inconsistent outings at Rickwood, Bridges was a player to be watched. He went on to a 16-year career, advancing to the major leagues with the St. Louis Cardinals, New York Yankees, and Washington Senators.[21]

Howe News Bureau standings in early June had Birmingham (6–5) trailing Indianapolis (11–2) and Kansas City (2–1).[22] Released with those standings were individual statistics. The league's best batter was Henry Aaron (.483), shortstop for the Indianapolis Clowns. Aaron also led the league in runs, hits, total bases, home runs, and RBIs. In addition, he was tied with Castille in doubles. The leading pitcher was Richardson (4–0). Birmingham's top hitter was Kimbro (.380).[23]

On a long, poorly reported road trip that included stops in Cincinnati, Louisville and Indianapolis, Birmingham won a least five games, two from Philadelphia and three from Chicago.[24] The team returned home in early June for a series with the Stars, managed by Oscar Charleston. New names on the Birmingham roster included Willie Brown, shortstop; Hiram Gaston, pitcher; and Arthur McLemore, a 16-year-old left-hander from the Acipco team.[25]

Philadelphia pitcher Willie Gaines, 24, from Tuscaloosa, was now in his fourth season with the Stars. He was a three-year World War II Navy veteran and was said to have played in the Negro Southern League, also.[26]

Rain washed out the second game on June 8, but Birmingham won the opener, 9–8, in 10 innings. Wesley "Doc" Dennis hit two home runs, driving in five runs. The first was a 392-foot drive over the center field wall. The second, with a man on, won the game in the bottom of the tenth. The crowd was reported at 4,355, more than a thousand more than had turned out for Opening Day.[27]

Birmingham returned to the road afterward, playing Memphis in such locales as Nashville, Little Rock, Tuscaloosa, and Greenville and Greenwood, Mississippi.

Howe News Bureau Standings through June 18: Indianapolis (17–8), Birmingham (19–13), and Kansas City (10–7).

Hank Aaron (.374) of the Clowns was the top batter for the fourth consecutive week.

Ted Richardson (6–0) was the top pitcher. Aaron also led in hits and RBIs and was tied with Eddie Brooks in runs scored. Brooks and "Doc" Dennis were tied in total bases; Dennis was the home run leader with six.[28]

By the time the Black Barons returned to Rickwood on June 20 to face Winfield Welch's Chicago American Giants, they had a new manager. George Scales was gone and second baseman Eddie Brooks had been named acting manager. Birmingham won the series opener, 4–3, with a new pitcher, Ulysses Hollimon, throwing a six-hit complete game.[29]

On Sunday, it was all Chicago and practically all-Leroy Handcock. The right fielder scored two runs and drove in two in the first game. In the second, he drove in five runs, three with a triple and two with a single. The Giants won both games, 7–3 and 12–1, before a crowd of 3,246. Otha Bailey caught the first game, as usual, but the backstop for the second game was the venerable Pepper Bassett.[30]

While Chicago was in town, Brooks was replaced with a permanent manager. He was Russell "Columbus" Ewing, sometimes misidentified as Ewing Russell. One such misidentification appears in a photograph of the 1936 Cincinnati Tigers in their last year as an independent team before joining the Negro American League. That photograph caption identification was perpetuated by other writers.[31]

Marcel Hopson, in the *Birmingham World*, presented a brief biography of Russell: "His name is Russell Ewing, a native of Nashville, Tenn. From the interview, I learned that Mr. Russell has behind him a colorful background of 13 years of managership of pro and semi-pro baseball teams. From 1938 to 1939 the husky Tennessean managed the Louisville (Ky.) Black Colonels. Later he skippered the Nashville Cubs and piloted them to the 1940 Negro Southern League championship. He left the Cubs in 1950."[32] The 1940 reference is doubtful because there was no Negro Southern League operating that year.[33]

With the managerial change came news that two starters were no longer on the team. Shortstop Irvin Castille and left fielder "Bobby" Robinson had both had been released. Rumors said that Castille and someone in the front office "failed to see eye-to-eye." As for Robinson, rumors cited a salary issue. "The top echelon didn't believe Bobby's services were worth the existing amount." Management was not forthcoming with additional information. Marcel Hopson lamented the departures, especially Robinson. "Just like 'Pepper' Bassett, Robinson was a sort of loveable legendary figure at Rickwood. To fans, he was an old likeable 'land mark' of Rickwood Field history," he wrote. "Now that Robby is gone, Basset is the only spark left on the team to remind fans of once thorough-bred [sic] Black Barons."[34]

Robinson landed on his feet, though. A few weeks later, he wrote a letter to a friend in Birmingham, saying he and pitcher Ted Richardson were playing in Manitoba, Canada.[35]

After another poorly reported week away, the Black Barons returned home with the Indianapolis Clowns after having just beaten them in Chattanooga.[36] The Clowns had clinched the East division for the second year in a row. Birmingham was second but several games behind.[37] There was good news for Birmingham fans, though. Bill Greason, a World War II veteran called back into service for the Korean War, had been discharged from the Marines and was expected to rejoin the team.[38]

Perhaps encouraged by the Greason news, Birmingham played well on Sunday afternoon. With Taylor Smith throwing an eight-hitter, they shut out the Clowns, 7–0. Sam Williams pitched an eight-hitter in the second game, winning 6–2. Dennis and Bassett hit home runs before a crowd of 5,409. Bassett's blow came with a man on and was reported to have traveled 492 feet over the right field wall. There was no explanation for that distance calculation. The current right field wall is 392 feet from home plate. A diagram of the field in a 1949 Birmingham Barons program shows the distance to be 334 feet ending where the "colored bleachers" began. Nor was there any reference to the fact that such a distance would have eclipsed Walt Dropo's famous 467-foot shot in 1948.[39]

Still, that was three wins in a row, and Greason was expected back by the middle of the month.[40]

On the Indianapolis roster was Andy "Wrong Way" Watts, who played third base for Birmingham in 1950. Marcel Hopson recalled that Watts came by his nickname while with the Black Barons: "Watts is the player who created much attention during a Sunday game sometime ago at Rickwood when, instead of heading home, he reversed the bases and collided with a mate on second base. His mate had just belted a long-hit triple. Since Watts, at that time, was considered a budding rookie on the team, fans attributed his costly blunder to the roaring excitement and noise in the park."[41] The description at the time was slightly different, but the collision with the teammate was real. Watts, an Ensley native, played on a championship service team during World War II and joined Cleveland after the war, hitting a home run the first time he played in Cleveland Stadium.[42]

Standings through July 4 had Indianapolis (26–14) and Birmingham (28–21) in front.[43] A week later the *Chicago Defender* declared that Indianapolis (27–17) and Chicago (28–22) were the first-half winners. Curiously, the standings were published as a unit rather than by East and West divisions. Under that system, Birmingham (24–26) was listed in fifth place.[44]

There was a new batting leader, Jim Jones (.376) of Philadelphia. Henry Aaron was gone, having a signed with Eau Claire in the Northern League. Kimbo led in total bases, hits, doubles, and triples. T.W. Richardson (6–0) was still the pitching leader, although he had likely jumped to Canada by this time.[45]

Birmingham and Indianapolis made a paired road trip afterward through Tennessee, Kentucky, and West Virginia. After splitting off from the Clowns, the Black Barons went to Chicago and won a double-header from the American Giants.[46]

What did not materialize in July, however, was the return of Bill Greason. Reportedly, he and Birmingham management could not come to terms on salary. He was said to be in Mexico after his discharge from the U.S. Marines. Actually, he had gotten a better deal. He signed a contract with Oklahoma City in the Texas League, where he had a sparkling 9–1 record.[47]

As Greason was entering Organized Ball, another former Black Baron was leaving it. Ed "Stainless" Steele was given his release after appearing in 47 games with Denver in the Western League and 22 games with Hollywood in the Pacific Coast League. An injury was contributory.[48]

While the team was on a month-long road trip, "Sou" Bridgeforth took care of the local fans with interesting barnstorming games. On July 20, the Stockham and Ensley teams from the city industrial league squared off. Stockham, which won 7–1, got to play the touring Cuban All-Stars in the second game. The Cubans won 11–4.[49]

The following weekend, Bridgeforth brought in the Zulu Giants and Canadian All-Stars. This particular group of Zulu Giants was said to be in their 16th year, operating out of Louisville, Kentucky. Like their predecessors from the 1930s, they promised to "give the affair a bizarre appearance as they go through their games while wearing grass skirts." The Zulus were founded by a veteran ballplayer named Charlie Henry in the 1930s.[50] It was his idea to put the players in grass skirts.[51] By 1952, it seems likely that the talent pool for arduous barnstorming was greatly diminished compared to the 1930s. There was better pay and more stability in other venues, especially with the openings in the minor leagues and Canada.

The Canadians were "luminaries of the Manitoba, Dakota and Western Canadian Leagues, who have crossed the border and are doing a nation-wide tour against all competition."[52] Although those Canadian leagues attracted a number of black players from the United States, they were still predominantly white leagues.[53]

The Canadians were unquestionably the superior team, swamping the Zulus, 21–2, in the first game. They won the second by a smaller score of 6–5. One of the Canadian stars was former Black Baron Johnny Cowan, who had a home run, triple and two singles.[54] Cowan had played with the Elmwood Giants in the 1951 Mandak League.[55] Other Birmingham connections on the Canadian team were Ace "Skeet" Griggs, Frank Evans, Harry Barnes, and Freddie Sheppard. Evans, who played two years with Cleveland and then went to the Mandak League, later became the Black Barons' final league manager.[56] Barnes caught for Birmingham for a number of years. Sheppard was manager of the All-Stars. Only 533 attended the game.[57]

The Black Barons, in first place, returned home to play Memphis on August 10. It was a good homecoming. Birmingham won both games. With Bassett, Kimbro, and Dennis hitting home runs, Birmingham won the first, 5–3. Taylor Smith, a former Tuskegee Institute pitcher, struck out 12. Willie Scruggs held Memphis to three hits in the second as the Black Barons won, 5–0, before a crowd of 1,350.[58] Howe's new statistics report had Kimbro and Jim Jones tied for the batting lead with .348 averages. Thompson (9–4) was third among pitching leaders.[59]

A single game was scheduled at Rickwood Field on Thursday night. It was announced that Pepper Bassett would be catching for Birmingham. "Bassett, who some quarters say is getting too old to work behind the plate, will get out the old rocking chair and take his seat behind home plate to do his catching chores," reported the *Birmingham News*.[60] Because of rain, local fans didn't get to see Pepper do his stunt, but the uninitiated sportswriter Alf Van Hoose told Bassett's story: "Pep didn't bring along his chair for his declining days—he brought along the rocking chair as catching paraphernalia. The young rookie knew that he had to bring along something beside a .300 batting average to gain attention so he used the chair...." Van Hoose said the rocking chair, an "annual" treat for fans, was on hold because the next two Birmingham games were with Kansas City, and they were much too important for gimmickry. He said the Black Barons would like for Bassett to continue his home run streak against the Monarchs. Bassett had homered in his last two games at Rickwood.

Although he had enjoyed catching Satchel Paige in the 1930s, Bassett said his favorite player was actually Birmingham's most recent fan favorite, Willie Mays:

> Willie broke in with us when he was only 16 and I tried to help him a lot. I didn't have to help him in the field, he was good enough out there already.
>
> I did try to help him with his batting a little. You know he's still a kid yet. He's still not reached his peak yet. Makes me feel good when I notice he's doing so well that I might have helped him a little.
>
> I was too old to try for the majors when they let us in baseball, so I guess I sorta figure Willie's my boy.[61]

In late August, there was a dichotomy of baseball integration news. Dave Hoskins, the first black to play in the Texas League, called by some "the savior of the Texas League," was honored in Fort Worth. He was credited with adding 92,850 to league attendance compared with the year before. A total of 164,301 fans had seen his 30 appearances. In South Carolina, a different scene played out. David Mobley, 22, was signed by the Rock Hill Chiefs of the Tri-state League. League President Bobby Hipps had asked Rock Hill not to enter the league's first Negro in a game. Rock Hill ignored the request and played Mobley in a home game on August 26. A day later, Mobley was dropped by the Chiefs. Club officials said the move was made "to maintain harmony within the league."[62] A headline in the *Decatur Daily* said Mobley was a former Black Baron, although that is not substantiated.[63] The author's research has found only an Ira Lee Mobley with the Birmingham club in 1953.

On August 17, the 20th annual East–West Game was played in Chicago. Buster Haywood of Indianapolis was the East manager while Winfield Welch led the West. Five Birmingham players—Eddie Brooks, Doc Dennis, Henry Kimbro, Otha Bailey, and Frank Thompson—were on the East squad, which lost, 7–3. Thompson, the starter, lasted but two innings, giving up all seven runs. However, his teammates committed three errors in a disastrous six-run third inning.[64]

After the all-star break, the Black Barons returned home for two single games with Kansas City and won both. With Smith pitching a four-hitter and striking out eight, Birmingham won on Tuesday, 5–2. Ed Steele, back with the Black Barons after his brief stint in Organized Baseball, and 18-year-old Carl Long hit "sizzling" doubles to pace the hitting attack. The next night, Frank "Hoss" Thompson struck out nine Monarchs and got two hits at the plate as the Black Barons won, 10–3.[65]

Thompson had changed nicknames over the course of his career. When he started with the New Orleans Black Pelicans in 1945, and for the next few years, he was known as "Groundhog." He was still "Groundhog" with Memphis in 1950, but when he joined Baltimore in 1951 he became "Hoss."[66] Both names showed up throughout 1952.

With the second-half title and a playoff spot against first-half winner Indianapolis in the balance, the Black Barons came home to play a double-header with Memphis. Birmingham won the first game, 14–8. Thompson pitched a one-hit, 4–0 shutout in the six-inning nightcap, called because of darkness.[67]

The Howe News Bureau's final, but unofficial, standings were Birmingham (23–15) followed by Indianapolis (18–16) and Chicago (16–15).[68]

Roy Williams (.347) of Chicago won the batting crown. Birmingham's top batters were Steele (.380, but in only 16 games) and Kimbro (.341 in 82 games). Birmingham leaders included Kimbro in runs and doubles, Dennis in hits and RBIs, and Long in triples. The leading pitcher was T.W. Richardson with a 12–5 record.[69] Obviously, a season-long confusion over Ted Richardson and T.W. Richardson stretched even to the Howe offices, since T.W. Richardson, the Birmingham pitcher earlier in the season, was now supposed to be in Canada.

While awaiting the championship series with Indianapolis, the Black Barons played a series of exhibitions with the Harlem Globetrotters, managed by Winfield Welch, now in his 26th year of professional baseball. Birmingham won the first game, 5–4, getting an unexpected boost from Willie Mays, who had a single and walked twice. Mays, who was on active duty in the Army, was home on a three-day pass from Fort Eustis, Virginia.[70]

Mays did not play in the other games, having "promised Army buddies he'd be back in Norfolk to play with them."[71]

Although promoted as the Negro World Series, the event was really just the Negro American League championship series.[72] The title was to be determined in a best seven out of twelve games series. The games would be played throughout the South "where the September weather is more favorable."[73] The opening game festivities on September 14 included a show by the Clowns' King Tut and Boogie Woogie Frisco, and music from the Fairfield Industrial High School band. Birmingham's lineup:

Thomas Butts, ss	"Pijo" King, lf
Eddie Brooks, 2b	Wiley Griggs or Frank Russell, 3b
Henry Kimbro, cf	Pepper Bassett or Otha Bailey, c
Wesley Dennis, 1b	Taylor Smith, Frank Thompson,
Edward Steele, rf	Theodore Richardson, Sammie C. Williams,
Carl Long, cf	Joseph Chestnut and Manny Cartledge, p[74]

The published lineups resurrected the Richardson confusion. Ted Richardson was listed with Indianapolis and Theodore Richardson with Birmingham. T.W. "Ted" Richardson is listed on both rosters in *The Negro Leagues Book*. An exhaustive study by Jay-Dell Mah, co-author of a book on black players in Canada, suggests but does not definitely confirm that T.W. Richardson and Ted Richardson were two different players.[75] Although "Ted" and "T.W." both appear in game reports, it appears from Mah's work that T.W. Richardson played for Birmingham, while Ted played for Indianapolis. Birmingham's Richardson was one of the league's better pitchers, compiling a 12–5 record by mid–August. He was one of six Black Barons selected for the East-West All-Star game and pitched four scoreless innings in the game.[76]

At the end of the lineups listing, it was noted that Irving Castille was a utility infielder.[77] Only two innings were played before a steady rain washed the first game all away.[78]

The playoff games were held in multiple cities. The *Pittsburgh Courier* called it a "Negro World Series barnstorming tour," listing 10 games to be played in 10 days in 10 cities. After Birmingham, the scheduled venues were Memphis, Little Rock, Hot Springs, Nashville, Knoxville, Welch and Bluefield, West Virginia, and Newport News and Norfolk, Virginia. The paper reported that other "championship contests" would be played in Columbus (Georgia), Atlanta, Mobile, Biloxi, and New Orleans, "with the schedule set to take care of any games which might be washed out by inclement weather."[79] When the series returned to Birmingham on October 3, it was reported that the Black Barons had won five out of nine games thus far. The scores had ranged from a 3–1 pitching duel in Columbus to a 20–1 Birmingham blowout in Bluefield.

There was no game-by-game coverage of the series in the local newspapers. When the teams returned to Rickwood Field for a Friday night game, billed as tenth in the series, the newspapers listed the previous games by score and location but with no details. However, only eight of the reported nine games were reported in even that brief format. The list of cities and scores is of questionable accuracy. For example, it was stated that Birmingham won, 10–1, in Nashville. However, the *Tennessean* reported the game, including a line score, as 12–0.[80] The Rickwood game proved to be another hitting match with Birmingham winning, 13–11. The two teams had 31 hits total. Bassett hit a home run. Unfathomably, Birmingham now reportedly led six games to five.[81]

The final game—the twelfth in some reports—was scheduled for the following Sunday at Rickwood. Like the Globetrotters game a few weeks earlier, Birmingham got a boost from a home boy who had been away. Bill Greason, after playing with Oklahoma City in the Texas League, was back in Birmingham. Joining his old team, he pitched the Black Barons to a 3–1 triumph and the 1952 championship. The only run off Greason was unearned. Alonzo Perry won the game with a two-run triple in the eighth.[82]

It should be noted that nearly two weeks later *The Chicago Defender* recognized Indianapolis as the playoff winner. In its edition of October 18, the newspaper reported on Indianapolis' 5–0 win in New Orleans with the following lead: "Syd Pollock's Indianapolis Clowns captured the Negro American League playoff series against the Birmingham Black Barons by taking seven out of 12 games." The Birmingham newspapers treated that game as merely another in the series. Both *The Birmingham News* and *The Birmingham World* reported on the following games in Birmingham as concluding the playoffs with Birmingham winning the pennant.

Much of Birmingham's success came from an outstanding defense. The *Chicago Defender* reported later that the Black Barons led the NAL with double plays, compiling 84 to 63 for second-place Indianapolis. The success was boosted by the arrival of Thomas "Pee Wee" Butts, who replaced William "Cap" Brown at shortstop.[83]

Finally, the usual postseason exhibitions brought the championship season to a close. Roy Campanella's barnstorming all-star team, featuring Larry Doby, Hank Thompson, George Crow, Joe Black, and Willie Mays, played a series of games in Birmingham and other cities.[84]

A postscript on the 1952 season: In March, the *Pittsburgh Courier* announced that it had put together a panel of experts to select an all-time Negro leagues team. Former players, coaches, managers, owners, and sportswriters made up the 24-member selection panel. Those among them with Birmingham connections were Larry Brown (catcher, 1921, 1923), William "Dizzy" Dismukes (manager, 1924, 1938), Willie Wells (shortstop-manager, 1941), Satchel Paige (pitcher, 1927–30), and Willie Foster (pitcher, 1925). Foster, the half-brother of Negro leagues founder Rube Foster, appeared in one game with Birmingham in 1925, throwing a no-hitter against Chicago. Also selected were Sam Bankhead, one of the five Birmingham baseball-playing brothers, and Monte Irvin, an Alabama native and future National Baseball Hall of Fame selectee. Honorable mention former Black Barons included "Mule" Suttles, George Scales, and "Double Duty" Radcliffe. Montgomery Grey Sox outfielder "Turkey" Stearnes was also on the list.[85]

25

A Four-Team League (1953)

Once again Birmingham had a new manager. Taking charge was Jesse "Hoss" Walker, the team's 1941–43 shortstop. A native of Austin, Texas, Walker had been playing professionally since the late 1920s. His stops include Nashville, Memphis, New York, and various Cincinnati-Indianapolis Clowns teams.[1]

The decline of black league ball was now like a snowball on a steep incline. The Chicago American Giants and the Philadelphia Stars, two great teams in black baseball, had folded.

The Negro American League could field only four teams for 1953—Birmingham, Indianapolis, Kansas City, and Memphis. League President Dr. J.B. Martin said there was a chance that Chicago and Philadelphia might be able to rejoin the league for the second half of the season. The league schedule was largely confined to Sunday double-headers and weekday barnstorming. The first half season opened on May 17 and closed the weekend of July 4–5.

The drain of the best black players into Organized Baseball continued. The *Chicago Defender* reported that nearly two dozen former NAL players were under OB contracts.[2]

Despite that, opportunities for black players were still far from satisfactory. Hot Springs, Arkansas, of the Class C Cotton States League found widespread opposition from the management of other teams when it signed brothers James and Leander Turgerson. League President Al Haraway ordered forfeiture of a May 20 game because of Hot Springs' action. However, George Trautman, president of the National Association, the minor league governing body, set aside the forfeitures and ordered the game replayed.[3] James Turgerson filed a $50,000 civil suit against the league but later dropped it.[4]

Birmingham owner William "Sou" Bridgeforth and General Manager Paul C. Jones announced that spring training would be on the Alabama State campus in Montgomery. Bridgeforth said contracts had been received from Otha Bailey, Wesley "Doc" Dennis, Tommy Butts, Eddie Robins, and others. He had also signed a non-ballplayer to help inspire the team. "Papa" Walter Lightfoot, "a stirring harmonica player," had been hired to travel with the club. "Lightfoot can really shake 'em up … and the players should be real groovy this year," he said.[5]

While the Black Barons were working out, another black baseball man in Birmingham had a new job. Arthur T. Williams, a 1932 Parker High School graduate, was signed by the Cleveland Indians as a scout, working under the supervision of future Hall of Famer Joe Sewell. Williams later served as Black Barons general manager.[6]

Returning players included first baseman Dennis; outfielders Henry Kimbro, "Pijo" King, and Carl Long; the double-play combination of Butts and Eddie Brooks; catcher Bailey; utility infielder Irving Castille; and pitchers Frank Thompson, Wallace Guthrie, James

Hollins, and Taylor Smith. A pitcher who looked good in camp was Minski Cartledge. He was referred to as a new player, but he had actually pitched some the year before as Manny Cartledge.[7] Another newcomer was Ray Haggins, a 23-year-old power hitter from Piper and Bessemer.[8] He was later a mainstay with the Memphis Red Sox.[9]

The exhibition season opened with Memphis at Rickwood Field. Birmingham won, 7–3, before "a surprisingly good, but chilled crowd of 1,481." King, Brooks, and Kimbro all had good days at the plate. Cartledge started and struck out four. He was relieved by Thompson, who also struck out four.[10]

On May 3, Kansas City opened a five-game exhibition series at Rickwood. Subsequent games were played in North Alabama. The Monarchs, under Manager Buck O'Neil, had a shortstop who was getting widespread attention from major league scouts. His name was Ernie Banks. "Ernie looks great on ground balls either to his right or left and he has a powerful throwing arm," said O'Neil.[11] Banks, of course, went on to a Hall of Fame career with the Chicago Cubs.

Birmingham won both games on Sunday, 3–2 and 2–1. The wins gave Birmingham ten victories in eleven exhibition starts.[12] The sweep had sportswriter Marcel Hopson looking forward to a good season, especially because of the team's hustle: "They move on and off the field with lightning-like pace between innings … not like the dropping-off lice movement of seasons gone by."[13]

The next weekend the Black Barons made it 19 wins in 23 exhibition games, beating Memphis twice in Birmingham.[14] The two clubs then did exhibition stops together in Mississippi and Arkansas before returning to Memphis for the NAL opener on May 17.[15]

The *Pittsburgh Courier* reported that Birmingham looked very strong during the exhibition season. Manager Walker said he believed the Black Barons had "enough youth with some steady veterans to make us real pennant contenders this year."[16]

Birmingham swept the Red Sox and returned home with a five-game winning streak. In the opener at Memphis, Don Johnson, the 17-year-old pitcher from the city industrial league, held the Red Sox to five hits. Brooks hit a home run in the first inning and Birmingham never trailed.[17]

The home opener in Birmingham was Friday, May 22. Pregame ceremonies included music from the Fairfield Industrial High School band under the direction of Professor Eugene Woods, accompanied by "a luscious corps of high-stepping majorettes." The local team was predicted to be "one of the best that has been put together here in many years."[18] Unfortunately, that was not the case. Despite the great exhibition season and an equally impressive start the first couple of weeks of the season, the Black Barons faltered badly as the season progressed. The starting lineup:

Birmingham

Tommy Butts, ss	Irvin Castille, 3b
Eddie Brooks, 2b	Carl Long, cf
Henry Kimbro, lf	Otha Bailey, c
Edward Steele, rf	Don Johnson or Frank Thompson, p[19]
Wesley "Doc" Dennis, 1b	

Birmingham won the Friday game, 4–2. Frank Thompson pitched well before a crowd of 3,095 fans.[20] Two Sunday games were split, with Memphis hitting three Birmingham pitchers hard in the 9–5 first game. The Black Barons won the six-inning second game, 8–3. Dennis drove in three runs with a triple and two singles. Memphis had taken an early

3–1 lead when Raymond Haggins, the former U.S. Pipe Shop slugger, hit a 350-foot homer over the right field bleachers.[21]

The two teams then played in Gadsden, Montgomery, and Russellville before picking up new opponents. Birmingham hooked up with Indianapolis in Sikeston, Missouri, playing at least eight games with the Clowns. Still playing second base for the Clowns was Toni Stone, now 22 years old. She was said to be "getting her share of base hits off opposing pitchers since the '53 season opened."[22] Indeed, as one sportswriter gushed: "She gives not an inch of ground as she executes double plays with finesse of a Jackie Robinson. She's agile, has good baseball instinct, and knows what a Louisville Slugger is for. Her timely batting has amazed baseball experts from coast to coast."[23] As always, the Clowns had King Tut, the chief merrymaker, and "a crackerjack ball club to give the Barons the stiffest competition they have yet faced."[24]

Birmingham won, 3–2, on Saturday. Thompson pitched a seven-hitter, striking out eight and walking three. Carl Long, the 18-year-old center fielder, hit a three-run homer for the winning margin. Long's blow, over the left field bleacher wall, was estimated at 400 feet.[25]

On Sunday, they split two games before 6,304 fans, said to be the largest Black Barons crowd at Rickwood Field since 1949. Birmingham won the first game, 6–5. Indianapolis scored four in the first inning and coasted, 7–1, in the second game.[26]

Don Johnson was reported to have won eleven consecutive games, eight exhibitions and three league starts. However, one writer noted that the team had not "been hitting the ball up to expectations." Manager Walker said a key to Birmingham's success was excellent defensive play from Brooks and Butts.[27]

If the four Negro American League clubs were struggling to keep black baseball alive, President Dr. J.B. Martin felt like the league was in good enough shape for him to take a vacation. He went to London for the coronation of Queen Elizabeth II, then boarded the ocean liner *Queen Mary* for a tour of Europe with family members. The trip was cut short when he became ill in Paris and spent four days "in the American hospital there."[28]

Although the NAL had shrunk to only four teams, and Birmingham was playing inconsistently, attendance at Black Barons games was up dramatically in early June. The large turnout for the Clowns series put attendance at 23,229 for only seven playing dates. That compared with a total attendance of 35,014 for 15 playing dates in 1952. The figures were released by Rickwood Field officials. It was noted that the 1952 season had a number of cloudy and rainy days, whereas the 1953 weather had been good.[29]

The Black Barons and Clowns left Birmingham and barnstormed in Tennessee and Kentucky. Then Birmingham changed partners, playing the Monarchs in Kansas City.[30]

On June 2, William "Dizzy" Dismukes, the 1938 Black Barons manager, was in town for a different purpose. Scouting for the New York Yankees, he signed pitcher Don Johnson, 17, to a minor league contract, just a week after his graduation from Brighton High School. Johnson, "regarded as the brightest prospect to leave the Negro league since Outfielder Willie Mays went away to the New York Giants in 1950," was assigned to the Olean, New York, club in the Class D Pony League. Johnson was 6–2, 178 pounds. "I like his coolness, his poise," said Dismukes. "He showed me a world of natural stuff and he's got style, class." Dismukes also signed Marshall Gilbert, an 18-year-old former Woodlawn High School first baseman. He was assigned to Owensboro, Kentucky, in the Class D Kitty League.[31] Johnson's combined exhibition and regular season record was an impressive 12–0.[32]

Sports columnist Marion E. Jackson wrote that Dismukes's role with the Yankees marked a change in attitude for the New York club that "had shown reluctance in signing a Negro or Jew." He said Dismukes had been given fertile territory:

> In Birmingham's Rush Hotel, a two-story building, where downstairs the clatter of billiard balls fills the air day and night, William (Dizzy) Dismukes surveys the South's best known baseball hunting grounds. That is the Jefferson County area of Bessemer, Brighton, Acipco, Stockham, Pipe Shop, Avondale, etc., which has spawned so many baseball notables.
>
> From Dismukes' headquarters on 18th Street, once one of America's most colorful street [*sic*] and immortalized by Octavius Roy Cohen in *Saturday Evening Post*, a steady stream of horsehide hopefuls come seeking the so-called golden chance....[33]

It is strange that Jackson would cite Cohen's short stories. Today, they would be considered blatantly racist, written in dialect, promoting buffoonish behavior as the norm among Africa-American characters. Indeed, there was occasionally some sense of shared humor in *Amos and Andy*, but nothing of that sort in Cohen's work.[34]

While Johnson was being signed, his teammates were in Pulaski, Tennessee, beating Indianapolis, 18–10. Cartledge won in relief and hit a three-run homer.[35]

Howe News Bureau standings for June 10 had Birmingham (13–6) a half game behind Kansas City (13–5).[36]

The Black Barons returned home on June 13, reportedly leading by half a game now. The home stand was a disaster. The Monarchs won all three games. Ernie Banks and Ernie Johnson each hit towering home runs.[37]

Birmingham left town afterward and was unreported for about ten days. Standings through June 23 showed Kansas City (17–7) and Birmingham (16–11).[38] They returned home on June 27 for a three-game series with Memphis. This home stand was a disaster, also.

After a rainout on Saturday night, the Red Sox won, 4–2 and 2–1, on Sunday. Former Birmingham catcher Lloyd "Pepper" Bassett hit a 381-foot home run to left-center field in the opening game win. The losses ended Birmingham's hopes for winning the first half. In addition to losing pitcher Don Johnson, the club had been slowed by injuries to Butts and Long.[39]

They closed the first half in Memphis, breaking even. Birmingham won, 10–6, and Memphis won, 4–3. In the second game, Isaac Harris saved the game for Memphis after the Black Barons drove 15-year-old Charley Pride from the mound in the third inning.[40] Pride became a Black Baron in 1954.[41]

As the second half got under way, Toni Stone and Indianapolis returned to Birmingham. The Clowns won a Saturday night game, and Birmingham won two on Sunday before a crowd of 3,800. Lefthander Kelly Searcy held the Clowns to just three hits in winning the first game, 7–2. In the second, "Doc" Dennis hit a 400-foot home run to spark a 4–2 victory.[42] None of the game reports mentioned Stone's performance.

Attempting to bolster the sometimes struggling team, General Manager Jones signed two new players in July. They were 24-year-old rookie outfielder J.D. Lewis from Laurel, Mississippi, and veteran outfielder William Scott, a former Philadelphia Stars player.[43]

In late July it was announced that 17-year-old Carl Long had been named to the East squad for the annual all-star game. Long, hitting .350, was one of the youngest players ever selected for the classic.[44]

While the Black Barons were on an East and Midwest swing, a group of former players booked a weekend at Rickwood Field for games with the Willie Mays All-Stars. Proceeds from the games were to go to the Negro Tuberculosis Association. Mays, still in the Army and also with an ankle injury, was questionable. His players, largely from North Carolina, included former Black Barons Louis Gillis, Rufus Gibson, John Cowan, Buddy Ivory, Freddie Shepard, Jim Canada, and Harry Barnes.[45] Also listed on the roster and said to be former Black Barons were Columbus Ragland, Elijah Craig, and Robert Baldwin, although their service has not been confirmed.[46]

Mays did not play. His ankle was "still in a cast after he broke a small bone in an Army game in Virginia 10 days ago." They didn't need him. The All-Stars won, 7–2 and 10–7. The star was Willie "Red" Harris, a 17-year-old Birmingham boy with the All-Stars. He hit two runs in the second game.[47]

While away, the Black Barons dropped five of eight games to Indianapolis along the East Coast. Second-half standings through August 5 showed Kansas City (16–7) running away with the second half from Indianapolis (11–10), Birmingham (7–11), and Memphis (5–11).[48] From mid–July to early August, Kansas City won 17 straight, topping the 14-in-a-row they had in the first half.[49]

Individual figures had two Birmingham players among the top hitters, newcomer Ira Mobley (.412) and "Doc" Dennis (.343). Mobley did not have enough at bats to qualify for the lead, though. Kimbro led in stolen bases and Brooks in triples.[50]

Before a crowd estimated at only 10,000, the East won the East–West Game at Comiskey Park in Chicago, 5–1. Forty players had been selected from among the four teams. The game, long a showcase for the best Negro league players, fell short this year. "No one apparently was overly impressed despite the fact that the players made a sincere and honest effort to give them a skillful, well-played game," reported the *Pittsburgh Courier*.[51]

Six Birmingham players appeared in the game: Butts, Brooks, Dennis, Kimbro, Castille, and Long.[52]

On August 22–23, Birmingham returned home to face the Monarchs. The visitors quickly showed why they were running away with the NAL race. They held Birmingham to three hits on Saturday night, winning 6–4. "Extra entertainment … was furnished by the acrobatic family, called the Flying Nesbits." They were loudly applauded for their seventh-inning show.[53] Russell Nesbitt and his wife and son toured the country in the 1950s, performing at baseball games and also warming up crowds before Harlem Globetrotters basketball games.[54]

Birmingham managed a split on Sunday, pulling out the nightcap, 8–1, after blowing a four-run lead in the first game.[55]

Second-half standings through August 19 showed Kansas City (21–8) far ahead. The other three teams were all under .500. Birmingham (7–13) was in third place. Kansas City finished with an overall league and barnstorming record of 79–21.[56]

Birmingham's leading batter was Mobley with .356 in 21 games. Through 50 games, "Doc" Dennis hit .344 with seven home runs and 48 RBIs. Minksi Cartledge (5–2) was Birmingham's best pitcher. There is confusion over Mobley's first name. Listed as Ira in the standings, he was called Chesley in a July game against Indianapolis. The names Al and Johnny also appeared at least once each.[57] However, his obituary on the findagrave.com Web site lists him as Ira Lee Mobley, Sr., a native Mississippian whose early baseball training came from the great Buck O'Neil.[58]

The season schedule ended on Labor Day weekend, but there was no report on the final games.[59]

26

Playing with Pride (1954)

The 1954 season saw the return of a familiar figure to Birmingham. General Manager Paul C. Jones announced that the new manager of the team would be Willie Wells, one of the all-time great Negro leagues shortstops. Wells, who had played with the Black Barons in 1941, was "a keen student of the game and … expected to produce a hustling team." He had most recently been playing and managing in the Canadian Mandak League.[1]

Wells promised a successful season. "From what I've heard of the Barons personnel, there is no reason for us not winning ball games. I'll insist that the boys give me everything they have. If they put out, we'll do okay," he said.[2]

Jones said that he had received contracts for Wesley "Doc" Dennis, the home run hitting first baseman; Eddie Brooks, the hustling shortstop; and Danny Wright and Minski Cartledge, right-handed pitchers. He said he a had also signed 19-year-old Bessemer left-hander, who was a prime prospect, and expected to have pitcher Frank "Hoss" Thompson on board soon.[3]

Wells, like Jesse Walker, his predecessor, was a native of Austin, Texas. His career had started in 1923 with the San Antonio Black Aces. He spent seven years with the St. Louis Stars and also had great years with Kansas City, Chicago, Homestead, and others. Historian James Riley calls Wells simply "the best shortstop in black baseball during the 1930s and early 1940s." Wells was inducted in the Hall of Fame at Cooperstown in 1997. He is also in the Cuba and Mexico baseball halls of fame.[4]

The Negro American League regained a little of its old strength with six teams in 1954. Joining Birmingham were Indianapolis, Kansas City, Memphis, the Detroit Stars, and the Louisville Clippers. The new Detroit franchise belonged to Ted Rasberry, who had no league experience but owned a successful semipro team in Grand Rapids, Michigan. The Louisville franchise was owned by a group of businessmen, two of whom were in Birmingham.[5]

The addition of Detroit and Louisville was a key factor in the league's not folding altogether, according to sportswriter Bill Nunn, Jr. He wrote that Kansas City and Indianapolis, the two biggest draws in the league, had been on the verge of dropping out and playing independent ball. "The possibility of bringing new life into the lagging East–West Game and the realization that that withdrawal of their two teams would kill the only remaining symbol of organized baseball among Negroes was what finally convinced Tom Baird, Monarch owner, and Syd Pollack, head man of the Clowns, that they should go along. Both of these teams made money in 1953," wrote Nunn.[6]

Rasberry came to the league with enthusiasm and ideas. He immediately began picking the better players from his Grand Rapids Black Sox for the preliminary stocking of the

The 1954 Black Barons at Sulphur Dell Park in Nashville. Front row, from left: Jim Zapp, Danny Wright, Ralph Brown, Eddie Brooks, "PeeWee" Jenkins, Otha Bailey, John Kennedy, Elliott "Jr." Coleman, Richard "Red" Wright. Back row: Charley Pride, Kelly Searcy, Willie "Curley" Williams, Frank "Hoss" Thompson, Clarence "Pijo" King, Jesse Mitchell, Bill "Fire Ball" Beverly, Sidney Bunch, Willie Wells (courtesy of the Friends of Rickwood Field).

Stars. The other players would remain in Grand Rapids, ostensibly on a farm team. This was a rare but not unheard-of idea in black baseball. The Nashville Cubs in the Negro Southern League had played a similar role to the Elite Giants when they moved to Baltimore.[7] Rasberry also reverted to a plan used by the original Detroit Stars in the 1920s. Although Detroit was home base, the team would play games throughout the state. He scheduled a week-long series with Louisville in Grand Rapids, Muskegon, Battle Creek, Lansing, and Saginaw.[8]

Rasberry's influence in the league was extended even further when he bought out Baird's interest in the Kansas City Monarchs.[9]

The Clippers were owned by Robert "Bob" Williams and Arthur A. Williams. They were president and general manager, respectively, although still operating a business in Birmingham. The manager of the new team was Homer "Goose" Curry.[10]

Spring training for Birmingham moved from the Alabama State campus in Montgomery to Sulphur Dell Park in Nashville, the well-known home of the white Southern Association Nashville Vols. A "baseball school" was scheduled a week before the players reported, "open to any youngster who believes he has the required ability to make an impressionable showing."[11]

Returning players included catcher Otha Bailey, outfielder Clarence "Pijo" King, and pitcher Kelly Searcy. General Manager Jones went to New York in April and returned, not with new ball players, but with comedians. He announced that he had signed the Chocolateers, a comedy team that was appearing at the Palace Theater. The troupe would travel with baseball teams throughout the season.[12] A swing dance trio of the same name had made some movies in the 1930s and 1940s. It is not clear if there was a relationship between comedians and the dancers.[13]

By May there was no mention of the comedy team. Instead, the Flying Nesbitts acrobat act was said to be traveling with the team.[14] Not to be outdone, Rasberry signed catcher Lloyd "Pepper" Bassett and his rocking chair. Louisville hired "Dub, the Midget Clown, as an added attraction."[15] Indianapolis had two women players, Connie Morgan and Mamie "Peanut" Johnson.

Just how far would showmanship go as black baseball struggled to survive? Perhaps, just as far as necessary. Two umpires working games between Indianapolis and Kansas City became an attraction unto themselves. Mark Van Bureau, working behind the plate, quickly became known for his booming voice that carried to the far reaches of the ballpark. Bob Motley, working the bases, was an even bigger show: "When a play is made, the arbiter rushes to the base, leaps high into the air and then comes down or up into a split with safe or out sign."[16]

But there were new Birmingham baseball players, too. Among them were Alonzo Daniels, a smooth-fielding shortstop; William Holscroff, 6-foot-3 first baseman; John Coleman, 17-year-old pitcher; and John Kennedy, second baseman.[17] Another was catcher Henry L. "Red" Wright, the son of a former pitcher with Nashville, Cleveland, and Columbus.[18]

While the Black Barons trained out of state, another team trained in Birmingham. Rasberry sent his Detroit Stars south to prepare for their first season. Jake Robinson was the manager.[19] As opening day drew near, Arthur Williams announced that he had signed former Black Barons Ed Steele and Frank Evans, as well as Buddy Ivory, a shortstop who had played with the Globetrotters. Ivory came out of the Birmingham industrial league.[20]

On April 25, an exhibition game between the Clippers and Black Barons was set at Rickwood Field. The game, sponsored by the Girl Scouts of Birmingham, was to be a tribute to Bob Williams, president of the Clippers.[21]

Williams was described as a beloved sports figure known "throughout the Birmingham area for his untiring efforts in trying to bring to Birmingham the best that is in the sports circle. He has also been associated with underprivileged boys around the town and has given his services as well as money to every cause."[22]

Birmingham won, 5–0, with three pitchers—Sugar Cain, Minski Cartledge, and Kelly Searcy—holding the Clippers to four hits. Wesley Dennis was leading Birmingham batters in spring training

NashvilleTennessean,
April 18, 1954

Advertisement promoting the Chocolateers Comedy Act at a Negro American League game. From the *Nashville Tennessean*, 18 April 1954.

with six home runs. A weak spot was second baseman Eddie Brooks's sore arm, but Johnny Kennedy had "capably filled" the spot so far.[23] Attendance for the game was 2,500.[24]

Although racial barriers were dropping at ballparks all over the country, many restrictions remained in place in the South. In Birmingham, there were still no integrated teams playing at Rickwood. However, the 1954 season did see a significant change in seating accommodations. An unsigned article in the *Huntsville Mirror* stated that changes in the city ordinance prohibiting mixed teams were coming, along with better seating for Negro fans. Several major league exhibition games with mixed-race teams were scheduled in April. Black fans were being allotted 452 box seats on the third base side, 2,415 left field bleacher seats, and 780 seats in the section known as Glennon Gardens. A separate entrance was also announced for them on the 11th Street West side of the ballpark.[25]

On Thursday, April 1, the St. Louis Cardinals and Chicago White Sox played at Rickwood Field, the first time blacks and whites had played baseball together in Birmingham. The Brooklyn Dodgers and Milwaukee Braves followed on Friday and Saturday. Three consecutive days of racially mixed baseball were played in Birmingham, Alabama, with "no racial flareup," according to the headline in the *Chicago Defender*. The paid attendance was 2,950.[26]

And how did the crowd handle the integrated game? There was little mention of it except for a piece written by Alf Van Hoose under the headline of "Was it major or bush, show?" Van Hoose's answer: "Birmingham fans were big-time in their first view of Negro players on a major league club. A ballplayer was a ballplayer.... If that was bush league stuff, I'll take the other kind."[27]

Overall, there were 37 African American players on major league teams on Opening Day. Only the New York Yankees, Detroit Tigers, Boston Red Sox, and Philadelphia Phillies were without black players.[28]

Birmingham looked impressive in its exhibition games, winning nine out of 12 as Opening Day neared. Shortstop Curley Williams, outfielder Clarence King, second baseman John Kennedy, and infielder Ralph Crosby drew notice. Crosby, 20 years old and the property of the New York Giants, was said to be "destined to be a star with the Giants in a few years. He is a smooth fielder and has a strong throwing arm." Despite his strong points, Crosby never advanced beyond Class C in the minor leagues.[29]

Opening Day was on Saturday, May 15, and it brought with it another appearance of women baseball players. Mamie "Peanut" Johnson and Connie Morgan had been pleasing crowds and performing adequately throughout the preseason. Johnson was said to have pitched four scoreless innings while Morgan played well at second base. Surprisingly, there was no mention of the usual pregame ceremonies such as a high school band or first-pitch honoree.

Birmingham scored four runs in the ninth to beat Indianapolis, 4–3. The Black Barons trailed 3–0 and had only one hit for eight innings. Danny Wright got the win in relief of William Beverly. They only gave up three total hits, but they walked 12 batters. The victory came before a slim crowd of only 1,200 paid admissions, possibly the smallest Opening Day crowd ever to that point.[30] However, Marcel Hopson later placed the crowd at 3,299.[31]

Regardless, attendance at Sunday's games was clearly much bigger, with estimates ranging from 6,000 to 10,000 fans, many of them there likely to see Indianapolis's "$10,000 female second baseman." The games were split, and Morgan was impressive. She "electrified" the fans "when she went far to her right to make a sensational stop of a scorcher labeled 'base-hit,' flipped to shortstop Bill Holder and stared a lighting double play ... at bat she walked in two appearances." Indianapolis won the first game, 10–5, and Birmingham the second, 9–8.[32]

On Monday night in Mobile, the Black Barons won, 4–3.[33] Back home on Thursday, Beverly's curveball mastery beat Kansas City, 4–1.[34]

But success had been costly. In the Thursday game, "Doc" Dennis was spiked on the foot, an injury so severe the doctor ordered him to the sidelines for two weeks. Dennis had hit 14 home runs during exhibition games and the opening series with Indianapolis. On the positive side, Manager Wells was pleased with the work of a right-hander Frank [*sic*] Pride, who had beaten both the Clowns and the Monarchs. He held Kansas City to three hits.[35]

After the Kansas City series, sportswriter Marcel Hopson addressed what he said was the growing trend of league teams taking their own umpires on the road. How their use was regulated was not explained. A line score from the Birmingham-Indianapolis series listed the umpires as "Van Buren of the Clowns," and locals James V. Tyus, Parker Austin, and Poindexter Williams. Hopson said Kansas City had also brought its own umpire, and the Black Barons were planning to take their man on the road.

Interestingly, a decision by Van Buren in favor of Birmingham caused a great uproar in one of the games. "The Clowns put so much heat behind their umpire [Van Buren]" that he suggested to the ruling umpire-behind-the-plate (Tyus) that he change the decision which he (Van Buren) had made. When Tyus decided to let the decision stand, Van Buren "fired a barrage of unpleasant make-your-face-look-ugly words at him, out on the playing field at that."[36]

The mascot umpire theme must have played out quickly because subsequent series with Memphis and Louisville at Rickwood saw only the regular local trio working.[37]

The first weekend in June brought in Memphis. Birmingham won two out of three, winning the Saturday night game, 5–4, with a run in the ninth. On Sunday, Memphis swamped the Black Barons, 12–1, with local boy Raymond Haggins driving in two runs. Birmingham won the nightcap, 8–5.[38]

After something of a slow start, the Black Barons found a rhythm in June, winning nine of 10 games, raising their record to 16–7, and taking first place from Memphis.

In mid–June, Birmingham was scheduled to start a series with Detroit, but the Stars were unable to get to town for the Saturday game. Birmingham hosted the Red Sox again, winning 9–4. The next day Detroit arrived, and they split a double-header.[39]

The first half ended with a home holiday series with Louisville. Birmingham won on Saturday night, 5–4. They divided the July 4 double-header. Louisville won the first game, 9–8. First baseman and Parker High graduate Charlie Dees scored the winning run in the eighth inning. He also drove in two runs with a double. And another Birmingham boy, Buddy Ivory, hit a 350-foot two-run homer over the right field bleachers. Birmingham won the five-inning second game, 5–1. Searcy held the visitors to two hits, and Dennis hit a 375-foot homer over the left field fence.[40]

Dees went on to play in Organized Ball for nine years, including three in the majors. In a 2010 interview, he said he played with the Black Barons for one year, possibly 1955. However, that service has not been confirmed by newspaper accounts. The author wonders if Dees, like Willie Mays, might have been an occasional player while attending high school.[41]

The Louisville victories put Birmingham (24–14) ahead of second-place Louisville (22–22), according to the *Birmingham World*.[42]

Yet, Birmingham owner Bridgeforth was not satisfied with the 24–14 record and the first- half title. As the second half got under way, he signed William Breda, a fast outfielder from Louisiana who had played with Kansas City. Breda "immediately established his worth as he went to deep center to pull down a would-be triple" in an exhibition game in Kentucky.[43]

There was also a change at the top. In mid–July, General Manager Paul Jones announced that Jesse "Hoss" Walker was back as manager. There was no explanation for the departure of Willie Wells, who had guided the team from spring training to the first-half title. Walker, who managed the club the previous year, had the team off to a 5–2 record after taking over.[44]

First baseman "Doc" Dennis was batting well after recovering from his foot injury. Dennis, who started playing in 1942 with Baltimore, was having his career-best season. By July 5 he was said to have hit 25 home runs and was projected to lead the league for the second year in a row.[45]

However, Howe News Bureau statistics in mid–July gave the home run lead to George Wanamaker of Indianapolis with a mere eight. Dennis's home run totals obviously included exhibition games. In fact, no Birmingham player was listed among the leaders at that time. The top batter was Johnny Williams (.396) of Louisville. Ray Haggins was the RBI leader with 41.[46] In early August, Wanamaker was still the home run leader with 11.[47]

In late July, the Clowns beat Birmingham, 8–5, at Salisbury, Maryland, and 4–3 at Milford, Delaware, in a day-night double-header. The wins put Oscar Charleston's team on top in the second-half race.[48]

Birmingham had opened the second-half season winning two out of three from Memphis at Rickwood. The Red Sox won on Saturday night, but Kelly Searcy and Frank Thompson pitched complete games on Sunday, winning 9–1 and 1–0, respectively.[49]

Then there was little reported on the team's whereabouts until Detroit came in on July 25.

Birmingham won both games at Rickwood. Frank Thompson limited the Stars to three hits in the 4–1 opener. Searcy and Beverly combined to win the second game, 7–5.[50]

Looking toward the annual East–West All-Star game, NAL President Dr. J.B. Martin made an impassioned plea for continued support of the league. In an interview with Luix Virgil Overbea of the Associated Negro Press news service, Martin said the game featured "the stars of tomorrow" each year. Further, he said future black major leaguers "must get their training in the NAL." Martin's premise was simple and to the point: "It is difficult to name a single player in big time baseball who did not get his start in Negro baseball. You never heard of a big league club giving an untried Negro high school student a big bonus to play with it. Look at Willie Mays. The Birmingham Black Barons took him out of high school before the Giants saw him."[51]

Overbea offered his own view of the status of black baseball. He wrote that he supported the East–West Game, but if Chicago did not provide support, it should move to another city. The NAL should be supported on its merits, with fans kept abreast of its players and activities. He also said that "women ball players would be better off in women's leagues." Finally, Overbea set the stage for the NAL's demise: "White baseball moguls are not altogether convinced about Negroes in baseball. When they do accept them freely, then the NAL should close shop, but not until then. Today, the NAL is a necessity, so it is up to the fans to support it."[52]

On August 8, Birmingham, reportedly back in first place after winning nine of their last 12 games, faced Memphis at Rickwood. They won both games. Danny Wright pitched a no-hitter in the 5–0 second game. Wright, "laughing and clowning the whole seven-inning route, walked three Red Sox, hit another, and one man got on first on an error by Doc Dennis on a dropped throw which would have completed a double play." Dennis gave Wright the only run he needed when he hit a home run over the 380-foot wall in right-center.[53]

Howe News Bureau standings in mid–August showed Indianapolis (12–6), Birmingham (14–10), and Memphis (12–12). The other three teams were all below .500. Johnny Williams (.394) of Louisville continued as the batting leader. Mike Hulemard (5–0) of Birmingham was the pitching leader.[54]

The division for the East–West Game had players from Louisville, Kansas City, and Memphis on Buck O'Neil's East squad. West Manager Oscar Charleston drew from Birmingham, Indianapolis, and Detroit. Black Barons on the team were second baseman Eddie Brooks, first baseman Wesley "Doc" Dennis, catcher Otha Bailey, shortstop John Kennedy, and pitcher Frank Thompson. Bessemer's Ray Haggins, the Memphis right fielder, was on the West squad.[55]

For the fourth straight year, the West won, combining good pitching and strong hitting for an 8–4 victory. Dennis hit a home run in the third inning. Brooks scored the East's final run after singling in the fifth. Thompson started, pitched three innings and left with the score tied. Russ J. Cowans, covering the game for the *Chicago Defender*, said Kennedy "stood out in the field … with several sparkling plays to cut off West hits." The crowd was a disappointing 10,000.[56]

On August 29. Birmingham split a double-header with Memphis, winning the first game, 6–1, and losing the second, 8–3. Wright won the first game, throwing a four-hitter. Charley Pride, playing left field, and Eddie Brooks hit home runs.[57]

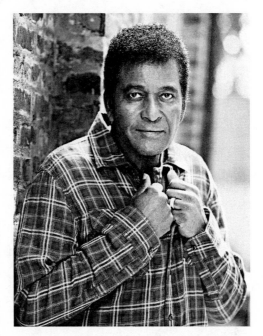

Pride's appearance in the Birmingham lineup came with an apocryphal story. It has been widely told for years Pride was traded to Birmingham for a team bus. Here is the way Pride related the incident in an interview: "I was with the Louisville Clippers, a new team in the league, and they needed money. They sold me and Jesse Mitchell … to the Black Barons for money to buy a team bus."[58]

The following year Pride returned to Memphis, where he closed out his career. His return to Memphis came from his having been released by Birmingham, according to Gail Jordan, daughter of "Sou" Bridgeforth. In 2009 she was interviewed when Bridgeforth was posthumously inducted into the Limestone County Sports Hall of Fame. She recalled: "I remember one time daddy took me to Ryman Auditorium (old Grand Ole Opry) to see Charley Pride receive a country music award for his song 'Kiss an Angel

Pride, along with Louisville Clippers teammate Jesse Mitchell, was traded to the Black Barons in 1954, in exchange for a team bus (photograph by Be De Rienzo; courtesy Music City Records).

Good Morning.' He later told me that he had to release Charley from the team, not because of his playing ability but because he kept everyone up all night on those long bus rides with his singing. His players were always too tired to play the next day."[59]

Pride returned to Birmingham in 1999 to sing the National Anthem at the fourth annual Rickwood Classic, a Birmingham Barons game played at Rickwood Field each year.[60] His statistics for his brief tenure with the Black Barons, according to the Howe News Bureau final numbers, were a pitching record of 4–3 with an earned run average of 4.13. His batting average was .242.

Indianapolis, riding the bat of Wanamaker, won

William "Sou" Bridgeforth, a 1950s owner of the Black Barons when Charley Pride was on the team (courtesy Harriet Bridgeforth Jordan).

Willie Mays speaking at the youth baseball field named in his honor in his hometown of Fairfield, Alabama, circa 2009 (courtesy Faye Davis and Birmingham Public Library Archives).

the second half. He led the league in total bases and was tied in RBIs and home runs.[61] Howe's final unofficial standings were Indianapolis (23–9), Memphis (24–17), and Birmingham (22–22). Released at the same time were final first- half standings. Again, Indianapolis (20–13) was the champion. Birmingham (19–16) was third.[62]

As 1954 saw a slow thawing of black-white relations in Birmingham—in baseball, at least—John T. McLaughlin, the white mayor of Fairfield, said he wholeheartedly endorsed the suggestion that Willie Mays be acknowledged in his hometown. He wanted to welcome Mays back to Fairfield "with city wide ceremonies in his honor."[63]

27

Gatemouth Moore and White Owners (1955)

As the 1955 season was gearing up, there were two things on the mind of sportswriter Herman "Steeple Jack" Taylor: The ownership of the Black Barons and the treatment of black fans at Rickwood Field. One of these issues had some resolution; the other did not.

During the offseason, ownership of two Negro American League teams went from Negroes to whites. The Kansas City Monarchs passed into the hands of white businessman Tom Y. Baird. In Birmingham, William "Sou" Bridgeforth sold his club to Syd Lyner and Floyd Meshad.[1]

Writing in the *Birmingham World*, Marion E. Jackson noted that there had long been "interracial … ownership and business managership" in the Negro American league. This had manifested itself as "frontship (Negroes using white capital and posing as owners)." There had also been some white business managers.[2]

Jackson attributed much of the decline in black baseball to not only integration but also the lack of black-owned ballparks. "Negro baseball never learned the lesson of the Negro newspaper. Negro-owned newspapers found survival difficult until they began to own their printing shops. Likewise Negro-owned baseball clubs have the best chance of survival where racial capital owns the ball park,"[3] he wrote.

In an effort to offset community unhappiness over the loss of black control of the Black Barons, management announced the hiring of the Rev. Dwight "Gatemouth" Moore as vice president.[4]

A well-known evangelist, gospel singer, and radio announcer, Moore was a high-profile choice. He had been a successful blues singer with such hits as "Baby, I Ain't Mad at You" and "Did You Ever Love a Woman?" Moore had a bandstand conversion at Chicago's Club DeLisa in 1948. He gave up secular music and turned to gospel.[5] One might not have expected such a religious experience some years earlier. On the night of April 23, 1940, the Rhythm Club in Natchez, Mississippi, caught on fire, killing 292 party-goers in the Moneywasters Social Club. Among the victims were noted band leader Walter Barnes and nine members of the Royal Creolians. Moore was one of three band member survivors of the nightclub fire. "The only reason I survived was because I was outside, in the bus, with a girl," Moore said in an interview years later.[6]

A contemporary account of the fire does not support that widely quoted story. *The Call*, Kansas City's black newspaper, covered the tragedy extensively. A front-page sidebar said five band members survived, none of whom was named Moore. Of course, there could have been a subsequent update of casualty and survivor lists, which was not published in *The Call*.[7]

Regardless, the hiring of the flamboyant Moore was praised. "This is a very fine gesture…. For years we have advocated home rule for our baseball club," wrote sports writer Taylor in *The Mirror*, a Huntsville, Alabama-based weekly newspaper.

At the same time, Taylor decried the fact that some major league clubs would bypass Birmingham on their way back north from spring training "because of the ugly law on the statute books banning mixed competition between Negroes and whites." The three exhibition games of the previous year notwithstanding, Birmingham officials continued to enforce rigidly not only the competition law but also Jim Crow seating in the stands.

"Negroes are allowed to sit in the bleachers and other spots at Rickwood while the Barons are playing but people have started to stay at home and more will stay at home this year. We are tired of going to Rickwood and sit[ting] over 350 feet away from the actual play … what worsens the situation, no Negros are allowed to play with the [white] Barons. When that time comes, you will see a terrific flow of Negro fans back to Rickwood field."[8]

Unfortunately, that time would not come in the life of those Birmingham Barons. Facing dwindling attendance, frequent franchise shift, and a reluctance to accept integration, the white Southern Association folded after the 1961 season.[9]

In 1964 the Southern League was formed, drawing from Southern Association and South Atlantic League franchises. Black athletes were part of the league.[10] Among them, playing for the Birmingham Athletics, was pitcher Stan Jones. He had played for the Black Barons in 1957, the only player to appear on both all-black and integrated Birmingham rosters.[11]

Meanwhile, there was still Black Barons baseball to be played despite the presence of white owners. Sid Lyner, or Lynor, was an automobile dealer. His name appeared in print with both spellings, but he is not listed in any Birmingham City Director for the time period. Floyd Meshad was a cemetery and funeral home owner who had been the first football coach at John Carroll Catholic High School. Moore was given "full power of the Black Barons and this prophet-style baseball magnate may become the new Barnum of Baseball," wrote columnist Marion E. Jackson.[12]

Moore, like blues singer Clarence "Gatemouth" Brown, got his nickname from a voice that served him well as a musician before getting the call to the ministry. When he assumed his role as the front man for the Black Barons, he was well known in the community as a minister and disk jockey.[13]

A native of Topeka, Kansas, he started singing in church, but by age 16 he was touring with the great Ma Rainey. He rode around Birmingham in a "fire engine red Cadillac" and, his ministry notwithstanding, was known for a flamboyant lifestyle.[14]

Small wonder Jackson envisioned a "Bible, blues and baseball" phenomenon in Birmingham.[15] And there were signs, it might happen. The first signing by the new ownership was a prominent manager.

Homer "Goose" Curry's career spanned four decades. He started as a pitcher in the late 1920s, playing four different times with Memphis. As pitcher-outfielder, he played in Nashville, Indianapolis, Philadelphia, Newark, New York, and Louisville.

Curry was a good all-round player and a capable manager. Even in the twilight of his career, he was a good choice for the 1955 Black Barons. One report said every other manager in the league had played under Curry at some time.[16] Even so, it was not an assignment that lasted even until opening day. By May 1, Curry was gone and veteran first baseman Jim Canada was named manager. There was no explanation for Curry's sudden departure.

Ironically, Curry, not Canada, appeared in the 1955 team photograph published the day before the season opened. Obviously, Curry's departure had been sudden.[17]

A Montgomery native, Canada's name often appears in Negro leagues reports as Canady. He played first base with Birmingham in 1936, 1937, and 1946. His career also included stops in Jacksonville, Memphis, Atlanta and Baltimore.[18]

The Birmingham team had organized at Hopkins Field near the U.S. Pipe Shop in north Bessemer. It then returned to Montgomery for spring training. The Black Barons had used the Alabama State campus for spring training for six years before going to Nashville in 1954.[19]

The Reverend Moore's early signees included all-star first baseman Wesley "Doc" Dennis (still called NAL home run king) and second baseman Eddie Brooks, the 1954 fielding leader. Leading the pitchers was Kelly Searcy, the 21-year-old left-hander from Nashville, being scouted by three major league clubs.[20]

The Negro American League announced that Opening Day was May 1 with the first half ending July 4. Disturbingly, once again it was a four-team league—Birmingham, Detroit, Kansas City, and Memphis.[21]

Birmingham opened at home against Kansas City. Promotional activities began with a parade sponsored by the new Black Barons Boosters Club. Participants included bands "with high stepping majorettes," Boy Scouts, businesses, and "outstanding celebs from all over the county." A banquet was held honoring the players and former players at Bob's Savoy Café.[22]

Henry Bayliss, 1949-50 infielder for the Black Barons, played for a number of teams in the Negro Leagues and the integrated minor leagues (courtesy Faye Davis and Birmingham Public Library Archives).

Another new promotion was Moore's Knothole Gang, an effort to get kids out to the ballpark. Open to children up to sixteen years of age, the group would have other activities such as "picnics, hikes, free movies and other fine treats" throughout the summer. Moore said some 1,000 children had been signed up for the program.[23]

There were no reports on Birmingham's exhibition game schedule. The first reference to any game was the announcement of Opening Day. Advance tickets to the game were available at Charles T. Mabry's Store and at the club headquarters, 1517½ Fourth Avenue North.[24]

But on Sunday, the Monarchs did the most celebrating, winning 8–3 before a crowd of 6,500. Third baseman Henry Bayliss, a 1949–50 Black Baron, drove in three runs with two doubles.[25]

Striving to put a positive spin on the bad start, one sportswriter opined, "The Black Barons have a young team this year and it probably took this game to give them the advantage of correcting their mistakes before the season gets in full swing."[26]

Marcel Hopson addressed some concerns other than the one-sided loss: the behavior of some fans in the stands, and the behavior of some ball players on the field. Regarding the fans, he wrote: "Those juice-sipping, violent-minded men and women, who like to engage in fisticuffs and physical combat when the heat of the sunshine sets afire the ingredients of that stinging booze in their bellies, should restrain themselves in the ball park, until they get home, and let the peace-loving, true baseball fans enjoy Sunday's diamond festivities without fear that they will be greeted by a flying booze bottle or given 'illegal surgery' with a swinging switchblade knife intended for someone else...."

As for the ballplayers, he criticized an unseemly approach to the game: "[A] ball player does not make himself 'popular' with the majority of fans if he consumes most of the two-hour baseball game on Sunday afternoon threatening the umpires, unnecessarily stalling the progress of play, or 'playing poorly' because he is mad with his manager.... He becomes the 'darling' of the fans when he plays his best, keeps the game moving at a fast pace and conducts himself orderly." Hopson said if that approach could be taken, then the NAL, said to be dying, might yet survive.[27]

There was no report on the team again until it returned home on May 13 and blasted Detroit, 15–7. John Kennedy and Jesse Mitchell hit triples, Dennis added a three-run homer, and Frank McCollum pitched a complete game.[28]

Again, the team seemed to disappear until Thursday, May 19, when they played Memphis at Rickwood. Minksi Cartledge was the loser as Memphis won, 3–1.[29]

Despite at least two known losses, a month later there was a remarkable report on the team. The Black Barons were said to be 6–1 and in first place. With exhibition games added in, the overall record was said to be 26–2. Birmingham had won 16 straight exhibition games before losing. Although none of those numbers are substantiated, one sportswriter extolled the team as Birmingham's best since 1948. With a starting lineup of "Doc" Dennis at first, Eddie Brooks at second, John Kennedy at shortstop, and Rufus Gibson at third, the team had "the league's best infield." The outfield was comprised of Roy Williams in left, Stanley Williams in right, and Jesse Mitchell in center. Mitchell was "setting the league on fire with his hitting and catching, and is being scouted every day."[30]

Meanwhile, "unofficial sources" told Hobson that Jim Canada had been released as manager. Hobson said there was talk of replacing him with James "Dizzy" Chambers, a well-known Birmingham industrial leaguer and current manager of the semipro 24th Street Red Sox.[31]

On June 5, Kansas City and Satchel Paige came to Rickwood. Although now out of the major leagues, Paige's career was far from over. In Birmingham he was matched with a new Black Barons pitcher named Sam Fulton. "Nobody knows how old Satchel is and he won't tell. Black Barons fans are well aware that Fulton is only 15," reported the *Birmingham News*. Preceding the game was one "with Willie Mays League 10 and 11-year-olds."[32]

The Black Barons struck early, scoring two in the second and two in the third in a 10–7 victory. Paige was relieved in the fourth inning. Gibson paced Birmingham with a triple and a single. Relief pitcher Searcy struck out seven. It was Birmingham's fourth straight over Kansas City, strengthening its hold on first place.[33]

In June, President Martin announced that the East–West Game would return to Chicago, nullifying a February decision to move the game to Kansas City. A group of owners had sided with Kansas City owner Tom Baird for the change. Later, Martin mustered enough support to secure another vote and keep the game at Comiskey Park.[34]

As often in the past, there was virtually no reporting of how the team fared when it was away. However, when Birmingham returned to Rickwood for a Sunday, July 10, double-header with Memphis, the team was described as the league's first-half champions. The advance story on the games noted that "well known sports figure" Floyd Meshad was now the sole owner of the Black Barons.[35] Another change was on the field. Second baseman Eddie Brooks was now manager of the team.[36] "Steeplejack" Taylor said Brooks was taking over "after a near collapse of the team" that practically assured that Detroit would win the second half.[37]

Birmingham won both games from Memphis, taking the opener, 8–6, as Dennis and Gibson hit home runs. William Cox hit a homer in the five-inning, darkness-shortened second. Willie Harris, who came out of the local YMCA industrial league, hit two home runs for Memphis. A crowd of 2,800 saw the Black Barons boost their first-place lead.[38]

The following Sunday, Detroit was the opponent. "Gatemouth" Moore announced that there would be additional attractions such as acrobats and a beauty pageant. The Flying Nesbitts were led by family patriarch Russell Nesbitt. He received some notoriety by hand-walking down forty-seven flights of Washington Monument stairs before being halted by security guards.[39] Also, there would be the crowning of Miss Black Baron, from "a group of some of the most beautiful girls in the Birmingham district." The winner would receive an all-expense paid trip to the East–West Game in Chicago.[40]

Powered by John Williams's early two-run homer, Birmingham won the first game, 8–3, before a crowd of 5,000. Detroit won the five-inning second game 8–1. Miss Catherine Peterson was crowned Miss Black Baron.[41]

A week later, in a move as dramatic as his arrival, "Gatemouth" Moore resigned. He said he needed more time for his religious activities. The loss was lamented by *The Mirror* sportswriter, presumably Herman "Steeplejack" Taylor:

> This now leaves the Black Barons owned and operated by whites with no Negro serving in an official capacity.
> The Rev. Moore, during his tenure in office, had built up quite a following and revised the old slogan: "Boost Your Black Barons." No team in the Negro American League has been able to lure the crowd to their home games like the people poured into Rickwood....[42]

Six Black Barons were selected for the East–West Game. Of course, the fact that there were only four teams in the league increased the number of selections for each team. Birmingham's group included Rufus Gibson, Eddie Brooks, John Kennedy, Otha Bailey, and Minski Cartledge, and John Williams.[43]

The West scored two runs in the seventh inning to win, 2–0. Cartledge, the third pitcher for the East, took the loss. Satchel Paige started for the West but a reliever got the win.[44] It was the West's fifth win in a row. Bailey "turned in a stellar job behind the plate" for the East.[45]

Another Birmingham visit from Satchel Paige and the Monarchs was scheduled for Sunday, August 7. Paige, reportedly earning $40,000 in his return to the NAL, was to face another youthful pitcher, 19-year-old Elliott Coleman.[46] Another black Little League game preceded the NAL game. Music was provided by the Rhythm in Blues Boys throughout the afternoon. The Birmingham lineup:

Eddie Brooks, 2b	William Cox, lf
John Kennedy, ss	Jessie Mitchell, cf
John Williams, rf	Otha Bailey, c
Rufus Gibson, 3b	Elliott Coleman, p
"Doc" Dennis, 1b	Brewster, p[47]

Paige and Enrique Maroto limited Birmingham to just three hits in a 5–2 win. Paige, now nearing 50 years old, started, struck out three, and walked one in four innings of work. Coleman struck out five and walked one, but the Monarchs bunched hits in two innings.[48]

Whether it was cause-and-effect or pure coincidence, after Moore's departure, the Black Barons went into a severe slump. After winning the first half "in a breeze," they lost seven games to Detroit and saw the Stars take over the second-half league lead. "Steeplejack" Taylor speculated that the players were unhappy about the sudden loss of Moore from the management. "From the way that the fellows are playing all signs are pointing in that direction," he wrote. In the Detroit series, the Stars scored 51 runs and had 107 hits.[49]

Second-half chances were further diminished a few days later when pitcher Kelly Searcy went to the Baltimore Orioles. The purchase price was not announced. Taylor wrote that the sale of Searcy added to fan speculation about the future of the ball club, coming after Canada's and Moore's departures.[50]

Near the end of season, local fans got at least one pleasant Sunday afternoon when Birmingham beat Kansas City, 10–2. McCollum gave up eight hits "but was very effective when the chips were down." He had a shutout going until the fifth, when a throwing error allowed a run to score. Birmingham batters backed McCollum with a four-run first inning.[51]

If there was a playoff between Birmingham and Detroit for the overall championship, it was not reported locally. There was the usual fall exhibition season, though.

Artie Wilson's Pacific Coast League All-Stars and the Willie Mays All-Stars played exhibition games at Rickwood Field in September and October.[52] Another fall game was between the Major League All-Stars and the Negro League All-Stars. An estimated 7,000 fans saw the major leaguers win, 6–1, behind the five-hit pitching of Brooklyn pitcher Don Newcombe. Hank Aaron and Ernie Banks hit home runs for the big leaguers. Aaron's shot "cleared the fence back of the bleachers in left field" and Banks lined his into the left field seats, bringing in Willie Mays, who had singled. The battery for the NAL team was Jehosie Heard and Otha Bailey.[53]

Others on the major league squad were Junior Gilliam, Hank Thompson, Joe Black, Sam Jones, Brooks Lawrence, and George Altman, all blacks who had made it to the big time. There were no white players on the team, reflecting the mixed picture that still existed in race and baseball.

A final note on the 1955 baseball season:

In July, Bill Greason was involved in an unusual play in Houston in a game against San Antonio. Bob Caffrey of San Antonio was on second when Greason threw a wild pitch that sailed over catcher Hal Smith's head. It struck a concrete rail behind home plate on the fly and rebounded back toward the field. Greason, rushing in to cover home plate, caught the ball on the fly, whirled and tagged out Caffrey, who was trying to score from second.[54]

28

Black Barons or Giants? (1956)

It was almost time for spring training and the overriding question was who would represent Birmingham in the Negro American League. Was it to be the familiar Birmingham Black Barons or would it be a new team called the Birmingham Giants?

In March, it looked as if the latter would be the case. "The new owner of the Birmingham Black Barons, Dr. Anderson Ross, stated that the Black Barons name was changed to avoid legal complications, the name Black Barons had been copyright [sic] by Floyd Meshad, the previous owner," wrote Herman "Steeplejack" Taylor in the *Huntsville Mirror*.[1]

"This is certainly very strange all these years since 1929 [sic] the Birmingham Club had operated as the Black Barons, even though they have had four owners since 1945. During that time no one bothered to copyright a team's name. Why was it copyrighted last year?" Taylor continued.[2]

All of this tumbled into the public spectrum rather suddenly. On March 15, the *Birmingham News* reported a spectacular announcement from Floyd Meshad, the Black Barons' owner. Meshad said he had signed a contract with Satchel Paige for the living legend to join the team as pitcher and manager.[3]

A month later Meshad was out of the picture, in which Paige may or may not have ever been involved. The franchise and equipment had been sold to Ross of Memphis. Meshad reportedly had withdrawn from the Negro American League for the 1956 season. There was no reference to the copyright issue, just a report that Ross would operate the team as the Birmingham Giants.[4]

Finally, Scott News Syndicate columnist Marion E. Jackson put the controversy in perspective:

> The "Birmingham Giants" was the title given to the 1956 Negro American League entry. However, the "Birmingham Black Barons" title had been registered by the 1955 owners of the NAL Birmingham franchise. Dates at Rickwood Field had been secured by the "Black Barons" and the NAL's "Birmingham Giants" had the franchise but not the [Rickwood] field. The "Black Barons" title had fallen into the hands of white ownership and business management. The "Birmingham Giants" were Negro-owned and Negro business managed. Both teams had Negro field managers.
>
> Leroy (Satchel) Paige was brought in to manage the Black Barons. Jim Canada was snatched up to pilot the Birmingham Giants. Fan sentiment began to murmur in support of the Giants, who were fieldless....

Led by Birmingham Barons General Manager Eddie Glennon,, the stalemate was brought to an end. The Birmingham Black Barons name and NAL franchise were sold to Ross along with playing dates at Rickwood.[5]

Meanwhile, the Negro American League had its own problems, having deteriorated to four teams twice in three years. With split seasons scheduled to open on May 20 and close July 4, the league was again comprised of Birmingham, Detroit, Kansas City, and Memphis. In Birmingham, Jim Canada was once again to be the manager.[6]

Business Manager Arthur Williams announced the team had opened its headquarters and business office in the Blue Note Hotel, 1704½ Fourth Avenue North. He said the team would do its spring training in Columbus, Mississippi, and that Canada had 24 players lined up for inspection.[7]

While the name controversy had raged, no one seemed to recall C.I. Taylor and the original Birmingham Giants in the early 20th century. Nor did anyone reference 1934, when Bill Perkins managed another Birmingham Giants team in the Negro Southern League.[8] But by Opening Day the name was settled, and "the old reliable Birmingham Black Barons" officially opened the NAL schedule on Sunday, May 20, at Rickwood Field. Canada's club would face Ed Steele's Detroit Stars.[9]

The "new" Black Barons team would be untested, "made up of young ball players from the greater Birmingham area." The industrial league continued to provide fresh talent such as Glenn Finley, a right-hander who had played with the Ensley Steelers. He came with a medium fastball and a good change of pace "that keeps most hitters off their stride."[10]

Gone was Wesley "Doc" Dennis, the husky first baseman who had thrilled Rickwood fans since 1952. Although his baseball career, which dated to 1942, was over, Dennis became an outstanding tournament-winning golfer.[11]

Spring training reports were sparse. The team played exhibitions in different cities, working its way to Birmingham for a May 6 game with defending champion Kansas City.[12] The Monarchs were under a new owner. Ted Rasberry purchased the team in the offseason and brought in veteran Olan "Jelly" Taylor as manager.[13]

General Manager Williams asserted that the locals would be "the greatest squad ever assembled under the Black Barons banner." He said the team was "loaded with young talents" clustered around seasoned veterans down the middle.[14] Williams, a Parker High School graduate, had been involved in baseball for a number of years. He managed a semipro team in Kentucky and played with Knoxville in the Negro Southern League. He had also scouted for the Cleveland Indians.[15]

Whether the word "great" would prove appropriate or not, the Black Barons did whip Kansas City, 10–3. A young right-hander named Joe Elliott struck out 10 and allowed only six hits. The Birmingham offense was led by new first baseman Billy Joe Moore, who drove in four runs with two doubles.[16]

Again, the team vanished from the local sports news radar for two weeks. On May 19, the *Birmingham Post-Herald* reported Birmingham would go into Opening Day with 15 wins in 18 exhibition games.[17]

Opening the season, the Black Barons won one of the more memorable games at Rickwood. Trailing 9–0, Birmingham erupted for 15 runs in the seventh inning. No details of the explosive inning were reported, but Rufus Gibson had a home run, double, and single, while Frank Marsh hit a triple and three singles. Birmingham won, 16–9.[18]

"Steeplejack" Taylor said both teams demonstrated a lot of speed, but also some fielding deficiencies such as outfielders failing to back each other up. He wrote that Birmingham had signed Frank Sienna, a former Indianapolis Clowns player, and Sienna had "played a very important part in rattling the Detroit pitcher when he took up his position in the coaching box along the first base line in the seventh inning." Taylor said Sienna was from Tampa and was of "Spanish descent."[19]

No player by that name shows up in online data bases. However, Cuban native Pedro Sierra signed a contract with Indianapolis at the age of 16 in 1954. He played with the Clowns for a year and then with the Detroit Stars from 1955 to 1958. There are no references to his having played for Birmingham other than Taylor's.[20]

The opener took so long to complete (55 minutes for the seventh inning, four hours for the game) that insufficient daylight remained for a scheduled second game. Instead, the crowd watched the Flying Nesbitts, back for another season.[21]

In Huntsville on Monday night, Detroit won by an identical score. Other games were played in Chattanooga, Lanett, and Decatur.[22]

Kansas City returned to Rickwood on May 27, their first appearance since the 10–3 exhibition game. Birmingham returned home with a new manager. Jim Canada had been relieved of his duties on May 21 while the team was in Huntsville. It was not clear if Canada's release was related to the team's loss to Detroit, 16–9, that night. The new manager was Jesse "Hoss" Walker, the 1941–43 shortstop and 1953–54 manager.[23]

Writing about Walker, the *Huntsville Mirror* also extolled the merits of three of Birmingham's young players, Jesse Mitchell, Frank Marsh, and Billy Joe Moore. Mitchell, a 20-year-old center fielder, was said to have "the strongest throwing arm since Willie Mays. This young lad is fleet afoot and pack [sic] a wallop, he is now batting a respectable .346." Marsh, actually misidentified as "Morris," was also a 20-year-old outfielder. Williams said Marsh was "ready for minor league competition with a batting average of .315." First baseman Moore was said to be a powerful hitter who needed just a little more fielding experience to move up.[24]

Mitchell spent most of his career with Birmingham, but finished with Kansas City. Former Monarch Jim Robinson described Mitchell as "one of the finest center fielders I've ever seen in my life. He was smooth; he reminded me so much of Paul Blair. He used to play right behind second base and Jessie Mitchell was the same kind of center fielder … he was so graceful."[25] Mitchell joined the Black Barons in 1954, playing four years.[26] His brother, Johnny Mitchell, played with Birmingham in the 1950s. He was an outfielder also.[27]

Marsh later was graduated from Grambling and taught school in his native Mobile for many years. He was the first black player for the Johnson City Cardinals of the Appalachian League. In his profile on the Negro Leagues Baseball Museum web page, he is said to have led the team in batting average, RBIs, hits, stolen bases and singles. However, he shows up on the 1954 Johnson City roster as appearing in just 44 games and leading in no categories.[28]

Moore is an enigma. He flirted with the NAL batting title the entire season, finally overtaking John Kennedy of Kansas City. Final published figures in early September showed Moore (.373) and Kennedy (.356).[29] After that sensational season, Moore vanished from black baseball. He does not show up in any of the spring training or regular season newspaper stories in 1957, nor does he appear on the roster of any of the other Negro American League teams. Nor does Birmingham sportswriter Marcel Hopson mention the previous season's best player.

There is some information on the route he took to get to Birmingham. Moore was born on May 28, 1930, in Clinton, Oklahoma. In 1948 he was sentenced to fifteen years in the Oklahoma state penitentiary on burglary charges. While incarcerated, he became a prison standout in several sports. In 1952 he batted .390 with 46 home runs. In 1953 it was .389 with 20 home runs. He came to the attention of New York Yankee scouts Joe McDermott and Tom Greenwade, the man who discovered Mickey Mantle. The Yankees secured a sixty-day leave for Moore to join the Class C Grand Forks club in the Northern League at a salary of $250 a month. If he made good with the club, he would remain on parole until his scheduled release date of May 25, 1955. According to the U.S. Social Security Death Index and the U.S. Find A Grave Index, Billy J. Moore died in Atoka, Oklahoma, in 2006. However, the obituary in the *Atoka County Times* is for a 76-year-old white attorney, who was born in Telephone, Texas, also on May 28, 1930. Billy Joe Moore, the baseball player, remains an enigma.[30]

On May 27, Birmingham beat Kansas City, 6–5, in a game that was tied four times and lasted 15 innings. It required four hours and 35 minutes to complete. The *Birmingham World* reported the crowd at 2,201.[31] According to the *Birmingham Post-Herald* and the *Birmingham News*, the game was 13 innings, followed by a 2–1 Kansas City win in a five-inning second game. In 1956, it seemed, the Black Barons could not keep from creating controversy off the field. Sportswriter Taylor reported that a beauty pageant held at the game would be done over "because of the large amount of protest resulting from the selection."[32]

The Monarchs and Black Barons then played out a long and tiring road trip through Alabama, Mississippi, and Tennessee.[33] On June 3, Birmingham changed opponents, splitting a twin bill with the Red Sox in Memphis. Marsh hit two home runs.[34]

But that trip was easy compared with one in late July and early August. That itinerary, paired first with Kansas City and then Detroit, included Alabama, Florida, Georgia, Tennessee, and North Carolina.[35] There were sometimes cancellations and changes in the schedule, but rarely a day off even then. Hops like Huntsville to Indianapolis to Demopolis, Alabama, with a nine-inning game or possibly a double-header played each day, must have been exhausting.

A June 10 double-header at Rickwood Field held a lot of fan anticipation as Memphis came in just a game and a half behind first-place Birmingham. The excitement was heightened by the prospect of a matchup between Memphis southpaw Ace Robinson and Birmingham right-hander Joe Elliott. In a previous meeting earlier in the season, the game had gone 13 innings with each pitcher striking out 14 batters.[36]

An added attraction was apparently the do-over of the controversial beauty pageant. Memphis won the first game, 7–4, as Birmingham committed five errors. The Black Barons won the rain-soaked five-inning second game, 4–1. The losing pitcher was Charley Pride. There was no report on the beauty pageant.[37]

Howe News Bureau statistics on June 30 saw Billy Joe Moore (.391) leading the league in hitting, as well as in hits, total bases, triples, and RBIs.[38] Kansas City (4–2) was in first place, followed by Detroit (7–2), Memphis (3–3), and Birmingham (4–7). Obviously either the Kansas City or Detroit record was erroneous.[39]

Most of the reported games in June were with Memphis, a number of them at Rickwood. They split a June 24 double-header with Memphis winning the first game, 8–5. Charley Pride hit one of three homers. Pride did not fare so well in the nightcap, losing a 4–1 decision to James Berry.[40]

The following Sunday, John Henry Williams and James Hall hit home runs as Birmingham won, 9–7. Again, Pride started the game for Memphis and struggled, although the losing pitcher was likely a reliever. A partial box score published in the *World* included the umpires. Joe Wilson was behind the plate; the base officials were Parker "Chest" Austin and Poindexter Williams.[41]

No final first-half standings were published. Birmingham opened the second half in an unreported series with Memphis. In late July, former Black Baron John Kennedy, now with Kansas City, took over the batting race, hitting an even .400. Moore (.393) was second, and Otha Bailey (.349), known more for his fielding, had moved up to fifth. Moore continued to lead in hits and triples and was tied in total bases and doubles.[42]

On a road trip with Kansas City, Birmingham won twice in Indianapolis, thereby taking a one-game lead over the Monarchs. The wins gave Birmingham four out of seven in the series. It concluded in North Carolina, and Detroit became Birmingham's new partner.[43] Very few results were reported.

The Black Barons finally returned home on August 3. On Friday, they beat Ed Steele's front-running Detroit Stars in Leeds. John Henry Williams had three hits, Willie Wyatt had two, and Frank Marsh hit an inside-the-park home run.[44] A Sunday double-header was split.[45]

As the series progressed in other cities, Birmingham took a five-games-to-two edge. Among the wins was a 17–7 game at Huntsville on August 6. Some 1,400 paid attendance fans saw Wiley Griggs, "enjoying the best year of his Negro American League career," hit two home runs. He had five RBIs. Marsh hit a grand slam home run in the sixth, and Mitchell had a two-run triple and a single. Frank Nichols, a 24-year-old rookie pitcher from Bessemer, was credited with the win.[46]

In early August, Moore (.394) regained the batting lead. Bailey (.330) was fifth. Moore also continued to lead in hits. Detroit (6–1) was in first place, followed by Kansas City (2–1), Birmingham (2–2), and Memphis (1–6).[47]

With the general decline of the league overall came a further diminishing of its classic event in Chicago. The East–West Game, played at Comiskey Park for 23 years, was also going to be played in other cities. There would be three 1956 games: Chicago, August 12; Birmingham, August 19; and New Orleans, August 26. The East players were from Birmingham and Detroit, the West from Kansas City and Memphis.

Birmingham General Manager Arthur Williams told the *Birmingham World* that he had "worked long and had a difficult time in persuading NAL President Martin and other league officials" to agree to playing one of the games in Birmingham.[48]

There was a decided Black Baron flavor to the event aside from playing in Birmingham. Three of the four managers and coaches had played for Birmingham during their careers. The East manager was Ed Steele, assisted by Jesse "Hoss" Walker. The West manager was Homer "Goose" Curry, assisted by Olan "Jelly" Taylor.[49] However, before the first game was played, there had been a coaching change. Walker was replaced as Birmingham manager by 20-year-old outfielder John Henry Williams, who subsequently became the West assistant.[50]

The players, 45 total, were selected by club owners, managers, and coaches, and approved by Martin. The dispersal was Memphis, 14 players; Kansas City, nine; Birmingham, 11; and Detroit, 11. The Birmingham players with uniform numbers were Charles Williams (11) and Claude Barnes (6), pitchers; Otha Bailey (4) and Jim Hall (8), catchers; Billy Joe Moore (15), 1b; Roscoe Mangun (2), 2b; Wiley Griggs (16), 3b; William Wyatt (14), ss; John Williams (11), of; and Frank Marsh (1), of.[51]

At Chicago, the East won, 11–5, before a crowd estimated at 8,000 by the *Chicago Tribune*.[52]

The Birmingham game was set for 2:30 p.m. Advance tickets were available at Temple Pharmacy, 402 North 17th Street, and Brock's Drug Store, corner of 18th Street and North Fourth Avenue. President Martin was enthusiastic about the Birmingham game: "We should have a great Classic…. Our league has some great material, both in pitching and the hitting departments. Our club owners report that several of the All-Stars are definitely big league material…. I certainly would like to see all Negro American League fans, especially those in Birmingham, to turn out and give these up and coming youngsters the support they deserve."[53]

In an eight-inning game, called because of darkness, the West evened the series, 5–4, scoring four runs on five hits in the seventh inning. Bailey, who had a single, a double, and two RBIs, was named Most Valuable Player by "major league scouts on hand."[54] The scouts were reported to be Jack Sanford, New York Giants; John B. Harris, Baltimore Orioles; Joe Sewell and chief scout Laddie [Placek], Cleveland Indians; Tom Baird, Kansas City Athletics; Buddy "Red" Lewis, St, Louis Cardinals.; and an unidentified Brooklyn representative.[55]

The attendance was disappointing. The anticipation of 8,000 to 10,000 fans was likely hampered by weather. "It did not rain at Rickwood Field but the over-all heavy clouds, thunder claps and scattered showers led many fans to believe that it was raining throughout Jefferson County," reported the *Birmingham World*. The attendance was 2,088.[56]

On the eve of the game, Howe News Bureau issued new league statistics. Moore (.376) continued to lead John Kennedy (.356). Bailey (.350) was fourth. Charlie Barnes (6–1) was the pitching leader.[57]

There was no report in the New Orleans newspapers to indicate the third all-star game was played.

Birmingham was to close the regular season with a lengthy Kansas City series in various cities in Mississippi, Tennessee, and Indiana. However, those games did not happen. Instead, there were Negro American League all-star games in each of those cities.[58]

Although the league had held on and completed the season, it had been a very difficult year and likely not profitable for any of the clubs. "Reducing the league to four clubs widened the 'jumps' [distance between where games are played]. Schedule making is tough and booking hard. Club owners are stubborn. They are taking a financial beating but will try to stick it out," reported the *Birmingham World*.[59] The writer said officials were looking for new cities to bolster the league. Mobile, Nashville, and New Orleans were mentioned as the primary prospects.[60]

Then there was the question of who won the pennant. On August 11, the *Birmingham World* reported that Birmingham held a three-game lead in the standings.[61] On September 7 the newspaper said Birmingham held a 5–2–1 record against Kansas City in the season's final series, although evidence of those games is not there. The series was to close out in Chattanooga and Durham and Asheville, North Carolina.[62]

To add to the season-ending confusion, Howe averages published in the *Birmingham World* on September 5 listed the following second-half records: Memphis (6–5), Kansas City (6–5), Birmingham (11–10) and Detroit (11–13). There was no indication that they were final standings. If so, Memphis and Kansas City tied for the second-half title. There had been no report on who won the first half. Nor was there any mention of playoffs to determine a final champion.

The individual batting title apparently was won by Billy Joe Moore (.373), followed by John Kennedy (.356). Otha Bailey (.344) was fourth.[63] Those were the last statistics published in the *World* in 1956. They were not reported as final statistics, though, and 1956 is among the years for which Howe's final official statistics are missing.

29

The Negro American League Rebounds (1957)

The Negro American League, refusing to buy into its many obituaries, came back a bit stronger in 1957. With a returning nucleus of Birmingham, Detroit, Kansas City, and Memphis, it added two members for a six-team lineup. The new teams were the New Orleans Bears and the Mobile Havana Cuban Giants. (The Mobile club was referred to as Longshoremen on several occasions by the *Birmingham World*.) The East–West All-Star game would return to Chicago, again with three teams providing players for each side. Eastern clubs were Birmingham, Detroit, and Mobile. In the West were Kansas City, Memphis, and New Orleans.[1]

Birmingham General Manager Arthur Williams said that the league could possibly jump to eight clubs if the Indianapolis Clowns gave up independent ball. He said a Pensacola, Florida, team was interesting in becoming the eighth member.[2]

In May, however, there was stunning news out of Kansas City. Ted Rasberry, the Michigan businessman, who now owned the Monarchs, announced that they would not be playing home games in the local Municipal Stadium. The team, faced with competition for fans from the Kansas City Athletics, transplanted from Philadelphia in 1955, had become more of a road team.[3] Rasberry's announcement reneged on a promise to return the team to Kansas City.

The following week, John L. Johnson, sports editor of *The Call*, wrote a blistering column about the demise of the famous franchise under Rasberry's ownership. He opened his column with this sentence: "This will be the last time I shall ever write about the Kansas City Monarchs—a team that once filled a yearning void in our baseball emptiness…."[4] Johnson was true to his word. The few references to the Monarchs over the next five years were brief reports from the Howe News Bureau or the Associated Negro Press. Although the club was still referred to as the Kansas City Monarchs, that city saw no more black baseball.

The league continued with six teams, but that was sufficient for sportswriter Marcel Hopson. He wrote that the potential for restoring interest had been crushed by too much familiarity the year before:

> We are hoping that Negro American League officials will act wisely and draft their schedules sanely and not have a team showing up too often in the same ball park during any one given period. If they desired to keep the faithful fans they now have and at the same time regain the old fans and new admirers, they had better space those playing dates for teams…. One team should not show up every other Sunday (three times every month) unless the other teams make appearances in between those dates…. One year Rickwood fans suffered from an over-dose of too much Memphis Red Sox….[5]

Of course, in those four-team years, schedule makers had a difficult task in providing a variety of team appearances.

Williams announced that Jim Canada was returning as manager; Shelley "Play Boy" Stewart, a popular radio station announcer, was named radio publicity chairman; Cleve Horn, veteran owner-manager of the semipro Graystone Gray Sox of Fairfield, would be the team's scout; and businessman and civic leader Dr. A.G. Gaston would represent the team at the league meeting in Memphis.[6]

Spring training was at the Brown Station Baseball Park, located between Hallman Gardens and Brown Station in Bessemer. Again, the team held a clinic and tryout camp sessions at Acipco's Sloss Field Baseball Park.[7]

Expected returning players were third baseman Wiley Griggs, outfielder Jesse Mitchell, catcher Otha "Bill" Bailey, and pitchers Edward Barnes, Fred Jackson, and James Baldwin.[8]

Bailey was in his sixth straight season with the Black Barons. A native of Huntsville, the 5-foot-6, 150-pound catcher was noted for his good arm, steady bat and ability to handle pitchers. After attracting attention as a semipro player in Huntsville in 1949, Bailey got a trial with the Black Barons, but was released. He then signed with Chattanooga in the Negro Southern League. In 1951 he was with the Houston Eagles. Starting as backup to Herman Bell and Pepper Bassett, he eventually took over the starting role. "There is little doubt that he has one of the strongest and most accurate throwing arms in the business," noted a sportswriter. Bailey was lauded for his hustle and total lack of fear when defending the plate against much bigger base runners.[9]

Potential newcomers included: Roy Barnett, 21, of Sylacauga, and James Osbern, 17, of Lynch, Kentucky, outfielders; Arthur Curtis Brown, 16, of Meridian, Mississippi, and Herchel Brown, 19, of Appalachia, Virginia, pitchers; Clarence Johnson, 17, of Bessemer, infielder; John Green, 20, of Lincoln, Alabama, and Willie McGhee, 19 of Birmingham, catchers; Willie Lee McClure, 19, of Huntington, West Virginia, infielder-outfielder; and Curtis White, 19, of Tuscaloosa, position not specified.[10]

More potentials were touted by General Manager Williams as the first exhibition game neared. High on his list were "Earnest Yeatts, 21, outfielder-infielder, from Tennessee State University; James Gross, 20, 'sensational all-around player'; Jess Boss, 18, of Birmingham, 'who readily reminds local fans of the famous shortstop of yesteryears, "Pee Wee" Butts'; Robert Bolden, 21, industrial league outfielder; Donnie Harris, 19, from Ullman High School and Alabama A&M; James 'Jake' Sanders, catcher from Fairfield Industrial High School; and Willie Smith, 19, left-handed pitcher from Anniston, Alabama."[11]

Smith was actually 18 years old. Picked up from a semipro team in Anniston, he played for the Black Barons for four years, then signed a major league contract with Detroit. "We heard the Black Barons were coming through and got up an all-star team to play them," he recalled in an interview. "I pitched against them. I was only 16 years old. I came on in the fourth inning and gave up one hit in five innings They didn't believe I was only 16. Their manager [Jim Canada] asked if I was interested in going on a barnstorming tour with them. I told him I'd have to think about it. It was really the next year [1957] before I did it."[12]

Again, coverage of exhibition games was sparse. On April 28, before a crowd of 1,898, Birmingham beat Detroit, 10–6, for what was reported to be its second straight exhibition win. Three pitchers combined for the win, giving up 11 hits. William Wyatt and Donnie Harris each drove in four runs. Wyatt's came on two triples and a single.[13]

The partial box score published in the *Birmingham World* was the only local one found for the entire 1957 season. The Birmingham lineup was:

Robert Baldwin, 1b
William Wyatt, 2b
Jesse Mitchell, lf
John Williams, rf
Wiley Griggs, 3b
Donnie Harris, cf
Otha Bailey, c
Jess Bass, ss
Stanley Jones, p
Edward Barnes, p
Joe Elliott, p[14]

Sportswriter Marcel Hopson said Harris's sensational performance was most remarkable, given his background. Ullman High School had no baseball team, so he learned the game in the industrial league. His mentor was James "Dizzy" Chambers, the defining coach for a number of outstanding industrial league players. Before joining the Black Barons, Harris played a year for Coach George H. Hopson at Alabama A&M.

Marcel Hopson noted that only two black high schools in Jefferson County had baseball teams. He credited the success of Harris and other youngsters of that period to the industrial league managers and "non-profitting individuals as Willie J. Harris,

Willie Smith, outstanding pitcher and outfielder from 1957 to 1960. He later played eight years in the major leagues and two in Japan (author's collection).

Warren "Pete" Chatman, Warren B. Mills, Sr., the Rev. James Darnell, C.B. Bailey, William Johnson of Enon Ridge, and Eugene Thomas of East Thomas. "Through the years these men and other civic minded community leaders have come home from their daily employment and spent afternoons and off-days organizing boys of their respective communities into competitive junior baseball league teams," he wrote.[15]

Opening Day was Sunday, May 19, a double-header against Memphis. General Manager Williams was said to be "seeking the services of a popular high school band and a colorful elementary school band" for the opening ceremonies. Once again Birmingham games would feature the Flying Nesbitts acrobatic team. This year there was the added attraction of Betty Alexander, a 15-year-old Birmingham girl, joining the troupe.[16]

Birmingham won, 9–4. Mitchell hit a two-run inside-the-park home run. The ball traveled 400 feet, striking the fence. Harris hit a bases-loaded triple. The second game was halted by darkness in fourth inning.[17]

There were no more reports on the team until the first weekend in June. They had beaten the new Mobile team in games played in Bessemer and Huntsville, although no details were given.[18] Howe News Bureau standings in early June had Detroit in first, followed by Memphis and Birmingham. The integrity of the standings was questionable, however, as they showed Kansas City and New Orleans having played but a single game while other teams had played five or more.[19] Jim Banks (.485) of Memphis was the leading batter. Jesse Mitchell (.370) was fourth.[20]

On June 9, the Mobile Cubans made their first appearance at Rickwood Field and took a 10–0 thumping from the Black Barons. Stanley Jones of Bessemer pitched a three-hitter, giving Birmingham 17 wins in 20 games.[21] Mobile found life a hassle off the field, also. Two of the players were arrested that night on suspicion of being white. The two players—Dominic Williams Turesellino, 19, and Eugene Frederick Gelke, 21—were said to be Cubans who spoke no English. They were arrested when police saw them "wandering around" the Trailways bus depot. They lacked proper identification and had not been registered with the other players at the Zanzibar Hotel. Assistant Police Chief J.C. Lance said it was not possible at the time of their arrest to determine if the two men were "Cuban Negroes" or "White Cubans." They were booked on "suspicion of possibly violating Birmingham's racial sports laws."[22]

Afterward, the Black Barons went on the road for 10 days, playing in Texas, Missouri, Virginia, and Illinois. They were reported to be leading the NAL with a 19–3 record.[23]

Returning home on June 23, they beat Memphis, 5–2, as Joe Elliott won his fifth game against no losses. Elliott, considered the team's best reliever, got a rare start and excelled. The team was now said to be 24–5.[24]

After beating Memphis in Pulaski, Tennessee, in late June, they went to New Orleans for a Sunday Beauticians Day game at Pelican Stadium. An estimated 500 barbers and beauticians were in the city for the 38th annual convention of the National Beauty Culturists League.[25]

The Fourth of July was celebrated at Rickwood with a three-team double-header. The Black Barons defeated the New Orleans Bears, 8–3, in the first game and Memphis, 7–5, in the second. Ivory had an inside-the-park home run. The two wins gave Birmingham the first-half title. Their record was now a sensational 34–7 or possibly 29–4.[26] The numbers varied with the different publications, but the team was unquestionably one of the best to wear the Birmingham uniform.

Howe News Bureau statistics at the break saw Memphis's Banks (.434) still leading all hitters. Birmingham's Wyatt (.321) was fifth.[27]

After the holiday, Birmingham joined Kansas City for a swing through Virginia, West Virginia, and North Carolina. On July 7, Birmingham won, 4–3, in Richmond. Elliott pitched 13 innings, giving up only four hits. Bailey doubled in the winning run.[28]

Because of poor reporting, it is difficult to determine if Birmingham was as dominant in the second half. When they returned home on July 14, they lost a double-header to Kansas City at Rickwood.[29]

Rebounding, the Black Barons won, 14–3, in Huntsville on Monday night and left on another poorly reported road trip. Mitchell hit a grand slam home run in New Orleans in one of the few games reported.[30] But the big excitement had occurred two days earlier when Curtis White, a 19-year-old rookie left-hander from Tuscaloosa, pitched a no-hitter against the Red Sox in Meridian, Mississippi. Smith's triple brought in both runs in the 2–0 victory.[31]

They played a single home game with Indianapolis on July 22, winning 10–9. They came from behind with a five-run fifth inning. Ivory hit a three-run homer in the seventh to tie the game.[32]

Soon after, Birmingham and Detroit made an extended swing through the Midwest. Two games that were reported were notable. On July 31, likely in Iowa or Kansas, Birmingham won, 7–2, on the all-round play of Willie Smith. The rookie pitcher struck out nine and hit a bases-loaded double. Second baseman Wyatt also drove in three runs.[33] A few nights later, rookie center fielder Harris was the star. He "fielded sensationally" and hit a grand-slam home run. He also scored what proved to be the winning run with a triple in the 13th inning.[34] Those were the team's last known results until nearly mid–August.

Returning to a single-game format, the 25th anniversary East–West Game was played in Chicago on July 28. Although it was the 25th anniversary, in fact there had been more than thirty games played. Two games were played in 1939, 1942, 1946, 1947, 1958, and 1956. Interestingly, the usually reliable web site www.baseball-reference.com acknowledges all of the two-game years except 1956. Only the Chicago game is listed for that year. Two former Black Barons were managers William "Dizzy" Dismukes for the West and Ed Steele for the East.[35] Dismukes was now in his 49th year of pro baseball. The selection process had changed from fan voting to administrative selection. Each team submitted nine players for possible inclusion on the rosters.[36]

Birmingham starters were shortstop William Wyatt and center fielder Jesse Mitchell.[37] The West won, 8–5, before a crowd estimated at 7,000. Promoters had hoped to pull in 15,000 by returning to Chicago for the anniversary contest.[38]

Birmingham's next reported game was on Sunday, August 11. They beat Detroit, 9–7, before an estimated 3,000 fans at Rickwood. The win put the Black Barons back on top in the second-half race. Mitchell led the 14-hit attack with three hits, one an inside-the-park home run. Jones got the win, his ninth against two losses, but needed relief help from Elliott in the sixth when the Stars loaded the bases. Elliott then threw third strikes past two batters to end the threat.[39]

By the following Sunday, the Black Barons were paired with Kansas City. They split a double-header at Grand Rapids, Michigan, then headed back home leading by three and a half games.[40] En route, they stopped in Vincennes, Indiana, where Kansas City won, 1–0. Curtis White pitched a three-hitter in the loss.[41]

On that Midwestern swing, the Black Barons stopped in Anderson, Indiana, for an exhibition game with a local team, the Anderson Falstaffs. Birmingham had beaten the Falstaffs, 5–0, on an earlier swing through the region. Joe Elliott pitched a four-hitter, striking out nine, and John Williams led a 12-hit attack with a double and three singles. The Falstaffs won the rematch, 5–4.[42]

The win over the Falstaffs brought some new names into play. The box score in the local newspapers listed the following lineup for Birmingham: John Mitchell, rf; Harris, 1b; Smith, lf; Jim Mitchell, cf; Gongs, 2b; Ivory, 3b; Bass, ss; Wright, c; Barnes, p; and Cotton, lf. Gongs, Cotton, and Wright were not

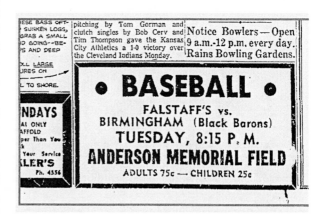

Advertisement from the *Anderson (IN) Herald*, 20 August 1957.

previously recorded for Birmingham in 1957. Gongs is almost certainly a misspelling of Wiley Griggs. No first names have been found for Cotton and Wright. The two Mitchells are a puzzle because the player previously noted with that last name was Jess Mitchell, also an outfielder.[43]

Birmingham returned to Rickwood Field on August 25 to split two games with Memphis.[44] They were the final reported NAL games for 1957. Birmingham almost certainly won both halves of the East Division pennant race. There was no indication that a playoff was held with the West Division winner.

Birmingham was to be at Rickwood on September 8 for another three-team doubleheader. In the first game the Black Barons would face the New Orleans Crescent Bears. The winner of that game would play the industrial league all-stars in the nightcap.[45] If the games were played, there was no report in the local newspapers.

30

Contraction (1958)

In early March, General Manager Arthur Williams announced that the 1958 Birmingham Black Barons spring training camp would open around March 29 at Sloss Field. As customary in recent years, the formal opening would be preceded by a rookie school for new prospects.[1] The Sloss location reflected the declining economics of black baseball. There would be no more spring training away from Birmingham.

There was a lot of uncertainty in the Negro American League. The spring meeting had been postponed due to the illness of Dr. W.S. Martin, vice president and owner of the Memphis Red Sox. Williams said Martin's health would likely determine when the meeting was rescheduled.[2] There was speculation that the league, with six teams committed, might even expand to eight. Homer "Goose" Curry was "toying" with the idea of purchasing the Detroit franchise. There was also "a renewed red hot report that former Black Baron president Tom H. Hayes, Jr. is entertaining the idea of returning to the NAL with another team."

The preliminary lineup of teams was Birmingham, Memphis, Kansas City, Detroit, and the New Orleans Bears.[3]

However, when the league meeting was finally held on March 29, there were just four teams: Birmingham, Detroit, Kansas City, and Memphis. The season would open on May 25 and close on Labor Day with the Fourth of July being the usual first- and second-half break. Arthur Dove, a businessman from Raleigh, North Carolina, requested a franchise for that city, but league President Dr. J.B. Martin said five teams would create a schedule imbalance. Dove said there was a possibility of a Baltimore request, but the responsible person was unable to attend the meeting. Martin said if the two approached the league later, they might be admitted as associate members for 1958 with full membership possible in 1959.[4]

The league also discussed an invitation from a New York City promoter to schedule some NAL games there. The white major league Brooklyn Dodgers and New York Giants had moved to California, leaving only the New York Yankees in the city. That scenario might prove profitable to the NAL.

As all of these potentialities simmered, Birmingham moved toward spring training without a field manager. Williams hinted that he might take the field himself with last year's manager Jim Canada serving as a coach.[5]

Meanwhile, Williams was busy signing players. One of his first moves was to bring back Joe Elliott, the 21-year-old right-hander who was reported to have a pitched a no-hitter against the Indianapolis Clowns the year before. Confirmation of the no-hitter has not been found. Elliott had finished with a 12–3 record, but there was no mention of the no-hitter in the sparse reportage of the 1957 season. In fact, the only reported game with

Indianapolis was won by Birmingham, 10–9, not likely a no-hitter.[6] Williams said other returning players were catcher Otha Bailey, center fielder Joseph Mitchell, right fielder Johnny Williams, and third baseman Wiley Griggs. The big hole he had to fill was second base, William Wyatt's contract having been purchased by the Cleveland Indians.[7]

At the rookie tryout camp, several home-grown prospects were declared to be "promising standouts." They included Bobby Gene Sanders, 19, infielder from Centreville, Alabama; from Birmingham, Felix Riddel, 19, outfielder; Robert Somersville, 19, right-handed pitcher; Walter Griggs, 20, outfielder; and Richard Colvin, 21, outfielder, 21.[8]

Wyatt's spot was filled with a familiar face by the time exhibition season opened. Back in a Black Barons uniform was Rufus Gibson, the all-star infielder who had played on the 1951, 1955, and 1956 teams.[9]

The Black Barons won their opening exhibition game on April 20, defeating Memphis, 3–2. Willie Smith, Joe Elliott, and Stanley Jones combined on a two-hitter.[10]

The team played another game with Memphis, winning 4–1. There was little other coverage until the May 25 Opening Day double-header with Detroit.[11]

The game at Rickwood Field was preceded by a Saturday morning parade featuring five local high school bands and an estimated 350 Little League baseball players.[12]

Arthur Williams, now identified as owner as well as general manager, decided against adding field manager to his duties. Instead, he brought back Canada, now in his third decade of baseball.[13] Canada subsequently had led the team to a 13–0 exhibition record.[14]

But Detroit dominated before a crowd of 7,000. Joe Childress, although outpitched by Jones, took a 3–2 win in the opener. Childress allowed five hits and struck out eight, while Jones allowed only three hits and struck out 10. The visitors were ahead, 6–1, when the second game was called for darkness after four innings.[15]

There were no further reports until June 15 when the Black Barons returned home to play Memphis. General Manager Williams announced that there would be a "sack and chemise" contest, reflecting the latest women's fashion. Also, the selection of Miss Black Baron of 1958 was planned.[16]

On the generally unreported road trip, Birmingham had won a bizarre double-header at Welch, Virginia (*sic*). The opponent was not identified but it was likely Memphis. The scores were 27–8 and 11–3. Shortstop Billy Sanders had four home runs and first baseman James Ivory three in the twin bill. Williams said several players had been shaken up on the road trip when the team's bus driver swerved to keep the vehicle from going over a 440-foot embankment.[17]

The games were actually in Welch, West Virginia, and the bus accident is almost certainly one that Willie Smith recalled some years later after he had made it to the major leagues:

> I remember one time when we were in the mountains … and the driver fell asleep at the wheel. One player was awake up front and yelled at him. We were lucky he turned the wheel the right way. He was about six inches from going off the side of the mountain.
>
> As it was, he ran right into the side of the mountain. I woke up and got out and there was this big mountain in front of me. I said, "I quit. If you people want to get killed, you can, but you're not going to kill me."[18]

Smith said he left the team for a time, but "love of the game" brought him back.[19] According to the official statistics released by the Howe News Bureau, he finished the season with a 6–2 record, recording two shutouts and 2.67 earned-run averages. His batting average in 15 games was .458.

Miss Black Baron still had not been selected two weeks later, though. Williams announced that the selection would be during the Sunday, June 29, games with the Detroit Clowns. The winner was to receive a trip to Chicago for the East–West Game.

There was no report on the games with Memphis at Rickwood, but as the two teams prepared for a paired road trip, Arthur Williams announced a managerial change. He said Jim Canada was demoted to scout duty. Replacing him in the dugout was John Henry Williams. Arthur Williams stated that "the Black Barons have a youth movement on, and Canada did not fit into the youth plans. He was also guilty of club rules and regulation violations."[20] It was the second time young Williams had been drafted to finish out the season as manager of the team. A similar situation had occurred in 1956 when he was just 20 years old.[21]

In late June, owner Williams announced the signing of 18-year-old Glenn Finley, a right-handed pitcher from Miles College. The institution had no formal team, but basketball coach Oscar Catlin had been "tutoring a squad of interested school-connected athletes in community games." Catlin, a Morehouse graduate who had a long career as a high school and college coach in the Birmingham area, said he hoped to field a regular team at Miles in 1959.[22] Unfortunately, Finley was "extremely Wild" and a "Big disappointment" in four starts and one relief appearance. He was said to have an extremely sore arm, too. Williams released the collegian shortly after signing him.[23]

On July 2, the *Birmingham World* published NAL statistics that had a Detroit third baseman named Baker leading the league with a .429 batting average. Strangely, no player named Baker was listed in the Howe News Bureau's final averages. Detroit's third baseman was Joseph Henry, who batted .284. Reflecting the greatly diminished schedule for a four-team league, the leaders in hits were tied with just 11 each after a full month of play.[24]

The Howe standings were Kansas City (3–1), Memphis (10–5), Detroit (5–4), and Birmingham (1–5). Note that total wins (19) do not equal total losses (15). Standings posted a week later were radically different: Detroit (7–5), Memphis (6–4), Birmingham (6–6), and Kansas City (5–9).[25]

Balanced standings (36 total games) were published in mid–July. They were Detroit (10–7), Memphis (8–5), Birmingham, (12–13), and Kansas City (6–11). The disparity in total games played was not explained. In individual statistics, Birmingham outfielder John Williams (.352) was the batting leader, followed by Detroit's Vern Thomas (.348). Williams also led in hits, runs, and total bases. Willie Harris of Birmingham was tops in doubles and tied in triples. Pitchers Stan Jones and Willie Smith were the leaders in innings pitched and strikeouts, respectively.[26]

The anemic coverage of the NAL continued throughout July and August with only six scores being reported in the local newspapers. Five of those contests were with Detroit and the other was with Memphis. The Memphis game saw Birmingham return to Yankee Stadium.[27] Birmingham beat the Red Sox, 6–4, on July 27 before a crowd of 13,614. The game was part of a long road trip that paired the two clubs in several other major league parks, including Briggs Stadium in Detroit, Ebbets Field in Brooklyn, Shibe Park in Philadelphia, and Memorial Stadium in Baltimore.[28]

Howe News Bureau standings on July 23 were Memphis (13–9), Birmingham (14–13), Kansas City (16–18), and Detroit (12–15). Birmingham's rookie infielder Billy Gene Sanders (5) was the home run leader. Frank McCollum of Kansas City, a 1955 Black Baron, had thrown the season's only no-hitter, beating Memphis, 5–2, on the Fourth of July.[29]

By early August, Birmingham (15–18) had dropped to last place. Memphis (17–13) was first, followed by Kansas City (23–22) and Detroit (13–17). Birmingham was third in team batting, but first in fielding. Individually, pitcher Willie Smith (.458) was the club's top hitter. His pitching record was 6–2 with 58 strikeouts and 19 walks.[30]

With so few NAL games being reported, it is difficult to gauge the popularity of the four teams. However, all of baseball was seeing a decline in attendance. Organized Ball's minor leagues had peaked with 438 teams in 59 leagues during the boom years after World War II.[31] By 1958 the total had plummeted to 172 baseball cities in 24 leagues.[32] The cause of the decline was multi-faceted. The rapid growth of television had people staying home to watch a variety of entertainment options never before available. The spread of air conditioning in individual homes made staying at home much easier in hot weather, especially in the humid South. Where the baseball park had been a part of the urban environment, it was not so in the suburbs, where many people were moving. And finally, the dramatic sudden-death playoff between the New York Giants and Baltimore Colts for the 1958 National Football League championship signaled a changing dynamic in America's sports interest.[33]

As owners added supplemental attractions such as comedy routines and acrobats to pull in fans, sometimes there were innovations that changed the nature of the game itself. One of those changes was presented at Rickwood in July. While the Black Barons were on the road, Kansas City and Detroit offered fans a "fast" game in the opener of their twin bills. Fast games had been played occasionally in other leagues. The five-inning contest was played "with unlimited substitutions, batters getting two strikes and three balls, pitchers resting between innings and the like." Kansas City won a regular league game, 15–2. Detroit won the "fast" game, 3–1.[34]

The East–West Game was scheduled for August 24, again at Comiskey Park in Chicago. The event was dedicated to the great players who had participated in the first game twenty-five years earlier. Marcel Hopson, writing in the *Birmingham World*, said he had seen "ink waves" of notations on Josh Gibson, Satchel Paige, Turkey Stearnes, Frank Duncan, and others. He said two Birmingham heroes were being overlooked: "They are Cafeman Poindexter (P.D.) Williams and George (Mule) Suttles, former members of the 1932 edition of the Birmingham Black Barons ... that year, Williams, a catcher, and Suttles, who shifted back and forth from first base to outfield, were members of the West team."[35] Suttles played in four East–West games, but Williams never made the roster, according to Larry Lester's history of the Classic.[36] Also, Suttles was with Birmingham from 1923 to 1925.

Poindexter Williams was born in Alabama in 1897. When the first industrial league team picked up the temporary nickname of the Coal Black Barons, he was the catcher. He made his professional debut with Chicago and Detroit in 1921. He was with the Black Barons from 1923 to 1929.[37] He was a playing manager in 1923 and 1928, strangely suffering broken legs in both seasons.[38] In 1930–31, he played with Louisville and Nashville, returning to Birmingham in 1932. His playing career ended with Nashville and Homestead in 1933, but he returned as Black Barons manager in 1935.[39]

Suttles' career highlights are covered elsewhere in this book.

Although little publicized, a second East–West Game was played at Yankee Stadium. Willie Smith was the winning pitcher in both games. The East won in Chicago, 4–3. Birmingham outfielder Brown Jackson won the game with a three-run home run. The East won, 6–5, in New York.[40]

On September 6, the *Birmingham World* published one of the most bizarre stories of the season. The paper reported that the Black Barons had won the second-half championship by virtue of winning a Rickwood double-header over Detroit on August 31. General Manager Arthur Williams was quoted as saying it was team's first NAL championship since 1940. Further, Williams said the Black Barons won both halves of the 1958 season, finishing with a record of 84 wins and 17 losses.[41]

It is unclear where Williams might have been when the Black Barons were playing in the Negro Leagues World Series in 1943, 1944, and 1948. Likewise in 1952, when Birmingham defeated Indianapolis in the championship playoff. Also, Birmingham likely won both halves in 1957. Finally, Birmingham did not make the playoffs in 1940.

It is difficult to find any rational explanation for the publication of the story, Certainly, Marcel Hopson and his editors knew better. With the 1958 season being one of the ones for which the final Howe News Bureau averages are available, it is easy to factually dismiss the story and Williams's assertions. At first glance, it appeared that Memphis had finally won a championship, but that turned out not to be the case. Unofficial standings published on October 18 were Memphis (17–13, .567), Kansas City (30–24, .556), Birmingham (15–19, .441), and Detroit (21–26, .447).

When the official records were released a few weeks later, Memphis was demoted and the Kansas City Monarchs had won yet another championship. The official standings were Kansas City (30–24–2, .556), Memphis (18–15–1, .545), Detroit (21–26–1, .447), and Birmingham (15–19–0, .441)[42]

Birmingham outfielder-manager John Williams (.357) won the batting championship, edging out Harold Hair (.355) of Kansas City. He was the only Black Baron among the leaders.[43]

Among the pitchers, Willie Smith (6–2) and Willie Gross (4–1) were team leaders.[44]

League officials scheduled a postseason review of 1958 in October. Marcel Hopson said the meeting would likely focus on putting the league "on a better operational basis," and certainly on cutting down on the enormous travel jumps around the nation.[45]

31

A Brief Reprieve (1959)

Just as the Negro American League, once again reduced to four teams, looked like it was taking its last breath in 1958, there was a brief resurgence. There were six clubs again in 1959. Joining Birmingham, Detroit, Kansas City, and Memphis were the Newark Eagles and the Raleigh Tigers.[1] With new blood, league President Dr. J.B. Martin predicted a revival of black baseball: "I believe we'll have our best season since the war years when all clubs in the league made money."

Opening Day was Sunday, May 17. Martin announced that four league double-headers were scheduled for Yankee Stadium during the season.[2]

The Black Barons, once again, had new out-of-town ownership. In January it was announced that Dr. Andrew Ross had sold the team to an eight-man syndicate in Chicago. Heading the group was former manager Winfield S. Welch, now traveling secretary with one of the Harlem Globetrotter teams. No price was disclosed for the deal, which was transacted at the NAL's winter meeting in Chicago.[3]

As spring training got under way at Sloss Field, one of the team's all-time favorites returned as manager. Lorenzo "Piper" Davis, who had help train such players as Willie Mays, Artie Wilson, Bill Greason, Bill Powell, Alonzo Perry, and Ed Steele, was back in the dugout.

"The versatile Davis, hoping to rebuild the club around youth and for his old manager, now franchise owner, Winfield Welch, is putting the squad together in daily workouts," reported the *Birmingham News*.[4] Davis, manager of the club for part of 1947 and all of 1948–49, had gotten his start under Welch in 1943.[5]

Davis, just finishing a nine-year minor league career that included long stays in the Pacific Coast League and the Texas League, said he might suit up himself and play "wherever I can help the club." Veterans in camp included outfielder John Williams, pitcher Willie Smith, and catcher Otha Bailey, back for his eighth season. Davis said two rookies looking good in early work were shortstop Bobby Sanders and unrelated outfielder Jake Sanders.[6]

Two other prospects were Anthony Lloyd of Fairfield, a Tuskegee Institute graduate, and Earnest Harris, Western High School graduate and Miles College student.[7]

After a home game rainout, Birmingham joined Memphis for a five-game exhibition series in Mississippi and Alabama.[8] Birmingham returned home for an exhibition game with Kansas City on May 10. Pitchers Pete Munford, Joe Elliott, and Willie Smith combined for a four-hit, 8–4 win. Second baseman Lloyd and shortstop Sanders each had two hits.[9]

Kansas City's "home" opener with Birmingham was played in Athens, Georgia, the Monarchs having abandoned Kansas City the year before. Kansas City won, 4–0.[10]

Birmingham's home opener a week later was promoted as the Black Barons' 40th season. Actually it was the 40th anniversary of black professional baseball in Birmingham. There had been no Black Barons teams in 1933, 1934, and 1939. Marcel Hopson's pregame story in the *Birmingham World* credited sportswriter Zipp Newman as the first to call the team Black Barons, although it was not an official name.[11] The spirited event was expected to draw many former Black Barons.

Two known living members of the 1919 formative team were catcher Poindexter "P.D." Williams, now a café owner, and first baseman George McAllister, who was living in Woodlawn. Other "identified members of the team" included John Kemp, Charles "Twosides" Wesley, Buford "Geechie" Meredith, John Henry Russell, Joe Mitchell, June Moon, "Cuban" Rousella, Harry Salmon, and Sam Streeter.[12]

Some Hobson observations were of questionable accuracy. He said promoters of the team over the years included William "Kid Wonder" Sharp, Bob Woods, and Frank Perdue. Hotel man Alfred "Fredo" Walker was said to have been the owner in 1934–35 with Anthony Cooper as his manager and John Dock as team secretary. He said Sam Crawford managed the team in 1921. In fact, Crawford was manager just briefly in 1924. The 1934 manager was likely Bill Perkins and the 1935 manager was Poindexter Williams, possibly replaced by George McAllister.

The anniversary observance was scheduled for Friday, May 22. Dr. John W. Nixon, prominent Ensley dentist and a noted soloist, was selected to throw out the first pitch. Music was by the Fairfield Industrial High School Band under Louis Rutland.[13]

The league president appealed for fans to support the Negro American League teams. Noting that there were now 56 black players in the major leagues, he said, "This is the reason we are determined to keep the Negro American League alive so that we can continue to train young Negro players for these big leagues…. We are looking forward to doing much better this year in baseball than we have in the last eight years and we can do it with your help."[14]

The Friday game was apparently rained out because Hopson reported the Sunday double-header as Opening Day. Birmingham won both, 8–3 and 3–1, with Smith and Munford pitching complete games. Left fielder John Mitchell hit a 375-foot three-run home run and Brown Jackson a 407-foot triple. In the second game, Mumford struck out twelve and walked only one, holding the visitors to four hits.[15]

A reported 3,300 fans saw the game in spite of a "Game of the Week" on national television and a radio broadcast of the white Barons' Southern Association game that afternoon.

Marcel Hopson urged support for the team, saying Manager Davis was taking talented young players and building a team "that will last more than one year, two years or a brief period." Taking on the naysayers about the young team, he wrote, "I am quite sure that many of us backward thinking folk would like to see the Black Baron squad loaded with a bunch of ancient linamint-rubbing [*sic*], old popular 'has-been' former ball players who are almost too old to sit in the grandstands. But Mr. Davis cannot build a representative properly functioning ball club with past tense, 'has-been' players who might not be able to hold a ball or bat in their hands even if it were handed to them by another person's hand. Sure, some of the youngsters are going to make mistakes. But, tell me, who has not?"[16]

Although there was grumbling about a lack of flashy, long-ball hitters, Hopson noted that in the double-header Willie "Red" Harris and Brown Jackson each had four hits, two of them triples; James Ivory had a double and a triple; and John Mitchell hit a home run. Birmingham's record was 4–1 after the sweep.[17]

There was no news locally on the team between the Detroit games and a return to Rickwood the weekend of June 6–7. The new Newark team came in with a 3–7 record, but showed surprising strength at the plate on Saturday night, winning 14–11. Birmingham won the opener on Sunday, 14–4, with Willie Smith throwing a five-hitter and striking out nine. Smith also starred at the plate, driving in three runs with two singles and a triple. Harris had four RBIs with two singles and a home run. The second game was called after three innings.[18] Birmingham's record was reported at 16–3.[19]

The next day Newark and Birmingham left town for games in North Alabama, Kentucky, Tennessee, and Arkansas. On June 21, Birmingham played two in Memphis, then paired with the Red Sox in Arkansas, Oklahoma, and Mississippi.[20]

Again, local newspaper cover was negligible, but a report from a game in Paris, Texas, provided a little insight into the club's finances. A Juneteenth game, sponsored by the Paris Baseball Club, drew 505 paying customers, "with the white and Negro fans divided almost evenly." The local club made $168 while Memphis and Birmingham shared $252.60. The Paris club president was so pleased with the outcome that he said he was bringing the same two teams back for a July 4 game.[21] However, Birmingham was in Indiana that day, playing Kansas City.

By the time the Black Barons returned home to begin a series with Raleigh, Brown Jackson (.300) was eighth in league hitting. Jesse Mitchell (.372) of Kansas City was first.[22]

The Raleigh team was organized in the 1940s, playing independent ball in the Carolinas. In 1948 it became an associate member of the Negro Southern League. Organized Ball players who got their start in Raleigh included Charlie Neal of the Los Angeles Dodgers and Wes Covington of the Milwaukee Braves.[23]

On a Ladies Night at Rickwood, the Black Barons trounced the Tigers, 10–4. Smith pitched another complete game, striking out 10. Again, he was formidable at bat, hitting a single and a triple. Mitchell and Ernest "Onk" Harris each had two hits. Harris also made "several fielding gems against the center field wall."[24]

On Sunday, Birmingham swept two, 10–3 and 8–1. Phil Welch gave up a few hits in the opener, and Munford gave up four in the second game. Harris, who was being watched by major league scouts, had three hits and three RBIs. Welch (7–2) struck out seven. Mumford (6–2) struck out 11.[25]

With the wins, Birmingham's record was 25–7. They had been in first place much of the 1959 season, and Marcel Hopson chastised fans for their lack of support. The team had drawn only 592 fans for Ladies Night game and 1,729 for a Sunday double-header. In a rambling column, Hopson wrote:

> Now tell me, fickle and some-timey Birmingham fans, what's the big excuse? The Black Barons currently boast five hitters batting the ball over the .300 mark, among them Willie Smith, the best pitching and best hitting hurling [*sic*] in the NAL today. Smith is the second top batter in the league with a .375 average. He is followed by Manager Piper Davis with .333, first baseman Willie "Red" Harris, .323; Bobby Sanders, .317. And right fielder Brown Jackson, .316. What more do you fans want? Now is the time … to show our deep appreciation for a winning team by coming out in attendance record-breaking numbers at Rickwood Field. There were no cloudy skies or rain Friday night nor Sunday afternoon. Where were you? Don't blame the [Floyd] Patterson-[Ingmar] Johansson fight for keeping you home. Remember, we know Joe Louis was not fighting! There were no TV showings of the fight. Anyway where were you so-called Black Barons fans. Prove yourselves by filling up the park.[26]

But lagging attendance was not just in Birmingham. It was era of ebbing interest for baseball, with television no doubt one factor. A letter-writer in one of the daily newspapers complained of poor attendance at white Barons games. He said the third-place Barons of 1948 had drawn more fans than the 1958 championship team.[27]

Although they lost to Kansas City at Indianapolis, the Black Barons (25–8) had a six-game lead over the Monarchs.[28]

They returned to Birmingham for a double-header with Kansas City on July 12, an event that would include the crowning of Miss Black Baron of 1959. The winner would get a trip to the East–West Game in Chicago. Coordinating the event was James "Dizzy" Chambers, who announced that the contestants would be judged in swimsuits. Contestants had to be 18 years old or older. First, second and third prizes would be awarded.[29]

Marcel Hopson made another appeal for fan support: "A team cannot exist or operate successfully without the financial support of the community through the paid attendance gates at the park. Organized baseball has left many cities and towns when they failed to get the necessary fan support at the ticket gates. We don't want to lose the Black Barons do we?"[30]

Rattling the Jim Crow cage, Hopson added: "When high schools are closed for the summer, the Black Barons provide the only wholesome sports amusement in the Birmingham area. If they leave us, we will have nothing, since Kiddie Land Park and other tax-supported better swimming pools, parks and playgrounds are barred to the Negro segment of the Birmingham-Jefferson County communities. Let us not put less than 5,000 paid fans at the Birmingham-Kansas City game."[31]

The Black Barons (26–9) were in first place. There was speculation that Kansas City would start a Birmingham boy in one of the important July 12 games at Rickwood. Aubrey Grigsby, of Woodlawn, in the last reported figures was 2–0 with 17 strikeouts for the Monarchs. He had played three years in the YMCA Industrial Baseball League in Birmingham.[32]

The Monarchs gained a game, winning the opener, 11–6. The right fielder for Kansas City was Fairfield's Jake Sanders. Birmingham won the five-inning nightcap, 2–0. Smith allowed only two hits, struck out four, but walked an unusually high five batters. Ivory drove in both Birmingham runs.[33]

The attendance was a disappointing 1,630 paid admissions. But a week later, it was determined that the person at Rickwood providing the numbers had erred. The corrected paid crowd was put at 4,387.[34]

During the pregame ceremonies, Lillian Sellers, of 125 North 15th Court, was named Miss Birmingham Black Barons. The 22-year-old was sponsored by Mr. And Mrs. W.M. Owens, owners of the Eagle's Café, 2610 North 16th Street.[35] But the crowning was not without controversy. "Dizzy" Chambers reported "that some former team officials dropped discouraging hints around where some of the interested young women could get [hear] them." Chambers said the critics had cut the field of contestants from 11 to four by the time the event was held.[36]

The next weekend, Memphis came in for three games. Birmingham won the Friday night game, 9–4. "Onk" Harris had three hits, one of them a 350-foot home run into the right field bleachers.[37]

With the win, Birmingham (32–14) was 12 games ahead of the Monarchs. They split on Sunday, Smith pitching a five-hit 4–1 win in the opener.[38]

Harris, a product of Western High School in Ensley and the industrial league, was among the top hitters and fielders in the league. The talent combination had watchers projecting him for Organized Ball in 1960. "Harris makes sensational fielding gems with apparent ease and is rated the fastest base runner in the Negro American League today," wrote

Hopson. "On a steal, he scampers far ahead of a pick-off throw. He is usually sitting on a base when the ball gets there, no matter how fast the oval is fired. Friday night, at the crack of the bat, he jet-rodded to far left center field and back-handed a would-be two-run triple hit off the wall 390 feet away."[39]

Harris got his chance with the Detroit Tigers and Philadelphia Phillies, but never moved beyond Class C. He played in 33 games at Bakersfield, California, in 1960, batting .191. The days of jumping from the Negro leagues to Organized Ball were about over. Only the rare ball player like Willie Smith would make it.[40]

In Howe News Bureau statistics in late July, John Williams (.377) of Detroit was the leading hitter. No Birmingham player was among the leaders.[41]

Birmingham and Memphis played on a road trip in North Alabama, Tennessee, Kentucky, and Missouri, winding up on East–West Game weekend.[42]

The West won, 8–7, in the 11th inning with Mumford getting the win. Birmingham players played key roles in the win. The East led 1–0, but the West got a five-run inning sparked when a misjudged Willie Smith fly to center resulted in an inside-the-park home run. Earnest Harris scored the winning run. The attendance was around 8,000 and included John H. Johnson, publisher of *Ebony* and *Jet*. He threw out the first pitch.[43]

There was no report on games after the all-star break until Birmingham and Memphis played on August 21–23. Memphis won Friday and Sunday games at Rickwood Field. The Friday game was a United Negro College Fund double-header. The first game featured all-star teams from the YMCA Industrial League.[44] The Western stars, managed by James "Slicks" Threatts, defeated Joe Allen's East team, 4–0. Memphis won, 7–4, in 11 innings.[45]

Manager Piper Davis's pennant-winning year came to an end on Monday, August 24, in Chattanooga. The Black Barons beat Memphis, 7–5, in the season's final game.[46]

There was no indication of any kind of postseason playoff, probably because Birmingham had so dominated the entire season.[47]

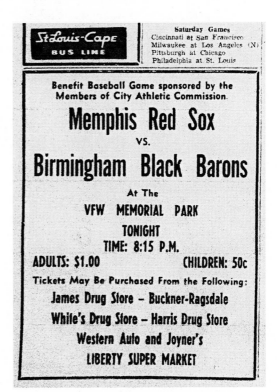

Advertisement from the *Sikeston (MO) Daily Standard*, 7 August 1959.

32

Last Team Standing?
(1960–62)

1960

When spring arrived in 1960, it was obvious that the Negro leagues were beyond even life support. They were essentially over. This chapter is a recounting of the end, and the author's whimsical assertion that the Birmingham Black Barons were the last team standing in the Negro American League.

Despite the championship in 1959, it had to be painfully clear to Birmingham fans that black baseball was in about gone. The 1959 East–West Game had attracted only an estimated 8,000 patrons, and there had been no postseason play. The regular season itself did not start until May 17, and it ended on August 24 rather than the traditional attendance-boosting Labor Day weekend.[1]

Of course, there was dramatic progress for African American baseball players. As the major leagues opened spring training, there were sixty black and Caribbean players on the rosters. The last holdout to integration, the Boston Red Sox, had signed infielder Jerry "Pumpsie" Green and pitcher Earl Wilson.[2]

Undaunted, the NAL announced that the league would operate with six teams. In addition to Birmingham, the lineup would include the Memphis Red Sox, Kansas City Monarchs, Detroit Stars, New Orleans Bears, and the New Orleans Crescent Bears. Dr. J.B. Martin was reelected as president and secretary, "but the body refused to elect him as treasurer." There was no explanation for that decision. Elected treasurer and vice president was Ted Rasberry, the Grand Rapids, Michigan, businessman who owned the Stars and the Monarchs.[3]

General Manager Arthur Williams brought Jim Canada back for his fifth stint as manager. Opening Day was set for Sunday, May 22, although that was later moved back a week. Spring training would begin on April 29.[4]

Again, Black Barons management held tryouts for aspirants. All youngsters between the ages of sixteen and twenty were invited to the Saturday session at Sloss Field Baseball Park. Williams said the participants should bring their own gloves, shoes and "an old uniform" if they had access to one."[5]

The exhibition season opened against Raleigh.[6] Birmingham won, 4–2, in a game that saw the return of Alonzo Perry. He had been playing in Mexico since 1955. He was a power hitter, leading the league in RBIs three times. After his production slipped, his salary was cut, so he returned to Birmingham.[7]

A three-team exhibition was played at Rickwood Field on May 15. Birmingham won both games, defeating the New York Royals, 4–3, and Indianapolis Clowns, 2–1. Phil Welch and Willie Smith were the winning pitchers. Hitting stars were left fielder John Mitchell and center fielder Brown Jackson. The estimated attendance was 5,200.[8]

That was the focus of Marcel Hopson's column in the *Birmingham World* afterward: "Gleefully gazing at Rickwood almost packed from right field to the far left field bleachers with spectators, former B. Barons officials and team players openly commented: 'My, my! Where have all these people (fans) been for the past two or three years?'" Hopson wondered if the turnout was a one-time thing for the Clowns or if it would be sustained.[9]

Moving Opening Day back a week was not the only change happening in the NAL. In mid–May, it was announced that the Memphis Red Sox, Birmingham's chief rival for decades, had folded. Dr. B.B. Martin told reporter Sam Brown of the *Memphis World* that the team had been "a losing proposition for the past four or five years, and the team, or rather, I, lost approximately $12,000 last year." Martin said he could have survived with the sale of two players to Organized Ball. However, catcher Isaac Barns and outfielder Bill White were unable to make it at the new level. Both had been returned, apparently negating the sale.[10] Memphis's place was taken by a resurrection of the Philadelphia Stars.[11]

For the May 29 opener with Kansas City, Williams presented this lineup:

John Mitchell, lf	Carl Lewis, 1b
Jesse Bass, 2b	Otha Bailey, c
James Ivory, ss	Clifford Dubose, 3b
Brown Jackson, rf	Phil Welch, p[12]
Harry Robinson, cf	

Actually, lefthander Willie Smith, now in his fourth season with the Black Barons, started the opener, shutting down Kansas City, 2–1, and striking out 15 batters.

It was Smith's final game with Birmingham. Immediately afterward, it was announced that he had been sold to the Chicago White Sox for a reported $10,000. He left the team with a spring and regular season record of 5–1 and 44 strikeouts in 57 innings. He was 14–4 the year before.[13] He was also one of the team's best hitters, playing both first base and outfield on his on-pitching days. His batting average was .450.[14]

After two weeks on the road, the team returned home for a double-header with Raleigh. Birmingham won both games, 13–4 and 14–10. Third baseman A.G. Westbrook drove in nine runs on three doubles and a single in the double-header. The wins put Birmingham in first place.[15]

The Raleigh pitcher in the first game was former Black Baron Bill Greason. It was one of the worst outings of Greason's career. In six innings, Birmingham batters got fourteen hits and seven bases on balls. He was ejected from the game for protesting the umpire's decision on a balk.[16]

Two weeks later, Birmingham hosted New Orleans in a Miles College building fund benefit. The school's marching band under Director Iva "Ike" Williams provided music between innings.[17] There was the added attraction of Mrs. Martha Doris Parker and the Daredevils of Pratt City, a "dazzling five-member acrobatic stunt troupe." Birmingham entered the games in first place.[18]

Birmingham won, 13–8, but the festive occasion was spoiled by rainy weather. Only 1,624 fans were counted. James Palmore, in relief of Welch, struck out nine and walked five. At bat, he had four hits and drove in four runs. Jackson drove in four runs on three hits.

Despite the bad weather, Arthur Williams was able to present Miles College officials with a check for $131.09.[19]

By early July, it there had been more changes in the NAL, and they were not positive. There now appeared to be only five teams in the league—Birmingham, Raleigh, Kansas City, Philadelphia, and New Orleans, which had changed owners. Birmingham's ownership had changed also. Wardell B. Jackson of Champaign, Illinois, had acquired the team "when it was reported that the previous owner apparently failed to carry out the financial obligations of an owner."[20]

Officials announced a new all-star game to be played at Rickwood on July 31. The opponents would be the league leader as of July 24 and a squad drawn from among the other four teams. There would also be a Miss Birmingham Black Barons competition.[21]

Birmingham hosted the Philadelphia Stars on July 10. Although no standings had been published, Kansas City was reportedly in first place. Birmingham (14–3) was second.[22] After sweeping the Stars, 5–3 and 3–2, the Black Barons were confusingly said to be 21–4. The second game lasted only five innings because of a Sunday curfew. Marcel Hopson wrote that some fans were irate over the stoppage although the ordinance had been in place for many years. "Fans had been able to enjoyed on ful [sic] nine-inning game and five innings of a second game. What more do they want? … Many fans feel that a game should be played until it is so dark, one cannot tell a bat from a ball." Hopson did chide stadium management for not reminding fans of the curfew law.[23]

Another double-header with Philadelphia followed two weeks later. General Manager Williams announced that by winning either game, Birmingham would be in first place and host for the all-star game. Sondra Williams (or Willingham) had been selected Miss Black Baron. She would "reign at the All-Star Game" and also would represent Birmingham at the East–West Game in Chicago. Second place went to Vivian Wilson and third place to Geraldine Boykin. The winner was "Williams" in the *World* and "Willingham" in the *News*. The win, witnessed by an estimated 5,000 fans, put Birmingham five games ahead.[24]

But the date changed. It was moved to August 14, a week before the East–West game. Williams said the Black Barons were available but the three teams—suggesting that the league was now down to four teams—that would provide the all-stars were not. They were all on a three-team barnstorming tour of California and other western states. He said they were contractually bound to continue the tour.[25]

Birmingham's role as host was cinched by splitting with Philadelphia, according to the *Birmingham News*. No standings had been reported since early July. The NAL All-Stars would be managed by New Orleans Manager Wesley Baron. Miss Vivian Wilson of Enon Ridge was named to throw out the first pitch in the game. She had been runner-up in the miss Black Baron competition. There was no mention of title holder Sondra Williams/Willingham or the previously announced runners-up.[26]

Birmingham fans would also see some new players. Added to the roster from Knoxville were Ernie Westfield, a six-foot,19-year-old right-handed pitcher, and Harold Subbeth, a 5-foot-11 catcher. Another new pitcher was James Bogans, a lefthander from Alexandria, Louisiana. Utility infielder Johnny Gilliam was released.[27]

Working toward the all-star game, the Black Barons split another double-header with Philadelphia, reportedly boosting their record to 34–10. On July 31, they defeated the Brooklyn Cuban Giants, 9–5.[28]

The August 14 all-star game ended in a 10-inning 2–2 tie, halted by the Sunday curfew.[29]

Looking toward East–West Game, Wendell Smith wrote in the *Pittsburgh Courier* that the game had long since lost its luster. At one time it was the showcase of outstanding black baseball players. Now, like the Negro leagues themselves, the all-star game was a victim of the Negro's progress. With major and minor league rosters burgeoning with black stars, the NAL talent pool was severely reduced. But league President Martin pleaded for the game's survival. "The East–West classic should not be permitted to die now. It served a great purpose when the Negro player needed it the most. We should perpetuate this event if for no other reason than its historical significance. It has been the Negro ball player's NAACP," said Martin.[30]

Martin also told the *Courier* that major league baseball had approached him for the second time with a proposed deal to subsidize a four-team Negro American League. Martin said a National League club had offered to finance the league in exchange for first call on the league's talent. He turned it down. A similar offer from an American League club was now on the table. Martin said he would make a decision after the all-star game.[31] Whether the offer was rejected or withdrawn, no deal was made. The NAL would struggle on for two more years, then die quietly.

The projected lineup for the game had three players from Raleigh and six from Birmingham in the East starting lineup. The Black Barons were shortstop Jesse Bass, third baseman James Ivory, right fielder Brown Jackson, centerfielder John Mitchell, pitcher Ernie Westfield, and a left fielder named Morris.[32]

The West won, 8–4, before a crowd estimated at only 5,000.[33] It was the last East–West game played at Comiskey Park, where the all-star event had begun in 1933. West shortstop Ike Brown of Kansas City went on to play for the Detroit Tigers in 1969. He was the last Negro leagues player signed by a major league team.[34]

The regular season ended with Kansas City at Rickwood Field on Labor Day. The games were split, with Birmingham winning, 8–1, and losing, 2–0, in five innings.[35]

There was no mention of who won the Negro American League pennant race. Most reports during the season had Birmingham in the lead, but Kansas City was a contender, also.

A postseason highlight for Birmingham fans came on a Sunday in October. Negro all-stars from the major leagues appeared at Rickwood in a four-city tour of Alabama. The managers were Hank Aaron of the Milwaukee Braves and Al Smith of the Chicago White Sox.[36]

1961

The first news of the Black Barons in 1961 was the annual tryout camp for youngsters 16 years of age and older. The session was held at Rough Rock Park in Bessemer. Participants were expected to provide their own shoes and gloves. General Manager Wardell Jackson also reported that veteran Jim Canada would be back as field manager.[37] The first appearance of the team before local fans would be an April 9 exhibition game.[38]

Dr. J.B. Martin of Memphis continued as Negro American League president. He announced in April that Opening Day for the four-team league would be Sunday, May 28, with Detroit at Raleigh and Kansas City at Birmingham. The East–West Game was moving from Chicago to New York. It would be played at Yankee Stadium under the sponsorship of an Elks organization.[39]

There was virtually no coverage of the regular season in Birmingham media. But there was a lot of reportage on the barnstorming Indianapolis Clowns, now in their 31st year. J. Earle Hensley, a local promoter, brought in the Clowns for two games at Rickwood Field. They played the New York Royals on April 30 and May 14. The May date was later revised to a double-header. The Black Barons and the Royals would play the first game, with the winner facing the Clowns.[40]

Among the stars on the Clowns team were "Natureboy Williams, comical first base-man; Ambidextrous Grant Greene, who can play any position with either hand; the Great Yogi; Crazylegs Battles; playing manager Carl Forney, and other top flight major league prospects." Two 1960 Clowns were said to have signed minor league contracts.[41]

For unexplained reasons, the first game lasted only five innings. New York beat Phil Welch, 2–1. The Clowns then shelled the Royals, 9–2, in the second game.[42]

The first Birmingham regular season game reported locally came in June and was not at Rickwood Field but in Lanett, Alabama. The independent Atlanta Stars beat Birmingham, 9–8.[43] It was, in fact, the only regular season game reported at all.

That same week a former Black Baron's name was in the news. Winfield Welch, 1941–46 manager, now scouting for the Philadelphia Phillies, was in Atlanta searching for talent in Georgia and Alabama. He said signings had been limited thus far because he only signed those "he thinks can make the grade." Elaborating, Welch said, "There is very little money in the minor leagues, and when I sign a ballplayer, I want to have every confidence that he can go all the way. You can ruin a kid's life by signing him if his qualifications are doubtful. I do not sign just to show officials I am working. I am going all the season without coming up with the right man, but meanwhile I am looking at every prospect possible with a critical eye."[44]

Another former Birmingham manager died in June. William "Dizzy" Dismukes, 71, died in Campbell, Ohio. A Birmingham native, he managed the Black Barons twice. The first time was in 1924 when Sam Crawford started the season but had a dispute with owner Joe Rush.[45] Charles Wesley took over until Dismukes was signed.[46] About two months later, he was released. Joe Hewitt finished the season.[47] Dismukes returned as manager-pitcher in 1938.[48]

Results for NAL games in 1961 are so sparse that it is difficult even to ascertain who was actually in the league. The Center for Negro Leagues Baseball Research compiled rosters for the Detroit Stars and Kansas City, while the author compiled a limited roster for Birmingham.[49] There is no roster for Raleigh.

Results for only three Birmingham games were found for the entire season. These are games with the Clowns and Atlanta Stars above, and a playoff game against Kansas City, which is examined further below.

In early August, James Edward "Dizzy" Chambers, a veteran of the Birmingham indus-trial leagues, was named general manager of "the league leading" Birmingham Black Barons. Chambers, still pitching at the age of 43, was public address announcer for Black Barons games for 15 years.[50]

Chambers said he was bringing the NAL All-Stars to Birmingham on Sunday, August 13, for a double-header with the Black Barons. There were no details on the composition of the all-star team and the circumstances that would bring it to Birmingham.[51] Nor is there any further report on the game.

The annual East–West Game was played in New York in conjunction with the 62nd annual convention of the International Benevolent and Protective Order of Elks. Managers were Sherm Brewer for the West and Frankie Fleming for the East. The West team won, 7–1. The starting pitcher for the East was none other than Satchel Paige, now a reported 55 years old. He pitched three scoreless innings, allowing only an infield single. Paige had been on the East roster in the very first East–West game in 1933.[52]

Although there was little to determine first- and second-half winners, Birmingham and Kansas City met for the NAL championship in a series beginning in Birmingham on Saturday, September 23. Birmingham won the opening game, 4–1. The second game was set the following day, but not at historic Rickwood Field. It was played at Sloss Field in Acipco. Games three and four were scheduled in Kansas City on September 30 and October 1.[53]

The outcome of the second game was unreported, as were the results of any additional games if, indeed, they were played. Even the *Birmingham World* and *The Call* failed to report on it. However, the *Birmingham News* reported on September 30 that fifth game in the series would be played the next day at Sloss Field, and that the Black Barons were leading three games to one.[54]

1962

In the final season of the Negro American League, the Birmingham Black Barons opened their spring training at Westfield Park on April 15. The camp was conducted by Mack Curry, a Bessemer resident and "well known baseball figure in Birmingham." Coming out to help with "the conditioning work" was Lorenzo "Piper" Davis. There was also the annual tryout session for anyone 16 or older.

Back for another season were first baseman James Ivory, second baseman Jessie Bass, outfielders Harry Robinson, Earnest Harris and Frank Evans, and catchers Otha Bailey and Harry Barnes.[55]

Selected to lead the 1962 team was Ted "Double Duty" Radcliffe. New General Manager Karl E. Wilken said Radcliffe would arrive around May 1 to take over the training sessions. He was currently in the Chicago area, where he had been scouting for the Cleveland Indians. The *Pittsburgh Courier* reported that Radcliffe had managed Birmingham to four pennants in five years during the 1930s. In fact, he played for four years in the 1940s and never served as manager.[56]

Nor did he serve in 1962. When the season opened, right fielder Frank Evans was the manager. A native of Linden, Alabama, in Marengo County, Evans had been playing pro baseball since 1937. He played with Memphis, Kansas City, Detroit, Philadelphia, and Cleveland in the Negro leagues. He also played in the minor leagues for two years and one year in the Canadian Mandak League.[57]

Wilken, the new general manager, was a native of Decatur, Illinois. The 46-year-old was a former minor league pitcher, major league scout, and business manager of several ball clubs. His duties included organizing "a nation-wide procurement system" for owner Wardell Jackson's organization. Jackson owned both Birmingham and Philadelphia clubs. Strangely, the both were referred to as "All Negro traveling baseball teams." There was no mention of league affiliation. Further, it was reported that Birmingham was "considering a three weeks foreign tour" during the season.[58]

Sportswriter Marcel Hopson found the changes in management a positive step. In the past, he wrote, "Many felt that questionable conduct at the general and field managerial level often made parents shudder to think of suggesting that their talented sons seek employment on the team in recent years."[59]

It was reported in early May that Birmingham had bid successfully for the annual Negro American Professional Baseball League all-star game. It was called the North–South game rather than the traditional East–West Game. A second all-star game was planned later in Chicago or Kansas City.[60]

The first exhibitions were scheduled May 13 against the Atlanta Stars. Wilken said the Black Barons would showcase rookie pitching sensation Ernest Williams, a 21-year-old right-hander from Jasper. His height and weight were 6-foot-3 and 205 pounds. Of more interest locally was the news that Alonzo Perry, Jr., would be in the outfield, giving catcher Otha Bailey an opportunity to play with both father and son.[61]

The star for the locals was third baseman Henry Elmore, who had four hits and four runs batted in. Williams pitched a three-hitter in the 5–3 victory. A second game was called after four innings. There was no mention of the younger Perry.[62]

There were no reports during spring training on the makeup of the Negro American League. An article in the *Birmingham World* in June indicated that Ted Rasberry owned two league members, Kansas City and Detroit. He also owned the Harlem Satellites basketball team. Rasberry said he would have tryout camps in Birmingham and Memphis to find new players for his teams.[63]

The Center for Negro League Baseball Research has 1962 rosters for Birmingham, Kansas City, and Raleigh. Philadelphia was called an associate member.

During the season, Birmingham also played the Atlanta Stars and, curiously, the Memphis Red Sox. There was no explanation for the apparent resurrection of the team that had folded two years earlier. The *Birmingham Post-Herald* referred to Birmingham's games with Atlanta, Philadelphia, and Memphis as Negro American League games.

Opening Day was set for Sunday, May 27, at Rickwood Field against longtime rival Kansas City.

The *Birmingham News* reported that the 1962 team would be "the youngest in the history of the ball club" with only four veterans: second baseman Rufus Gibson, left fielder John Henry Williams, catcher Otha Bailey and right fielder/manager Frank Evans. Top newcomers were first baseman Alonzo Perry, Jr., shortstop Robert Cardwell, and center-fielder Edwards Stubbs.[64] Perry was 17 years old, and Cardwell and Stubbs were 18. Williams was the starting pitcher. Birmingham businessman Dr. A.G. Gaston threw out the first pitch.[65]

The new season opened auspiciously as Birmingham won both games, 9–1 and 6–4. The second game was held to five innings by the Sunday curfew. Williams pitched a two-hitter in the first game.[66]

The following Sunday brought Philadelphia to town. Behind the hitting of Gibson, who drove in three runs with two doubles, Birmingham won the opener, 5–4. The second game was stopped by the Sunday curfew.[67]

Playing at home for the third consecutive Sunday, Birmingham hosted third-place Raleigh on June 10. Birmingham (9–2) was in the first place. Raleigh was 7–6. The games were not covered in the local newspapers. There was a report of a win over Raleigh on Monday, June 18. Alonzo Perry, Jr., hit a home run in the 10th inning. The location of the game was not given.

On June 24, the Black Barons were at home for a double-header against the Atlanta Stars. Rookie second baseman Billy Sartis (.314) was leading the team in hitting. Melvin

Roach was selected to pitch the opening game against Atlanta's unbeaten Calvin Ray. Atlanta won, 6–5, and the second game was rained out. The Black Barons then left on "a lengthy road jaunt." It must have been extremely long because the team was not seen again in Birmingham until August.[68]

During the hiatus, the Harlem Stars and Kansas City played at Rickwood. Satchel Paige pitched for the Stars, working three innings in relief. He gave up two runs and struck out five. Goose Tatum was a pinch runner. The game end in 12-inning tie, called because of darkness.[69]

The Black Barons returned home on August 12 for two games with mysterious Memphis. An added attraction was a Twist contest, a dance sensation at the time. Again, there was no mention of the folding of the Red Sox in 1960. Had the ream been revived or was this another team using the same name? Ernest Williams, now 13–4, and Charley Lacey were scheduled to start for Birmingham. The Memphis pitchers would be former Black Barons Charley Pride and Frank "Groundhog" Thompson.[70] According to various sources, Pride retired from baseball in 1960 to concentrate on his music career. His last recorded competition was with Missoula in the Pioneer league. He had tryouts with major league teams in 1961 and 1962, but he had sustained injuries to his pitching arm.

There was no report on the games in local newspapers.

The Indianapolis Clowns found Birmingham a profitable venue, returning for a third appearance on August 26 while select Black Barons were in Kansas City for the East–West Game.[71]

President J.B. Martin had announced that the 30th annual all-star game would be played in Kansas City. Martin said Kansas City had been asking for the game for several years.[72] The *Birmingham News* reported five Birmingham players selected for the game.[73]

The final East–West Game was played after the conclusion of the regular season. Before the game, Jackie Robinson, Frank Duncan, New Allen, and Satchel Paige were honored in a special ceremony. The West team won, 5–2. The managers were Sherwood Brewster for the West and Frank Evans for the East.[74]

In August, Marcel Hopson lashed Black Barons leadership:

> Poor functioning in both the departments of field manager and general manager literally killed organized professional baseball in Birmingham for the past three years ... in order to restore the Birmingham Black Barons to their lofty positions in the minds of and hearts of loyal Jefferson County fans, some qualified competent men will have to be brought into the picture from outside of the state to fill the field and general manager posts. The men will have to be of such lofty caliber so the youngsters will look up to them with respect and with willing obedience to produce on the field of play for them.[75]

Charley Pride, who went on to a great singing career after playing with the Black Barons and the Memphis Red Sox (photograph by Dan Stroud; courtesy Charley Pride).

Indirectly citing the Black Barons' long road trips, Hopson said without appearances by the Clowns, Kansas City, and Harlem Stars, "baseball would have been noticeably extinct in the confines of Birmingham."[76]

Despite all of the confusion over league membership, somehow there had been an NAL season in 1962. In September, it was reported that Birmingham and Kansas City would begin a seven-game playoff for the championship. The series would begin on Saturday, September 23, at Sloss Field. Other Birmingham home games would be on September 24, September 30, and October 1. Games in Kansas City were not listed.[77]

There was no coverage of the first two games, but their apparent outcome was reported the following week. The *Post-Herald* said Birmingham had won the first two games, 4–1 and 13–4.[78] There was no report on the remainder of the series in Birmingham papers. Sportswriter Marcel Hobson, always a champion of the Black Barons in the 1950s, never mentioned the playoffs in his "Hits and Bits" column. Nor did *The Call*, the African American newspaper in Kansas City.

Based on the *known* results of the Negro American League's final playoffs, the author has declared the Birmingham Black Barons as the Last Team Standing in Negro *league* baseball.

With the season over, Frank Evans said owner Wardell Jackson loaded the Black Barons uniforms and equipment on the team bus and carried it all back to his home in Champaign, Illinois. The only thing left of the Black Barons in Birmingham was memories.[79]

In March 2014, two youth baseball fields at Stephens Park in Montevallo, Alabama, were named for former Black Barons Raymond Haggins and Clifford DuBose (courtesy of the DuBose family).

Afterward

While 1962 was the final year for the Negro American League, it was not the final year for some of the black baseball teams. The Black Barons and the Philadelphia Stars, both owned by Jackson, barnstormed together in 1963. Pitcher Leroy Miller recalled: "We barnstormed all over Illinois, Memphis, Little Rock, Danville [Virginia], Tennessee, and all over the East. About the middle of the season, Jackson had me go [to] the Philadelphia Stars team. They played out West. We went through the Dakotas, played all over Canada and came out in Washington State."[80]

Rochell Broome said Jackson kept his barnstorming teams on the road for several more years. The ultimate survivor, though, was the Indianapolis Clowns. That team, emphasizing sideshow more than baseball, did not disband until 1989.[81]

Appendix A

Year-by-Year Standings, Spring Training Sites, Opening Day Attendance, First-Pitch Honorees, No-Hitters, No-Hitters Against, East–West Game All-Stars

Year by Year

The final Negro American League records were all compiled by the author except for 1948–50, 1952–54, and 1958, which were drawn from the Howe News Bureau Official Records. No effort has been made to distinguish between first and second-half results because of the inconsistency of published results. The league designations are: NSL, Negro Southern League; NNL, Negro National League; NAL, Negro American League; and "ind," independent.

Year	LG/POS	W	L	T	PCT	
1920	NSL, 4th	43	39	0	.524	league games
		46	39	0	.541	all games
1921	NSL, 4th	61	56	0	.521	league games
		61	56	0	.521	all games
1922	NSL, 8th	29	41	0	.414	league games
		32	41	0	.438	all games
1923	NSL, 1st	26	9	0	.743	1st half
	NNL, 8th	21	24	3	.467	2nd half
		47	33	3	.588	all games
	Won first half, second half canceled.					
1924	NNL, 6th	41	41	0	.500	league games
		44	42	0	.512	all games
1925	NNL, 7th	29	62	0	.319	league games
		35	65	0	.350	all games
1926	NSL, 1st	55	21	0	.724	league games
		5	2	3	.714	playoffs
		64	27	5	.703	all games
	Won first half, defeated Memphis for championship.					
1927	NNL, 2nd	49	42	2	.538	league games
		0	4	0	.000	playoffs
		56	48	0	.538	all games
	Won second half, lost to Chicago in championship series.					
1928	NNL, 5th	46	54	0	.460	league games
		48	55	1	.466	all games

Year	LG/POS	W	L	T	PCT	
1929	NNL, 6th	36	56	0	.391	league games
		46	61	1	.430	all games
1930	NNL, 5th	45	51	0	.469	league games
		52	52	0	.500	all games
1931	NSL, 3rd	32	32	0	.500	league games
		36	39	0	.480	all games
1932	NSL, na	11	7	1	.611	league games
		15	15	1	.500	all games
	Did not play second half.					
1933	ind	4	13	0	.235	all games
1934	NSL, na	9	8	0	.529	league games
		11	18	1	.379	all games
1935	NSL, na	3	6	0	.333	league games
		3	6	0	.333	all games
1936	NSL, 1st	17	6	0	.739	league games
		25	8	0	.758	all games
1937	NAL, 5th	17	21	0	.447	league games
		19	21	0	.475	all games
1938	NAL, 7th	12	34	0	.261	league games
		14	36	0	.280	all games
1939	no team					
1940	NAL, 5th	16	19	0	.457	league games
		19	22	0	.463	all games
1941	NAL, 3rd	28	14	0	.667	league games
		47	23	1	.671	all games
1942	NAL, 3rd	20	18	0	.526	league games
		30	27	0	.526	all games
1943	NAL, 1st	15	9	0	.625	league games
		3	2	0	.600	playoffs
		4	5	1	.444	World Series
		36	27	2	.571	all games
	Defeated Chicago for NAL championship, lost to Homestead in World Series.					
1944	NAL, 1st	38	19	0	.667	league games
		1	4	0	.200	World Series
		52	34	0	.605	all games
	Won both halves, lost to Homestead in World Series.					
1945	NAL, 2nd	39	25	0	.609	league games
		57	31	0	.648	all games
1946	NAL, 2nd	35	25	0	.583	league games
		54	31	0	.635	all games
1947	NAL, 3rd	45	27	0	.625	league games
		63	36	0	.636	all games
1948	NAL, 1st	55	21	0	.724	league games
		5	2	1	.714	playoffs
		1	4	0	.200	World Series
		67	37	0	.644	all games
	Defeated Kansas City for NAL championship, lost to Homestead in World Series					
1949	NAL, 3rd	47	42	0	.528	league games
		66	44	0	.600	all games
1950	NAL, 2nd	52	25	0	.675	league games
		59	33	0	.641	all games

Year	LG/POS	W	L	T	PCT	
1951	NAL, na	16	22	0	.421	league games
		17	22	0	.436	all games
1952	NAL, 1st	52	36	0	.591	league games
		6	4	0	.600	playoffs
		60	41	0	.594	all games

Won first half, played Indianapolis in disputed championship series.

Year	LG/POS	W	L	T	PCT	
1953	NAL, 2nd	28	34	0	.452	league games
		30	35	0	.462	all games
1954	NAL, 3rd	41	38	1	.519	league games
		41	38	1	.519	all games
1955	NAL, na	9	6	0	.600	league games
		9	7	0	.563	all games
1956	NAL, na	18	13	0	.581	league games
		18	13	0	.581	all games
1957	NAL, na	21	8	0	.724	league games
		22	9	0	.710	all games
1958	NAL, 4th	15	19	0	.441	league games
		15	19	0	.441	all games
1959	NAL, 1st	16	13	0	.552	league games
		17	13	0	.567	all games

Won NAL championship.

Year	LG/POS	W	L	T	PCT	
1960	NAL, na	11	3	0	.786	league games
		13	3	0	.813	all games
1961	NAL, na	0	1	0	.000	league games
		1	0	0	1.000	playoffs
		1	2	0	.333	all games

Won only NAL playoff game reported.

Year	LG/POS	W	L	T	PCT	
1962	NAL, na	4	1	0	.800	league games
		2	0	0	1.000	playoffs
		6	1	0	.857	all games

Won only NAL playoff games reported.

Spring Training Sites

1920	Undetermined	1936	Birmingham, Acipco Field
1921	Undetermined	1937	Birmingham, Acipco Field
1922	Smith's Park, Smithfield	1938	Birmingham, Sloss Field
1923	Tidewater Diamond, behind Terminal Stadium [Ensley?]	1939	no team
1924	Birmingham, Rickwood Field	1940	Jackson, Mississippi
1925	Gadsden	1941	Shreveport, Louisiana
1926	Gadsden	1942	Algiers, Louisiana
1927	Gadsden	1943	Birmingham, Sloss Field
1928	Columbus, Georgia, Fort Benning	1944	Birmingham, Sloss Field and Rickwood Field
1929	Columbus, Georgia, Fort Benning	1945	Birmingham, site not identified
1930	Columbus, Georgia, Fort Benning	1946	Birmingham, Sloss Field
1931	Birmingham, Vineville College [Miles College]	1947	Orlando, Florida
1932	Birmingham, Stockton Field [*sic*; Stockham?]	1948	Montgomery, Alabama State campus
1933	Not in league, independent team?	1949	Montgomery, Alabama State campus
1934	Diamond at 12th Street and 8th Avenue	1950	Montgomery, Alabama State campus
		1951	Montgomery, Alabama State campus
		1952	Montgomery, Alabama State campus
		1953	Montgomery, Alabama State campus
1935	Birmingham, Sloss Field	1954	Nashville, Tennessee, Sulphur Dell

1955	Montgomery, Alabama State,and	1958	Birmingham, Sloss Field
	Hopkins Field, North Bessemer	1959	Birmingham, Sloss Field
1956	Columbus, Mississippi	1960	Probably Birmingham, Sloss Field
1957	Bessemer, Brown Station Baseball	1961	Undetermined
	Park	1962	Birmingham, Westfield Park

Opening Day Attendance

In the years in which two figures appear, the first number is from the *Birmingham News* and the second is from the *Birmingham Reporter* (1929) or the *Birmingham* World (after 1934).

Year	Date	Opponent/Score	Attendance
1920	May 3	New Orleans 5, Birmingham 3	5,000
1921	April 25	Birmingham 8, Montgomery 1	5,000
1922	May 1	Memphis 2, Birmingham 1	4,000
1923	April 30	Birmingham 4, Memphis 0	8,500
1924	April 28	Birmingham 6, Cubans 3	10,600
1925	April 27	Chicago 15, Birmingham 6	10,000
1926	May 10	Birmingham 5, Memphis 1	8,000
1927	April 25	Birmingham 5, Cubans 4	10,000
1928	May 14	Memphis 4, Birmingham 1	7,500
1929	April 29	Birmingham 6, Cubans Stars 2	6,000 (10,000)
1930	April 28	Birmingham 4, Cuban Stars 1	8,000
1931	May 18	Birmingham 5, Chattanooga 3	NA
1932	April 25	Pittsburgh 5, Birmingham 3?	NA
1933	—	not in league	NA
1934	May 20	Birmingham 5, Memphis 4	2,000
		Birmingham 10, Memphis 4	
1935	April 29	Atlanta 3, Birmingham 2	NA
1936	May 10	Birmingham 4, Nashville 1	2,000
1937	May 9	Kansas City 7, Birmingham 1	4,000
		Kansas City 10, Birmingham 1	
1938	May 1	Chicago 5, Birmingham 0	4,000
		Chicago 6, Birmingham 1	
1939	no team		
1940	May 12	Kansas City 6, Birmingham 0	8,500
		Birmingham 5, Kansas City 3	
1941	May 11	Kansas City 9, Birmingham 3	NA
		Kansas City 5, Birmingham 3	
1942	May 10	Birmingham 9, Jacksonville 2	9,000
		Jacksonville 6, Birmingham 3	
1943	May 30	Birmingham 6, Memphis 2	12,000
		Birmingham 10, Memphis 1	
1944	May 4	Birmingham 7, Kansas City 2	11,000
		Birmingham 3, Kansas City 0	
1945	May 6	Cleveland 4, Birmingham 0	NA
		Birmingham 9, Cleveland 3	
1946	May 9	Birmingham 7, Cleveland 2	7,000 (11,000)
1947	May 10	Birmingham 5, Kansas City 2	7,000
1948	May 1	Birmingham 11, Cleveland 2	7,625 paid (10,000)
1949	April 30	Birmingham 3, Houston 1	4,636
1950	May 11	Memphis 15, Birmingham 3	4,918
1951	May 4	Birmingham 6, New Orleans 5	3,554
1952	May 16	Birmingham 4, Memphis 3	3,155
1953	May 22	Birmingham, Memphis 2	3,095
1954	May 15	Birmingham 4, Indianapolis 3	1,200 (3,299)

Year	Date	Opponent/Score	Attendance
1955	May 1	Kansas City 8, Birmingham 3	6,500
1956	May 6	Birmingham 16, Detroit 9	NA
1957	May 19	Birmingham 9, Memphis 4	NA
		Second game 4 innings (darkness)	
1958	May 25	Detroit 3, Birmingham 2	7,000
1959	May 24	Birmingham 8, Detroit 3	NA
		Birmingham 3, Detroit 1	
1960	May 22	Birmingham 2, Kansas City 1	5,000
		Kansas City 8, Birmingham 5	
1961	May 14?	New York Royals 2, Birmingham 1?	NA
1962	May 27	Birmingham 9, Kansas City 1	
		Birmingham 6, Kansas City 4	NA

First Pitch

1920–25	NA
1926	Bishop B.G. Shaw, received by Pastor Goodgame
1927–34	NA
1935	Bishop B.G. Shaw
1936	Thelma Smith, Parker High School student with highest grade point average
1937–38	NA
1939	no team
1940	NA
1941	Mrs. Matilda Folkes
1942	Emory O. Jackson, *Birmingham World* editor; receiver Principal W.B. Johnson of Parker High School
1943	Fairfield Industrial High School Principal E.J. Oliver
1944	NA
1945	FIHS Principal E. J. Oliver
1946	William "Sweet" Conley, "well-liked Fourth Avenue bondsman"
1947	W.H. Hollis, president of the Negro Business League
1948–49	NA
1950	Rev. J.W. Goodgame, pastor, Sixth Avenue Baptist Church; Poindexter D. Williams, receiver
1951	NA
1952	E.W. Barker, executive director, 18th Street YMCA.
1953–61	NA
1962	A.G. Gaston

No-Hitters

Tue. July 26, 1921	John Juran, Birmingham 4, Atlanta 0 John Kemp, catcher
Sun. July 12, 1925	Robert Poindexter, Birmingham 6, @Chicago 0 Poindexter Williams, catcher
Wed. Aug. 5, 1925	Willie Foster, Birmingham 5, @Detroit 0 Poindexter Williams, catcher
Mon. Aug. 28, 1926	Harry Salmon, Birmingham, 8 Albany 0 Poindexter Williams, catcher
Wed. July 27, 1928	Robert Poindexter, Birmingham, 6 Chicago 0 Bill Perkins, catcher
Sat. July 18, 1931	Walter Calhoun, Birmingham 11, Fort Benning 0 @Rickwood _____ Carter, catcher

Sat. July 31, 1948   Jimmie Newberry, Birmingham 4, Cleveland 0, @Dayton, Ohio,
                      Pepper Bassett, catcher
May 1949   Jimmie Newberry, Birmingham W, Louisville L
                      catcher NA
Sun. Aug. 8, 1954   Danny Wright, Birmingham, 5 Memphis 0 (7 innings)
                      catcher NA
Fri. Jul 19, 1957   Curtis White, Birmingham 2, Memphis 0, @Meridian, Miss.
                      catcher NA
1957   Joe Elliott vs. Indianapolis, unconfirmed
1959   Stan Jones, unconfirmed

No-Hitters Against

Sat. June 28, 1926   Bill Gatewood, Albany 7, Birmingham 0
                      John Charleston, catcher
Sat. Sept. 5, 1931   Homer Curry, Memphis 3, Birmingham 1
                      Otis Henry, catcher
Wed. Aug. 8, 1951   Leander Turgerson, Indianapolis 15, Birmingham 1
                      Sam Sands, catcher

East–West Game All-Stars

1938	Parnell Woods, ph		Piper Davis, 2b
1940	Parnell Woods, 3b		Bill Greason, p
	Tommy Sampson, 2b	1950	Alonzo Perry, 1b
1941	Lyman Bostock, 1b		Pepper Bassett, c
	Tommy Sampson, 2b		Ed Steele, lf
	Dan Bankhead, p		Bill Powell, p
1942 (Chicago)	Tommy Sampson, 2b	1951	Henry Kimbro, cf
	Lloyd Davenport, ph		Wesley Dennis, 1b
1942 (Cleveland)	Tommy Sampson, 2b		Ed Steele, rf
	Alvin Gipson, p		Norman Robinson, lf
1943	Lester Lockett, lf	1952	Eddie Brooks, 2b
	Tommy Sampson, 2b		Wesley Dennis, 1b
	Gread McKinnis, p		Henry Kimbro, cf
1944	Artie Wilson, ss		Otha Bailey, c
	Ted Radcliffe, c		Frank Thompson, p
1945	Lester Lockett, lf	1953	Peewee Butts, ss
1946 (Washington)	Artie Wilson, ss		Eddie Brooks, 2b
	Piper Davis, 2b		Wesley Dennis, 1b
1946 (Chicago)	Artie Wilson, ss		Henry Kimbro, rf
	Piper Davis, 2b		Irwin Castille, 3b
1947 (Chicago)	Artie Wilson, ss		Carl Long, lf
	Piper Davis, 2b		Otha Bailey, c
1947 (New York)	Artie Wilson, ss		Manny Cartlege, p
	Piper Davis, 2b	1954	Eddie Brooks, 2b
	Pepper Bassett, c		Wesley "Doc" Dennis, 1b
1948 (Chicago)	Artie Wilson, ss		Otha Bailey, c,
	Piper Davis, 2b		Frank Thompson, p.
	Bill Powell, p		John Kennedy, ss
1948 (New York)	Artie Wilson, ss	1955	Elliott "Junior" Coleman, p
	Piper Davis, 2b		Eddie Brooks, 2b
	Pepper Bassett, c		Otha Bailey, c
1949	Jose Burgos, ss		Manny Cartledge, p
	Herman Bell, ph		Rufus Gibson, 3b

	Al "Johnny" Mobley, 1b		Wiley Griggs, 3b
	John Williams, rf		James "Sap" Ivory, 1b-35
	Jesse Mitchell (?)		Brown Jackson, lf
1956	Claude Barnes, p		Jessie Mitchell, rf
	Otha Bailey, c		Bob Saunders, ph-ss
	Wiley Griggs, 3b-2b (2)		Willie Smith, p
	Jim Hall c	1959	Ernest "Onk" Harris, cf
	Willie Ivory, 2b		James "Sap" Ivory, inf
	Frank Marsh, cf-rf (2)		Pete Mumpford, p
	Gene Johnson, 1b		Bobby Sanders, ss
	Roscoe Mangun, 2b		Willie Smith, p
	Bill Moore, 1b (2)		John Mitchell, cf (?)
	Charlie Williams, p (2)	1960 *Starters*:	John Mitchell, cf
	John Williams, 2b (2b)		Ernie Westfield, p
	William Wyatt, 2b-ss (2)		Jesse Bass, ss
	Jesse Mitchell (?)		James "Sap" Ivory, 3b
1957	Otha Bailey, c		Willie Harris, lf
	Joe Elliott, p		Brown Jackson, rf
	Donnie Harris, cf	*Substitutes*:	Herbert Paymond, p
	Jesse Mitchell, lf		Waite (Walter) Stoves, c
	John Williams, lf		Phillip Welch, p
	Danny Wright, p		Gus Westbrook, inf
	William Wyatt, 2b	1961	Frank Evans, manager
1958	Otha Bailey, c		James "Sap" Ivory, 3b
	Jessie Bass, pr-3b	1962	Frank Evans, manager

Appendix B
Birmingham Black Barons
All-Time Roster

This comprehensive roster was compiled by the author largely from newspaper reports. The names preceded by an asterisk (*) were confirmed to have actually played in a game for Birmingham. Those without the asterisk may very well have played also, but confirmation was not found. The roster also includes the 1933 Birmingham Monarchs/Foxes/Black Barons and the 1934 Birmingham Giants with those players designated by # and + symbols, respectively.

For the 1948 season, the Internet site www.baseball-reference.com listed several players that the author had not found in his research. Since those names came with some statistical data, they are included. For the 1949 season the opposite occurred. The web site listed only four players, whereas the author had 22 confirmed players. Several players for the 1960 and 1962 seasons were added from rosters compiled by the Center for Negro Leagues Baseball Research. The positions played are in parentheses with (x) representing one undetermined.

Administrative

Adams, Oscar W., 1926–27 president
Allen, Gus, 1935 owner
Atkins, Joseph, 1950 traveling secretary, 1951 secretary
Bennings, A.G., 1926 club official, 1927 secretary and business manager, 1928 club official, 1930 club official
Bridgeforth, William "Sou," 1952–54 owner
Buchanon, Oscar, 1926 club official
Chambers, James "Dizzy," 1961 general manager by early August
Chisholm, C___, 1935 assistant manager
Cobb, L.S.N., 1932 owner
Frazier, Lige, 1933 president
Graham, L.J., 1946–47 traveling secretary
Gray, Molton H. 1935 business manager
Hayes, Thomas Jr., 1940–51 owner, purchased club from NAL, December 1939
Hensley, Earl, 1952 publicist
Holt, Jesse, 1942 trainer
Jackson, R.T., 1926 secretary, 1927 secretary (also NNL board member), 1928–29 president, 1929 president
Jackson, Wardell B., 1960 owner, 1961 owner-general manager, 1962 president
Johnson, Charles, 1931 official.
Johnson, Levi, 1941 publicity director

Paul C. Jones, 1952 business manager, 1953–54 general manager
Lincoln, C. Eric, 1948 traveling secretary
+ Keys, Ludie, 1934 owner
King, Baby Lee, 1923 business manager
Kritzkey, W.N., 1926 pre-season owner
Lyner, Sid, 1955 co-owner
Meshad, Floyd, 1955 co-owner, 1956 owner
Moore, Dwight "Gate Mouth," 1955 vice president
Moore, Henry L., 1937 owner
Patterson, William B., 1925 secretary-bookkeeper
Perdue, Frank, 1930 owner, + 1934 owner
Pollard, Nathaniel, 1949 traveling secretary; 1950 traveling secretary, preseason
Ross, Dr. Anderson, 1956 owner, 1957 owner?, 1958 owner?
Rush, Joe, 1923 owner, 1924 owner, 1925 owner and president; 1926 owner?
Saperstein, Abe, 1939–45 co-owner
Shepard, Freddie, 1946 traveling secretary
Strawbridge, H___, 1926 treasurer, 1928 secretary
Strawbridge, W___, 1927 secretary
Walker, Charles, 1934 secretary
Walker, Freddo, 1934, owner?
Welch, Winfield, 1959 owner
Wilken, Karl E., 1962 general manager
Williams, Arthur J., 1955 business manager, 1956–57 general manager, 1958 owner, 1960 general manager
Williams, C.E., 1944 publicist

Managers (16)

+ Andrews, Herman, 1934?
Brooks, Eddie, 1952 (acting manager by June 17), 1955 (by mid–July)
Canada, James, 1955–1957, 1960–61, 1958 manager-scout
Crawford, Sam, 1924 (fired April 28), 1925 (by May 15)
Curry, Homer, 1955 pre-season
Davis, Lorenzo "Piper," 1947–49, 1959
Dismukes, William "Dizzy," 1924, 1938
Evans, Frank, 1962
Gatewood, Bill, 1927, 1930 (by July 23)
Harris, Vic, 1950
Hewitt, Joe, 1924
Jones, Reuben, 1927
McAllister, George, 1932, 1935
Meredith, Buford "Geechie," 1931
Nash, George, 1933
Patterson, W.B., 1925
+ Perkins, W.G., "Bill" 1934 preseason
Perdue, Frank, 1920–22 owner-manager
Rush, Joe, 1926?
Russell, Ewing, 1952 (by June 24)
Sampson, Tommy, 1946–47
Scales, George, 1952
Smith, Clarence, 1926, 1930
Springer, ___, 1933?
Steele, Ed, 1951

Taylor, Candy Jim, 1940
Walker, A(ndrew) M., 1936–37
Walker, Jesse "Hoss," 1953–54, 1956 (by early June), 1954 (by mid–July)
Welch, Winfield, 1941–45
Wells, Willie Sr., 1954
Wesley, Charles "Twosides," 1923–24, 1928–29
Williams, John Henry, 1956 (by July 27), 1958 (by June 16)
Williams, Poindexter, 1923, 1928, 1932, 1935

Players

A

Alexander, ___ (x) 1929 preseason
* Alexander, Chuff (2b-ss-lf-rf) 1927–28
Alexander, Ted (rhp) 1949
* Allen, Buddy (cf) 1940
* Alvin, January (of) 1929
* Anderson, ___ (p) 1952
Anderson, Andy (of) 1948 preseason
* Anderson, Arianthal (p-of) 1947
* Anderson, Hank (cf-rf) 1931
* Anderson, Theodore "Bubbles" (2b) 1924
Anderson, William (of) 1931
* Andrews, C.F. "Jabbo" (rf-p) 1930–31, 1940
*+ Andrews, Herman (of) 1930, 1934 (rf-mgr?) 1940
* Arnold, ___ "Toots" (lhp) 1946
* Ash, Rudolph, (p-rf-lf) 1921
Ashby, Earl (c) 1946–47
* Austin, Frank (rhp) 1930
Avery, ___ "Top" (p), 1947 preseason

B

Bailey, Otha (c) 1952–62
Baldwin, Robert (x) 1920s or 1930s?
* Baldwin, Robert (1b) 1957
Bames, ___ (c) 1937
+ Bankhead, ___ (x) 1934
* Bankhead, ___ (ss) 1935
* Bankhead, Dan (rhp-inf) 1940–42
* Bankhead, Fred (ss, 2b) 1935–38
* Bankhead, Joe (rhp) 1948
* Bankhead, Sam (2b-ss-2b) 1931–32
* Barber, Sammy (p) 1940
* Barker, ___ (p) 1949
* Barnes, (c) 1937
* Barnes, ___ (p) 1936
* Barnes, ___ (c) 1956
* Barnes, Charlie "Red" (p) 1955
Barnes, Claudie (rhp) 1948 preseason
* Barnes, Edward "Red" (p) 1957
# Barnes, Harry (x) 1933

* Barnes, Harry (c) 1935–38, 1942
Barnes, Harry (rhp) 1936
* Barnes, Harry Jr. (c) 1961, 1962 preseason
* Barnes, Red (p) 1962
* Barnett, Roy (of) 1957
* Bass, Jessie (Willie?) (2b-ss) 1957–62
* Bass, Leroy "Red" (c)
* Bassett, Lloyd "Pepper" (c) 1944–52
* Batson, ___ (c) 1924
* Batts, Richard "Pike" (lhp) 1949
* Bayliss, Henry (inf) 1949–50, 1951 preseason
* Bealle, ___ (p) 1931
# Bell, ___ (c) 1933
* Bell, Charley   (lhp) 1929
* Bell, Fred (rf-lf) 1923
* Bell, Herman (c) 1943, 1945–50, 1951 preseason
Bell, J___ (of) 1938
Bell, James "Cool Papa" (x) 1942?
Bell, John (x) 1928
* Bell, Johnny (p) 1930 [Julian Bell?]
* Bell, Julian "Jute" (rhp) 1929–30
Bell, William "Lefty" (lhp) 1950 preseason
* Benjamin, ___ (x) 1935
+ Benjamin, Jerry (cf-1b) 1934
* Bennett, ___ (ph) 1930
* Bennett, Bradford (cf) 1942
Bennett, Don (of) 1930
Bennett, John (of) 1930
* Bennington, ___ (p) 1958
* Berdine, Leo "Eight Rock" (rhp-of) 1926–31 [always Birdine and Burdine in the newspapers]
Bernard, Thomas (ss) 1956 preseason
* Berry, James (p) 1955–56
* Bester, Walter (rhp) 1946
* Beverly, Bill (rhp) 1952 preseason, 1954–55
* Beverly, Charles "Hooks" (lhp) 1925–26
* Billingsley, Clarence (James?) (p) 1960 [probably Lawrence]
* Billingsley, Lawrence (p) 1958, (p) 1959 preseason, (p) 1960

Billingsley, Sam (p) 1958
* Bissant, John (rf) 1940
Black, Dan, (c) 1952 preseason
* Black Diamond (p) 1929 [see Robert Pipkin]
* Black, Good (2b) 1935 [likely a nickname]
* Blackman, Clifford (rhp) 1938
* Blackmore, Willie (inf-c) 1951
* Blackwell, Charles (lf) 1925
Blair, Bill (lhp) 1948 preseason
* Bland, ___ (c) 1941
Blue, ___ (p) 1922, preseason
* Bogans, James (lhp) 1960
* Bolden, James (rhp) 1946–47, 1952, 1962?
* Bolden, Robert (inf) 1957
* Bonds, ___ (c) 1935 [probably Harry Barnes]
# Bonner, ___ (p) 1933
* Booker, Nathaniel "Nay" (rhp) 1949, 1950
  preseason
* Boone, Alonzo (rhp) 1932, 1944–46
* Boone, Oscar (c) 1940
* Boothe, ___ (p) 1919
# Borden, ___ (c-lf-ss) 1933
* Borden, J___ (3b-lf-rf-p) 1932–33
* Bostock, Lyman Sr. (1b) 1940–43, 1946, 1954
Boulware, Willie (x) 1951 preseason
* Boyd, Erwin (p), 1935
* Bozeard, Sam (p) 1960
* Bradford, Bill (rf-cf) 1942
* Bradshow, ___ (x) 1931
* Brandon, Mack (lf) 1951
* Branham, Luther (2b-3b-ph-lf) 1949
* Breda, Bill (cf) 1954
Bremble, ___ (2b) 1931
* Brewster, ___ (p) 1955
Brewster, Jack (p) 1956 pre-season
* Brickford, ___ (c) 1951 [probably Blackmore]
Bridges, Marshall (p) 1951 preseason
Britton, ___ (p) 1958
* Britton, John (3b) 1944–49
* Brizzle, James (cf) 1947
Brooks, Eddie (2b-mgr) 1952–55
* Brown, ___ (3b) 1920
# Brown, ___ (cf) 1933
* Brown, ___ (p) 1937
* Brown, A___ (c) 1923
Brown, Alex (3b) 1951 preseason
* Brown, Arthur Curtis (p) 1957
* Brown, Bob (x) 1959
Brown, Charles, (rhp) 1949
* Brown, John "Slats" (p) 1947
* Brown, Larry, c 1921, 1923
* Brown, Ralph (ss-2b) 1954
* Brown, Roger (3b), 1960

* Brown, William "Cap" (ss) 1952
Brown, Willie (2b), 1953 preseason
Bruton, Jack "Dizzy" (p-of-1b) 1936–38,
  1940 [brother of Pit Bruton]
* Bruton, Pit "Daffy" (p) 1936, 1937 preseason
  [brother of Jack Bruton]
Bryant, ___ (x) 1933
* Budini, ___ (lf) 1926
* Buford, James? "Black Bottom" (3b) 1931
Buggess, Cain D. (1b) 1949 preseason
* Bumble, ___ (2b) 1931
* Bumpus, Earl (lhp) 1944–45
* Bunch, Sidney (rf) 1952, 1953 preseason,
  1954, 1955 preseason, 1962
* Burdine, "Eight Rock" [see Leo Berdine]
Burgess, Cain D. (1b), 1949–50 preseason
* Burgos, Jose (ss) 1949–50, 1951 preseason
* Burke, ___ (p) 1957
* Buroughs, ___ (p) 1940 [probably Burris]
* Burris, Samuel (p) 1938, 1940
* Burton, Richard (p) 1940
* Burton, Samuel (3b-2b-1b-lf) 1940
* Bush, Val J. (2b-of) 1962
* Button, ___ (x) 1958
* Butts, Thomas "Pee Wee" (ss) 1952–53
* Bynum, C.F. (ss) 1930

C

+ Cabness, William (x) 1934
Cain, Fred (p) 1952 preseason
* Cain, Marion "Sugar" (p) 1954
# Caldwell, ___ (p) 1933
* Calhoun, ___ (p) 1926
# Calhoun, Walter (rf-p) 1933
* Calhoun, Walter (p-of) 1931–33, + 1934?
* Callaway, ___ (of) 1925 preseason
# Campbell, ___ (ph-lf) 1933
* Canada, James (1b-mgr) 1936–37, 1947?,
  1951, 1952 preseason, 1955–58, 1960–61
  [often misspelled Canady]
Candidate, ___ (1b) 1933 [probably James
  Canada]
+ Candidate, James (inf) 1934 [probably
  James Canada]
* Canella, ___ (ph) 1920
* Cannon, Richard (p) 1932
* Cardenas, Francisco "Panchito" (c-lf)
  1920–21
* Cardwell, Robert (ss) 1962
* Carlisle, Matthew "Lick" (ss-2b) 1931–33, +
  1934
* Carlyle, ___ (2b) 1935 [probably Matthew
  Carlisle]

+ Carlyle, Walter (2b) 1934
* Carr, Cliff (3b) 1935
* Carter, ___ (p-2b) 1931
* Carter, ___ (3b-ss) 1932 [likely Elmer]
* Carter, ___ (ph-1b) 1938
* Carter, ___ (p) 1941
* Carter, ___ (ph) 1943
* Carter, A___ (p-3b-ss) 1931
* Carter, Elmer "Willie" (ss-1b) 1930–31, 37
* Carter, Ernest "Spoon" (rhp) 1931–32,
    + 1934, 1949
Carter, George, (x) 1952 preseason
* Carter, J___ (p) 1931
* Carter, Nick (p) 1930
* Carter, Willie (x), 1930
* Carter, Z___ (2b-3b) 1931
Cartledge, Robbie "Manny," "Minski" (rhp)
    1952–55
* Cartwright, Claiborne (cf) 1951
* Cason, John (c) 1920, 1923
* Casselberry, Jaycee (c) 1960.
Castille, Irwin (ss-3b-of) 1951–53
* Casey, ___ (c) 1923 [probably John Cason]
Cates, Joe (x) 1930
Cephus, Goldie "Groundhog" (ss) 1937
* Chambers, James E. "Dizzy" (mgr) 1961,
    1963
* Charleston, John "Red" (c) 1920, 1923
* Charlton, John (x) 1920 [probably John
    Charleston]
Chatman, ___ (p) 1933
* Chatman, ___ (x) 1955
* Chestnut, Joe (p) 1952
Chinn, Joe (x) 1950 preseason
* Chism, Elijah (lf-2b) 1947, 1951
* Chism, Joe (2b), 1951
* Christian, ___ (c) [1923 [probably John
    Charleston]
* Clark, ___ (lf) 1931
* Clark, Marcell, (c) 1941
Clarke, Fred (x), 1951 preseason
* Clemmons, ___ (ph) 1920
* Coleman, ___ (ss) 1936 [Melvin?]
* Coleman, Elliott "Jr." (rhp) 1954–55
* Coleman, Joe "Lefty" (lhp) 1954
Coleman, John (p), 1954–55
* Coleman, ___ "Junior" (p) 1955 [see Elliott
    Coleman]
Coleman, Melvin (ss-c) 1937
Coleman, Sylvester (c), 1924 preseason
College, ___ (x) 1933
* Collier, Leonard (lhp) 1951
* Collins, Atkins "Yak" (p) 1935

+ Collins, Frank (p) 1934
* Collins, Willie "Rip" (rhp) 1950–51
Colvin, Richard (of) 1958 preseason
Cooley (Colley), Norris L. (of) 1951 preseason
Cooley, Willie Lee (x) 1951 preseason
Cooley, Walter (p) 1933
* Cooley, Walter (c-3b-rf) 1931, #1933
Cooper, ___ (of) 1934
* Cooper, Andy (x) 1928 [released May 3]
+ Cooper, Anthony (cf-ss) 1934
* Cooper, Anthony (ss-lf [released early in
    season, said to have played last year]
* Cooper, Anthony "Runt," "Peewee" (ss-of)
    1928–31, 1934
* Cooper, B___ (p) 1931
* Cooper, S___ (lf) 1928; (ss) 1929 [probably
    Anthony Cooper]
* Cornelius, Willie "Sug," "Fork" (rhp) 1930
Cotton, ___ (lf) 1957
Cowan, Johnny (3b) 1933
+ Cowan, Johnny (3b) 1934
* Cowan, Johnny (3b) #1933, + 1934, 1935–
    36, 1950
* Cox, ___ (cf) 1936
* Cox, William (lf) 1955
Craig, Elijah (x) [probably "Lefty" below]
* Craig, ___ "Lefty" (lhp) 1937
* Crawford, ___ (cf) 1924 preseason
# Crawford, ___ (rf) 1933
Crawford, David (1b) 1948 preseason
* Crawford, Sam (rhp-mgr) 1924–25, 1938
+ Crawford, Willie (of) 1934
Creasy, Dewey (inf), 1924 preseason
* Crosby, Ralph (ss-3b) 1954
* Crutchfield, Jimmy (of-c) 1930
* Cunningham, Harry (p) 1932
* Curry, Homer "Goose" (rhp-mgr) 1955
    preseason
Curry, Willie (c) 1955
* C…well, ___ (lf) 1933

D

* Daily, James (1b) 1945 [likely misidentified
    Piper Davis]
* Dallas, Porter (3b) 1929
Dalton, Rossie (c) 1940
* Daniels, ___ (ph) 1926
* Daniels, Alonzo (inf) 1954
* Daniels, Fred (rhp-ph-lf) 1923–27
Daniels, Fred (inf) 1954
* Daniels, Jim (p) 1943
* Davenport, Lloyd "Ducky" (of) 1941–42

* Davis, ___ (p-lf-1b-cf) 1925
* Davis, ___ (3b) 1925
* Davis, ___ (2b) 1932
* Davis, ___ (lf) 1935
* Davis, A___ (ss-ph) 1925
* Davis, Dixie (lf-ss) 1926
* Davis, John (p) 1928
* Davis, Lorenzo "Piper" (inf-mgr) 1942–50, 1959
* Davis, Lorenzo, Jr. (c) 1959
Davis, Raymon (p) 1961?
Davis, Ross (p) 1942
* Davis, Saul "Dixie" (ss-3b) 1925–26
+ Davis, William (x) 1934
+ Dawson, ___ (ph) 1934
* Dawson, Johnny (c) 1941 preseason, 1942
* Dean, Nelson (rhp) 1927–28
* Dedrick, ___ (rf) 1919
* DeJarnette, Sol (p) 1919
* Dennis, Wesley "Doc" (1b) 1952–55
* Dials, Odem "Lou" (lf) 1928
* Dickey, John "Steel Arm" (lhp-rf) 1921
* Dismukes, William "Dizzy" (rhp-mgr) 1924, 1938
* Dixon, Frank (3b-p) 1950
* Dixon, George (c) 1924
* Dogan, ___ (p) 1960
# Dokes, ___ (ph-lf) 1933 [Dukes?]
* Doon, Pat [see Padrone]
* Dougherty, ___ (p) 1923
* Douglas, Jesse (of, inf) 1941–42
* Dozier, Willie (2b-rf) 1920
* Drake, Andrew (c) 1932
* DuBose, Clifford (3b) 1960
# Dukes, ___ (ss) 1933
* Dukes, Tommy (c) 1931
* Dunkins, "Ishkooda," "Stringbean" (rhp) 1938
* Dunn, ___ (x) 1955
* Dunn, Alphonse "Blue" (1b-of) 1942–43
* Duran, ___ (lhp, 1922 [see Eli Juran]
* Duran, B___ (p) 1922–23 [see John Juran]
* Durand, B___ (p) 1923 [see John Juran]
Durand, E___ (p) [see Eli Juran]
* Durant, ___ (p) [see Eli Juran]]
* Durant, Jimmy (p) [see Johnny Juran]
* Durant, M___ (1b) 1923 [probably Johnny Juran]
* Dykes, A. J. (2b) 1929

E

Eatmon, Elbert "Lefty" (lhp) 1937–38
* Ea"on, E___ (rf) 1941 [Eatmon?]

* Edwards, Jesse "Johnny" (2b-3b) 1920
* Edwards, ___ (x) 1922
* Edwards, ___ (3b-lf-cf) 1925
* Edwards, Jesse (rhp-inf) 1923–25, 1931
* Edwards, Phillip (p) 1948
* Ellington, ___ (p) 1922
Elliot, Jesse (inf) 1948 preseason
* Elliot, Joe (rhp) 1956–58
* Ellis, ___ (c) 1935
* Ellis, Joe (2b) 1956
* Ellis, Rocky "Rube" (lhp) 1942, 1944
* Elmore, Henry (3b) 1962
* El Petros (1b) 1947
* Ervin, ___ (p) 1935
* Ester, Tory (p) 1962
* Evans, ___ (1b) 1941
* Evans, ___ (p) 1942
* Evans, Felix "Chin" (rhp-of) + 1934, (p) 1949
* Evans, Frank (of-mgr) 1950 preseason, 1955, 1961–62

F

Fain, Clifton (of) 1949 preseason
* Fairly, Johnny (of) 1962
* Farrar, ___ (p) 1956
* Farrell, ___ (p) 1956
* Felder, Kendall (inf) 1945
Fellows, ___ (p) 1937
* Fenner, John (p) [see John Finner]
Ferguson, Bob (util) 1938
* Ferrell, Willie (rhp) 1936–37, 1942
* Fiall, George (ss),1929
# Fields, ___ (ss) 1933
* Fields, Benny (cf-ss) 1936
* Fields, James (cf-rf) 1935
Fields, Wilmer (p) 1949 preseason
* Finner, John (rhp) 1925
* Finley, Glenn (rhp) 1956, 1958
* Fleachie, ___ (c) 1956
Flintory, Lee (x) 1948 preseason
* Ford, ___ (3b-ss) 1938
Foreman, Sylvester (c) 1924 preseason
Forge, Willie (p) 1959 preseason
Foster, Willie (lhp) 1925
Frazier, Albert (x) 1933 [brother of Severne Frazier]
Frazier, Severne? (x) 1933 [brother of Albert Frazier
Fulcher, Robert (p) 1940
* Fulton, Sam (p) 1955

G

Gaiton, Arthur, (rhp) 1950 preseason

Galloway, ___ (lf) 1921 preseason

* Garrett, ___ (cf) 1930

Garrett, Frank (of) 1949 preseason

Garrett, Homer (x) 1951 preseason

* Gaston, Hiram (lhp) 1952–53

Gaston, Isaac (ss) 1949

* Gatewood, Bill (rhp-mgr) 1927, 1930

* Gay, Herbert (p) 1930

* Gibson, Ralph "Rufus" (2b-ss) 1951, 1955–56, 1962

Gibson, Ted (c) 1942 preseason?

Gilers, ___ (of) 1928

* Gilliam, Elijah "Pete" (rhp) 1962

* Gilliam, Johnny (inf) 1960

* Gillis, Louis "Sea Boy" (c) 1951, 1952 preseason

* Gilyard, Luther (1b) 1942

* Gimes, ___ (2b) [see Jiminez]

* Giminez, ___ (2b) [see Jiminez]

* Gipson, Alvin "Buster" (rhp) 1941–46, 1947?

Gipson, Ben (x) 1948 preseason

* Givens, Mack (p) 1951

* Glass, ___ (c) 1925

* Glass, Carl (lhp) 1923

* Glover, Walter "Lefty" (lhp) + 1934, 1936, 1937 preseason

Godfrey, Sr., James Edward "Cleve" (x) 1951

* Golden, Charlie (p-of) 1947

* Good Black (2b) 1935

* Gordon, ___ (p) 1920 [probably Gordon Ziegler]

* Gordon, Herman (x) 1924 preseason

* Gougis, ___ (p) 1942

Graham, Milton, (c) 1956 preseason

* Gray, ___ (1b) 1921

* Gray, ___ (p) 1921

Gray, Lefty (lhp) 1924 preseason

* Gray, Will (lf) 1924 preseason

* Greason, Bill, (rhp) 1948–52

* Green, ___ (1b) 1925

* Green, Curtis (lhp) 1923

Green, Joe (c) 1957 preseason

* Gregory, Pete (p) 1940

* Gresham, ___ (rf-p) 1935

Griffin, ___ (x) 1947

Griffin, ___ (p) 1958

* Griffin, ___ (c) 1959

* Griffin (Griffith?), Robert (c) 1958

* Griggs, Acie "Skeet" (cf) 1951

* Griggs, Wiley "Diamond Jim" (inf) 1948–58, 1959 preseason

* Griggsby, Aubrey (x) 1958

* Grimes, ___ (c) 1921

* Grissim, Charles, (x) 1950

* Gross, James (p) 1957–60

Gurley, E.C. (x) 1929 [probably James Gurley]

* Gurley, E.G., (x) 1927 [probably James Gurley]

* Gurley, James Earl (rf-ph) 1927, 1929

* Guthrie, Wallace (lhp) 1953 [Guthrie Wallace?]

H

Haggins, Raymond (p-of) 1953 preseason

* Hair, Harold (3b) 1953

* Hairston, Clyde (c-inf) 1944

Hairston, Sam (c) 1944

* Hairston, Harold (rhp) 1953

* Haley, Granville "Red" (3b-2b) 1928

* Hall, James (c-rf) 1952 preseason, 1956

* Hall, Perry (3b-c-of) 1928

* Hamilton, ___ (lf) 1925 [probably Eppie Hampton]

Hamilton, George (c) 1929

* Hamilton, J.H. "Spade" (3b-ss-2b) 1927

* Hamilton, L___ (lf) 1925

* Hampton, Eppie (c-ph) 1925, 1929

Hampton, Marcellus (x) 1929

Hancock, Eddie (p) 1952 preseason

* Hardy, Paul James "Greyhound" (c-of) + 1934, 1940–43, 1945?

* Hardy, Paul (c) 1959

* Harper, David T. (of) 1946

* Harper, Ed (c) 1919

* Harper, Walter (c) 1923

* Harrell, Billy (ss) 1951

Harris, ___ (x) 1933

* Harris, Curtis (p-1b-2b) 1926

* Harris, Donnie (cf) 1957

* Harris, Ernest "Onk" (cf) 1959, 1961–62

* Harris, Horace (x) 1932 preseason

Harris, Lonnie (rf) 1954 preseason

Harris, Oscar (p) 1949 preseason

* Harris, Paul, (1b) 1951

Harris, Roger (inf) 1942

Harris, Ross (x) 1942 preseason

* Harris, Sammy Jr. (lf-rf) 1942

Harris, Samuel (p) 1940

* Harris, Willie "Red" (of) 1958–60, 1962

Harriston, Clyde (c-inf) 1944

* Harvey, Bob (2b) 1945

* Hayes, ___ (p) 1928
* Haynesworth, R.L. (x) 1935
* Haywood, Albert "Buster" (c) 1940
* Heard, Jehosie "Jay" (lhp) 1946–48
* Henderson, ___ (c) 1925
* Henderson, ___ (p) 1925
* Henderson, Ben (rhp) 1937
* Henderson, Lenon (3b-ss) 1932
Henry, Leo "Preacher" (p), 1947 preseason
Hester, Tommy (James?) (of) 1952 preseason
* Hewitt, Joe (2b-ss, mgr) 1924
* Hicks, ___ (x) 1923 preseason
* Higgins, Barney (p) 1946
Hill, Sam (lf) 1956 preseason
Hill, Willie (of) 1949 preseason
* Hill, Willie (p) 1958
* Holden, Carl (c) 1960
* Hollimon, Ulysses (p) 1950 preseason, 1952, 1954
* Hollingsworth, Curtis (lhp) 1946–48, 50
* Hollins, ___ "Pop-Eye" (rhp) 1936
* Hollins, James (p) 1953
* Holloway, ___ (ss) 1962
* Holly, ___ (p) 1949 [probably Curtis Hollingworth]
* Holscroff, William (inf) 1954
* Holston, ___ (p) 1937
* Holt, Will (of) 1920–22
* Honeycroft, William (inf) 1954
* Honeycutt, Albert (lhp) 1963
Horn, ___ (2b) 1925
Hosey, Bob (x) 1952 preseason
Hough, William (p) 1949 preseason
* Houlemard, Michael (lhp) 1954
Houser, William (p) 1949 preseason
Houston, Nathaniel (p) 1929 preseason
* Howard, A___ "Red" (lf) 1936 [probably Carl Howard]
* Howard, B___ (lf) 1936 [probably Carl Howard]
* Howard, Carl (lf) 1936
* Howard, Herman "Red" (lhp-of) 1936–37, 1940
Howard, Percy (c) 1947 preseason
* Howard, S___ (1b) 1935
* Howard, William "Bill" (1b-2b) 1931, # 1933
* Huber, ___ (cf-lf) 1931 [Hubert?]
*Huber, John "Butch" (rhp) 1943–45
* Hunter, ___ (x) 1943 [probably John Huber]
* Hyatt, ___ (3b) 1930 [probably Cowen Hyde]
* Hyde, Cowen (2b) 1930

I

* Ivory, James (1b) 1957–61 1b, 1962?

J

* Jackson, ___ (2b) 1920 [possibly Stanford Jackson]
Jackson, ___ (x) 1936 preseason
* Jackson, ___ (c) 1938
* Jackson, A. Matthew (ss) 1934
* Jackson, Bennie (x) 1958
# Jackson, Bozo (x) 1933
* Jackson, Brown (rf) 1958–60
* Jackson, Fred (p) 1953
* Jackson, Fred (of) 1955
* Jackson, Fred (p) 1956 preseason, 1957
* Jackson, Mack (3b) 1935
* Jackson, Stanford (ss) 1923
* Jackson, Tommy (p) 1953–54
January, Alvin (of) 1929 preseason
* Jasper, John (p) 1932
Jeffrey, ___ (of) 1931
*Jeffries, James "Lefty" (lhp-rf-pr) 1926–28, 1931
* Jemes, ___ (2b) 1920 [see Jiminez]
* Jeminez, ___ (2b) 1920 [see Jiminez]
* Jenkins, ___ (p) 1922.
* Jenkins, James (Paul?) "Pee Wee" (rhp) 1952, 1954
* Jerry, ___ (3b-2b) 1931
* Jessup, Gentry (rhp) 1940–41
Jiles, Jennie (lhp) 1956 preseason
Johnson, ___ (c) 1921
Johnson, ___ (of) 1928
+ Johnson, ___ (lf-rf) 1934
* Johnson, ___ (rf-cf-lf) 1935
* Johnson, ___ (ph) 1936
* Johnson, ___ (p) 1956
* Johnson, ___ (x) 1958
Johnson, ___ (p) 1958
* Johnson, ___ (rf) 1919
* Johnson, ___ (p) 1927
Johnson, Burton (of) 1938 preseason
* Johnson, Charles (c) 1953
Johnson, Charlie (p) 1952 preseason, 1953
* Johnson, Clarence (inf) 1957
* Johnson, Claude (3b) 1929–30
* Johnson, Donald (rhp) 1953
# Johnson, Hamp (cf-rf) 1933, + 1934, 1935
* Johnson, Hamp (cf) 1946
* Johnson, Ivory (p) 1930
* Johnson, J.D. "James" (p) 1952
Johnson, Jimmy (p) 1942 preseason

* Johnson, John (p) 1941
* Johnson, John W. (lhp) 1927
* Johnson, L___ (ss-2b) 1941 [possibly Leaman Johnson]
* Johnson, Leaman (3b) 1943
* Johnson, Lee (c) 1941 [same as Leaman Johnson?]
* Johnson, Leroy (p) 1950–52
Johnson, Morris (x) 1930
* Johnson, R___ (lf) 1938 [probably Burton Johnston]
* Johnson, Robert (p) 1956
* Johnson, Noble (c-3b-ph) 1929
* Johnson, ___ "Slim" (x) 1941 [probably same as John Johnson]
* Jones, ___ (rf) 1919
# Jones, ___ (lf) 1933
* Jones, ___ (p) 1935
* Jones, ___ (ph) 1940
Jones, ___ (cf) 1946 [likely Hamp Johnson]
*+ Jones, Arthur "Mutt" (rhp-ss-ph) 1925, # 1933, + 1934
# Jones, B___ (ph) 1933
+ Jones, Bill (p) 1934
* Jones, C___ (or G___?) (f) 1925
+ Jones, C___ (p) 1934
* Jones, Cecil, (cf) 1928
* Jones, Collis (pr-lf-cf) 1944–45
Jones, Fate (of) 1950 preseason
Jones, Fred (p) 1949 preseason
Jones, Hurley (p) 1931
* Jones, Lucien (lf) 1928 [likely Reuben Jones]
* Jones Reuben (rf-mgr) 1923–28
* Jones, Stanley (rhp) 1956–58 p, 1959 preseason
+ Jones, W___ (rf-cf) 1934
* Joseph, Newt (3b-2b-ss) 1924 preseason, 1925
Joseph, William (2b) 1925
* Juanelo, John [see Juanelo Mirabel]
June, Mitchell (inf) 1949 preseason
* Juran, ___ (p) 1922, 1925 [Eli or John Juran]
* Juran, B___ (p) [see John Juran]
* Juran, D___ (p) 1923 [Eli or John Juran]
* Juran, Eli "Lefty," "Eagle" (lhp-of) 1921–24, 1925 preseason
* Juran, Johnny "Bubba," "Buck" (rhp-of) 1921–24
* Juran, P___ (p) 1921 [Eli or John Juran]
* Juran, T___ (p) 1921 [Eli or John Juran]
* Juran, ___ (p) 1926 [Eli or John Juran]

K

* Keepy, ___ (2b) 1935
* Keglar, Walter (p) 1960
* Kelly, Walter (p) 1953
* Kemp, ___ (cf) 1931
* Kemp, ___ (ss) 1935
Kemp, Charles, 1952, preseason, from Huntsville
* Kemp, John (cf-lf) 1920–23, 1924?, 1926
Kennedy, Jim (1b) 1951
* Kennedy, John (3b-ss) 1954–55
* Keyes, ___ (p) 1942
* Kimbro, Henry (of) 1952–53
* Kimbroe, ___ (c) 1936
* Kines (Kiner?), ___ "Lefty" (lhp) 1951
* King, Clarence "Pijo" (of) 1947 preseason, 1948–50, 1951 preseason, 1952–54
King, Sim (p) 1951 preseason
+ Kirchfield, ___ (x) 1934
Knox, Jimmy (inf) 1937 preseason

L

Lacey, Charles (p) 1962
* Lamar, ___ (3b) 1952
* Lamar, Clarence (ss-3b) 1937, 1942, 1943 preseason
Landford, Charles (c) 1937 preseason
* Laurent, Milton (2b) 1932
Lawsson, Nathaniel (of) 1951 preseason
* Lee, Willie (lf) 1956
* Levenson, ___ (p) 1960
* Levy, Thomas (x) 1929
* Lewis, ___ (c) 1922 preseason
* Lewis, A.D. (1b) 1937
* Lewis, Carl (1b) 1960
* Lewis, J.D. (of) 1953
* Lillie, ___ (util) 1925
* Lily, John (lf) 1926
* Lilly, Roosevelt (p) 1949 preseason, 1951
* Lindsay, James (inf) 1943 [Lindsey?]
* Lindsey, Leonard (1b) 1943 [probably James Lindsay]
* Listach, Nora (rf) 1941
Little, Jess (lf) 1956 preseason
* Lloyd, Anthony (2b) 1959
* Locke, Eldridge (p) 1951
* Lockett, Lester "Buck" (ss, 3b, of) 1938, 41–46
Lockhart, ___ (x) 1923 preseason
* Long, Carl (of) 1952–53
* Long, Grady (x) 1935

* Longley (Langley), ___ (3b) 1941
Louden, Louis "Tommy" (c) 1945

M

* Maddox, Forest "One Wing" (p-of) 1920–21, 1923
Madison, Robert (p) 1942 preseason
* Mangle, ___ "Rip" (p) 1956 [same as Mangrum?]
* Mangrum, ___ "Rip" (2b) 1956 [same as Mangle?]
Manning, __ (x) 1936 preseason
Marbury, Jimmy (of) 1948 preseason
* Markham, John "Buster" (p) 1941–45
Marsh, Frank (lhp) 1949 preseason
* Marsh, Frank (1b) 1954–55?, 1956
Marshall, Jack (p) 1929
* Martini, ___ (c) 1920
* Mason, ___ (p), 1922
* Maston, ___ (ph) 1946
Matthews, Jesse (inf) 1942 preseason
* Maya, ___ (p) 1935
* Mays, W.H. (lf-cf-3b) 1935
* Mays, Willie "Sonny Boy" (of) 1948–50, 1952
* McAllister, ___ (1b) 1919 [probably George McAllister]
+ McAllister, ___ (1b) 1934 [probably George McAllister]
McAllister, Chip (x) 1945 preseason
* McAllister, George (1b-c) 1922–29, 1931–32, 1935
* McBride, Fred (3b-1b) 1940
* McBride, T___ (ph) 1940 [probably same as Fred]
McCall, Henry "Butch" (1b) 1938, 1944 preseason
* McCall, William (lhp) 1924
McClinic, Nat (x) 1948 preseason
* McClure, Willie Lee (inf-of) 1957
* McCullom, Frank Jr. (rhp) 1955, 1956 preseason, 1960
* McCormack, ___ (ss) 1919
* McCormick, ___ (3b) 1931
* McCormick, Bob (ss-3b-lf) 1920–22
* McDuffie, Terris (lf-cf) 1930–31, # 1933
* McEntire, ___ (lf) 1919
* McHaskell, ___ (2b) 1929
* McIntosh, ___ (lf) 1919
* McIntyre, ___ (ss) 1926
McKenzie, ___ (ph) 1948 preseason
McKey, James (ph) 1940

* McKinnis, Gready "Lefty" (lhp) 1941–43
* McLauren, Felix (of) 1942–45
* McLemore, Arthur (lhp) 1952
* McNealy, Joe (rf) 1946
# Mc...sw...wan, ___ (3b) 1933
# Mc'wain, ___ (3b) 1933
* Mead, ___ (c) 1928 [probably Lewis Means]
* Means, Lewis (c) 1923–24, 1926, 1928
Means, Woodrow (x) 1951 preseason
* Meed, Phillip (p) 1958
* Meredith, Buford "Geechie," (2b-ss-3b-mgr) 1920–29, 1931
* Meyers, ___ (2b) 1919
* Michaels, ___ (p) 1954
* Mickey, James (3b-ss) 1940
Middleton, Charles (2b) 1929 preseason
* Miles, ___ (2b) 1920
Miles, Jonas (p) 1943 preseason
* Miller, ___ (p) 1925
* Miller, ___ (x) 1931
* Miller, ___ (ss) 1942
Miller, A___ (of) 1928
* Miller, C.B. "Bob" (3b-2b) 1923, 1927
Miller, Dempsey (p) 1931
Mills, ___ (x) 1933
* Mirabal, Juanelo (rhp-of-3b) 1920–21
* Mitchell, ___ (rf) 1919
* Mitchell, ___ (cf) 1922
* Mitchell, ___ (of) 1923
* Mitchell, ___ (p) 1925
* Mitchell, ___ (2b) 1935
* Mitchell, ___ (p) 1935
* Mitchell, Alonzo "Hooks," "Bo" (rhp) 1937–38
* Mitchell, Jesse (of) 1954–57
* Mitchell, Jim (cf) 1957
* Mitchell, Jodie (p) 1935
Mitchell, Joe (of) 1923 [same as Joe Mitchell Reed?]
* Mitchell, Joe "Goose" (rf) 1926
*Mitchell, Johnny (of) 1958–60
Mitchell, Leonard (2b) 1930
* Mitchell, Otto (3b-2b) 1930
* Mitchell, Robert (of) 1923
* Mitchell, Wild Bill (p) 1935
* Mobley, Ira Lee (rf) 1953
* Montalvo, Estaban (lf) 1920
Montrell, ___ (of) 1924 preseason.
* Moody, Blanchette (p) 1940 [same as Frank?]
* Moody, Frank (p) 1940 [same as Blanchette?]

* Moody, Lee (of-1b) 1946–47
* Moon, ___ (rf) 1919
* Moore, ___ (p) 1923
* Moore, Billy Joe (1b) 1956, 1957 1b preseason?
Moore, Boots (p) 1948 preseason
Moore, C.C. (p) 1947 preseason
Moore, John (ss) 1929
* Moore, Ralph "Square" (p) 1923, 1925
Morgan, ___ (of) 1928
* Morgan, Leon (p-rf) 1928
Morgan, William (p) 1948
* Morney, Leroy (ss-3b-1b) 1942–44
* Morris, ___ (rf) 1921
+ Morris, ___ (p) 1934
* Moses, Joe (c) 1955
+ Mosley, ___ (rf) 1934
* Mosley "Hog" (3b) 1935
* Moss, ___ (p) 1922
* Mott, ___ (3b-lf) 1931
* Mullen, A___ (rf) 1928
Mullins, N___ (x) 1928
* Mumford, Pete (rhp) 1959
Murphy, ___ (p) 1930
* Murphy, Al (p) 1937
Murray, ___ "Lefty" (lhp) 1929
* Murray, ___ (p) 1938
* Myals, ___ (2b) 1920

N

* Nash, George (p-lf-mgr) 1928, 1932, # 1933, + 1934, 1935 [George and William Nash are possibly the same person]
Nash, Lafayette (p) 1944 [probably Fay Washington]
* Nash, William (lhp) 1928, 1932–33 (p-lf) + 1934
Nesbitt, Frank (inf) 1949 preseason
* Neve, J.L. (p) 1949 [probably Jimmie Lee Newberry]
* Newberry, Jimmie Lee (rhp) 1943–50
* Nichols, Frank (p) 1956
* Nixon, Willie (Billy) (of) 1940–41
* Norman, ___ (1b) 1919

O

* Oden, Johnny Webb (3b-ss) 1926–29
* Oliver, ___ (rf-2b-c) 1931, 1934
* Oliver, James (x) 1945
# Oliver, Martin (2b-rf-c) 1932, # 1933, + 1934
* Orange, Grady (ss) 1925
* Osbern, James (inf-of) 1957

* Osley, Julius "Snooks" (p) 1938
* Owens, Dewitt (ss-of) 1926–28, 1930, 1936–38
* Owens, Sylvester (2b) 1935
* Owens, Willie (x) 1935

P

* Pardee, John (c) 1925
* Padrone, Juan (lhp) 1923
* Paige, Holly (of) 1950
* Paige, Leroy "Satchel" (rhp) 1927–30
* Palm, Clarence (c) 1927
* Palmore, (rf) 1962
* Palmore (Paramore), James (p) 1960
* Palmore, Robert (p) 1962
* Paramore, Herbert (p) 1960 [see Herbert Paymon]
* Pardee, John (c) 1925
Parker, Tom (of) 1945
* Parnell, Roy "Red" (rf-rhp) 1927–28
Parsley, Paul (2b) 1952 preseason
* Patterson, ___ (c) 1906
* Patterson, Willie "Pat" (c-3b) 1951, 1955, 1957
* Paymon, Herbert (p) 1960–61
Payne, ___ (of) 1928
* Pearson, David (of-p) 1962
* Pennington, Art (of) 1945
* Perkins, ___ (3b) 1929 [probably Bill Perkins]
* Perkins, ___ (1b-c-rf) 1941
+ Perkins, Bill (c-mgr) 1934 preseason?
* Perkins, Bill (c) 1928, 1930, 1945
Perkins, Charlie (lhp) 1944 preseason
* Perkins, G. Robert (x) 1928
* Perry, Alonzo (rhp-1b) 1946?, 1947–50, 1951?, 1960
* Perry, Alonzo Jr. (of-1b) 1962
Perry, Elisha (1b), 1947 preseason
Perry, James (p) 1947 preseason
Pervis, ___ (p) 1937
* Peterson, ___ (p-cf) 1931
Peterson, ___ (x) 1936 preseason
+ Peterson, Harvey (lf) 1934
* Peterson, Harvey (lf-3b-c) 1932, 1934
* Petway, Charlie (ss-3b-of) 1931
* Phelps, Roy (cf) 1945
Phillips, ___ (p) 1927
* Phillips, ___ (p) 1952
* Phillips, Carlin (inf) 1942
* Pickens, ___ (lhp) 1920–22
Pickett, Charles A. (1b) 1948 preseason

Pickins (Pickens), Douglas (rf) 1951 preseason

Pierson, ___ (p) 1947

* Pines, Felix Jr. (x) 1951

Pinkston, Alfred (of) 1950 preseason

* Pipkin, Robert "Black Diamond," "Lefty" (lhp) 1928–29, 1932 preseason?, 1940, 1942

* Pitts, ___ 1919

* Poindexter, Robert (rhp-of) 1924–28

* Pollard, Nat (rhp) 1946–48, 1950, 1951 preseason, 1962

Porter, Dallas (x) 1928

* Posey, Jeff "Ray" (p-ph) 1935–36

Powell, Melvin (of) 1941

* Powell, William "Bill," "Mutt" (rhp) 1946–50, 1951 preseason, 1952

Preda, William (of) 1955 preseason

* Price, Willie Lee (p) 1951

* Pride, Charley (rhp-of) 1954

Pride, Ralph (of) 1955 pre-season

* Purdue (Perdue), Billy (p) 1959

Q

* Quicksey, ___ (3b-c-of) 1936–37

R

Radcliff, Alex (3b) 1942 preseason?

* Radcliffe, Ted "Double Duty" (c-rhp) 1942, 1944–45

* Ramsey, ___ (p) 1943

* Ramsey, Lamon (rhp) 1951

* Rassler, ___ (p) 1921

* Ray, John (lf-cf) 1937, 1945

* Redd, Ulysses "Gumbo" (ss) 1940–41

Reed, Eugene (2b) 1945 preseason

Reed, Fleming (3b) 1952 preseason

Reed, J.A. (x) 1941 preseason

Reed, Joe Mitchell (x) 1923

Reed, Leo (p) 1943 preseason

* Reed, Walter (p) 1942

* Reynolds, James (1b-c) 1946

* Rhodes, ___ (c) 1921

* Richardson, ___ (c-3b) 1924

* Richardson, ___ (c) 1927

* Richardson, ___ (p) 1954

* Richardson, John (p) 1924

Richardson, R___ (p) 1954

* Richardson, T.W. "Ted" (lhp-of) 1952–53

* Riddell (Ridgell?), Felix (of) 1958

* Rigby, Charles (x) 193

* Riley, Jim (ph-2b) 1945

* Roach, Melvin (rhp) 1962

* Robertson, ___ (p) 1936

* Robertson, Charles "Rags" (lhp) 1923, 1925

* Robinson, ___ (lhp) 1925

* Robinson, Bobby (3b) 1927

* Robinson, Charles (p) 1925

* Robinson, Harry (cf) 1960–61, 1962 pre-season

Robinson, John H. (of) 1948 preseason

* Robinson, Melvin (cf) 1963

* Robinson, Norman "Bobby" (of) 1945?, 1947–52

* Robinson, William (3b) 1927

* Rochelle, ___ (cf) 1920 [same as Rochette? Rosella?]

* Rochette, ___ (cf) 1920 [same as Rochelle? Rosella?]

Rodgers, Glen (of), 1950 preseason

* Rodgers, William "Nat" (rf-lf) 1930

* Rogers, ___ (p) 1920 [possibly Rodriguez]

* Rogers, Nat (ph) 1942

Rogers, William (of) 1930

* Rodriguez, Conrado "Red," (p) 1920

* Roland, Carl (c) 1926

Ronsell, ___ (of) 1929

Roosevelt, ___ (ph) 1948 preseason

* Rosella, B___ (cf) 1919–20 [Rochelle?, Rouselle?]

Rosser, William (p) 1949 preseason

* Roth, Herman (c) 1925

Rouselle, ___ (2b-cf) 1921 [Rosella? Rochette?]

Roussell, Edwin "Jimsy" (cf) 1928–29

Rowe, ___ (p) 1933

* Rudolph, ___ (p) [see Rudolph Ash]

* Ruffing, ___ (x) 1955

* Russell, J.H. (3b-ss) 1919–21

* Russell, Frank "Junior" (of-rhp) 1952–53

* Rutledge, ___ (p) 1960

S

* Salmon, Harry "Fish" (rhp-of) 1920–21, 1923–1932

* Sampson, Emanuel "Eddie" (rf) 1941, 1943?, 1946

* Sampson, Tommy (2b) 1940–47

* Samson, ___ (p) 1920 [probably Harry Salmon]

* Sanders, Bobby Gene (rhp-ss) 1958–59

* Sanders, James "Jake" (c-of) 1957, 1959

* Sartis, Billy (2b) 1962

* Saunders, Leo (ss) 1940

* Saylor, Alfred "Greyhound" (c-1b-rhp) 1941–45

* Scott, ___ (of) 1947
Scott, C___ (p) 1937
* Scott, Joe (1b) 1947 preseason, 1948–49
* Scott, John (lf) 1944
* Scott, Leroy (p) 1953
* Scott, William "Bill" (of) 1953
Scruggs, H.C. (c) 1924 preseason
* Scruggs, William C. "Willie" (rhp) 1949, 1952, 1958
* Seals, ___ (1b) 1919
* Searcy, Kelly (lhp) 1949 preseason, 1950–51, 1952 preseason, 1953–55
* Seay, Dick (2b) 1930
* Sellers, ___ [see Suttles]
* Sellers, G___ [see Suttles]
* Sewell, James (ss) 1955, 1956 preseason
* Shackleford, John G. (3b-2b) 1930
* Shanks, Hank (1b) 1927
Sharpe, "Pepper" (p-of) 1947 preseason
* Shaw, Herbert (ph-of) 1942
Sheeler, Willie (ss) 1955 preseason
* Sheffield, ___ (of) 1922 preseason
* Shepard, Freddie (rhp-of) 1945–46
Sheppard, Tommy (of) 1945
Sheppard, Lee (p) 1929 preseason
* Sheppard, Ray (ss-3b) 1924, 1928–29
* Sherman, ___ (p) 1926 [probably Harry Salmon]
* Sherman, J.L. (p) 1951
* Sienna, Frank (p) 1956 [probably Pedro Sierra]
* Simon, ___ (p-rf-cf) 1923, 1926 [probably Harry Salmon]
Simpson, Herbert (of) 1942 preseason
* Sims, ___ (2b) 1938
Small, ___ (p) 1928 [probably Owen Smaulding]
* Smallwood, Dewitt "Woody" (of) 1954
* Smaulding, Owen (p) 1928
* Smith, ___ (p) 1919
* Smith, ___ (1b-lf-cf) 1921
* Smith, ___ (cf-c-lf-ss) 1926
* Smith, ___ (c) 1932
* Smith, ___ (rf-ss) 935
* Smith, ___ (lf-cf-rf) 1942
* Smith, Buster (1b) 1932–33
* Smith, C___ (2b) 1926
# Smith, Carl (c) 1933
Smith, Carl (c-1b) 1938
* Smith, Charles (p) 1957
* Smith, Clarence (2b-cf-c-lf-ss-mgr) 1926, 1929–30
Smith, Don (p) 1953

Smith, H___ (ss) 1933
* Smith, Howard (util) 1935
* Smith, J___ (1b) 1942
* Smith, Jesse (of) 1930
* Smith, John (util) 1935
Smith, John (of) 1942
Smith, John (c) 1943 preseason
Smith, Johnny (2b) 1950 preseason, 1951 preseason
Smith, ___ "Lefty" (p)
* Smith, Quincy (of) 1945–46
* Smith, Robert "Bob" (c-ph-rf) 1930–1
* Smith, T___ (lf-cf-1b) 1931
# Smith, T___ (1b) 1933
* Smith, Taylor (rhp) 1952–53, 1958
* Smith, Willie (lhp-of) 1957–60
* Snead, Bill (lhp) 1927 [Jim? Joe?]
* Sneed, E___ (x) 1927
* Sneed (Snead), Eddie (lhp-of) 1940–42
Snell, Jim (x) 1927 preseason
Somersville, Robert (rhp) 1958 preseason
* Sotalongo, ___ (c) 1920
* Spearman, Clyde (rf) 1943 [brother of Jake Spearman]
* Spearman, Jake (x) 1943 [brother of Clyde Spearman]
* Spencer, Joseph B. "Joe" (ss-2b) 1942, 1945
* Spencer, Willie (of) 1941
Stafford, Hubert (p) 1929 preseason
* Stankie, Eddie (rf) 1951
* Starks, Jim (x) 1945
* Staton, Ollie (rhp) 1951–52
* Steele, Ed (rf-mgr) 1941 preseason, 1942–1953, 1955 preseason
Steele, Willie (of) 1958 preseason
* Stephens, Jess (x) 1935
* Stephenson, ___ (lhp-cf) "Lefty" 1925 [Stevenson?]
* Stevenson, "Lefty" (p) 1925 [Stephenson?]
Stewart, Leon (of) 1942
Stewart, Lionel (x) 1942 preseason
Stock, Martin (x) 1929
Stone, Edward (2b) 1945 preseason
* Stoves, Walter (c) 1960
* Stratton, Leroy (3b) 1923–25, 31
* Streeter, Sam (lhp) 1923–25, 1927–28, 1930–31
* Stubbs, Edward (cf) 1962
* Subbeth, Harold (c) 1960
* Sudduth (of) 1925 [probably Suttles}
* Sullivan, ___ (p) 1937
* S'van, ___ (cf) 1931 [Sullivan?]
* Suttles, George "Mule" (of-1b) 1923–25

T

Talbert, Andrew (inf) 1947 preseason

Talley, Sterling (ss) 1948 preseason, 1949 preseason

* Tantaros (Tantanos), ___ (c) 1920
* Tate, Roosevelt "Speed" (cf) 1932
* Tatum, Reese "Goose" (1b-of) 1941–42
* Taylor, ___ (cf) 1919
* Taylor, ___ (cf) 1925 [Tyler?]
* Taylor, ___ (p) 1920
* Taylor, ___ (1b) 1921 [possibly Matthews Taylor]
* Taylor, Candy Jim (ph-mgr) 1940
* Taylor, G ___ (rf) 1920

Taylor, John (of) 1943, 1945

Taylor, Johnny (c) 1947 preseason

*Taylor, Mathews (1b) 1920

Taylor, Olan "Jelly" (x) 1934

Taylor, Raymond (x) 1944 preseason

* Terry, ___ (p) 1947 [probably Perry]
* Thomas, ___ (rf) 1925 [probably James Thomson]
* Thomas (x) 1955

Thomas, Alonzo (of) 1949 preseason

* Thomas, Dan (cf-ph-lf) 1940
* Thomas, Dave "Frisco" (1b-lf) 1929–30
* Thomas, David (x) 1928

Thomas, Frank (p) 1945 [probably Frank Thompson]

+ Thomas, Hazel (p) 1934

Thomas, J___ (of) 1946–47

* Thomas, John (p) 1953
* Thomas, John Henry (cf) 1946
* Thomas, L___ (c) 1929–30
* Thomas, Walter (cf-lf) 1947
* Thompson, Frank "Groundhog" "Hoss" (lhp) 1945, 1952–54
* Thompson, Harold R. (of) 1929
* Thompson, James (cf) 1924–25, 1927–28

Thompson, Samuel (ss) 1929 preseason

* Thompson, Stoney (x) 1927 [see James Thompson]
* Threats, C___ (p) 1935
* Threatt, ___ (cf) 1935

Thurston, ___ (p) 1938

* Tibbs, ___ (ph) 1923 [probably Tubbs]

Tipton, ___ (x) 1942

* Tolbert, ___ (c) 1940

Tolbert, ___ (x) 1941 preseason

* Tooley, ___ (3b) 1931 [probably Walter Cooley]
* Town, George (c) 1927

Town(e)s, Leonard (lhp) 1950 preseason

* Trammel, Nat (1b) 1930
* Trehearn, ___ (1b) 1945

Tubbs, ___ (of) 1923 [probably "Black Babe Ruth" Tubbs]

* Tubbs, ___ "Black Babe Ruth" (1b-rf) 1920–22

Turner, Arthur (of) 1949 preseason

Turner, Carl (x) 1944 preseason

* Turner, E.C. (3b) 1930
# Turner, Joe (x) 1933

Turner, Ted (rhp) 1948 preseason

Tyler, "Steel Arm" (of) 1925

* Tyson, ___ (ph-1b-c) 1938
* Tyson, Armand "Cap" (3b-2b-c) 1936, 1940–41

U

Underwood, ___ (3b) 1959 preseason

V

* Vance, Columbus "Hy" (lhp) 1927, 1930–31, #1934
* Veal, Robert, Sr. (p) 1931 [from Birmingham]
* Veal, Robert, Jr. (batboy) 1948
+ Vines, ___ (p) 1934

Vines, Eddie (1b-3b) 1940 preseason

W

* Waddy, ___ (x) 1937 [probably David Whatley]
* Wair, Willie (1b) 1925
* Walker, Jesse "Hoss" (ss-mgr) 1941–43, 19513–54, 1956
* Walker, Robert "Bob" (rhp) 1935–36
* Wallace, Guthrie (p) 1953 [Wallace Guthrie?]
* Ward, Thomas "Pinky" (cf) 1927
* Ware, John (p) 1941

Warmack, James (x) 1923 preseason

* Warner, __ (p) 1920
* Warren, Jesse (1b-lf) 1942
+ Washington, John (1b) 1934

Washington, Lafayette "Fay" (rhp) 1944–45

* Watson, ___ (c) 1922–23
* Watson, ___ (c) 1935

Watson, ___ (p) 1935

* Watson, David (rhp) 1922–23
* Watts, Andy (3b) 1950, 1951 preseason
* Watts, Richard "Dick" (p) 1949–50
* Weaver, ___ (3b) 1919

* Webster, Charles (of) 1950
* Welch, Phil "Smut" (p) 1958–61
* Welch, Winfield S. (of-mgr) 1941–45
* Wells, Willie Sr. (ss-mgr) 1941, 1954
* Wesley, Charles "Two Sides" (2b-mgr) 1919, 1923–24, 1925 preseason, 1928–29
* Wesley, Eugene (c-cf) 1920.
* Wesley, T___ (c-rf) 1920 [probably Charles Wesley]
* West, Charlie (of-inf) 1942
+ West, Jim (1b) 1934
* West, Jim (1b-ph) 1930, 1932, 1945, 1947
* West, Ollie (rhp) 1946
* Westbrook, A.G. (3b) 1960
* Westfield, Ernie (rhp) 1960
* Whaley, ___ (s) 1919
* Whatley, David "Hammer Man" (rf-cf) 1936–38
* White, ___ (rf) 1935
White, Buster (c) 1924 preseason
* White, Curtis (p) 1957
* Wiley, Joe (lf) 1948
* Wilkes, ___ (rf) 1922
* Williams, ___ (p) 1919
* Williams, ___ (3b-ss-lf) 1921
Williams, ___ (of), 1938
* Williams, ___ (ph) 1935
Williams, B___ (of-1b) 1938
* Williams, Benny Ray (3b) 1963
* Williams, C___ (c) 1924 [probably Poindexter Williams]
* Williams, Charles (inf-p) 1956
* Williams, Chester (inf) 1929
Williams, David (Davis) (p) 1951 preseason
* Williams, Ernest (rhp) 1961–62
* Williams, Findale (rf) 1927
Williams, Gerald (ss) 1922 preseason
* Williams, ___ "Honeyboy" (lf-3b-ss) 1921
* Williams, Ira (ss) 1929 preseason
* Williams, John Henry (p) 1941
Williams, John (x) 1944 preseason
* Williams, John Henry "Stanky" (2b-of-mgr) 1951–59, 1962
* Williams, Johnny (p) 1955
* Williams, L___ (p) 1923
* Williams, M___ (lf-rf)
Williams, Nish (c-of) 1937
* Williams, P___ (ph) 1935
* Williams, Poindexter (c-2b-mgr) 1923–29, 1932, 1935
* Williams, Roy "Curley" (lf) 1955
* Williams, Samuel T. "Sam" (rhp) 1947–50, 1951 preseason, 1952

* Williams, Stanley (rf) 1955
* Williams, T___ (c) 1919
Williams, Willie (p) 1941
* Williams, Willie C. "Curley" (ss-rf) 1954, 1955 preseason
* Williford, ___ (ss) 1926
* Willis, Charles "Coop" (cf) 1950, 1951 preseason
* Willis, Ed (x) 1928
* Willis, Jim (rhp) 1928
* Wilson, ___ (c) 1926
* Wilson, ___ (ss) 1936
* Wilson, ___ (cf) 1941
* Wilson Arthur "Artie" (ss) 1944–48
Wilson, James (of) 1940 preseason
* Wilson, Jay (inf) 1945, 1948 [probably Artie Wilson]
* Wilson, T___ (cf) 1941
* Winston, ___ (c) 1921
* Wolfe, Alex (p) 1959
* Woodal, ___ (p) 1922
Woodruff, Joe (p) 1956 preseason
* Woods, ___ (x) 1955
* Woods, Parnell (3b) 1936–38, 1940
* Wooten, Nathaniel (p) 1955
+ Worthington, ___ (1b) 1934 [probably John Washington]
* Wrencher, ___ (1b) 1935
* Wright, Charley (p) 1931
* Wright, Danny (rhp) 1953–54
* Wright, ___ (c) 1957
* Wright, Henry (c) 1954
* Wright, Richard (c) 1954
* Wyatt, William "Willie" (ss) 1956–57

Y

* Yeatts, Earnest (inf-of) 1957
* Young, ___ (p) 1919
* Young, ___ (p) 1920
* Young, ___ (rhp) 1922
* Young, Leandy (c-of) 1944–45
Young, Wilbur (p) 1945 [probably Willie Young]
* Young, Willie (lhp) 1945

Z

* Zapp, Jim (of) 1948, 1952 preseason, 1954
* Zeigler, Gordon (lhp) 1919–20, 1923
Zomphier, Charles (3b) 1927

Chapter Notes

Introduction

1. William J. Plott, *The Negro Southern League: A Baseball History 1920–1951* (Jefferson, NC: McFarland, 2015), 7–8; Dick Clark and Larry Lester, *The Negro Leagues Book* (Cleveland: Society for American Baseball Research, 1994), 15–16.
2. *Ibid.*
3. Leslie Heaphy, *The Negro Leagues 1869–1960* (Jefferson, NC: McFarland, 2003), 211.
4. Robert W. Peterson, *Only the Ball Was White* (Englewood Cliffs, NJ: Prentice-Hall, 1970).
5. Larry Powell, *Black Barons of Birmingham: The South's Greatest Negro League Team and Its Players* (Jefferson, NC: McFarland, 2009).
6. *Birmingham World*, 6 July 1945.
7. Email letter from Raymond J. Nemec, 5 September 2010.
8. *Birmingham Reporter*, 25 May 1929.
9. *Birmingham World*, 8 July 1941.
10. *Ibid.*, 29 July 1941.
11. *Pittsburgh Courier*, 27 July 1929.
12. *Birmingham World*, 30 April 1946.
13. Harold Wentworth and Stuart Berg Flexner, *Dictionary of American Slang* (New York: Thomas Y. Crowell Company, 1960), 171.
14. *Birmingham World*, 18 April 1941.
15. *Montgomery Advertiser*, 21 August 1920.
16. *Birmingham News*, 11 July 1920.
17. *Atlanta Constitution*, 4 September 1920.
18. *Birmingham News*, 18 July 1920.
19. *Atlanta Daily World*, 23 July 1936.

Chapter 1

1. *Birmingham News*, 8 July 1919.
2. *Birmingham World*, 20 May 1959.
3. *Ibid.*, 3 August 1948.
4. *Montgomery Advertiser*, 27 April 1927.
5. *Ibid.*
6. Bill O'Neal, *The Southern League: Baseball in Dixie 1885–1994* (Austin: Eakin Press, 1994), 2; Marshall D. Wright, *The Southern Association in Baseball, 1885–1961* (Jefferson, NC: McFarland, 2002), 5.
7. Bill Plott, "The Southern League of Colored Baseballists," *Baseball Research Journal* (Cleveland: Society for American Baseball Research, 1974).
8. *Birmingham Reporter*, 16 May 1908.
9. Leroy "Satchel" Paige (as told to David Lipman), *Maybe I'll Pitch Forever* (Garden City, NY: Doubleday, 1961), 20–23.
10. James A. Riley, *The Biographical Encyclopedia of the Negro Baseball Leagues* (New York: Carroll & Graf, 1994), 763–64.
11. Paul Debono, *The Indianapolis ABCs* (Jefferson, NC: McFarland, 1997), 27–8.
12. Riley, *Biographical Encyclopedia*, 763–64.
13. *Pittsburgh Press*, 29 February 1928.
14. *Birmingham News*, 5 August 1923.
15. DeBono, *The Indianapolis ABCs*, 27–8.
16. DeBono, *The Indianapolis ABCs*, 73.
17. *Ibid.*, 92–3; Riley, *Biographical Encyclopedia*, 763–64.
18. *Birmingham News*, 5 August 1923.
19. *Birmingham Reporter*, 20 March 1915.
20. *Ibid.*, 15 April 1915.
21. *Ibid.*, 20 April 1916.
22. *Birmingham Reporter*, 15 April 1916.
23. *Ibid.*, 15 April 1916.
24. *Ibid.*, 5, 19 July 1919.
25. *Birmingham News*, 8 July 1919.
26. *Ibid.*, 17 July 1919.
27. *Ibid.*, 18 July 1919.
28. *Birmingham News*, 22 July 1919; *Birmingham Reporter*, 26 July 1919.
29. *Birmingham News*, 23 July 1919.
30. Wright, *The Southern Association in Baseball 1885–1961*, 201.
31. *Birmingham News*, 24 July 1919.
32. *Ibid.*, 25 July 1919.
33. *Ibid.*, 12 August 1919.
34. *Ibid.*, 28 August 1919.
35. *Ibid.*, 29 August 1919.
36. *Birmingham News*, 2 September 1919; *Birmingham Reporter*, 6 September 1919.
37. *Birmingham News*, 3 September 1919.
38. *Birmingham News*, 9 September 1919; *Birmingham Reporter*, 13 September 1919.
39. *Birmingham News*, 12 September 1919.
40. *Birmingham News*, 17, 18 September 1919; *Birmingham Reporter*, 20 September 1919.
41. *Birmingham News*, 23, 24, 25 September 1919; *Birmingham Reporter*, 27 September 1919.
42. Reel 12, Tuskegee Institute microfilm collection of newspaper clippings, Alabama Department of Archives and History, Montgomery, AL.
43. *Birmingham News*, 11, 12 July 1919.
44. *Ibid.*, 6 June 1920.
45. *Birmingham News*, 29 April 1923.

Chapter 2

1. John Holway, *The Complete Book of Baseball's Negro Leagues: The Other Half of Baseball History* (Fern Park, FL: Hastings House, 2001), 139; Dick Clark and Larry Lester, eds., *The Negro Leagues Book* (Cleveland: Society for American Baseball Research, 1974), 160.

2. *Ibid.*

3. *Ibid.*

4. *Atlanta Independent*, 6 March 1920.

5. *Chicago Defender*, 6 March 1920.

6. *Ibid.*, 203–26.

7. *Montgomery Advertiser*, 9 May 1920.

8. *Atlanta Constitution*, 20 May 1920.

9. *Ibid.*, 1 July 1920.

10. *Atlanta Independent*, 6 March 1920.

11. *Chicago Defender*, 17 April 1920.

12. *Atlanta Constitution*, 26 April 1920.

13. *Pensacola Journal*, 30 April 1920.

14. *Montgomery Advertiser*, 1 May 1920; *Times-Picayune*, 4 May 1920.

15. *Atlanta Constitution*, 15 August 1920.

16. *Montgomery Advertiser*, 1, 2 May 1920.

17. *Birmingham News*, 2 May 1920.

18. *Ibid.*, 4 May 1920.

19. *Ibid.*, 5 May 1920.

20. *Ibid.*

21. *Ibid.*, 28 June 1920.

22. livefromthesurfaceofthemoon.blogspot.com, 16 June 2010; Certificate of Death, State of Georgia File Number 21319.

23. *Birmingham News*, 16 May 1920.

24. *Birmingham Reporter*, 29 May 1920.

25. *Birmingham News*, 20 May 1920.

26. *Ibid.*, 30 May 1920.

27. *Atlanta Constitution*, 23 May 1920.

28. *Birmingham News*, 3 June 1920.

29. *Knoxville Journal*, 3 June 1920; *Knoxville Sentinel*, 3 June 1920.

30. *Birmingham News*, 8 June 1920.

31. *Montgomery Advertiser*, 23 July 1920.

32. Riley, *Biographical Encyclopedia*, 748.

33. *Birmingham News*, 9 June 1920.

34. *Ibid.*, 10 June 1920.

35. *Birmingham City Directory 1920–21* (Birmingham: R.L. Polk & Co., 1902), 1198; *Birmingham City Directory* (Birmingham: R.L. Polk & Co., 1921), 613, 840.

36. *Birmingham News*, 6 June 1920.

37. *Times-Picayune*, 21 July 1920.

38. *Birmingham News*, 22, 23, 24 June 1920.

39. *Ibid.*, 7 July 1920.

40. *Knoxville Journal*, 7 July 1920; *Knoxville Sentinel*, 7 July 1920.

41. *Knoxville Journal and Tribune*, 76 July 1920.

42. *Ibid.*, 7 July 1920.

43. *Ibid.*, 25 July 1920.

44. *Ibid.*, 30 July 1920.

45. *Ibid.*, 19 June, 2; July 1920.

46. *Ibid.*, 2 July 1920.

47. *Birmingham News*, 27, 28 July 1920.

48. *Ibid.*, 15 August 1920.

49. *Ibid.*, 7 September 1920.

50. *Times-Picayune*, 24 May 1920.

51. *Birmingham News*, 18 July 1920.

52. *Knoxville Journal and Tribune*, 6 September 1920.

53. *Ibid.*, 12 September 1920.

54. *Knoxville Journal and Tribune*, 30 August 1920.

55. *Ibid.*

56. *Ibid.*, 6 September 1920.

57. *Knoxville Sentinel*, 27 September 1920; *Pensacola Journal*, 28 September 1920.

58. Negro Leagues Researchers and Authors Group, privately published statistics, 15 January 2005.

59. Riley, *Biographical Encyclopedia*, 555.

60. *Ibid.*, 11 July 1920.

61. *Ibid.*, 7 September 1920.

62. *Ibid.*, 22 February 1921; *Atlanta Independent*, 3 March 1921.

63. *Birmingham News*, 26 April 1921.

64. Riley, *Biographical Encyclopedia*, 122.

65. baseball-reference.com/bullpen/Larry_Brown_%28Negro_Leagus%29, last update on 2 May 2013; Riley, *Biographical Encyclopedia*, 122–23.

66. *Sporting News*, 22 April 1972; *Birmingham News*, 8 April 1972.

67. *Birmingham News*, 26 April 1921.

68. *Ibid.*, 27 April 1921.

69. *Ibid.*, 28 April 1921.

70. *Ibid.*, 29 April 1921.

71. Riley, *Biographical Encyclopedia*, 555.

72. *Birmingham News*, 1 May 1921.

73. *Chattanooga Daily Times*, 12 May 1921.

74. *Knoxville Journal and Tribune*, 23 May 1921.

75. *Birmingham News*, 8 May 1921; *Chattanooga Daily Times*, 11 June 1921.

76. *Birmingham News*, 5, 8 May 1921.

77. Riley, *Biographical Encyclopedia*, 223.

78. *Birmingham News*, 19 May 1921.

79. *Chicago Defender*, 11 June 1921.

80. *Birmingham News*, 26 May 1921.

81. *Ibid.*, 12 June 1921.

82. *Nashville Banner*, 30 July 1921.

83. *Birmingham News*, 30 July 1921.

84. *Ibid.*

85. *Ibid.*, 27 July 1921.

86. *Birmingham News*, 2–3, 8 August 1921; *Montgomery Advertiser*, 7, 8 August 1921.

87. *Montgomery Advertiser*, 21 August 1921.

88. *Birmingham News*, 29 May 1921.

89. *Ibid.*, 5 June 1921.

90. *Birmingham Age-Herald*, 20 June 1921.

91. *Birmingham News*, 4 September 1921.

92. *Nashville Tennessean*, 14 September 1921.

93. *Montgomery Advertiser*, 28 August 1921.

94. *Nashville Banner*, 14 September 1921.

95. *Ibid.*, 15 September 1921.

96. *Ibid.*, 17, 19–20 September 1921.

97. Plott, *The Negro Southern League*, 33.

98. https://www.bhamwiki.com/w/Joseph_Riley_Smith, last modified on 13 April 2011.

99. *Birmingham News*, 30 April 1922.

100. Riley, *Biographical Encyclopedia*, 558.

101. *Birmingham News*, 2 May 1922.

102. *Ibid.*

103. *Ibid.*, 28 May 1922.

104. *Ibid.*, 25 June 1922.

105. *Chicago Defender*, 1 July 1922.

106. *Ibid.*, 10 June 1922.

107. *Chattanooga Daily Times*, 21 June 1922.

108. *Commercial Appeal*, 12 July 1922.

109. *Nashville Banner*, 30 July 1922.

110. *Commercial Appeal*, 7 August 1922.

111. *Ibid.*

112. *Ibid.*, 10 September 1922.

113. *Montgomery Journal*, 19 August 1922.

114. *Chicago Defender*, 7 September 1922.

Chapter 3

1. *Birmingham News*, 23 April 1923.
2. *Ibid.*, 28 April 1923.
3. *Ibid.*, 8 April 1923.
4. *Ibid.*, 29 April 1923.
5. Riley, *Biographical Encyclopedia*, 753.
6. *Birmingham News*, 28 April 1923.
7. *Ibid.*, 1 May 1923; *Birmingham Age-Herald*, 1 May 1923.
8. Author interview with Willie Young, 16 May 1999, Birmingham, AL.
9. *Birmingham World*, 27 May 1959.
10. *Buffalo Evening News*, 20 June 1925.
11. *Birmingham News*, 2, 3 May 1923.
12. *Ibid.*, 5 May 1923.
13. *Birmingham Age-Herald*, 5 May 1923.
14. *Birmingham News*, 6 May 1923.
15. *Commercial Appeal*, 13 May 1923.
16. *Birmingham News*, 27 May 1923.
17. *Ibid.*, 7 June 1923.
18. *Ibid.*, 10 June 1923.
19. *Ibid.*, 28 June 1923.
20. Albert L. Scipio, *The 24th Infantry at Fort Benning* (Silver Spring, MD: Roman Publications, 1986).
21. *Birmingham News*, 27 June 1923.
22. *Ibid.*, 1 July 1923.
23. *Ibid.*, 11 July 1923.
24. *Birmingham News*, 15 July 1923.
25. *Times-Picayune*, 7 July 1923.
26. *Pittsburgh Courier*, 4 August 1923.
27. *Chicago Defender*, 4 August 1923.
28. *Birmingham News*, 15 July 1923.
29. Clark and Lester, *The Negro Leagues Book*, 160.
30. *Chicago Defender*, 28 July 1923.
31. *Birmingham News*, 20 July 1923.
32. *Chicago Defender*, 28 July 1923.
33. *Birmingham News*, 21 July 1923.
34. *Pittsburgh Courier*, 28 July 1923.
35. *Birmingham Age-Herald*, 22 July 1923.
36. *Ibid.*, 25 July 1923.
37. *Ibid.*, 22 July 1923.
38. *Birmingham News*, 28 July 1923.
39. *Ibid.*
40. *Birmingham Age-Herald*, 27 July 1923.
41. *Birmingham News*, 29 July 1923.
42. *Birmingham Age-Herald*, 2 August 1923.
43. *Birmingham News*, 3 August 1923.
44. *Ibid.*, 5 August 1923.
45. *Ibid.*, 7 August 1923.
46. *Birmingham Age-Herald*, 8 August 1923.
47. *Birmingham News*, 8 August 1923.
48. *Ibid.*, 19 August 1923.
49. *Ibid.*
50. Riley, *Biographical Encyclopedia*, 753.
51. *Birmingham News*, 19 August 1923.
52. *Ibid.*
53. *Birmingham Age-Herald*, 20 August 1923.
54. *Birmingham News*, 22 August 1923.
55. *Birmingham Age-Herald*, 21 August 1923.
56. *Birmingham News*, 22 August 1923.
57. *Ibid.*, 23 August 1923.
58. *Birmingham News*, 23 August 1923.
59. *Ibid.*, 2 September 1923.
60. *Birmingham Age-Herald*, 3 September 1923.
61. *Birmingham News*, 4 September 1923.
62. *Birmingham News*, 5 September 1923.
63. *Ibid.*, 6 September 1923.
64. *Ibid.*
65. *Ibid.*, 9 September 1923.
66. *Ibid.*, 11 September 1923.
67. *Ibid.*, 14 September 1923.
68. *Ibid.*, 19 September 1923.
69. *Ibid.*
70. *Ibid.*, 20 September 1923.
71. Clark and Lester, *The Negro Leagues Book*, 160; Holway, *The Complete Book of Baseball's Negro Leagues*, 175.

Chapter 4

1. *Birmingham News*, 30 March 1924; *Chicago Defender*, 15 March 1924; Riley, *Biographical Encyclopedia*, 1997–98.
2. *Birmingham News*, 30 March 1924.
3. *Ibid.*, 6 June 1924.
4. Riley, *Biographical Encyclopedia*, 203.
5. *Ibid.*, 27 April 1924.
6. *Birmingham News*, 24 April 1924.
7. *Ibid.*, 29 April 1924.
8. *Ibid.*
9. *Ibid.*, 1 May 1924.
10. *Ibid.*, 4 May 1924.
11. *Ibid.*, 6 May 1924.
12. Riley, *Biographical Encyclopedia*, 630, 537.
13. *Birmingham News*, 7 May 1924.
14. *Ibid.*, 4 May 1924.
15. *Indianapolis Star*, 10, 11, 12 May 1924.
16. *Ibid.*, 12 May 1924.
17. *Ibid.*, 18 May 1924.
18. *Ibid.*, 20 May 1924.
19. *Ibid.*, 21 May 1924.
20. *Ibid.*, 29 May 1924.
21. *Ibid.*, 27 May 1924.
22. *Ibid.*, 28 May 1924.
23. *Ibid.*, 30, 1 May 1924.
24. *Ibid.*, 8 June 1924; *Commercial Appeal*, 1, 2, 3, 4 June 1924.
25. *Ibid.*, 10 June 1924.
26. *Ibid.*, 11 June 1924.
27. *Ibid.*, 23 June 1924; *Chicago Defender*, 21, 28 June 1924.
28. *Ibid.*, 6 July 1924.
29. *Ibid.*, 12 July 1924.
30. *Ibid.*, 8 July 1924.
31. *Ibid.*, 9–10 July 1924.
32. *Ibid.*, 11 July 1924.
33. *Ibid.*, 21 June 1924.
34. *Ibid.*, 15 July 1924.
35. *Ibid.*
36. *Ibid.*, 18 July 1924.
37. *St. Louis Post-Dispatch*, 27 July 1924; *Chicago Defender*, 26 July 1924.
38. http:///en.wikipedia.org/wiki/Turkey_Stearnes, last revised on 7 August 2015.
39. *Birmingham News*, 29 July, 1 August 1924.
40. *Ibid.*, 1 August, 3 August 1924.
41. *Commercial Appeal*, 4 August 1924.
42. *Birmingham News*, 6 August 1924.
43. *Chicago Defender*, 23 August 1924; *Detroit Free Press*, 24, 25, 27 August 1924.
44. *Pittsburgh Courier*, 6 September 1924.
45. *Birmingham News*, 2 September 1924.
46. *Ibid.*, 5 September 1924.
47. *Ibid.*, 4 September 1924.

48. *Ibid.*, 6 September 1924.
49. *Ibid.*, 7 September 1924.

Chapter 5

1. *Birmingham News*, 5 April 1925; *Chicago Defender*, 7 March 1925.
2. *Birmingham News*, 5 April 1925; *Chicago Defender*, 21 March 1925.
3. *Birmingham News*,19 April 1925; *Chicago Defender*, 25 April 1925.
4. *Ibid.*, 26 April 1925.
5. *Ibid.*
6. *Ibid.*
7. *Ibid.*, 28 April 1926.
8. *Ibid.*
9. *Birmingham News*, 1 May 1925; *Chicago Defender*, 2 May 1925.
10. *Birmingham News*, 4 May 1925; *St. Louis Post-Dispatch*, 3 May 1925; *Indianapolis Star*, 10–13 May 1925.
11. *Birmingham News*, 15 May 1925.
12. *Ibid.*, 17 May 1925; *Chicago Defender*, 23 May 1925.
13. *Birmingham News*, 19 May 1925.
14. *Ibid.*, 20 May 1925.
15. *Ibid.*, 21 May 1925.
16. *Birmingham News*, 28 May 1925; *Chicago Defender*, 30 May 1925.
17. *Ibid.*, 31 May 1925.
18. *Chicago Defender*, 6 June 1925.
19. *Detroit Free Press*, 6, 7, 8, 9, 10, 11 June 1925.
20. *Ibid.*, 20 June 1925.
21. *Birmingham News*, 8 July 1925.
22. *Ibid.*, 9 July 1925.
23. *Birmingham* News, 12, 13, 14 July 1925; *Chicago Defender*, 18 July 1925.
24. *Indianapolis Star*, 19–20 July 1925.
25. *Birmingham News*, 19 July 1925.
26. *Ibid.*, 21 July 1925; *Chicago Defender*, 18 July 1925; *Birmingham News*, 19 July 1925.
27. *Ibid.*, 22 July 1925.
28. *Ibid.*, 23 July 1925.
29. *Chicago Defender*, 1, 8 August 1925.
30. *Birmingham News*, 6 August 1925; *Detroit Free Press*, 2, 3, 5 June 1925.
31. *Birmingham News*, 5 August 1925.
32. *Chicago Defender*, 8 August 1925.
33. *Birmingham News*, 12 August 1925; *Chicago Defender*, 22 August 1925.
34. *Ibid.*, 23 July 1925.
35. *Ibid.*, 16 August 1925.
36. *Ibid.*
37. *Ibid.*, 17 August 1925.
38. *Birmingham News*, 17 August 1925; Riley, *Biographical Encyclopedia*, 800.
39. *Birmingham News*, 19 August 1925.
40. *Ibid.*, 20 August 1925.
41. *Ibid.*, 27 August 1925.
42. *Chicago Defender*, 12 September 1925.
43. *Ibid.*, 20 September 1925.

Chapter 6

1. *Chicago Defender*, 3 April 1926; *Pittsburgh Courier*, 3 April 1926.
2. *Pittsburgh Courier*, 10 April 1926; www.tennessee encyclopedia.net/entry.php?rec=1144, last updated 24 February 2011.
3. *Birmingham Reporter*, 6 March 1926.
4. *Ibid.*
5. *Ibid.*
6. *Ibid.*
7. www.encyclopediaofalabama.org/aticle/h-1665.
8. *Birmingham Reporter*, 3 March 1926.
9. *Ibid.*, 13 March 1926.
10. Plott, *The Negro Southern League*, 54.
11. *Ibid.*, 3 April 1926.
12. Riley, *Biographical Encyclopedia*, 720.
13. *Birmingham Reporter*, 3 April 1926.
14. *Birmingham Reporter*, 17 April 1926; *Birmingham News*, 2 May 1926.
15. *Chattanooga Daily Times*, 2 May 1926.
16. https://search.ancestry.com/collections/6135/records/273841; https://search.ancestry.com/collections/2469/records/98254993.
17. *Ibid.*, 3–5 May 1926.
18. *Commercial Appeal*, 8, 9, 10 May 1926.
19. *Birmingham Reporter*, 8 May 1926; *Chicago Defender*, 15 May 1926.
20. *Birmingham Reporter*, 1 May 1926.
21. *Ibid.*, 8 May 1926.
22. *Birmingham Reporter*, 18 May 1926; *Birmingham News*, 11 May 1926.
23. *Birmingham Reporter*, 15 May 1926.
24. *Ibid.*
25. *Ibid.*; *Birmingham News*, 11, 12, 13 May 1926.
26. *Chattanooga Daily Times*, 16 May 1926.
27. Riley, *Biographical Encyclopedia*, 309–10.
28. *Birmingham Reporter*, 6 June 1926; *Birmingham News*, 18, 19 May 1926.
29. *Birmingham News*, 27, 28 May 1926.
30. *Ibid.*, 28, 29, 30, 31 May 1926.
31. *Ibid.*, 1 June 1926.
32. *Ibid.*
33. *Chicago Defender*, 12 June 1926; *Atlanta Independent*, 10 June 1926; *Birmingham Reporter*, 12 June 1926.
34. *Birmingham Reporter*, 5 June 1926.
35. *Ibid.*, 12 June 1926.
36. *Commercial Appeal*, 6 June 1926.
37. *Ibid.*, 3 July 1926.
38. *Albany Herald*, 28 June 1926.
39. *Chicago Defender*, 17 July 1926.
40. *Albany Herald*, 24 May 1926.
41. *Chicago Defender*, 26 June 1926.
42. *Commercial Appeal*, 19, 28 June 1926.
43. *Birmingham News*, 20 June 1926.
44. *Knoxville Journal*, 28 June 1926.
45. *Times-Picayune*, 13 July 1926.
46. Telephone interview with Claude Walker, September 1998.
47. *Birmingham News*, 11 June 1926.
48. *Times-Picayune*, 21 May 1926.
49. *Birmingham News*, 18 July 1926.
50. *Ibid.*
51. *Ibid.*, 9 September 1926.
52. *Ibid.*, 26-, 27, 28 July 1926.
53. *Ibid.*, 27, 28, 29, 30, 31 August 1926, 1 September 1926.
54. *Ibid.*, 19 September 1926.
55. *Ibid.*, 12 September 1926.
56. Riley, *Biographical Encyclopedia*, 248.
57. *Commercial Appeal*, 22 September 1926.
58. *Birmingham News*, 12 September 1926; *Commercial Appeal*, 12 September 1926.

59. *Birmingham News*, 13 September 1926; *Commercial Appeal*, 13 September 1926.
60. *Birmingham News*, 14 September 1926; *Commercial Appeal*, 14 September 1926.
61. *Birmingham Reporter*, 18 September 1926.
62. Paul Dickson, *The Dickson Baseball Dictionary*, 3rd ed. (New York: W.W. Norton, 2009), 292.
63. *Birmingham News*, 22 September 1926; *Commercial Appeal*, 22 September 1926; Paul Dickson, *The Dickson Baseball Dictionary*, 292.
64. *Birmingham News*, 23 September 1926.
65. *Birmingham News*, 24 September 1926; *Commercial Appeal*, 24 September 1926.
66. *Birmingham News*, 27 September 1926; *Commercial Appeal*, 27 September 1926.
67. *Birmingham News*, 29 September 1926; *Commercial Appeal*, 29 September 1926.
68. *Birmingham News*, 30 September 1926; *Commercial Appeal*, 30 September 1926.
69. *Birmingham News*, 30 September 1926.
70. Clark and Riley, *The Negro Leagues Book*, 160–62.

Chapter 7

1. *Birmingham News*, 12 September 1926.
2. *Ibid.*, 17 April 1927.
3. *Birmingham News*, 17 April 1927.
4. *Birmingham Reporter*, 29 April 1927.
5. *Birmingham News*, 19 April 1927.
6. *Ibid.*, 20 April 1927.
7. *Ibid.*, 21 April 1927.
8. *Ibid.*, 22 April 1927.
9. *Ibid.*, 24 April 1927.
10. *Ibid.*, 26 April 1927.
11. *Ibid.*, 30 April 1927.
12. *Ibid.*, 1 May 1927.
13. *Ibid.*, 3 May 1927.
14. *Ibid.*, 4 May 1927.
15. *Ibid.*, 5, 6 May 1027.
16. *Birmingham Reporter*, 18 June 1927.
17. *Birmingham News*, 11, 12 May 1927.
18. *Ibid.*, 16, 17, 18 May 1027.
19. *Birmingham News*, 22, 23, 24, 25, 26 May 1927; *St. Louis Post-Dispatch*, 26, 27 May 1927.
20. *Birmingham News*, 27, 30 May 1927.
21. *Ibid.*, 29 May 1927.
22. *Birmingham Reporter*, 18 June 1927.
23. *Birmingham News*, 29 May 1927.
24. *Ibid.*
25. *Ibid.*, 31 May 1927.
26. *Ibid.*, 1, 2, 3 June 1927.
27. *Ibid.*, 5 June 1927.
28. *Ibid.*, 7 June 1927.
29. *Ibid.*, 8 May 1927.
30. *Ibid.*, 9 June 1927.
31. *Ibid.*, 10 June 1927.
32. *Ibid.*, 13 June 1927.
33. *Commercial Appeal*, 13, 14, 16 June 1927; *Birmingham News*, 13 June 1927.
34. *Ibid.*, 19–20 June 1927.
35. *Ibid.*, 26–27 June 1927.
36. *Birmingham Reporter*, 2 July 1927.
37. *Birmingham News*, 6 July 1927.
38. *Ibid.*
39. *Ibid.*, 23 July 1927.
40. *Ibid.*, 30 July 1927.
41. *Ibid.*, 17 July 1927.
42. *Ibid.*, 10 July 1927.
43. *Ibid.*, 12 July 1927.
44. *Commercial Appeal*, 17, 18, 19, 20, 21 July 1921; *Birmingham News*, 17, 20, 22 July 1927.
45. *Birmingham News*, 26, 27, 28 July 1927.
46. *Ibid.*, 28 July 1927.
47. *Birmingham Reporter*, 20 August 1927.
48. *Birmingham News*, 31 July 1927.
49. *Ibid.*, 2 August 1927.
50. *Ibid.*, 3 August 1927.
51. *Ibid.*, 7 August 1927.
52. *Ibid.*, 10 August 1927.
53. *Birmingham Reporter*, 20 August 1927.
54. *Birmingham News*, 14 August 1927.
55. *Ibid.*, 15 August 1927.
56. *Ibid.*, 16 August 1927.
57. *Birmingham Reporter*, 20 August 1927.
58. *Birmingham News*, 27, 28, 29, 30, 31 August, 2 September 1927; *Chicago Tribune*, 28 August, 1 September 1927.
59. *Birmingham News*, 1 September 1927.
60. *Ibid.*
61. *Ibid.*, 4 September 1927.
62. *Ibid.*, 6 September 1927.
63. *Ibid.*, 8 September 1927.
64. *Ibid.*, 9 September 1927.
65. *Ibid.*, 11 September 1927.
66. *Ibid.*, 13 September 1927.
67. *Ibid.*, 14 September 1927.
68. *Ibid.*, 15 September 1927.
69. *Ibid.*, 16 September 1927.
70. *Birmingham Reporter*, 17 September 1927.
71. *Ibid.*
72. *Birmingham News*, 18 September 1927.
73. *Ibid.*, 20 September 1927.
74. *Ibid.*, 21 September 1927.
75. *Birmingham Reporter*, 24 September 1927.
76. *Ibid.*, 24–25 September 1927.
77. Clark and Lester, *The Negro Leagues*, 164.
78. *Birmingham Reporter*, 1 October 1927.

Chapter 8

1. *Birmingham News*, 17 May, 13 June, 17 August 1928.
2. *Ibid.*, 23 June 1928.
3. *Ibid.*, 14 April 1928.
4. *Ibid.*, 22 September 1928.
5. *Pittsburgh Courier*, 7 April 1928.
6. *Birmingham Reporter*, 14 April 1928.
7. *Ibid.*, 22 September 1928.
8. *Birmingham Reporter*, 21 April 1928; *Birmingham News*, 20 April 1928.
9. *Birmingham Reporter*, 28 April 1928; *Birmingham Age-Herald*, 18 April 1928.
10. *Birmingham Reporter*, 5 May 1928; *Birmingham News*, 1 May 1928.
11. *Birmingham Reporter* 12 May 1928; *St. Louis Post-Dispatch*, 29 April, 1–2 May 1928.
12. *Birmingham News*, 6 May 1928; *Chicago Defender*, 12 May 1928.
13. *Birmingham News*, 15 May 1928; *Birmingham Reporter*, 12 May 1928.
14. *Birmingham Reporter*, 12 May 1928.
15. *Birmingham News*, 13 May 1928.
16. *Ibid.*, 15 May 1928.

17. *Ibid.*, 16 May 1928.
18. *Ibid.*, 17 May 1928.
19. *Ibid.*, 22 May 1928.
20. *Ibid.*, 23 May 1928.
21. *Ibid.*, 29 May 1928.
22. *Ibid.*, 30–31 May 1928.
23. *Birmingham Reporter*, 26 May 1928.
24. *Ibid.*, 2 June 1928.
25. Riley, *Biographical Encyclopedia*, 619.
26. *Birmingham Reporter*, 2 June 1928.
27. *Ibid.*, 9 June 1028.
28. *Birmingham News*, 3 June 1928.
29. *Birmingham Reporter*, 30 June 1928.
30. Riley, *Biographical Encyclopedia*, 734.
31. *Birmingham Reporter*, 2 June 1928.
32. *Birmingham News*, 7 June 1928.
33. *Ibid.*, 8 June 1928.
34. *Birmingham News,* 28 June 1928; *Chicago Defender*, 7 July 1928.
35. Riley, *Biographical Encyclopedia*, 537, 730.
36. *Ibid.*, 630.
37. *Chicago Defender*, 21 June 1930; *Birmingham Age-Herald*, 21, 22 June 1928.
38. *Birmingham News*, 12 July 1928.
39. *Ibid.*, 17 July 1928.
40. *Ibid.*, 21 July 1928; *St. Louis Post-Dispatch*, 22 July 1928; *Birmingham Age-Herald*, 2, 23, 24, 25 July 1928.
41. *Birmingham News*, 16 August 1928.
42. *Ibid.*, 21 August 1928.
43. *Ibid.*, 23 August 1928.
44. *Ibid.*
45. *Ibid.*, 27 August 1928.
46. *Ibid.*, 28, 29 August 1928.
47. *Ibid.*, 31 August 1928.
48. *Chicago Defender*, 8 September 1928; *Birmingham News*, 4 September 1928.
49. *Birmingham News*, 9, 10, 11 September 1928; *Detroit Free Press*, 10, 11 September 1928; *Pittsburgh Courier*, 15 September 1928.
50. *Birmingham Reporter*, 1 September 1928.
51. *Ibid.*, 22 September 1928.

Chapter 9

1. *Birmingham News*, 14 April 1929.
2. Clark and Lester, *The Negro Leagues Book*, 160.
3. *Birmingham News*, 14 April 1929; *Chicago Defender*, 2 March 1929; *Birmingham Reporter*, 13 April 1929.
4. *Birmingham Reporter*, 20 April 1929; *Birmingham News*, 14 April 1929.
5. *Birmingham News*, 27 April 1929; *Commercial Appeal*, 27 April 1929.
6. *Birmingham News*, 29 April 1929; *Commercial Appeal*, 28–29 April 1929.
7. *Birmingham Reporter*, 27 April 1929; *Birmingham News*, 28–29 April 1929.
8. *Birmingham News*, 13 July 1932.
9. *Ibid.*, 28 April 1929.
10. *Chicago Defender*, 27 September 1930; Riley, *Biographical Encyclopedia*, 561–2; www.seamheads.com/NegroLgs/player.php?playerID=monta01.est&tab=pit.
11. www.baseball-reference.com/register/player.fcgi?id=montal000est.
12. *Birmingham News*, 29 April 1929.
13. *Birmingham News*, 30 April 1929; *Birmingham Reporter*, May 1929.
14. *Birmingham News*, 3 May 1929.
15. *Commercial Appeal*, 29 April 1929; *Birmingham News*, 6, 8 May 1929.
16. *Ibid.*, 18 May 1929; *Battle Creek Enquirer*, 16–18 May 1929.
17. *Birmingham News*, 21 May 1929; *Detroit Free Press*, 19–21 May 1929.
18. *Birmingham Reporter*, 25 May 1929.
19. *Ibid.*, 15 June 1929.
20. *Ibid.*
21. *Birmingham News*, 26, 27, 28, 29 May 1929; *St. Louis Post-Dispatch*, 26, 28 May 1929.
22. *Birmingham Reporter*, 1 June 1929.
23. *Ibid.*, 8 June 1929; *Pittsburgh Courier*, 29 June 1929.
24. *Ibid.*, 8 June 1929.
25. *Commercial Appeal*, 14 July 1929.
26. *Birmingham News*, 3 September 1929.
27. Riley, *Biographical Encyclopedia*, 537.
28. *Birmingham Reporter*, 8 June 1929; *Chicago Defender*, June 1929; *Birmingham News,* 31 May 1929.
29. *Birmingham News*, 8 June 1929.
30. *Ibid.*
31. *Ibid.*
32. *Ibid.*, 11 June 1929.
33. *Birmingham Reporter*, 15 June 1929.
34. *Birmingham News*, 12 June 1929; Riley, *Biographical Encyclopedia*, 93–94.
35. *Birmingham News*, 16 June 1929.
36. *Birmingham News*, 20 June 1929; *Birmingham Age-Herald*, 22 June 1929.
37. *Ibid.*, *Chicago Defender*, 29 June 1929.
38. *Birmingham News*, 25 June 1929.
39. *Ibid.*, 30 June, 1 July 1929.
40. *Birmingham News,* 28 June 1929; *Pittsburgh Courier*, 27 July 1929.
41. *Pittsburgh Courier*, 3 August 1929.
42. *Birmingham Reporter*, 10 August 1929.
43. *Ibid.*, 17 August 1929.
44. *Ibid.*, 24 August 1929.
45. *Ibid.*, 29 June 1929.
46. *Birmingham Reporter*, 29 June 1929.
47. *Chicago Defender*, 13 July 1929; *Birmingham Age-Herald*, 10 July 1929.
48. *Birmingham Age-Herald*, 15, 22 July 1929; *Birmingham News*, 21 July 1929; *Chicago Defender*, 13, 20, 27 July 1929; *Detroit Free Press*, 15, 17, 19, 21 July 1929.
49. *Birmingham News*, 26 July 1929.
50. *Birmingham Reporter*, 3 August 1929.
51. *Birmingham Reporter*, 3 August 1929.
52. *Detroit Free Press*, 15 July 1929.
53. *Birmingham News*, 7 August 1992.
54. *Ibid.*, 8 August 1929.
55. *Birmingham News*, 18 August 1929; *Chicago Defender*, 18 August 1929; *Detroit Free Press*, 19, 21 August 1929.

Chapter 10

1. *Birmingham Reporter*, 25 January 1930.
2. *Pittsburgh Courier*, 13 December 1930; Riley, *Biographical Encyclopedia*, 292.
3. *Pittsburgh Courier*, ibid.
4. *Birmingham Reporter*, 25 January 1930; Clark and Lester, *The Negro Leagues Book*, 160.
5. *Chicago Defender*, 12 April 1930.
6. *Pittsburgh Courier*, 29 March 1930.

7. *Birmingham Reporter*, 15 March 1930.
8. *Ibid.*, 29 March 1930.
9. *Chicago Defender*, 19 April 1930; *Birmingham News*, 27 April 1930.
10. *Birmingham Reporter*, 29 March 1930.
11. *Chicago Defender*, 26 April 1930; https://emn.wikipedia.org/wiki/Vitaphone, last modified on 15 August 2017.
12. *Birmingham World*, 9 September 1941.
13. *Birmingham Reporter*, 12 April 1930.
14. *Ibid.*, 19 April 1930.
15. *Ibid.*
16. *Birmingham News*, 18 May 1930; Riley, *Biographical Encyclopedia*, 547; Clark and Lester, *The Negro Leagues Book*, 103.
17. *Birmingham Reporter*, 29 March 1930.
18. Clark and Lester, *The Negro Leagues*, 103.
19. Riley, *Biographical Encyclopedia*, 201–02.
20. *Birmingham Reporter*, 26 April 1930.
21. *Birmingham News*, 29 April 1930; *Birmingham Reporter*, 3 May 1930.
22. *Ibid.*, 30 April, 1 May 1930; *Ibid.*, 3 May 1930.
23. *Birmingham News*, 2 May 1930.
24. *Ibid.*, 18 May 1930.
25. *Commercial Appeal*, 11 May 1930.
26. *Nashville Tennessean*, 14 May 1930.
27. *Ibid.*, 14–15 May 1930.
28. *Ibid.*, 15 May 1930.
29. *Pittsburgh Courier*, 7 June 1930.
30. *Birmingham News*, 18 June 1930.
31. *Birmingham News*, 23–24, 26–27 May 1930; *Birmingham Reporter*, 17 May 1930.
32. *Birmingham News*, 22 May 1930.
33. *Birmingham Reporter*, 24 May 1930.
34. *Ibid.*
35. *St. Louis Post-Dispatch*, 30–31 May 1930; *Birmingham Reporter*, 31 May 1930; *Birmingham News*, 30–31 May, 1 June 1930; *Chicago Defender*, 7 June 1930; *Birmingham Age-Herald*, 30, 31 May 1930.
36. *Birmingham News*, 1 June 1930; *Chicago Defender*, 7 June 1930; *Birmingham Age-Herald*, 2 July 1930.
37. *Birmingham Reporter*, 31 May 1930.
38. Riley, *Biographical Encyclopedia*, 134.
39. *Commercial Appeal*, 27 June 1930.
40. *Birmingham Reporter*, 31 May 1930.
41. Riley, *Biographical Encyclopedia*, 706.
42. *Birmingham Reporter*, 14 June 1930; *Birmingham Age-Herald*, 9, 10 June 1930.
43. *Ibid.*, 28 June 1930.
44. *Chicago Defender*, 14 June 1930.
45. *Battle Creek Enquirer*, 13, 14 June 1930; *Chicago Defender*, 14 June 1930; *Detroit Free Press*, 15, 16, 18 June 1930; *Birmingham Age-Herald*, 16, 17, 18 June 1930.
46. *Pittsburgh Courier*, 28 June 1930; Riley, *Biographical Encyclopedia*, 537, 630.
47. *Chicago Defender*, 21 June 1930.
48. *Commercial Appeal*, 26 June 1930.
49. *Birmingham News*, 24, 25, 26, 27 June 1930.
50. *Chicago Defender*, 12 July 1930.
51. *Ibid.*, 19 July 1930.
52. *Birmingham News*, 16 July 1930; *Birmingham Reporter*, 19 July 1930.
53. *Birmingham News*, 19 July 1930; *Birmingham Reporter*, July 1930.
54. *Birmingham News*, 23 July 1930; *Birmingham Reporter*, 26 July 1930.
55. *Birmingham News*, 24 July 1930; *Birmingham Reporter*, 26 May 1930.
56. *Birmingham News*, 25 July 1930.
57. Riley, *Biographical Encyclopedia*, 598.
58. *Birmingham News*, 30 July 1930; *Birmingham Reporter*, 2 August 1930.
59. *Birmingham News*, 6 August 1930.
60. *Chicago Defender*, 3 August 1930.
61. *Birmingham News*, 3, 7, 8 August 1930; *Birmingham Reporter*, 9 August 1930.
62. *Chicago Defender*, 16 August 1930.
63. *Birmingham Reporter*, 23 August 1930.
64. *Ibid.*, 2 July 1930.
65. *Birmingham News*, 3 September 1903; *Birmingham Reporter*, 6 September 1930.

Chapter 11

1. Clark and Lester, *The Negro Leagues Book*, 161–62.
2. Plott, *The Negro Southern League*, 82.
3. *Arkansas Gazette*, 28 June, 12 July 1931.
4. *Birmingham News*, 31 March 1931.
5. *Birmingham Reporter*, 7 March 1931; *Chicago Defender*, 14 March 1931.
6. *Birmingham News*, 3 March 1931.
7. *Birmingham Reporter*, 21 March 1931.
8. *Commercial Appeal*, 5 April 1931.
9. *Birmingham News*, 19 April 1931.
10. *Ibid.*, 26 April 1931; *Birmingham Reporter*, 11, 25 April 1931.
11. *Commercial Appeal*, 22 July 1931.
12. *Birmingham News*, 19 April 1931.
13. *Ibid.*, 26 April 1931.
14. *Ibid.*
15. *Birmingham Post-Herald*, 17 May 1962.
16. Riley, *Biographical Encyclopedia*, 784–85.
17. *Birmingham News*, 28 April 1931.
18. *Ibid.*
19. *Birmingham News*, 28 April 1931.
20. Riley, *Biographical Encyclopedia*,784–85.
21. *Birmingham News*, 29 April 1931.
22. Dickson, *The Dickson Baseball Dictio*nary, 763.
23. *Birmingham Reporter*, 2 May 1931.
24. *Alabama Journal*, 3 April 1931.
25. *Montgomery Advertiser*, 1 May 1931.
26. *Montgomery Advertiser*, 2 May 1931; *Alabama Journal*, 4, 5, 6, 7 May 1931; *Birmingham Reporter*, 16 May 1931; *Chattanooga Daily Times*, 15, 16, 17 May 1931.
27. *Birmingham Reporter*, 16 May 1931
28. *Birmingham News*, 17 May 1931.
29. *Birmingham Reporter*, 16 May 1931.
30. *Birmingham News*, 19 May 1931.
31. *Ibid.*; *Birmingham Reporter*, 23 May 1931.
32. *Ibid.*, 20 May 1931; *Birmingham Reporter*, 23 May 1931.
33. *Ibid.*, 24 April 1931.
34. *Birmingham News*, 24 May 1931.
35. *Birmingham Reporter*, 30 May 1931.
36. *Ibid.*, 2 June 1931.
37. *Birmingham Reporter*, 6 June 1931.
38. *Arkansas Gazette*, 4, 5 June 1931.
39. *Ibid.*, 13, 14 June 1931.
40. *Chicago Defender*, 4 July 1931.
41. *Arkansas Gazette*, 28 June 1931.
42. *Chicago Defender*, 20 June 1931.
43. *Commercial Appeal*, 15, 16 June 1931; *Detroit Free Press*, 20, 21, 22, 23, 24 June 1931; *Chattanooga Daily Times*, 29 June 1931.

44. *Alabama Journal*, 17 June 1931; *Birmingham Reporter*, 27 June 1931.
45. *Birmingham Reporter*, 27 June 1931; https://en.wikipedia.org/wiki/Cramton_Bowl, last modified on 12 August 2017.
46. *Commercial Appeal*, 5, 6 July 1931.
47. *Birmingham News*, 28 June 1931; *Birmingham Reporter*, 4 July 1931.
48. *Birmingham Reporter*, 11 July 1931.
49. www.encyclopediaofalabama.org/article/h-2392.
50. *Birmingham News*, 15 July 1931.
51. *Pittsburgh Courier*, 18 July 1931.
52. *Birmingham News*, 19 July 1931; *Birmingham Reporter*, 25 July 1931.
53. *Nashville Banner*, 27 July 1931.
54. *Ibid.*, 13, 14 August 1931.
55. *Birmingham News*, 2 August 1931.
56. *Birmingham Reporter*, 8 August 1931.
57. *Nashville Tennessean*, 24 July, 26 August 1931.
58. *Commercial Appeal*, 9, 18 September 1931.
59. *Ibid.*, 21 September 1931.
60. *Nashville Tennessean*, 26 August 1931.
61. *Ibid.*, 1 September 1931.
62. *Monroe Star-News*, 7, 8, 9, 10 September 1931.

Chapter 12

1. Clark and Lester, *The Negro Leagues Book*, 161–64.
2. Plott, *The Negro Southern League*, 91.
3. Riley, *Biographical Encyclopedia*, 186.
4. *Birmingham Reporter*, 16 January 1932; Certificate of Death, Alabama Center for Health Statistics, 17 January 1932, official copy issued on 27 August 1998.
5. *Birmingham Reporter*, 16 January 1932.
6. *Ibid.*, 9 April 1932; *Chicago Defender*, 12, 19 April 1932.
7. *Commercial Appeal*, 23, 24, 25 April 1932.
8. *Chicago Defender*, 7 May 1932; *Courier-Journal*, 30 April, 1, 2, 3, 4 May 1932.
9. *Chicago Defender*, 14 May 1932.
10. *Pittsburgh Courier*, 9 July 1932.
11. *Commercial Appeal*, 12 May 1932.
12. *Birmingham Reporter*, 7 May 1932.
13. *Montgomery Advertiser*, 14, 15, 16, 17 May 1932.
14. *Ibid.*, 14, 15, 16, 17, 18 May 1932.
15. Riley, *Biographical Encyclopedia*. 50–54.
16. *Ibid.*, 52.
17. *Ibid.*, 51.
18. *Ibid.*, 52.
19. *Ibid.*
20. *Monroe News-Star*, 22 May 1932.
21. *Ibid.*, 21, 22, 23 May 1932.
22. *Birmingham Age-Herald*, 25 May 1932.
23. *Pittsburgh Press*, 29 May 1932; *Chicago Defender*, 4 June 1932; *Cleveland Plain Dealer*, 30, 31 May 1932.
24. *Chicago Defender*, 6 August 1932.
25. *Ibid.*, 27 August 1932.
26. *Pittsburgh Courier*, 4 June 1932.
27. Clark and Lester, *The Negro Leagues Book*, 17.
28. *Ibid.*, 26 June 1932.
29. *Monroe Morning World*, 6 July 1932; *Atlanta Daily World*, 6 July 1932; *Chicago Defender*, 9 July 1932.
30. *Atlanta Daily World*, 22 July 1932.
31. *Ibid.*
32. *Chicago Defender*, 23 July 1932.
33. *Pittsburgh Courier*, 9 July 19323; *Atlanta Daily World*, 8 July 1932.
34. *Pittsburgh Courier*, 9 July 1932.
35. *Chicago Defender*, 30 July 1932.
36. *Knoxville News-Sentinel*, 26 June 1932.
37. *Montgomery Advertiser*, 3, 4, 5, 6, July 1932.
38. *Knoxville News-Sentinel*, 26 June 1932.
39. *Chicago Defender*, 30 July 1932.
40. *Montgomery Advertiser*, 13 August 1932.
41. *Ibid.*
42. *Ibid.*, 20 August 1932.
43. *Monroe Morning World*, 6, 9, 19 August 1932.
44. *Ibid.*, 21, 22, 23, 24 August 1932.
45. *Ibid.*, 28, 29, 30, 31 August 1932.
46. *Chicago Defender*, 13 August 1932.
47. *Pittsburgh Courier*, 20 August 1932.
48. *Pittsburgh Courier*, 20 August 1932.
49. *Ibid.*, 19 September, 7 October 1932.
50. *Monroe Star-News*, 11, 12, 13 September 1932.

Chapter 13

1. *Atlanta Daily World*, 8 June 1932.
2. *Chicago Defender*, 22 April 1933.
3. Riley, *Biographical Encyclopedia*, 577; Bob Luke, *The Baltimore Elite Giants: Sport and Society in the Negro Baseball League* (Baltimore: Johns Hopkins University Press, 2009), 24.
4. Plott, *The Negro Southern League*, 105–06.
5. https://en.wikipedia.org/wiki/J_B_Martin, last modified on 13 January 2017.
6. *Commercial Appeal*, 10 May 1933; *Montgomery Advertiser*, 4 May, 28 June 1933.
7. *Chicago Defender*, 8 April 1933.
8. *Birmingham Reporter*, 15 April 1933.
9. *Chicago Defender*, 20 May 1933; *Montgomery Advertiser*, 29 July 1933; *Birmingham Reporter*, 29 April 1933.
10. *Birmingham Reporter*, 6 May 1933.
11. *Montgomery Advertiser*, 4 May 1933; Riley, *Biographical Encyclopedia*, 534–36.
12. *Montgomery Advertiser*, 4, 5, 6, 7 May 1933.
13. *Commercial Appeal*, 10 May 1933.
14. *Ibid.*, 14 May 1933.
15. *Ibid.*, 15, 16 May 1933.
16. *Chicago Defender*, 20 May 1933.
17. *Commercial Appeal*, 15 May 1933.
18. *Birmingham Reporter*, 27 May 1933.
19. *Ibid.*, 3 June 1933.
20. *Pittsburgh Courier*, 10 June 1933.
21. *Montgomery Advertiser*, 1 July 1933.
22. *Ibid.*, 4 July 1933.
23. *Times-Picayune*, 17, 18, 19 June 1933.
24. *Ibid.*, 20 June 1933.
25. *Montgomery Advertiser*, 29, 30, 31 June 1933.
26. *Times-Picayune*, 5, 6, 7 August 1933.
27. Plott, *The Negro Southern League*, 106.
28. *Arkansas Gazette*, 21 April, 21 September 1933.
29. *Monroe Star-News*, 11, 12 April 1933.
30. *Ibid.*, 17 April 1933.
31. *Jackson Clarion-Ledger*, 23 April 1933.
32. *Jackson Clarion-Ledger*, 28 May 1933.
33. *Chicago Defender*, 6 May, 6, 10, 24 June 1933; *Pittsburgh Courier*, 10 June, 8 July 1933.
34. *Pittsburgh Courier*, 7 October 1933.
35. *Commercial Appeal*, 30 June 1933; *Chicago Defender*, 24 June 1933.
36. *Chicago Defender*, 12 August 1933.
37. *Ibid.*

38. *Arkansas Gazette*, 19 August 1933.
39. *Arkansas Gazette*, 9, 10 September 1933.
40. *Chicago Defender*, 26 August 1933.
41. *Times-Picayune*, 3 September 1933.
42. *Ibid.*, 3, 4, 5 September 1933.
43. *Ibid.*, 9 September 1933.
44. *Chicago Defender*, 16 September 1933.
45. *Times-Picayune*, 18 September 1933.9
46. *Ibid.*
47. *Ibid.*, 26 September 1933.

Chapter 14

1. *Pittsburgh Courier*, 3 February 1934; *Birmingham News*, 13 July 1932.
2. *Pittsburgh Courier*, 10 February 1934.
3. *Ibid.*
4. *Ibid.*, 3 February 1934.
5. *Ibid.*, 3 March 1934; *Atlanta Daily World*, 1 April 1934.
6. *Ibid.*, 31 March 1934.
7. *Chicago Defender*, 7 April 1934.
8. *Ibid.*, 7 October 1933.
9. *Times-Picayune*, 21 April 1934.
10. *Birmingham News*, 20 May 1934.
11. *Birmingham Post*, 27 April 1934.
12. *Birmingham News*, 26 April 1934.
13. *Courier Journal*, 17 May 1934.
14. *Birmingham News*, 26 April 1934.
15. *Nashville Globe and Independent*, 30 March 1934; *Pittsburgh Courier*, 31 March 1934.
16. *Birmingham News*, 26 April 1934.
17. *Ibid.*, 28 April 1934.
18. *Ibid.*, 29, 30 April 1934.
19. Riley, *Biographical Encyclopedia*, 75.
20. *Ibid.*, 195.
21. *Ibid.*, 447.
22. *Birmingham News*, 13 May 1934.
23. *Atlanta Daily World*, 6 May 1934.
24. *Ibid.*
25. *Birmingham News*, 14, 1 May 1934.
26. *Ibid.*, 15 May 1934.
27. *Ibid.*, 16 May 1934.
28. Riley, *Biographical Encyclopedia*, 619; https://www.baseball-reference.com/register/players.fcgi?id=perkin000bil.
29. *Atlanta Daily World*, 21 April 1934.
30. *Ibid.*, 5, 6, 8 May 1934.
31. *Chicago Defender*, 9 June 1934.

Chapter 15

1. *Pittsburgh Courier*, 6 April 1935; *Chicago Defender*, 6 April 1935.
2. *Chicago Defender*, 13 April 1935.
3. www.athletics.morehouse.edu/sports/2010/11/22/btharvey.aspx?id=10.
4. *Atlanta Daily World*, 28 June 1936.
5. *Ibid.*, 18 April 1935.
6. *Birmingham News*, 28 April 1935.
7. *Atlanta Daily World*, 10 April 1935.
8. *Ibid.*
9. *Ibid.*, 28 April 1935.
10. Plott, *The Negro Southern League*, 127; John Klima, *Willie's Boys: The 1948 Birmingham Black Barons, the Last Negro League World Series, and the Making of*

a Baseball Legend (Hoboken, NJ: John Wiley and Sons, 2009), 20.
11. *Ibid.*, 28 April 1935.
12. *Ibid.*, 30 April 1935.
13. *Ibid.*, 1 May 1935.
14. www.encyclopediaofarkansas.net, last updated on 11 December 2008; Riley, *Biographical Encyclopedia*, 648–50.
15. *Chicago Defender*, 2 March 1935.
16. *Chicago Defender*, 22 June 1935; *Times-Picayune*, 13 June 1935.
17. *Atlanta Daily World*, 20 March 1935.
18. *Ibid.*, 18 April 1935.
19. *Ibid.*, 3 June 1935.
20. *Ibid.*, 4 June 1935.
21. *Birmingham News*, 1 May 1935.
22. *Alabama Journal*, 27 April 1935.
23. *Birmingham News*, 3 May 1935.
24. Luke, *The Baltimore Elite Giants*, 16; *Pittsburgh Courier*, 16 February 1935.
25. *Birmingham News*, 1 May 1935.
26. *Ibid.*, 3 May 1935.
27. *Ibid.*, 19 May 1935.
28. *Atlanta Daily World*, 17, 18, 19 May 1935.
29. *Ibid.*, 17 May 1935.
30. *Ibid.*, 18 May 1935.
31. *Ibid.*
32. *Ibid.*, 19 May 1935.
33. *Birmingham News*, 20 May 1935.
34. *Ibid.*, 3 June 1935.
35. *Montgomery Advertiser*, 28 August 1935.
36. *Ibid.*, 28 August 1935.
37. *Ibid.*, 29 August 1935.
38. *Atlanta Daily World*, 12 March 1935.
39. *Chicago Defender*, 27 July 1935.
40. *Chattanooga Daily Times*, 23 June 1935.
41. *Chattanooga Daily Times*, 2 September 1935; *Atlanta Daily World*, 12 March 1935.
42. *Monroe Star-News*, 26 May 1935.
43. *Atlanta Daily World*, 18 June 1935.
44. *Ibid.*, 2 September 1935.
45. *Ibid.*, 21 June 1935.
46. *Ibid.*, 28 August 1935.
47. *Monroe Star-News*, 20 September 1935.
48. *Atlanta Daily World*, 2 September 1935.
49. *Ibid.*
50. *Ibid.*, 7 September 1935.
51. *Atlanta Daily World*, 14 September 1935; *Pittsburgh Courier*, 28 September 1935; Clark and Lester, *The Negro Leagues Book*, 115–17.
52. *Atlanta Daily World*, 16 September 1935.
53. *Ibid.*
54. *Ibid.*, 3 October 1935.

Chapter 16

1. *Birmingham News*, 10, 12 June 1936.
2. Riley, *Biographical Encyclopedia*, 807.
3. *Birmingham World*, 20 August 1948.
4. www.wikipedia.org/wiki/Numbers_game, last modified 2 January 2017.
5. *Ibid.*
6. *Ibid.*
7. Holway, *The Complete Book of Baseball's Negro Leagues*, 361, 364.
8. www.ancestry.com, 1940 United States Federal Census.

9. *Birmingham News*, 5 April 1936.
10. *Ibid.*
11. *Ibid.*
12. *Ibid.*, 19 April 1936.
13. *Chicago Defender*, 11 April 1936.
14. *Ibid.*, 4 April 1936.
15. *Birmingham News*, 5 April 1936.
16. *Nashville Banner*, 24 April 1936.
17. *Chicago Defender*, 11 April 1936.
18. *Atlanta Daily World*, 15 April 1936.
19. *Ibid.*, 3 May 1936.
20. *Ibid.*, 12 May 1936.
21. *Ibid.*, 14 May 1936.
22. *Chattanooga Daily Times*, 26 April 1936.
23. *Nashville Banner*, 15 May 1936.
24. *Kentucky New-Era*, 8 June 1936.
25. Riley, *Biographical Encyclopedia*, 129–30; *Birmingham News*, 19 April 1936.
26. *Birmingham News*, 19 April 1936.
27. *Ibid.*
28. Riley, *Biographical Encyclopedia*, 395–97.
29. https://www.baseball-refernce.com/register/player.fcgi?id=howard000er; https://www.baseball-refrence.com/register/players.fcgi?id=howard00wil.
30. https://www.semheads.com/NegroLgs/players.php?ID=2412.
31. *Montgomery Advertiser*, 18 April 1936.
32. *Ibid.*, 19 April 1936.
33. *Birmingham News*, 26 April 1936.
34. *Ibid.*, 27 April 1936.
35. *Ibid.*, 3 May 1936.
36. *Ibid.*
37. *Ibid.*, 7 May 1936.
38. *Ibid.*, 10 May 1936.
39. *Ibid.*, 8, 10 May 1936.
40. *Ibid.*, 11 May 1936.
41. *Ibid.*, 11 May 1936.
42. Riley, *Biographical Encyclopedia*, 831–32.
43. *Birmingham News*, 12 May 1936.
44. *Ibid.*, 15 May 1936.
45. *Ibid.*, 14 May 1936
46. *Ibid.*, 15 May 1936.
47. *Atlanta Daily World*, 18 May 1936.
48. *Birmingham News*, 22 May 1936.
49. *Atlanta Daily World*, 20 May 1936.
50. Riley, *Biographical Encyclopedia*, 828.
51. *Birmingham News*, 25 May 1936.
52. *Commercial Appeal*, 11 May 1936; *Nashville Tennessean*, 15 May 1936.
53. *Birmingham News*, 28 May 1936.
54. *Atlanta Daily World*, 29 May 1936.
55. *Birmingham News*, 31 May 1936.
56. *Ibid.*, 31 May 1936.
57. *Ibid.*
58. *Ibid.*, 10, 12 June 1936.
59. *Ibid.*, 14 June 1936.
60. *Ibid.*
61. *Ibid.*
62. *Ibid.*, 15 June 1936.
63. *Ibid.*, 16 June 1936.
64. *Atlanta Daily World*, 12 July 1936.
65. *Ibid.*, 30 August 1936.
66. *Birmingham News*, 9 July 1936.
67. *Ibid.*, 10 June 1936.
68. *Atlanta Daily World*, 1 August 1936.
69. *Ibid.*, 16 July 1936.
70. *Birmingham News*, 2 August 1936.
71. *Ibid.*, 3 August 1936.
72. *Ibid.*, 17 August 1936.
73. *Ibid.*, 3 May 1936.
74. *Montgomery Advertiser*, 11 April 1936.
75. *Ibid.*, 13 April 1936.
76. *Ibid.*, 11 May 1936.
77. *Ibid.*, 24 June 1936.
78. *Ibid.*

Chapter 17

1. Clark and Lester, *The Negro Leagues Book*, 17, 161–62.
2. *Chicago Defender*, 29 June 1940.
3. *Pittsburgh Courier*, 31 October 1936.
4. *Ibid.*
5. *Chicago Defender*, 12 February 1937.
6. *Birmingham News*, 21 March 1937.
7. *Ibid.*, 25 April 1937.
8. *Ibid.*, 26 April 1937.
9. *Ibid.*, 9 May 1937.
10. *Ibid.*, 16 May 1937.
11. *Ibid.*, 17 May 1937.
12. *Chicago Defender*, 29 May, 5 June, 10 July 1937.
13. *Ibid.*, 17 July 1937.
14. *Ibid.*, 21 August 1938.
15. https://en.wikipedia.org/wiki/St._Louis_Stars_(baseball), last modified on 15 November 2016; Riley, *Biographical Encyclopedia*, 736.
16. *Chicago Tribune*, 22, 23, 24, 25 May 1937; *Call*, 5 June 1937.
17. *Ibid.*, 5 June 1937.
18. *Birmingham News*, 7 June 1937.
19. *Ibid.*, 27 June 1937; *Pittsburgh Courier*, 26 June 1937.
20. *Birmingham News*, 27 June 1937.
21. *Ibid.*, 5 July 1937.
22. *Chicago Defender*, 10 July 1937.
23. *Birmingham News*, 28 June 1937.
24. *Ibid.*, 5, 6, July 1937; *Chicago Defender*, 10 July 1937.
25. *Birmingham News*, 16, 19 July 1937.
26. *Ibid.*, 15 August 1937.
27. *Ibid.*, 16, 17 August 1937.
28. *Chicago Defender*, 14 August 1937.
29. Holway, *The Complete Book of Baseball's Negro Leagues*, 341–43.
30. *Chicago Defender*, 17 July 1937.
31. *Ibid.*, 7 August 1937.
32. *Ibid.*, 14 August 1937.
33. *Birmingham News*, 23 August 1937; *Pittsburgh Courier*, 14 August 1937.
34. *Birmingham News*, 1 May 1938.
35. *Ibid.*, 29 April 1938.
36. *Birmingham World*, 22 July 1961.
37. *Ibid.*
38. *Birmingham News*, 12 July 1924.
39. *Pittsburgh Courier*, 18 April 1936.
40. https://www.baseball-reference.com/register/team.cgi?id=cb2f294d.
41. *Birmingham News*, 22 May 1938.
42. *Chicago Defender*, 26 March 1938.
43. *Ibid.*, 26 February 1938.
44. *Birmingham News*, 1 May 1938.
45. *Chicago Defender*, 26 February 1938.
46. Riley, *Biographical Encyclopedia*, 406–07, 629–30.
47. *Birmingham News*, 1 May 1938.
48. *Ibid.*, 29 April 1938.

49. https://baseball-referencecom/register/player.rcgi?id=Dunkin000esc.

50. *Birmingham News*, 2 May 1938.

51. *Birmingham Age-Herald*, 9, 10 May 1938.

52. *Chicago Defender*, 2 April 1938.

53. *Ibid.*, 16 April 1938.

54. *Birmingham Age-Herald*, 6 May 1938.

55. *Atlanta Daily World*, 16 May 1938.

56. *Birmingham News*, 23 May 1938.

57. *Ibid.*

58. *Birmingham Age-Herald*, 30 May 1938.

59. *Chicago Defender*, 11 June 1938; *Birmingham Age-Herald*, 6 June 1938.

60. *Chicago Defender*, 18 June 1938.

61. *Ibid.*

62. *Ibid.*, 20 June 1938.

63. *Birmingham News*, 20, 21 June 1938; *Birmingham Age-Herald*, 20 June 1938; *Chicago Defender*, 25 June 1938.

64. *Birmingham News*, 21 June 1938.

65. *Chicago Defender*, 2 July 1938.

66. *Ibid.*, 30 July 1938.

67. *Ibid.*, 6 August 1938.

68. *Ibid.*, 13 August 1938; *Birmingham News*, 8 August 1938.

69. *Chicago Defender*, 2 July 1938.

70. *Ibid.*, 9 July 1938.

71. *Ibid.*

72. *Ibid.*, 23 July 1938.

73. *Ibid.*, 30 July 1938.

74. *Ibid.*, 20 August 1938.

75. Larry Lester, *Black Baseball's National Showcase: The East–West All-Star Game, 1933–1953* (Lincoln: University of Nebraska Press, 2001), 118–19.

76. *Ibid.*, 27 August 1938.

77. *Ibid.*, 10 September 1938.

78. *Ibid.*

79. *Ibid.*, 17 September 1938.

80. *Ibid.*

81. *Ibid.*, 30 September 1938.

82. *Ibid.*, 1 October 1938.

83. *Ibid.*, 17 December 1938.

84. Brent Kelley, *Voices From the Negro Leagues: Conversations with 52 Baseball Standouts of the Period 1924–1960* (Jefferson, NC: McFarland, 1998), 87.

85. *Birmingham News*, 4 September 1938.

86. *Ibid.*, 832; http://www.baseball-reference.com/register.cgi?id=whatle000dav; Riley, 832.

Chapter 18

1. Riley, *Biographical Encyclopedia*, 786; Holway, *The Complete Book of Baseball's Negro Leagues*, 359.

2. *Birmingham News*, 29 April 1939.

3. *Ibid.*, 1, 5, 13 August 1939, 8 September 1939.

4. *Ibid.*, 17 December 1939.

5. *Chicago Defender*, 20 January, 3 February 1940.

6. *Chicago Defender*, 20 April 1940.

7. *Birmingham News*, 8 May 1940.

8. *Ibid.*

9. *Ibid.*, 12 May 1940.

10. *Ibid.*

11. *Ibid.*, 13, 14 May 1940.

12. Riley, *Biographical Encyclopedia*, 562.

13. https://www.baseball-reference.com/register/plyer.fcgi?id=moody-002fra; https://baseball=reference.com//register/team.cgi?id=fc7525ed.

14. *Birmingham News*, 13 May 1940.

15. *Ibid.*, 19 May 1940

16. *Ibid.*, 20 May 1940.

17. *Ibid.*, 3, 4 June 1940.

18. *Chicago Defender*, 15 June 1940.

19. *Ibid.*, 22 June 1940; Riley, *Biographical Encyclopedia*, 765.

20. *Birmingham News*, 23 June 1940.

21. *Ibid.*, 24 June 1940.

22. *Ibid.*, 26, 27 June 1940.

23. *Ibid.*, 1 July 1940; *Chicago Defender*, 6 July 1940.

24. Riley, *Biographical Encyclopedia*, 629, 786; DeBono, *The Indianapolis ABCs*, 117; *Chicago Defender*, 6 July 1940.

25. *Birmingham News*, 6 July 1940.

26. Riley, *Biographical Encyclopedia*, 559.

27. *Birmingham News*, 5, 6 July 1940.

28. *Ibid.*, 8 July 1940; *Chicago Defender*, 20, 27 July 1940.

29. *Chicago Defender*, 27 July 1940

30. *Birmingham News*, 29 July 1940.

31. *Ibid.*, 5 August 1940; *Chicago Defender*, 10 August 1940.

32. Lester, *Black Baseball's National Showcase*, 151.

33. *Birmingham News*, 18 August 1940.

34. Holway, *The Complete Book of Baseball's Negro Leagues*, 375.

35. Riley, *Biographical Encyclopedia*, 764.

36. *Chicago Defender*, 13 February 1943.

37. *Birmingham News*, 2 May 1941.

38. *Birmingham World*, 1 April 1941.

39. *Ibid.*, 7 March 1941.

40. *Ibid.*, 25 April 1941; *Pittsburgh Courier*, 26 April 1941.

41. *Birmingham World*, 2 April 1941.

42. *Ibid.*, 30 May 1941.

43. *Birmingham News*, 5 May 1941.

44. *Birmingham World*, 2 May 1941.

45. *Birmingham News*, 13 May 1941.

46. *Birmingham World*, 1 May 1941.

47. *Birmingham News*, 15, 22, 23 May 1941.

48. *Birmingham World*, 23 May 1941.

49. *Birmingham News*, 26 May 1941; *Birmingham World*, 27 May 1941.

50. *Birmingham World*, 1 May 1941.

51. *Ibid.*, 6 June 1941.

52. *Ibid.*, 9 June 1941.

53. *Ibid.*, 11 June 1941.

54. *Ibid.*, 27 June 1941.

55. *Ibid.*, 30 June 1941.

56. *Ibid.*, 2 July 1941.

57. *Ibid.*, 5 July 1941.

58. *Daily Times*, 5 July 1941; *Winnipeg Tribune*, 17, 21, 22 July 1941; *Minneapolis Star*, 15 July 1941.

59. *Birmingham World*, 22 August 1941.

60. *Star Tribune*, 16 August 1941.

61. Lester, *Black Baseball's National Showcase*, 169; *Pittsburgh Courier*, 26 July 1941.

62. *Birmingham News*, 27 July 1941.

63. *Ibid.*, 28 July 1941.

64. *Ibid.*, 29 July 1941.

65. *Ibid.*, 1 August 1941.

66. *Birmingham News*, 17 August 1941; *Birmingham World*, 25 July 1941.

67. *Birmingham World*, 26 August 1941.

68. *Ibid.*, 22 August 1941.

69. *Ibid.*, 2 September 1941.

70. *Birmingham News*, 14 September 1941.

71. Clark and Lester, *The Negro Leagues Book*, 129, 165; Holway, *The Complete Book of Baseball's Negro Leagues*, 383.

72. *Birmingham World*, 7 April 1942.

73. *Ibid.*, 5 June 1942.

74. *Ibid.*, 21 September 1941.

75. https://www.baseball-reference.com/register/team.cgi?id=79022e9e; Holway, T*he Complete Book of Baseball's Negro Leagues*, 384.

Chapter 19

1. *Birmingham News*, 5 April 1942.

2. *Ibid.*, 8 May 1942.

3. *Ibid.*, 27 July 1942.

4. *Ibid.*, 30 July 1942.

5. *Chicago Defender*, 3 January 1942.

6. *Birmingham World*, 7 April 1942.

7. *Birmingham News*, 5 April 192.

8. Holway, *The Complete Book of Baseball's Negro Leagues*, 392.

9. *Birmingham World*, 10 May 1942.

10. *Birmingham News*, 20 April 1942.

11. *Ibid.*, 3 May 1942.

12. *Pittsburgh Courier*, 16 May 1942.

13. *Birmingham News*, 9 May 1942; *Birmingham World*, 8 May 1942; *Birmingham Age-Herald*, 8 May 1942.

14. *Birmingham News*, 9 May 1942.

15. *Birmingham World*, 12 May 1942.

16. *Birmingham News*, 11 May 1942; *Birmingham World*, 12 May 1942.

17. *Chicago Defender*, 23 May 1942.

18. *Birmingham News*, 11 May 1942.

19. *Birmingham World*, 2 June 1942.

20. https://en.wikipedia.org/wiki/Lyman_Bostock_Sr., last modified on 22 April 2016 at 17:34.

21. http://seamheads.com/NegroLgs/player.php?playerID=gilya0lut.

22. http://search.ancstry.com/cgi-bin/sse.dll?_phsrc=nZb29&_phstart=successSource&usePUBJs=true&gss=angs-g&new=1&rank=1&msT=1&gsfn=luther&gsfn_..]

23. *Birmingham News*, 17 May 1942.

24. *Ibid.*, 18 May 1942.

25. *Ibid.*, 7 June 1942.

26. *Ibid.*, 8 June 1942.

27. *Ibid.*, 28 June 1942.

28. www.ameshistory.org/exhibits/evens/rationing.htm.

29. *Birmingham News*, 28 June 1942.

30. *Ibid.*, 3 July 1942.

31. *Ibid.*

32. *Ibid.*, 5 July 1942.

33. *Ibid.*, 6 July 1942.

34. *Birmingham World*, 7 July 1942.

35. *Birmingham News*, 18 July 1942.

36. *Ibid.*, 20 July 1942.

37. *Birmingham World*, 14, 24 July 1942.

38. *Birmingham World*, 7 August 1942.

39. *Birmingham News*, 26 July 1942.

40. *Ibid.*, 27 July 1942.

41. *Ibid.*, 23 August 1942.

42. *Ibid.*, 17 August 1942.

43. *Ibid.*, 24 August 1942.

44. *Ibid.*, 17 September 192.

45. *Ibid.*, 20 September 1942.

46. *Ibid.*, 21 September 1942.

47. *Ibid.*, 27 September 1942.

48. *Birmingham News*, 27 September 1942.

49. *Ibid.*, 28 September 1942.

50. *Ibid.*, 4 October 1942.

51. www.baseballinwartime.com/negro.htm.

52. *Chicago Defender*, 13 February 1943.

53. *Montgomery Advertiser*, 17 May 1943.

54. *Chicago Defender*, 13 February 1943.

55. *Ibid.*, 6 March 1943.

56. *Ibid.*

57. *Ibid.*, 13 March 1943; *Pittsburgh Courier*, 13, 20 March 1943.

58. *Chicago Defender*, 3 April 1943.

59. *Ibid.*, 15 May 1943.

60. Clark and Lester, *The Negro Leagues Book*, 163.

61. *Birmingham News*, 6 June 1943.

62. *Birmingham World*, 30 March 1943.

63. *Pittsburgh Courier*, 3 April 1943.

64. *Ibid.*

65. *Birmingham News*, 2 May 1943.

66. *Birmingham News*, 3 May 1943.

67. *Ibid.*

68. *Ibid.*, 4 May 1943.

69. *Ibid.*, 7 May 1943.

70. *Montgomery Advertiser*, 8 May 1943.

71. *Pittsburgh Courier*, 1 May 1943.

72. *Ibid.*, 8 May 1943.

73. *Ibid.*, 12 June, 3 July 1943.

74. *Cincinnati Enquirer*, 17 May 1938.

75. *Birmingham News*, 24 May 1943; *Pittsburgh Courier*, 29 May 1943.

76. *Birmingham News*, 30 May 1943.

77. *Ibid.*

78. *Birmingham News*, 31 May 1943.

79. *Ibid.*, 6 June 1943.

80. *Ibid.*, 7 June 1943.

81. *Ibid.*, 11 June 1943.

82. *Ibid.*, 6 June 1943.

83. *Ibid.*, 14 June 1943.

84. *Ibid.*, 3 July 1943.

85. *Chicago Tribune*, 21 June 1943.

86. *Ibid.*, 5 July 1943.

87. *Birmingham News*, 25 July 1943.

88. *Ibid.*

89. *Ibid.*, 26 July 1943.

90. *Ibid.*, 30 July 1943.

91. *Ibid.*, 30 July, 2 August 1943; www.uso.org/history.aspx; *Pittsburgh Courier*, 14 August 1943.

92. Lester, *Black Baseball's National Showcase*, 220.

93. *Birmingham News*, 1 August 1943.

94. *Ibid.*, 2 August 193.

95. *Winnipeg Tribune*, 9, 10, 11, 12 August 1943; *Minneapolis Star*, 6, 9 August 1943; *Minneapolis Star-Tribune*, 11, 12, 13 August 1943.

96. *Ibid.*, 16 August 1943.

97. *Ibid.*, 20 August 1943.

98. Clark and Lester, *The Negro Leagues Book*, 125–30; *Birmingham News*, 22 August 1943.

99. *Birmingham News*, 23 August 1943; *Birmingham Age-Herald*, 23 August 1943.

100. Riley, *Biographical Encyclopedia*, 632–33.

101. *Birmingham News*, 30 August 1943.

102. *Ibid.*, 10 September 1943.

103. *Ibid.*, 14 September 1943.

104. *Ibid.*, 15, 16, 18 September 1943; *Pittsburgh Courier*, 25 September 1943.

105. *Birmingham News*, 19 September 1943.

106. *Ibid.*

107. Riley, *Biographical Encyclopedia*, 485; Clark and Lester, *The Negro Leagues Book*, 132.
108. *Birmingham News*, 19 September 1943.
109. *Ibid.*, 20 September 1943; *Pittsburgh Courier*, 25 September 1943.
110. *Birmingham News*, 20 September 1943.
111. *Ibid.*, 30 September 193.
112. *Birmingham World*, 23 February 1949.
113. www.wikipedia.org/wiki/Ted_Radcliffe, last modified on 4 April 2014.
114. *Pittsburgh Post-Gazette*, 22 September 1943; *Birmingham News*, 22 September 1943.
115. *Birmingham News*, 24 September 1943; *Baltimore Sun*, 24 September 1943.
116. *Birmingham News*, 25 September 1943.
117. *Ibid.*, 27 September 1943; *Pittsburgh Courier*, 2 October 1943.
118. *Birmingham News*, 29 September 1943.
119. *Ibid.*, 30 September 1943; *Indianapolis News*, 30 September 1943.
120. *Birmingham News*, 1, 5, October 1943.
121. *Ibid.*, 3 October 1943.
122. *Ibid.*, 4 October 1943; *Pittsburgh Courier*, 9 October 1943.
123. *Birmingham News*, 6 October 1943.
124. *Ibid.*, 8, 11, 1943.
125. *Pittsburgh Courier*, 2 October 1943.
126. *Ibid.*, 16 October 1943.
127. *Birmingham News*, 1, 7 April 1944.
128. *Birmingham World*, 1 March 1944.
129. Clark and Lester, *The Negro Leagues Book*, 163; *Pittsburgh Courier*, 11 March 1944; *Chicago Defender*, 11 March 1944.
130. *Chicago Defender*, 3, 18 March 1944.
131. *Birmingham World*, 14 March 1944.
132. *Pittsburgh Courier*, 11 March 1944
133. *Ibid.*
134. *Birmingham World*, 21 March 1944; Riley, *Biographical Encyclopedia*, 829.
135. *Pittsburgh Courier*, 8 April 1944.
136. *Birmingham World*, 4 April 1944.
137. *Birmingham News*, 14 April 1944.
138. *Birmingham News*, 3 April 1944; *Birmingham World*, 4 April 1944.
139. *Ibid.*, 10, 17 April 1944; *Birmingham World*, 4, 11 April 1944.
140. *Birmingham News*, 1 May 1944; *Birmingham World*, 2 May 1944.
141. *Pittsburgh Courier*, 13 May 1944.
142. *Birmingham News*, 8 May 1944.
143. *Birmingham News*, 11 May 1944.
144. *Birmingham World*, 9 May 1944.
145. *Ibid.*
146. *Ibid.*, 19 May 1944.
147. *Birmingham News*, 15 May 1944.
148. *Pittsburgh Courier*, 27 May 1944.
149. *Birmingham News*, 29 May 1944; *Birmingham World*, 30 May 1944.
150. *Birmingham World*, 6 June 1944.
151. *Chicago Defender*, 3, 17, 24 June 1944; *Birmingham News*, 5, 8, 10, 12 June 1944; *Birmingham World*, 6 June 1944.
152. *Birmingham World*, 9 June 1944.
153. www.wikipedia.org/wiki/Rationing_in_the_United_States.
154. *Birmingham News*, 26 June 1944.
155. *Birmingham World*, 6 June 1944.
156. *Birmingham News*, 3 July 1944.
157. *Pittsburgh Courier*, 15 July 194.
158. *Chicago Defender*, 22 July 1944.
159. www.wikipedia.org/wiki/Bessie_Smith.
160. *Birmingham World*, 21 July 1944; Riley, *Biographical Encyclopedia*, 571–72.
161. *Ibid.*
162. *Birmingham World*, 1 August 1944.
163. *Ibid.*
164. *Birmingham News*, 30 July 1944.
165. *Ibid.*, 24 July 1944.
166. Holway, *The Complete Book of Baseball's Negro Leagues*, 415; Clark and Lester, *The Negro Leagues Book*, 134.
167. *Birmingham News*, 7 August 1944.
168. *Ibid.*, 18 August 1944.
169. *Ibid.*, 15 August 1944.
170. *Ibid.*, 22 August 1944.
171. *Birmingham News*, 6 September 1944.
172. *Birmingham News*, 19 September 1944; *Chicago Defender*, 16 September 1944.
173. *Chicago Defender*, 9 September 1944.
174. *Pittsburgh Courier*, 16 September 1944.
175. *Birmingham News*, 17 September 1944.
176. *Pittsburgh Courier*, 23 September 1944; Riley, *Biographical Encyclopedia*, 448.
177. *Birmingham News*, 17 September 1944.
178. *Ibid.*, 19 September 1944; *Birmingham World*, 19 September 1944; *Pittsburgh Courier*, 23 September 1944.
179. *Birmingham News*, 20 September 1944; *Chicago Defender*, 30 September 1944.
180. *Birmingham News*, 22 September 1944; *Birmingham World*, 22 September 1944; *Chicago Defender*, 30 September 1944.
181. *Birmingham News*, 24 September 1944; *Pittsburgh Post*, 24 September 1944.
182. *Pittsburgh Courier*, 30 September 1944.
183. *Birmingham News*, 25 September 1944; *Pittsburgh Courier*, 30 September 1944; *Pittsburgh Post-Gazette*, 2 September 1944.
184. *Birmingham World*, 6 October 1944; *Chicago Defender*, 7 October 1944.
185. *Chicago Defender*, 7 October 1944.
186. www.baseballinwartime.com.
187. *Chicago Defender*, 3, 17 March 1945.
188. *Ibid.*, 3 March 1945.
189. *Ibid.*, 3 June 1945.
190. *Birmingham World*, 3 April 1945; *Chicago Defender*, 17 March 1945; *Pittsburgh Courier*, 10 March 1945.
191. *Pittsburgh Courier*, 17 March 1945.
192. *Birmingham News*, 6 April 1945.
193. *Birmingham World*, 24 April 1945.
194. Riley, *Biographical Encyclopedia*, 110–11.
195. *Birmingham World*, 13 March 1945.
196. *Chicago Defender*, 31 March 1945.
197. *Birmingham News*, 2 May 1945.
198. *Birmingham World*, 24 April 1945.
199. *Ibid.*, 11 May 1945.
200. *Ibid.*, 4 May 1945.
201. *Birmingham News*, 7 May 1945.
202. *Birmingham World*, 11 May 1945.
203. *Chicago Defender*, 19, 26 May 1945.
204. *Birmingham News*, 1 June 1945.
205. *Birmingham News*, 20 May 1945.
206. *Ibid.*, 2 June 1945.
207. *Ibid.*, 27 May 1945.
208. *Chicago Defender*, 26 May 1945.
209. *Birmingham News*, 28, 31 May 1945.

210. *Ibid.*, 4 June 1945.
211. *Ibid.*, 6 June 1945.
212. *Atlanta Daily World*, 5 June 1945.
213. *Birmingham News*, 7 June 1945.
214. *Ibid.*, 6, 11 June 1945.
215. William Plott, interview with Willie Young, Birmingham, AL, 16 May 1999.
216. *Chicago Defender*, 16 June 1945.
217. *Ibid.*
218. *Ibid.*, 7 July 1945.
219. *Ibid.*, 14 July 1945.
220. *Birmingham News*, 24 June 1945.
221. *Ibid.*, 16 September 1945.
222. www.wikipedia.org/wiki/Jim_Gilliam, last modified 1 February 2015; www.baseball-reference.com/players/g/gilliji01.shtml.
223. *Birmingham News*, 25 June 1945; *Pittsburgh Courier*, 30 June 1945.
224. *Ibid.*, 30 April 1930.
225. www.pitchblackbaeball.com/nlotmluistiant.html; www.baseball-reference.com/player/t/tiantlu01.shtml; Riley, *Biographical Encyclopedia*. 784–85.
226. *Birmingham News*, 2 July 1945.
227. *Ibid.*, 4 July 1945.
228. *Commercial Appeal*, 5 July 1945.
229. *Birmingham News*, 16 August 1945.
230. Clark and Lester, *The Negro Leagues Book*, 163.
231. *Journal and Guide*, 20 July 1945.
232. *Chicago Defender*, 28 July 1945.
233. *Ibid.*
234. *Birmingham News*, 20 August 1945.
235. *Birmingham World*, 24 August 1945.
236. *Birmingham News*, 16 September 1945.
237. *Ibid.*, 17 September 1945.
238. *Ibid.*, 20 September 1945.
239. Clark and Lester, *The Negro Leagues Book*, 165.
240. *Birmingham News*, 24, 25 September 1945.
241. *Chicago Defender*, 1, 13 October 1945.
242. www.wikipedia/wiki/World_War_II, last modified on 9 February 2015.

Chapter 20

1. *Pittsburgh Courier*, 12 January 1946.
2. *Ibid.*, 5, 26 January 1946.
3. *Ibid.*, 6, 13 April 1946; Riley, *Biographical Encyclopedia*, 638.
4. *Chicago Defender*, 5 January 1946; *Pittsburgh Courier*, 5 January 1946.
5. *Birmingham News*, 7 April 1946.
6. Riley, *Biographical Encyclopedia*, 692–93; http://www.baseball-reference.com/bullpen/Tommy_Sampson; http://coe.k-state.edu/annex/nlbmuseum/history/players/sampson.html.
7. *Birmingham News*, 9 March 1946.
8. *Birmingham World*, 22 January 1946.
9. *Pittsburgh Courier*, 9 March 1946.
10. *Birmingham News*, 9 March 1946.
11. *Birmingham World*, 15 March 1946.
12. *Birmingham News*, 24 March 1946.
13. *Ibid.*, 22 March 1946.
14. *Ibid.*, 30 April 1946.
15. *Birmingham News*, 27 April 1946.
16. Riley, *Biographical Encyclopedia*, 512.
17. *Birmingham News*, 25 March 1946.
18. *Pittsburgh Courier*, 6 April 1946.
19. *Ibid.*

20. William Plott, telephone interview with Al Smith, c. 18 June 1997.
21. *Pittsburgh Courier*, 13 April 1946.
22. https://en.wikipedia.org/wiki/Eddie_Klep, last modified on 29 December 2016.
23. William Plott, telephone interview with Ethel Klep, c. 17 June 1997.
24. *Ibid.*, telephone interview with Joseph Klep, c. 17 June 1997.
25. Chuck Brodsky, "The Ballad of Eddie Klep" from *Letters in the Dirt* (Red House Records, 1999).
26. *Birmingham News*, 7 August 1950.
27. *Chicago Defender*, 20 April 1946.
28. *Birmingham World*, 7 May 1946.
29. *Ibid.*, 30 April 1946.
30. *Ibid.*, 3 May 1946.
31. *Birmingham News*, 6, 7 May 1946; *Pittsburgh Courier*, 11 May 1946.
32. *Birmingham News*, 8 May 1946.
33. *Birmingham World*, 30 April, 3 May 1946.
34. *Ibid.*, 30 April 1946.
35. *Birmingham News*, 9 May 1946.
36. *Birmingham World*, 3 May 1946.
37. *Ibid.*, 10 May 1946; *Birmingham News*, 10 May 1946.
38. *Birmingham News*, 11 May 1946.
39. *Ibid.*
40. *Ibid.*, 12, 13 May 1946.
41. *Birmingham World*, 17 may 1946.
42. http://en.wikipeid.org/wiki/Oscar_Adams, last modified on 27 March 2015.
43. *Commercial Appeal*, 13, 14 May 1946.
44. *Ibid.*, 15 May 1946.
45. *Ibid.*, 17 May 1946.
46. *Ibid.*, 20 May 1946.
47. Riley, *Biographical Encyclopedia*, 770.
48. *Birmingham News*, 27 May 1946.
49. *Birmingham World*, 31 May 1946.
50. *Birmingham News*, 28, 29 May 1946.
51. *Gadsden Times*, 30 May 1946.
52. *Birmingham World*, 4 June 1946; *Birmingham News*, 28 May 1946.
53. *Birmingham News*, 4, 5, 6, 7 June 1946; *Birmingham World*, 4 June 1946.
54. *Birmingham World*, 4 June 1946.
55. *Ibid.*, 4, 7 June 1946.
56. *Birmingham News*, 10 June 1946; *Birmingham World*, 11, 14 June 1946.
57. Plott, *The Negro Southern League*, 145.
58. *Ibid.*, 156.
59. *Montgomery Advertiser*, 1, 4, 5, 6, 11 June 1946.
60. *Birmingham News*, 17 June 1946; *Birmingham World*, 21 June 1946.
61. *Birmingham News*, 24 June 1946.
62. *Birmingham World*, 25 June 1946.
63. *Ibid.*
64. Clark and Lester, *The Negro Leagues Book*, 163; *Birmingham News*, 5 July 1946; *Birmingham World*, 5 July 1946.
65. *Birmingham World*, 9, 12 June 1946.
66. *Ibid.*
67. *Ibid.*, 23 July 1946; *Post-Standard*, 29 July 1946.
68. *Birmingham World*, 16, 19 July 1946.
69. *Ibid.*, 23 July 1946.
70. *Ibid.*, 9 August 1946.
71. *Birmingham News*, 1 August 1946; *Birmingham World*, 12 July, 9 August 1946.
72. *Birmingham News*, 5, 9 August 1946; *Birmingham World*, 13 August 1946.

73. *Birmingham News*, 12 August 1946.
74. *Birmingham World*, 16 August 1946; Lester, *Black Baseball's National Showcase*, 274–79.
75. Lester, *Ibid.*
76. *Birmingham News*, 16 August 1946.
77. *Birmingham World*, 20 August 1946.
78. *Birmingham News*, 19 August 1946.
79. *Ibid.*, 26 August 1946.
80. *Chattanooga Daily Times*, 21 August 1946.
81. *Birmingham World*, 6 September 1946.
82. *Ibid.*, 3, 9 September 1946.
83. *Ibid.*, 8 October 1946; Clark and Lester, *The Negro Leagues Book*, 15.
84. *Birmingham News*, 28 September 146.
85. *Ibid.*, 29 September 1946.
86. *Ibid.*, 25 April 1947.
87. *Ibid.*, 29 September 1946.
88. *Ibid.*, 30 September 1946; *Birmingham World*, 4 October 1946.
89. *Birmingham World*, 11, 15 October 1946.
90. *Ibid.*, 18 October 1946.
91. *Chicago Defender*, 21 September 1946.
92. *Birmingham World*, 6 September 1946.
93. *Ibid.*, 10 January 1947.
94. *Ibid.*, 18 March 1947.
95. *Birmingham News*, 13 April 1947.
96. *Birmingham World*, 7 February 1947.
97. *Ibid.*, 11 March 1947.
98. Clark and Lester, *The Negro Leagues Book*, 162.
99. *Chicago Defender*, 8 March 1947.
100. Riley, *Biographical Encyclopedia*, 697.
101. *Chicago Defender*, 8 March 1947.
102. *Ibid.*, *Pittsburgh Courier*, 8 March 1947.
103. Riley, *Biographical Encyclopedia*, 648.
104. *Birmingham World*, 25 March, 1 April 1947.
105. *Ibid.*, 18 April 1947.
106. *Birmingham News*, 30 April 1947.
107. *Birmingham World*, 1 May 1943.
108. *Ibid.*, 13 May 1947.
109. *Ibid.*, 6, 9 May 1947.
110. *Ibid.* 13 May 1947.
111. *Birmingham News*, 4 May 1947.
112. *Birmingham World*, 13 May 1947.
113. *Birmingham News*, 9 May 1947.
114. *Birmingham World*, 6 May 1947.
115. *Ibid.*, 13 May 1947.
116. *Ibid.*, *Birmingham News*, 11 May 1947.
117. *Birmingham News*, 12 May 1947.
118. *Birmingham World*, 20 May 1947.
119. *Ibid.*
120. *Ibid.*, 20 May 1947; *Chicago Defender*, 24 May 1947; *Pittsburgh Courier*, 24 May 1947.
121. *Birmingham World*, 20 May 1947.
122. *Ibid.*, 27 May 1947.
123. *Birmingham News*, 26 May 1947.
124. *Ibid.*, 29 May 1947.
125. *Ibid.*, 2 June 1947; *Birmingham World*, 3 June 1947.
126. *Birmingham News*, 4 June 1947; *Birmingham World*, 6, 13 June 1947.
127. *Birmingham World*, 17 June 197.
128. *Ibid.*, *Birmingham News*, 16 June 1947.
129. *Birmingham News*, 18, 19, 20 June 1947.
130. *Birmingham World*, 6 June 1947.
131. *Ibid.*, 10, 17 June 1947.
132. *Ibid.*, 20 June 1947.
133. *Ibid.*, 27 June 1947.
134. *Birmingham News*, 27 June 1947.

135. *Birmingham World*, 1, 4 July 1947.
136. *Birmingham News*, 2 July 1947.
137. *Ibid.*, 17 July 1947.
138. *Birmingham World*, 22 July 1947.
139. *Birmingham News*, 5 July 1947.
140. *Birmingham World*, 15 July 1947.
141. *Ibid.*, 11 July 1947; *Birmingham News*, 7 July 1947.
142. *Birmingham News*, 11 July 1947.
143. *Birmingham World*, 21 July 1947.
144. *Ibid.*, 29 July 1947.
145. *Ibid.*, 29 June 1947; Lester, *Black Baseball's National Showcase*, 294.
146. Lester, *Black Baseball's National Showcase*, 301–02.
147. *Birmingham World*, 29, 30 July, 1 August 2947; *Birmingham News,* 30 July 1947.
148. *Birmingham News*, 3 August 1947; http://sabr.org/bioproj/person/211ac89e; www.baseball-reference.com/register/player.cgi?id=hairston001sam.
149. http://sabr.org/bioproj/person/211ac89e.
150. *Birmingham News*, 17 September 1947.
151. http://sabr.org/bioproj/person/211ac89e.
152. www.pitchblackbaseball.com/nlotm_Sam%20Hairston.html.
153. Holway, *The Complete Book of Baseball's Negro Leagues*, 415.
154. Riley, *Biographical Encyclopedia*, 346.
155. https://topic.revolvy.com/topic.Third-generation%20Major%20League%20Baseball%20families&item_type=topic; http://en.wikipedia.org/wiki/Ed_Delahanty, last modified on 4 February 2015, at 22:35.
156. *Birmingham News*, 4 August 1947; *Birmingham World*, 5 August 1947.
157. *Birmingham World*, 8, 12 August 1947.
158. *Ibid.*, 12 August 1947.
159. *Ibid.*, 12, 15 August 1947.
160. *Birmingham News*, 4 August 1947.
161. *Ibid.*, 17 August 1947.
162. *Birmingham World*, 22 August 1947.
163. *Ibid.*, 26 August 1947.
164. *Ibid.*, 29 August 1947.
165. *Ibid.*, 22 August 1947; *Birmingham News* 2, 5 August 1947.
166. Riley, *Biographical Encyclopedia*, 693.
167. *Birmingham World*, 2 September 1947.
168. https://en.wikipedia.org/wiki/Minnie_Minoso; https://baseball-reference.com/register/player.cgi?id=minoso001sat.
169. *Birmingham News*, 14 September 1947.
170. Riley, *Biographical Encyclopedia*, 65–66.
171. *Birmingham News*, 15 September 1947.
172. *Birmingham World*, 10 February 1948; *Pittsburgh Courier*, 14 February 1948.
173. Lester, *Black Baseball's National Showcase*, 295, 302; *Birmingham World*, 29 July 1947.

Chapter 21

1. *Birmingham World*, 20 February 1948; *Pittsburgh Courier*, 10 January 1948.
2. *Birmingham News*, 16 April 1948.
3. *Ibid.*, 23 February 1948; *Pittsburgh Courier*, 28 February 1948.
4. *Birmingham News*, 18 February 1948; *Birmingham World*, 20 February, 19 March 1948.
5. *Birmingham News*, 25 April 1948.
6. *Ibid.*, *Birmingham World*, 30 March 1948.

7. *Birmingham World*, 13 January 1948.

8. Clark and Lester, *The Negro Leagues Book*, 163; *Birmingham World*, 13 January 1948.

9. *Birmingham World*, 13 January 1948

10. *Ibid.*, 16 March 1948.

11. *Ibid.*, 24 February 1948.

12. *Ibid.*, 30 April 1948.

13. *Ibid.*, 27 February 1948.

14. *Ibid.*, 30 March 1948.

15. *Ibid.*, 6 April 1948.

16. *Ibid.*

17. *Ibid.*, 30 April 1948; *Pittsburgh Courier*, 1 May 1948; *Birmingham News*, 2 May 1948.

18. *Birmingham News*, 2 May 1948; *Birmingham World*, 4 May 1948; *Pittsburgh Courier*, 8 May 1948.

19. *Birmingham World*, 27 April 1948; www.baseball-reference.com/nlb/player.cgi?id+longle000ray.

20. *Birmingham News*, 3 May 1948; *Birmingham World*, 4 May 1948.

21. *Ibid.*

22. *Birmingham World*, 7, 11 May 1948.

23. *Birmingham News*, 10 May 1948.

24. *Ibid.*, 14, 16 May 1948.

25. *Ibid.*, 17 May 1948.

26. *Birmingham World*, 21 May 1948.

27. *Birmingham World*, 18 May 1948; *Pittsburgh Courier*, 29 May 1948.

28. *Ibid.*, 21 May 1948.

29. Riley, *Biographical Encyclopedia.*

30. *Birmingham News*, 19 May 1948; *Birmingham World*, 21 May 1948.

31. *Birmingham World*, 21 May 1948.

32. *Chicago Defender*, 29 May 1948.

33. *Birmingham News*, 21 May 1948; *Birmingham World*, 25 May 1948.

34. *Birmingham News*, 24 May 1948; *Birmingham World*, 25 May 1948.

35. *Birmingham News*, 25, 26 May 1948; *Birmingham World*, 28 May 1948.

36. *Birmingham World*, 28 May 1948.

37. *Birmingham News*, 4 June 1948.

38. *Birmingham News*, 27 May 1948; *Birmingham World*, 29 June 1948.

39. *Birmingham World*, 1 June 1948.

40. *Ibid.*

41. *Birmingham News*, 31 May 1948.

42. *Birmingham News*, 2 June 1948; *Times-Picayune*, 3 June 1948; *Birmingham World*, 4 June 1948.

43. *Birmingham News*, 8 June 1948; *Birmingham World*, 8 June 1948.

44. *Pittsburgh Courier*, 5 June 1948.

45. *Birmingham News*, 8, 11 June 1948; *Birmingham World*, 25 June 1948.

46. *Ibid.*, 18 June 1948.

47. *Birmingham News*, 14 June 1948; *Birmingham World*, 18 June 1948.

48. *Birmingham News*, 21 June 1948; *Birmingham World*, 22 June 1948.

49. *Birmingham News*, 22 June 1948.

50. *Ibid.*, 23, 24, 25 June 1948.

51. *Ibid.*, 28 June 1948.

52. *Ibid.*, 2 July 1948.

53. Bill Plott, interview with Piper Davis, Montevallo, AL, 24 February 1983.

54. *Chattanooga Daily Times*, 30 May 1948; Klima, *Willie's Boys*, 94.

55. *Birmingham World*, 20 July 1948.

56. *Ibid.*, 2 July 1948.

57. *Ibid.*

58. *Birmingham News*, 5 July 1948; *Birmingham World*, 6 July 1948.

59. *Birmingham World*, 9 July 1948.

60. *Ibid.*

61. *Birmingham News*, 7, 10 July 1948; *Birmingham World*, 20 July 1948.

62. *Birmingham World*, 20 July 1948; *Birmingham News*, 22 July 1948.

63. *Birmingham World*, 23 July 1948.

64. *Birmingham World*, 27 July 1948.

65. www.baseball-almanac.com.

66. *Times-Picayune*, 10 May 1948.

67. *Birmingham World*, 20 July 1948.

68. *Birmingham World*, 27 July 1948.

69. Riley, *Biographical Encyclopedia*, 407–08.

70. *Birmingham News*, 26 July 1948; *Birmingham World*, 28 July 1948.

71. *Birmingham News*, 29 July 1948; *Birmingham World*, 28 July 1948.

72. *Birmingham News*, 28 July 1948.

73. *Alabama Citizen*, 31 July 1948.

74. *Ibid.*, 14 August 1948; *Birmingham World*, 3 August 1948.

75. *Birmingham World*, 30 July 1948; sabr.org/bioproj/person/62d6502.

76. *Ibid.*, 10 August 1948; *Birmingham News*, 8 August 1948.

77. *Birmingham News*, 9 August 1948.

78. *Birmingham World*, 13 August 1948.

79. *Ibid.*

80. *Birmingham News*, 13 August 1948.

81. *Ibid.*, 14 August 1948; *Birmingham World*, 30 July 1948.

82. *Birmingham News*, 16 August 1948; *Birmingham World*, 17 August 1948.

83. *Birmingham World*, 3, 6 August 1948; *Birmingham News*, 19 August 948.

84. *Birmingham World*, 30 July 1948.

85. *Ibid.*, 3 August 1948.

86. *Ibid.*, 17 August 1948.

87. *Ibid.*, 24 August 1948; *Birmingham News*, 20 August 1948.

88. *Birmingham World*, 24 August 1948.

89. *Ibid.*, 31 August 1948; *Birmingham News*, 30 August 1948.

90. *Birmingham World*, 7 September 1948.

91. *Birmingham World*, 10 September 1948.

92. *Ibid.*, 14 September 1948; *Birmingham News*, 12 September 1948; *Pittsburgh Courier*, 18 September 1948.

93. *Birmingham News*, 13 September 1948; *Birmingham World*, 14 September 1948.

94. *Birmingham News*, 13 September 1948.

95. *Ibid.*, 16 September 1948; *Birmingham World*, 17 September 1948.

96. *Birmingham News*, 20, 23 September 1948; *Birmingham World*, 24 September 1948; *Pittsburgh Courier*, 25 September, 2 October 1948.

97. *Birmingham News*, 24 September 1948.

98. *Birmingham World*, 21 September 1948.

99. *Birmingham News*, 26 September 1948.

100. *Call*, 1 October 1948; *Birmingham News*, 27 September 1948; *Birmingham World*, 28 September 1948.

101. *Birmingham News*, 29 September 1948; *Birmingham World*, 28 September 1948.

102. *Birmingham News*, 30 September 1948; *Birmingham World*, 1 October 1948.

103. *Birmingham News*, 1 October 1948.

104. *Ibid.*, 4 October 1948; *Times-Picayune*, 4 October 1948; *Chicago Defender*, 2 October 1948; *Birmingham World*, 24 October 1948; *Pittsburgh Courier*, 9 October 1948.

105. *New Orleans Item*, 5 October 1948; *Times-Picayune*, 5 October 1948; *Louisiana Weekly*, 9 October 1948; *Pittsburgh Courier*, 16 October 1948.

106. *Birmingham World*, 5 October 1948.

107. *Birmingham News*, 6 October 1948; *Birmingham Age-Herald*, 6 October 1948; *Chicago Defender*, 16 October 1948.

108. *Birmingham News*, 13 October 1948; *Birmingham World*, 15 October 1948.

109. *Chicago Defender*, 19 February 1949.

110. Clark and Lester, *The Negro Leagues Book*, 15–16.

111. *Chicago Defender*, 19 February 1949; *Birmingham World*, 18 February 1949.

112. *Birmingham World*, 18 February 1949.

113. *Ibid.*

114. *Chicago Defender*, 19 February 1949.

115. *Birmingham News*, 27 April 1949; *Chicago Defender*, 23 April 1949.

116. *Birmingham World*, 11 March 1949.

117. *Ibid.*, 22 April 1949.

118. *Chicago Defender*, 23 April 1949.

119. *Birmingham World*, 22 April 1949.

120. *Ibid.*, 21 June 1949.

121. *Journal and Guide*, 11 March 1949.

122. *Birmingham World*, 26 August 1949.

123. *Ibid.*, 22 March 1949.

124. *Ibid.*, 8 April 1949.

125. *Ibid.*, 25 March 1949.

126. *Ibid.*

127. *Ibid.*, 13 February 1949.

128. *Birmingham News*, 1, 17 April 1949.

129. *Birmingham World*, 3 Mach 1949.

130. *Ibid.*, 4 February 1949.

131. *Ibid.*, 8 February 1949.

132. *Birmingham News*, 1, 17 April 1949; *Birmingham World*, 3, 10, 22 March 1949.

133. *Birmingham World*, 29 March 1949.

134. *Birmingham News*, 1 May 1949.

135. *Birmingham World*, 3 May 1949.

136. *Ibid.*, 6 May 1949; *Birmingham News*, 6 May 1949.

137. *Alabama Citizen*, 14 May 1949.

138. *Birmingham News*, 10 May 1949; *Birmingham World*, 10 May 1949.

139. *Birmingham World*, 10 May 1949.

140. *Birmingham News*, 23 May 1949; *Birmingham World*, 27 May 1949.

141. *Birmingham World*, 27 May 1949.

142. *Ibid.*, 24, 27 May 1949; *Birmingham News*, 22, 24, 26 May 1949.

143. *Birmingham News*, 24 May 1949.

144. *Ibid.*, 26 May 1949; *Birmingham World*, 27 May 1949.

145. *Birmingham News*, 27 May 1949.

146. *Ibid.*, 30 May 1949; *Birmingham World*, 31 May 1949.

147. *Birmingham World*, 10 June 1949; *Birmingham News*, 9 June 1949.

148. *Birmingham World*, 7 June 1949.

149. *Ibid.*, 14 June 1949; *Birmingham News*, 12 June 1949.

150. *Birmingham News*, 13 June 1949.

151. *Birmingham World*, 14 June 1949.

152. *Birmingham News*, 14 June 1949.

153. *Ibid.*, 20 June 1949.

154. *Ibid.*, 21 June 1949.

155. *Birmingham World*, 21 June 1949.

156. *Ibid.*

157. *Ibid.*

158. *Ibid.*, 24 June 1949.

159. *Birmingham World*, 1 July 1949.

160. *Ibid.*, 5 July 1949.

161. *Birmingham World*, 5 July 1949.

162. *Birmingham World*, 15 July 1949.

163. *Ibid.*, 8 July 1949; *Birmingham News*, 5 July 1949.

164. *Birmingham News*, 10 July 1949.

165. www.bhamwiki.com/w/Walt_Dropo; http://www.ryan-gluesing.com/travel/baseball/rickwoodtour.htm, last updated 20 February 2009.

166. *Birmingham News*, 8 July 1949; *Birmingham World*, 8 July 1949.

167. *Birmingham World*, 12 July 1949.

168. *Ibid.*, 12 July 1949; *Birmingham News*, 11 July 1949.

169. *Birmingham News*, 23 July 1949.

170. Ackmann, *Curveball: The Remarkable Story of Toni Stone*, 30–31.

171. *Birmingham World*, 29 July 1949.

172. *Ibid.*, *Birmingham News*, 28 July 1949.

173. *Birmingham News*, 31 July 1949.

174. *Ibid.*, 1 August 1949.

175. *Ibid.*, 9 August 1949.

176. Clark and Lester, *The Negro Leagues Book*, 297.

177. *Ibid.*, 24 September 1949.

178. Riley, *Biographical Encyclopedia*, 620–21.

179. *Ibid.*, 897.

180. *Birmingham News*, 15 August 1949.

181. *Ibid.*, 14 August 1949.

182. Lester, *Black Baseball's National Showcase*, 335–6; *Baltimore Sun*, 6 August 1949.

183. *Birmingham World*, 9 August 1949.

184. *Ibid.*, 16, 23 August 1949; *Birmingham News*, 18 August 1949.

185. *Birmingham News*, 22 August 1949.

186. *Birmingham World*, 26, 30 August 1949.

187. *Birmingham News*, 29, 30 August 1949.

188. *Birmingham World*, 6 September 1949.

189. *Birmingham World*, 13 September 1994.

190. *Talladega Daily Home*, 18 October 1949.

191. *Birmingham News*, 19 October 1949.

192. *Ibid.*, 7 October 1949.

193. Riley, *Biographical Encyclopedia*, 359–60.

194. *Birmingham World*, 21 June 1949.

195. *Ibid.*, 19 July 1949.

196. *Ibid.*, 26 August 1949

197. *Chicago Defender*, 28 August 1949.

Chapter 22

1. *Birmingham World*, 7 October 1949.

2. Riley, *Biographical Encyclopedia*, 359–61.

3. *Birmingham World*, 10 March 1950.

4. *Ibid.*, 23 May, 13 June 1950.

5. Clark and Lester, *The Negro Leagues Book*, 163.

6. *Birmingham World*, 21 June 1949.

7. www.wikipedia.org/wiki/History_ofbaseball_in_the_United-States,last modified on 12 February 2015; James R. Walker and Robert V. Bellamy, Jr., *Center Field Shot: A History of Baseball on Television* (Lincoln and London, University of Nebraska Press, 2008).

8. *Birmingham News*, 14, 16, 17 April 1950.

9. *Ibid.*, 2 April 1950.
10. *Birmingham World*, 10, 14 March 1950; *Chicago Defender*, 11 March 1950.
11. *Birmingham World*, 28 March 1950; *Tuscaloosa News*, 25 March 1950.
12. *Birmingham News*, 2 April 1950.
13. *Birmingham World*, 31 March 1950
14. *Birmingham News*, 2, 28 April 1950.
15. *Birmingham World*, 28 April 1950.
16. *Ibid.*, 12 May 1950.
17. *Ibid.*, 9 May 1950.
18. *Ibid.*
19. *Ibid.*, 19 May 1950.
20. *Ibid.*, 12 May 1950.
21. *Ibid.*, 15 May 1950.
22. *Ibid.*, 19 May 1950.
23. *Birmingham News*, 25 May 1950; *Birmingham World*, 26 May 1950.
24. *Ibid.*
25. *Birmingham News*, 26, 27 May 1950; *Birmingham World*, 30 May 1950.
26. *Birmingham News*, 2 June 1950.
27. *Ibid.*
28. *Ibid.*, 10 June 1950.
29. *Ibid.*
30. *Birmingham World*, 30 May 1950.
31. *Ibid.*, 2 June 1950.
32. *Birmingham News*, 30, 31 May 1950, 1 June 1950.
33. *Birmingham World*, 6 June 1950.
34. *Birmingham News*, 7 June 1950.
35. *Chicago Defender*, 10 June 1950.
36. *Birmingham News*, 13 June 1950.
37. *Chicago Defender*, 17 June 1950.
38. *Ibid.*, 24 June 1950.
39. *Birmingham World*, 13 June 1950.
40. *Birmingham News*, 19 June 1950; *Birmingham World*, 20 June 1950.
41. *Birmingham World*, 23 June 1950.
42. Barry Swanton, *The Mandak League: Haven for Former Negro League Ballplayers, 1950–1957* (Jefferson, NC, McFarland, 2006, 144).
43. *Birmingham News*, 22 June, 25 September 1950; *Chicago Defender*, 1 July 1950.
44. *Birmingham News*, 22 June 1950.
45. *Birmingham World*, 20 June 1950.
46. *Ibid.*, 27 June 1950.
47. *Chicago Defender*, 1 July 1950.
48. *Birmingham News*, 26 June 1950; *Birmingham World*, 27 June 1950.
49. *Ibid.*, 1 July 1950.
50. *Ibid.*, 5 July 1950.
51. *Birmingham World*, 7 July 1950; *Chicago Defender*, 22 July 1950.
52. *Birmingham World*, 11 July 1950.
53. *Ibid.*, 14 July 1950.
54. *Ibid.*, 11 July 1950.
55. *Ibid.*
56. *Birmingham News*, 21 July 1950.
57. Clark and Lester, *The Negro Leagues Book*, 281.
58. www.thebaseballcube.com/players/profile.asp?P=willie-mays.
59. *Birmingham World*, 18 July 1950; William J. Plott, interview Charles Willis, Birmingham, AL, 23 August 2010.
60. *Birmingham News*, 19, 20 July 1950; *Birmingham World*, 21 July 1950.
61. *Birmingham News*, 23, 24 July 1950; *Birmingham World*, 25 July 1950.

62. *Birmingham World*, 4 August 1950.
63. *Birmingham News*, 6 August 1950.
64. *Chicago Defender*, 12 August 1950.
65. *Birmingham News*, 7 August 1950; *Birmingham World*, 8 August 1950; *Chicago Defender*, 12 August 1950.
66. *Birmingham News*, 7 August 1950; *Pittsburgh Courier*, 12, 19 August 1950.
67. *Birmingham News*, 7 August 1950.
68. Riley, *Biographical Encyclopedia*, 169.
69. *Birmingham News*, 10 August 1950; *Birmingham World*, 8 August 1950.
70. *Birmingham World*, 11 August 1950.
71. *Birmingham News*, 10 August 1950; *Birmingham World*, 8 August 1950.
72. *Birmingham News*, 16 August 1950; Riley, *Biographical Encyclopedia*, 746.
73. *Birmingham World*, 27 June 1950; *Atlanta Daily World*, 7 July 1950.
74. *Ibid.*, 22 August 1950.
75. *Birmingham World*, 15 August 1950.
76. Lester, *Black Baseball's National Showcase*, 359.
77. *Birmingham World*, 22 August 1950.
78. *Ibid.*, 29 August 1950.
79. *Birmingham News*, 23 September 1950; *Chicago Defender*, 16 September 1950.
80. *Chicago Defender*, 12 August 1950.
81. *Ibid.*, 16 September 1950.
82. *Birmingham News*, 10 September 1950.

Chapter 23

1. https://en.wikipedia.org/wiki/Ed_Steele, last modified on 19 June 2017; https://www.baseball-reference.com/register/player.fcgi?id=steele01edw.
2. Clark and Lester, *The Negro Leagues Book*, 163; *Alabama Citizen*, 10 February 1951; *Birmingham World*, 1 May 1951.
3. *Alabama Citizen*, 13 January 1951.
4. *Birmingham World*, 1 May 1951.
5. www.quora.com/Was-there-a-draft-in-the-U.S.-during-the-Korean-War-Why.
6. *Birmingham World*, 27 February 1951.
7. *Birmingham News*, 8 April 1951.
8. *Ibid.*
9. *Ibid.*, 15 April, 3 May 1951.
10. *Birmingham World*, 23 March 1951.
11. *Birmingham News*, 8 April 1951.
12. *Birmingham World*, 16 March 1951.
13. *Ibid.*, 30 March 1951.
14. *Ibid.*
15. Riley, *Biographical Encyclopedia*, 167–68; *Birmingham News*, 22 April 1951.
16. *Birmingham News*, 23 April 1951.
17. *Birmingham World*, 24 April 1951.
18. *Birmingham News*, 3 May 1951.
19. *Pittsburgh Courier*, 5 May 1951.
20. *Birmingham World*, 4 May 1951.
21. *Ibid.*, 15 May 1951.
22. *Birmingham News*, 5 May 1951; *Birmingham World*, 8 May 1951.
23. *Birmingham News*, 7 May 1951; *Birmingham World*, 8 May 1951.
24. *Birmingham World*, 11 May 1951.
25. *Birmingham News*, 12, 13 May 1951.
26. *Birmingham News*, 25 May 1951; *Birmingham World*, 29 May 1951.
27. *Birmingham News*, 26 May 1951.

28. *Birmingham News*, 28 May 1951; *Birmingham World*, 29 May 1951.

29. *Birmingham World*, 1 June 1951.

30. *Birmingham News*, 15 June 1951.

31. *Birmingham World*, 12, 22 June 1951.

32. *Birmingham News*, 1 July 1951; *Birmingham World*, 17 July 1951.

33. *Birmingham News*, 2 July 1951; *Birmingham World*, 3 July 1951

34. *Ibid.*, 17 July 1951; *Pittsburgh Courier*, 7 July 1951.

35. *Chicago Defender*, 7 July 1951.

36. Riley, *Biographical Encyclopedia*, 209–11.

37. *Birmingham World*, 17 July 1951.

38. Peter Filichia, *Professional Baseball Franchises, From the Abbeville Athletics to the Zanesville Indians* (New York: Facts on File, 1993), 299; www.sabr.org/bioproj/person/aee4d9d3; Clark and Lester, *The Negro Leagues*, 320.

39. *Birmingham News*, 16 July 1951.

40. *Ibid.*, 23 July 1951.

41. Plott, *The Negro Southern League*, 199–200.

42. *Birmingham News*, 29 July 1951.

43. Riley, *Biographical Encyclopedia*, 149–50, 693.

44. *Birmingham News*, 30 July 1951; *Birmingham World*, 31 July 1951.

45. *Birmingham News*, 9 August 1951; *Chicago Defender*, 1 September 1951.

46. Riley, *Biographical Encyclopedia*, 793–94; baseball-reference.com,/register/player.cgi?id=tugers001lea.

47. *Birmingham World*, 10 August 1951; *Chicago Defender*, 11 August 1951.

48. *Birmingham News*, 13 August 1951; *Birmingham World*, 14 August 1951; *Chicago Defender*, 18 August 1951.

49. *Birmingham News*, 20 August 1951; *Birmingham World*, 24 August 1951.

50. *Birmingham World*, 21 August 1951.

51. *Ibid.*

52. *Ibid.*, 31 August 1951.

53. *Birmingham News*, 2 September 1951.

54. *Birmingham News*, 5 September 1951;www.coe.k-state.edu/annex/nlbemuseum/history/players/Wilson.html; www.baseball-almanac.com/awards/International_League_mvp.shtml.

55. *Birmingham World*, 7 September 1951; *Birmingham News*, 4 September 1951.

56. *Birmingham World*, 4 September 1951.

57. *Chicago Defender*, 18 August 1951.

Chapter 24

1. Riley, *Biographical Encyclopedia*, 699–701.

2. *Ibid.*, 50, 107–88; Luke, *The Baltimore Elite Giants*, 131.

3. http://lcsjpf.com/view.php?id=36.]

4. Christopher D. Fullerton, *Every Other Sunday* (Birmingham, AL: R. Boozer Press, 1999), 101.

5. https://baseball-reference.com/register/player.fcgi?id=steele001edw; Riley, *The Biographical Encyclopedia of Baseball's Negro Leagues*, 741.

6. www.attheplate.com/wcbl/intercounty_league, html; Riley, *Biographical Encyclopedia*, 741.

7. Clark and Lester, *The Negro Leagues Book*, 163; *Pittsburgh Courier*, 1 March 1952.

8. *Alabama Citizen*, 2 May 1952.

9. *Birmingham News*, 6 April 1952; *Birmingham World*, 7 March 1952; *Pittsburgh Courier*, 15 March 1952.

10. *Birmingham News*, 12 April 1952; *Alabama Citi-zen*, 8 April 1952; *Birmingham World*, 8 April 1952; *Chicago Defender*, 12 April 1952.

11. *Birmingham News*, 27 April 1952.

12. Riley, *Biographical Encyclopedia*, 139–140; *Birmingham World*, 18 April, 2 June 1952.

13. *Birmingham World*, 18 April 1952.

14. *Birmingham News*, 13 May 1952; *Birmingham World*, 9 May 1952; *Chicago Defender*, 10, 17 May 1952; *Pittsburgh Courier*, 10 May 1952.

15. *Birmingham World*, 16 May 1952.

16. *Ibid.*

17. Riley, *Biographical Encyclopedia*,778–79.

18. https://www.baseball-reference.com/bullpen/Groundhog_Thompson.

19. *Birmingham News*, 17 May 1952; *Birmingham World*, 20 May 1952.

20. *Birmingham World*, 27 May 1952.

21. Clark and Lester, *The Negro Leagues Book*, 316.

22. *Ibid.*, 3 June 1952.

23. *Ibid.*

24. *Ibid.*, 6 June 1952.

25. *Birmingham News*, 6, 8 June 1952.

26. *Ibid.*

27. *Birmingham News*, 9 June 1952; *The Mirror*, 14 June 1952; *Birmingham World*, 6 June 1952.

28. *Birmingham World*, 24 June 1952; *Pittsburgh Courier*, 28 June 1952.

29. *Birmingham News*, 21 June 1952; *Birmingham World*, 24 June 1952.

30. *Birmingham News*, 23 June 1952; *Birmingham World*, 24 June 1952.

31. Brent Kelley, *The Negro Leagues Revisited* (Jefferson, NC: McFarland, 2000), 48; Riley, *Biographical Encyclopedia*, 686.

32. *Birmingham World*, 24 June 1952.

33. Plott, *The Negro Southern League*, 142.

34. *Birmingham World*, 24 June 1952.

35. *Ibid.*, 25 July 1952.

36. *Birmingham News*, 7 July 1952.

37. *Birmingham News*, 4 July 1952; Clark and Lester, *The Negro Leagues* Book, 163.

38. *Birmingham News*, 6 July 1952.

39. https://Wikipedia.org/wikie/Ricckwood_Field; 1949 Birmingham Barons program, courtesy of Clarence Watkins.

40. *Birmingham News*, 7 July 1952; *Birmingham World*, 8 July 1952.

41. *Birmingham World*, 4 July 1952.

42. Riley, *Biographical Encyclopedia*, 823.

43. *Birmingham World*, 15 July 1952.

44. *Chicago Defender*, 12 July 1952.

45. *Birmingham World*, 15 July 1952; *Pittsburgh Courier*, 5 July 1952.

46. *Birmingham World*, 18 July 1952.

47. Clark and Lester, *The Negro Leagues Book*, 320.

48. *Birmingham World*, 25 July 1952; Clark and Lester, *The Negro Leagues Book*, 304; Riley, *Biographical Encyclopedia*, 740.

49. *Birmingham News*, 18, 21 July 1952.

50. Riley, *Biographical Encyclopedia*, 376.

51. *Birmingham News*, 27 July 1952.

52. *Ibid.*, 25 July 1952.

53. www.attheplate.com/wcbl/intercounty_league, html; https://en.wikipedia.org/wiki/Mandak_League.

54. *Birmingham News*, 28 July 1952.

55. Riley, *Biographical Encyclopedia*, 195; Swanton, *The ManDak League*, 14, 91.

56. Swanton, *The ManDak League*, 100–101.

57. *Birmingham News*, 28 July 1952; *Mirror*, 19 July 1952; *Birmingham World*, 29 July 1952.

58. *Birmingham News*, 11 August 1952.

59. *Pittsburgh Courier*, 9 August 1952.

60. *Birmingham News*, 13 August 1952.

61. *Ibid.*, 19 August 1952.

62. *Decatur Daily*, 27, 28 August 1952.

63. *Ibid.*, 27 August 1952.

64. *Chicago Defender*, 23 August 1952; Lester, *Black Baseball's National Showcase*, 372–74.

65. *Birmingham News*, 20, 21 August 1952; *Birmingham World*, 22 August 1952.

66. Clark and Lester, *The Negro Leagues Book*, 138, 149.

67. *Birmingham News*, 25 August 1952; *Birmingham World*, 26 August 1952.

68. *Birmingham World*, 9 September 1952.

69. *Ibid.*

70. *Birmingham News*, 7 September 1952.

71. *Ibid.*, 8 September 1952.

72. *Birmingham World*, 9 September 1952.

73. *Ibid.*, 12 September 1952.

74. *Birmingham News*, 13 September 1952.

75. Barry Swanton and Jay-Dell Mah, *Black Baseball Players in Canada: A Biographical Dictionary 1881–1960* (Jefferson, NC: McFarland, 2009), 138–140.

76. www.attheplate.com/wcbl/intercounty_league, html; *Birmingham News*, 24 August 1952.

77. *Birmingham News*, 13 September 1952.

78. *Ibid.*, 15 September 1952.

79. *Pittsburgh Courier*, 13 September 1952.

80. *Birmingham News*, 30 September 1952; *Tennessean*, 19 September 1952.

81. *Birmingham News*, 4 October 1952.

82. *Ibid.*, 6 October 1952.

83. *Chicago Defender*, 23 May 1953.

84. *Decatur Daily*, 16 October 1952.

85. *Pittsburgh Courier*, 19 April 1952.

Chapter 25

1. *Birmingham World*, 17 April 1953; Riley, *Biographical Encyclopedia*, 809–10.

2. Clark and Lester, *The Negro Leagues Book*, 152, 163; *Pittsburgh Courier*, 19 April 1953; *Chicago Defender*, 18 April, 9 May 1953.

3. *Birmingham News*, 7 June 1953.

4. *The Decatur Daily*, 14 July, 8 December 1953.

5. *Birmingham World*, 24 March 1953; *Chicago Defender*, 4 April 1953.

6. *Birmingham World*, 24 March 1953.

7. *Birmingham News*, 19 April 1953.

8. *Birmingham World*, 17 April 1953.

9. William Plott, interview with Raymond Haggins, Montevallo, AL, April 1994.

10. *Ibid.*, 21 April 1953; *Birmingham News*, 20 April 1952.

11. *Birmingham World*, 28 April 1953.

12. *Ibid.*, 5 May 1953.

13. *Ibid.*, 8 May 1953.

14. *Ibid.*, 12 May 1953.

15. *Ibid.*

16. *Pittsburgh Courier*, 2, 9 May 1953.

17. *Birmingham World*, 29 May 1953; *Pittsburgh Courier*, 30 May 1953.

18. *Birmingham News*, 21 May 1953; *Birmingham World*, 19, 22 May 1953.

19. *Birmingham World*, 22 May 1953.

20. *Ibid.*, 26 May 1953; *Birmingham News*, 23 May 1953.

21. *Birmingham World*, 26 May 1953.

22. *Birmingham News*, 29 May 1953.

23. *Birmingham World*, 29 May 1953.

24. *Birmingham News*, 29 May 1953.

25. *Birmingham News*, 2 June 1953.

26. *Ibid.*, 2 June 1953; *Mirror*, 6 June 1953.

27. *Pittsburgh Courier*, 6, 13 June 1953.

28. *Chicago Defender*, 13, 17 June 1953.

29. *Birmingham* World, 5 June 1953.

30. *Ibid.*, 2 June 1953; *Chicago Defender*, 13 June 1953.

31. *Birmingham News*, 3 June 1953; *Chicago Defender*, 13 June 1953.

32. *Birmingham World*, 5 June 1953.

33. *Birmingham World*, 9 June 1953.

34. https://en.wikipedia.org/wiki/Octavus.Roy_Cohen.

35. *Birmingham News*, 3 June 1953.

36. *Birmingham World*, 16 June 1953.

37. *Birmingham News*, 14, 15 June 1953.

38. *Birmingham World*, 30 June 1953; *Pittsburgh Courier*, 4 July 1953.

39. *Birmingham World*, 30 June 1953; *Mirror*, 4 July 1953; *Chicago Defender*, 27 June 1953.

40. *Birmingham World*, 7 July 1953.

41. baseball-reference.com/bullpen/Charley_Pride, last modified 24 December 2011.

42. *Mirror*, 18 July 1953; *Birmingham World*, 14 July 1953.

43. *Chicago Defender*, 18 July 1953.

44. *Birmingham News*, 18 July 1953.

45. *Ibid.*, 28 July 1953.

46. *Ibid.*, 30 July 1953.

47. *Ibid.*, 3 August 1953.

48. *Birmingham World*, 11 August 1953; *Pittsburgh Courier*, 1 August 1953.

49. *Pittsburgh Courier*, 8 August 1953.

50. *Birmingham World*, 11 August 1953.

51. *Pittsburgh Courier*, 22 August 1952.

52. *Baltimore Sun*, 17 August 1953.

53. *Birmingham News*, 23 August 1953.

54. *Washington Post*, 28 November 2001.

55. *Birmingham World*, 25 August 1953.

56. *Pittsburgh Courier*, 29 August, 12 September 1953.

57. *Mirror*, 22 August 1953; *Birmingham World*, 28 August 1953.

58. https://findagrave.com.cgi-bin/fg.cgi?page=gr&Grid=72284652.

59. *Birmingham World*, 8 September 1953.

Chapter 26

1. *Birmingham World*, 9 March 1954; Swanton and Mah, *Black Baseball Players in Canada*, 175.

2. *Pittsburgh Courier*, 13 May 1954.

3. *Birmingham World*, 9 March 1954.

4. Riley, *Biographical Encyclopedia*, 826–8; https://en.wikipedia.org/wiki/Willie_Wells.

5. Clark and Lester, *The Negro Leagues Book*, 163; *Pittsburgh Courier*, 10 April 1954.

6. *Pittsburgh Courier*, 20 March 1954.

7. Luke, *The Baltimore Elite Giants*, 81; Plott, *The Negro Southern League*, 170.

8. *Chicago Defender*, 10 April 1954.

9. Heaphy, *The Negro Leagues*, 1869–1960, 96.

10. *Ibid.*, 3 April 1954.
11. *Ibid.*, 27 March 1954; *Chicago Defender*, 3 April 1954; *Birmingham World*, 23 March 1954.
12. *Chicago Defender*, 17 April 1954.
13. www.weirdwildrealm.com.
14. *Ibid.*, 15 May 1954.
15. *Ibid.*, 29 May 1954.
16. *Ibid.*, 12 June 1954.
17. *Ibid.*, 24 April 1954.
18. *Ibid.*, Riley, *Biographical Encyclopedia*, 883.
19. *Chicago Defender*, 10 April 1954; *Pittsburgh Courier*, 10 April 1954.
20. *Chicago Defender*, 1 May 1954; *Birmingham World*, 3 March 1954.
21. *Birmingham News*, 25 April 1954; *Chicago Defender*, 3 April 1954; *Pittsburgh Courier*, 3 April 1954.
22. *Mirror*, 1 May 1954.
23. *Birmingham News*, 26 April 1954; *Birmingham World*, 27 April 1954; *Mirror*, 1 May 1954.
24. *Mirror*, 1 May 1954.
25. *Ibid.*, 6 February 1954.
26. *Birmingham News*, 2 April 1954.
27. *Ibid.*
28. *Pittsburgh Courier*, 17 April 1954.
29. *Ibid.*, 15 may 1954; www.baseball-reference.com/register/player.fcgi?id+crosby001ral.
30. *Birmingham News*, 16 May 1954; *Birmingham World*, 18 May 1954.
31. *Birmingham World*, 16 July 1954.
32. *Birmingham News*, 17 May 1954; *Chicago Defender*, 29 May 1954; *Pittsburgh Courier*, 29 May 1954.
33. *Chicago Defender*, 29 May 1954.
34. *Birmingham News*, 21 May 1954; *Birmingham World*, 25 May 1954.
35. *Ibid.*, 5 June 1954.
36. *Birmingham World*, 25 May 1954.
37. *Ibid.*, 8 June, 9 July 1954.
38. *Birmingham World*, 8 June 1954; *Birmingham News*, 7 June 1954.
39. *Birmingham World*, 22 June 1954; *Birmingham News*, 21 June 1954.
40. *Birmingham World*, 6 July 1954.
41. Bill Plott, telephone interview with Charlie Dees, 30 October 2010.
42. *Birmingham World*, 6 July 1954; *Pittsburgh Courier*, 3 July 1954.
43. *Chicago Defender*, 10, 17 July 1954.
44. *Ibid.*, 24 July 1954.
45. *Ibid.*, 10, 17 July 1954; Riley, *Biographical Encyclopedia*, 229.
46. *Chicago Defender*, 24 July 1954.
47. *Chicago Defender*, 31 July 1954.
48. *Ibid.*, 31 July 1954.
49. *Birmingham World*, 13 July 1954; *Birmingham News*, 11, 12 July 1954.
50. *Birmingham World*, 27 July 1954; *Birmingham News*, 26 July 1954.
51. *Chicago Defender*, 7 August 1954.
52. *Ibid.*
53. *Birmingham News*, 9 August 1954; *Chicago Defender*, 21 August 1954; *Pittsburgh Courier*, 21 August 1954.
54. *Birmingham World*, 17 August 1954.
55. *Chicago Defender*, 21 August 1954.
56. *Ibid.*, 28 August 1954.
57. *Birmingham News*, 30 August 1954; *Birmingham World*, 31 August 1954.
58. Bill Plott, telephone interview with Charley Pride, May 1999.
59. http://lcshof.com/view.php?id=36.
60. *Birmingham News*, 9 May 1999.
61. *Chicago Defender*, 11 September 1954.
62. *Birmingham World*, 14 September 1954; *Pittsburgh Courier*, 4, 25 September 1954.
63. *Ibid.*, 14 August 1954.

Chapter 27

1. *Chicago Defender*, 19 April 1955; *Birmingham World*, 15 March 1955; *Birmingham Post-Herald*, 17 February 1997; https://en.wikipedia.org/Birmingham_Black_Barons,last modified on 4 February 2016.
2. *Birmingham World*, 19 April 1955.
3. *Ibid.*
4. *Ibid.*, 15 April 1955.
5. https://en.wikipedia.org/wiki/Gatemouth_Moore, last modified on 4 February 2016; http://www.msbluestrail.org/blues-trail-markers/gatemouth-moore.
6. http://www.ponderosastomp.com/music_more.php/48/Gatemouth+Moore; *Birmingham World*, 15 April 1955; www.jazzhouse.org; www.lib.berkeley.edu; www.pondersosastomp.com; www.wikipedia.org.
7. *Call*, 3 May 1940.
8. *Mirror*, 19 March 1955.
9. https://en.Wikipedia.org/wiki/Southern_Association, last modified 20 December 2015; Wright, *The Southern Association in Baseball*, 546.
10. Wright, *The Southern Association in Baseball*, 557.
11. https://basesball-eference.com/register/player.cgi?id=jones-001sta; *Mirror*, 25 April 1964.
12. *Birmingham World*, 15 April 1955.
13. *Ibid.*
14. *Ibid.*; www.jazzhouse.org; www.lib.berkeley.edu; www.pondersosastomp.com; www.wikipedia.org.
15. *Birmingham World*, 15 April 1955.
16. *Mirror*, 26 March 1955.
17. *Ibid.*, 30 April 1955.
18. Riley, *Biographical Encyclopedia*, 149–50.
19. *Birmingham World*, 5 April 1955.
20. *Mirror*, 26 March 1955.
21. *Birmingham World*, 8 April 1955.
22. *Mirror*, 30 April 1955; *Birmingham World*, 26 April 1955.
23. *Mirror*, 30 April 1955.
24. *Mirror*, 30 April 1955.
25. *Ibid.*, 7 May 1955; *Birmingham World*, 3 May 1955.
26. *Mirror*, 7 May 1955.
27. *Birmingham World*, 6 May 1955.
28. *Ibid.*, 17 May 1955.
29. *Birmingham World*, 24 May 1955.
30. *Ibid.*, 27 May 1955; *Mirror*, 4 June 1955.
31. *Birmingham World*, 3 June 1955.
32. *Birmingham News*, 5 June 1955.
33. *Birmingham World*, 10 June 1955.
34. *Pittsburgh Courier*, 11 June 1955.
35. *Birmingham News*, 8 July 1955.
36. *Birmingham World*, 15 July 1955.
37. *Mirror*, 20 August 1955.
38. *Birmingham World*, 15 July 1955.
39. *Ibid.*
40. *Mirror*, 16 July 1955.
41. *Mirror*, 2 July 1955; *Birmingham World*, 22 July 1955.
42. *Mirror*, 30 July 1955.

43. *Birmingham World*, 19 July 1955; *Pittsburgh Courier*, 6 August 1955.

44. *Birmingham World*, 2 August 1955.

45. *Mirror*, 6 August 1955; *Pittsburgh Courier*, 30 July 1955.

46. *Birmingham News*, 8 July 1955.

47. *Ibid.*, 7 August 1955.

48. *Birmingham World*, 12 August 1955.

49. *Mirror*, 20 August 1955; *Pittsburgh Courier*, 20 August 1955.

50. *Mirror*, 27 August 1955.

51. *Ibid.*, 10 September 1955; *Birmingham World*, 6 September 1955; *Birmingham News*, 5 September 1955; *Birmingham Age-Herald*, 5 September 1955.

52. *Birmingham World*, 6 September 1955; *Birmingham News*, 26 September 1955.

53. *Birmingham News*, 27 October 1955.

54. *Pittsburgh Courier*, 23 July 1955.

Chapter 28

1. *Mirror*, 17, 31 March 1956; *Pittsburgh Courier*, 24 March 1956.

2. *Mirror*, 31 March 1956.

3. *Birmingham News*, 15 March 1956.

4. *Ibid.*, 11 April 1956.

5. *Birmingham World*, 1 June 1956; *Pittsburgh Courier*, 7 April 1956.

6. *Mirror*, 31 March 1956.

7. *Pittsburgh Courier*, 3 March 1956.

8. Plott, *The Negro Southern League*, 9, 115–16.

9. *Mirror*, 21 April 1956.

10. *Mirror*, 21 April 1956.

11. Riley, *Biographical Encyclopedia*, 229.

12. *Birmingham News*, 4 May 1956.

13. Riley, *Biographical Encyclopedia*, 770; *Birmingham World*, 1 May 1956.

14. *Mirror*, 5 May 1956.

15. *Birmingham World*, 24 March 1956.

16. *Birmingham News*, 7 May 1956.

17. *Birmingham Post-Herald*, 19 May 1956.

18. *Mirror*, 26 May 1956.

19. *Ibid.*

20. www.sportscelebs.com, http://www.baseballinlivingcolor.com/player.php?card=15.

21. *Birmingham News*, 21 May 1956; *Mirror*, 26 May 1956; *Birmingham Post-Herald*, 21 May 1956.

22. *Birmingham World*, 25 May 1956.

23. *Ibid.*

24. *Birmingham World*, 2 June 1956.

25. Kelley, *The Negro Leagues Revisited*, 311–12.

26. *Birmingham News*, 19 September 2010.

27. http://coe.k-state.edu/annex/nlbemuseum/history/players/Mitchell.html.

28. http://coe.k-state.edu/annex/nlbemuseum/history/playes/marsh.htmil; http://www.baseball-reference.com/register/leader.cgi?id+e4408a80; http://www.baseball-refernce.com/register/leader.cgi?id+cb8df6f8.

29. http://www.oocities.org/colosseum/field/1538/lastgame.hetml.

30. www.diamondsinthedust.com; *Muskegon Chronicle*, 12 June 1956; U.S. Social Security Death Index, 1935–2014; *Atoka County Times*, 11 October 2006.

31. *Birmingham World*, 1 June 1956.

32. *Mirror*, 2 June 1956; *Birmingham Post-Herald*, 28 May 1956; *Birmingham News*, 28 May 1956; *Pittsburgh Courier*, 9 June 1956.

33. *Birmingham World*, 25 May 1956.

34. *Birmingham News*, 4 June 1956.

35. *Birmingham World*, 25 July 1956.

36. *Ibid.*, 8 June 1956.

37. *Mirror*, 16 June 1956; *Birmingham Post-Herald*, 11 June 1956.

38. *Birmingham News*, 1 July 1956.

39. *Pittsburgh Courier*, 23 June 1956.

40. *Birmingham News*, 25 June 1956.

41. *Birmingham World*, 7 July 1956; *Birmingham Post-Herald*, 1 July 1956.

42. *Birmingham World*, 25 July 1956.

43. *Ibid.*, 1 August 1956.

44. *Birmingham Post-Herald*, 4 August 1956.

45. *Birmingham World*, 8 August 1956.

46. *Ibid.*, 11 August 1956.

47. *Pittsburgh Courier*, 4 August 1956.

48. *Birmingham World*, 1 August 1956.

49. *Ibid.*, 28 July 1956; *Birmingham News*, 12 August 1956.

50. *Birmingham World*, 1 August 1956.

51. *Ibid.*, 4 August 1956.

52. *Chicago Tribune*, 13 August 1956; *Birmingham World*, 18 August 1956; *Pittsburgh Courier*, 8 June 1956.

53. *Birmingham World*, 11 August 1956.

54. *Ibid.*, 22 August 1956; *Birmingham News*, 20 August 1956.

55. *Birmingham World*, 25 August 1956; *Birmingham Post-Herald*, 20 August 1956.

56. *Birmingham World*, 25 August 1956.

57. *Birmingham News*, 19 August 1956.

58. *Indianapolis Star*, 25 August 1956; *Greenwood Commonwealth*, 29 August 1956; *Tennessean*, 31 August 1956; *Jackson Sun*, 24 August 1956.

59. *Birmingham World*, 4 August 1956.

60. *Ibid.*

61. *Ibid.*, 11, 15 August 1956.

62. *Birmingham World*, 7 September 1956.

63. *Ibid.*, 5 September 1956.

Chapter 29

1. *Birmingham World*, 13 March 1957; *Pittsburgh Courier*, 8 June 1957; *Call*, 26 April 1957.

2. *Birmingham World*, 13 March 1957.

3. https://en.wikipedia.org/wiki/History_of_the_Oakland_Athletics, last modified on 7 January 2018; *Call*, 31 May 1957.

4. *Call*, 31 May 1957.

5. *Ibid.*, 18 May 1957.

6. *Ibid.*, 13 March 1957.

7. *Ibid.*

8. *Ibid.*

9. Riley, *Biographical Encyclopedia*, 44; *Mirror*, 14 September 1957.

10. *Birmingham World*, 10 April 1957.

11. *Ibid.*

12. Bill Plott, interview with Willie Smith in Anniston, AL, 10 December 1993.

13. *Birmingham News*, 29 April 1957; *Birmingham World*, 1 May 1957.

14. *Birmingham World*, 1 May 1957.

15. *Ibid.*, 4 May 1957.

16. *Ibid.* 18 May 1957.

17. *Ibid.*, 25 May 1957; *Birmingham News*, 20 May 1957; *Birmingham Post-Herald*, 20 May 1957; *Mirror*, 25 May 1957.

18. *Birmingham World*, 8 June 1957.
19. *Ibid.*, 12 June 1957.
20. *Birmingham News*, 9 June 1957.
21. *Ibid.*, 10 June 1957; *Birmingham World*, 15 June 1957.
22. *Birmingham World*, 15 June 1957.
23. *Birmingham News*, 12 June 1957.
24. *Ibid.*, 24 June 1957; *Birmingham World*, 29 June 1957.
25. *Pittsburgh Courier*, 29 June 1957.
26. *Birmingham News*, 5 July 1957; *Birmingham Post-Herald*, 5 July 1957; *Birmingham World*, 3 July 1957.
27. *Birmingham News*, 7 July 1957.
28. *Ibid.*, 8 July 1957; *Birmingham World*, 13 July 1957.
29. *Birmingham Post-Herald*, 15 July 1957.
30. *Ibid.*, 22 July 1957; *Birmingham News*, 22 July 1957.
31. *Birmingham Post-Herald*, 20 July 1957.
32. *Ibid.*, 25 July 1957; *Birmingham News*, 23 July 1957; *Birmingham World*, 27 July 1957.
33. *Birmingham Post-Herald*, 1 August 1957.
34. *Ibid.*, 5 August 1957.
35. *Pittsburgh Courier*, 27 July 1957; *Birmingham World*, 27 July 1957; www.baseball-refernce.com, last modified on 1 December 2014.
36. *Birmingham World*, 20 July 1957; *Pittsburgh Courier*, 8, 22, 29 July 1957.
37. *Birmingham World*, 27 July, 3 August 1957.
38. *Ibid.*, 3 August 1957; *Pittsburgh Courier*, 27 July, 3 August 1957; *Chicago Tribune*, 29 July 1940.
39. *Mirror*, 17 August 1957.
40. *Birmingham News*, 19 August 1957.
41. *Ibid.*, 21 August 1957.
42. *Anderson Daily Bulletin*, 24, 25 July, 20, 21 August 1957.
43. *Ibid.*, 25 July, 21 August 1957; *Anderson Daily Bulletin*, 25 July, 21 August 1957.
44. *Birmingham World*, 31 August 1957.
45. *Birmingham World*, 31 August 1957.

Chapter 30

1. *Birmingham World*, 8 March 1958.
2. *Ibid.*
3. *Ibid.*, 22 March 1958
4. *Ibid.*, 2 April 1958; *The Call*, 23 May 1958.
5. *Birmingham World*, 8 March 1958.
6. *Birmingham News* 23 July 1957; *Birmingham Post-Herald*, 25 July 1957.
7. *Birmingham World*, 8 March 1958.
8. *Ibid.*, 22 March 1958.
9. *Mirror*, 26 April 1958.
10. *Ibid.*, 26 April 1958; *Birmingham World*, 26 April 1958.
11. *Birmingham World*, 10 May 1958; *Birmingham Post-Herald*, 12 May 1958.
12. *Birmingham News*, 18 May 1958.
13. Riley, *Biographical Encyclopedia*, 149.
14. *Birmingham News*, 18 May 1958.
15. *Birmingham World*, 31 May 1958.
16. *Ibid.*, 14 June 1958.
17. *Ibid.*
18. *Anniston Star*, 23 January 1970.
19. *Ibid.*
20. *Birmingham Post-Herald*, 28 June 1958.
21. *Birmingham News*, 27 July 1956.
22. *Birmingham World*, 2 July 1958.
23. *Ibid.*, 12 July 1958.
24. *Ibid.*, 2 July 1958.

25. *Ibid.*, 9 July 1958.
26. *Ibid.*, 16 July 1958.
27. *Ibid.*, 12 July 1958.
28. *Ibid.*, 12 July, 6 August 1958.
29. *Ibid.*, 23 July 1958.
30. *Ibid.*, 6 August 1958.
31. Lloyd Johnson and Miles Wolfe, editors, *The Encyclopedia of Minor League Baseball* (Durham, NC: Baseball America, 1993), 239–45.
32. *Ibid.*, 294–96.
33. *Ibid.*, 263.
34. *Birmingham News*, 20 July 1958; *Birmingham Post-Herald*, 21 July 1958.
35. *Birmingham World*, 26 July 1959.
36. Lester, *Black Baseball's National Showcase*, 434–38.
37. http://baseball-reference.com/register/player.cgi?id=willia000poi; *Birmingham News*, 22 July 1919.
38. *Ibid.*, 19 August 1923, 17 May 1928.
39. http://baseball-reference.com/register/player.cgi?id=willia000poi.
40. *Pittsburgh Courier*, 6 September 1958; https://www.baseball-reference.com/bullpen/East-West_Game.
41. *Birmingham World*, 9 September 1958.
42. Official 1958 Negro American League Records, Howe News Bureau, Chicago, IL, mimeographed copy in author's possession.
43. *Birmingham World*, 18 October 1958.
44. *Ibid.*
45. *Birmingham World*, 6 September 1958.

Chapter 31

1. *Memphis World*, 22 April 1959; *Pittsburgh Courier*, 26 March 1959.
2. *Memphis World*, 23 April 1959.
3. *Birmingham News*, 2–3 January 1959.
4. *Birmingham News*, 12 April 1959; *Mirror*, 4 April 1959.
5. *Birmingham World*, 21 March 1959.
6. *Birmingham News*, 12 April 1959.
7. *Mirror*, 4 April 1959.
8. *Ibid.*, 29 April 1959.
9. *Ibid.*, 16 May 1959.
10. *Ibid.*, 16 May 1959.
11. *Ibid.*, 20 May 1959.
12. *Birmingham Reporter*, 16 January 1932.
13. *Birmingham World*, 20 May 1959.
14. *Ibid.*, 23 May 1959.
15. *Ibid.*, 27 May 1959.
16. *Ibid.*, 30 May 1959.
17. *Ibid.*, 30 May 1959.
18. *Ibid.*, 10 June 1959.
19. *Ibid.*, 13 June 1959.
20. *Ibid.*
21. *Paris News*, 19, 21 June 1959.
22. *Birmingham World*, 24 June 1959.
23. *Ibid.*, 29 June 1959.
24. *Ibid.*, 1 July 1959.
25. *Ibid.*, 4 July 1959.
26. *Ibid.*
27. *Ibid.*, 3 June 1959.
28. *Ibid.*, 8 July 1959.
29. *Ibid.*
30. *Ibid.*
31. *Ibid.*
32. *Ibid.*, 11 July 1959.
33. *Ibid.*, 18 July 1959.

34. *Ibid.*, 22 July 1959.
35. *Ibid.*, 15 July 1959.
36. *Ibid.*
37. *Ibid.*, 22 July 1959.
38. *Ibid.*
39. *Ibid.*, 22 July 1959.
40. Larry Powell, *Black Barons of Birmingham* (Jefferson, NC: McFarland, 2009): 56; www.baseball-reference.com/register/player.fcgi?id=harris002ear.
41. *Ibid.*, 29 July 1959.
42. *Ibid.*, 1, 4 August 1959.
43. *Birmingham World*, 15 August 1959; *Pittsburgh Courier*, 22 August 1959; *Chicago Tribune*, 10 August 1959.
44. *Mirror*, 1 August 1959; *Birmingham World*, 29 July 1959; *Birmingham World*, 13 August 1959.
45. *Birmingham World*, 29 August 1959.
46. *Ibid.*
47. *Birmingham News*, 5 September 1959.

Chapter 32

1. *Birmingham World*, 15, 29 August 1959.
2. *Ibid.*, 4 May 1960.
3. *Ibid.*, 23 April 1960; *Call*, 6 May 1960.
4. *Birmingham World*, 23 April, 21 May 1960; *Pittsburgh Courier*, 7 May 1960.
5. *Birmingham World*, 6 April 1960; *Mirror*, 12 March 1960.
6. *Birmingham World*, 6 April 1960.
7. *Hattiesburg American*, 5, 9 May 1960; *Mirror*, 7 May 1960; www.baseball-refrence.com/bullpen/Alonzo_Perry, last modified on 10 May 2015.
8. *Ibid.*, 18, 21 May 1960.
9. *Ibid.*, 21 May 1960.
10. *Ibid.*, 21 May 1960; *Mirror*, 7 May 1960.
11. *Birmingham World*, 21 May 1960.
12. *Ibid.*, 28 May 1960; *Mirror*, 28 May 1960.
13. *Birmingham World*, 4 June 1960; *Birmingham News*, 30 May 1960; *Mirror*, 4 June 1960.
14. *Birmingham World*, 4 June 1960.
15. *Ibid.*, 18 June 1960; *Birmingham News*, 13 June 1960; *Mirror*, 18 June 1960.
16. *Birmingham World*, 18 June 1960.
17. *Ibid.*, 18 June 1960; *Birmingham News*, 13 June 1960; *Mirror*, 18 June 1960.
18. *Birmingham World*, 25 June 1960.
19. *Ibid.*, 2 July 1960; *Birmingham News*, 27 June 1960; *Mirror*, 2 July 1960.
20. *Birmingham World*, 2 July 1960.
21. *Ibid.*
22. *Ibid.*, 9 July 1960.
23. *Ibid.*, 16 July 1960.
24. *Ibid.*, 23 July 1960; *Birmingham News,* 11 July 1960.
25. *Birmingham World*, 30 July 1960.
26. *Ibid.*
27. *Ibid.*, 23, 30 July 1960.
28. *Ibid.*, 30 July, 6 August 1960; *Mirror*, 30 July 1960.
29. *Birmingham World*, 20 August 1960; *Birmingham News*, 14, 15 August 1960.
30. *Pittsburgh Courier*, 6 August 1960.
31. *Ibid.*
32. *Pittsburgh Courier*, 20 August 1960
33. *Birmingham World*, 27 August 1960; *Pittsburgh Courier*, 20 August, 3 September 1960.
34. https://klmitchell.com/2015/12/01/ernest-westfield-one-of-the-lst-negro-league-all-stars.

35. *Ibid.*, 20 August 1960; *Birmingham News*, 6 September 1960.
36. *Birmingham News*, 20 October 1960.
37. *Birmingham World*, 25 March 1961.
38. *Ibid.*, 5 April 1961.
39. *Pittsburgh Courier*, 22 April 1961.
40. *Birmingham World*, 18 March, 5, 12 April 1961, 6 May 1961.
41. *Ibid.*, 17 June 1961.
42. *Birmingham World*, 20 May 1961; *Pittsburgh Courier*, 3 June 1961.
43. *Birmingham World*, 1 July 1961.
44. *Ibid.*, 5 July 1961.
45. *Ibid.*, 19, 22 July 1961; *Birmingham New*, 19 April 1924.
46. *Birmingham News*, 12 July 1924.
47. *Chicago Defender*, 23 August 1924.
48. *Birmingham World*, 19 July 1961.
49. www.cnlbr.org/Portals/O/%20Negro%20American%20League%20(1958–62).pdf.
50. *Mirror*, 5 August 1961.
51. *Ibid.*
52. *Birmingham World*, 30 August 1961; *Pittsburgh Courier*, 12 August 1961; Lester, *Black Baseball's National Showcase*, 29.
53. *Birmingham News*, 24 September 1961.
54. *Ibid.*, 1 October 1961.
55. *Birmingham News*, 15 April 1962; *Birmingham World*, 7 April 1962.
56. *Birmingham News*, 25 April 1962; *Pittsburgh Courier*, 5 May 1962.
57. https://en.wikipdia.org/wiki/Frank_Evans_(baseball) last modified 29 May 2016; http://www.baseball-reference.com/bullpen/Frank_Evans last modified on 11 February 2013; Swanton, *The ManDak League*, 100–101.
58. *Mirror*, 10 February 1962.
59. *Birmingham World*, 14 April 1962.
60. *Birmingham News*, 4 May 1962; *Pittsburgh Courier*, 12 May 1962.
61. *Birmingham News*, 13 May 1962.
62. *Ibid.*, 14 May 1962; *Birmingham Post-Herald*, 14 May 1962.
63. *Birmingham World*, 13 June 1962.
64. *Birmingham News*, 25 May 1962.
65. *Ibid.*, 27 May 1962.
66. *Ibid.*, 28 May 1962; *Birmingham Post-Herald*, 28 May 1962.
67. *Birmingham Post-Herald*, 4 June 1962.
68. *Birmingham News*, 22, 25 June 1962.
69. *Birmingham News*, 6 August 1962; *Mirror*, 11 August 1962.
70. *Birmingham News*, 10, 11 August 1962; *Birmingham Post-Herald*, 11 August 1962.
71. *Birmingham News*, 19 August 1962.
72. *Birmingham World*, 22 August 1962.
73. *Birmingham News*, 10 August 1962.
74. https://www.baseball-reference.cm/bullpen/East-West_Game; www.cnlbr.org/Portals/O/RL/East-West%20All%20Star%20Game%20Summaries.pdf.
75. *Birmingham World*, 4 August 1962.
76. *Ibid.*
77. *Birmingham Post-Herald*, 22 September 1962.
78. *Ibid.*, 29 September 1962.
79. www.cnlbr.org/Portals/O/RL/Player%20Interviews.pdf.
80. *Ibid.*
81. www.cnlbr.org/Portals/O/RL/History%20of%20the%20Indianpaolis%20Clowns.pdf.

Bibliography

Newspapers

Alabama

Alabama Citizen (Tuscaloosa)
Alabama Journal (Montgomery)
Anniston Star
Birmingham Age-Herald
Birmingham Journal
Birmingham Ledger
Birmingham News
Birmingham Post
Birmingham Post-Herald
Birmingham Reporter
Birmingham Times
Birmingham World
Centreville Press
Daily Home (Talladega)
Daily Mountain Eagle (Jasper)
Decatur Daily
Gadsden Times
Gadsden Times & Daily News
Huntsville Mirror
Huntsville Times
Marion Times-Standard
Mobile News-Item
Mobile Press
Mobile Press-Register
Mobile Register
Montgomery Advertiser
Selma Times-Journal
Tuscaloosa News

Arkansas

Arkansas Democrat (Little Rock)
Arkansas Gazette (Little Rock)

Delaware

Morning News (Wilmington)
News Journal (Wilmington)

District of Columbia

Washington Post

Florida

Florida Times-Union (Jacksonville)
Pensacola Journal

Georgia

Albany Herald
Atlanta Daily World
Atlanta Independent
Atlanta Journal
Augusta Chronicle
Constitution (Atlanta)
Macon News
Macon Telegraph
Moultrie Observer
Savannah Morning News
Savannah Press
Thomasville Daily Enterprise
Waycross-Journal-Herald

Illinois

Chicago Daily Tribune
Chicago Defender
Decatur Herald

Indiana

Anderson Daily Bulletin
Anderson Herald
Evansville Courier
Indianapolis News
Indianapolis Star
Muncie Evening News
Star Press (Muncie)
Times (Hammond)

Iowa

Daily Times (Davenport)
Des Moines Register
Des Moines Tribune

Kentucky

Courier-Journal (Louisville)
Kentucky New-Era (Hopkinsville)

Lexington Herald
Lexington Leader
Owensboro Inquirer

Louisiana

Alexandria Daily Town Talk
Louisiana Weekly (New Orleans)
Monroe Morning World
Monroe News-Star
New Orleans Item
Shreveport Journal
Shreveport Times
Times-Picayune (New Orleans)

Maryland

Baltimore Sun

Michigan

Battle Creek Enquirer
Detroit Free Press
News-Palladium (Benton Harbor)
Press-Herald (St. Joseph)

Minnesota

Minneapolis Star
Star-Tribune (Minneapolis)

Mississippi

Commercial-Dispatch (Columbus)
Delta Democrat (Greenville)
Greenwood Commonwealth
Hattiesburg American
Jackson Clarion-Ledger
Meridian Star

Missouri

Call (Kansas City)
Daily Standard (Sikeston)
St. Louis Post-Dispatch
St. Louis Star
Sporting Life (St. Louis)
Sporting News (St. Louis)

Nebraska

Beatrice Daily Sun

New York

Buffalo Evening News
New York Times
Post-Standard (Syracuse)

North Carolina

Asheville Citizen
Asheville Citizen-Times
Asheville Times
Raleigh News & Observer

Ohio

Akron Beacon-Journal
Alliance Review
Cincinnati Enquirer
Cleveland Plain Dealer
Columbus Citizen Journal
Columbus Dispatch
Dayton Daily News
Dayton Herald
Dayton Journal
Times Recorder (Zanesville)

Pennsylvania

Delaware County Daily Times (Chester)
Evening News (Harrisburg)
Harrisburg Patriot-News
Harrisburg Sunday Courier
Harrisburg Telegraph
Philadelphia Daily News
Philadelphia Enquirer
Pittsburgh Courier
Pittsburgh Post-Gazette
Pittsburgh Press

South Carolina

Charleston News & Courier

South Dakota

Daily Argus-Leader (Sioux Falls)

Tennessee

Chattanooga Daily Times
Chattanooga Free Press
Commercial Appeal (Memphis)
Jackson Sun
Knoxville Herald
Knoxville Journal & Tribune
Knoxville News-Sentinel
Knoxville Sentinel
Memphis Avalanche-Appeal
Memphis World
Nashville Banner
Nashville Globe & Independent
Nashville Tennessean
Public Guide (Knoxville)

Texas

Austin American-Statesman
Paris News

Virginia

Daily Press (Newport News)
Journal and Guide (Norfolk)
Richmond Times-Dispatch

West Virginia

Wheeling Register

Canada (Manitoba)

Winnipeg Tribune

Books

Aaron, Hank. *I Had a Hammer.* Lonnie Wheeler, ed. New York: HarperCollins, 1991.

Ackmann, Martha. *Curveball: The Remarkable Story of Toni Stone.* Chicago: Lawrence Hill, 2010.

Aiello, Thomas. *The Kings of Casino Park: Black Baseball in the Lost Season of 1932.* Tuscaloosa: University of Alabama Press, 2011.

Ashe, Arthur. *A Hard Road to Glory: The History of the African American Athlete,* volumes 1 and 2. New York: Amistad, 1988.

Bailey, Richard. *They Too Call Alabama Home: African American Profiles, 1880–1999.* Montgomery, AL: Pyramid, 1999.

Bak, Richard. *Turkey Stearnes and the Detroit Stars: The Negro Leagues in Detroit, 1919–1933.* Detroit: Great Lakes, 1994.

Bankes, James. *The Pittsburgh Crawfords.* Dubuque, IA: Wm. C. Brown, Dubuque, 1991.

Barra, Allen. *Rickwood Field: A Century in America's Oldest Ballpark.* New York: W.W. Norton, 2010.

Black, Art. *Showdown at Rickwood: Ray Caldwell, Dizzy Dean and the Early Years of America's Oldest Ball Park.* Birmingham: Blue Rooster Press, 2017.

Brashler, William. *Josh Gibson: A Life in the Negro Leagues.* New York: Harper and Row, 1978.

Bruce, Janet. *The Kansas City Monarchs: Champions of Black Baseball.* Lawrence: University Press of Kansas, 1985.

Bush, Frederick C., and Bill Nowlin, eds. *Bittersweet Goodbye: The Black Barons, the Grays, and the 1948 Negro League World Series.* Phoenix, AZ: Society for American Baseball Research, 2017.

Chalk, Ocania. *Black College Sports.* New York: Dodd, Mead, 1976.

Charlton, Jim, and Mike Shatzkin. *The Ballplayers.* New York: Arbor House, 1990.

Clark, Dick, and Larry Lester, eds. *The Negro Leagues Book.* Cleveland: Society for American Baseball Research, 1994.

Cook, Ben. *Good Wood: A Fan's History of Rickwood Field.* Birmingham, AL: A.H. Cather, 2005.

Darnell, Tim. *The Crackers: Early Days of Atlanta Baseball.* Athens, GA: Hill Street Press, 2003.

Debono, Paul. *The Indianapolis ABCs.* Jefferson, NC: McFarland, 1997.

Dickson, Paul. *The Dickson Baseball Dictionary,* 3rd ed. New York: W.W. Norton, 2009.

Dixon, Phil, and Patrick Hannigan. *The Negro Baseball Leagues: A Photographic History.* Mattituck, NY: Amereon House, 1992.

Einstein, Charles. *Willie's Time: Baseball's Golden Age.* Carbondale: Southern Illinois University Press, 1979.

Faulkner, David. *Nine Sides of the Diamond: Baseball's Great Glove Men on the Fine Art of Defense.* New York: Times Books, 1990.

Filichia, Peter. *Professional Baseball Franchises: From the Abbeville Athletics to the Zanesville Indians.* New York: Facts On File, 1993.

Fullerton, Christopher. *Every Other Sunday.* Birmingham, AL: R. Boozer Press, 1999.

Gisclair, S. Derby. *Baseball in New Orleans.* Charleston, SC: Arcadia, 2004.

Grabowski, John. *Willie Mays.* New York: Chelsea House, 1990.

Gregorich, Barbara. *Women at Play: The Story of Women in Baseball.* New York: Harcourt Brace, 1993.

Guzman, Jessie Parkhurst, ed. *1952 Negro Year Book.* New York: Wm. and Wise, 1952.

Hano, Arnold. *Willie Mays: The Say-Hey Kid.* New York: Bartholomew House, 1961.

Heaphy, Leslie A. *The Negro Leagues, 1869–1960.* Jefferson, NC: McFarland, 2003.

Henderson, Edwin Bancroft. *The Negro in Sports.* Washington, D.C.: Associated Publishers, 1939.

Heward, Bill, with Dimitri V. Gat. *Some Are Called Clowns: A Season with the Last of the Great Barnstorming Baseball Teams.* New York: Thomas Y. Crowell, 1974.

Hogan, Lawrence. *Shades of Glory: The Negro Leagues and the Story of African-American Baseball.* Washington, D.C.: National Geographic, 2006.

Holway, John B. *Black Diamonds: Life in the Negro Leagues from the Men Who Lived It.* Westport, CT: Meckler, 1989.

_____. *Blackball Stars: Negro League Pioneers.* Westport, CT: Meckler, 1988.

_____. *Bullet Joe and the Monarchs.* Washington, D.C.: Capital Press, 1984.

_____. *The Complete Book of Baseball's Negro Leagues: The Other Half of Baseball History.* Fern Park, FL: Hastings House, 2001.

_____. *Josh and Satch: The Life and Times of Josh Gibson and Satchel Paige.* Westport, CT: Meckler, 1991.

_____. *Smokey Joe and the Cannonball.* Washington, D.C., 1983.

_____. *Voices from the Great Black Baseball Leagues.* New York: Dodd, Mead, 1975.

Irvin, Monte, and James A. Riley. *Nice Guys Finish First.* New York: Carroll and Graf, 1995.

Johnson, Lloyd, and Miles Wolff, eds. *The Encyclopedia of Minor League Baseball.* Durham, NC: Baseball America, 1993.

Kelley, Brent. *"I Will Never Forget."* Jefferson, NC: McFarland, 2003.

_____. *The Negro Leagues Revisited: Conversations with 66 More Baseball Heroes.* Jefferson, NC: McFarland, 1998.

_____. *Voices from the Negro Leagues, Conversations with 52 Baseball Standouts.* Jefferson, NC: McFarland, 1998.

Klima, John. *Willie's Boys: The 1948 Birmingham Black Barons, the Last Negro League World Series, and the Making of a Baseball Legend.* Hoboken, NJ: John Wiley and Sons, 2009.

Laing, Jeffrey Michael. *Bud Fowler: Baseball's First Black Professional.* Jefferson, NC: McFarland, 2013.

Lebovitz, Hal, with Satchel Paige. *Pitchin' Man:*

Satchel Paige's Own Story. Cleveland: Cleveland News, 1948.

Lester, Larry. *Black Baseball's National Showcase: The East-West All-Star Game, 1933–53*. Lincoln: University of Nebraska Press, 2002.

Lowry, Philip J. *Green Cathedrals: The Ultimate Celebrations of All 173 Major League and Negro League Ballparks Past and Present*. Boston: Addison-Wesley, 1993 Reprint Edition.

Luke, Bob. *The Baltimore Elite Giants: Sport and Society in the Age of Negro League Baseball*. Baltimore, MD: Johns Hopkins University Press, 2009.

Mays, Willie, with Charles Einstein. *Born to Play Ball*. New York: G.P. Putnam's Sons, 1955.

Mays, Willie, with Lou Sahadi. *Say Hey: The Autobiography of Willie Mays*. New York: Simon & Schuster, 1988.

McCann, Kevin D. *Jackson Diamonds, Professional Baseball in Jackson, Tennessee*. Dickson, TN: Three Star Press, 1999.

McNary, Kyle P. *Ted "Double Duty" Radcliffe: 36 Years of Pitching and Catching in Baseball's Negro Leagues*. St. Louis, MO: McNary, 2005.

Michaeli, Ethan. *Chicago Defender: How the Legendary Black Newspaper Changed America*. Boston and New York: Houghton Mifflin Harcourt, 2016.

Newman, Zipp, and Frank McGowan. *House of Barons*. Birmingham, AL: Cather Brothers, 1948.

O'Neal, Bill. *The Southern League*. Austin, TX: Eakin Press, 1994.

Overmyer, James. *Queen of the Negro Leagues: Effa Manley and the Newark Eagles*. Lanham, MD: Scarecrow, 1998.

Paige, Leroy, as told to David Lipman. *"Satchel": Maybe I'll Pitch Forever*. Garden City, NY: Doubleday, 1961.

Peterson, Robert. *Only the Ball Was White: A History of Legendary Black Players and All-Black Professional Teams*. Englewood Cliffs, NJ: Prentice-Hall, 1970.

Plott, William J. *The Negro Southern League: A Baseball History, 1920–1951*. Jefferson, NC: McFarland, 2015.

Porter, David D. *Biographical Dictionary of American Sports: Baseball*. Westport, CO: Greenwood, 1987.

Powell, Larry. *Black Barons of Birmingham: The South's Greatest Negro League Team and Its Players*. Jefferson, NC: McFarland, 2009.

Pride, Charley, with Jim Henderson. *Pride: The Charley Pride Story*. New York: William Morrow, 1994.

Retort, Robert D. *Pictorial Negro League Legends Album*. New Castle, PA: Commercial Printing, 1992.

Ribosky, Mark. *A Complete History of the Negro Leagues*. Secaucus, NJ: Carol, 1995.

_____. *Don't Look Back: Satchel Paige in the Shadows of Baseball*. New York: Simon & Schuster, 1994.

Riley, James A. *All-Time All-Stars of Black Baseball*. Cocoa, FL: TK Publishers, 1983.

_____. *The Biographical Encyclopedia of the Negro Baseball Leagues*. New York: Carroll and Graf Publishers, 2002.

_____. *Dandy, Day and the Devil: A Trilogy of Negro League Baseball*. Cocoa, FL: TK Publishers, 1987.

Robinson, "Slow" Frazier, with Paul Bauer. *Catching Dreams: My Life in the Negro Baseball Leagues*. Syracuse, NY: Syracuse University Press, 1999.

Rogosin, Donn. *Invisible Men: Life in the Negro Leagues*. New York: Atheneum, 1993.

Ruggles, William B. *The History of the Texas League of Professional Baseball Clubs, 1888–1951*. N.p.: Texas Baseball League, 1951.

Rust, Art. *Get That Nigger Off the Field: An Oral History of Black Ballplayers from the Negro Leagues the Present*. New York: Delacorte, 1976.

Scipio, L. Albert. *The 24th Infantry at Fort Benning*. Silver Spring, MD: Roman Publications, 1986.

Shatzkin, Mike, ed. *The Ballplayers*. New York: Arbor House William Morrow, 1990.

Shirley, David. *Satchel Paige: Baseball Great*. New York: Chelsea House Publishers, 1993.

Spatz, Lyle, ed. *The SABR Baseball List and Record Book*. Scribner's, New York, London, Toronto and Sydney, 2007.

Swanton, Barry. *The ManDak League: Haven for Former Negro League Ballplayers, 1950–1957*. Jefferson, NC: McFarland, 2006.

Swanton, Barry, and Jay-Dell Mah. *Black Baseball Players in Canada: A Biographical Dictionary, 1881–1960*. Jefferson, NC: McFarland, 2009.

Trouppe, Quincy. *Twenty Years Too Soon*. Los Angeles: SandS Enterprises, 1977

Tygiel, Jules. *Baseball's Great Experiment: Jackie Robinson and His Legacy*. New York: Oxford University Press, 1983.

Walker, James R., and Robert V. Bellamy, Jr. *Center Field Shot: A History of Baseball on Television*. Lincoln: University of Nebraska Press, 2008.

Watkins, Clarence. *Baseball in Birmingham*. Charleston, SC, Chicago, IL, Portsmouth, NH, and San Francisco, CA: Arcadia, 2010.

_____. *Baseball in Memphis*. Charleston, SC, Chicago, IL, Portsmouth, NH, and San Francisco, CA: Arcadia, 2012.

_____. *Baseball in Montgomery*. Charleston, SC, Chicago, IL, Portsmouth, NH, and San Francisco, CA: Arcadia, 2017.

Wentworth, Harold, and Stuart Berg Flexner, comps. *Dictionary of American Slang*. New York: Thomas Y. Crowell, 1960.

Wheeler, Lonnie. *If I Had a Hammer; The Hank Aaron Story*. New York: HarperCollins, 1991.

White, Sol. *Sol White Baseball Guide*. Philadelphia: H. Walter Schlicter, 1907; reprint, Columbia, SC: Camden House, 1984.

_____. *Sol White's History of Colored Base Ball, with Other Documents on the Early Black Games, 1886–1936*. Introduction by Jerry Malloy. Lincoln, NE: University of Nebraska Press, 1995.

Whitehead, Charles A. *A Man and His Diamonds: The Story of Rube Foster*. New York: Vantage, 1980.

Wolff, Rick, ed. dir. *The Baseball Encyclopedia*, 9th ed. New York: Macmillan, 1993.

Wright, Marshall D. *The Southern Association in Base-ball:1885–1961.* Jefferson, NC: McFarland, 2002.

Young, A.S. "Doc." *Great Negro Baseball Stars and How They Made the Major Leagues.* New York: A. S Barnes, 1953

_____. *Mets from Mobile, Cleon Jones and Tommie Agee.* New York: Harcourt Children's Books, 1970.

_____. *Negro Firsts in Sports.* Chicago: Johnson, 1963.

Periodicals

Aiello, Thomas. "The Fading of the Greys: Black Baseball and Historical Memory in Little Rock." *Arkansas Historical Quarterly,* Winter 2006, 360–84.

"America's Only Negro Daily," *Negro Digest,* December 1945, 67–8.

"Base Ball." *Aluminum Bulletin,* June 1920, 10–11.

"Baseball Future." *Negro Digest,* March 1944, 41.

Bates, Bryna L. "The New Migration to the South." *Ebony,* September 1998, 58–63.

Brashler, William. "The Honky Writer." *Newsweek,* February 20, 1978, 21.

Chadwick, Bruce. "Color Blind Collectibles." *Topps Magazine,* Fall 1992, 42–43.

Cohen, Haskell. "Ace of Diamonds." *Negro Digest,* July 1944, 31–33.

Craft, David. "Memphis Red Sox Spotlighted in New Video." *Sports Collectors Digest,* June 12, 1998, 130–31.

Cummiskey, Joe. "Baseball's Biggest Drawing Card." *Negro Digest,* August 1944, 69–70.

"Diamond Dazzler." *Negro Digest,* October 1946, 56.

Frank, Stanley. "No Diamond Dimout." *Negro Digest,* July 1943, 17–18.

Fullerton, Chris. "Striking Out Jim Crow." *The Reader,* February–March 1995, 1–2.

Harwell, Ernie. "Found: A Popular Umpire." *Negro Digest,* April 1944, 10.

"Homerun Josh." *Negro Digest,* October 1945, 79.

Horick, Tandy. "They Might Have Been Heroes: Memories of Nashville and the Glory Days of Baseball's Negro Leagues." *Nashville Scene,* May 2, 1996, 23–30

"Josh the Basher." *Negro Digest,* September 1943, 45–6.

"Judy Johnson (1899–1989." *Negro Digest,* June 26, 1989.

Kessler, Gene. "Boogie on the Diamond." *Negro Digest,* February 1946, 9–10.

"The Legend of Bismarck, N.D." *Negro Digest,* November 1944, 83–85.

Lewis, Lloyd. "Hesitation Ball." *Negro Digest,* January 1945, 37–38.

Mann, Arthur. "24 Letter-Man." *Negro Digest,* May 1946, 31–35.

Monroe, Al. "Panic Is Seen Within the Ranks of Organized Baseball." *Abbott's Monthly,* August 1932.

_____. "What IS the Matter with Baseball?" *Abbott's Monthly,* April 1932.

Morse, George C. "Iron Men of Baseball." *Negro Digest,* September 1946, 23–66.

The National Pastime. Society of American Baseball Research, Cleveland, Ohio, 1975–2009.

"No Average Ball Players." *Negro Digest,* August 1943, 91–2.

Paige, Satchell. "My Biggest Baseball Day," as told to Ernest Mehl. *Negro Digest,* May 1943, 7–10.

Plott, Bill. "The Southern League of Colored Base Ballists." *Baseball Research Journal,* 1974.

Reynolds, James E. "The Batboy Who Swung for Equality." *Sports Illustrated,* July 2, 1990.

Rosengarten, Theodore. "Reading the Hops, Recollections of Lorenzo Piper Davis and the Negro Baseball League." *Southern Exposure,* Summer/Fall 1977.

Rozin, Skip. "Two Worlds." *Topps Magazine,* Fall 1992, 36–39.

Rushin, Steve. "A Life Well-Lived." *Sports Illustrated,* January 20, 2003, 15.

Smith, Shelley. "Remembering Their Game." *Sports Illustrated,* July 6, 1992.

Smith, Wendell. "Baseball on Diplomatic Rocks." *Negro Digest,* 71–2.

Turkin, Hy. "Foul Bawl." *Negro Digest,* April 1945, 35–6.

_____. "No Black Ball for Black Jackie." *Negro Digest,* March 1946, 41–43.

Woodward, Stanley. "Satchel's Ambition." *Negro Digest,* August 1943, 41–43.

Miscellaneous

Alabama Center for Health Statistics, death certificate for Buford Meredith.

Correspondence and research assistance from Clint Chaffin, Moultrie, GA (April 26, 1995).

The Courier, newsletter for the Negro Leagues Committee of the Society for American Baseball Research, 1999–2018.

Fullerton, Christopher. "Striking Out Jim Crow: The Birmingham Black Barons." Master's thesis, University of Mississippi, 1994; later expanded and published as *Every Other Sunday.*

Gerlach, Larry R. "Baseball's Other 'Great Experiment': Eddie Klep and the Integration of the Negro Leagues." Advance copy of then unpublished paper.

Joyce, Allan E. "The Atlanta Black Crackers." Master's thesis, Emory University, Atlanta, GA, 1975.

Letter from Cliff McCarthy, Dunstable, MA, grandson of C.H. McCarthy, president of the Negro Southeastern League in 1921 (January 16, 1993, apparently early correspondence about 5 years previous.)

SABR Journal, Society of American Baseball Research, Cleveland, Ohio, 1982–2018.

13th Annual Induction Ceremony and Banquet program, March 17, 2003, Alabama High School Sports Hall of Fame. Montgomery, AL: Alabama Printers, 2003.

VHS/DVD

Black Diamonds, Blues City: Stories of the Memphis Red Sox. Video produced by John R. Haddock

and Steven J. Ross, University of Memphis, 1998.
Safe at Home. Atlanta Public Television, 1974. (Connie Ward Cameron, producer?)
Swingin' Timber. Video on the Claybrook Tigers. Directed by David D. Dawson, University of Arkansas, Fayetteville, 2001.

Compact Disk

Brodsky, Chuck. *Letters in the Dirt*. Red House Records ASIN B000001BB3, 1999.
Fullerton, Christopher D., and Been Cook. *Every Other Sunday: Interviews with Birmingham Black Barons*. Produced by Barry Brooks.

Papers

Harmon, David. "That Other Baseball Team: The Atlanta Black Crackers and the World of Southern African American Baseball." NASSH Convention, Auburn University, May 26, 1996.
Plott, Bill. "The Negro Southern League, 1920–50: A Baseball History." Alabama Department of Archives and History, July 21, 2016.
_____. "Negro Southern League 1920–50." SABR Negro Leagues Committee Conference, Harrisburg, PA, August 7, 1998.

Internet Sources

agatetype.typepad.com (blog)
ameshistoricalsociety.org, official web page of the Ames, Iowa, Historical Society.
arkbaseball.com
astrosdaily.com
attheplate.com
baseball-almanac.com
baseball-fever.com
baseball-reference. com
baseballhistoryblog.com
baseballinlivingcolor.com
baseballinwartime.com
baseballlibrary.com
bhamwiki.com
blackathlete.net
blackusa.com
chicagogobaseballmuseum.org
cincysports.net
cnlbr.org, Center for Negro League Baseball Research.
coe.ksu.edu/nlbemuseum
connection.ebscohost.com/c/articles/51320347/only-negro-acrobat-troupe
encyclopediaofarkansas.net, Arkansas history and culture.
examiner.com
fantasypros911.com
georgiaencyclopedia.org
highbeam.com
historicbaseball.com
HMdb.org
hutchnews.com
indystar.com

jazzhouse.org
leagle.com/decisions/1964800205A2d595_1796 NESBITT%20v.%20UNITED%STATES
lib.berkeley.edu
miamitimesonline.com
monroemonarchs. com
montgomeryal.gov, official web site for City of Montgomery, Alabama.
morehouse.edu
msbluestrail.org/blues-trail-markers/gatemouth-moore
msnbc.com
negro-baseball-league.com
negroleaguebaseball.com
nlbpa.com, official site of Negro Leagues Baseball Players Association
nuweb.neu.edu
nytimes.com
pepeprgame.com
pitch.com
pitchblackbaseball.com
pittsburgh.pirates.m.b.com
ponderosastomp.com
princetonpartners.com/hunting-broadway-tickets-led-birmingham-black-barons
sabr.bioproj.org
seamheads.com
siouxcityghosts.com
siouxcityhistory.org
smoaky.com
sporttaco.com
tennesseeencyclopedia.net
thegrio.com
u-s-history.com
usd281.com/pages/townteam/baseball5.html
webcache.googleusercontent.com
weirdwildrealm.com
weldbham.com/blog/2015/02/03/reclaiming-history-birmingham-black-barons.
westegg.com, The Inflation Calculator, created by S. Morgan Friedman.
wikipedia.org

Interviews

All interviews were conducted by the author. Some were formal question-and-answer sessions either in person or by telephone; others were casual visits at conferences, receptions, banquets and other public occasions. Almost all of them yielded additional information of value on Negro leagues baseball.

Otha Bailey, Birmingham, AL, 16 May 1999.
Ralph Banks, telephone interview, 10 September 1998.
Lyman Bostock, Sr., Birmingham, AL, 16 June 1993; telephone interview, June 1997.
"Birmingham Sam" Brison, Birmingham, AL, 3 June 2010.
John Brown, telephone interview, 18 June 1997.
Joe Caffee, telephone interview, 6 June 2003.
Bill "Ready" Cash, Harrisburg, PA, 8 August 1998.
Cato Clowney, telephone interview, 26 July 2012
Bubba Cunningham, Montgomery, AL, 5 October 1997.

Bennie Daniels, telephone interview, 1 June 1996.

Lorenzo "Piper" Davis, Montevallo, AL, 24 February 1983.

Charlie Dees, telephone interview, 30 October 2010.

Henry Elmore, Birmingham, AL, 17 February 2011.

Frank Evans, Birmingham, AL, 13 August 2009, 3 June 2010.

Severn Frazier, telephone interview, 11 January 1992.

Severn Frazier, Jr., telephone interview, 13 October 1998.

Jesse Gosha, Montgomery, AL, 26 September 1997; telephone interview, 2 September 1998.

Willie Grace, telephone interview, 16 June 1997.

Bill Greason, Birmingham, AL, 1 February 1995.

Bennie L. Griggs, Birmingham, AL, 6 June 2002.

Wiley Griggs, Birmingham, AL, 14 April 1995.

Raymond Haggins, Montevallo, AL, 15 April 1994.

James Hannon, Montgomery, AL, 26 September 1997.

Sam Jethroe, telephone interview, 18 June 1997.

Mamie "Peanut" Johnson, Harrisburg, PA., 8 August 1998.

Ethel Klep, telephone interview, 17 June 1997.

Joseph Klep, telephone interview, 17 June 1997.

Mrs. Elnora Frazier Lee, telephone interview, 5 November 1998.

Tony Lloyd, Birmingham, AL, 3 June 2010.

Buck O'Neil, Asheville, NC, 7 July 1996.

David Pope, telephone, interview, 18 July 1996.

Charley Pride, telephone interview, 6 May 1999; Birmingham, AL, 16 May 1999.

"Double Duty" Radcliffe, Montgomery, AL, 17 August 1996.

Norman "Bobby" Robinson, undated Jerry Malloy Conference, SABR Negro Leagues Committee.

Tommy Sampson, telephone, 18 June 1997.

Jake Sanders, Birmingham, 17 February 2011.

Al Smith, Cleveland Buckeyes, telephone, 18 June 1997.

Willie Smith, Anniston, AL, 20 January 1970, 10 December 1993.

Thomas "High Pockets" Turner, Harrisburg, PA, 8 August 1998.

Bob Veale, Montevallo, AL, February 24, 1983; Birmingham, AL, 20 May 1998.

Claude Walker, telephone interview, 20 September 1998.

Ernest Waters, telephone interview, 20 September 1998.

Bessie Williams, telephone interview, 4 February 2004.

Charles L. "Coot" Willis, telephone interview, 23 August 2010.

Artie Wilson, telephone interview, 20 July 1996.

Bill Wilson, telephone interview and correspondence, various dates, September 1998.

Willie Young, Birmingham, AL, 16 May 1999.

Index

Numbers in *bold italics* indicate pages with illustrations